Lecture Notes in Computer Science 6376

Commenced Publication in 1973
Founding and Former Series Editors:
Gerhard Goos, Juris Hartmanis, and Jan van Leeuwen

D1666336

Michael Goesele   Stefan Roth
Arjan Kuijper   Bernt Schiele
Konrad Schindler (Eds.)

Pattern Recognition

32nd DAGM Symposium
Darmstadt, Germany, September 22-24, 2010
Proceedings

 Springer

Volume Editors

Michael Goesele
Stefan Roth
TU Darmstadt, Dept. of Computer Science
Fraunhoferstr. 5, 64283 Darmstadt, Germany
E-mail: {sroth,goesele}@cs.tu-darmstadt.de

Arjan Kuijper
Fraunhofer Institute for Computer Graphics Research (IGD)
Fraunhoferstr. 5, 64283 Darmstadt, Germany
E-mail: arjan.kuijper@igd.fraunhofer.de

Bernt Schiele
MPI Informatik
Campus E1 4, 66123 Saarbrücken, Germany
schiele@mpi-inf.mpg.de

Konrad Schindler
ETH Zurich
Photogrammetry and Remote Sensing
Wolfgang-Pauli-Str. 15, 8093 Zurich, Switzerland
E-mail: schindler@geod.baug.ethz.ch

Library of Congress Control Number: 2010934415

CR Subject Classification (1998): I.5, I.4, I.3.5, I.2.10, I.4.1, I.2.6, F.2.2

LNCS Sublibrary: SL 6 – Image Processing, Computer Vision, Pattern Recognition, and Graphics

ISSN   0302-9743
ISBN-10   3-642-15985-0 Springer Berlin Heidelberg New York
ISBN-13   978-3-642-15985-5 Springer Berlin Heidelberg New York

springer.com

© Springer-Verlag Berlin Heidelberg 2010
Printed in Germany

Typesetting: Camera-ready by author, data conversion by Scientific Publishing Services, Chennai, India
Printed on acid-free paper   06/3180

Preface

On behalf of the organizing committee, we would like to welcome you to Darmstadt and DAGM 2010, the 32nd Annual Symposium of the German Association for Pattern Recognition.

The technical program covered all aspects of pattern recognition and, to name only a few areas, ranged from 3D reconstruction, to object recognition and medical applications. The result is reflected in these proceedings, which contain the papers presented at DAGM 2010. Our call for papers resulted in 134 submissions from institutions in 21 countries. Each paper underwent a rigorous reviewing process and was assigned to at least three program committee members for review. The reviewing phase was followed by a discussion phase among the respective program committee members in order to suggest papers for acceptance. The final decision was taken during a program committee meeting held in Darmstadt based on all reviews, the discussion results and, if necessary, additional reviewing. Based on this rigorous process we selected a total of 57 papers, corresponding to an acceptance rate of below 45%. Out of all accepted papers, 24 were chosen for oral and 33 for poster presentation. All accepted papers have been published in these proceedings and given the same number of pages. We would like to thank all members of the program committee as well as the external reviewers for their valuable and highly appreciated contribution to the community. We would also like to extend our thanks to all authors of submitted papers; without their contribution we would not have been able to assemble such a strong program.

The technical program was complemented by a workshop on "Pattern Recognition for IT Security", which was organized by Stefan Katzenbeisser, Jana Dittmann and Claus Vielhauer, as well as by four tutorials given by renowned experts:

- "Sparse Linear Models: Reconstruction and Approximate Bayesian Inference" by Matthias Seeger
- "Computer Vision on GPUs" by Jan-Michael Frahm and P.J. Narayanan
- "Color in Image and Video Processing" by Joost van de Weijer
- "MAP Inference in Discrete Models" by Carsten Rother

In addition to the presentations from the technical program, we were also proud to have had three internationally renowned invited speakers at the conference:

- Richard Szeliski (Microsoft Research Redmond)
- Yair Weiss (The Hebrew University of Jerusalem)
- Andrew Zisserman (University of Oxford)

Due to its success at DAGM 2009 in Jena, we again organized the Young Researchers' Forum at DAGM 2010 to promote scientific interaction between excellent young researchers and our community. This year the contributions of six students were accepted, who presented their Bachelor or Master thesis work during the conference and interacted with our community. Their participation was kindly supported by Daimler.

We would like to extend our sincere thanks to everyone who helped with making DAGM 2010 in Darmstadt a success. We are indebted to Ursula Päckel, Suzana Alpsancar and Carola Eichel for their help with all organizational matters, to Silke Romero and Nils Balke for web support and technical assistance, to Sebastian Koch and Fabian Langguth for assembling the proceedings and creating the registration system, our students and PhD students for many miscellaneous things along the way, to Fraunhofer IGD for providing the rooms for the PC meeting, workshop as well as the tutorials free of charge, and to Microsoft for offering the CMT conference management system for free.

We would also like to sincerely thank all our sponsors for their financial support, which helped to keep the registration fees as low as possible, especially those of the student attendees. In particular, we would like to thank our Platinum sponsor Daimler, our Gold sponsors Bosch and MVTec Software GmbH, our Silver sponsors ISRA Vision and Toyota, as well as our Bronze sponsor Microsoft Research. We appreciate their donations to our community, which values and recognizes the importance of these contributions to our field.

We were happy to host the 32nd Annual Symposium of the German Association for Pattern Recognition in Darmstadt and look forward to DAGM 2011 in Frankfurt.

September 2010

Michael Goesele
Stefan Roth
Arjan Kuijper
Bernt Schiele
Konrad Schindler

Laudatio for Gerald Sommer, Chairman of DAGM 2006–2009

Dear members of the German Pattern Recognition Society (DAGM),

The Darmstadt symposium on Pattern Recognition is the first meeting of our society after Gerald Sommer's chairmanship. It is my pleasure to thank my predecessor Gerald Sommer for his service to our society during the last three years as chairman and before that as vice chairman and as head of the technical committee. He has fostered a climate of openness for new pattern recognition challenges beyond our core scientific interests in computer and robot vision; for example, machine learning has found a natural home in our society. His emphasis on mathematical rigor and his insistence that pattern recognition has to solve relevant problems will guide us beyond his tenure as DAGM chairman. Together with my colleagues on the DAGM board I hope that we can rely on his advice in the future and we wish him all the best for the years to come.

Joachim M. Buhmann
Chairman DAGM e.V.

Organization

General Chairs

Arjan Kuijper   Fraunhofer IGD
Bernt Schiele   TU Darmstadt and MPI Informatics

Program Chairs

Michael Goesele   TU Darmstadt
Stefan Roth   TU Darmstadt

Workshop and Tutorial Chair

Konrad Schindler   TU Darmstadt and ETH Zürich

Program Committee

Horst Bischof	TU Graz
Thomas Breuel	TU Kaiserslautern
Joachim Buhmann	ETH Zürich
Wolfram Burgard	Universität Freiburg
Hans Burkhardt	Universität Freiburg
Daniel Cremers	TU München
Andreas Dengel	DFKI
Joachim Denzler	Universität Jena
Peter Eisert	HU Berlin
Michael Felsberg	Linköping University
Gernot Fink	TU Dortmund
Boris Flach	CMP Prague
Uwe Franke	Daimler AG
Matthias Franz	FH Konstanz
Wolfgang Förstner	Universität Bonn
Dariu Gavrila	Daimler AG and University of Amsterdam
Peter Gehler	ETH Zürich
Michael Goesele	TU Darmstadt
Fred Hamprecht	Universität Heidelberg
Wolfgang Heidrich	University of British Columbia
Joachim Hornegger	Universität Erlangen
Xiaoyi Jiang	Universität Münster
Bernd Jähne	Universität Heidelberg
Reinhard Koch	Universität Kiel
Arjan Kuijper	Fraunhofer IGD

Bastian Leibe	RWTH Aachen
Hendrik Lensch	Universität Ulm
Helmut Mayer	Universität der Bundeswehr München
Rudolf Mester	Universität Frankfurt
Klaus-Robert Müller	TU Berlin
Nassir Navab	TU München
Hermann Ney	RWTH Aachen
Björn Ommer	Universität Heidelberg
Gunnar Rätsch	MPI Tübingen
Bodo Rosenhahn	Universität Hannover
Stefan Roth	TU Darmstadt
Volker Roth	Universität Basel
Carsten Rother	Microsoft Research Cambridge
Bernt Schiele	TU Darmstadt and MPI Informatics
Konrad Schindler	TU Darmstadt and ETH Zürich
Christoph Schnörr	Universität Heidelberg
Gerald Sommer	Universität Kiel
Peter Sturm	INRIA
Christian Theobalt	MPI Informatics
Klaus-Dietz Tönnies	Universität Magdeburg
Thomas Vetter	Universität Basel
Joachim Weickert	Universität des Saarlandes

External Reviewers

H. Ackermann	P. Fechteler	K.I. Kim
B. Andres	J. Fehr	M. Klodt
B. Bartczak	G. Floros	U. Koethe
M. Baust	B. Frank	C. Kofler
J. Behr	A. Frick	K. Kolev
R. Bensch	S. Gehring	D. Kondermann
A. Bigdelou	S. Grewenig	R. Kümmerle
R. Bohnert	S. Grzonka	A. Ladikos
D. Borth	A. Guevara	F. Larsson
M. Breuss	P. Gwosdek	B. Lau
N. Brieu	J. Hedborg	P.H. D. Le
A. Bruhn	A. Hilsmann	L. Leal-Taixé
N. Canterakis	M. Hofmann	A. Lehmann
C. Conrad	S. Ilic	C. Leistner
S. Demirci	M. Jaeger	R. Lenz
P. Drewe	M. Jehle	S. Lieberknecht
S. Ebert	F. Kellner	F. Lindner
L. Ellis	J. Keppler	X. Lou
M. Enzweiler	M. Kettern	L. Ma
S. Esquivel	M. Keuper	D. Mai

Prizes 2009

Olympus Prize

The Olympus-Award 2009 was given to

Carsten Rother

for his outstanding work in the field of image segmentation using statistical methods, and his ability to transfer scientific results into real-life products.

DAGM Prizes

The main prize for 2009 was awarded to

Bastian Goldlücke and Daniel Cremers: A Superresolution Framework for High-Accuracy Multiview Reconstruction

Pascal Paysan, Marcel Lüthi, Thomas Albrecht, Anita Lerch, Brian Amberg, Francesco Santini and Thomas Vetter: Face Reconstruction from Skull Shapes and Physical Attributes

Further DAGM prizes for 2009 were awarded to

Martin R. Oswald, Eno Töppe, Kalin Kolev and Daniel Cremers: Nonparametric Single View Reconstruction of Curved Objects Using Convex Optimization

Christian Walder, Martin Breidt, Heinrich H. Bülthoff, Bernhard Schölkopf and Cristobal Curio: Markerless 3D Face Tracking

The DAGM Young Researchers' Prize was awarded to

Falko Kellner, Christian-Albrechts-Universität Kiel:
Environment Modelling and Object Segmentation Using an Actively Steered Time-of-Flight Camera

DAGM Young Researchers' Forum 2010

The following contributions were accepted into the DAGM Young Researchers' Forum 2010

Angela Eigenstetter, TU Darmstadt:
Multi-Cue Pedestrian Classification with Partial Occlusion Handling

Martin Hofmann, University of Illinois:
Dense Spatio-temporal Motion Segmentation for Tracking Multiple Self-occluding People

Tim Pattinson, Stuttgart University:
Quantification and Description of Distance Measurement Errors of a Time-of-Flight Camera

Jens Rannacher, Heidelberg University:
Realtime 3D Motion Estimation on Graphics Hardware

Marcus Rohrbach, TU Darmstadt:
Visual Knowledge Transfer Using Semantic Relatedness

Robert Wulff, Christian-Albrechts-Universität Kiel:
Image-Based 3D Documentation in Archeology

Table of Contents

Geometry and Calibration

Poster Session I

Recognition

Learning and Optimization

Applications

Poster Session II

Motion

Low-Level Vision and Features

Surfaces and Materials

3D Reconstruction Using an n-Layer Heightmap

David Gallup[1], Marc Pollefeys[2], and Jan-Michael Frahm[1]

[1] Department of Computer Science, University of North Carolina
{gallup,jmf}@cs.unc.edu
[2] Department of Computer Science, ETH Zurich
marc.pollefeys@inf.ethz.ch

Abstract. We present a novel method for 3D reconstruction of urban scenes extending a recently introduced heightmap model. Our model has several advantages for 3D modeling of urban scenes: it naturally enforces vertical surfaces, has no holes, leads to an efficient algorithm, and is compact in size. We remove the major limitation of the heightmap by enabling modeling of overhanging structures. Our method is based on an an n-layer heightmap with each layer representing a surface between full and empty space. The configuration of layers can be computed optimally using a dynamic programming method. Our cost function is derived from probabilistic occupancy, and incorporates the Bayesian Information Criterion (BIC) for selecting the number of layers to use at each pixel. 3D surface models are extracted from the heightmap. We show results from a variety of datasets including Internet photo collections. Our method runs on the GPU and the complete system processes video at 13 Hz.

1 Introduction

Automatic large-scale 3D reconstruction of urban environments is a very active research topic with broad applications including 3D maps like Google Earth and Microsoft Bing Maps, civil planning, and entertainment. Recent approaches have used LiDAR scans, video, or photographs, acquired either from ground, aerial, or satellite platforms [1,2,3,4,5]. In this work, we focus on reconstructions from street-level video, which has higher resolution than aerial data, and video cameras are significantly less expensive than active sensors like LiDAR.

To process in a reasonable time, computational efficiency must be considered when modeling wide-area urban environments such as entire cities, since millions of frames of video are required for even a small town [3]. Even if a (cloud) computing cluster is used, efficiency is of great concern since usage of such systems is billed according to processing time. In addition to computational efficiency, the models need to be compact in order to efficiently store, transmit, and render them.

Gallup et al. [6] introduced a method, which uses a heightmap representation to model urban scenes. See Figure 1 for an example. The method takes depthmaps as input and fits a heightmap to a volume of occupancy votes. In contrast to other volumetric methods [7], the heightmap model has several advantages. First, it enforces that walls and facades are strictly flat and vertical,

M. Goesele et al. (Eds.): DAGM 2010, LNCS 6376, pp. 1–10, 2010.

Sample Input Images   Sample Input Depthmaps

Heightmap   3D Model Geometry   Textured 3D Model

Fig. 1. Our system uses a heightmap model for 3D reconstruction. Images courtesy of Gallup et al.[6].

Fig. 2. Examples of n-layer heightmaps

since they appear as discontinuities in the heightmap. Second, the heightmap represents a continuous surface and does not allow for holes. Third, because the height estimate is supported by the entire vertical column, no regularization is necessary, leading to a highly parallel and efficient computation. Fourth, heightmaps can be stored and transmitted efficiently using depthmap coding algorithms.

However, the major limitation of the method is the inability to model overhanging structures. Thus awnings, eves, balconies, doorways, and arches are either filled in or missed entirely. While some loss of detail is to be expected in exchange for a robust and compact representation, this is a major weakness.

In this paper we adopt the heightmap approach and improve upon it in the following ways: First we introduce a multi-layer representation to handle overhanging structures. Second, the cost function for heightmap estimation is derived from probability. We address the overhanging structure problem by extending the method of [6] to an n-layer heightmap. Each layer represents a surface between full and empty space. Some examples are shown in Figure 2. The positions of the n layers at each heightmap pixel can be computed optimally using dynamic programming. We also include the Bayesian Information Criterion (BIC) as a model selection penalty to use additional layers only when necessary. In [6], the cost function for heightmap estimation was defined in an ad-hoc manner. We show how this cost function can be derived from probabilities. This derivation also allows us to incorporate the BIC in a principled way.

As in [6], our method also runs on the GPU, and the complete system can process video at 13 Hz. We have demonstrate our approach on several challenging street-side video sequences. Results show a clear improvement over [6], particularly on overhanging structures and trees.

Another data source for urban 3D reconstruction is images downloaded from photo sharing websites such as Flickr. In this case data acquisition is free but is subject to the interests of the website community, and thus datasets are usually limited to popular tourist locations. Camera poses can be computed using techniques such as Snavely et al. [8] and the more recent methods of [9,10]. Dense stereo and surface modeling were achieved by Goesele et al. [11] and recently by Furukawa et al. [12]. We apply our extended heightmap approach to 3D reconstruction from community photo collections as well. Our approach is much simpler and faster, and yet results are surprisingly good.

2 Related Work

Recent approaches employ simplified geometries to gain robustness [13,1,14,15]. Cornelis et al.[13] produce compact 3D street models using a ruled surface model. Similar to the heightmap model, this assumes that walls and facades are vertical. Furukawa et al.[14] presented a Manhattan-world model for stereo, where all surfaces have one of three orthogonal surface normals. Sinha et al.[15] employ a general piecewise-planar model, and Gallup et al.[6] uses a more general piecewise-planar model that can also handle non-planar objects. Our approach uses a simplified geometry and is far more general than [13,15], and more efficient and compact than [14,6]. It effectively models buildings and terrain, but also naturally models cars, pedestrians, lamp posts, bushes, and trees.

In our approach we use the probability occupancy grid of the scene from the robotics literature [16,17]. The occupancy of each voxel is computed by bayesian inference, and our derivation is similar to that of Guan et al.[18]. We model the measurement distribution as a combination of normal and uniform distrubutions in order to better handle outliers. Robustness to outliers is critical since our input measurements are stereo depthmaps.

Dense 3D reconstruction for photo collections has first been explored by Goesele et al.[11] and by Furukawa et al.[19]. Images on the web come from a variety of uncontrolled settings, which violate many of the assumptions of stereo such as brightness constancy. Goesele et al. and Furukawa et al. take great care to select only the most compatible images, starting from points of high certainty and growing outward. Our approach on the other hand relies on the robustness of the heightmap model and results in a much simpler and faster algorithm.

Merrell et al. [20] proposed a depthmap fusion from video employing the temporal redundancy of the depth computed for each frame. It obtains a consensus surface by enforcing visibility constraints. The proposed heightmap fusion in contrast does not require a confidence measure due to the benefits of the vertical column regularization.

3   Method

The proposed n-layer heightmap generalizes the single layer heightmap. A single layer heightmap defines a surface, which is the transition from occupied space to empty space. In an n layer heightmap, each layer defines a transition from full to empty or vice versa. The number of layers needed to reconstruct a scene can be determined with a vertical line test. For any vertical line, the number of surfaces that the line intersects is the number of layers in the scene. In our approach, the user must give the number of layers beforehand, although model selection may determine that fewer layers are sufficient.

The input to our method is a set of images with corresponding camera poses and their depthmaps. The depth measurements from each camera are used to determine the occupancy likelihood of each point in space, and an n-layer heightmap is fit. Using a heightmap for ground-based measurements has the advantage that the estimated parameter, height, is perpendicular to the dominant direction of measurement noise. This is ideal for urban reconstruction where vertical walls are of particular interest.

We will now present our novel method for reconstructing scenes using an n-layer heightmap. This method consists of the following steps:

- Layout the volume of interest.
- Construct the probabilistic occupancy grid over the volume.
- Compute the n-layer heightmap.
- Extract mesh and generate texture maps.

The volume of interest for heightmap computation is defined by its position, orientation, size, and resolution. Heightmap computation assumes the vertical direction is known, which can be extracted from the images itself. Besides that constraint, the volume of interest can be defined arbitrarily. For processing large datasets like video of an entire street, it makes sense to define several volumes of interest and process them independently. For video, a frame is chosen as reference, and the volume of interest is defined with respect to the camera's coordinate system for that frame. Reference frames are chosen at irregular intervals where the spacing is determined by overlap with the previous volume. Our video data also contains GPS measurements, so the camera path is geo-registered, and the vertical direction is known. For photo collections, the vertical direction can be found using a heuristic derived from photography practices. Most photographers will tilt the camera, but not allow it to roll. In other words, the x axis of the camera stays perpendicular to gravity. This heuristic can be used to compute the vertical direction as a homogeneous least squares problem as shown in [21]. The size and resolution of the volume are given as user parameters.

The next step is to compute the probabilistic occupancy grid over the volume of interest. Since the heightmap layers will be computed independently for each vertical column of the volume, the occupancy grid does not need to be fully stored. Only each column must be stored temporarily, which keeps the memory requirement low. We will first derive the occupancy likelihood for each voxel independently. Voxel occupancy is in fact not independent since it must obey the layer constraint, and we will later show how to compute the layers for a column of voxels using dynamic programming. The variables used in our derivation are summarized as follows:

- O_p: a binary random variable representing the occupancy of voxel p.
- $Z_p = Z_1 \ldots Z_k$: depth measurements along rays intersecting p from cameras $1 \ldots k$.
- z_{min}, z_{max}: depth range of the scene.
- σ: depth measurement uncertainty (standard deviation).
- S: depth of surface hypothesis.
- $L_x = l_1 \ldots l_n$: configuration of layers at point x in the heightmap. l_i is the vertical position of layer i.

For simplicity we have assumed that all depth measurements have the same uncertainty σ although this is not a requirement.

We will now derive the likelihood for O_p. We will drop the subscript p until multiple voxels are considered for dynamic programming.

$$P(O|Z) \propto P(Z|O)P(O) \tag{1}$$

$$P(Z|O) = \prod_{i=1\ldots k} P(Z_i|O) \tag{2}$$

Equation 2 states our assumption that the measurements are independent. We use the occupancy prior $P(O)$ to slightly bias the volume to be empty above the camera center and full below. This helps to prevent rooftops extending into empty space since the cameras don't observe them from the ground.

To determine $P(Z_i|O)$ we will follow [18] and introduce a helper variable S which is a candidate surface along the measurement ray. The depth measurement can then be formulated with respect to S.

$$P(Z_i|O) = \int_{z_{min}}^{z_{max}} P(Z_i|S,O)P(S|O)dS \tag{3}$$

$$P(Z_i|S,O) = P(Z_i|S) = \begin{cases} \mathcal{N}(S,\sigma)|_{Z_i} & \text{if inliner} \\ \mathcal{U}(z_{min},z_{max})|_{Z_i} & \text{if outlier} \end{cases} \tag{4}$$

$$= \rho\mathcal{N}(S,\sigma)|_{Z_i} + (1-\rho)\mathcal{U}(z_{min},z_{max})|_{Z_i} \tag{5}$$

The measurement model is a mixture of a normal distribution $\mathcal{N}$ and uniform distribution $\mathcal{U}$ to handle outliers. $\mathcal{N}|_Z$ is the disribution's density function evaluated at Z. ρ is the inlier ratio, which is a given parameter. $P(S|O)$ is the surface formation model defined as follows where $\epsilon \to 0$ and z_p is the depth of the voxel.

$$P(S|O) = \begin{cases} 1/(z_{max}-z_{min}) & \text{if } S < z_p - \epsilon \\ (1-z_p/(z_{max}-z_{min}))/\epsilon & \text{if } z_p - \epsilon \leq S \leq z_p \\ 0 & \text{if } S > z_p \end{cases} \tag{6}$$

This model states that the surface must be in front of the occupied voxel, but not behind it. We will also need the measurement likelihood given that the voxel is empty, which we will denote by $\neg O$. The derivation is the same, replacing O with $\neg O$, except the surface formation model is

$$P(S|\neg O) = 1/(z_{max} - z_{min}). \tag{7}$$

We will now define our n-layer model and show how to recover it with dynamic programming. We will derive the likelihood of L_x which is the layer configuration at pixel x in the heightmap. This pixel contains a vertical column of voxels, which we will denote as O_i where i is the height of the voxel ranging from 0 to m.

$$P(L|Z) \propto P(Z|L)P(L) \tag{8}$$

$$P(Z|L) = \prod_{i=0}^{l_1-1} P(Z|O_i) \prod_{i=l_1}^{l_2-1} P(Z|\neg O_i) \dots \prod_{i=l_n}^{m} P(Z|\neg O_i). \tag{9}$$

$$P(L) = \prod_{i=0}^{l_1-1} P(O_i) \prod_{i=l_1}^{l_2-1} P(\neg O_i) \dots \prod_{i=l_n}^{m} P(\neg O_i). \tag{10}$$

Note that the measurement likelihoods alternate between the full condition $P(Z|O_i)$ and the empty condition $P(Z|\neg O_i)$ as dictated by the layer constraint. Also note that the number of layers is assumed to be odd, giving the final product the empty condition. This is true for outdoor urban scenes. For indoor scenes, an even number of layers could be used.

We will now define our cost function C by taking the negative log-likelihood of $P(L|Z)$, which will simplify the dynamic programming solution.

$$C = -ln\ P(Z|L)P(L) = -\sum_{i=0}^{l_1-1} (ln\ P(Z|O_i) + ln\ P(O_i)) \tag{11}$$

$$-\sum_{i=l_1}^{l_2-1} (ln\ P(Z|\neg O_i) + ln\ P(\neg O_i)) \dots \tag{12}$$

To simplify the sums over the layers we will define the following:

$$I_a^b = -\sum_{i=a}^{b} (ln\ P(Z|O_i) + ln\ P(O_i)) \tag{13}$$

$$\bar{I}_a^b = -\sum_{i=a}^{b} (ln\ P(Z|\neg O_i) + ln\ P(\neg O_i)). \tag{14}$$

The sums I_0^b (resp. $\bar{I}$) for all b can be precomputed making it easy to compute $I_a^b = I_0^b - I_0^{a-1}$ (resp. $\bar{I}$).

We can now write our cost function recursively in terms of C_k which is the cost only up to layer k.

$$C_k(l) = \begin{cases} I_{l'}^l + C_{k-1}(l') & \text{if } odd(k) \\ \bar{I}_{l'}^l + C_{k-1}(l') & \text{if } even(k) \end{cases} \tag{15}$$

$$l' = \arg\min_{l' \le l} C_{k-1}(l') \tag{16}$$

$$C_0(l) = 0 \tag{17}$$

The original cost function is then $C = C_n(m)$ where n is the number of layers and m is the number of voxels in the vertical column.

The layer configuration that minimizes C can be computed with dynamic programming. In order for this to be true, the problem must exhibit *optimal substructure* and *overlapping subproblems* [22]. The problem has optimal substructure because of the independence between non-adjacent layers, i.e. an optimal configuration of layers $1 \ldots i-1$ will still be optimal regardless of the position of layer i. (As in C_k, we consider only the voxels below the layer.) The overlapping subproblems occur since computing the optimal position of any layer greater than i requires computing the optimial configuration of layers $1 \ldots i$. Therefore, the optimal configuration can be solved with dynamic programming. The recursive formulation in Equation 19 lends easily to the table method, and the solution can extracted by backtracking.

Many parts of the heightmap will not need all n layers. The extra layers will be free to fit the noise in the measurements. To avoid this, we incorporate the Bayesian Information Criterion (BIC).

$$C_{BIC} = -ln\ P(Z|L)P(L) + \frac{1}{2}n\ ln\ |Z_x| \tag{18}$$

$|Z_x|$ is the number of measurements interacting with the heightmap pixel x. The first part of the equation is exactly C and the second part adds a penalty of $ln\ |Z_x|$ for every layer in the model. We can add this penalty into our recursive formulation by adding $ln\ |Z_x|$ at each layer unless the layer position is the same as the preceding layer.

$$C_k^{BIC}(l) = \begin{cases} I_{l'}^l + C_{k-1}(l') + T(l \ne l')\frac{1}{2}ln\ |Z_x| & \text{if } odd(k) \\ \bar{I}_{l'}^l + C_{k-1}(l') + T(l \ne l')\frac{1}{2}ln\ |Z_x| & \text{if } even(k) \end{cases} \tag{19}$$

Thus model selection is performed by prefering layers to *collapse* unless there is sufficient evidence to support them. The table required to solve the problem is of size $m \times n$, and the sum variables are of size m. Therefore the algorithm takes $O(mn)$ time and space per heightmap pixel, and the whole heightmap takes $O(whmn)$ time and $O(wh + mn)$ space.

4 Results

We have tested our n-layer heightmap method on street-level video datasets and photo collections downloaded from the web. For the video datasets, the camera

Fig. 3. Original photos and depthmaps computed from Internet photo collections

poses and depthmaps were computed with the real-time system of Pollefeys et al.[3]. To compute the camera poses for the photo collections, we used the method of Li et al.[9]. The output of their approach also gives a clustering of the images which can be used to select compatible views for stereo. We computed a depthmap for each photograph by selecting the 20 views in the same cluster with the most matched and triangulated SIFT points in common. Stereo is performed on the GPU using a simple NCC planesweep. Results are shown in Figure 3.

From these inputs we used our n-layer heightmap system to obtain a 3D reconstruction in the form of a texture-mapped 3D polygonal mesh. Texture mapping the mesh is a non-trivial problem, however, we did not focus on this in our method. We have used a simple method to reconstruct the appearance at each point on the surface. Each point is projected into all cameras, a 3-channel intensity histogram is constructed. The histogram votes are weighted by a guassian function of the difference between the measured depth and the heightmap model's depth, which helps to remove the influence of occluders. The final color is the per-channel median and is easily obtained from the histograms.

Figure 4 shows the improvement gained by using multiple layers in the heightmap. Overhanging structures are recovered while the clean and compact nature of the reconstruction is preserved. Figures 5 show the results of the reconstructions from video. Figures 6 show the results of the reconstructions from photo collections.

Our system can process video at 13.33 Hz. Computing a 3-layer 100x100 heightmap with 100 height levels from 48 depthmaps takes only 69 ms to on the GPU. The other steps are not as fast as we did not focus as much on optimizing them. Converting the heightmap into a mesh takes 609 ms, and generating texture maps takes 1.57 seconds. The total time for processing a heightmap is 2.25 seconds. However, heightmaps only need to be computed about every 30 frames of video. (All frames are used for depthmaps.) Therefore our system can process video at 13.33 frames per second. Reconstructing photo collections is more

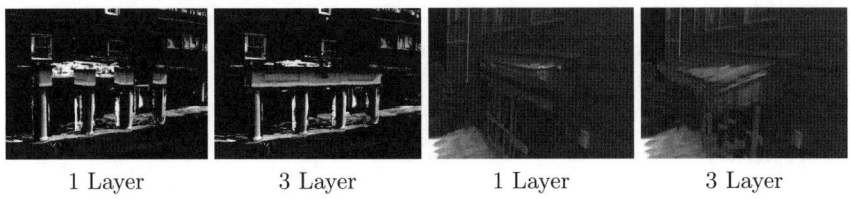

| 1 Layer | 3 Layer | 1 Layer | 3 Layer |

Fig. 4. 1-layer and 3-layer reconstructions

Fig. 5. 3D reconstructions from video

Original   Model   Model

Fig. 6. 3D reconstructions from internet photo collections

challenging. Each scene takes 20-30 minutes, and most of that time is spent computing NCC stereo.

5   Conclusion

We proposed a novel n-layer heightmap depthmap fusion providing a natural way to enforce vertical facades while providing advantageous structure separation. The main advantage of the proposed approach is the generality of the modeled geometry. The regularization along the vertical direction allows the heightmap fusion to effectively suppress depth estimation noise. Our fusion is computationally efficient providing real-time computation. We demonstrated the proposed method on several challenging datasets downloaded from the Internet.

References

1. Cornelis, N., Leibe, B., Cornelis, K., Gool, L.V.: 3d urban scene modeling integrating recognition and reconstruction. IJCV (2008)
2. Früh, C., Jain, S., Zakohr, A.: Data processing algorithms for generating textured 3d building facade meshes from laser scans and camera images. IJCV (2005)
3. Pollefeys, M., et al.: Detailed real-time urban 3d reconstruction from video. Int. Journal of Computer Vision (IJCV) (2008)
4. Zebedin, L., Bauer, J., Karner, K., Bischof, H.: Fusion of feature- and area-based information for urban buildings modeling from aerial imagery. In: Forsyth, D., Torr, P., Zisserman, A. (eds.) ECCV 2008, Part IV. LNCS, vol. 5305, pp. 873–886. Springer, Heidelberg (2008)
5. Xiao, J., Quan, L.: Image-based street-side city modeling. In: Siggraph Asia (2009)
6. Gallup, D., Frahm, J.M., Pollefeys, M.: Piecewise planar and non-planar stereo for urban scene reconstruction. In: CVPR (2010)
7. Zach, C., Pock, T., Bischof, H.: A globally optimal algorithm for robust tv-l1 range image integration. In: ICCV (2007)
8. Snavely, N., Seitz, S.M., Szeliski, R.: Photo tourism: Exploring photo collections in 3d. In: SIGGRAPH, pp. 835–846 (2006)
9. Li, X., Wu, C., Zach, C., Lazebnik, S., Frahm, J.M.: Modeling and recognition of landmark image collections using iconic scene graphs. In: Forsyth, D., Torr, P., Zisserman, A. (eds.) ECCV 2008, Part I. LNCS, vol. 5302, pp. 427–440. Springer, Heidelberg (2008)
10. Agarwal, S., Snavely, N., Simon, I., Seitz, S.M., Szeliski, R.: Building Rome in a day. In: ICCV (2009)
11. Goesele, M., Snavely, N., Curless, B., Hoppe, H., Seitz, S.M.: Multi-view stereo for community photo collections. In: ICCV (2007)
12. Furukawa, Y., Curless, B., Seitz, S.M., Szeliski, R.: Towards internet-scale multi-view stereo. In: CVPR (2010)
13. Cornelis, N., Cornelis, K., Van Gool, L.: Fast compact city modeling for navigation pre-visualization. In: Computer Vision and Pattern Recognition (CVPR) (2006)
14. Furukawa, Y., Curless, B., Seitz, S.M., Szeliski, R.: Manhatten-world stereo. In: Proceedings IEEE CVPR (2009)
15. Sinha, S.N., Steedly, D., Szeliski, R.: Piecewise planar stereo for image-based rendering. In: Proceedings IEEE ICCV (2009)
16. Margaritis, D., Thrun, S.: Learning to locate an object in 3d space from a sequence of camera images. In: ICML (1998)
17. Pathak, K., Birk, A., Poppinga, J., Schwertfeger, S.: 3d forward sensor modeling and application to occupancy grid based sensor fusion. In: IROS (2007)
18. Guan, L., Franco, J.S., Pollefeys, M.: 3d object reconstruction with heterogeneous sensor data. In: 3DPVT (2008)
19. Furukawa, Y., Curless, B., Seitz, S.M., Szeliski, R.: Towards internet-scale multi-view stereo. In: CVPR (2010)
20. Merrell, P., Akbarzadeh, A., Wang, L., Mordohai, P., Frahm, J.M., Yang, R., Nister, D., Pollefeys, M.: Real-Time Visibility-Based Fusion of Depth Maps. In: Proceedings of International Conf. on Computer Vision (2007)
21. Szeliski, R.: Image alignment and stitching: A tutorial. Microsoft Research Technical Report (2005)
22. Cormen, T.H., Leisorson, C.E., Rivest, R.L., Stein, C.: Introduction to Algorithms. The MIT Press, Cambridge (2001)

Real-Time Dense Geometry from a Handheld Camera

Jan Stühmer[1,2], Stefan Gumhold[2], and Daniel Cremers[1]

[1] Department of Computer Science, TU München
[2] Department of Computer Science, TU Dresden

Abstract. We present a novel variational approach to estimate dense depth maps from multiple images in real-time. By using robust penalizers for both data term and regularizer, our method preserves discontinuities in the depth map. We demonstrate that the integration of multiple images substantially increases the robustness of estimated depth maps to noise in the input images. The integration of our method into recently published algorithms for camera tracking allows dense geometry reconstruction in real-time using a single handheld camera. We demonstrate the performance of our algorithm with real-world data.

1 Introduction

Reconstructing the geometry of the environment from a hand-held camera is among the classical topics in computer vision. While sparse reconstructions of a finite number of tracked points can easily be done in real-time [1,2], the fast computation of dense reconstructions from a moving camera remains an open challenge.

Traditionally there are two complementary approaches to estimating dense geometry, namely the reconstruction of depth maps (often called 2.5d reconstructions) from stereo image pairs and the reconstruction of full $3D$ structure from multiple images. While we have observed substantial advances in dense $3D$ reconstruction from multiple images, many of these approaches are to date not real-time capable [3,4]. Moreover, they typically require a larger number of around 30 calibrated images making them unsuited for live scene reconstructions from a single moving camera. On the other hand, there exist many approaches to reconstructing dense depth maps from pairs of images [5,6]. While these approaches were shown to provide excellent results on dense depth estimation, they are typically too computationally intense for real-time applications, moreover, they are rather noise sensitive since they only exploit two images.

In this paper, we propose a variational approach for computing dense depth maps from multiple images with real-time performance. The key idea is to adopt recently developed high-accuracy optic flow algorithms [7] to the problem of depth map estimation from multiple images. Depth maps are computed by sequential convex optimization by means of a primal-dual algorithm. In particular, we prove that the primal variables can be efficiently computed using a sophisticated thresholding scheme. To obtain optimal performance, the dense depth

M. Goesele et al. (Eds.): DAGM 2010, LNCS 6376, pp. 11–20, 2010.

maps are computed in coarse-to-fine-manner on the GPU while the camera co-ordinates are simultaneously computed on the CPU using recently developed algorithms. Our experiments demonstrate that the algorithm allows to compute dense high-quality depth maps from a moving camera in real-time. Moreover, our quantitative evaluation confirms that using multiple images substantially improves the noise-robustness of estimated depth maps.

After submission of this manuscript we became aware that the problem of reconstructing depth maps from a handheld camera was independently addressed in the recent work of Newcombe and Davisson [8]. In the latter work, the authors first estimate an optical flow field from consecutive images and subsequently use this flow field to update a depth map. In contrast, we propose a variational approach which directly provides a depth field. This seems more appropriate to us: Why estimate a 2D motion vector for each pixel, if - apart from the camera motion - the considered scene is static? One consequence of the proposed solution to directly determine the depth field is that our algorithm is real-time capable on a single graphics card whereas the approach of Newcombe and Davison needs several seconds per frame on two GPUs.

2   Robust Estimation of Depth Maps from Images

In Section 2.1 we introduce our mathematical framework for computing dense depth maps for the simpler case of two input images. In Section 2.2 we extend this formulation and introduce a novel variational approach for estimating depth maps from multiple images. In Section 2.3 we propose a primal-dual algorithm which substantially generalizes the one of Zach et al and which allows to efficiently minimize the proposed functional.

First we give an introduction to our notation. Let us assume a given set of gray value images $\{I_i : \Omega_i \to \mathbb{R}\}$ with $i \in \{0, \ldots, N\}$ that were taken from different viewpoints with the same camera. Let us further assume, that the corresponding camera poses (location and orientation of the camera) and the projection $\pi : \mathbb{R}^3 \to \mathbb{R}^2$ that projects from homogeneous coordinates to pixel coordinates are known. The depth map h, that should be estimated, is a scalar field which is defined with respect to the coordinate frame of one of the images. Let us denote this camera image without loss of generality as I_0 such that $h : \Omega_0 \to \mathbb{R}$ assigns a depth value to every pixel of I_0. By using homogeneous 2D coordinates $\mathbf{x} = (x_1, x_2, 1)^T \in \Omega_0$ we can express the position of each 3D surface point $\mathbf{X}$ of the depth map by multiplying the homogeneous 2D vector by the depth value: $\mathbf{X}(\mathbf{x}, h) := h(x_1, x_2) \cdot \mathbf{x}$.

Note that the above position vector is relative to the coordinate frame of I_0. The projection of such a 3D point $\mathbf{X}$ onto another image plane Ω_i can be achieved by $\pi(\exp(\hat{\xi}_i) \cdot \mathbf{X})$, where ξ_i is the camera pose for each image relative to the coordinate frame of I_0. The camera poses are given in so called *twist coordinates* $\xi \in \mathbb{R}^6$. The *hat-operator* transforms ξ_i such that the *twist* $\hat{\xi}_i \in se(3)$ gives the exponential coordinates of the rigid-body motion that transforms the coordinate frame of I_0 into the coordinate frame of I_i.

2.1   Stereo Estimation Using Two Images

Let us introduce our mathematical framework for the simplest case, when two images are provided. To estimate a heightmap h from these two images we propose the following variational formulation consisting of an L_1 data penalty term and an L_1 total variation (TV) regularization of the depth map

$$E(h) = \lambda \int_{\Omega_0} \left| I_1\big(\pi\big(\exp(\hat{\xi}_1)\,\mathbf{X}(\mathbf{x},h))\big)\big) - I_0\big(\pi(\mathbf{x})\big)\right| d^2\mathbf{x} + \int_{\Omega_0} |\nabla h|\, d^2\mathbf{x}, \quad (1)$$

where the data term $I_1\big(\pi\big(\exp(\hat{\xi}_1)\,\mathbf{X}(\mathbf{x},h))\big)\big) - I_0\big(\pi(\mathbf{x})\big)$ measures the difference of the image intensities of I_0 and the image intensities that are observed at the projected coordinates in I_1. Above data term is motivated by the *Lambertian* assumption, that the observed intensity is independent of the viewpoint as long as the same surface point is observed in both views. The TV-norm regularizer allows to preserve discontinuities in the depth map, e.g. at object boundaries, while the robust data term lowers the sensitivity towards outliers in cases where objects are invisible by occlusion or when the input images are affected with noise. In the following we will use the simplified notation $I_1(\mathbf{x},h)$ for $I_1\big(\pi\big(\exp(\hat{\xi}_1)\,\mathbf{X}(\mathbf{x},h))\big)\big)$.

We begin with a linearization of $I_1(\mathbf{x},h)$ by using the first order Taylor expansion, i.e.

$$I_1(\mathbf{x},h) = I_1(\mathbf{x},h_0) + (h - h_0)\frac{d}{dh}I_1(\mathbf{x},h)\Big|_{h_0} \quad (2)$$

where h_0 is a given depth map. The derivative $\frac{d}{dh}I_1(\mathbf{x},h)$ can be considered as a directional derivative in direction of a differential vector on the image plane that results from a variation of h It can be expressed as the scalar product of the gradient of $I_1(\mathbf{x},h)$ with this differential vector, i.e.

$$\frac{d}{dh}I_1(\mathbf{x},h) = \nabla I_1(\mathbf{x},h) \cdot \frac{d}{dh}\pi\big(\exp(\hat{\xi})\,\mathbf{X}(\mathbf{x},h)\big). \quad (3)$$

The differential vector mentioned above needs to be calculated with respect to the chosen camera model.

Using the linear approximation for $I_1(\mathbf{x},h)$ and by reordering the integrals the energy functional (Eq. 1) now reads

$$E(h) = \int_{\Omega_0}\Big\{\lambda\underbrace{\Big|I_1(\mathbf{x},h_0) + (h-h_0)\frac{d}{dh}I_1(\mathbf{x},h)\Big|_{h_0} - I_0(\mathbf{x})\Big|}_{\rho_1(\mathbf{x},h_0,h)} + |\nabla h|\Big\}\,d^2\mathbf{x}. \quad (4)$$

Though this energy functional is much simpler than the original functional (Eq. 1), the task of minimizing it is still difficult, because both the regularization term and the data term are not continuously differentiable.

We introduce an auxiliary function u that decouples the data term and the regularizer, leading to the following convex approximation of Eq. 4:

$$E_\theta = \int_\Omega \Big\{|\nabla u| + \frac{1}{2\theta}(u-h)^2 + \lambda\,|\rho_1(h)|\Big\}\,d^2\mathbf{x}, \quad (5)$$

where θ is a small constant and $\rho_1(h)$ denotes the current residual of the data term (by omitting the dependency on h_0 and $\mathbf{x}$). It is immediate to see that for $\theta \to 0$ the minimization of the above functional results in both h and u being a close approximation of each other.

This minimization problem can be solved efficiently in real-time by minimizing the data term with a simple thresholding scheme and using a primal dual algorithm for the minimization of the ROF energy [9].

2.2 Extension to Multiple Images

Let us now consider the case when multiple input images are given. In the previous section we formulate our energy model for the classical stereo task in case of two images. Compared to previous approaches that employ the epipolar constraint by using the fundamental matrix the main difference is that here we formulate the data term relative to the coordinate system of one specific view and use the perspective projection to map this coordinate system to the second camera frame. This makes it easy to incorporate the information from other views by simply adding up their data terms. We propose the following energy functional to robustly estimate a depth map from multiple images

$$E(h) = \lambda \int_\Omega \sum_{i \in \mathcal{I}(\mathbf{x})} |\rho_i(\mathbf{x}, h)| \, d^2\mathbf{x} + \int_\Omega |\nabla h| \, d^2\mathbf{x} \qquad (6)$$

where $\mathcal{I}(\mathbf{x})$ contains the indices of all images for which the perspective projection $\pi(\exp(\hat{\xi}_i) \cdot \mathbf{X}(\mathbf{x}, h))$ is inside the image boundaries. With $\rho_i(\mathbf{x}, h)$ we denote the residual of the linearized data term for image I_i

$$\rho_i(\mathbf{x}, h) = I_i(\mathbf{x}, h_0) + (h - h_0) I_i^h(\mathbf{x}) - I_0(\mathbf{x}), \qquad (7)$$

where $I_i^h(\mathbf{x})$ is a simplified notation for the derivative $\frac{d}{dh} I_i(\mathbf{x}, h) \Big|_{h_0}$.

By using the above functional we should expect two benefits. First of all algorithms using only two images are not able to estimate disparity information in regions that are occluded in the other view or simply outside of its image borders. The use of images from several different views should help in these cases because information from images where the object is not occluded can be used. The use of the L_1-norm in the data terms allows an increased robustness towards outliers in cases where objects are occluded. The second benefit of using multiple images is the increased signal to noise ratio that provides much better results when the input images are affected by noise, which is a typical property of image sequences acquired by webcams or consumer market camcorders.

This functional is more complicate to solve because the data term consists of the sum of absolute values of linear functions, that cannot be minimized using the simple thresholding scheme proposed in [7]. In [4] the authors extend the thresholding scheme to data terms of the form $\sum_i |x - b_i|$, with a set of constants $\{b_i \in \mathbb{R}\}$. Unfortunately the data term in the proposed functional is not of such form. Nevertheless, we will show in the next section that the thresholding concept can be generalized to a substantially larger class of functionals.

2.3   Generalized Thresholding Scheme

In this section we provide a substantial generalization of the thresholding scheme which also applies to multiple images and more sophisticated data terms.

We decouple the smoothness and data term by introducing an auxiliary function u and get the following convex approximation of Eq. 6:

$$E_\theta = \int_\Omega \left\{ |\nabla u| + \frac{1}{2\theta}(u - h)^2 + \lambda \sum_{i \in \mathcal{I}(\mathbf{x})} |\rho_i(\mathbf{x}, h)| \right\} d^2\mathbf{x}, \qquad (8)$$

The above functional is convex so an alternating descent scheme can be applied to find the minimizer of E_θ:

1. For h being fixed, solve

$$\min_u \int_\Omega \left\{ |\nabla u| + \frac{1}{2\theta}(u - h)^2 \right\} d^2\mathbf{x} \qquad (9)$$

This is the ROF energy for image denoising [10,9].

2. For u being fixed, solve

$$\min_h \int_\Omega \left\{ \frac{1}{2\theta}(u - h)^2 + \lambda \sum_{i \in \mathcal{I}(\mathbf{x})} |\rho_i(\mathbf{x}, h)| \right\} d^2\mathbf{x} \qquad (10)$$

This minimization problem can be solved point-wise.

A solution for the minimization of the the ROF energy, the first step in our alternating scheme, was proposed in [9], that uses a dual formulation of Eq. 9. For the convenience of the reader we reproduce the main results from [9].

Remark 1. The solution of Eq. 9 is given by

$$u = h - \theta \operatorname{div} \mathbf{p}, \qquad (11)$$

where $\mathbf{p} = (p_1, p_2)$ is a vector field and fulfills $\nabla(\theta \operatorname{div} \mathbf{p} - h) = |\nabla\theta \operatorname{div} \mathbf{p} - h|\mathbf{p}$, which can be solved by the following iterative fixed-point scheme:

$$\mathbf{p}^{k+1} = \frac{\mathbf{p}^k + \tau \nabla(\operatorname{div} \mathbf{p}^k - h/\theta)}{1 + \tau |\nabla(\operatorname{div} \mathbf{p}^k - h/\theta)|}, \qquad (12)$$

where $\mathbf{p}^0 = \mathbf{0}$ and the time step $\tau \le 1/8$.

The second step of the alternation scheme, Eq. 10, can be solved point-wise, but shows some difficulties as it is not continuously differentiable. Nevertheless we provide a closed-form solution by generalizing the thresholding concept to data terms of the form $\sum_i |a_i\, x - b_i|$.

By taking a look at Eq. 7 we see, that for fixed h_0 and $\mathbf{x}$ the residuals of the linearized data terms ρ_i can be expressed in the general form of linear functions, $\rho_i(\mathbf{x}, h) = a_i h + b_i$, with $a_i := I_i^h(\mathbf{x})$ and $b_i := I_i(\mathbf{x}, h_0) - h_0 I_i^h(\mathbf{x}) - I_0(\mathbf{x})$. The absolute valued functions $|\rho_i(h)|$ are differentiable with respect to h except at their critical points, where a function equals zero and changes its sign. Let us denote those critical points as

$$t_i := -\frac{b_i}{a_i} = -\frac{I_i(\mathbf{x}, h_0) - h_0 I_i^h(\mathbf{x}) - I_0(\mathbf{x})}{I_i^h(\mathbf{x})}, \qquad (13)$$

where $i \in \mathcal{I}(\mathbf{x})$.

At these points Eq. 9 is not differentiable, as the corresponding ρ_i changes its sign. Without loss of generality we can assume that $t_i \leq t_{i+1}$, i.e. we obtain a sorted sequence of $\{\rho_i : i \in \mathcal{I}(\mathbf{x})\}$, that is sorted by the values of their critical points. In order to avoid special cases we add $t_0 = -\infty$ and $t_{|\mathcal{I}(\mathbf{x})|+1} = +\infty$ to this sequence.

Proposition 1. *The minimizer of Eq. 10 can be found using the following strategy: If the stationary point*

$$h_1 := u - \lambda\theta \left(\sum_{i \in \mathcal{I}(\mathbf{x}):i \leq k} I_i^h(\mathbf{x}) - \sum_{j \in \mathcal{I}(\mathbf{x}):j > k} I_j^h(\mathbf{x}) \right) \qquad (14)$$

lies in the interior of (t_k, t_{k+1}) for some $k \in \mathcal{I}(\mathbf{x})$, then $h = h_1$. Else the minimizer of Eq. 10 can be found among the set of critical points:

$$h = \arg \min_{h_2 \in \{t_i\}} \left(\frac{1}{2\theta}(u - h)^2 + \lambda \sum_{i \in \mathcal{I}(\mathbf{x})} |\rho_i(\mathbf{x}, h_2)| \right). \qquad (15)$$

Proof. Eq. 10 is differentiable with respect to h in the interior of intervals (t_k, t_{k+1}). Let us assume that the stationary point

$$h_1 := u - \lambda\theta \sum_{i \in \mathcal{I}(\mathbf{x})} \left(\text{sgn}\left(\rho_i(\mathbf{x}, h_1)\right) I_i^h(\mathbf{x}) \right) \qquad (16)$$

exists and lies in the interior of the interval (t_k, t_{k+1}), then

$$\sum_{i \in \mathcal{I}(\mathbf{x})} \left(\text{sgn}\left(\rho_i(\mathbf{x}, h_1)\right) I_i^h(\mathbf{x}) \right) = \sum_{i \in \mathcal{I}(\mathbf{x}):t_i < h_1} I_i^h(\mathbf{x}) - \sum_{j \in \mathcal{I}(\mathbf{x}):t_j > h_1} I_j^h(\mathbf{x}) \quad (17)$$

$$= \sum_{i \in \mathcal{I}(\mathbf{x}):i \leq k} I_i^h(\mathbf{x}) - \sum_{j \in \mathcal{I}(\mathbf{x}):j > k} I_j^h(\mathbf{x}). \quad (18)$$

This stationary point exists, iff it stays in the interior of (t_k, t_{k+1}) for some k. If none of the proposed stationary points stays in the interior of its corresponding interval, the minimizer of Eq. 10 resides on the boundary of one of the intervals, i.e. it can be found among the set of critical points $\{t_i\}$. $\qquad \square$

3   Implementation

Because the linearization of the data term (Eq. 7) only holds for small displacements of the projected coordinates, the overall innovation of the depth map is limited. To overcome this, the energy minimization scheme is embedded into a coarse-to-fine approach: Beginning on the coarsest scale a solution h is computed. This solution is used as new point h_0 for the linearization on the next finer scale. By using this scheme we not only employ an iterative linearization, but also utilize the multi-scale approach to avoid convergence into local minima. When processing a consecutive sequence of input images, an initialization of the coarsest scale can be achieved by transforming the depth map computed in the preceding frame to the current camera pose, thus utilizing the sequential property of the input data.

We embedded our method into a recently published camera tracking approach, that allows tracking of a handheld camera in real-time [11]. An integral part of this camera tracker is the storage of *keyframes*. While the pose for the current camera image needs to be estimated in real-time, and thus contains a significant amount of noise in the pose estimation, the camera pose associated to each keyframe can be refined iteratively, leading to very accurate estimates for the keyframes. Instead of using subsequent images with noisy real-time pose estimates, our approach enables to estimate a depth map in a similar fashion to the strategy employed in the camera tracker, by estimating the depth map using the current camera image and the N closest keyframes to the current pose. By using the much better camera pose estimates of the keyframes, the amount of noise in the camera poses is minimized.

Fig. 1. Dense depth maps computed from images of a hand-held camera

4   Experimental Results

High-accuracy dense depth maps from a hand-held camera: The proposed algorithm allows to compute dense depth maps from a moving camera. Figure 1 shows the reconstruction result from 5 input images. In contrast to the commonly used structure-and-motion algorithms [1,2], the proposed method computes a dense geometry rather than the location of sparse feature points. Another example is given in Figure 2 that shows the reconstruction result of an office scene. Note the accurate reconstruction of small-scale details like the network cable.

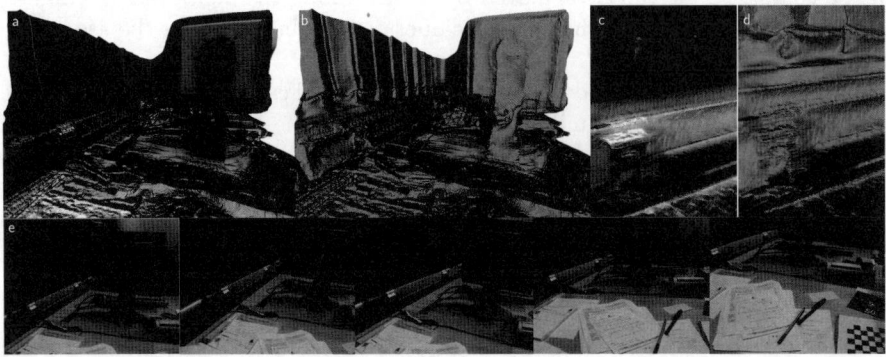

Fig. 2. Textured (a,c) and untextured geometry (b,d). Note the accurate reconstruction of small-scale details like the network socket and cords. (e) Images.

Realtime geometry reconstruction: The proposed primal-dual scheme can be efficiently parallelized on the GPU. The joint estimation of camera motion on the CPU allows for live dense reconstructions of the scene. Clearly there is a trade-off between speed and accuracy of the reconstructed geometry. Figure 3 shows reconstruction results from 5 input images with different parameter settings and for different resolutions of the resulting depth map. For evaluation we used a standard personal computer equipped with a NVidia GTX 480 graphics card and implemented our method using the CUDA framework. With high quality parameter settings, an accurate reconstruction of the scene can be computed at 1.8 frames per second (fps). A slightly less accurate reconstruction can be obtained at 11.3 fps. In both cases, the input images and reconstructed depth map have a resolution of 640×480 pixels. By reducing the resolution of the computed depth map, even realtime performance can be reached with 24 fps at a depth map resolution of 480×360. In the two latter cases, a slightly different numerical scheme is used: a number of 4 internal iterations is performed before the data is exchanged with other blocks of the parallelized implementation, resulting in small blocking artifacts visible in the reconstruction.

Table 1. Parameter settings for different frame rates

Quality Setting	High	Medium	Low
Pyramid Levels	24	10	7
Pyramid Scale-Factor	0.94	0.8	0.7
Iterations per Level	120	70	70
Internal Iterations	1	4	4
Frames per Second	1.8	11.3	24

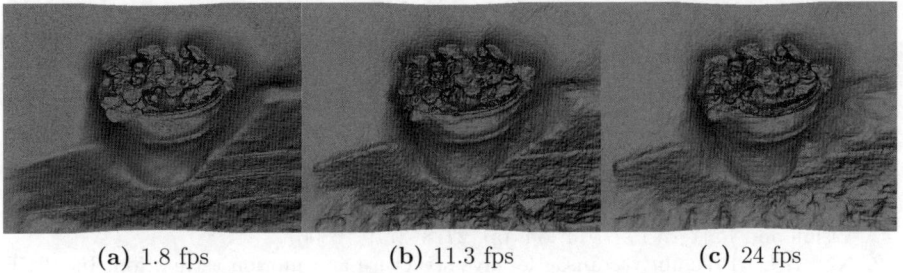

(a) 1.8 fps   (b) 11.3 fps   (c) 24 fps

Fig. 3. Trade-off between speed and accuracy

Quantitative evaluation of the noise robustness: In contrast to traditional stereo approaches, the proposed framework makes use of multiple images in order to increase the robustness of the reconstruction. Figure 4 shows the reconstruction error $\epsilon = \frac{\int_\Omega (h_\sigma - h_{\sigma=0})^2 \, d\mathbf{x}}{\int_\Omega h_\sigma^2 \, d\mathbf{x} + \int_\Omega h_{\sigma=0}^2 \, d\mathbf{x}}$ as a function of the noise level σ. In contrast to the two-frame formulation, the integration of multiple frames is substantially more robust to noise.

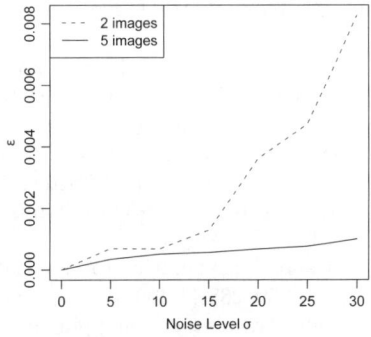

Fig. 4. Reconstruction error ϵ as a function of the noise level σ. The integration of multiple images is significantly more robust to noise.

5 Conclusion

We proposed a variational method to compute robust dense depth maps from a handheld camera in real-time. The variational approach combines a robust regularizer with a data term that integrates multiple frames rather than merely two. Experimental results confirm that the integration of multiple images substantially improves the noise robustness of estimated depth maps. The nonlinear and non-convex functional is minimized by sequential convex optimization. To this end, we adapt a primal-dual algorithm originally proposed for optical flow to the problem of depth map estimation, and show that the primal update can be solved in closed form by means of a sophisticated thresholding scheme. While the camera motion is determined on the CPU, the depth map is estimated on the GPU in a coarse-to-fine manner, leading to dense depth maps at a speed of 24 frames per second.

References

1. Jin, H., Favaro, P., Soatto, S.: Real-time 3-d motion and structure of point-features: A front-end for vision-based control and interaction. In: Int. Conf. on Computer Vision and Pattern Recognition, pp. 2778–2779 (2000)
2. Nister, D.: Preemptive ransac for live structure and motion estimation. In: IEEE Int. Conf. on Computer Vision, pp. 199–206 (2003)
3. Kolev, K., Cremers, D.: Continuous ratio optimization via convex relaxation with applications to multiview 3d reconstruction. In: CVPR, pp. 1858–1864. IEEE, Los Alamitos (2009)
4. Zach, C., Pock, T., Bischof, H.: A globally optimal algorithm for robust TV-L^1 range image integration. In: IEEE Int. Conf. on Computer Vision, Rio de Janeiro, Brazil. LNCS. IEEE, Los Alamitos (2007)
5. Pock, T., Schoenemann, T., Graber, G., Bischof, H., Cremers, D.: A convex formulation of continuous multi-label problems. In: Forsyth, D., Torr, P., Zisserman, A. (eds.) ECCV 2008, Part III. LNCS, vol. 5304, pp. 792–805. Springer, Heidelberg (2008)
6. Slesareva, N., Bruhn, A., Weickert, J.: Optic flow goes stereo: A variational method for estimating discontinuity-preserving dense disparity maps. In: Kropatsch, W.G., Sablatnig, R., Hanbury, A. (eds.) DAGM 2005. LNCS, vol. 3663, pp. 33–40. Springer, Heidelberg (2005)
7. Zach, C., Pock, T., Bischof, H.: A duality based approach for realtime TV-L1 optical flow. In: Hamprecht, F.A., Schnörr, C., Jähne, B. (eds.) DAGM 2007. LNCS, vol. 4713, pp. 214–223. Springer, Heidelberg (2007)
8. Newcombe, R.A., Davison, A.J.: Live dense reconstruction with a single moving camera. In: Int. Conf. on Computer Vision and Pattern Recognition (2010)
9. Chambolle, A.: An algorithm for total variation minimization and applications. J. Math. Imaging Vis. 20(1-2), 89–97 (2004)
10. Rudin, L.I., Osher, S., Fatemi, E.: Nonlinear total variation based noise removal algorithms. Phys. D 60(1-4), 259–268 (1992)
11. Klein, G., Murray, D.: Parallel tracking and mapping for small AR workspaces. In: Proc. Sixth IEEE and ACM International Symposium on Mixed and Augmented Reality (ISMAR 2007), Nara, Japan (November 2007)

From Single Cameras to the Camera Network: An Auto-Calibration Framework for Surveillance

Cristina Picus, Branislav Micusik, and Roman Pflugfelder

Safety and Security Department
AIT Austrian Institute of Technology

Abstract. This paper presents a stratified auto-calibration framework for typical large surveillance set-ups including non-overlapping cameras. The framework avoids the need of any calibration target and purely relies on visual information coming from walking people. Since in non-overlapping scenarios there are no point correspondences across the cameras the standard techniques cannot be employed. We show how to obtain a fully calibrated camera network starting from single camera calibration and bringing the problem to a reduced form suitable for multi-view calibration. We extend the standard bundle adjustment by a smoothness constraint to avoid the ill-posed problem arising from missing point correspondences. The proposed framework optimizes the objective function in a stratified manner thus suppressing the problem of local minima. Experiments with synthetic and real data validate the approach.

1 Introduction

Camera networks in surveillance systems can easily count hundreds of cameras. The contextual information available within the network is currently not used in practice, as maintenance of an updated map turns out to be a very expensive procedure. Therefore the integration of information from single cameras occurs only locally and completely relies on the human operator. Automatic integration of contextual and geometric information on a large scale just from visual information would dramatically amplify the potential of such networks: not only maintenance would be much easier, but also the automation of surveillance tasks would profit of it. For reason of costs and efficiency, cameras are typically installed in sparse networks with *non-overlapping* fields of view and hence large visual gaps. The absence of point correspondences among camera views is a problem for calibrating the network in a first step and, as a consequence, tasks such as handovering of moving objects between cameras are much harder [1].

In this paper we introduce a framework which aims at an auto-calibration of *non-overlapping* cameras in surveillance scenario just by observing walking people, see Fig. 1. We start with the fully uncalibrated case without information neither about internal nor external camera parameters. Currently we do not deal with the trajectory association problem and always consider a single trajectory. We assume motion on a common ground-plane as it is often the case in realistic scenarios and synchronized video streams.

M. Goesele et al. (Eds.): DAGM 2010, LNCS 6376, pp. 21–30, 2010.

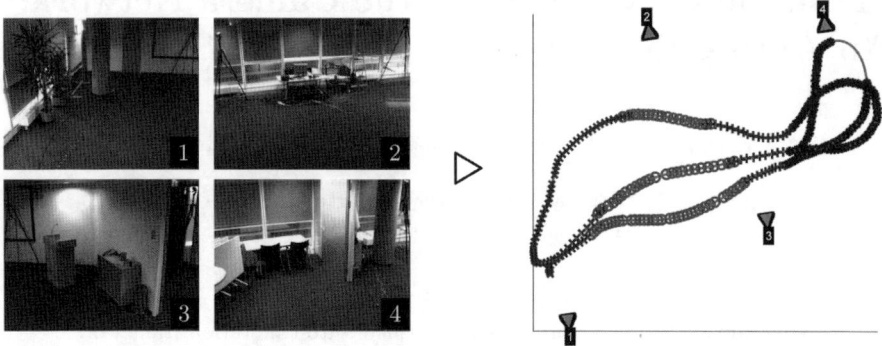

Fig. 1. Goal of the paper: calibrating non- or slightly-overlapping surveillance cameras from observing a moving object and expressing the cameras in one coordinate frame

As a result the cameras are expressed in one coordinate frame with estimated focal lengths, see Fig. 1. We purely rely on visual information, especially on detecting and tracking people. The reason is that in many cases, using special calibration targets or manually established fiducial points is not possible or is too impractical for non-experts. On the other hand we typically have a long video footage from each camera observing walking persons containing enough information to perform the calibration off-line without having an access to the cameras and without any knowledge of camera properties. The difficulty of the problem being solved here is underlined by the fact that there are *no point correspondences* across the camera views and hence *no standard calibration technique* known in Structure from Motion (SfM) community can be applied [2].

The contribution of the paper is three-fold and lies in introducing a stratified auto-calibration framework: *(i)* we propose to pre-calibrate the cameras independently from observing a frontally oriented person at different locations [3]. We recognized that this technique chooses a local coordinate system in such a way that it advantageously brings the problem of the following multi-view camera calibration to a reduced form where problem of local minima is greatly suppressed. *(ii)* we show that the method [4] for calibrating top view cameras at constant height from observing a moving object works for generally mounted cameras with varying focal lengths. The proposed stratified auto-calibration method allows bringing the problem very close to an optimal solution w.r.t. Gaussian image noise. *(iii)* we extend the standard bundle adjustment (BA) optimizing over all the parameters except focal length [5] by a smoothness constraint enforced on the trajectory. It allows solving the originally ill-posed problem when some points on the trajectory are not seen at all and when the most of the points are seen by at most one camera.

Our method is a first step towards a self-calibrating network that configures itself solely by detecting human activity in the environment. The reconstruction of the scene geometry provides the essential information needed to robustly solve visual surveillance tasks such as detection in single cameras [6] or multiple-camera tracking [7]. It reduces on the one hand computational burden when

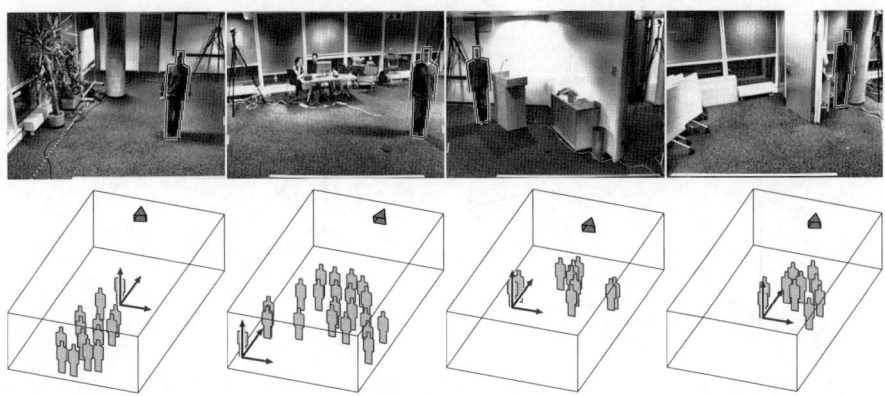

Fig. 2. The single camera pre-calibration step. Four cameras are independently pre-calibrated by [3] from an observed and automatically detected person (top row) standing at different locations. The calibrations are related to different local coordinate systems by $[\tilde{\mathbf{R}}^i, \tilde{\mathbf{t}}^i]$ shown in the bottom views of the 3D plots.

detecting and tracking people, and on the other hand it reduces significantly spurious false positive detections by enforcing the geometrical constraints.

Related Work. Calibration frameworks for overlapping cameras with known internal camera parameters can be traced back in literature to Lee et al. [8]. Planar trajectories in camera triplets are used to estimate the plane-induced inter-camera homographies, camera rotations and camera centers by non-linear trajectory alignment. The approach was further improved by successive dense alignment of the images [9] and additional vanishing points [10]. The most relevant framework for non-overlapping cameras assumes calibrated, top view cameras. Similar to BA, an objective function based on known planar trajectories can be formulated. Although the problem is ill-posed, additional regularization by assuming smooth trajectories allows estimation of camera rotation, camera centers and trajectory's location simultaneously. The approach was also augmented for moving cameras and unknown trajectory association [11] and has also been improved in efficiency [12] by splitting the solution search space into parts corresponding to visible and not visible parts of the trajectory. This paper basically extends this approach for uncalibrated cameras, general camera views and slightly non-planar trajectories to make it applicable in surveillance scenarios.

2 Network Calibration Framework

The calibration pipeline operates in three basic steps: first, a pre-calibration estimates the camera intrinsics and their calibration w.r.t. a local coordinate system [3]. Second, the local systems are aligned to a common reference frame using a Maximum A Posteriori (MAP) estimate of both camera parameters and

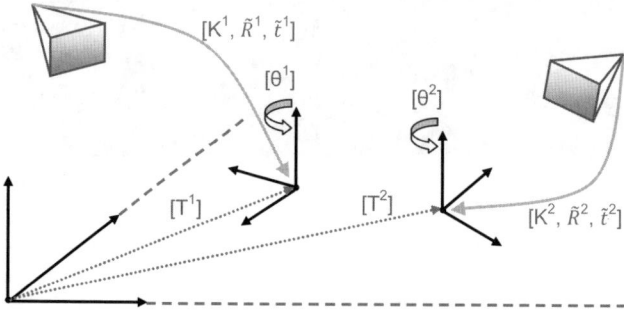

Fig. 3. The estimated camera parameters after pre-calibration $[\mathsf{K}^i, \tilde{R}^i, \tilde{\mathbf{t}}^i]$ refer to different local ground-plane reference systems, which can be aligned to the global reference system by a 2D translation and a rotation about the vertical axes $\mu^i = [\mathbf{T}^i, \theta^i]$.

trajectory after mapping on the ground-plane [4]. The combined solution of the pre-calibration and alignment step is used as initialization of a local optimization procedure which extends the standard BA [5] to non-overlapping cameras.

2.1   Pre-calibration

The pre-calibration delivers for each ith camera its focal length f^i, rotation $\tilde{R}^i$, and translation $\tilde{\mathbf{t}}^i$ w.r.t. a coordinate system placed on the ground plane with one axis perpendicular to it, as shown in Fig. 2. The coordinate system is given by one of the person positions.

We adopt the method for calibrating single cameras just by observing a person [3]. Typically one can automatically select frontal poses, e.g. by the HOG detector [13], possibly containing outliers and feed that into the method of [3]. The method has been shown to outperform techniques calibrating a single camera just from vanishing points [14] or similarly from human foot-head homology [15]. Further the method is advantageous in two aspects: first, it does not require any special calibration target, just a person standing at different locations in parallel and approximately frontal poses, therefore not necessarily parallel to the image plane. Second, coordinate systems of single cameras are related up to 1D rotation and 2D translation on the ground plane. That allows us to reduce the space of unknowns when trying to express all the cameras in one coordinate system shown in Fig. 3. For each camera we need then to search for 3 parameters (1 for rotation angle and 2 for translation) instead of 7 (1 for focal length, 3 for rotation angles and 3 for translation) in the general case. Note, that the translations $\tilde{\mathbf{t}}^i$ are already estimated with the correct scale if the same person is used for calibration of all the cameras.

2.2   Ground-Plane Alignment

The alignment of the local ground-plane coordinate systems is done using the information provided by a moving target in the image view and assumptions about its trajectory. The image point $\mathbf{u}$ is first projected to the point $\mathbf{y}$ onto the ground plane by $[\tilde{\mathbf{R}}^i, \tilde{\mathbf{t}}^i]$ estimated with the pre-calibration. Then we apply simultaneous trajectory reconstruction and network calibration [4]. Although this is thought for general positioning of the cameras given the local homography, the experiments in [4] are restricted to the top camera view scenario with all cameras at the same height. This is to avoid pre-calibration and the determination of the focal length, which however could potentially break the assumption of planarity of the 2D trajectory on which the method is based. In Sec. 3 we show that the method works even if the planarity condition is only approximately fulfilled.

Following Rahimi et al. we define a MAP criterion to determine the ground-plane trajectory $\mathbf{x}$ and camera parameters $\mu = [\mathbf{T}, \theta]$ as represented in Fig. 3

$$[\mathbf{x}^*, \mu^*] = \arg\max_{\mathbf{x},\mu} p(\mathbf{y}|\mathbf{x}, \mu)p(\mathbf{x})p(\mu). \qquad (1)$$

The first term in Eq. (1) is the likelihood of the target's measurements, while $p(\mathbf{x})$ and $p(\mu)$ are the a priori distribution of trajectory and camera parameters respectively. The likelihood criterion is based on minimization of the reprojection error. Contrary to standard BA in SfM, which always considers overlapping views, in the non-overlapping case when part of the trajectory is unseen the contribution from $p(\mathbf{x})$ is essential to gain enough constraints for solving the optimization. This is defined using a linear Gaussian Markov dynamics to describe the state transition of the target $\mathbf{x}_t \rightarrow \mathbf{x}_{t+1}$. Finally, the last term in Eq. (1) is used to fix one of the cameras at the origin of the global reference system.

The advantage of setting the non-linear optimization problem coming from Eq. (1) in a reduced parameter space is that in many cases it is possible to find a satisfying solution even with arbitrary initial conditions. This is not the case in the general optimization by BA. To the best of our knowledge, currently there are no alternative closed-form techniques for non-overlapping cameras to deal with the non-linearity coming from the rotation parameters [7]. We follow Rahimi et al. and set the initialization of all cameras and trajectory points to the origin of the reference systems.

2.3   Bundle-Adjustment for Non-overlapping Cameras Scenario

Bundle adjustment [5] as the standard optimization method is used as the last step of 3D reconstruction problems to find a local solution which is optimal under Gaussian measurements noise. The general reconstruction problem is to find, starting from an approximate estimate of the solution and given the temporal sequence of 3D points $\mathbf{X}_1 \ldots \mathbf{X}_T$ and the set of projections $\mathbf{u}_t^i$ of the point visible at time instance t in the camera i, the camera parameters and the 3D points that minimize the reprojection error between predicted and observed image points. This requires the solution of a non linear least square problem over a large parameter space. In the usual reconstruction at least some of the 3D points are observed from multiple views, which provide the necessary constraints to infer the reciprocal location of the cameras. In the non-overlapping camera scenario such constraints are missing. Analogue to the approach of Rahimi et al. for a planar trajectory we generalize BA to the non-overlapping case by using the smoothness constraint.

The data term is represented by the squared reprojection error computed using the Mahanalobis distance $\|.\|_{\Sigma_U}$ with measurement covariance Σ_U

$$d_U^2 = \sum_t \sum_i \delta(i,t) \left\| \mathbf{u}_t^i - \lambda \mathsf{K}^i \left[\mathsf{R}^i \ \mathbf{t}^i \right] \mathbf{X}_t \right\|_{\Sigma_U}^2. \tag{2}$$

Here λ stands for the scale and K, R and $\mathbf{t}$ for the camera intrinsic calibration matrix, the rotation and translation w.r.t. the world coordinate system [2], the latter derived by composing the local $\tilde{\mathsf{R}}^i$ and $\tilde{\mathbf{t}}^i$ with the parameters from the plane alignment $[\mathbf{T}^i, \theta^i]$. The indicator function $\delta(i,t)$ takes the value 1 at times t in which the target is detected in camera i, otherwise 0. In the implementation we parametrize the rotations in terms of unit quaternions, as they are known to have a more stable numerical behavior than Euler angles [16]. Smoothness is enforced on the trajectory by minimizing the second derivative

$$\|\mathbf{X}_{t+1} - 2\mathbf{X}_t + \mathbf{X}_{t-1}\|_2 \to 0. \tag{3}$$

Given the temporal sequence of 3D points $\mathbf{X} = [\mathbf{X}_1 \ldots \mathbf{X}_T]^\top$, the smoothness term corresponding to the temporal constraint is defined as

$$d_X^2 = \mathbf{X}^T \mathsf{G}^T \mathsf{G} \mathbf{X}, \tag{4}$$

where G is defined as the stack over all time stamps of the matrices G_t

$$\mathsf{G}_t = \sqrt{\Sigma_X^{-1}} [0_{3\times3}, \ldots, \underbrace{\mathbf{I}_{3\times3}}_{t-1}, \underbrace{-2\mathbf{I}_{3\times3}}_{t}, \underbrace{\mathbf{I}_{3\times3}}_{t+1}, \ldots, 0_{3\times3}]. \tag{5}$$

with smoothness covariance Σ_X. Finally, the minimization problem w.r.t. $\mathbf{X}$, the camera rotations $\mathsf{R} = \{\mathsf{R}^i\}$ and translations $\mathbf{t} = \{\mathbf{t}^i\}$ is defined by the sum of the data and smoothness terms

$$[\mathbf{X}^*, \mathsf{R}^*, \mathbf{t}^*] = \arg\min_{\mathbf{X}, \mathsf{R}, \mathbf{t}} d_U^2(\mathbf{X}, \mathsf{R}, \mathbf{t}) + d_X^2(\mathbf{X}). \tag{6}$$

The covariance matrices of the data and smoothness terms are the model parameters. We use diagonal matrices and set the variance associated to the data term a few orders of magnitude smaller than that of the smoothness term. Therefore the minimization of the reprojection error is the leading criterion of the reconstruction if points are observed in at least one image view and the smoothness constraint is the only criterion when observations are missing.

3   Experiments

To establish the limits of the approach for camera calibration a set of experiments on both synthetic and real data is carried out.

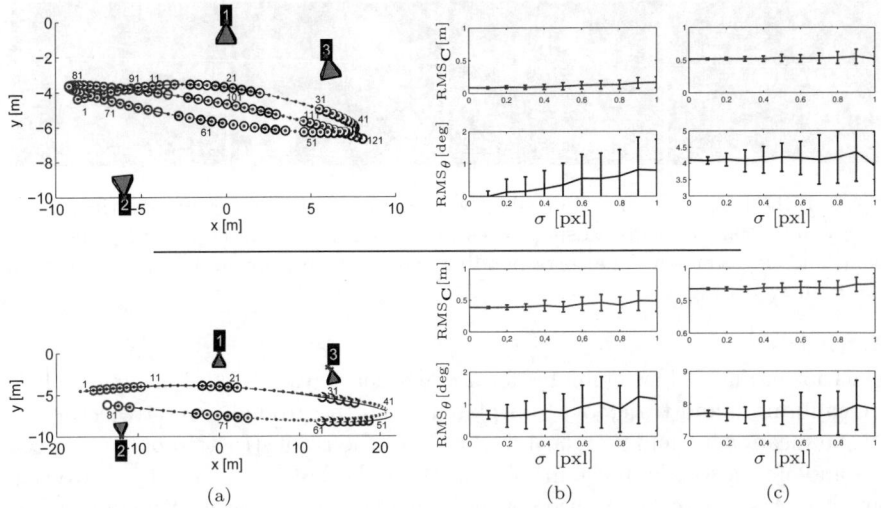

Fig. 4. Estimating camera parameters $[\mathbf{T}^i, \theta^i]$ and trajectory reconstruction for slightly (top) and largely (bottom) non-overlapping synthetic camera setup. (a) Top-view of the reconstructions. The true and estimated camera centers are shown by red crosses connected by red lines. The true and reconstructed trajectories are plotted by a blue line and connected red dots respectively. Circles mark the points observed by the cameras. (b) The RMS error on camera center localization and angle estimation vs. image noise level. (c) The same but with 3D noise added to the trajectory.

Synthetic Data. We emulate a three camera scenario, each camera observing a part of a synthetic spline curve located in the $z = 0$ plane. The quality of the reconstruction is strongly influenced by deviations of the trajectory from the Markov dynamics used to model it.

We evaluate the quality of calibration by ground-plane alignment in two realizations of the synthetic scenario, represented in the first column (a) of Fig. 4. In the first case, called slightly non-overlapping, the gap between the field of view of the cameras is of one up to few meters, while in the second case distances are about 5 to 10 meters. Camera centers and rotations are known up to translation and rotation on the ground-plane $[\mathbf{T}^i, \theta^i]$. Fig. 4 shows qualitatively a good agreement between ground-truth and reconstruction, even though in the second example the sharp turn is reproduced with less accuracy than other parts of the trajectory because it falls outside the field of view.

We evaluate the camera localization, which is the most relevant cue in surveillance applications, by computing average and standard deviation of the RMS error for different realization of the same trajectory, obtained by adding a Gaussian noise to the trajectory points observed in the camera views. This noise emulates the noisy detections in the image data. Each trajectory is sampled 50 times for each noise level with standard deviation between 0 and 1 pixel. Moreover, we compare the two cases with and without a uniform noise added to the 3D trajectory. A 3D noise of standard deviation $\sigma = 20$ cm and 40 cm is added to the two

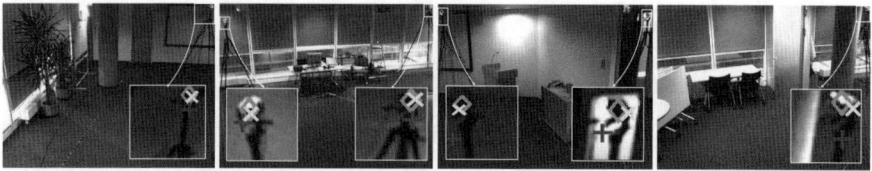

Fig. 5. LED-light experiment in a slightly overlapping case. '◊' ground-truth epipoles, '+' projected camera centers using the estimated parameters after ground-plane alignment, and '×' after BA. The corresponding camera calibration and trajectory estimation is shown in Fig. 1.

scenarios in Fig. 4. This emulates for a real scenario the effect of inaccurate local pre-calibration and trajectory non-planarity on the ground-plane trajectory.

The mean value and standard deviation of the reconstruction of camera centers and of rotations is shown in columns (b) and (c) of Fig. 4. For almost overlapping cameras, the reconstruction of the camera centers is, even with added Gaussian noise, in the range of 10 cm. The error increases in the full non-overlapping case to about 50 cm. The estimate of the error on the angle is comparable in the two scenarios, in the range up to 2 degrees without 3D noise and up to 9 degrees with added 3D noise.

Real Data. In the real experiments we consider the full pipeline in a setup equivalent to the almost overlapping scenario of the synthetic experiment. The full calibration uses detections from a moving LED-light source, although in this step a head-shoulder detector could be used instead. We choose the LED-light in order to find the upper limits of accuracy of our method independently of the precision of the detector. However in generating the trajectory no special attention was paid in having it perfectly planar. Therefore, although the detection of the LED-light source is sub-pixel accurate, the up and down motion of the human hand holding the light partially reproduces the inaccuracy of the detector.

Fig. 1 shows the indoor scenario made up of four cameras. We measure with a laser based device the distance between camera centers $\mathbf{C}$ with a precision of ± 10 cm. The fields of view overlap in order to be able to mark manually the epipoles. An epipole e is related to the estimated parameters by $e = -\mathbf{KRC}$. Epipoles are used as ground-truth giving implicitly information about rotations and camera centers. The cameras have a resolution of 640×480 pxl and are synchronized by an external trigger. The lens distortion is negligible as we used $1/2''$ normal lens with $1/3''$ cameras. The LED-light spots are automatically detected with subpixel precision. Few detections fall in the overlap area between the cameras.

We perform two experiments: in the first one we include detections in the overlap area while in the second one we eliminate them manually, in order to fall into the slightly non-overlapping scenario equivalent to the first case in Fig. 4. For the overlapping case, the full reconstruction after BA is shown in Fig. 1. The

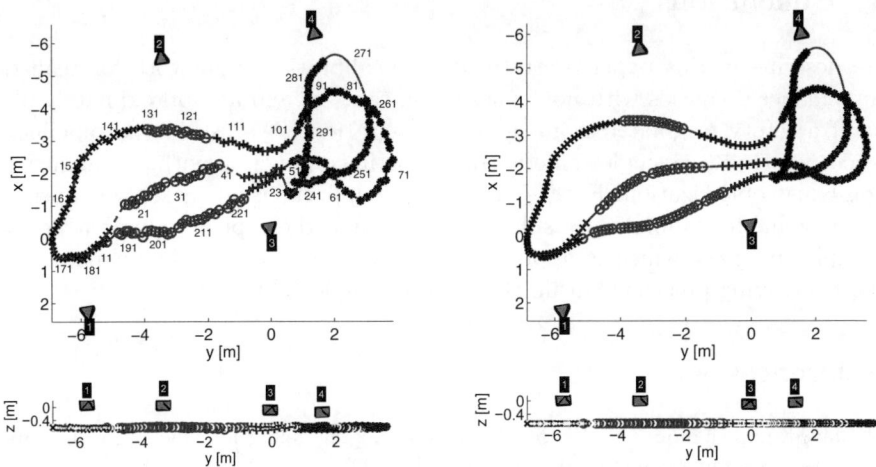

Fig. 6. LED-light experiment in a fully non-overlapping case. Top- and side-views of camera calibrations and trajectory reconstruction before (left) and after (right) bundle adjustment.

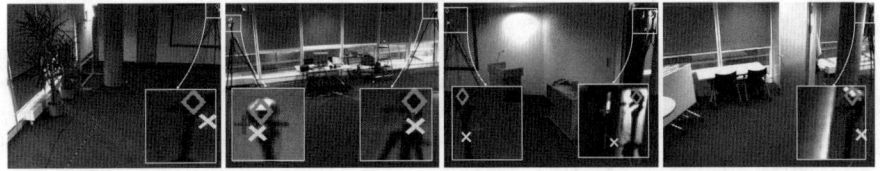

Fig. 7. Epipole analysis for non-overlapping case from Fig. 6. See caption of Fig. 5.

target detections are mapped by the local homographies to a noisy trajectory on the ground plane. As the ground-plane alignment enforces planarity of the reconstructed 3D trajectory, it is not able to match continuously the trajectory from one camera to the other and moreover the reconstructed trajectory is noisy. The result of the last optimization step in Fig. 1 is instead a smooth trajectory which is as expected slightly non planar. Moreover, the corrections of the BA in this scenario improves noticeably the estimate of the epipoles, as shown in Fig. 5. The average error on the estimated distance between the cameras is about 50 cm.

Reconstruction in the non-overlapping scenario is shown in Fig. 6. There is a good qualitative agreement of both experiments in terms of the reconstructed trajectory and camera centers. However, the epipoles are estimated with less accuracy and the BA is not able to improve the result of the ground-plane alignment, Fig. 7. The reason for that is evident: even with few points in the overlapping area, triangulation provides stronger support to the correct solution then the smoothness constraint for the non-overlapping case.

4   Conclusions

We describe in this paper a stratified auto-calibration framework for realistic surveillance scenarios with non-overlapping cameras and an approximately planar trajectory originated from human observations. We use in the pipeline a recently introduced single camera calibration in conjunction with an augmented non-linear optimization. For the method to support visual tasks, we expected an error in the calibration result not larger than the typical volume a person occupies in space which is approximately $1\,\mathrm{m} \times 1\,\mathrm{m} \times 2\,\mathrm{m}$. The experiments show satisfying precision within this limit of applicability.

References

1. Javed, O., Shafique, K., Shah, M.: Appearance modeling for tracking in multiple non-overlapping cameras. In: Proc. CVPR (2005)
2. Hartley, R.I., Zisserman, A.: Multiple View Geometry in Computer Vision. Cambridge University Press, Cambridge (2004)
3. Micusik, B., Pajdla, T.: Simultaneous surveillance camera calibration and foot-head homology estimation from human detections. In: Proc. CVPR (2010)
4. Rahimi, A., Dunagan, B., Darrell, T.: Simultaneous calibration and tracking with a network of non-overlapping sensors. In: Proc. CVPR (2004)
5. Triggs, B., McLauchlan, P., Hartley, R., Fitzgibbon, A.: Bundle adjustment - a modern synthesis. In: Triggs, B., Zisserman, A., Szeliski, R. (eds.) ICCV-WS 1999. LNCS, vol. 1883, pp. 298–375. Springer, Heidelberg (2000)
6. Hoiem, D., Efros, A.A., Hebert, M.: Putting objects in perspective. In: Proc. CVPR (2006)
7. Pflugfelder, R., Bischof, H.: Localization and trajectory reconstruction in surveillance cameras with non-overlapping views. PAMI 32(4), 709–721 (2009)
8. Lee, L., Romano, R., Stein, G.: Monitoring activities from multiple video streams: Establishing a common coordinate frame. PAMI 22(8), 758–767 (2000)
9. Stein, G.: Tracking from multiple view points: Self-calibration of space and time. In: Proc. CVPR. (1999)
10. Jaynes, C.: Multi-view calibration from planar motion trajectories. Image and Vision Computing (IVC) 22(7), 535–550 (2004)
11. Sheikh, Y., Li, X., Shah, M.: Trajectory association across non-overlapping moving cameras in planar scenes. In: Proc. CVPR (2007)
12. Rudoy, M., Rohrs, C.E.: Simultaneous sensor calibration and path estimation. In: IEEE Asilomar Conf. on Signals, Systems, and Computers (2006)
13. Dalal, N., Triggs, B.: Histograms of oriented gradients for human detection. In: Proc. CVPR (2005)
14. Lv, F., Zhao, T., Nevatia, R.: Self-calibration of a camera from video of a walking human. In: Proc. ICPR (2002)
15. Krahnstoever, N., Mendonca, P.R.S.: Bayesian autocalibration for surveillance. In: Proc. ICCV, pp. 1858–1865 (2005)
16. Lourakis, M.A., Argyros, A.: SBA: A Software Package for Generic Sparse Bundle Adjustment. ACM Trans. Math. Software 36(1), 1–30 (2009)

Active Self-calibration of Multi-camera Systems

Marcel Brückner and Joachim Denzler

Chair for Computer Vision
Friedrich Schiller University of Jena
{marcel.brueckner,joachim.denzler}@uni-jena.de

Abstract. We present a method for actively calibrating a multi-camera system consisting of pan-tilt zoom cameras. After a coarse initial calibration, we determine the probability of each relative pose using a probability distribution based on the camera images. The relative poses are optimized by rotating and zooming each camera pair in a way that significantly simplifies the problem of extracting correct point correspondences. In a final step we use active camera control, the optimized relative poses, and their probabilities to calibrate the complete multi-camera system with a minimal number of relative poses. During this process we estimate the translation scales in a camera triangle using only two of the three relative poses and no point correspondences. Quantitative experiments on real data outline the robustness and accuracy of our approach.

1 Introduction

In the recent years multi-camera systems became increasingly important in computer vision. Many applications take advantage of multiple cameras observing a scene. Multi-camera systems become even more powerful if they consist of *active* cameras, i. e. pan-tilt zoom cameras (Fig. 1). For many applications, however, the (active) multi-camera system needs to be calibrated, i. e. the intrinsic and extrinsic parameters of the cameras have to be determined. Intrinsic parameters of a camera can be estimated using a calibration pattern [1] or camera self-calibration methods for a rotating camera [2,3]. The focus of this paper is on (active) extrinsic calibration which consists of estimating the rotation and translation of each camera relative to some common world coordinate system.

Classical methods for extrinsic multi-camera calibration need a special calibration pattern [1] or user interaction like a moving LED in a dark room [4,5]. From a practical point of view, however, a pure self-calibration is most appealing. Self-calibration in this context means that no artificial landmarks or user interaction are necessary. The cameras estimate their position only from the images they record. An example for self-calibration of a *static* multi-camera system is the work of Läbe and Förstner [6]. Given several images they extract point correspondences and use these to estimate the relative poses. Another example is the graph based calibration method proposed by Bajramovic and Denzler [7] which considers the uncertainty of the estimated relative pose of each camera pair. However, both methods are designed for static cameras and do not use the benefits of active camera control.

M. Goesele et al. (Eds.): DAGM 2010, LNCS 6376, pp. 31–40, 2010.
© Springer-Verlag Berlin Heidelberg 2010

Fig. 1. A multi-camera system (left) consisting of six pan-tilt zoom cameras (white circles). The cameras are mounted near the intersection of the pan and tilt axes (right).

Sinha and Pollefeys [8] suggest a method where each pan-tilt zoom camera builds a high resolution panorama image. These images are used for relative pose estimation. However, these huge images can contain many ambiguities which affect the extraction of correct point correspondences. The calibration method of Chippendale and Tobia [9] defines an observer camera which searches for the continuously moving other cameras. If the observer spots some other camera the relative pose between the two cameras is extracted by detecting the circle shape of the camera lens and tracking some special predefined camera movements. The applicability and accuracy of this method highly depends on the distance between the cameras.

One of the biggest problems in extrinsic camera calibration is extracting *correct* point correspondences between the camera pairs. This problem is called wide baseline stereo and several approaches can be found in the literature [10,11]. However, if the cameras have very different viewpoints on a scene, projective influences and occlusions complicate or make it impossible to establish correct point correspondences. Active cameras could use rotation and zoom to reduce these projective influences.

In this paper, we present a method which uses active camera control to calibrate a multi-camera system consisting of pan-tilt zoom cameras. After an initial coarse calibration which uses the common field of view detection of Brückner et al. [12] to reduce ambiguities in the point correspondence detection, the best relative pose for each camera pair is selected based on its probability. Hence we present an image based probability distribution for relative poses. Given the initial poses, each camera pair rotates and zooms in a way that the points of view of the two cameras are very similar. The resulting similar camera images significantly simplify the problem of establishing new point correspondences which are used to reestimate the relative poses. In a final step we use the relative poses and their probabilities to calibrate the complete multi-camera system from a minimal set of relative poses. In order to estimate the scale factors of the relative poses in a camera triangle, we use only two of the three relative poses and we do not need any triple point correspondences. Instead we use active camera control and our image based probability distribution for relative poses. This reduces the number of relative poses needed for the complete calibration and totally avoids outlier point correspondences. The remainder of this paper is organized as follows: in Section 2 we introduce some basics and notation. Our method is described in Section 3. In Section 4 we present and discuss our experiments. Conclusions are given in Section 5.

2 Basics

2.1 Camera Model and Relative Pose between Cameras

A world point $\boldsymbol{X}_w$ is projected to the image point $\boldsymbol{x} \overset{\text{def}}{=} \boldsymbol{K}\boldsymbol{R}_{ptu}\left(\boldsymbol{R}_i\boldsymbol{X}_w + \boldsymbol{t}_i\right)$, where $\boldsymbol{R}_i, \boldsymbol{t}_i$ are the extrinsic camera parameters (rotation and translation), $\boldsymbol{K}$ is the pinhole matrix [13] and $\boldsymbol{R}_{ptu}$ is the rotation of the pan-tilt unit. We assume the pan and tilt axes to be identical to the Y and X axes of the camera coordinate system, respectively. Throughout the paper we use image points which are normalized with respect to the camera and pan-tilt rotation $\tilde{\boldsymbol{x}} \overset{\text{def}}{=} \boldsymbol{R}_{ptu}^{-1}\boldsymbol{K}^{-1}\boldsymbol{x}$. From this point on, when talking about the camera orientation and position we actually mean $\boldsymbol{R}_i, \boldsymbol{t}_i$ with no pan-tilt rotation $\boldsymbol{R}_{ptu} = \boldsymbol{I}$. The relative pose between two cameras i and j is defined as $\boldsymbol{R}_{i,j} \overset{\text{def}}{=} \boldsymbol{R}_j\boldsymbol{R}_i^{-1}$ and $\boldsymbol{t}_{i,j} \overset{\text{def}}{=} \boldsymbol{t}_j - \boldsymbol{R}_j\boldsymbol{R}_i^{-1}\boldsymbol{t}_i$.

2.2 Common Field of View Detection

Common field of view detection consists of deciding which image pairs show a common part of the world. We will briefly describe the probabilistic method of Brückner et al. [12] which gave the best results in their experiments.

Given two camera images, the difference of Gaussian detector [11] is used to detect interest points $\mathcal{C}_i = \{\tilde{\boldsymbol{x}}_1, \ldots, \tilde{\boldsymbol{x}}_n\}$ and $\mathcal{C}_j = \{\tilde{\boldsymbol{x}}_1', \ldots, \tilde{\boldsymbol{x}}_{n'}'\}$. For each point $\tilde{\boldsymbol{x}}_i$, the SIFT descriptor $\mathbf{des}(\tilde{\boldsymbol{x}}_i)$ is computed [11]. These descriptors are used to construct a conditional correspondence probability distribution for each $\tilde{\boldsymbol{x}}_i$

$$p\left(\tilde{\boldsymbol{x}}_j' \mid \tilde{\boldsymbol{x}}_i\right) \propto \exp\left(-\frac{d_d^{i,j} - d_N(\tilde{\boldsymbol{x}}_i)}{\lambda_d\,d_N(\tilde{\boldsymbol{x}}_i)}\right) , \tag{1}$$

where λ_d is the inverse scale parameter of the exponential distribution, $d_d^{i,j} = \mathrm{dist}(\mathbf{des}(\tilde{\boldsymbol{x}}_i), \mathbf{des}(\tilde{\boldsymbol{x}}_j'))$ is the Euclidean distance between the descriptors of the points $\tilde{\boldsymbol{x}}_i$ and $\tilde{\boldsymbol{x}}_j'$, and $d_N(\tilde{\boldsymbol{x}}_i) = \min_j(d_d^{i,j})$ denotes the distance of the nearest neighbor of the point $\tilde{\boldsymbol{x}}_i$. Each of the resulting conditional probability distributions $p(\tilde{\boldsymbol{x}}_j' \mid \tilde{\boldsymbol{x}}_i)$ has to be normalized such that $\sum_{\tilde{\boldsymbol{x}}_j' \in \mathcal{C}_j} p(\tilde{\boldsymbol{x}}_j' \mid \tilde{\boldsymbol{x}}_i) = 1$ holds.

The conditional probability distributions are used to calculate the normalized joint entropy which is defined as

$$H(\mathcal{C}_i, \mathcal{C}_j) \overset{\text{def}}{=} -\frac{1}{\eta} \sum_{\tilde{\boldsymbol{x}}_i \in \mathcal{C}_i} \sum_{\tilde{\boldsymbol{x}}_j' \in \mathcal{C}_j} p(\tilde{\boldsymbol{x}}_i)p\left(\tilde{\boldsymbol{x}}_j' \mid \tilde{\boldsymbol{x}}_i\right) \log\left(p(\tilde{\boldsymbol{x}}_i)p\left(\tilde{\boldsymbol{x}}_j' \mid \tilde{\boldsymbol{x}}_i\right)\right) , \tag{2}$$

where $\eta = \log(nn')$ is the maximum joint entropy and $p(\tilde{\boldsymbol{x}}_i)$ is a uniform distribution if no prior information about the interest points is available. A low joint entropy $H(\mathcal{C}_i, \mathcal{C}_j)$ indicates similar images. For further details the reader is referred to [12].

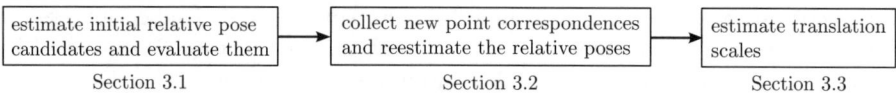

Fig. 2. The three steps of our multi-camera calibration method. Each step is described in the indicated Section.

3   Active Multi-camera Calibration

We calibrate an active multi-camera system consisting of c pan-tilt zoom cameras. For each camera the intrinsic parameters for different zoom steps are assumed to be known. Our calibration method consists of three steps which are illustrated in Fig. 2: an initial relative pose estimation with an evaluation of the relative poses, an optimization of these relative poses and a final estimation of the translation scale factors. Each step uses active camera control in a different way and to a different extent.

3.1   Initial Relative Pose Estimation and Evaluation

Given the intrinsic parameters, each camera records as many images as necessary to cover its complete environment. Now each camera pair searches for image pairs sharing a common field of view (Section 2.2). This search can be viewed as a prematching of point correspondences which considers the local environment of each interest point. Hence, it decreases the chance of ambiguities disturbing the point matching process. Between each of these image pairs point correspondences are extracted using the difference of Gaussian detector, the SIFT descriptor, the Euclidean distance, and the two nearest neighbors matching with rejection as proposed by Lowe [11].

Based on all extracted point correspondences of a camera pair we estimate the relative pose using the five point algorithm [14]. An important point is that the translation of these relative poses can only be estimated up to an unknown scale factor. For the complete calibration of a multi-camera system consistent scale factors for all translations have to be estimated.

In order to increase the robustness against outliers we embed the five point algorithm into a RANSAC scheme [15]. As distance measure we use the closest distance between two viewing rays

$$d_e^{i,j}\left(\tilde{\boldsymbol{x}}_i, \tilde{\boldsymbol{x}}_j'\right) \overset{\text{def}}{=} \min_{\lambda_i, \lambda_j} \left\| \left(\lambda_i \boldsymbol{R}_{i,j}\tilde{\boldsymbol{x}}_i + \frac{\boldsymbol{t}_{i,j}}{\|\boldsymbol{t}_{i,j}\|_2}\right) - \lambda_j \tilde{\boldsymbol{x}}_j' \right\|_2 \quad \text{with} \quad \lambda_i, \lambda_j > 0 . \quad (3)$$

Since we normalize the translation to unit length, it is possible to define the inlier threshold relative to the camera distance. The scale factors λ_i and λ_j need to be positive which affects the direction of the viewing rays and is similar to the constraint of 3D points to lie in front of both cameras.

Instead of selecting a single best pose, we select the m_p best poses based on the number of inliers. Since most of these poses are quite similar, we additionally constrain the selection to take only relative poses that satisfy a minimum rotation difference θ_R and translation difference θ_t to the already selected relative poses.

Now, each camera pair i, j performs the following procedure for each of its m_p relative pose candidates. First, the two cameras are rotated in a way that they look into the same direction and their optical axes are aligned (or a setup as close as possible to this). Camera i has to look in the direction $-\boldsymbol{R}_{i,j}\boldsymbol{t}_{i,j}$ and camera j looks at $-\boldsymbol{t}_{i,j}$. From each of the resulting camera images interest points are extracted. Now, the cameras repeat the first step, but in the opposite direction. The result of this procedure is a set of interest points $\mathcal{C}_i$ and $\mathcal{C}_j$ for each of the two cameras i and j. Given these interest point sets we want to evaluate the relative pose candidate. Therefore we calculate the probability

$$p\left(\boldsymbol{R}_{i,j}, \boldsymbol{t}_{i,j}\right) \propto \sum_{\tilde{\boldsymbol{x}}_i \in \mathcal{C}_i} \sum_{\tilde{\boldsymbol{x}}'_j \in \mathcal{C}_j} p\left(\boldsymbol{R}_{i,j}, \boldsymbol{t}_{i,j} \mid \tilde{\boldsymbol{x}}'_j, \tilde{\boldsymbol{x}}_i\right) p\left(\tilde{\boldsymbol{x}}'_j \mid \tilde{\boldsymbol{x}}_i\right) p\left(\tilde{\boldsymbol{x}}_i\right) , \qquad (4)$$

where $p\left(\boldsymbol{R}_{i,j}, \boldsymbol{t}_{i,j} \mid \tilde{\boldsymbol{x}}'_j, \tilde{\boldsymbol{x}}_i\right) \overset{\text{def}}{=} \exp\left(-d_e^{i,j}\left(\tilde{\boldsymbol{x}}_i, \tilde{\boldsymbol{x}}'_j\right) / \lambda_e\right)$ is an exponential distribution using the distance measure of (3) and the inverse scale parameter λ_e, $p\left(\tilde{\boldsymbol{x}}'_j \mid \tilde{\boldsymbol{x}}_i\right)$ is the conditional correspondence probability of (1) and $p\left(\tilde{\boldsymbol{x}}_i\right)$ is a uniform distribution if no prior information about the interest points is available. We note that this probability distribution can also be viewed as an image similarity measure which is based on image and geometric information. For each camera pair the relative pose candidate with the highest probability is selected.

3.2   Actively Optimizing the Relative Poses

Given the initial relative poses $\boldsymbol{R}_{i,j}, \boldsymbol{t}_{i,j}$ we optimize these poses by steering each camera pair in a way that it can easily establish new point correspondences.

As mentioned in Section 1, the biggest problem in finding correct point correspondences are projective influences. These influences depend on the relation between camera distance and scene distance and the difference in the viewing directions between the cameras. To reduce these influences we first rotate the two cameras in a way that their optical axes are aligned as described in Section 3.1. Additionally we search for the zoom step z of the backmost camera i with the highest image similarity by

$$\underset{z}{\operatorname{argmin}} \, H\left(\mathcal{C}_i\left(z\right), \mathcal{C}_j\right) , \qquad (5)$$

where $\mathcal{C}_i\left(z\right)$ is the interest point set of camera i at zoom step z and $H\left(\mathcal{C}_i, \mathcal{C}_j\right)$ is the normalized joint entropy (2). Again, this procedure is repeated for the opposite direction and yields in an interest point set for each camera. Similar to the initial calibration we extract point correspondences and use these to estimate the relative pose. Since we expect the descriptors of two corresponding points to be very similar due to the high similarity of the camera images, we choose a stricter rejection threshold for the two nearest neighbors matching than in the initial calibration. The estimated relative poses are evaluated as described in Section 3.1. For each camera pair the reestimated relative pose will only be used if it has a higher probability than the initial relative pose.

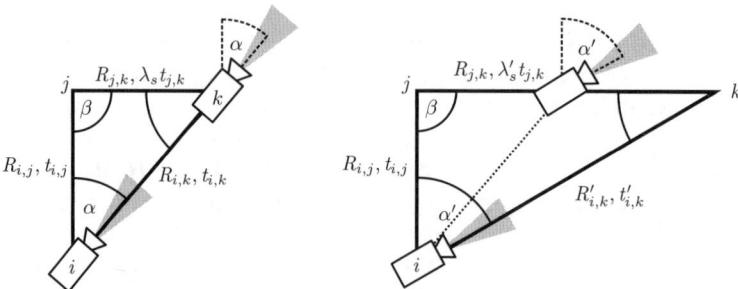

Fig. 3. A camera triangle (i, j, k). Cameras i and k rotate with angle α around the plane normal of the camera triangle. The scale λ_s depends on the angle α. There will be only one angle α where the optical axes of both cameras are aligned (left). At this point the triangle is correctly scaled. In all other cases the cameras will not look into the same direction and the scaling between the relative poses is incorrect (right).

3.3   Estimation of the Translation Scale Factors

At this point of our calibration we have for each camera pair i, j a relative pose $\boldsymbol{R}_{i,j}, \boldsymbol{t}_{i,j}$ and a probability of this pose $p\left(\boldsymbol{R}_{i,j}, \boldsymbol{t}_{i,j}\right)$. We do not know the correct scale factor of each translation. Scaling a relative pose always means scaling the translation. The final calibration can only be estimated up to one common scale factor [13]. In order to estimate the scale factors in a camera triangle, traditional methods use either all three relative poses in the triangle [6,7] or they try to establish point correspondences between all three camera images [13]. Our proposed method uses only two of the three relative poses and does not need any point correspondences at all. Instead we use active camera control and the probability distribution of (4). This reduces the number of required relative poses and totally avoids the chance of outlier point correspondences.

The final calibration is represented by a relative pose graph where each vertex represents a camera and each edge represents the relative pose between two cameras. Two vertices i and j are *simple connected* if there exists a path between them and they are called *triangle connected* if there exists a path of triangles between them [7]. The important difference is that only triangle connected subgraphs have a consistent scaling. In the beginning this graph has no edges. The following procedure is repeated until the graph is triangle connected.

We search for the camera triangle (i, j, k) which has the highest product of the probabilities of two of its relative poses $p\left(\boldsymbol{R}_{i,j}, \boldsymbol{t}_{i,j}\right) p\left(\boldsymbol{R}_{j,k}, \boldsymbol{t}_{j,k}\right)$ and no edge between the two vertices i and k. We now simultaneously estimate the third relative pose $\boldsymbol{R}_{i,k}, \boldsymbol{t}_{i,k}$ and all translation scale factors of the triangle. This is done by rotating camera i and k simultaneously around the plane normal of the camera triangle. In the beginning both cameras look into the direction defined by the translation $\boldsymbol{t}_{i,j}$. Now, we search for the rotation angle α that

$$\max_{\alpha} p\left(\boldsymbol{R}_{i,k}, \boldsymbol{t}_{i,k}\left(\alpha\right)\right) \text{ with } \boldsymbol{R}_{i,k} \stackrel{\text{def}}{=} \boldsymbol{R}_{j,k}\boldsymbol{R}_{i,j} \text{ and } \boldsymbol{t}_{i,k}\left(\alpha\right) \stackrel{\text{def}}{=} \boldsymbol{R}_{j,k}\boldsymbol{t}_{i,j} + \lambda_s \boldsymbol{t}_{j,k} ,$$

$$(6)$$

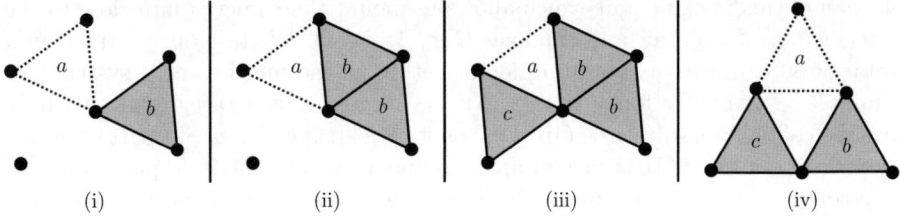

Fig. 4. Situations that can occur when inserting a camera triangle into the relative pose graph. The inserted triangle a has doted lines. Existing triangles are gray and share the same letter if they are in a triangle connected subgraph.

where we assume $\|t_{i,j}\|_2 = \|t_{j,k}\|_2$, the scale factor $\lambda_s \overset{\text{def}}{=} \sin(\alpha) / \sin(\Pi - \alpha - \beta)$ arises from the law of sines and $\beta \overset{\text{def}}{=} \arccos\left(\left(t_{i,j}^{\mathrm{T}} t_{k,j}\right) / \left(\|t_{i,j}\|_2 \|t_{k,j}\|_2\right)\right)$ is the angle between the translation vectors $t_{i,j}$ and $t_{k,j}$. The probability $p\left(R_{i,k}, t_{i,k}\left(\alpha\right)\right)$ is the probability of (4). There will be only one rotation angle α where the two cameras i and k look exactly into the same direction. For a clearer understanding the described relations are visualized in Fig. 3. The procedure is repeated in the opposite direction which results in estimating the inverse relative pose $R_{k,i}, t_{k,i}$. Again, we decide between these two poses based on their probability.

If the relative poses and scales of a camera triangle are known, it is inserted into the graph. We distinguish four different situations when inserting a new relative pose triangle into the relative pose graph. These four situations are illustrated in Fig. 4. The first situation is the trivial case of inserting a single triangle without conflicting edges. In the second case the inserted triangle shares a common edge with a triangle connected subgraph. This situation requires a rescaling of the triangle. The scale factor is defined by the relation between the translation lengths of the two common edges (the translation direction of these is identical). The third case creates a triangle connection between two prior simple connected parts of the graph. This requires rescaling the triangle and one of the two graph parts. The relative pose triangle in the fourth case cannot be inserted because it is impossible to correctly rescale the participating subgraphs. After inserting a camera triangle into the graph we need to check if two edges of some camera triangle are in the same triangle connected sub graph. In this case the relative pose of the third edge results from the poses of these two edges.

We note that several single camera triangles can be inserted before some of them build a triangle connected subgraph which reduces error propagation.

4   Experiments and Results

4.1   Experimental Setup

In our experiments we use a multi-camera system consisting of six Sony DFW-VL500 cameras with a resolution of 640×480 pixels. Each camera is mounted on a Directed Perception PTU-46-17.5 pan-tilt unit. We use a slightly modified version of this pan-tilt unit which allows to mount the camera quite close to the intersection of the pan and tilt axes (Fig. 1, right). We test our method on a total of 30 calibrations with 5 different setups of the multi-camera system. An example setup can be found in Fig. 1 (left). In order to generate ground truth we use the calibration software of the University Kiel [16] which uses a pattern based calibration method [1] with non-linear refinement. The intrinsic parameters of five zoom steps of each camera are estimated using the self-calibration method of [3]. The radial distortion of the images is corrected using the two parameter radial distortion model of [17]. As explained in Section 3.3, we can only calibrate up to a common scale factor. In order to compare our calibration with the ground truth, we scale our calibration result by the median of the factors $\|t_{i,j}^{\mathrm{GT}}\|_2/\|t_{i,j}\|_2$ of all camera pairs i, j, where $t_{i,j}^{\mathrm{GT}}$ is the ground truth translation.

For the common field of view detection we use $\lambda_d = 0.5$ and $m_r = 71$ as suggested by Brückner et al. [12]. Each camera records 20 images in order to cover its complete environment. For each camera pair we use the $m_i = 20$ image pairs with the highest image similarity. From each of these image pairs 25 point correspondences are extracted using a nearest neighbor rejection threshold of 0.8 as suggested by Lowe [11]. This results in a maximum of $m_c = 500$ point correspondences for each camera pair. We use 50000 RANSAC iterations and an inlier threshold of 0.005 for the initial relative pose estimation. For each camera pair we save the $m_p = 5$ best poses according to the number of inliers and a minimum rotation and translation difference of $\theta_R = \theta_t = 2°$. We set the inverse scale parameter λ_e of the exponential distribution in (4) to 0.005. The choice of this parameter is not that critically as additional experiments show. For the matching during the optimization process we use a stricter nearest neighbor rejection threshold of 0.6.

4.2   Results

We present our calibration results in Fig. 5 using box plots (the box depicts the 0.25 and 0.75 quantiles, the line in the middle is the median and crosses are outliers, for further details please refer to [18]). In the upper row we show the rotation errors in degree. The bottom row displays the translation errors in degree or millimeters depending on the calibration step. We plot the errors of the relative poses for the initial calibration (initial, Section 3.1), after the evaluation and optimization step (opt., Section 3.2) and of the absolute camera poses for the final calibration (final, Section 3.3). We also distinguish whether we used the five zoom steps (zoom) or not (no zoom). For comparison we also present results of the passive uncertainty based calibration method of Bajramovic and Denzler [7] (passive). We manually rotate the cameras to ensure that they share a common field of view for this passive method.

The results show that each step refines the calibration and outliers are rejected. We achieve a final median rotation error of 0.9 degree and a median translation error of about 68 millimeters for the method using zoom. In the case of no zoom the results are slightly worse. In comparison to the passive approach we reach a similar rotation and a much lower translation error.

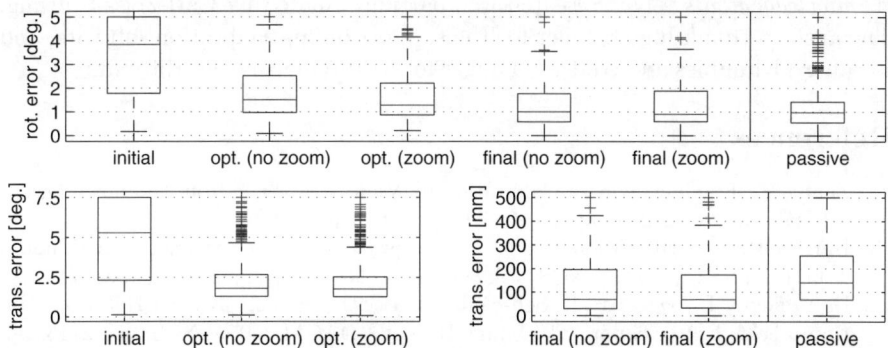

Fig. 5. Top: the rotation error during the different calibration steps in degree. Bottom: the translation error in degree or millimeters depending on the calibration step. For comparison we also present the results of the passive calibration approach of [7] (passive). The results of the initial calibration and some outliers are truncated.

Since we assume the pan and tilt axes to be identical to the Y and X axes of the camera, we also investigated the rotation error between the pan-tilt unit and the camera. We note that a (small) rotation between the camera and the pan-tilt unit has a higher impact on normalized point coordinates extracted from zoomed images. In order to rate the magnitude of this rotation we estimate it with the hand-eye calibration method of Tsai and Lenz [19]. The mean rotation between pan-tilt unit and camera in our experiments is 0.995°.

We also investigate the repeatability of the camera zoom by switching between the zoom steps and calibrating the intrinsic parameters several times. The calculated coefficients of variation for the intrinsic parameters lie in a magnitude of 10^{-3} which indicates good repeatability.

Calibrating a multi-camera system consisting of six cameras takes about 70 minutes in the current (serial) implementation. However, since many steps could be parallelized the runtime could be improved significantly.

5   Conclusions

We presented a method which uses active camera control for calibrating a multi-camera system consisting of pan-tilt zoom cameras. In order to evaluate a relative pose we introduced a probabilistic measure (4) which incorporates image and geometric information. Relative poses were optimized by rotating each camera pair in a way that simplifies the problem of extracting correct point correspondences. The final calibration process was based on these relative poses and their probabilities. The scale factors in each camera triangle were estimated using our probabilistic measure and active camera control. This allowed to reduce the number of necessary relative poses. Our experiments demonstrated the robustness and high accuracy of our approach. We achieved a median rotation error of 0.9° and a median translation error of 68 mm (Fig. 5). In our future work we hope to improve our calibration by considering the hand-eye calibration.

Acknowledgements. This research was partially funded by Carl-Zeiss-Stiftung. The authors thank Ingo Schiller for the support on his calibration software, and Bernhard Klumbies and Andreas Langer for modifying the pan-tilt units.

References

1. Zhang, Z.: Flexible Camera Calibration by Viewing a Plane from Unknown Orientations. In: Proceedings of the ICCV, pp. 666–673 (1999)
2. Hartley, R.: Self-calibration from multiple views with a rotating camera. In: Eklundh, J.-O. (ed.) ECCV 1994. LNCS, vol. 800, pp. 471–478. Springer, Heidelberg (1994)
3. Bajramovic, F., Denzler, J.: Self-calibration with Partially Known Rotations. In: Hamprecht, F.A., Schnörr, C., Jähne, B. (eds.) DAGM 2007. LNCS, vol. 4713, pp. 1–10. Springer, Heidelberg (2007)
4. Chen, X., Davis, J., Slusallek, P.: Wide area camera calibration using virtual calibration objects. In: Proceedings of the CVPR, vol. 2, pp. 520–527 (2000)
5. Svoboda, T., Hug, H., Van Gool, L.: ViRoom–Low Cost Synchronized Multicamera System and Its Self-calibration. In: Van Gool, L. (ed.) DAGM 2002. LNCS, vol. 2449, pp. 515–522. Springer, Heidelberg (2002)
6. Läbe, T., Förstner, W.: Automatic relative orientation of images. In: Proceedings of the 5th Turkish-German Joint Geodetic Days (2006)
7. Bajramovic, F., Denzler, J.: Global uncertainty-based selection of relative poses for multi camera calibration. In: Proceedings of the BMVC, vol. 2, pp. 745–754 (2008)
8. Sinha, S., Pollefeys, M.: Towards calibrating a pan-tilt-zoom cameras network. In: Proceedings of the IEEE Workshop on Omnidirectional Vision (2004)
9. Chippendale, P., Tobia, F.: Collective calibration of active camera groups. In: IEEE Conf. on Advanced Video and Signal Based Surveillance, pp. 456–461 (2005)
10. Matas, J., Chum, O., Urban, M., Pajdla, T.: Robust wide baseline stereo from maximally stable extremal regions. In: BMVC, pp. 384–393 (2002)
11. Lowe, D.: Distinctive Image Features from Scale-Invariant Keypoints. IJCV 60(2), 91–110 (2004)
12. Brückner, M., Bajramovic, F., Denzler, J.: Geometric and probabilistic image dissimilarity measures for common field of view detection. In: Proceedings of the CVPR, pp. 2052–2057 (2009)
13. Hartley, R., Zisserman, A.: Multiple View Geometry in Computer Vision. Cambridge University Press, Cambridge (2003)
14. Nistér, D.: An efficient solution to the five-point relative pose problem. PAMI 26, 756–770 (2004)
15. Fischler, M.A., Bolles, R.C.: Random Sample Consensus: a Paradigm for Model Fitting with Applications to Image Analysis and Automated Cartography. Communications of the ACM 24(6), 381–395 (1981)
16. Schiller, I.: MIP - MultiCameraCalibration, http://mip.informatik.uni-kiel.de/tiki-index.php?page=Calibration (Last visited on 22-04-2010)
17. Heikkila, J., Silvén, O.: A Four-step Camera Calibration Procedure with Implicit Image Correction. In: Proceedings of the CVPR, pp. 1106–1112 (1997)
18. McGill, R., Tukey, J., Larsen, W.A.: Variations of Boxplots. The American Statistician 32, 12–16 (1978)
19. Tsai, R.Y., Lenz, R.K.: A new technique for fully autonomous and efficient 3d robotics hand/eye calibration. IEEE Transactions on Robotics and Automation 5(3), 345–357 (1989)

Optimization on Shape Curves
with Application to Specular Stereo

Jonathan Balzer[1], Sebastian Höfer[2], Stefan Werling[2], and Jürgen Beyerer[2]

[1] King Abdullah University of Science and Technology (KAUST),
Geometric Modeling and Scientific Visualization Center, Thuwal 23955-6900,
Kingdom of Saudi Arabia
jonathan.balzer@kaust.edu.sa
[2] Lehrstuhl für Interaktive Echtzeitsysteme, Institute for Anthropomatics,
Karlsruhe Institute of Technology (KIT), Germany
{hoefer,werling,beyerer}@ies.uni-karlsruhe.de

Abstract. We state that a one-dimensional manifold of shapes in 3-space can be modeled by a level set function. Finding a minimizer of an independent functional among all points on such a shape curve has interesting applications in computer vision. It is shown how to replace the commonly encountered practice of gradient projection by a projection onto the curve itself. The outcome is an algorithm for constrained optimization, which, as we demonstrate theoretically and numerically, provides some important benefits in stereo reconstruction of specular surfaces.

1 Introduction

1.1 Motivation

Some reconstruction methods in computer vision are plagued with non-uniqueness. Instead of a single solution, they return to the user an entire family of surfaces Γ that could have evoked the underlying observation(s) and therefore require some form of regularization. This paper specializes in families Γ_φ of a real parameter $c \in \mathbb{R}$. Initially, we notice that these are conveniently expressed in terms of level set functions $\varphi \in C^2(\mathbb{R}^3)$:

$$\Gamma_\varphi := \{\Gamma \subset \mathbb{R}^3 \mid \varphi(\boldsymbol{x}) = c, \boldsymbol{x} \in \Gamma\}. \tag{1}$$

Observe that φ does not necessarily represent a signed distance, for in that case all elements in Γ_φ would be scaled versions of each other. The set Γ_φ exhibits the structure of a one-dimensional shape space or, as we call it, *shape curve*, which gathers surfaces with the same trace in a joint equivalence class. Mathematically speaking, a level set function is Eulerian in nature, meaning that it references a global world coordinate system rather than a collection of local bases, and as such accounts for the quotient structure of shape spaces in a very desirable way.

Imposing a smoothness assumption is a widespread practice to select a unique element Γ^* from Γ_φ. But what if all its shapes on the curve are equally smooth?

M. Goesele et al. (Eds.): DAGM 2010, LNCS 6376, pp. 41–50, 2010.

To facilitate more sophisticated regularization schemes, a-priori knowledge may be expressed in terms of a *selector functional* $E : \Gamma_\varphi \mapsto \mathbb{R}$ in such a way that the sought-after surface

$$\Gamma^* = \arg\min E(\Gamma) \quad \text{subject to} \quad \Gamma \in \Gamma_\varphi. \tag{2}$$

A simple but effective strategy for the solution of the constrained optimization problem (2) with feasible region Γ_φ shall be the core of Section 2.2. An application of the proposed algorithm to the reconstruction of specular surfaces is discussed in Section 3.2.

1.2   Related Work

The monograph [1] provides a vast introduction to the analysis of shape spaces and functionals defined on them. In [2], Aubert *et al.* argue where and how this calculus has advantages over the classical variational approach in image processing. Among other things, they discuss segmentation by active contours which is aside from constraints the $2d$ counterpart of what will be presented below. Solem and Overgaard provide a framework for shape optimization under equality constraints, which heavily relies on gradient projection in infinite-dimensional Hilbert spaces [3].

2   Optimization on Shape Curves

2.1   Fundamentals

First, let us briefly recall a few essential concepts of shape calculus: Scalar normal velocity fields $v_n : \Gamma \mapsto \mathbb{R}$ may be regarded as "tangents" to a shape space at a "point" Γ. By the Hadamard-Zolésio theorem, every functional E possesses a unique *shape gradient* $g_E : \Gamma \mapsto \mathbb{R}$ such that the differential of E in the direction v_n can be written as the L^2-inner product $dE(\Gamma, v_n) = \langle g_E, v_n \rangle_{L^2(\Gamma)}$, cf. [1, p. 348f.]. Analogous to the finite-dimensional setting, an auxiliary functional E_φ can be used to implicitly rephrase (1) as $\Gamma_\varphi = \{\Gamma \subset D \mid E_\varphi(\Gamma) = 0\}$ and constrain a gradient descent by subtracting from its steps the components orthogonal to Γ_φ and thus parallel to g_{E_φ}. Unfortunately, a large class of side conditions, including the one discussed in Section 3, does not admit this kind of projection because both, E_φ as well as g_{E_φ} are zero on Γ_φ. For an illustration, consider the finite-dimensional example $S^1 = \{\boldsymbol{x} \in \mathbb{R}^2 \mid \varphi(\boldsymbol{x}) = (\|\boldsymbol{x}\| - 1)^2 = 0\}$. While as feasibility region the unit circle itself admits a projection along its normal field, this specific algebraic representation forbids it as $\nabla\varphi = \boldsymbol{0}$ on S^1. One speaks of insufficient *linear independence constraint qualification*, cf. [4, Definition 12.4].

2.2   The Algorithm

Even when well-defined, projected-gradient descents tend to accumulate errors as they progress so that one would have to unbias the *iterates* themselves towards the curve in regular intervals anyway [3]. One key observation is that for feasibility regions of the form (1), this amounts to normal field adaption: From the theory of implicit functions, we know that $\nabla\varphi$ is orthogonal to the iso-surfaces of φ and hence, after normalization, equal to their Gauss maps. The image $\tilde{\Gamma}$ of a regular surface Γ with unitary normal field[1] $\hat{n}$ under the projection onto Γ_φ must make

$$E_\varphi(\Gamma) = \int_\Gamma \frac{1}{2}\|\hat{n} - \nabla\varphi\|^2 d\Gamma \tag{3}$$

stationary. Assume now that $\tilde{\Gamma} = \Gamma + \tilde{v}_n\hat{n}$. If Γ was a plane and φ respectively $\nabla\varphi$ did not depend on the spatial variable $x \in \mathbb{R}^3$, the optimal normal perturbation $\tilde{v}_n$ could be directly found as solution of the Poisson equation

$$\Delta_\Gamma \tilde{v}_n = \operatorname{div} \nabla\varphi \tag{4}$$

on Γ, where Δ_Γ denotes the Laplace-Beltrami operator[2]. In the general case, update $\tilde{\Gamma} = \Gamma + \tilde{v}_n\hat{n}$ and solution of (4) must be iterated alternatingly. It can be shown that this procedure is equivalent to Newton's method applied to the nonlinear least squares formulation (3) of the projection subproblem, see the examples section in [5] for further details. Interweaving the projection and a descent with respect to the selector functional E, the following algorithm is obtained:

1. Start with some initial surface Γ_0.
2. Project Γ_k onto Γ_φ by minimization of (3).
3. Advect the result $\tilde{\Gamma}_k$ according to $\Gamma_{k+1} = \tilde{\Gamma}_k + \alpha_k v_n(\tilde{\Gamma}_k)\hat{n}(\tilde{\Gamma}_k)$ with v_n *any* descent direction of E and $\alpha_k \in \mathbb{R}$ an appropriate step size.
4. Terminate if $|E(\tilde{\Gamma}_k) - E(\tilde{\Gamma}_{k-1})|$ is below a fixed user-selected threshold, else set $k \leftarrow k + 1$ and continue with step 2).

The stopping criterion is justified because it involves a finite difference approximation to the derivative of the chained mapping $E(c) : \mathbb{R} \mapsto \mathbb{R}$, taking the curve parameter c to the value of E.

3   Application to Specular Stereo

3.1   Introduction

Shape from Specular Reflection[3] was originally described in [6] maybe earlier and proceeds roughly as follows: A camera images via the unknown specular object some areal light source, e.g. a liquid crystal display. The latter is capable

---

[1] Here and subsequently, unit vectors are marked with a hat, i.e. $\|\hat{x}\| = 1$.

[2] A comprehensive exposition of the Laplace-Beltrami operator as well as a convenient Eulerian tangential calculus can be found in [1, p. 360ff.].

[3] Also known as *Shape from Distortion* or, among measurement scientists, as *deflectometry*.

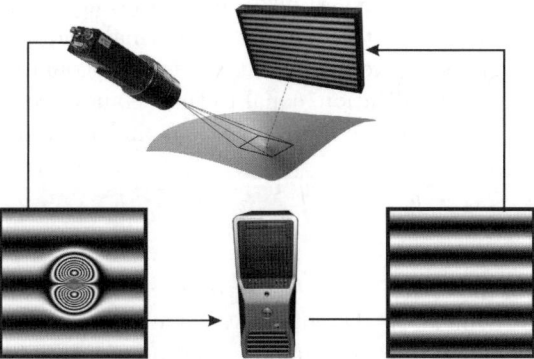

Fig. 1. Deflectometry principle for the high-precision measurement of specular surface shape: Every screen pixel identifies itself in the camera image by a unique sequence of gray values leading to robust correspondences between scene points and viewing directions

of displaying optical code words such that individual correspondences between pixels and observed scene points can be established, see Figure 1. Rising one abstraction layer, by Malus' and Dupin's law, the raw data is converted into a vector field $\hat{\boldsymbol{n}}_\mathrm{d}$ of desired unit normals on a subset $D \subseteq \mathbb{R}^3$ of the field of view, see Figure 2(a). Integrability provided, obviously $\hat{\boldsymbol{n}}_\mathrm{d}$ induces a shape curve of the form (1) via the partial differential equation (PDE) $\nabla \varphi = \hat{\boldsymbol{n}}_\mathrm{d}$, cf. [7]. To highlight the dependance of a shape curve Γ_φ on a normal field $\hat{\boldsymbol{n}}_\mathrm{d}$, we will subsequently use the notation $E_{\hat{\boldsymbol{n}}_\mathrm{d}}$ instead of E_φ for the associated projection functional (3). In the present context, regularization is understood as the selection of the level set of φ corresponding to the true physical mirror surface. In particular, the idea of *specular stereo* as introduced in [8] is to gain information by recording a series of different normal fields $\hat{\boldsymbol{n}}_\mathrm{d}^i$, $i \in \{1 \ldots, n\}$ with $n \geq 2$. As opposed to classical stereo on Lambertian surfaces, the key concept illustrated in Figure 2(a) is to correlate *solution candidates* through a generalized disparity $d : D \mapsto \mathbb{R}$ of their normal fields, *not* features in image data. For further details, the interested reader is encouraged to consult the survey [9] and the references therein.

3.2   Disparity Minimization on the Solution Manifold

We will strictly enforce the constraint that Γ^* must lie on the shape curve spanned by the mean normal field

$$\hat{\boldsymbol{n}}_\mathrm{d}^m = \frac{\boldsymbol{n}_\mathrm{d}^m}{\|\boldsymbol{n}_\mathrm{d}^m\|}, \quad \boldsymbol{n}_\mathrm{d}^m := \frac{1}{n} \sum_{i=1}^{n} \hat{\boldsymbol{n}}_\mathrm{d}^i. \tag{5}$$

It can be assumed that $\hat{\boldsymbol{n}}_\mathrm{d}^m$ is dense in D since we expect the result to lie inside the visual hull induced by the involved imaging sensors. This is favorable in view of the fact that for finite pattern generator areas, highly convex objects

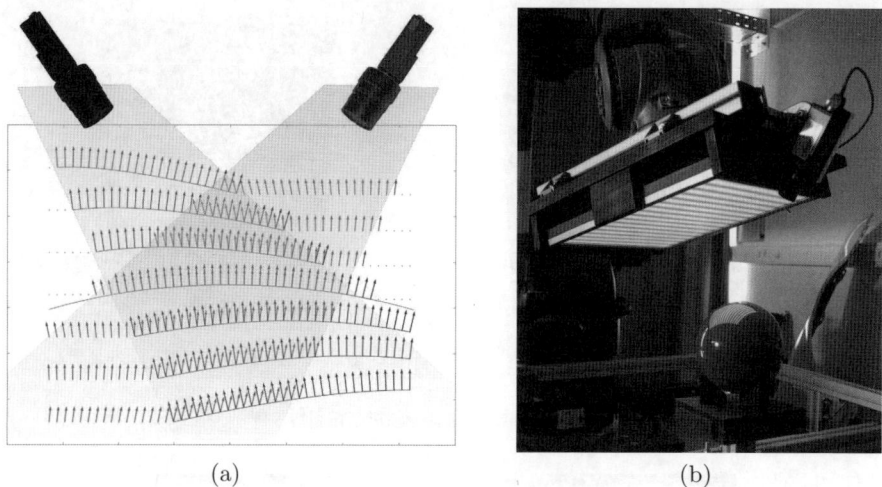

(a)   (b)

Fig. 2. (a) Principle of specular stereo: The true surface must run through the points where the generalized disparity between normal fields attains a minimum. (b) Our robot-based monocular stereo setup.

may require multiple measurements, see for example Figure 7(c). As selector functional we choose

$$E(\Gamma) := \int_\Gamma d(\boldsymbol{x})d\Gamma, \tag{6}$$

although a variety of alternatives is imaginable (e.g. individual normal error, distance to a known point, etc.). If we interpret the disparity d as Riemannian metric on $\mathbb{R}^3$ respectively Γ, then (6) is simply a minimal weighted-area surface functional with well-known shape gradient $g_E = \kappa d + \langle \nabla d, \hat{\boldsymbol{n}} \rangle$, cf. [1,2,10]. In homogenous regions where $\nabla d = 0$, the product of mean curvature κ and d decreases the value of E simply by shrinking the integral's domain of definition. We can drop it in our application and still maintain a, possibly less efficient, descent direction for E! The vanishing of ∇d is exactly what we want to achieve, all the while κ only introduces undesirable numerical stiffness into the descent equation. The remaining gradient term can be problematic in practice, as stochastic disturbances of d are amplified through differentiation. Thus, we only use it to estimate the correct sense of direction for v_n in step 3) of our algorithm by setting

$$v_n(\boldsymbol{x}) := \begin{cases} 1 & \text{if } \int_\Gamma \langle \nabla d, \hat{\boldsymbol{n}} \rangle d\Gamma < 0, \\ -1, & \text{else.} \end{cases} \tag{7}$$

After all, the only requirement on v_n is that it is some descent direction. Furthermore, if the elements of Γ_φ vary slowly enough, the identity function on Γ seems

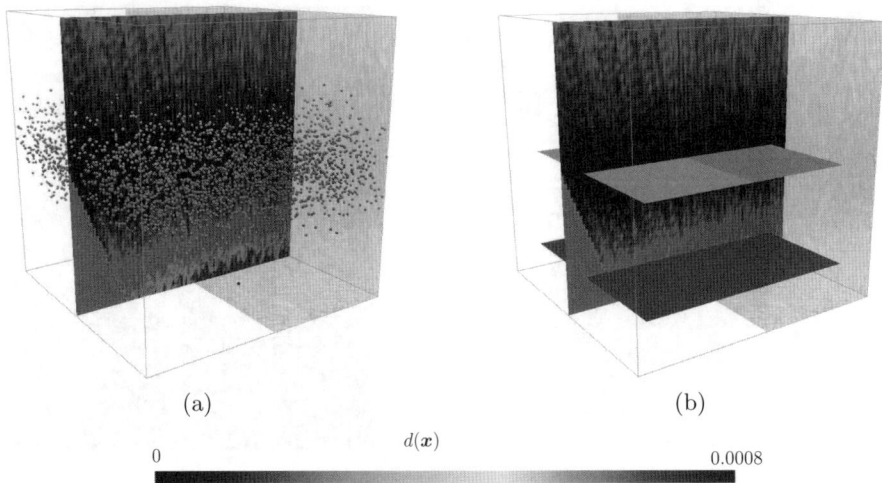

Fig. 3. (a) Pointwise reconstruction by voxel carving. The coloring reflects the distance of points in the cloud to the plane $z = 0$. (b) Reconstruction by our method: initial surface (dark) and limit surface (light). Enforcing a hard constraint can lead to high-quality results even under the influence of measurement noise, making extensive post-processing obsolete. Also shown are cross sections of the corrupted disparity field d : $D \mapsto \mathbb{R}$. Areas, where only one or no normal field at all is available and hence the disparity is not well-defined, are indicated by the color cyan.

to be a fairly good approximation of the shape gradient g_E always provided that $\Gamma \in \Gamma_\varphi$.

4   Experiments

4.1   Implementation

As we assumed the topology of Γ^* to be known in advance, we based the implementation on an explicit simplicial surface model, particularly a manifold mesh, which contains no self-intersections, hanging edges, t-junctions, or isolated vertices. This choice affords relatively low computational complexity compared to the level set method, which is to be favored when topological changes are expected to occur during the evolution. Still, although not mandatory, a full three-dimensional Cartesian lattice of size $100 \times 100 \times 100$ was maintained for visualization purposes. It actually suffices to attach measurement data to the evolving mesh via back-projection and compute all quantities specifying the descent direction in a tubular neighborhood around Γ_k (very similar to narrow band level set methods). The linear elliptic PDE (4) was handled by the finite-element method in our implementation. For control of the step sizes α_k, a simple Armijo backtracking strategy was employed, cf. [4, p. 37] for the technical details.

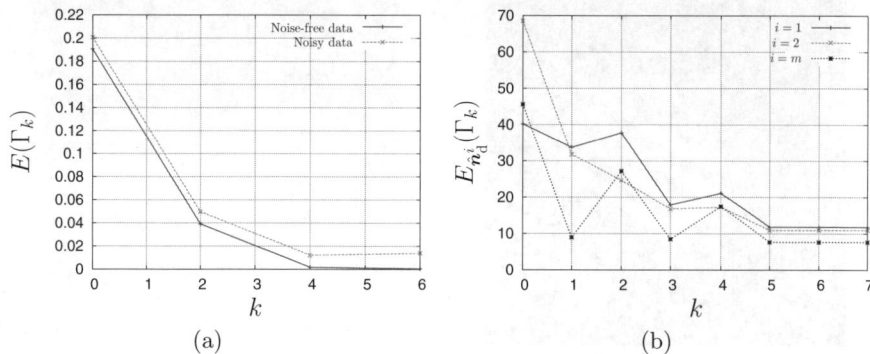

Fig. 4. (a) Value of the selector functional E over Γ_k progressing through Γ_φ. (b) The error between actual surface normals and the gradient of φ quantifies the distance of Γ_k from the constraint manifold Γ_φ. Also the error with respect to the individual fields $\hat{n}_d^1$ and $\hat{n}_d^2$ is decreasing. Re-projection occurs at odd steps, which have been inserted here for visualization only (a cycle of the proposed algorithm begins at even numbers).

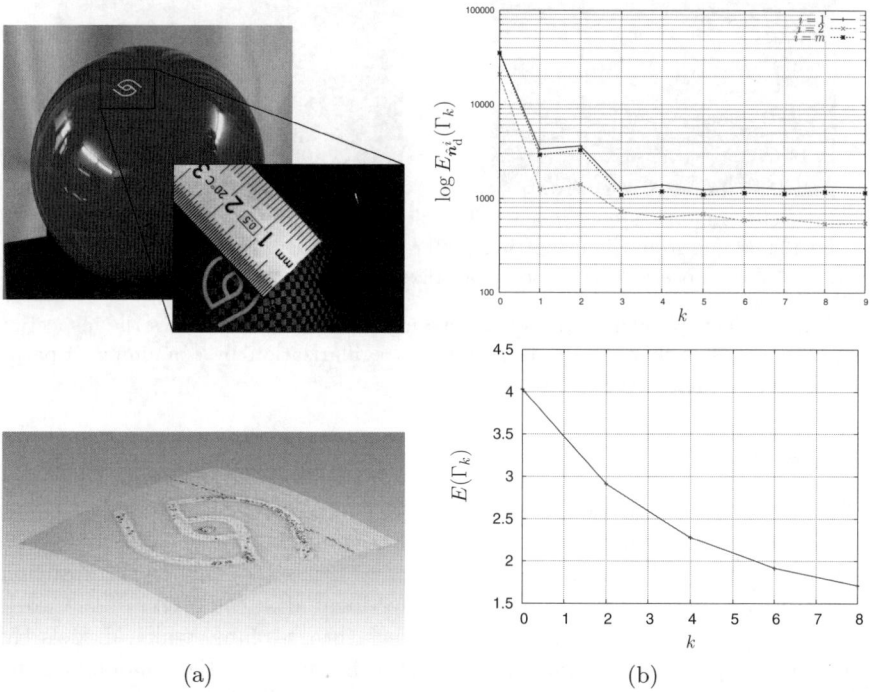

Fig. 5. (a) Partially specular bowling ball: Even sub-millimeter details like the embossed logo print are easily recovered. The color encodes the mean curvature of the reconstructed $3d$ model. (b) Convergence rates.

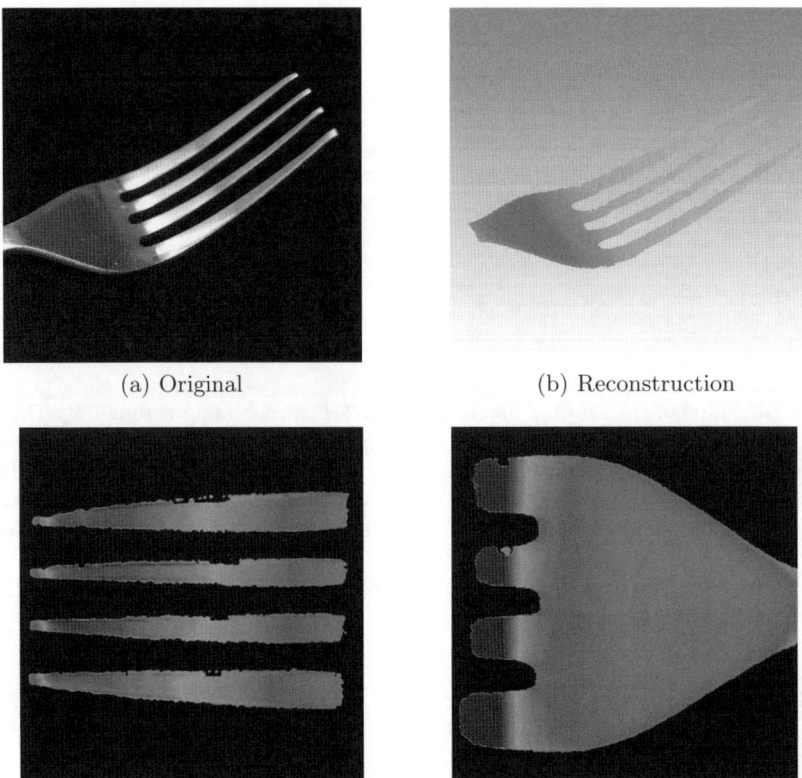

(a) Original   (b) Reconstruction

(c) Deflectometric stereo image: The color encodes the norm of the vector field emerging from the projection center of the camera and pointing to the locus of the observed scene point per pixel.

Fig. 6. Multiview specular stereo serves two main purposes: It enables the inspection of large or complex-shaped objects as well as regularization by examining disparity values in overlapping measure fields

4.2   Results

To be able to assess algorithm performance by comparison with ground truth, we synthesized the following benchmark by ray tracing: A pinhole camera observes the planar mirror $\Gamma^* = \{(x,y,z)^\top \in \mathbb{R}^3 \mid z = 10\}$ orthogonal to the principle axis. Sight rays, leaving the projection center located in the origin of the world coordinate system, are reflected and intersect the xy-plane, which models the controllable illumination. The surfaces in the induced solution manifold gradually develop from concave to convex with growing distance from the optical center. The original surface was regained effortlessly by voxel carving as described in [11]. However, superimposing every coordinate of $\hat{\boldsymbol{n}}_d^m$ with zero-mean Gaussian noise (standard deviation $\sigma = 0.5$) diminished reconstruction quality visibly, see Figure 3(a). Shape and disparity change only little within the solution manifold, still enough, though, to be relevant from the standpoint of optical

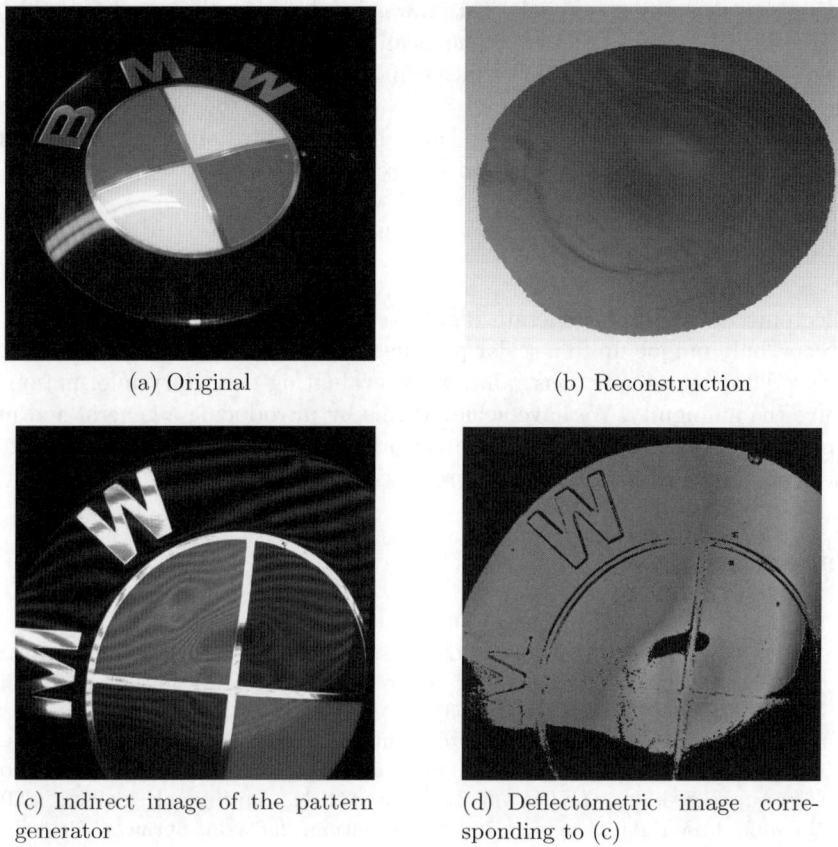

(a) Original

(b) Reconstruction

(c) Indirect image of the pattern generator

(d) Deflectometric image corresponding to (c)

Fig. 7. Partially specular emblem of a German auto brand: Figure (c) demonstrates that usually not all of the surface can be covered by one imaging constellation

metrology. It is precisely this low sensitivity that makes the pointwise approach so error-prone. Our method enforces two strong constraints as countermeasures: First, the context of points united in a regular surface is not resolved[4]. Second, a feasible surface must be coherent with the deflectometric measurement. This way, the mean squared distance error reduced from 0.13 to $1.38 \cdot 10^{-6}$. Besides the final reconstruction, one can observe in Figure 3(b) that, by definition (7), the disparity must not necessarily be dense in the computational domain D. Convergence rates are shown in Figure 4.

For our first real test object, the bowling ball depicted in Figure 5(a), the manufacturer specifies a mean curvature of $\kappa_d = 0.0125\ mm^{-1}$, acting as some form of ground truth here. Data were acquired in a monocular fashion with the help of our robot-mounted sensor head shown in Figure 2(b). The result by point-wise disparity minimization was degraded to a degree of unusability. We experienced in turn high robustness of our algorithm with respect to noise,

---

[4] Of course, one could argue that this is a disadvantage while recovering discontinuities.

although no smoothing or regularization was involved but the averaging of fields in Equation (5), refer to Figure 5. The mean curvature estimate of 0.0008 mm^{-1} for an arbitrarily chosen initial surface could be improved to as close as 0.01149 mm^{-1} to κ_d. This relative error of 8.7 % develops in the Voronoi area-based curvature estimator used and may be also due to calibration uncertainties. Two more practial examples are shown in Figures 6 and 7.

5   Conclusion

Deflectometric methods generate highly reliable shape information, which is, however, only unique up to a scalar parameter. It is thus very natural to enforce a strict data consistency constraint, while evaluating secondary information to resolve the ambiguity. We have achieved this by introducing a general and mathematically sound optimization framework, which could prove rewarding in other computer vision or optical metrology scenarios.

References

1. Delfour, M., Zolésio, J.P.: Shapes and Geometries. SIAM, Philadelphia (2001)
2. Aubert, G., Barlaud, M., Faugeras, O., Besson, S.: Image segmentation using active contours: Calculus of variations or shape gradients? SIAM Journal on Applied Mathematics 63(6), 2128–2154 (2003)
3. Solem, J., Overgaard, N.: A gradient descent procedure for variational dynamic surface problems with constraints. In: Paragios, N., Faugeras, O., Chan, T., Schnörr, C. (eds.) VLSM 2005. LNCS, vol. 3752, pp. 332–343. Springer, Heidelberg (2005)
4. Nocedal, J., Wright, S.: Numerical Optimization, 2nd edn. Springer, Heidelberg (2006)
5. Balzer, J.: Second-order domain derivative of normal-dependent boundary integrals. Journal of Evolution Equations (2010)
6. Sanderson, A., Weiss, L., Nayar, S.: Structured highlight inspection of specular surfaces. IEEE Transactions on Pattern Analysis and Machine Intelligence 10(1), 44–55 (1988)
7. Tarini, M., Lensch, H., Goesele, M., Seidel, H.P.: 3D acquisition of mirroring objects. Elsevier Graphical Models 67(4), 233–259 (2005)
8. Wang, Z., Inokuchi, S.: Determining shape of specular surfaces. In: The 8th Scandinavian Conference on Image Analysis, pp. 1187–1194 (1993)
9. Ihrke, I., Kutulakos, K., Lensch, H., Magnor, M., Heidrich, W.: State of the art in transparent and specular object reconstruction. In: STAR Proceedings of Eurographics (2008)
10. Goldlücke, B., Ihrke, I., Linz, C., Magnor, M.: Weighted minimal surface reconstruction. IEEE Transactions on Pattern Analysis and Machine Intelligence 29(7), 1194–1208 (2007)
11. Bonfort, T., Sturm, P., Gargallo, P.: General specular surface triangulation. In: Proceedings of the Asian Conference on Computer Vision, vol. 2, pp. 872–881 (2006)

Unsupervised Facade Segmentation Using Repetitive Patterns

Andreas Wendel, Michael Donoser, and Horst Bischof

Institute for Computer Graphics and Vision, Graz University of Technology
{wendel,donoser,bischof}@icg.tugraz.at

Abstract. We introduce a novel approach for separating and segmenting individual facades from streetside images. Our algorithm incorporates
prior knowledge about arbitrarily shaped repetitive regions which are detected using intensity profile descriptors and a voting–based matcher. In
the experiments we compare our approach to extended state–of–the–art
matching approaches using more than 600 challenging streetside images,
including different building styles and various occlusions. Our algorithm
outperforms these approaches and allows to correctly separate 94% of
the facades. Pixel–wise comparison to our ground–truth yields a segmentation accuracy of 85%. According to these results our work is an
important contribution to fully automatic building reconstruction.

1   Introduction

Large–scale image acquisition for geospatial mapping platforms such as Microsoft
Bing Maps or Google Maps requires appropriate data processing methods. While
early systems just showed raw photographies, more recent visualization techniques allow to superimpose data obtained from satellite imagery, aerial photography, and road maps. Modern systems use multiple–view images to analyze the
geometric properties of objects, resulting in 3D visualizations.

State–of–the–art methods [1] for 3D reconstruction are able to automatically
extract simple building models from aerial images. However, photographs taken
from an airplane offer limited view of building facades and therefore the reconstruction lacks details. This is depicted to the left in Figure 1 using a 3D model
obtained from Microsoft Bing Maps. In contrast, an image of the same location
taken from street–level can be found to the right. The advantages are obvious:
Streetside images can be obtained with higher spatial resolution and from a more
natural point of view than aerial images.

Recently, there has been increasing interest in using streetside imagery for
automatically deriving 3D building models [2,3]. Müller et al. [2] introduced an
approach on image–based procedural modeling. Given single facade images they
first determine the structure of a facade. Once they know about the hierarchical
subdivisions of the facade it is possible to replace architectural elements by
parameterizable models. This representation has several advantages: First, the
visual quality of the image is improved. Whether we scale or change the view
within the model, there is no limit in spatial resolution. Second, the approach

M. Goesele et al. (Eds.): DAGM 2010, LNCS 6376, pp. 51–60, 2010.

Fig. 1. Comparison between aerial and streetside imaging: While the 3D model obtained from Microsoft Bing Maps (**left**) lacks details, it is easy to recognize the New York Stock Exchange in the streetside image (**right**)

assigns semantical meanings to parts of the facade. This is important for future applications using city models, for instance if the entrance has to be located. Third, the huge amount of image data required to visualize an entire city can be reduced to a predictable number of parameters. This allows geospatial mapping systems to transmit high–quality data in a reasonable time across the web.

The availability of procedural modeling algorithms motivates the implementation of fully automatic streetside modeling pipelines. However, the gap between real–world data and assumptions in algorithms is big: State–of–the–art approaches for 3D modeling [2,3] require orthorectified images of a *single* facade as input. Since streetside data is in general acquired by cameras on top of a moving car, images are not rectified and may show multiple facades. The goal of our work is to close this gap by detecting and extracting single facade segments from streetside images. By our definition, two facades should be separated if a significant change in color or building structure can be detected. A single facade segment is therefore a coherent area in an image, containing *repetitive patterns* which match in color and texture.

The successful realization of this task does not only have an impact on automatic procedural modeling workflows but also supports other computer vision algorithms that cope with urban environments. For example, window detection is strongly simplified if applied to single facades because the appearance of windows is often similar. Our work contributes to this goal in two areas:

(1) Repetitive patterns. We analyze repetitive patterns by using contextual information rather than directly comparing features or raw image data. Besides, we compare our algorithm against various state-of-the-art feature matching approaches which we adapt for our purpose.

(2) Facade separation and segmentation. Building upon repetitive patterns discovered in streetside images, we show how to separate and segment facades. The approach is evaluated using 620 high–resolution streetside photographs, acquired by cameras on top of a moving car. The images offer total coverage of a city as seen from roads, but also include difficulties such as various building styles and occlusions.

2   Facade Separation and Segmentation Algorithm

Our algorithm for facade segmentation consists of three major steps: First, we detect repetitive patterns in streetside images by extending a method designed for wide–baseline matching (Section 2.1). The resulting pairs of interest points are then used in a bottom–up manner to separate facades (Section 2.2). Finally, we combine the knowledge about repetitive areas with state–of–the–art segmentation methods to obtain individual facade segments (Section 2.3).

2.1   Finding Repetitive Patterns

Matching of local features has been widely investigated but hardly ever applied to a *single* image. Most algorithms were originally developed for object recognition or wide–baseline matching where the task is to find the single best match to a descriptor in a second image. We choose the Scale–Invariant Feature Transform (SIFT) [4] to represent the category of local feature–based matching approaches. SIFT has been designed for finding correspondences among feature sets from different images. For single image operation a range of valid matches needs to be defined. However, finding a proper threshold turned out to be difficult as the descriptor either matched with structures across facade boundaries or it did not find enough matches within a facade.

Shechtman and Irani [5] presented an approach to match complex visual data using local self–similarities. They correlate a patch centered at the point of interest with a larger surrounding region and use the maximal correlation values within log–polar bins as descriptor. The benefit of this approach is the independence of representation, meaning that just the spatial layout or shape is important. However, this poses a problem for our needs: The most common repetitive patterns are windows and their shape is often similar in different facades. While the texture within the window often stays the same, the texture outside changes and should definitely influence the result.

Tell and Carlsson [6,7] developed a robust approach for wide–baseline matching. The basic idea is to extract intensity profiles between pairs of interest points and match them to each other. If these profiles lie on a locally planar surface such as a facade, any scale–invariant descriptor is also invariant to affine transformations. Fourier coefficient descriptors of the first image are then matched to descriptors of the second image, and votes are casted for the respective start- and endpoints of the matching intensity profiles. Maxima in the voting table are then considered as the best matches for the interest points of both images.

Within this work, we adapt the approach of [6] for finding repetitive patterns within a single image. We detect interest points in the image, namely Harris corners [8], and extract color intensity profiles on a straight line between them. This results in a graph which connects all interest points (nodes) to each other. To limit the complexity, we take only the nearest 30 neighbors into account.

Every RGB color channel contributes 20 values to the descriptor, sampled using bilinear interpolation in regular intervals along the line. Finally, the 60–dimensional descriptor is normalized. We achieve scale invariance by extracting

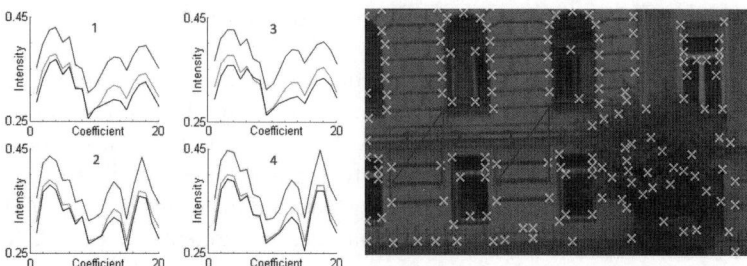

Fig. 2. We describe the image content between Harris corners by extracting intensity profiles with 20 values for every RGB color channel

a fixed amount of coefficients from interpolated, one–dimensional data. While illumination changes of small areas are also corrected by the interpolation, larger areas can be handled with the tolerance of the matching approach. Figure 2 visualizes some extracted intensity profiles and their origin in the image.

We use a kd–tree [9] for efficient matching of descriptors within a single image, tolerating ±5% deviation off the descriptor prototype for finding repetitive patterns. We do not consider matches with more than 10 descriptors involved because these features are not discriminative enough. The robustness of the approach is based on an additional voting step. All matching profiles vote for the similarity of the respective pair of start- and endpoints. Using this method, interest points which are in similar regions get more votes than two random points. We store a list of contributing profiles for every possible pair and increase the vote count only if a descriptor has not contributed to that correspondence so far. This is in a similar manner described in [7] and ensures that no bias is introduced in the voting matrix. For locating repetitive patterns in the voting matrix, we threshold the number of votes a correspondence received. A correspondence of interest points has to be supported by at least 3 of 30 intensity profiles (10%). One of the advantages of this voting process is the ability to match arbitrary areas of the image, as visualized in Figure 3(a).

For the purpose of our work, we can further restrain the previously found matches. Repetitive patterns on facades are unlikely to occur across the entire image, but also very close matches are not valuable. We therefore restrict the horizontal or vertical distance of the matches to avoid outliers. The final result of our algorithm for finding repetitive patterns in a single image can be seen in Figure 3(b). Note that only a small amount of interest point correspondences cross the boundary between the two facade segments, while we can find a large number within a segment.

2.2   Facade Separation

Facade separation is a task which has not received much attention in the past. Müller et al. [2] introduced an algorithm which is able to summarize redundant parts of a facade and thus subdivide images into floors and tiles. However, a

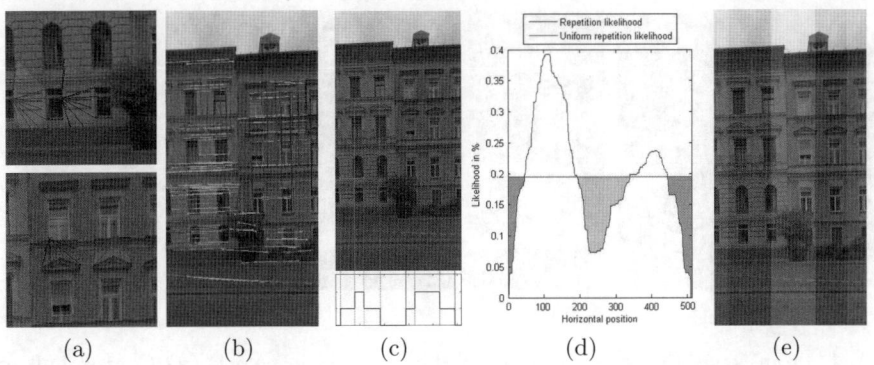

(a)   (b)   (c)   (d)   (e)

Fig. 3. From streetside data to separation (best viewed in color): **(a)** Matching of arbitrary areas **(b)** Detected repetitive patterns (color–coded lines) **(c)** Projection results in a match count along the horizontal axis **(d)** Thresholding the repetition likelihood with the uniform repetition likelihood **(e)** Resulting repetitive areas, separation areas (green), and unknown areas (red)

major limitation is the dependency on *single* facade images, and automatic processing fails for scenarios with blurry texture, low contrast, chaotic ground floors, and occlusions caused by vegetation. Other works on facade separation [3,10] are based on the evaluation of directional gradients, which did not proof to be robust for our datasets because it only works for highly regular facades.

The first stage of our facade segmentation algorithm provides interest point correspondences. We can now use these results to detect clusters of repetitive patterns. In this step we employ the Gravity Assumption, meaning that the majority of images in streetside datasets show facades where repetitions occur in horizontal direction and separations between facades in vertical direction. This allows us to project the lines between all pairs of matching interest points onto the horizontal axis and obtain the match count for every position on the horizontal axis. An illustration can be found in Figure 3(c). We normalize the match count to obtain the percentage of all matches at a given place on the horizontal axis, which we call the repetition likelihood.

Simply detecting minima on the repetition likelihood is not suitable for finding separation areas, as the global minimum would fail for panoramic images with multiple splits and local minima occur regularly between rows of windows. If all parts of the facade would contribute the same amount of repetitive patterns to the likelihood, we would get a uniform repetition likelihood. This value is an intuitive threshold, because areas where the likelihood is higher are more repetitive than average (*repetitive areas*) and areas where it is lower are less repetitive (*separation areas*). This fact is visualized in Figure 3(d). While repetitive areas are used for segmentation later on, separation areas mark the position where one facade ends and another starts. We also have to cope with the problem of narrow fields of view, i.e. few or no repetitions are visible in images that actually show a separation. We solve this by defining an *unknown area* on both sides of

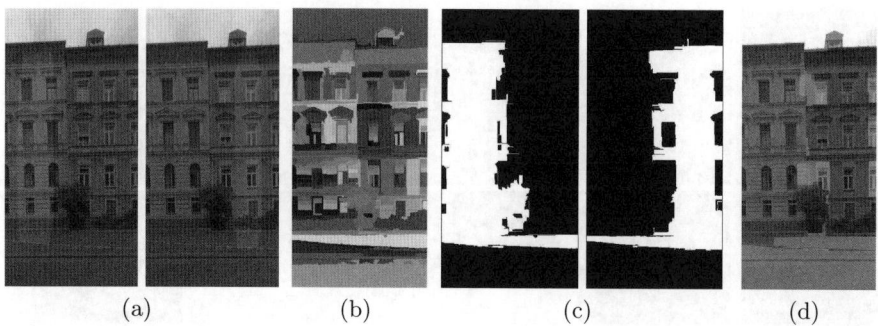

Fig. 4. From separation to segmentation (best viewed in color): **(a)** Convex hull of repetitive points as segmentation prior **(b)** Superpixel segmentation [11] **(c)** Combination of prior and appearance **(d)** Typical result

the image, starting at the image boundary and ending at the point where the first repetitive area is detected. Separation examples are given in Figure 3(e). The algorithm does not depend heavily on the quality of repetitive patterns but works well with several approaches, as the evaluation in Section 3.1 shows.

2.3 Facade Segmentation

For the task of facade segmentation it is important to consider both the continuity of segments and the underlying structure of facades. Popular unsupervised methods such as Normalized Cuts [12] or efficient graph–based segmentation [11] failed to provide satisfactory results on our data because they lack this prior knowledge. An approach which considers prior knowledge has been presented by Korah and Rasmussen [13], who assume that the pixels located around a window belong to the building wall. Their method also fails for our datasets as we do not have knowledge about the window grid and a significant part of facades does not have homogeneous texture.

In contrast, we want to incorporate repetitive areas as prior knowledge. Based upon the results of the separation stage, we process repetitive areas individually. An interest point is called repetitive point if it has some correspondence to another point. We assemble a set of all repetitive points within a repetitive area and compute a convex hull [14] for this set of points, as can be seen in Figure 4(a). The graph–based segmentation approach of [11] can be adjusted to deliver superpixels (oversegmentations), visualized in pseudo–colors in Figure 4(b). We further combine prior knowledge and superpixels to the binary masks in Figure 4(c). For all repetitive areas, we include those superpixels into the respective facade segment which overlap with the convex mask. After morphological post–processing, the final output of our algorithm are individually segmented facades as depicted in Figure 4(d).

3   Experiments and Results

Experimental evaluation is based on 620 images in total, which can be grouped in two single–frame datasets and one dataset with panoramic images. First, the US–style dataset contains 220 single–frame facade images. The main difficulties of the dataset are very similar facades and low image quality in the top third of the image. The second dataset consists of 380 frames with European–style buildings. Compared to the first dataset, lower buildings result in more visible parts of the facades. However, cars and trees occlude the facade and large parts of road and sky can be seen. Furthermore, facades are heavily structured and it is hard to obtain good segments for most of them. Finally, we manually selected 20 series (each of about 30 consecutive frames) to create the Panorama dataset. Panoramic stitching is important because it increases the field of view in the direction necessary for finding repetitive patterns. However, common algorithms such as Autostitch [15] regularly fail due to occlusions by vegetation and significant depth changes. While we cannot rely on fully automatic image stitching for large sequences, we still want to show the applicability of our algorithm.

We use precision and recall [16] to evaluate our algorithm and combine them by a harmonic mean to obtain the measure of effectiveness, also called F_1–measure. We obtained ground–truth by manually labeling individual facades. We estimate the point matching quality by clustering the matches and assigning them to ground–truth, resulting in a set of inliers and outliers for every segment. We only use the match precision (PR_{match}), as it is not possible to estimate the amount of false negatives required to compute the recall. Facade separation quality $F_{1,sep}$ is estimated by checking if the detected repetitive area lies within the ground–truth segment. More or less splits lower the effectiveness except when they occur in an unknown area. The facade segmentation quality $F_{1,seg}$ is estimated using a pixel–wise comparison between the automatically obtained segment and the ground–truth segment.

Our approach depends on the parameters of the Harris corner detector ($\sigma_D = 0.7$, $\sigma = 3.0$ for the European–style dataset and $\sigma = 2.0$ else) and the settings of the superpixel segmentation ($\sigma = 1.0, k = 100, min = 100$). All other parameters are defined with respect to the image scale. Facade segmentation using intensity profiles takes about 10s per frame in a MATLAB implementation and could be further improved by a proper implementation.

3.1   Comparison of Methods

The first experiment analyzes the influence of different profile descriptors. We compare our choice of using intensity profiles in RGB color space, as described in Section 2.1, to intensity profiles in different color spaces (Lab, grayscale), Fourier profiles as used by Tell and Carlsson [6], gradients as used in SIFT [4], and RGB histograms which neglect all spatial information.

The second experiment analyzes the influence of different methods for point matching on the quality of facade separation and segmentation. We compare our profile matching approach to the extended versions of SIFT descriptors [4], self–similarities [5], and raw patches of pixels. All methods are integrated in the workflow of the facade segmentation algorithm and differ only by the approach to repetitive pattern detection.

Table 1. Evaluation results as an average of all datasets. Our approach of intensity profiles in RGB color space performs best

620 images, 3 datasets	PR_{match}	$F_{1,sep}$	$F_{1,seg}$
Intensity profiles (RGB)	**72.8%**	**94.0%**	**85.4%**
Intensity profiles (Lab)	68.8%	89.6%	83.8%
Intensity profiles (gray)	67.2%	90.9%	83.6%
Fourier profiles (gray)	67.1%	89.8%	84.6%
Gradient profiles (gray)	51.0%	82.6%	80.3%
Histogram profiles (RGB)	51.8%	83.6%	81.3%
SIFT [4]	72.6%	86.6%	78.6%
Self–similarities [5]	63.9%	78.4%	70.2%
Raw patches of pixels	72.3%	92.4%	83.6%

Table 1 presents an overview of the average results on all datasets. According to these results our method performs better than any other intensity profile descriptor or any extended state–of–the–art method. Although the distance to its competitors is small there are two main reasons for using our method: First, it achieves the best matching precision combined with a number of correct repetitive patterns which is three times higher than for other methods. This increased support makes the repetition likelihood defined in Section 2.2 more robust. Second, our method is most tolerant regarding the appearance of repetitive patterns. Corresponding areas can be arbitrarily shaped and do not depend on scale or rotation.

3.2   Illustration of Results

After comparing the performance using objective measures we want to illustrate the results. Figure 5 shows the separation and segmentation of four consecutive images for the US- and European–style datasets. For better visualization, videos are provided online[1]. A typical result for multiple–facade separation and segmentation (Panorama dataset) can be found in Figure 6.

Separation problems occur if the field of view is too small. In such a case, a different column of windows is enough to indicate a different facade. Segmentation problems are mainly caused by repetitive patterns which are not part of the facade, such as power lines in the sky. The resulting segment is therefore too large and includes parts of the sky. Missing repetitive patterns at image boundaries lead to wrong segmentations as well.

---

[1] http://www.icg.tugraz.at/Members/wendel/

Fig. 5. Typical results for facade separation (**left**) and segmentation (**right**) for US–style facades (**top**) and European–style facades (**bottom**). The separation ground–truth is marked by red lines. It overlaps either with separation areas (green), or unknown areas (red) if not enough repetitive matches can be found.

Fig. 6. Typical results for multiple–facade separation (**top**) and segmentation (**bottom**) in the Panorama dataset

4   Conclusion

In this work we proposed an algorithm which closes the gap between real–world data and state–of–the–art procedural modeling approaches [2]. Our contributions are two–fold: First, we developed a novel algorithm for finding repetitive patterns in a single image. We compare contextual information using pairwise intensity profile descriptors and an intermediate step of vote casting. As a result, corresponding areas can be arbitrarily shaped and the matches are invariant to small illumination changes and affine transformations. Second, we presented a novel approach for facade separation and segmentation. Our algorithm achieves excellent results of 94.0% separation and 85.4% segmentation effectiveness, making our work an important contribution to fully automatic building reconstruction. Future research should focus on detecting occlusions such as vegetation and cars, as avoiding separations in these areas would improve the performance. Furthermore, our approach will be applied to texture segmentation and symmetry detection.

Acknowledgments. This work has been supported by the Austrian Research Promotion Agency (FFG) project FIT-IT CityFit (815971/14472-GLE/ROD) and project FIT-IT Pegasus (825841/10397).

References

1. Zebedin, L., Klaus, A., Gruber-Geymayer, B., Karner, K.: Towards 3d map generation from digital aerial images. Journal of Photogrammetry and Remote Sensing 60(6), 413–427 (2006)
2. Mueller, P., Zeng, G., Wonka, P., Gool, L.V.: Image-based procedural modeling of facades. ACM Transactions on Graphics 26(3) (2007)
3. Xiao, J., Fang, T., Zhao, P., Lhuillier, M., Quan, L.: Image-based street-side city modeling. ACM Transactions on Graphics 28(5) (2009)
4. Lowe, D.G.: Distinctive image features from Scale-Invariant keypoints. International Journal of Computer Vision (IJCV) 60(2), 91–110 (2004)
5. Shechtman, E., Irani, M.: Matching local Self-Similarities across images and videos. In: Proceedings of CVPR (2007)
6. Tell, D., Carlsson, S.: Wide baseline point matching using affine invariants computed from intensity profiles. In: Vernon, D. (ed.) ECCV 2000. LNCS, vol. 1842, pp. 814–828. Springer, Heidelberg (2000)
7. Tell, D., Carlsson, S.: Combining appearance and topology for wide baseline matching. In: Heyden, A., Sparr, G., Nielsen, M., Johansen, P. (eds.) ECCV 2002. LNCS, vol. 2350, pp. 68–81. Springer, Heidelberg (2002)
8. Harris, C., Stephens, M.: A combined corner and edge detector. In: Proceedings of the Alvey Vision Conference, vol. 15, p. 50 (1988)
9. Friedman, J.H., Bentley, J.L., Finkel, R.A.: An algorithm for finding best matches in logarithmic expected time. ACM Transactions on Mathematical Software 3(3), 209–226 (1977)
10. Hernandez, J., Marcotegui, B.: Morphological segmentation of building facade images. In: Proceedings of ICIP, p. 4030 (2009)
11. Felzenszwalb, P.F., Huttenlocher, D.P.: Efficient Graph-Based image segmentation. International Journal of Computer Vision (IJCV) 59(2) (2004)
12. Shi, J., Malik, J.: Normalized cuts and image segmentation. IEEE Transactions on Pattern Analysis and Machine Intelligence (PAMI) 22(8), 888–905 (2000)
13. Korah, T., Rasmussen, C.: Analysis of building textures for reconstructing partially occluded facades. In: Forsyth, D., Torr, P., Zisserman, A. (eds.) ECCV 2008, Part I. LNCS, vol. 5302, pp. 359–372. Springer, Heidelberg (2008)
14. Barber, C.B., Dobkin, D.P., Huhdanpaa, H.: The quickhull algorithm for convex hulls. ACM Transactions on Mathematical Software 22(4), 469–483 (1996)
15. Brown, M., Lowe, D.G.: Automatic panoramic image stitching using invariant features. International Journal of Computer Vision (IJCV) 74(1), 59–73 (2007)
16. Rijsbergen, C.J.V.: Information retrieval. Butterworth-Heinemann Newton, MA (1979)

Image Segmentation with a Statistical Appearance Model and a Generic Mumford-Shah Inspired Outside Model

Thomas Albrecht and Thomas Vetter

University of Basel

Abstract. We present a novel statistical-model-based segmentation algorithm that addresses a recurrent problem in appearance model fitting and model-based segmentation: the "shrinking problem". When statistical appearance models are fitted to an image in order to segment an object, they have the tendency not to cover the full object, leaving a gap between the real and the detected boundary. This is due to the fact that the cost function for fitting the model is evaluated only on the inside of the object and the gap at the boundary is not detected. The state-of-the-art approach to overcome this shrinking problem is to detect the object edges in the image and force the model to adhere to these edges. Here, we introduce a region-based approach motivated by the Mumford-Shah functional that does not require the detection of edges. In addition to the appearance model, we define a generic model estimated from the input image for the outside of the appearance model. Shrinking is prevented because a misaligned boundary would create a large discrepancy between the image and the inside/outside model. The method is independent of the dimensionality of the image. We apply it to 3-dimensional CT images.

1 Introduction

We present a novel statistical-model-based segmentation algorithm that addresses a recurrent problem in appearance model fitting and model-based segmentation: the "shrinking problem", see the "Examples of Failure" in [1] for instance. When statistical appearance models are fitted to an image in order to segment an object, they have the tendency not to cover the full object, leaving a gap between the real and the detected boundary. The model seems to shrink inside the real object, a typical example can be seen in Figure 3b. This is due to the fact that the cost function for fitting the model is evaluated only on the inside of the object and the gap at the boundary is not detected. The state-of-the-art approach to overcome this shrinking problem is to detect the object edges in the image and force the model to adhere to these edges [2]. While this can in fact prevent shrinking, it requires the accurate detection of the object boundary. But in many applications the boundary detection can be almost as difficult as the original segmentation task.

M. Goesele et al. (Eds.): DAGM 2010, LNCS 6376, pp. 61–70, 2010.

Here, we introduce a region-based method that aims at solving the shrinking problem without the need to explicitly detect edges. The idea is borrowed from the Mumford-Shah functional for image segmentation [3], and is widely used in the field of level set segmentation [4]: Instead of detecting edges, we try to partition the image into different regions. The edges are only implicitly determined as the boundary between these regions, see [5] for an illustrative explanation of this principle. While the original Mumford-Shah method seeks any regions that offer an optimal piecewise approximation of the image, in our case of appearance model fitting, we have a very strong preconception into what regions we wish to partition the image: The foreground object, which is an instance of our statistical appearance model, and the background, the area around the model. In this way, we combine some of the advantages of Mumford-Shah based level set segmentation and appearance model fitting.

Statistical appearance models are built from example data sets and model the shape and appearance of a specific object class. Typical object classes in the literature are faces, organs or bones. In some cases, the example data sets may offer representative data not only for the inside of the object but also for the background. In these cases, the background can be modeled in a similar way to the foreground, see [6], or the model can simply be enlarged to include some of the background information. This problem can be regarded as solved.

We on the other hand focus on cases where the example data sets do not provide representative data for the background. Even though it would be desirable to develop a complete model of an object and all possible backgrounds and adjacent objects, it is easier and often the only realistic option to focus on one object of interest at a time. Our main motivation is a femur bone model we developed from CT scans of isolated bones. In the scans, the bones are surrounded only by air, but in most practical applications, bones will be surrounded by soft tissue, adjacent bones, etc., see Figure 1. A similar situation is found in face modeling, where a model has to be fitted to faces without any prior knowledge about the background.

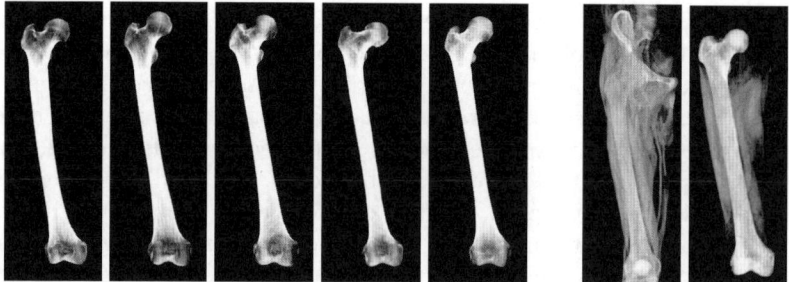

Fig. 1. On the left: a subset of the bones used to build the appearance model. The model is built from isolated bones. No useful information is available for the outside of the bones that could be used in real segmentation tasks such as segmenting the femur in the images on the right.

With no usable example data on the outside of the object, we look again to the Mumford-Shah functional [3], which is generic in the sense that it does not model regions based on examples. Instead, the appearance for the different regions is estimated form the input image itself. The original formulation of the functional proposes two possible ways to estimate the appearance for a given region from the intensity values: the mean intensity or a smoothed version of the image on that region. More sophisticated models have later been developed, see [4]. However, introducing and evaluating the different modeling techniques for different applications is beyond the scope of this paper and we introduce our method based on the simple models from [3].

Prior Work. Image segmentation remains one of the most important challenges in image analysis. When the objects of interest like for instance bones, organs or faces, cannot be identified by simple intensity thresholding, the most successful and intensively researched approach is to include prior knowledge in the form of a statistical shape model into the segmentation algorithms and allow only shapes than can be represented by this model as segmentation results. We can distinguish between algorithms with strict and those with relaxed shape constraints. The algorithm we propose here enforces a strict shape constraint, which means that the segmentation results have to strictly lie in the space of shapes modeled by the statistical model. Essentially, such a segmentation can also be regarded as a model fitting algorithm, as it optimizes only the pose and model parameters. In principle the strict shape constraint could be relaxed by one of the methods proposed in [6], but we have not yet implemented these methods.

There are two main segmentation frameworks that are commonly used as the basis for shape-model-constrained segmentation and our method combines features from both of them. The first is based on the active shape and appearance models as proposed by Cootes, Taylor et al. [1] or Blanz and Vetter [7]. The second framework is that of level set segmentation and is mostly based on the Mumford-Shah functional [3] and its level set formulation [5]. Instead of trying to summarize the extensive research performed in this area, we refer to the comprehensive reviews by Heimann et al. [6] and Cremers et al. [4]. Both frameworks share the distinction between edge- and region-based segmentation. Region-based methods have proven to be more robust and successful as they do not only consider local edge information, but rather complete regions like the inside and the outside of the segmented object, see [4,6].

Shape and Region Modelling. Conceptually, the main difference between the level set and active appearance model frameworks is the representation of the shapes. Active shape and appearance models represent shapes by discrete point sets or grids, while level set methods represent shapes by implicit (= level set) functions. Consequently, for including prior knowledge about an object class of shapes into the segmentation algorithm, appropriate statistical models have been proposed for each framework. Active shape and appearance models represent the class of shapes by deformations of a reference. New shapes are generated by linear combinations of example deformations. In order to determine these example deformations, the example data sets have to be brought into correspondence with a non-rigid registration algorithm. In level set methods, a class of shapes is modeled by linear combination of example level set functions. For this, the shapes do not need to be in correspondence but only rigidly aligned.

Further, the different shape model representations determine a different treatment of the image regions within the model. With correspondence information available, it is easy to transfer the image intensity or "appearance" of each example to the reference and build a separate linear model of appearances. For level set based models without correspondence information, such a straight-forward appearance modeling is not possible. Therefore, level set methods typically use intensity models estimated from the input image or histogram-based statistic that do not require correspondence information.

If we wish to use the statistical appearance information from the example data sets for the inside of the model and a generic model estimated from the input image on the outside, we have two possibilities: 1. Find a way to integrate a correspondence-based intensity model in the level set framework. 2. Integrate a generic input-image-based outside model into the active appearance model fitting. While the first possibility is an interesting research topic and may be the subject of a future paper, we take the second approach here. In this way the appearance model can be used in its original form and only needs to be complemented by an outside model.

2   Segmentation Method

In this section, we give a more detailed description of the models and show how they can be combined. Then, we show the feasibility of our approach on a few qualitative results. A thorough comparison with state of the art segmentation methods would require the implementation of many edge- and region-based segmentation methods, which is beyond the scope of this paper.

2.1   Inside Shape and Appearance Model

To build the inside appearance model, we need to acquire a representative collection of example data sets of the organ we wish to model. In our experiments, we acquired $n = 47$ CT data sets of isolated human femur bones. After a rigid pre-alignment, these are brought into correspondence with a non-rigid image registration method [8]. We single out one of the data sets as the reference and register all n data sets to this reference. This introduces a bias in the model towards the reference, but the interested reader can find strategies to remove or reduce this bias in [6]. Once the data sets are registered, a statistical shape and appearance model can be built along the lines of those proposed by Blanz and Vetter or Cootes and Taylor [7,1]. The registration algorithm produces n deformation fields $u_i : \Omega \to \mathbb{R}^d$ defined on the reference's image domain $\Omega \subset \mathbb{R}^d$, where the dimensionality d is of course typically 2 or 3. When we denote by

$\Gamma \subset \Omega$ the points on the inside of the reference shape, the inside of the target shapes is represented as

$$\Gamma_i = \{x + u_i(x) \,|\, x \in \Gamma\}, \tag{1}$$

i.e. Γ_i is a forward warp of Γ with $x + u_i(x)$. On the other hand, we can backward-warp the CT intensities ct_i of the targets to the reference as:

$$\widetilde{ct}_i(x) = ct_i(x + u(x)) \text{ for } x \in \Gamma_i. \tag{2}$$

In this way, the shape and the intensity information of all examples is available on the reference. In practice Γ is a finite set with $m := |\Gamma|$ elements, and each shape can be represented by a dm-dimensional vector $\mathbf{s}_i$ of coordinates and each appearance by an m-dimensional vector $\mathbf{t}_i$ of intensity values. From these, we can calculate mean vectors $\bar{\mathbf{s}}$ and $\bar{\mathbf{t}}$ and covariance matrices $\Sigma_s = \frac{1}{n}\mathbf{X}_s\mathbf{X}_s^T$, $\Sigma_t = \frac{1}{n}\mathbf{X}_t\mathbf{X}_t^T$, where $\mathbf{X}_s, \mathbf{X}_t$ are the mean free data matrices with columns $\mathbf{s}_i - \bar{\mathbf{s}}$ resp. $\mathbf{t}_i - \bar{\mathbf{t}}$. The actual statistical modeling consists of assuming multivariate normal distributions $\mathcal{N}(\bar{\mathbf{s}}, \Sigma_s)$, $\mathcal{N}(\bar{\mathbf{t}}, \Sigma_t)$ for the shape and intensity data. After a singular value decomposition of the data matrices:

$$\tfrac{1}{\sqrt{n}}\mathbf{X}_s = \mathbf{U}_s\mathbf{W}_s\mathbf{V}_s^T \text{ resp. } \tfrac{1}{\sqrt{n}}\mathbf{X}_t = \mathbf{U}_t\mathbf{W}_t\mathbf{V}_t^T, \tag{3}$$

we can represent the shapes and intensities of the statistical model as:

$$\mathbf{s}(\alpha) = \bar{\mathbf{s}} + \mathbf{U}_s\mathbf{W}_s\,\alpha =: \bar{\mathbf{s}} + \mathbf{Q}_s\,\alpha, \text{ and } \mathbf{t}(\beta) = \bar{\mathbf{t}} + \mathbf{U}_t\mathbf{W}_t\,\beta =: \bar{\mathbf{t}} + \mathbf{Q}_t\,\beta. \tag{4}$$

where α and β are coefficient vectors. Under the assumption of the above normal distributions, α and β are distributed according to $\mathcal{N}(0, \mathbf{I})$. While the 3D Morphable Model [7] was originally only defined *on* and not on the inside of the modeled 3D object and the active appearance model [1,6] was originally only introduced for 2D shapes, this is a straight-forward extension of these models. Such models are usually called PCA models as Equations (3) and (4) constitute a principal component analysis of the data matrices.

Segmentation with this statistical model is now performed by finding those coefficients α, β for which the difference between the shape and appearance associated with the vectors $\mathbf{s}(\alpha), \mathbf{t}(\beta)$ and the target object in the input image $\mathcal{I}(x)$ is minimal. In addition to the shape and appearance, we also need to estimate the pose of the object in the image, which can be represented by a rigid or similarity transform T_ρ with parameters ρ. The segmentation can be formulated as a minimization problem. For better readability we treat the vectors $\mathbf{s}, \mathbf{t}$ as continuous functions and write the problem as an integral:

$$E(\alpha, \beta, \rho) = \int_\Gamma \Big(\underbrace{(\bar{\mathbf{t}} + \mathbf{U}_t\beta)(x)}_{\text{model intensity}} - \underbrace{\mathcal{I}\big(T_\rho\,(\bar{\mathbf{s}} + \mathbf{U}_s\alpha)(x)\big)}_{\text{image intensity at model point}} \Big)^2 dx + \eta_s\|\alpha\|^2 + \eta_t\|\beta\|^2.$$

$$\tag{5}$$

The norms of α and β with weighting terms η_t, η_s act as regularization terms motivated by the normal distributions $\mathcal{N}(0, \mathbf{I})$ of α and β. The optimal parameters α, β, ρ can be sought with any standard optimization algorithm, and in this fashion the shape, appearance and position of any object that can be represented by the statistical model can be identified. However, only points on the inside of the model are considered and all points on the outside of the model are ignored, which can lead to the adverse effect of "shrinking" described in the introduction.

2.2   Mumford Shah Model

In their landmark paper [3], Mumford and Shah introduced what is now known as the Mumford-Shah functional for image segmentation, which seeks to simultaneously find an edge set C and a piecewise smooth approximation $\mathcal{J}$ of an input image $\mathcal{I} : \Omega \to \mathbb{R}$. In [5] Chan and Vese proposed a simplified version of this functional for the case that C is a closed contour (represented by a level set function) that separates the image domain Ω into an inside and an outside, $\text{in}(C)$ and $\text{out}(C)$ of C. In this case, the Mumford-Shah functional can be written as:

$$F(C, \mathcal{J}) = \lambda \int_{\text{in}(C)} (\mathcal{J}_{\text{in}} - \mathcal{I})^2 + \lambda \int_{\text{out}(C)} (\mathcal{J}_{\text{out}} - \mathcal{I})^2 + \mu \text{ length}(C) + \nu \int_{\Omega \backslash C} |\nabla \mathcal{J}|^2 , \quad (6)$$

where $\text{length}(C)$ denotes the length of the segment boundary C and acts as a regularization term. Typically, the functional is minimized with an interlaced algorithm. In every other iteration the boundary C is kept fixed and the image approximation $\mathcal{J}$ is optimized and in the next iteration $\mathcal{J}$ is fixed and C optimized. Mumford and Shah showed that if C is fixed, $\mathcal{J}$ optimizes the functional if and only if it satisfies the following elliptic boundary value problem with zero Neumann boundary conditions on each of the segments, here written out only for $\text{out}(C)$:

$$-\Delta \mathcal{J}_{\text{out}} = \frac{\lambda}{\nu} (\mathcal{I} - \mathcal{J}_{\text{out}}) \text{ on } \text{out}(C) \qquad \frac{\partial \mathcal{J}_{\text{out}}}{\partial n} = 0 \text{ on } \partial(\text{out}(C)). \quad (7)$$

This means that $\mathcal{J}$ has to be a smoothed version of $\mathcal{I}$ with sharp edges on the boundary C, which is why the functional is minimal when C coincides with edges in the image, while on the segments the image can be approximated well by smooth functions. The great advantage over methods based on actual edge detection is that when no sharp edges are present in the image, the minimizing edge set C will still separate the different regions in the image in an optimal way when $F(C, \mathcal{J})$ is minimized. If $\frac{\lambda}{\nu} \to 0$, the optimal approximation $\mathcal{J}$ is a piecewise constant function which takes on the mean value of the function $\mathcal{I}$ on each of the segments, i.e. $\mathcal{J}_{\text{out}} \equiv c_{\text{out}} = \frac{1}{|\text{out}(C)|} \int_{\text{out}(C)} \mathcal{I}$. More sophisticated approximation strategies for $\mathcal{J}_{\text{in,out}}$, e.g. based on texture can be found in [4].

This segmentation method separates those two regions which can be best approximated by mean intensities or smooth approximations. However, it is by no means guaranteed that these coincide with the organs we want to segment in the image.

2.3 Combining the Models

We now present a way to combine the prior knowledge of the statistical shape and appearance model and the generic ad-hoc modeling technique of the Mumford-Shah segmentation method. For the inside of the object, we use the appearance model exactly as described in Section 2.1. The outside Mumford-Shah model is derived from (6) with a few adjustments. First of all, we only use the terms concerning the outside region. The length term can be omitted as the regularization properties of the statistical model provide a superior regularization method.

The terms in Equation (6) are defined on a part of the input image domain, whereas Equation (5) is defined on a part of the reference domain. To seamlessly integrate the outside terms into the appearance model segmentation, we need to transform them to the reference domain. In Equation (5), the spatial transformation from the reference model to the image is given by $\Phi_{\alpha,\rho}(x) := T_\rho\,(\bar{\mathbf{s}}+\mathbf{Q}_s\alpha)(x)$. and thus the transformation ("change of variables") of the outside terms by:

$$
\lambda \int_{\text{out}(C)} (\mathcal{J}_{\text{out}} - \mathcal{I})^2 + \nu \int_{\text{out}(C)} |\nabla \mathcal{J}_{\text{out}}|^2 = \lambda \int_{\Phi_{\alpha,\rho}(\Gamma_{\text{out}})} (\mathcal{J}_{\text{out}} - \mathcal{I})^2 + \nu \int_{\Phi_{\alpha,\rho}(\Gamma_{\text{out}})} |\nabla \mathcal{J}_{\text{out}}|^2
$$

$$
= \lambda \int_{\Gamma_{\text{out}}} (\mathcal{J}_{\text{out}} \circ \Phi_{\alpha,\rho} - \mathcal{I} \circ \Phi_{\alpha,\rho})^2 \, |\det D\Phi_{\alpha,\rho}| + \nu \int_{\Gamma_{\text{out}}} |\nabla \mathcal{J}_{\text{out}} \circ \Phi_{\alpha,\rho}|^2 \, |\det D\Phi_{\alpha,\rho}|,
$$

$$(8)$$

where Γ_{out} is the outside of the model in the reference domain. In principal, Γ_{out} should be chosen so that $\Phi_{\alpha,\rho}(\Gamma_{\text{out}}) = \text{out}(C)$, but in practice, any neighborhood of Γ can be used. Then, contrary to the original integral from the Mumford-Shah functional, the transformed integral does not depend on the function or parameters we wish to optimize, which greatly simplifies the minimization. The only dependence remains in the determinant term from the transformation formula $|\det D\Phi_{\alpha,\rho}|$. However, this is where we introduce a simplifying approximation and assume $|\det D\Phi_{\alpha,\rho}| \equiv 1$, as it would be very time-consuming to compute the derivative of the deformations caused by the matrix $\mathbf{Q}_s$. Secondly, this term measures the volume change caused by $\Phi_{\alpha,\rho}$ and would allow the minimization of the functional simply by contracting the model, which is not desirable. Our proposed combined segmentation problem is then given as:

$$
G(\alpha, \beta, \rho) = \int_\Gamma \left((\bar{\mathbf{t}} + \mathbf{Q}_t\beta)(x) - \mathcal{I} \circ \Phi_{\alpha,\rho}(x) \right)^2 dx + \eta_s \|\alpha\|^2 + \eta_t \|\beta\|^2
$$

$$
+ \lambda \int_{\Gamma_{\text{out}}} (\mathcal{J}_{\text{out}} \circ \Phi_{\alpha,\rho} - \mathcal{I} \circ \Phi_{\alpha,\rho})^2 + \nu \int_{\Gamma_{\text{out}}} |\nabla \mathcal{J}_{\text{out}} \circ \Phi_{\alpha,\rho}|^2. \quad (9)
$$

The principal component matrix $\mathbf{Q}_s$ and mean vector $\bar{\mathbf{s}}$ used in $\Phi_{\alpha,\rho}$ have been defined only for the inside model Γ in Section 2.1. They need to be extended to the outside in order to calculate the outside terms of Equation (9). If the deformation fields u_i from which the model is calculated are defined on the entire image domain of the reference, which is the case for the registration algorithm we used, this extension can be performed in a straight-forward manner. The mean vector $\bar{\mathbf{s}}$ is naturally extended by the mean of the fields on Γ_{out}. The matrix $\mathbf{Q}_s$ can be extended by employing the same linear combination of the original deformation fields on the outside as on the inside. The linear combinations are stored in the matrix $\mathbf{V}_s$ from the singular value decomposition Equation (3), and we can compute the principal component's extension to Γ_{out} as $\mathbf{Q}_s = (\mathbf{X}_s - \bar{\mathbf{s}})\, \mathbf{V}_s$.

2.4   Implementation

The minimization of the functional G defined in Equation (9) is handled in an interlaced algorithm similar to that described in Section 2.2: We alternately calculate the ad-hoc model $\mathcal{J}_{\mathrm{out}}$ for the current parameters α, β, ρ, and find the parameters for the next iteration step with a standard optimization algorithm; we use the LBFGS optimizer [9]. $\mathcal{J}_{\mathrm{out}}$ needs to be calculated from the image intensities as the mean or according to the elliptic equation (7) (on Γ_{out} instead of $\mathrm{out}(C)$). Like the inside Γ, we represent Γ_{out} by an unstructured grid, and implemented a Gaussian smoothing with Neumann zero boundary conditions on this grid to approximate the solution of Equation (7). A more exact solution could be achieved by computing a finite element solution on this grid.

2.5   Results

We conclude by showing a few examples of bone segmentations that show the feasibility of segmentation with our proposed combined method and its advantages over the individual methods of level set and appearance model segmentation. As we are using a strict shape constraint, none of the segmentation results are perfect. They are only the best approximation within the space of the shape model that the optimization algorithm was able to find. We used the LBFGS algorithm with a landmark-based rigid alignment of the mean model as initialization. The method is not very sensitive to the parameters. For all experiments, we have chosen $\lambda = 1$, $\eta_s = 100$, $\eta_t = 10$. For the Gaussian smoothing of the outside model, we have used a variance that corresponds to $\nu = 300$.

Figure 2 illustrates the two proposed method for outside models. Only when the outside of the bone is very uniform as for instance in the case of isolated

Fig. 2. On the left: A CT slice with its approximation by the inside and outside model. The inside is an instance of the statistical model, while the outside is modeled as a smoothed version of the image intensities. On the right, the outside is modeled as the mean value of the outside intensities, which works best for uniform outside intensity.

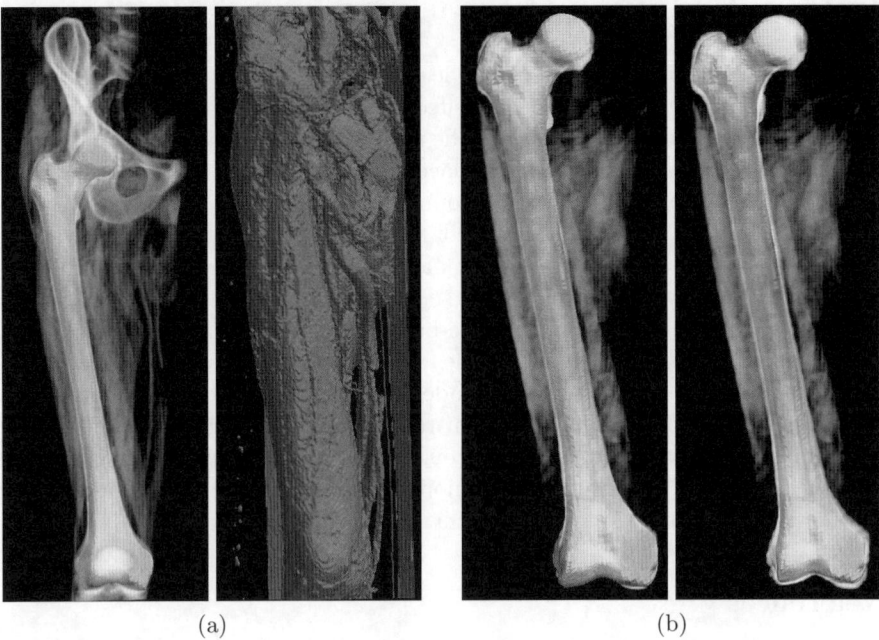

(a)   (b)

Fig. 3. Comparison of the our segmentation method with each of the original methods. The input images are shown in Figure 1. On the left in (a), the proposed method identifies to femur bone, whereas the original Mumford-Shah level set segmentation on the right separates air from not-air, and the segmentation boundary shows the muscle tissue and not the femur bone. On the left in (b), the proposed method identifies the femur as well as the model permits, while on the right the appearance model without outside model "shrinks" and leaves a small gap between the model and the real bone surface.

bones is the constant approximation by the mean preferable over the smooth approximation. Note that the aim of the outside model is not the perfect representation of the input image, that would of course be given by the unsmoothed image itself. The aim is to give a homogeneous representation of the outside which encourages the correct placement of the model boundary because any other placement would incur a higher cost in the functional from Equation (9).

In Figure 3a we see how our method can identify the femur in a CT image with soft tissue and other bones. In contrast, the Mumford-Shah level set segmentation finds the most prominent segment boundary in the image, that between air and everything that is not air. While this is the optimal boundary from the point of view of this segmentation method, it is not the boundary we are interested in if we wish to segment femur bones. In Figure 3b, we see another successful segmentation with our combined model, contrasted with a result of using only the inside appearance model. As expected, in this case, the segmentation leaves a narrow gap around the boundary of the model.

3 Discussion

We have showed that including an outside model term motivated by the Mumford-Shah functional can help reduce the effect of "shrinking" in active appearance model fitting/segmentation. Without the need of explicit edge detection, the outside model discourages the incorrect placement of the boundary. Obviously, this works best in regions where the foreground and background have distinct intensity values, but the correct separation of fore- and background should always be at least as good as without the outside model. We did not yet perform a quantitative comparison with state-of-the-art segmentation or model fitting algorithms. In fact, we think that a fine-tuned edge-based method may perform equally well or even better if the correct edges can be found. But we have shown that a region-based combined model can improve model-based segmentation while completely circumventing the difficult and often unstable problem of edge detection.

Possible future work includes a thorough quantitative comparison with state-of-the-art methods, the evaluation of more advanced outside region models, and ways to relax the strict shape constraint.

References

1. Cootes, T., Taylor, C.: Statistical models of appearance for medical image analysis and computer vision. In: Proc. SPIE Medical Imaging, vol. 4322, pp. 236–248 (2001)
2. Romdhani, S., Vetter, T.: Estimating 3d shape and texture using pixel intensity, edges, specular highlights, texture constraints and a prior. In: IEEE Computer Society Conference on Computer Vision and Pattern Recognition, CVPR 2005, vol. 2 (2005)
3. Mumford, D., Shah, J.: Optimal Approximations by Piecewise Smooth Functions and Associated Variational Problems. Center for Intelligent Control Systems (1988)
4. Cremers, D., Rousson, M., Deriche, R.: A Review of Statistical Approaches to Level Set Segmentation: Integrating Color, Texture, Motion and Shape. International Journal of Computer Vision 72(2), 195–215 (2007)
5. Chan, T.F., Vese, L.A.: Active contours without edges. IEEE Trans. Image Process. 10(2), 266–277 (2001)
6. Heimann, T., Meinzer, H.: Statistical shape models for 3D medical image segmentation: A review. Medical Image Analysis (2009)
7. Blanz, V., Vetter, T.: A morphable model for the synthesis of 3d faces. In: SIGGRAPH 1999: Proceedings of the 26th annual conference on Computer graphics and interactive techniques, pp. 187–194. ACM Press, New York (1999)
8. Dedner, A., Lüthi, M., Albrecht, T., Vetter, T.: Curvature guided level set registration using adaptive finite elements. In: Pattern Recognition, pp. 527–536 (2007)
9. Zhu, C., Byrd, R., Lu, P., Nocedal, J.: L-BFGS-B: Fortran subroutines for large-scale bound constrained optimization. ACM Transactions on Mathetmatical Software 23(4), 550–560 (1997)

Estimating Force Fields of Living Cells – Comparison of Several Regularization Schemes Combined with Automatic Parameter Choice

Sebastian Houben, Norbert Kirchgeßner, and Rudolf Merkel

Forschungszentrum Jülich, IBN-4, 52425 Jülich, Germany
{n.kirchgessner,r.merkel}@fz-juelich.de

Abstract. In this paper we evaluate several regularization schemes applied to the problem of force estimation, that is Traction Force Microscopy (TFM). This method is widely used to investigate cell adhesion and migration processes as well as cellular response to mechanical and chemical stimuli. To estimate force densities TFM requires the solution of an inverse problem, a deconvolution. Two main approaches have been established for this. The method introduced by Dembo [1] makes a finite element approach and inverts the emerging LES by means of regularization. Hence this method is very robust, but requires high computational effort. The other ansatz by Butler [2] works in Fourier space to solve the problem by direct inversion. It is therefore based on the assumption of smooth data with little noise. The combination of both, a regularization in Fourier space, has been proposed [3] but not analyzed in detail. We cover this analysis and present several methods for an objective and automatic choice of the required regularization parameters.

1 Introduction

Living cells in multicellular organisms, e.g. sponges, mice and men, are constantly experiencing and, most often, generating mechanical forces. These are essential in a plethora of physiological and pathological processes ranging from stem cell differentiation and tissue formation during embryogenesis to cell locomotion in the cellular immune response and cancer metastasis. Any attempt to quantitatively understand such processes crucially depends on spatially and temporally highly resolved measurements of cell forces. The first reliable technique to visualize forces of individual cells was pioneered by Harris et al. [4] who grew cells on a thin silicone sheet and observed wrinkles emerging under contracting cells. To estimate the acting traction forces the setup was slightly changed by replacing the silicone sheet with a solidly supported thin film of elastic material. Usually cross-linked polyacrylamide (PAA) [1] or polydimethylsiloxane (PDMS) [5], [6] are used. Fluorescent marker beads are embedded slightly below the surface. These markers can be localized by fluorescent light microscopy combined with digital image processing (c.f. Sect. 2). By comparison to a reference image where the cell has been removed mechanically and the rubber has reached its relaxed state the cell force induced deformations can be quantified (see Fig. 1).

M. Goesele et al. (Eds.): DAGM 2010, LNCS 6376, pp. 71–80, 2010.

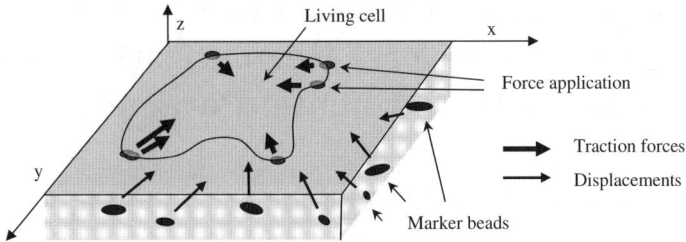

Fig. 1. Scheme of the experimental setup for traction force analysis. A cell is located on a thin rubber film with embedded marker beads and exerts forces on it. The position of the fluorescent beads can be detected with fluorescence microscopy and quantified by digital image processing (c.f. Sect. 2). The deformation vector field is subsequently used to estimate location and magnitude of the cell force (see Sect. 3). Please note that the proportions are not realistic.

To find a mathematical model that relates the measured deformations to the traction forces the silicone substrate layer is most often assumed to be infinitely thick, i.e., a linear elastic halfspace. Furthermore, the tractions are restricted to act only on the surface of the halfspace. This kind of problem was studied in elasticity theory by Boussinesq [7], [8] and found to satisfy the following Fredholm integral equation

$$\int_{\mathbb{R}^2\setminus\{y\}} G(y-x)f(x)dx = u(y) \text{ for each } y \in \mathbb{R}^2 \text{ or short } \mathcal{G}[f] = u , \quad (1)$$

where $u : \mathbb{R}^2 \mapsto \mathbb{R}^2$ denotes the deformation at a place y, $f : \mathbb{R}^2 \mapsto \mathbb{R}^2$ the force at a location x and G the Boussinesq Greens' Tensor

$$G(d) = \frac{3}{4\pi E|d|^3} \begin{pmatrix} |d|^2 + d_1^2 & d_1 d_2 \\ d_1 d_2 & |d|^2 + d_2^2 \end{pmatrix} \text{ with } d = (d_1, d_2)^T \in \mathbb{R}^2 . \quad (2)$$

For notational clarity we use the uncommon $\mathcal{G}[f]$ for the linear operator $\mathcal{G}$ acting on f. E is the rubber's Young modulus. Its Poisson ratio was found to be 0.5 [6] corresponding to an incompressible medium. Merkel et al [9] have shown that the assumption of an infinite halfspace has to be dropped if the layer thickness is less than 60 μm. Here a modified Greens' Tensor must be used, c.f. [9].

For both the finite and the infinite thickness case we must therefore invert a Fredholm integral equation, a procedure which is known to be ill-posed. It hence requires a regularization ansatz. We briefly introduce the methods of Dembo and Butler in Sects. 1.1 and 1.2, several possibilities combining both methods are discussed in Sect. 3.

1.1 Finite Element Method

To discretize the integral equation (1) Dembo used the manually marked cell outline and generated a quadrilateral mesh within for estimating traction densities. Cell forces are therefore restricted to the cell area. This is a reasonable assumption and limits the complexity of the emerging equation system. However, after discretization the LES is still ill-posed and normally even lacks a solution. To circumvent this Dembo made use of the regularization functional

$$||\mathcal{G}\,[f] - u||^2 + \lambda\Omega(f) \tag{3}$$

whose minimum is a force distribution f that compromises between the measured data set u and the operator Ω. In Dembo's method an entropy measure is used to prefer smooth force fields. The regularization parameter $\lambda \geq 0$ is used to adjust the expected complexity of the solution. Dembo's method is known to be highly accurate and profits from the restriction to the force application area, which stabilizes the algorithm and restrains the number of unknowns. Nevertheless, f is still high-dimensional and the minimization of the functional (3) is computationally expensive.

1.2   Fourier Method

Since the left-hand side of Equation (1) is a convolution, a transformation to Fourier space will reduce it to a simple product

$$\hat{G}(k)\hat{f}(k) = \hat{u}(k) \text{ for each } k \in \mathbb{R}^2 \ , \tag{4}$$

where $\hat{G}, \hat{f}, \hat{u}$ respectively denote the Fourier transforms of G, f, u and k is a two dimensional wave number. Note that for each k Equation (4) is a LES with two equations and two unknowns while the Dembo's LES is a system with $2n$ equations and $2m$ unknowns. Here the number of beads is denoted by n and m is the number of forces. The inversion of (4) is therefore very fast. However, for small k the matrix $\hat{G}$ is nearly singular and a good solution will hence crucially depend on noise-free data as mentioned by Butler et al [2].

2   Digital Image Processing

Several methods are currently in use to track fluorescent marker beads in micrographs. All of them are comparably fast, accurate and reliable. In our case we used a tracking algorithm that was implemented and described earlier [9]. Briefly, the method comprises two steps. First, an interactively marked sample bead of the reference image is fitted by a two dimensional Gaussian to obtain a template. This is then compared to the whole image by normalized cross-correlation. Local maxima of the thresholded correlation function are assumed to be probable bead positions. Second, from each of these initial positions in the reference image a template is taken and cross-correlated to a certain vicinity in the image of the strained rubber. Templates that are recognized above a preselected threshold are taken into account for the deformation vector field.

3   Regularization

In the following we suggest a combination of both Dembo's and Butler's method, a regularization in Fourier space, aiming to connect the stabilizing effects of the regularization approach with the fast computation of a fourier space scheme. Such a combined method has already been proposed by Sabass et al [3] albeit without quantitative analysis of the possible regularization schemes and with a manual choice of the regularization parameter. For this purpose we interpolate the scattered deformation vector field on a rectangular grid. Let g_x, g_y be the grid numbers and x_{min}, x_{max}, y_{min} and y_{max} minimum and maximum x- and y-coordinate of the n bead positions, respectively. By choosing

$$g_x := \left\lfloor \sqrt{n \frac{y_{max} - y_{min}}{x_{max} - x_{min}}} \right\rfloor \text{ and } g_y := \left\lfloor \frac{n}{g_x} \right\rfloor \tag{5}$$

we guarantee that the number of displacement vectors and the aspect ratio of the definition area stay approximately the same. Please note that by this choice the spatial resolution of our TFM method is already determined ($\lfloor x \rfloor :=$ $\max_{k \in Z, k \leq x}(k)$). In a next step we perform a FFT on the interpolated deformation field to obtain $\tilde{u}$ and[1] likewise wave numbers $k_{1,x}, k_{1,y}..., k_{n,x}, k_{n,y} \in \mathbb{R}$. We now approach equation (4) for these k. For convenience, let

$$\tilde{G} := \begin{pmatrix} \hat{G}(k_{1,x}) & & \\ & \ddots & \\ & & \hat{G}(k_{n,y}) \end{pmatrix} . \tag{6}$$

We retrieve the LES

$$\tilde{G}\tilde{f} = \tilde{u} . \tag{7}$$

A back transformation of its solution[2] $\tilde{f}$ gives a force density on the grid that $\tilde{u}$ was interpolated on. However, the blocks of $\tilde{G}$ are nearly singular for small values of k and must hence be regularized. For reasons of computational efficiency and convenient implementation we restrict ourselves to a slightly generalized version of the regularization procedure by Tikhonov [10]. In fact we make use of the following functional:

$$||\tilde{G}\tilde{f} - \tilde{u}||^2 + \lambda||L(\tilde{f} - f_0)||^2 , \tag{8}$$

where L is a quadratic matrix and f_0 is a vector of the same dimension as $\tilde{f}$. The minimum of this functional is known to be the solution of

$$(\tilde{G}^*\tilde{G} + \lambda L^*L)\tilde{f} = \tilde{G}^*\tilde{u} + \lambda L^*L f_0 \tag{9}$$

that is guaranteed to be unique if L is injective. Minimization of (8) is therefore unexpensively accomplished by direct inversion of (9). Choosing L and f_0 is

---

[1] $\tilde{u}$ is a vector containing x- and y- coordinates of the Fourier-transformed deformation vectors in the grid which is assigned linewise.

[2] $\tilde{f}$ is unique because $\tilde{G}$ is blockwise non-singular.

equivalent to selecting a suitable penalty term for equation (8). L is normally chosen to be a measure of a property that the solution is expected to have while f_0 can be understood to be an approximation of the solution itsself. There are procedures that allow the definition of an optimal L using a Bayesian approach with a prior of the solution's noise distribution. Because traction force patterns have never been measured by direct methods, the essential information for the Bayesian interpretation is unavailable. Instead we will evaluate several heuristic methods that are based on reasonable assumptions of location, formation and temporal evolution of the traction field.

3.1   Classic Approaches

A first attempt to stabilize (7) is to penalize high values of $\tilde{f}$ by setting $L = I$ as proposed by Tikhonov [10]. Since the equations that belong to small wave numbers are more instable than those to large ones, it also seems reasonable to penalize high Fourier coefficients for small wave numbers.[3] For this we made the following choices we call wave damp or wave damp square choosing

$$L_{ij} := \delta_{ij}\frac{1}{|k_i|} \qquad \text{or} \qquad L_{ij} := \delta_{ij}\frac{1}{|k_i|^2} \; . \qquad (10)$$

3.2   Temporal Smoothing

In many cases a series of cell and substrate images is made to record the cell's activity. If we assume that the difference of forces from image to image is small we can develop another penalty term. Let $t_1, ..., t_l \in \mathbb{R}$ be the points of time the images were made and $u^{(t_i)}$ the respective deformation and forces at those points of time. If we set

$$\bar{G} := \overbrace{\begin{pmatrix} \tilde{G} & & \\ & \ddots & \\ & & \tilde{G} \end{pmatrix}}^{l \text{ times}} \qquad \text{and} \qquad \bar{u} := \begin{pmatrix} u^{(t_1)} \\ \vdots \\ u^{(t_l)} \end{pmatrix} \qquad (11)$$

the solution of $\bar{G}\bar{f} = \bar{u}$ will give a force density estimation for the whole series of images. We can now introduce our assumptions of little difference by applying

$$L_{ij} := \delta_{ij} - \delta_{i(j-2n)} \; , \qquad (12)$$

i.e. the penalty term sums the differences between the fourier coefficients in one time step and the proceeding. Thus, the functional (8) will prefer solutions where the forces at the different points of time only change slightly.

---

[3] With ground truth we could isolate the critical frequencies for an optimal L.

3.3 Restriction to a Predefined Area

An important advantage of Dembo's finite element method is that it easily allows the force to be estimated only within a predefined area. By transforming the convolution (1) into Fourier space this seems to become impossible since the FFT algorithm works on a rectangular grid. However, it is possible to effectively restrict forces to a certain area by the following procedure. Let $1_C : \mathbb{R}^2 \mapsto \{0, 1\}$ be the indicator function for the cell area, i.e., $1_C(x)$ yields 1 if and only if x is within the cell area.

The procedure consists of two steps. First we solve equation (7) by a common regularization scheme (c.f. Sects. 3.1 and 3.2) to get a solution $\tilde{f}$. We now transform $\tilde{f}$ into spatial domain and multiply the result with 1_C. The product will be 0 outside the predefined area and return the estimated force pattern inside. Subsequently we retransform the product into Fourier space and call the final result f_0. In a second step we make use of the functional

$$||G\tilde{f} - \tilde{u}||^2 + \lambda||\tilde{f} - f_0||^2 \tag{13}$$

to get a solution that implicitly prefers a resemblance to the function f_0, i. e., it has no significant forces outside the marked cell area.

3.4 Objective Choice of the Regularization Parameter

Crucial to all regularization methods is the choice of the parameter λ that is supposed to balance the data discrepancy and the penalty term. Therefore it is of high importance to use well founded values for λ.[4] To automate this parameter choice without knowledge of the error several procedures have been proposed of which two proved especially useful for our case.

The heuristic idea of the L-curve criterion [11] is to find a λ that represents a trade-off between data fidelity and the penalty norm. This balance can be determined by examining the L-shaped curve $(||Gf_\lambda - u||, ||L(f_\lambda - f_0)||)$ where f_λ is the solution of (9) but for our purpose this method proved unstable. Instead we determine the functions $d(\lambda) = ||Gf_\lambda - u||$ and $p(\lambda) = ||L(f_\lambda - f_0)||$ and identify the λ values at which d has maximum and p has minimum derivative. The average of those two values subsequently provides a useful choice for the regularization parameter since it determines the value where the penalty starts to apply and the data is still sufficiently fitted by the model.

Another parameter choice yielding a very good performance is an adjusted cross-validation approach [12]. The cv-method splits the data set into a validation and computation set. A ratio of 25% to 75% is a common choice. While the computation set is used to calculate a solution for several choices of λ, these solutions are applied to the direct problem and the result is compared to the validation set. The solution that suits best is the one that most likely can explain the unused data and is therefore a reasonable choice.

---

[4] With the Bayesian approach that was previously mapped out, λ turns out to be optimally chosen as ratio of the squared deformation error and the squared error in the force field.

Since a cross-validation in Fourier space did not provide satisfying results we adapted it to work in position space. The computation set is interpolated on a grid, transformed into Fourier space and forces are estimated as described above. By equation (7) we are now able to compute the deformation vector field u_λ that would be observed if the estimation f_λ was accurate. u_λ is retransformed to position space and the difference d_λ to the grid-interpolated validation set is determined. The λ which minimizes d_λ is the parameter to choose. It is possible to repeat this procedure with another 25% validation set to stabilize the results. Thus, the cross-validation approach is very reliable but computationally expensive.

4   Experiments and Results

We evaluated our approach on several data to test it with ground truth and different levels of noise in displacement data. First we created a synthetic set of test data (see Fig 2, first row, left). The second situation was force fields of normal human epidermal keratinocytes (Young modul of substrate: 11 kPa) as retrieved by Tikhonov regularization and the L-curve criterion. (see Fig 2, first row, right). This enables us to test the traction estimation in a realistic situation. Both traction distributions served as ground truth for our second test on synthetic data with known ground truth and noise.

4.1   Simulations

Simulations were performed by adding normal distributed noise on ground truth displacements. For each noise level we performed the simulation with 20 different noise patterns. To avoid random fluctuations between the tested penalties and parameter determinations we used the same noise patterns for all simulations.

Noise levels were chosen as multiples of the occuring mean displacements in the test images. As the interpretation of this quantity is not obvious we show the displacement vector fields with the highest noise level in Fig. 2, second row. All tests were done with 7 different noise levels.

On all data we performed tests with the wave damp, squared wave damp, classical Tikhonov regularization and the temporal derivative as regularization penalties. For determination of the regularization parameter we used both, the L-curve criterion and the cross-validation approach with and without restricting the traction to the cell area.

4.2   Results

Results for the artificial test pattern are shown in Fig. 3. Wave damp and squared wave damp regularization generally show a linear dependence of estimation error on the noise level up to a certain point. The error without any regularization is also shown. The temporal derivative of the traction is therefore not well suited for estimation in Fourier space. This was surprising since for the well-known point

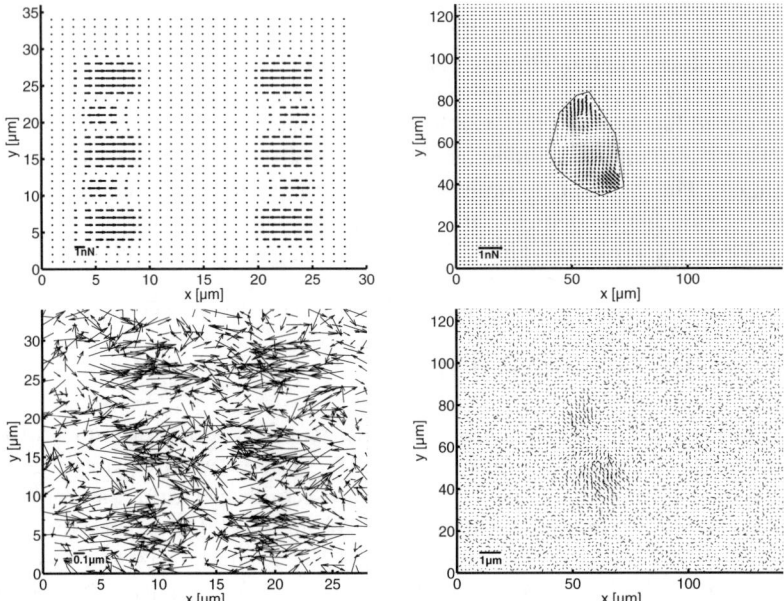

Fig. 2. Synthetic test data. First row: Defined traction patterns. Left: Artificial test pattern. Right: Estimated traction distribution of a normal human epidermal keratinocyte. Second row: Synthetic displacement data with maximum of added noise. Left: Displacements of artificial test pattern, standard deviation of noise: 0.14 μm. Right: Displacement of estimated traction distribution of a normal human epidermal keratinocyte, standard deviation of noise: 0.054 μm.

force traction estimation as mapped out in [3], we found it a stable improvement. Classical Tikhonov regularization combined with cross-validation yields best accuracy. This result is confirmed by the simulations with the realistic traction distribution (cf. Fig. 3, 3rd and 4th row). The squared wave damp regularization also provides good results for high noise levels.

For low noise the cross-validation is not suited for the choice of an appropriate regularization parameter which leads to high deviations (see Fig 3, 3rd row right, for noise lower than 2 times of the mean displacement $\lambda < 10^{-6}$, for higher noise levels $\lambda > 10^6$). The second step regularization restricting the forces to the cell area was able to enhance the results in several cases. Due to its low computational effort the second step should be considered whenever the force application area is known.

5   Discussion

In this paper we presented a systematic investigation of wave damp, wave damp squared, Tikhonov regularization and temporal derivative as penalties for traction estimation in Fourier space. The regularization parameter estimation was

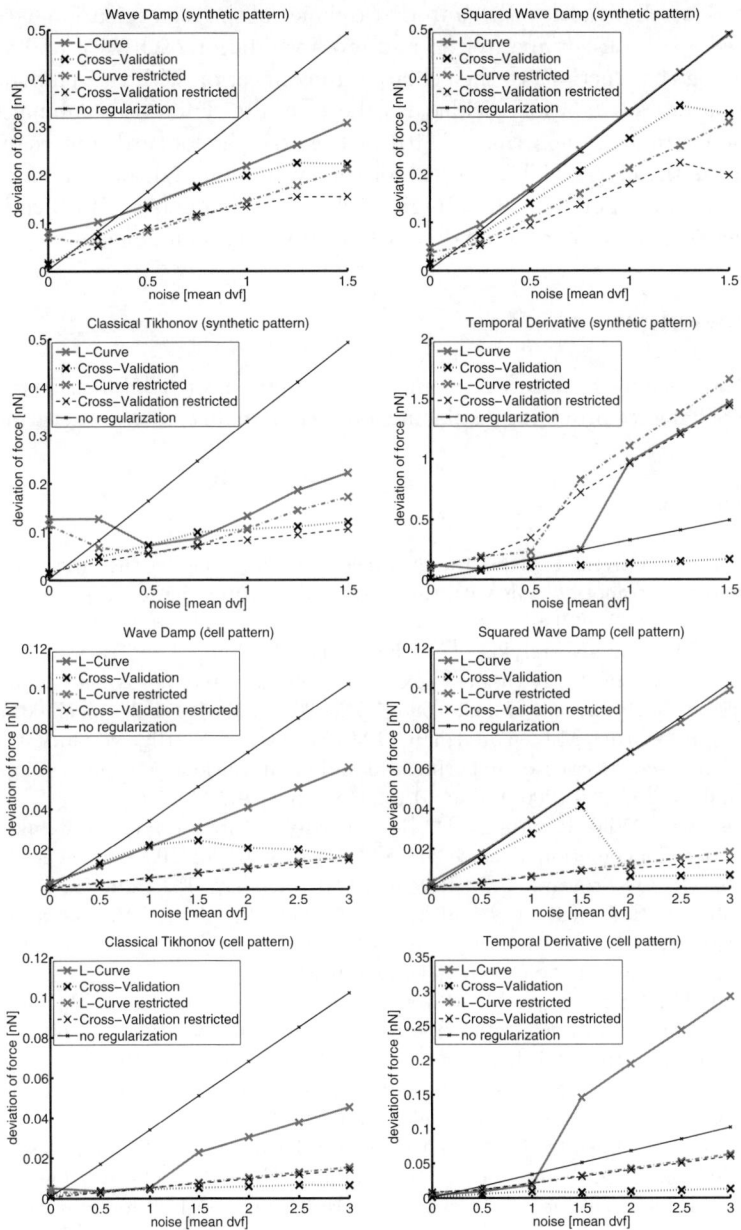

Fig. 3. Results of different penalty terms on the evaluation of artificial test data (first two rows) and a realistic traction distribution (last two rows) using different estimation methods for the regularization parameter λ. First row left: wave damp, right: wave damp squared. Second row left: Tikhonov, right: temporal derivative with 5 time steps considered, note the different scaling. Third row left: wave damp, right: wave damp squared. Fourth row left: Tikhonov, right: temporal derivative with 5 time steps considered, note the different scaling.

performed for all penalties with automatic choice of the regularization parameter λ inspired by the L-curve criterion and cross-validation each with and without constraining the tractions to the cell area. In connection with the Tikhonov regularization cross-validation yielded the best results. For this combination the estimation errors are less than a fifth of the straight forward, not regularized solution. As the choice of λ is critical for the evaluation of displacement data we see an important point in its automized choice. This enables an objective and reproducible evaluation of large data sets comprising many images.

Acknowledgements

The authors thank Hanno Scharr and Micah Dembo for helpful discussion and Claudia Schäfer for providing displacment data of human epidermal keratinocytes.

References

1. Dembo, M., Oliver, T., Ishihara, A., Jacobson, K.: Imaging the traction stresses exerted by locomoting cells with the elastic substratum method. Biophysical Journal 70, 2008–2022 (1996)
2. Butler, J.P., Tolic-Norrelykke, I.M., Fabry, B., Fredberg, J.J.: Traction fields, moments, and strain energy that cells exert on their surroundings. American journal of physiology, Cell physiology 282, C595–C605 (2002), doi:10.1152/ajpcell.00270.2001
3. Sabass, B., Gardel, M.L., Waterman, C.M., Schwarz, U.S.: High resolution traction force microscopy based on experimental and computational advances. Biophysical Journal 94, 207–220 (2008), doi: 10.1529/biophysj.107.113670
4. Harris, A.K., Wild, P., Stopak, D.: Silicone rubber substrata: a new wrinkle in the study of cell locomotion. Science 208, 177–179 (1980), doi: 10.1126/science.6987736
5. Balaban, N.Q., Schwarz, U.S., Riveline, D., Goichberg, P., Tzur, G., Sabanay, I., Mahalu, D., Safran, S., Bershadsky, A., Addadi, L., Geiger, B.: Force and focal adhesion assembly: a close relationship studied using elastic micropatterned substrates. Nature Cell Biology 3, 466–472 (2001)
6. Cesa, C.M., Kirchgeßner, N., Mayer, D., Schwarz, U., Hoffmann, B., Merkel, R.: Micropatterned silicone elastomer substrates for high resolution analysis of cellular force patterns. Rev. Sci. Instrum. 78, 034301-1–034301-10 (2007)
7. Boussinesq, J.: Applications des potentiels a l'etude de l'equilibre et du mouvement des solides elastiques. Gauthier-Villars, Paris (1885)
8. Landau, L.D., Lifshitz, E.M.: Lehrbuch der Theoretischen Physik: Elastizitaetstheorie, vol. 7. Akademie-Verlag, Berlin (1987); Deutsche Uebersetzung
9. Merkel, R., Kirchgeßner, N., Cesa, C.M., Hoffmann, B.: Cell force microscopy on elastic layers of finite thickness. Biophysical Journal 93, 3314–3323 (2007)
10. Tikhonov, A.N.: On the solution of ill-posed problems and the regularization method. Dokl. Akad. Nauk SSSR 151, 501–504 (1963)
11. Hansen, P.C.: Analysis of discrete ill-posed problems by means of the L-curve. SIAM Review 34, 561–580 (1992)
12. Wahba, G.: Spline models for observational data. SIAM, US (1990)

Classification of Microorganisms via Raman Spectroscopy Using Gaussian Processes

Michael Kemmler[1], Joachim Denzler[1], Petra Rösch[2], and Jürgen Popp[2]

[1] Chair for Computer Vision
[2] Institute of Physical Chemistry
Friedrich Schiller University of Jena

Abstract. Automatic categorization of microorganisms is a complex task which requires advanced techniques to achieve accurate performance. In this paper, we aim at identifying microorganisms based on Raman spectroscopy. Empirical studies over the last years show that powerful machine learning methods such as Support Vector Machines (SVMs) are suitable for this task. Our work focuses on the Gaussian process (GP) classifier which is new to this field, provides fully probabilistic outputs and allows for efficient hyperparameter optimization. We also investigate the incorporation of prior knowledge regarding possible signal variations where known concepts from invariant kernel theory are transferred to the GP framework. In order to validate the suitability of the GP classifier, a comparison with state-of-the-art learners is conducted on a large-scale Raman spectra dataset, showing that the GP classifier significantly outperforms all other tested classifiers including SVM. Our results further show that incorporating prior knowledge leads to a significant performance gain when small amounts of training data are used.

1 Introduction

In the fast-growing field of medical and biological science, the need for classifying microorganisms is rapidly increasing. There are many crucial tasks which demand an accurate classification method, such as the categorization of potentially pathogenic particles in clinical applications [1] or the identification of contamination conditions in clean room environments [2], to name just a few. The assortment of tools available for identifying microbes is broad, ranging from microscopic inspection [3] to advanced biochemical analysis [4]. Though, while the classification based on microscopic means using morphological information is only possible on a coarse level, most accurate biochemical methods require time consuming pre-processing steps for cultivating the media of interest. So-called "vibrational techniques" such as Raman spectroscopy offer an elegant way out of this dilemma by obtaining a "molecular fingerprint" of biological samples [2].

This work aims at introducing the Gaussian Process classifier to the field of vibrational spectroscopy. Although GP regression is well-known for the calibration of spectroscopic data [5], GP classification is, to our knowledge, new to the field of Raman spectroscopy. Moreover, we investigate the use of a-priori knowledge

M. Goesele et al. (Eds.): DAGM 2010, LNCS 6376, pp. 81–90, 2010.

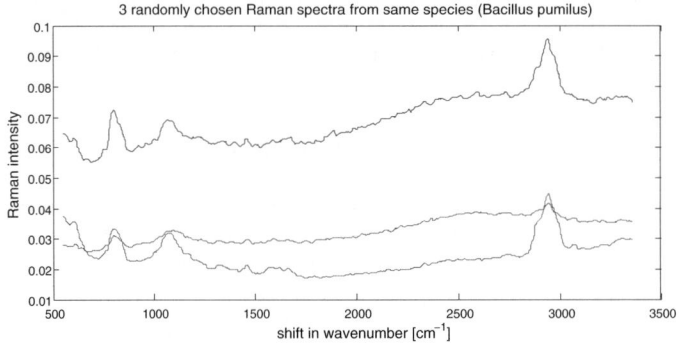

Fig. 1. Illustration of (pre-processed) Raman spectra and signal variations

by means of possible variations of Raman spectra, where we apply the approach of Peschke et al. [6] to the GP framework. Shortcomings of this approach as well as heuristics to overcome those issues are discussed.

This paper is organized as follows. In Sect. 2 we give a brief summary to Raman spectroscopy. Sect. 3 gives an introduction to GP classification. In Sect. 4 we formulate the notion of transformation invariant kernels and show how a-priori knowledge can be incorporated in the GP framework. In Sect. 5 we empirically demonstrate the performance of the GP classifier for Raman spectra categorization compared to other state-of-the-art classification techniques and investigate the effect of prior knowledge. Finally, we conclude and summarize our findings.

2   Classification of Raman Spectra

Raman spectroscopy is an optical technique for measuring the vibration of molecules. The sample under focus is irradiated with a narrow-band LASER and the scattered light is analyzed. Since shifts in wavenumber are strongly related to the vibrational state of molecules and shifts from all molecules are superimposed, we obtain a molecular fingerprint of the whole sample (c.f. Fig. 1). Since most microorganisms substantially differ in molecular decomposition it is assumed that they can be distinguished by means of their vibrational signature. Empirical results validate [2] that Raman spectra contain discriminative information and are suitable for categorization of even very similar microorganisms.

However, one major drawback is the occurrence of prominent background signals introduced by other optical phenomena such as fluorescence. One common technique to overcome this issue is to explicitly pre-process all spectra prior to training and learning. Alternatively, Peschke et al. [6] successfully apply an invariant kernel approach which implicitly incorporates possible background variations into the kernel for SVM and k-Nearest-Neighbor classification. In addition to assessing the suitability of the GP classifier to the field of Raman spectroscopy, this work aims at transferring the approach of [6] to the GP framework.

3   Gaussian Process Classification

This section gives a brief introduction to GP classification. Since the classification is motivated from non-parametric Bayesian regression, we first briefly introduce the regression case before we discuss the GP classifier.

3.1   The Regression Case

The regression problem aims at finding a mapping from input space $\mathcal{X}$ to output space $\mathbb{R}$ using labeled training data $\mathbf{X} = [\mathbf{x}_1, \ldots, \mathbf{x}_n] \in \mathcal{X}^n$, $\mathbf{y} = [y_1, \ldots, y_n]^T \in \mathbb{R}^n$. In the following it is assumed that the output is generated by a latent (non-observed) function $f : \mathcal{X} \to \mathbb{R}$ and an additive noise term ε, i.e. $y = f(\mathbf{x}) + \varepsilon$. Rather than restricting f to a certain functional family, we only assume that the function is drawn from a specific probability distribution $p(\mathbf{f}|\mathbf{X})$. This allows for a Bayesian treatment of our problem, i.e. we infer the probability of outputs y_* given new inputs x_* and old observations $\mathbf{X}, \mathbf{y}$ by integrating out the non-observed function values f_* and $\mathbf{f}$:

$$p(y_*|\mathbf{X}, \mathbf{y}, \mathbf{x}_*) = \int p(f_*|\mathbf{X}, \mathbf{y}, \mathbf{x}_*)\, p(y_*|f_*)\, df_* \tag{1}$$

$$p(f_*|\mathbf{X}, \mathbf{y}, \mathbf{x}_*) = \int p(f_*|\mathbf{X}, \mathbf{f}, \mathbf{x}_*)\, p(\mathbf{f}|\mathbf{X}, \mathbf{y})\, d\mathbf{f} \ . \tag{2}$$

The central assumption in GP regression is that all function values are jointly normally distributed, i.e. $\mathbf{f}|\mathbf{X} \sim \mathcal{N}(m(\mathbf{X}), \kappa(\mathbf{X}, \mathbf{X}))$. This distribution is solely specified by the mean function $m(\cdot)$ and covariance function $\kappa(\cdot, \cdot)$. When we additionally assume that the data is generated by zero mean independent Gaussian noise, i.e. $y \sim \mathcal{N}(f, \sigma_n^2)$, then we are able to solve the integrals in closed form. Using a zero mean GP, the predictive distribution (2) is again Gaussian with predictive mean $\mu_* = \mathbf{k}_*^T \left(\mathbf{K} + \sigma_n^2 \mathbf{I} \right)^{-1} \mathbf{y}$ and predictive variance $\sigma_*^2 = k_{**} - \mathbf{k}_*^T \left(\mathbf{K} + \sigma_n^2 \mathbf{I} \right)^{-1} \mathbf{k}_*$ using shortcuts $\mathbf{K} = \kappa(\mathbf{X}, \mathbf{X})$, $\mathbf{k}_* = \kappa(\mathbf{X}, \mathbf{x}_*)$, and $k_{**} = \kappa(\mathbf{x}_*, \mathbf{x}_*)$ and hence also implies that (1) is Gaussian.

3.2   From Regression to Classification

The goal in binary GP classification is to model a function which predicts a confidence for each class $y \in \{-1, 1\}$, given a feature vector $\mathbf{x}$. In order to make probabilistic inference about the output given a training set, we can directly apply the Bayesian formalism from equation (1) and (2). However, the key problem is that the assumption of Gaussian noise no longer holds since the output space is discrete. We could either ignore this issue and perform regression on our labels or we could use a more appropriate assumption of $p(y|f)$. Here we follow the latter approach using the cumulative Gaussian likelihood $p(y|f) = (2\pi)^{-\frac{1}{2}} \int_{-\infty}^{yf} exp\left(-0.5x^2\right) dx$. The disadvantage of this procedure is that our predictive distribution (2) no longer is a normal distribution. To overcome this issue, we follow the standard approach to approximate [7] the posterior

$p(\mathbf{f}|\mathbf{X}, \mathbf{y})$ with a normal distribution $\hat{p}$. We use Laplace's Method, i.e. the mean of $\hat{p}$ is set equal to the mode of $p(\mathbf{f}|\mathbf{X}, \mathbf{y})$ and the Hessian of $-\log p(\mathbf{f}|\mathbf{X}, \mathbf{y})$ is utilized as covariance matrix of $\hat{p}$. Moreover, by using the cumulative Gaussian as described above, equation (1) also turns out to be a cumulative Gaussian [8] and hence can be efficiently computed. Finally, appropriate hyperparameters θ^* of the covariance function can be efficiently found by marginal likelihood maximization, i.e. $\theta^* = \mathrm{argmax}_\theta p(\mathbf{y}|\mathbf{X}, \theta)$.

4   Prior Knowledge in GP Classification

As has been pointed out in Sect. 2, Raman spectra often contain undesirable information introduced by fluorescence or different measuring conditions. The resulting signal variations often pose a problem for most classifiers. This is especially the case in real scenarios where only small amounts of training data are available, since the possible variations are not sufficiently covered by the training set. One way to overcome this issue is to implicitly embed knowledge about possible signal variations into the learning algorithm. In this section we discuss how and to which extent this kind of prior information can be incorporated into the GP framework by means of Tangent Distance Substitution Kernels [9].

4.1   Tangent Distance Substitution Kernels

Many methods in machine learning are solely expressed via symmetric similarity functions κ, so-called kernels. These kernels $\kappa(\mathbf{x}, \mathbf{x}')$ are often positive definite in which case they can be interpreted as inner products $\kappa(\mathbf{x}, \mathbf{x}') = \Phi(\mathbf{x})^T \Phi(\mathbf{x}')$ in some feature space $\mathcal{Y}$ induced by a mapping $\Phi : \mathcal{X} \to \mathcal{Y}$. Many kernels used throughout the literature are also expressed in terms of Euclidean distances d. One possibility to introduce some degree of invariance into kernels is to replace Euclidean distances with distances that are invariant with respect to pattern variations. When specified beforehand, knowledge about expected pattern variations is thus some kind of prior information which can be incorporated into distances. In the following we use the regularized Mean Tangent Distance [9] TDMN_γ which results in a locally invariant distance measure:

$$\mathrm{TDMN}_\gamma^2(\mathbf{x}, \mathbf{x}') = \frac{1}{2}\left(\mathrm{TD1S}_\gamma^2(\mathbf{x}, \mathbf{x}') + \mathrm{TD1S}_\gamma^2(\mathbf{x}', \mathbf{x})\right) \tag{3}$$

$$\mathrm{TD1S}_\gamma^2(\mathbf{x}, \mathbf{x}') = \min_{\mathbf{p}} \ ||\mathbf{x} + \mathbf{T_x p} - \mathbf{x}'||_2^2 + \gamma||\mathbf{p}||_2^2 \ , \tag{4}$$

where $\mathrm{TD1S}_\gamma$ denotes the one-sided Tangent distance using regularization parameter γ. The latter Tangent distance computes the distance between $\mathbf{x}'$ and the first order approximation $\mathbf{T_x}$ of the variation manifold in which $\mathbf{x}$ resides (see Fig. 2). As detailed in [9], Tangent distances can be used in any possible distance-based kernel. In this paper, however, we will solely focus on the squared exponential (SE) kernel [8] with respect to some distance d:

$$\kappa_{\nu_1, \nu_2}(\mathbf{x}, \mathbf{x}') = \nu_1^2 \exp\left(-\frac{d^2(\mathbf{x}, \mathbf{x}')}{2\nu_2^2}\right) \ . \tag{5}$$

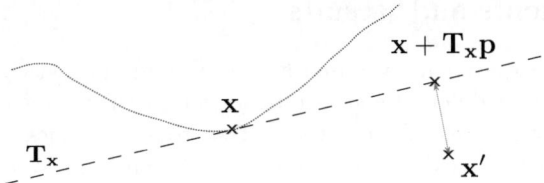

Fig. 2. Visualization of Tangent distance. Dotted red: Pattern variation manifold with respect to $\mathbf{x}$. Dashed blue: Tangent $\mathbf{T_x}$ of variation manifold with respect to $\mathbf{x}$. Solid green: Unregularized one-sided Tangent distance $\mathrm{TD1S}_0(\mathbf{x}, \mathbf{x}')$.

4.2 Invariant Kernels in GP Classification

GP methods can be related to kernel machines through their covariance function κ which describes the underlying similarity structure. One can therefore utilize invariant kernels such as (5) with $d = \mathrm{TDMN}_\gamma$ as a covariance function. By doing so, however, the theoretical assumptions behind the GP framework might be violated. This is due to the fact that the Tangent distance is not necessarily a metric distance. It can be shown [9] that in this case the above kernel is not positive definite and hence no valid covariance function for a GP.

To overcome this issue one could *explicitly enforce positive definiteness*. This is possible, e.g. by clipping off negative eigenvalues (CLIP), flipping negative values to its positive absolute value (ABS) or by adding a constant $c \geq |\lambda_{\min}|$ to all eigenvalues (SHIFT), where $\lambda_{\min}$ is the smallest algebraic eigenvalue of the kernel matrix. While the latter technique can be efficiently realized by Krylov subspace methods such as Lanczos algorithms, CLIP and ABS require a full eigendecomposition of the covariance matrix of the entire data.

To guarantee positive definiteness, one could also *reduce the set of possible tangents*. It can be shown [9] that by using tangents which are constant, i.e. independent of the input arguments $\mathbf{x}$, the Tangent distance is equal to a Mahalanobis distance which leads to positive (semi-)definite SE-kernels.

We could also ignore the indefiniteness of the covariance function. One result would be that variances might get negative. In order to construct a Gaussian distribution in the end, one could use heuristics to ensure positivity of the variance term, e.g. by setting negative values to zero (*negative variance cut-off heuristic*).

Although the Bayesian perspective gets lost using the latter approach, we can take a different view on the outcome. In GP regression, the moments μ_* and σ_*^2 of predictive Gaussian $p(f_* | \mathbf{X}, \mathbf{f}, \mathbf{x}_*)$ can be also derived from linear estimation [10] in some indefinite inner product (Kreĭn) space $\mathcal{K}$, where the predictive mean $\mu_* = \sum_k w_k \mathbf{f}_k$ is the linear Least Squares estimate with respect to the latent function values $\mathbf{f}$, and σ_*^2 is equal to the Least Squares objective at the corresponding stationary point $\mathbf{w}$. Using the Laplace Approximation, a similar relationship holds using a slightly modified set of latent function values. From this perspective, cutting off negative variances means that we are confident ($\sigma_*^2 = 0$) for estimates f_* in some regions of $\mathcal{K}$ that will result in negative Least Squares objective values σ_*^2.

5   Experiments and Results

In the following experiments we used a large Raman dataset consisting of 6707 spectra comprising 4 different genera (classes) and 10 species (sub-classes) which was captured over a period of 3 years. Due to the physics of the recording process, each spectrum exhibits a potentially different set of wavenumber shifts. We therefore crop the interesting region to the interval $\mathcal{I} = [540cm^{-1}, 3350cm^{-1}]$ that is shared among all samples. In order to work with fixed dimensions, we use quadratic interpolation to obtain the Raman intensity with respect to all integer wavenumbers $\omega \in \mathcal{I} \cap \mathbb{Z}$. In order to eliminate spike noise artifacts introduced by cosmic radiation, a running median (of size 21) is applied. For the sake of numerical stability, all spectra are either normalized to unit length or multiplied by a fixed constant $c = 8.5741 \times 10^{-5}$. In all experiments we used the (noise-free) GP classifier from Sect. 3.2 with kernel (5) whose parameters are tuned with marginal likelihood maximization (starting at $\nu = (1, 1)^T$, 10 iterations). To allow for multiple classes, a one-vs-all scheme based on predictive probabilities (1) is employed.

In this section, we will empirically validate the following hypotheses:

1. The GP classifier is suitable for classification of Raman spectra (Sect. 5.1).
2. For small training sets, a significant performance gain is achieved by incorporating prior information (Sect. 5.2).
3. A special treatment of indefinite kernels is not necessary for our task (Sect. 5.2).

5.1   Suitability for Raman Spectroscopic Categorization

In order to investigate whether the GP classifier is suitable for the categorization of Raman spectra, we compared it to four state-of-the-art classifiers: k-Nearest-Neighbor classifier (KNN), Randomized Decision Forests (RDF) and AdaBoost.MH [11] (ADA) with decision stumps, as well as Support Vector Machines [12] (SVM), where for the latter logistic regression is used to generate pseudo-probabilistic outputs. Particularly, we used KNN with $k = 1$ (best performance for this value of k), a gently randomized RDF (95% resampling probability, 250 random features per node) with 100 trees, and a SVM with rbf-kernel whose parameters were determined via leave-one-out (LOO) estimates on a 2x10 grid for trade-off parameter and bandwidth parameter.

It should be noted that results concerning the novel large dataset used in this work are not directly comparable to other work (e.g. [2]) since other datasets strongly differ in size and complexity and are generally not publicly available. An indirect comparison, however, is possible since we compare against SVM which is known to achieve very good results in the field of Raman spectroscopy [2]. Moreover, since fast LOO error estimates cannot be computed for all classifiers, we randomly chose 75% of the data for training and the remainder for testing. In order to yield a more robust performance estimate we repeated this procedure ten times.

The resulting ten average recognition rates for each classifier are illustrated in Fig. 3 where results for the genus level (4 classes) and species level (10 classes) are

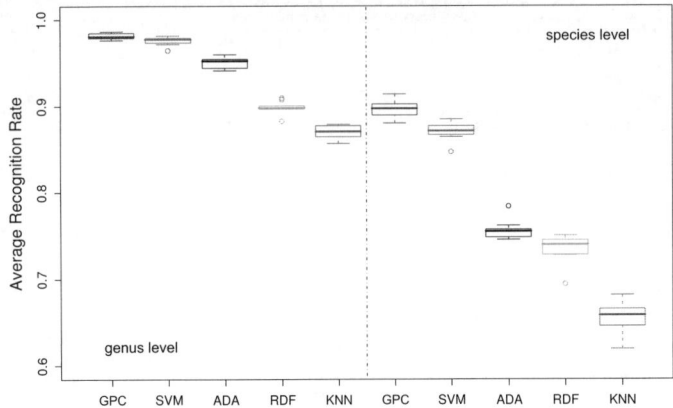

Fig. 3. Average recognition rates on the genus level (4 classes) and species level (10 classes) using ten repetitions with 75% of the data randomly chosen for training and the remainder for testing

given via Boxplots. They clearly show that the GP classifier (GPC) is suitable for our setting and provides significantly higher average recognition rates than the gold standard SVM (verified using t-test, $p < 0.05$). Please also note that all experiments were conducted with unit length normalized spectra, however, multiplication with a fixed constant yields analogous results in this setting.

5.2 Benefit of Prior Information

In the following we analyze different techniques from Sect. 4.2 to incorporate prior knowledge into the GP framework.

Negative Variance Cut-Off Heuristic. To evaluate the effect of prior knowledge we analyzed a different scenario, where only 10 spectra per class are utilized for training. We tested our GP classifier on the remaining spectra for different values of the crucial regularization parameter γ for both types of normalization. Instead of ten repetitions of the randomized partitioning scheme we performed one hundred trials. As in [6], we utilized the Tangent distance which is invariant to global scaling of spectra and slowly varying background signals which are modeled by a linear combination of Lagrange bases of degree $deg = 3$. Since the assumed variations are both linear in the parameters, the Tangent distance is no approximation but calculates the mean of exact (regularized) distances between variation manifolds and patterns (see Fig. 2).

From Fig. 4 we clearly see that we observe different behavior when different kinds of normalization are employed. Using the standard Euclidean kernel, the unit length normalization (unit) yields substantially better performances compared to raw features (raw) multiplied with normalization constant c. When using invariant kernels with negative variance cut-off heuristic, however, the results turn out to be completely different. In case of unit length normalization,

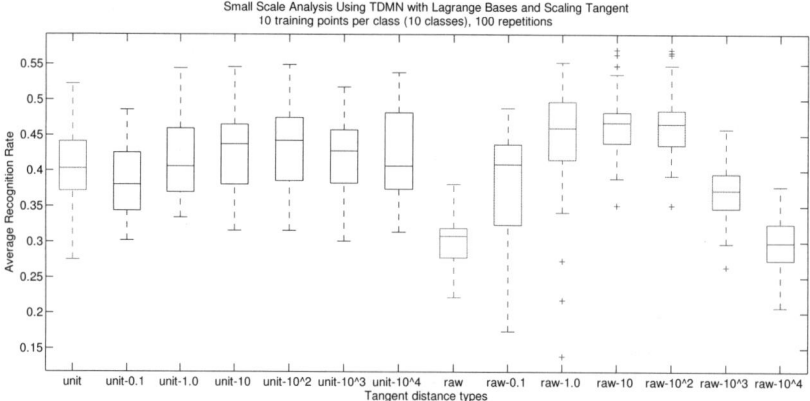

Fig. 4. Euclidean versus TDMN$_\gamma$-induced squared exponential kernel for different values of regularization parameter $\gamma \in \{0.1, 1, 10, 10^2, 10^3, 10^4\}$ and different normalizations (unit, raw). Labels containing a number correspond to invariant kernels, e.g. raw-10^3 corresponds to the kernel using raw data and regularization parameter $\gamma = 10^3$.

we only observe marginal improvements. This can be explained by the fact that we are applying an extra transformation to the spectra prior to using the invariant kernel. While the unit length transformation already provides a certain kind of scaling invariance, it simultaneously hinders the use of the transformation invariance that is embedded in the GP prior.

When using raw spectra, however, we observe a significantly higher performance gain compared to the Euclidean kernel (30.4% versus 46.8% on average). Moreover, using this normalization type leads to significantly higher average recognition rates than using unit length normalized data (3.5% for $\gamma = 10^2$).

It should be further noted that the benefit of using prior knowledge gets lost when using large amounts of training data, e.g. we even observed a performance drop of 2.5% compared to the non-invariant case when using 75% of the entire dataset for training.

Constant Tangents. We already discussed in Sect. 4.2 that Tangent distance with constant tangents leads to positive semi-definite SE-Kernels. Since the Lagrange bases used in our approach are independent of the Raman spectra, we obtain overall constant tangents by discarding the non-constant scaling tangent. To evaluate this approach which does not need any heuristics or approximation, we repeated the above experiments and still observed a substantial performance gain over the Euclidean kernel (30.4% versus 47.8% on average for raw spectra). Compared to the negative variance cut-off heuristic, the results are nearly the same. Therefore and due to space limitations, we omit further results regarding this experiment.

Positive Definite Approximations. As has been discussed in Sect. 4.2, the use of positive definite approximations is computationally prohibitive. We therefore

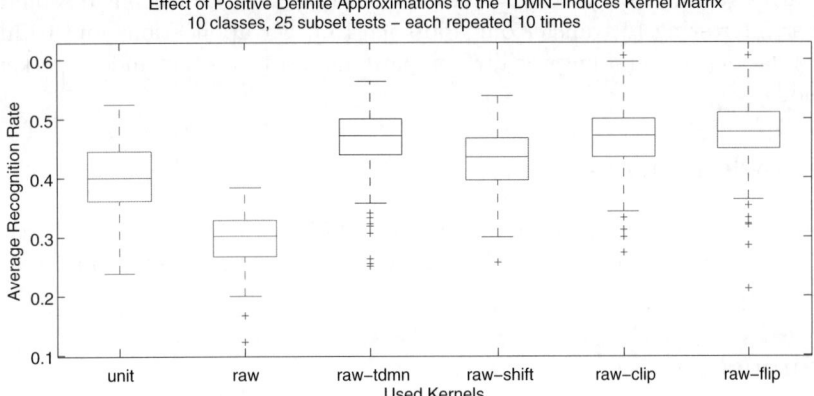

Fig. 5. Standard GP approach (unit, raw) and invariant GP heuristic (raw-tdmn) versus positive definite approximation methods (raw-shift, raw-clip, raw-flip)

adapted our experimental setting to accommodate for this fact. We randomly selected a fraction of 50 spectra for each category and trained the classifier with ten randomly chosen data points per category. Each such fraction was measured ten times. In order to obtain a measure for the entire dataset, this whole procedure was repeated 25 times. We thus ended up with a collection of 10×25 averaged recognition rates per classifier. We can see from Fig. 5 that no approximation substantially improved the invariant GP classifier (raw-tdmn) though non-positive eigenvalues occurred. Moreover, we can see that the rather fast SHIFT transform is even counterproductive, leading to a slightly decreased averaged performance (3%). The behavior of the SHIFT transform is even worse in large-scale training sets. E.g. when 75% of the data is used for training, we observe a performance drop of 55.8% compared to Euclidean kernels. This seems to be an inherent problem of this approximation method, as similar performances are reported for SVMs [13].

6   Conclusion and Future Work

This paper tackles the problem of Raman spectroscopic identification of microorganisms and introduces the Gaussian Process classifier to this field. In addition to the standard GP classifier we investigate the use of partially invariant covariance functions, where we embed known ideas from invariant kernel theory into the Gaussian Process framework. We highlight the shortcomings of this approach, i.e. that general GP classifiers are not able to cope with indefinite covariance matrices, and investigate methods to circumvent this issue. Empirical results show that the GP classifier outperforms state-of-the-art methods on a large Raman dataset. Moreover, for the case of few training samples a significant performance gain is achieved via Tangent distance based covariance functions incorporating prior knowledge from possible pattern variations. Our results show that investigating invariant GP methods can indeed be beneficial. It would be further interesting to transfer our approach to other applications and to highlight relationships and empirically compare our work to other indefinite kernel methods.

Acknowledgments

We want to especially thank Mario Krause and Michaela Harz from the Institute of Physical Chemistry at the FSU Jena for capturing the large Raman spectra dataset.

References

1. Buijtels, P., Willemse-Erix, H., Petit, P., Endtz, H., Puppels, G., Verbrugh, H., van Belkum, A., van Soolingen, D., Maquelin, K.: Rapid identification of mycobacteria by raman spectroscopy. Journal of Clinical Microbiology 46(3), 961–965 (2008)
2. Rösch, P., Harz, M., Peschke, K.D., Ronneberger, O., Burkhardt, H., Motzkus, H.W., Lankers, M., Hofer, S., Thiele, H., Popp, J.: Chemotaxonomic identification of single bacteria by micro-raman spectroscopy: Application to clean-room-relevant biological contaminations. Applied and Environmental Microbiology 71, 1626–1637 (2005)
3. Barrow, G., Feltham, R.: Cowan and Steel's Manual for the Identification of Medical Bacteria, 3rd edn. Cambridge University Press, UK (1993)
4. Amann, R., Fuchs, B.: Single-cell identification in microbial communities by improved fluorescence in situ hybridization techniques. Nature Reviews Microbiology 6, 339–348 (2008)
5. Chen, T., Morris, J., Martin, E.: Gaussian process regression for multivariate spectroscopic calibration. Chemometrics and Intelligent Laboratory Systems 87(1), 59–71 (2007)
6. Peschke, K.D., Haasdonk, B., Ronneberger, O., Burkhardt, H., Rösch, P., Harz, M., Popp, J.: Using transformation knowledge for the classification of raman spectra of biological samples. In: Proceedings of the 24th IASTED international conference on Biomedical engineering, Anaheim, CA, USA, pp. 288–293. ACTA Press (2006)
7. Nickisch, H., Rasmussen, C.E.: Approximations for binary gaussian process classification. Journal of Machine Learning Research 9, 2035–2078 (2008)
8. Rasmussen, C.E., Williams, C.K.I.: Gaussian Processes for Machine Learning. Adaptive Computation and Machine Learning. The MIT Press, Cambridge (2005)
9. Haasdonk, B.: Transformation Knowledge in Pattern Analysis with Kernel Methods. PhD thesis, Computer Science Department, University of Freiburg (2005)
10. Hassibi, B., Sayed, A., Kailath, T.: Linear estimation in krein spaces - part i: Theory. IEEE Transactions on Automatic Control 41(1), 18–33 (1996)
11. Casagrande, N.: Multiboost: An open source multi-class adaboost learner (2005), http://multiboost.sourceforge.net/
12. Joachims, T.: Making large-Scale SVM Learning Practical. MIT-Press, Cambridge (1999)
13. Chen, Y., Gupta, M.R., Recht, B.: Learning kernels from indefinite similarities. In: Proceedings of the 26th Annual International Conference on Machine Learning, pp. 145–152. ACM, New York (2009)

Robust Identification of Locally Planar Objects Represented by 2D Point Clouds under Affine Distortions

Dominic Mai, Thorsten Schmidt, and Hans Burkhardt

University of Freiburg, Computer Science Department
79110 Freiburg i. Br., Germany
{maid,tschmidt,burkhardt}@informatik.uni-freiburg.de

Abstract. The matching of point sets that are characterized only by their geometric configuration is a challenging problem. In this paper, we present a novel point registration algorithm for robustly identifying objects represented by two dimensional point clouds under affine distortions. We make no assumptions about the initial orientation of the point clouds and only incorporate the geometric configuration of the points to recover the affine transformation that aligns the parts that originate from the same locally planar surface of the three dimensional object. Our algorithm can deal well with noise and outliers and is inherently robust against partial occlusions. It is in essence a GOODSAC approach based on geometric hashing to guess a good initial affine transformation that is iteratively refined in order to retrieve a characteristic common point set with minimal squared error. We successfully apply it for the biometric identification of the bluespotted ribbontail ray *Taeniura lymma*.

1 Introduction

Euclidean motion of planar objects in 3D is equivalent to affine transformations in 2D if we assume parallel projection neglecting occlusion. It is often possible to robustly extract interest points from images that suffice to uniquely identify a class of objects or even individual entities [1,2,3]. The identity of two clouds under some transformation model can be established by a global invariant feature [2,4] or by aligning the two clouds [5]. Global features for point clouds like shape contexts [6] or features derived by integrating a local feature over the whole structure [4] are fast to compare as we only need to compute distances in the feature space. Such features, however, cannot deal well with outliers as every point affects the value in the feature space. Point registration performs much better in the presence of outliers: once a valid transformation is found, a similarity measure based on point correspondences is not affected. Rigid motion of non-planar objects generally requires the construction of a 3D model to be able to model the transformation in two dimensions [2]. In this paper we exploit the fact that many objects possess partly planar surfaces and therefore can be partly modeled with an affine transformation[7]. Sample applications are depicted in Fig. 1.

M. Goesele et al. (Eds.): DAGM 2010, LNCS 6376, pp. 91–100, 2010.

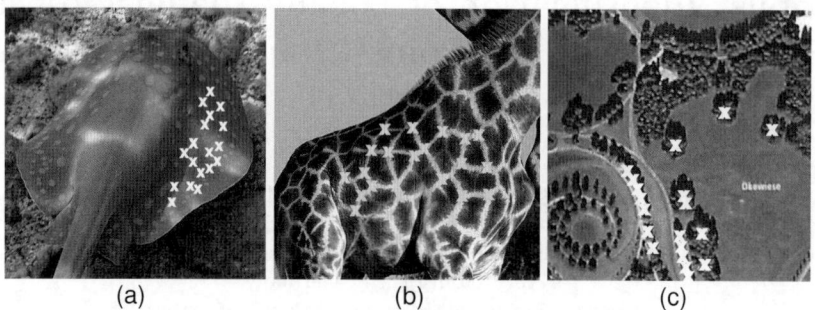

Fig. 1. Possible applications of the point registration algorithm include noninvasive wildlife monitoring (a,b) and place recognition in mobile robotics (c)

Formalization of the Problem. Let $\mathcal{C}$ be a point cloud containing points $p_i = (x, y, 1)^\mathrm{T}$ in homogeneous coordinates. Let the common point set of two clouds $\mathcal{C}_i$ under the affine transformation $\boldsymbol{A}$ be:

$$\mathcal{X}_{\boldsymbol{A}}(\mathcal{C}_1, \mathcal{C}_2) = \{(p_1, p_2) \mid p_1 \in \mathcal{C}_1, p_2 \in \mathcal{C}_2 : \|\boldsymbol{A}p_1 - p_2\| < \delta_{corr}\} \quad . \quad (1)$$

We assume a correspondence (p_1, p_2) if the Euclidean distance of p_2 and the transformed point p_1 is smaller than a threshold δ_{corr}. We define the *characteristic common point set*

$$\hat{\mathcal{X}}_{\boldsymbol{A}}(\mathcal{C}_1, \mathcal{C}_2) \subseteq \mathcal{X}_{\boldsymbol{A}}(\mathcal{C}_1, \mathcal{C}_2), \quad |\hat{\mathcal{X}}_{\boldsymbol{A}}(\mathcal{C}_1, \mathcal{C}_2)| \geq \#_{min} \quad (2)$$

as a subset of $\mathcal{X}_{\boldsymbol{A}}$, holding enough correspondences to identify the object that the point clouds originate from.

The minimum cardinality $\#_{min}$ of $\hat{\mathcal{X}}_{\boldsymbol{A}}(\mathcal{C}_1, \mathcal{C}_2)$ depends on the application. For biometric identification, $\#_{min}$ usually is a small value: The Battley System reports two fingerprints identical when seven correspondences between minutiae have been found[8], the seven most significant *Eigenface* coefficients suffice to describe a face[9].

A fast and well understood method for aligning point clouds is the *Iterative closest Point* algorithm[10] (ICP). The ICP needs a good initial alignment of the point clouds and is hence not suitable for our problem by itself, but it is useful to refine a transformation once a coarse initial guess has been made.

For recovering an affine transformation we need to find at least three corresponding points. Local descriptors like SIFT[1], Spin Images[7] or orientation of surface normals[11] are popular features to solve this task. In absence of such descriptors, one can use invariant features based on the geometric configuration of the points. [3,12,13] encode the points of a cloud relative to all possible 3 point bases and use a generalized hough voting to find a corresponding basis. Aiger et al.[14] use a feature based on area ratios to find a corresponding basis to a fixed basis of 4 points. A popular philosophy to speed up the search for correspondences is geometric hashing [3,11,12]: Points or groups of points are indexed with a feature that remains invariant under the assumed transformation. When using groups of points two additional problems arise: *1.* One has to make sure that the sampling strategy remains unaffected by the allowed transformations of the cloud. Sampling all $\binom{n}{3}$ combinations [3,12] is only practicable for small clouds. *2.* The feature for indexing also has to be invariant against permutations of the input – to the best of our knowledge none of the existing affine invariant features fulfills this property.

Contribution and Overview. In this paper we present a novel algorithm to find a characteristic common point set of two point clouds under the assumption of an affine transformation. Our contributions are:

1. a family of affine invariant descriptors T_ρ for sets of four points in arbitrary order based on area ratios,
2. a novel strategy to partition the point cloud into a linear number of those local four-point-neighborhoods based on a Voronoi decomposition, and
3. a point registration algorithm based on geometric hashing to identify a characteristic common point set.

The remainder of the paper is organized as follows: In Section 2 we will introduce the invariant mapping T_ρ, in Section 3 we present our cloud partition algorithm, and in section 4 we introduce the point registration based on the former two sections. In section 5 we show the applicability of our algorithm for the biometric identification of blue spotted ribbontail rays and conclude in Section 6.

2 Affine Invariants for 4 Points

An invariant mapping T of a pattern x is a function that maps all members of an equivalence class ϵ_G under a transformation group G into one point of the feature space:

$$x_i \stackrel{G}{\sim} x_j \Rightarrow T(x_i) = T(x_j) \quad . \tag{3}$$

As this necessary condition for invariance can already be achieved by a simple constant function that maps the same value to every input, we also require

$$T(x_1) = T(x_2) \Rightarrow x_1 \stackrel{G}{\sim} x_2 \quad , \tag{4}$$

which would assure completeness [15]. This is difficult to achieve and might also be difficult to prove in a domain with possibly infinite different patterns. We therefore aim to construct invariants with a high degree of *separability*, which is completeness on a subset of relevant patterns. Furthermore, we demand *continuity* of the invariant mapping T to be able to deal with noisy data, i.e. small changes in the pattern result in small changes in the feature space.

Four not all collinear points $p_i{}^1$

$$\boldsymbol{P} = \{p_1, p_2, p_3, p_4\} \tag{5}$$

---

[1] In homogeneous coordinates like in Eqn. 1.

define four triangles $\triangle_i$ with at most one degenerate triangle having an area of zero. We will call such a point set $\boldsymbol{P}$ a *4 point affine set* (4PAS). Without loss of generality we order the triangles ascending based on the area:

$$\text{Area}(\triangle_i) \leq \text{Area}(\triangle_j) \Leftrightarrow i < j. \tag{6}$$

The sequence of triangles with equal areas is not important. We compute six area ratios

$$R_{ij} = \frac{\text{Area}(\triangle_i)}{\text{Area}(\triangle_j)} \quad \forall i < j. \tag{7}$$

The Area ratio fulfills the following properties:

1. Due to the sorting, we have $R_{ij} \in [0, 1]$.
2. The area can be computed using the determinant which is a continuous function in the point coordinates. Hence the area ratio is also continuous. It can be shown that this also holds in the case of a change in the ordering of triangles caused by coordinate noise.
3. The area ratio $\frac{\text{Area}(\triangle_1)}{\text{Area}(\triangle_2)} = \frac{\text{Area}(\blacktriangle_1)}{\text{Area}(\blacktriangle_2)}$, with $\blacktriangle_i$ being an affine transformed version of $\triangle_i$, is invariant under affine transformations[16].

In the following, we will index the six ratios R_{ij} with a single index for ease of notation as the order is not important. We can now introduce the invariant mapping function $T_{\boldsymbol{\rho}} : \mathbb{R}^{3 \times 4} \rightarrow [0, 1]$

$$T_{\boldsymbol{\rho}}(\boldsymbol{P}) = T_{\boldsymbol{\rho}}(R_1, \ldots, R_6) = \frac{1}{6!} \sum_{\pi \in S_6} R_{\pi(1)}^{\rho_1} \cdot \ldots \cdot R_{\pi(6)}^{\rho_6} \quad . \tag{8}$$

The mapping $T_{\boldsymbol{\rho}}$ is a symmetric polynomial parameterized with a set of exponents $\boldsymbol{\rho} \in [0, \infty)^6$, i.e. the positive part of the $\mathbb{R}^6$. We need this restriction to assure that $R_{ij} \in [0, 1]$. In order to be invariant to a permutation of the input we integrate over the symmetric group S_6.

We want to use $T_{\boldsymbol{\rho}}$ as an indexing function for a hash table. Therefore we aim to find a parameterization $\boldsymbol{\rho}$ that yields an invariant distribution as uniform as possible, as this is optimal for hashing[13]. The shape of the distribution depends on the underlying population of 4PAS and the parameterization ρ. Fig. 2 illustrates the impact of the parameterization ρ. Note that the hashing will work with any kind of distribution, the degree of uniformity only has an impact on the number of candidates within a tolerance level. We did not elaborately analyze this part of the problem and choose $\rho = [1, 1, 0, 0, 0, 0]$ as parameterization for the further experiments, as it yields the most uniform distribution among the parameterizations tested.

3   Voronoi Decomposition

With geometric hashing, we want to establish an initial pairing between two 4PAS $\boldsymbol{P}$ that lie on a characteristic common point set (Eqn. 2) of two objects.

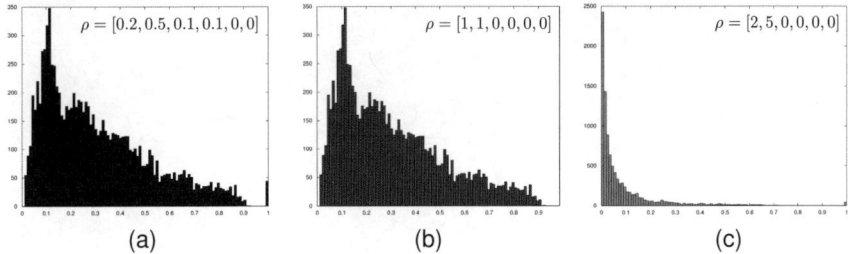

Fig. 2. The histograms show invariant distributions for 10.000 4PAS (see Sec. 3), sampled from a typical population of *Taeniura lymma* (see Sec. 5) under different parameterizations ρ. The distribution (c) is not suitable for hashing.

As we do not make any assumptions for the initial configurations of the point clouds, we need to partition the cloud into local neighborhoods[2] of four points independent of the cloud's orientation.

The *Voronoi decomposition* partitions the $\mathbb{R}^2$ into disjunct cells based on a set of centroids $\mathbf{c}_i$. For each cell holds that every point of the cell is closer to its centroid $\mathbf{c}_i \in \mathcal{C}$ than to every other centroid $\mathbf{c}_j \in \mathcal{C}$:

$$\mathcal{V}_{cell}(\mathbf{c}_i) = \{p \mid \forall j \neq i \ \ \|\mathbf{c}_i - p\| < \|\mathbf{p}_j - p\|\} \quad . \tag{9}$$

Note that all the $\mathcal{V}_{cell}(\mathbf{c}_i)$ are disjoint, but their union does not equal the $\mathbb{R}^2$ as the borders of the cells are not part of the cell. These borders are referred to as *Voronoi segments* and can be defined in the following way:

$$\mathcal{V}_{seg}(\mathcal{C}) = \mathbb{R}^2 \setminus \bigcup_{\mathbf{c}_i \in \mathcal{C}} \mathcal{V}_{cell}(\mathbf{c}_i) \tag{10}$$

These segments represent the borders of the distinct Voronoi cells. All points on a segment are equidistant to at least two Voronoi sites. The intersection points of the borders define a *Voronoi node*:

$$\mathcal{V}_{nodes}(\mathcal{C}) = \{\mathbf{v} \mid \exists \mathbf{c}_i, \mathbf{c}_j, \mathbf{c}_k \in \mathcal{C} : \|\mathbf{c}_i - \mathbf{v}\| = \|\mathbf{c}_j - \mathbf{v}\| = \|\mathbf{c}_k - \mathbf{v}\|\} . \tag{11}$$

We will construct the set $\mathcal{P}$ containing the 4PAS $\boldsymbol{P}$ by extracting the four nearest neighbors for every Voronoi node $\boldsymbol{v} \in \mathcal{V}_{nodes}(\mathcal{C})$ (See Fig. 3 for an illustration). The construction of a Voronoi decomposition takes $O(n \log(n))$ time and contains $O(n)$ Voronoi nodes. The distance queries are issued on a *kd-tree* that also takes $O(n \log(n))$ for construction and $O(log(n))$ for a nearest neighbor query. The overall preprocessing time for a point cloud hence is in $O(n \log(n))$.

This partitioning strategy is canonical for similarity transformations as relative point distances do not change. It therefore is also valid for affine distortions that do not contain strong skews or strong anisotropic scaling. The number of 4PAS $\in \mathcal{P}$ is linear in the number of points in the point cloud.

---

[2] The points of the characteristic common point set originate from a locally planar part of the object.

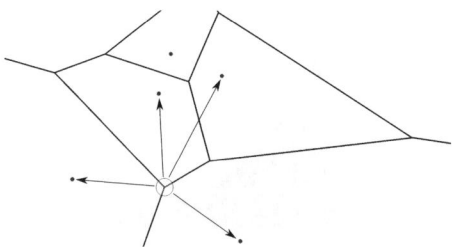

Fig. 3. A Voronoi node with its four nearest neighbors

4   Point Registration

The goal of the point registration is to find the affine transformation A that defines a characteristic common point set (Eqn.2) of two point clouds C_i. We use *geometric hashing* to establish an initial correspondence between two 4PAS that are indexed by the invariant T_ρ (Eqn. 8). This seed is used to compute an initial transformation which is iteratively refined to obtain the transformation that minimizes the quadratic error between the assumed point correspondences. This can be seen as a GOODSAC [17] approach as we make an informed guess (through hashing) for a good initial alignment. To achieve robustness against bin-jumping, we use a *kd-tree* for indexing the set of 4PAS instead of fixed bin sizes. For a 4PAS P_1 we consider every P_2 that lies within a certain tolerance δ as a candidate correspondence: $|T_\rho(P_1) - T_\rho(P_2)| \leq \delta$.

4.1   Pseudoinverse Matrix

We define the affine transformation A and two 4PAS:

$$A = \begin{pmatrix} a_1\ a_2\ a_3 \\ a_4\ a_5\ a_6 \\ 0\ \ 0\ \ 1 \end{pmatrix} \ , P_1 = \{p_1, \ldots, p_4\} \subset C_1, \quad P_2 = \{p_1, \ldots, p_4\} \subset C_2. \quad (12)$$

Without loss of generality we align $C_1 \rightarrow C_2$, i.e. $A(P_1) = P_2$, with point correspondences $p_1^i \sim p_2^i$. Therefore, we have to solve:

$$\underbrace{\begin{pmatrix} p_{1x}\ p_{1y}\ 1\ 0\ \ \ 0\ \ 0 \\ 0\ \ \ 0\ \ 0\ p_{1x}\ p_{1y}\ 1 \\ \vdots\ \ \vdots\ \ \vdots\ \ \vdots\ \ \ \vdots\ \ \vdots \\ p_{nx}\ p_{ny}\ 1\ 0\ \ \ 0\ \ 0 \\ 0\ \ \ 0\ \ 0\ p_{nx}\ p_{ny}\ 1 \end{pmatrix}}_{M} \underbrace{\begin{pmatrix} a_1 \\ a_2 \\ a_3 \\ a_4 \\ a_5 \\ a_6 \end{pmatrix}}_{a} = \underbrace{\begin{pmatrix} \tilde{p}_{1x} \\ \tilde{p}_{1y} \\ \vdots \\ \tilde{p}_{nx} \\ \tilde{p}_{ny} \end{pmatrix}}_{b}. \quad (13)$$

This overdetermined linear system of equations (Eqn. 13) encodes a point correspondence in two lines, as the x– and y–coordinates of a point each impose a condition. For the initial pairing, the number of correspondences is $n = 4$. It can be solved using the *Moore-Penrose Pseudoinverse* $\boldsymbol{M}^+$, minimizing the quadratic Euclidean error between the corresponding points:

$$\boldsymbol{a} = \boldsymbol{M}^+ \boldsymbol{b} \quad . \tag{14}$$

In general we do not know the corresponding points initially. Therefore we have to check all 4! permutations of $\boldsymbol{P}_1$ against $\boldsymbol{P}_2$. We return the candidate transformation with minimal error (Eqn. 15).

4.2   Iterative Refinement

Once we have an initial guess for the affine transformation $\boldsymbol{A}$, we iteratively add more correspondences to the Eqn. 13. We continue adding correspondences as long as a *maximum likelihood* classification of the error of $\boldsymbol{A}$ indicates its validity. We find the next correspondence by checking a small number k of candidates in the neighborhood of the already found correspondences and take the one with the smallest error (Alg. 1, lines 3 and 5). With this strategy, we find the next most likely corresponding points without explicitly specifying a threshold δ_{corr} (Eqn. 1). The goal of the refinement is to estimate the size of the common point set $\mathcal{X}_{\boldsymbol{A}}(\mathcal{C}_1, \mathcal{C}_2)$ that is implied by $\boldsymbol{A}$. We accept two objects as identical once its size reaches the application specific threshold $\#_{min}$. Naturally, the more common points we find, the more confident we can be about the identity of the objects.

We define the error of a mapping of two sets of n correspondences $\boldsymbol{K}_1 \rightarrow \boldsymbol{K}_2$ with respect to $\boldsymbol{A}$ as

$$e_{\boldsymbol{A}}(\boldsymbol{K}_1, \boldsymbol{K}_2) = \frac{1}{\eta^2} \sum_{i=1}^{n} \| \boldsymbol{A}(\boldsymbol{K}_1^i) - \boldsymbol{K}_2^i \|^2 \quad , \tag{15}$$

with normalizer η being the average distance of neighboring points in $\mathcal{C}_2$. We need to normalize the error to account for different scalings in the data. The error rises if the assumed correspondences can not be modeled well by an affine transformation which usually is the case if they do not originate from a common point set. This error measure enables us to to deal with noisy data well: By learning the distributions of the expected error of $\boldsymbol{A}$ for a given number of correspondences n, the registration algorithm adapts optimally to the noise-level present in the application. With *noise* we refer to errors in the point coordinates due to detector inaccuracies and not perfectly planar surfaces.

We have two classes: ω_{pos} for correspondences that originate from a common point set and ω_{neg} for assumed correspondences that do not originate from a common point set. We continue adding correspondences as long as maximum likelihood classification of the error $e_{\boldsymbol{A}}$ of the transformation

$$p(e_{\boldsymbol{A}} \mid \omega_{pos}, n) < p(e_{\boldsymbol{A}} \mid \omega_{neg}, n) \tag{16}$$

indicates its validity. The distributions $p(e_{\boldsymbol{A}} | \omega_{\{pos,neg\}}, n)$ for the positive and negative cases with n points have to be learned on a set of labeled correspondences originating from the population that we wish to work on.

Algorithm 1. $[K_1, K_2, A]$ = refineTransformation(A, C_1, C_2, K_1, K_2)

1: **for** $n \in 4, \ldots, \#_{min}$ **do**
2:     $\mu = \text{mean}(K_2)$ {center of gravity}
3:     $B \leftarrow \text{KNN}(C_2, K_2, k)$ {k nearest neighbors to K_2 on C_2}
4:     **for** $c_2 \in B$ **do**
5:         $c_1 = \text{KNN}(A \circ C_1, c_2, 1)$
6:         $K_1 \leftarrow c_1, K_2 \leftarrow c_2$ {add to correspondences}
7:         $A = \text{computeAFF}(K_1, K_2)$ {using Eqn. 14}
8:         **if** $p(e_A | \omega_{pos}, n) < p(e_a | \omega_{neg}, n)$ **then** {ML classification of quality}
9:             remove c_i from K_i
10:         **else**
11:             break
12:         **end if**
13:     **end for**
14:     **if** no new correspondence found **then**
15:         **return** K_1, K_2, A
16:     **end if**
17: **end for**

4.3   Complexity

The complexity of the registration algorithm is directly proportional to the size of the queue holding the candidate pairings. For each pairing we have to run the iterative refinement (Alg. 1) that runs at most $\#_{min}$ iterations. We can assume that this is a rather small value in real world applications (See Sect. 5). Therefore we estimate the cost of one refinement with $O(\#_{min})$. The size of the queue is dependent on the discrimination power of T_ρ and the noise level of the data. The best case, i.e. a characteristic common point set exists, is achieved in constant time. The worst case (negative matching on a repetitive pattern) is quadratic in the number of points as we have to try all possible pairings. The average case for the negative matching is linear in the number of points, if the hashing yields few possible candidate pairings. This usually is the case for random patterns.

5   Experiments

We test the algorithm for the biometric identification of the bluspotted ribbontail ray, working with a total of 42 underwater pictures from 6 different individuals (7 pictures each). We extract the point pattern using a multi scale LoG detector. The extracted point data contains nearly no false positives on the surface of the ray, but may contain lots of *outliers*. The average point cloud contains 140 points and is partitioned into 180 4PAS. We learn the positive distribution $p(e_A|\omega_{pos}, n)$ on one hand labeled set of 7 pictures for $n \in 4, \ldots, 21$, retrieving around 500 error measurements e_A for each n. The negative case ω_{neg} is learned on point clouds of two different individuals by sampling iteratively increasing neighborhoods of n points on the clouds.

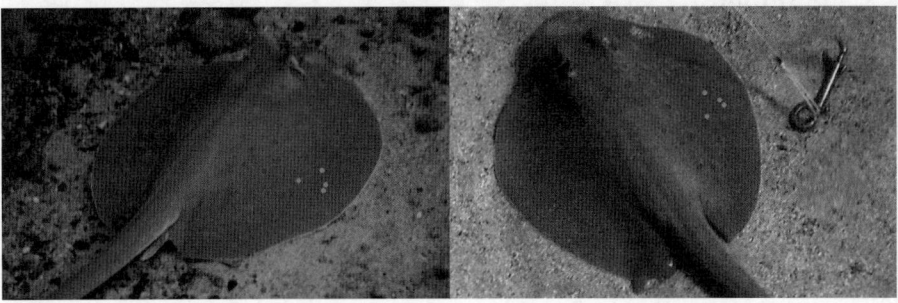

Fig. 4. A positively identified sting ray with its characteristic common point set (*red*) and the initial pairing of 4PAS (*green*)

We perform a pairwise comparison on the remaining 5 sets conducting a total of 595 tests. Fig. 5 shows the precision–recall diagram of our classification results. We achieve a precision of 1 with a recall of 0.75 which validates our algorithm for the biometric identification. With $\#_{min} = 17$ we would achieve perfect confidence on this population. The points that lie outside of the characteristic common point set can be regarded as outliers, although they most likely represent a real blue spot on the ray's surface – but not from the same planar surface patch. To the best of our knowledge, no other point registration algorithm exists that can handle point clouds under affine distortions with $\sim 90\%$ outliers in arbitrary initial positions.

For the positive cases we find the solution after an average of 69 pairings. The algorithm was implemented using MATLAB R2009a on a Intel Core 2 Duo. Absolute timings for the positive matching are ~ 3 sec. and ~ 15 sec. for the negative case. The learning of $p(e_A|\omega_{\{pos,neg\}}, n)$ takes less than one second for every n.

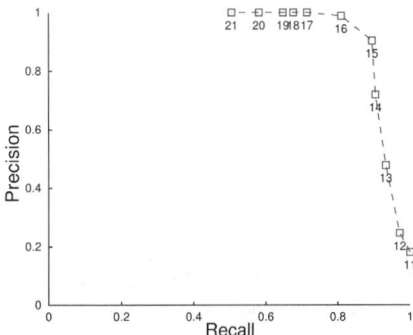

Fig. 5. A cardinality of $\#_{min} = 17$ for the characteristic common point set identifies an individual of *Taeniura lymma* unambiguously on our dataset

6   Conclusion

We presented a novel point registration algorithm for matching two dimensional point clouds originating from partly planar surfaces under affine distortions. It can handle a huge amount of outliers and is able to deal with noisy data well. We successfully apply it for the biometric identification of *Taeniura lymma*.

Acknowledgements

We would like to thank Jessica Weidenbörner[3] for the underwater pictures of Taeniura lymma and the anonymous reviewers for their helpful comments.

References

1. Lowe, D.G.: Distinctive image features from scale-invariant keypoints. International Journal of Computer Vision 60, 91–110 (2004)
2. Burghardt, T., Campbell, N.: Individual animal identification using visual biometrics on deformable coat patterns. In: ICVS 2007 (March 2007), doi:10.2390
3. Costa, M., Haralick, R., Shapiro, L.: Object recognition using optimal affine-invariant matching (1990)
4. Burkhardt, H., Reisert, M., Li, H.: Invariants for discrete structures - an extension of haar integrals over trf. groups to dirac delta functions. In: Rasmussen, C.E., Bülthoff, H.H., Schölkopf, B., Giese, M.A. (eds.) DAGM 2004. LNCS, vol. 3175, pp. 137–144. Springer, Heidelberg (2004)
5. Speed, C.W., Meekan, M.G., Bradshaw, C.J.a.: Spot the match - wildlife photo-identification using information theory. Frontiers in zoology 4, 2 (2007)
6. Belongie, S., Malik, J., Puzicha, J.: Shape matching and object recognition using shape contexts. IEEE Trans. Pattern Anal. Mach. Intell. 24(4), 509–522 (2002)
7. Lazebnik, S., Schmid, C., Ponce, J.: Semi-local affine parts for object recognition. In: BMVC, pp. 959–968 (2004)
8. Coetzee, L., Botha, E.C.: Fingerprint recognition in low quality images, vol. 26, pp. 1441–1460 (1993)
9. Turk, M.A., Pentland, A.P.: Face recognition using eigenfaces. In: IEEE Computer Society Conference on CVPR 1991, pp. 586–591 (1991)
10. Rusinkiewicz, S., Levoy, M.: Efficient variants of the icp algorithm. In: International Conference on 3D Digital Imaging and Modeling (2001)
11. Winkelbach, S.: Efficient methods for solving 3d-puzzle-problems. IT - Information Technology 50(3), 199–201 (2008)
12. Lamdan, Y., Schwartz, J., Wolfson, H.: Object recognition by affine invariant matching. In: CVPR 1988, pp. 335–344 (1988)
13. Wolfson, H., Rigoutsos, I.: Geometric hashing: An overview. CalSE 4(4), 10–21 (1997)
14. Aiger, D., Mitra, N.J., Cohen-Or, D.: 4-points congruent sets for robust surface registration. ACM Transactions on Graphics 27(3), #85, 1–10 (2008)
15. Burkhardt, H.: Transformationen zur lageinvarianten Merkmalgewinnung. In: Habilitation, Fortschrittbericht(Reihe 10, Nr.7). VDI-Verlag (1979)
16. Weiss, I.: Geometric invariants and object recognition. Int. J. Comput. Vision 10(3), 207–231 (1993)
17. Michaelsen, E., von Hansen, W., Kirchhof, M., Meidow, J., Stilla, U.: Estimating the essential matrix: Goodsac versus ransac. In: PCV 2006 (2006)

---

[3] jessica.weidenboerner@t-online.de

Model-Based Recognition of Domino Tiles Using TGraphs

Stefan Wirtz, Marcel Häselich, and Dietrich Paulus*

University of Koblenz-Landau
Department for Computer Science

Abstract. This paper presents a case study showing that domino tile recognition using a model-based approach delivers results comparable to heuristic or statistical approaches. The knowledge on our models is modeled in TGraphs which are typed, attributed, and ordered directed graphs. Four task-independent rules are defined to create a domain independent control strategy which manages the object recognition. To perform the matching of elements found in the image and elements given by the model, a large number of hypotheses may arise. We designed several belief functions in terms of Dempster-Shafer in order to rate hypotheses emerging from the assignment of image to model elements. The developed system achieves a recall of 89.4% and a precision of 94.4%. As a result we are able to show that model based object recognition is on a competitive basis with the benefit of knowing the belief in each model. This enables the possibility to apply our techniques to more complex domains again, as it was tried and canceled 10 years ago.

1   Introduction

Object detection using model-based image analysis is still a challenge. Although there has been research in this area for many years. It is widely excepted that knowledge of the object domain is needed to classify objects. For example, Google Earth provides lots of models of buildings which are designed in Geography Markup Language (GML) and Keyhole Markup Language (KML). These model descriptions deliver symbolic descriptions of buildings which may give new relevance to model-based image analysis, because plenty of models are available.

Several approaches try to find an algorithm which is general, robust and efficiently calculable. In this study we evaluate the *efficiency* and *robustness* of model-based object recognition in a *task-independent* pattern recognition system. Furthermore we introduce *belief functions* to achieve that goal. For this purpose we use exemplary domino tiles as a first manageable application domain.

One archetype of such a system is ERNEST [1], which is a pattern recognition system developed in 1980 employing semantic networks in several application domains, like building recognition [2] and speech understanding [3]. In our

* This work was partially funded by Deutsche Forschungsgemeinschaft (DFG) under grant PA 599/8-1.

M. Goesele et al. (Eds.): DAGM 2010, LNCS 6376, pp. 101–110, 2010.

approach, we use TGraphs [4] as a "light-weight"-ontology. TGraphs are a very general graph concept which is based on vertices and edges as first-class entities and includes types, attributes, and ordering for both. We store the meta-knowledge and instantiate concrete models using this knowledge, taking advantage of the fact that no large sets of samples are needed because the geometrical knowledge about domino tiles is directly used to construct the models. To find features in images we exploit the explicit knowledge given by the models. Therefore, we use a task-independent *activity-control*, which manages the application flow of the system. In this paper, we outline how our model-based system can be extended to work in any other application domain.

We introduce the related work in Section 2. Section 3 describes our approach in detail. There we give the exact definition of the task and describing our model of domino tiles as well as the designed belief functions. We show and discuss our experiments and results in Section 4. A summary and ideas for future work can be found in Section 5.

2   Related Work

In principle, the object detection task for domino tiles is simple; this problem has been used as a case study before, e.g. in [5]. A heuristic strategy is to detect circles and rectangles and count the circles in each half of the domino tile. Another approach is to apply *template matching* [6], which is widely used in face recognition. Bollmann et. al. [5] use template matching to identify domino tiles. The advantage of template matching is that it delivers a similarity measure, but it is neither rotation nor scale invariant.

Today, model-based approaches normally use statistics, appearance, shape or geometry, which mostly work without an explicit geometrical model schema [7,8]. In this work we only use models where the modeling of the objects is in a explicit form, like it is used in Computer Aided Design, which rather corresponds to the human view. We use domino tiles as an example to demonstrate and evaluate model-based approaches.

Using models for explicit knowledge representation, there are two main strategies how a controlling algorithm can handle the analysis process (cf. [9] p. 240ff). On the one hand, there is the *data-driven* strategy, where the segmentation objects, found in the image, serve as an initialization for the analysis. Based on the segmentation objects, the best possible model is sought. The *model-driven* strategy on the other hand works the other way round. Each model determines whether it is contained in the image or not and tries to locate its elements.

Hybrid forms are feasible and favored in most cases. We choose a hybrid approach where data-driven models become pre-evaluated and then we selectively search model-driven for segmentation objects. These strategies can be called task-independent because they do not refer to knowledge of the domain. Other systems exist which use ontologies such as OWL[1] and combine them with uncertain knowledge for finding concepts in a domain [10,11].

---

[1] http://www.w3.org/2004/OWL/

Uncertainty theories, such as Bayes [6], Dempster-Shafer [12] or fuzzy sets [12] define how to deal with uncertain, insecure or vague knowledge. They provide a representation formalism for uncertain information and reasoning strategies. The Dempster-Shafer as belief propagation is used by Hois in [13] and [10], where Neumann uses Bayesian compositional hierarchies for scene interpretation [14].

The knowledge-based processing strategy was popular in several areas, also in the image analysis, in the 80s. Semantic networks were introduced and successfully used for image and speech analysis [15,16,17]. The formalism ERNEST [17] combines representation of concepts in a graph, using sparse edge types, with a task-independent control of A*-basis. There the search for the best association can be considered as a path search which can also be performed if not all states are generated. This can be controlled by the A^*-algorithm [15].

An overview of knowledge-based systems for object recognition is given in [18]. Such systems need to be robust to errors in segmentation data as well as predominantly invariant to changes in image acquisition.

3   The Model-Based Approach

This paper describes a model-based approach to locate domino tiles in images, where Section 3.1 gives a formal specification of the task. The application flow of the system is to accomplish first a pre-evaluation of the models (3.2), where only the circles in each half of a rectangle are counted. Then the activity control (3.3) starts to recognize domino tiles with these model. The hypotheses of found domino tiles are evaluated for each assignment (3.4) and the entire model.

3.1   Specification

The recognition system in this case study works with several domino tiles and can handle wrong inputs.

Given
- a universe SEGMENT of all possible segmentation objects,
- a set RECT $\subset$ SEGMENT of all possible rectangles,
- a set CIRCLE $\subset$ SEGMENT of all possible circles,
- CIRCLE $\cap$ RECT $= \varnothing$
- a relation CONTAINS which describes if a segmentation objects contains another segmentation objects, CONTAINS $\subseteq$ SEGMENT$\times$SEGMENT,
- one domino tile rectangle $dr_1 \in$ RECT and its two halves $dr_2 \in$ RECT and $dr_3 \in$ RECT,
- a set P $\subset$ CIRCLE of possible pips with a specific position, with $|P| = 14$,
- a set LAYOUT of possible layouts, $|\text{LAYOUT}| = 28$, the number of possible domino tiles, and LAYOUT $\subset 2^P$,
- a set of Models M $= \{dr_1\}\times\{dr_2\}\times\{dr_3\}\times$LAYOUT, where $m \in$ M $\wedge m = (m_1, m_2, m_3, m_4)$ is a concrete model (see Sect. 3.2).

Input

- a set $S \subset$ SEGMENT, $S = R \dot\cup C$ with $R \subset$ RECT and $C \subset$ CIRCLE, of all segmentation objects found in the image,
- a threshold $\theta \in [0, 1]$, to set a belief limit of the hypotheses
- a total function $\text{Bel}_S : S \to [0, 1] \subset \mathbb{R}$, describing the belief in the segmentation object itself
- a total function $\text{Bel}_M : M \times (2^R \times 2^C) \to [0, 1] \subset \mathbb{R}$, describing the belief in the model assignment.

Output

- a set $M' \subset M$ of domino models, where $\forall\, m' \in M' \mid \text{Bel}_M(m', R', C') \geq \theta$, with $C' \in 2^C \wedge R' \in 2^R$,
- $\forall\, m' \in M'$
  - a set $R^{m'} \subset R$ of rectangles partially mapped to m'_1, m'_2 and m'_3, with $|R| < 4$, where $r_1 \in R^{m'}$ is assigned to the domino tile m'_1,
  - $\gamma_C^{m'} = C \rightarrowtail m'_4$,
  - $\forall\, c_1 \in C \mid c_1 \in \text{dom}(\gamma_C^{m'}) : r_1$ CONTAINS c_1
  - judgments $J^{m'}_{\text{local}_k} \in [0, 1]$, $k = 1, \ldots, L$ how well these mappings in detail could be established,
  - a total judgment $J^{m'} \in [0, 1]$ of the found models. These are calculated with Bel_M.

In this case study the judgment J is according to the belief of the Dempster-Shafer theory [19].

3.2   Model

The basis for the model-based object recognition system is, of course, the model itself. Therefore, we model the declarative knowledge in a generic scheme (see Fig. 1). The main elements of the model are the elements `TwoDGeometricObject` and `SemanticObject`, which are derived classes of the `GenericObject`, so we have a clear separation of semantic and geometric objects.

Two types of edges are defined in the schema. On the one hand, the `consists-Of` edge which describes that `TwoDGeometricObjects` are able to consist of other `TwoDGeometricObjects` and `SemanticObject` are able to consist of other `SemanticObjects`. A constraint to the schema is that `SemanticObjects` cannot consist of `TwoDGeometricObjects` and the other way round. On the other hand, the `isRepresentedBy` edge maps a `SemanticObject` to a `TwoDGeometricObject`. Every edge has the attribute `obligatory` to determine if the part or representation is obligatory to recognize the object.

In addition to declarative knowledge, we also model the procedural knowledge in the schema. Therefore, we need the three methods `initiate`, `limit` and `calculateBelief` for every element. The `initiate` method has the task to find

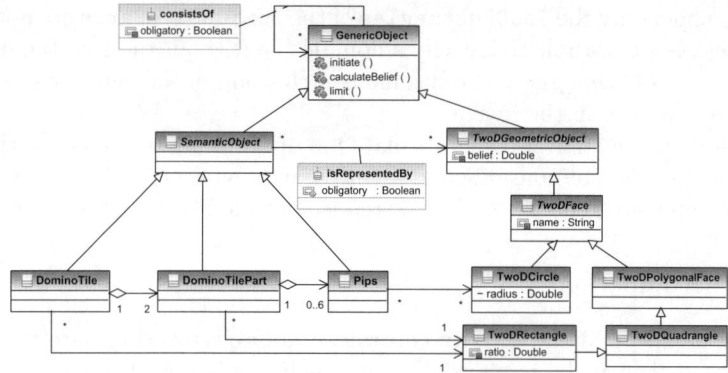

Fig. 1. UML diagram of the domino tile schema

its potential equivalents in the image and to provide them to the system. After a successful initialization, the `limit` method is needed to calculate with a given segmentation object, as initiation candidate, the resulting limiting, region of interest (*ROI*). This ROI is set to the further parts of the model, so that in further calculation steps only candidates within the ROI are considered. Finally, the `calculateBelief` method calculates the belief in the element. These belief functions vary widely and it is a scientific task to find adequate belief functions. In Section 3.4, the functions are described in more detail.

With this schema, we are able to construct concrete models. In this case study, we have 28 basic models, because we have 28 domino tiles.

3.3   Pragmatic of the System

A control system can now take these models and start with the analysis of the image. The developed system is inspired by ERNEST (see Sect. 2). In ERNEST six task-independent rules precisely define the computation of elements and instances. These rules are combined with graph search algorithms to handle the control problem. Our system has four task-independent rules.

Rule 1. If a `isRepresentedBy` edge belongs to the actual element, go to the `TwoDGeometricObject` of the `isRepresentedBy`-edge and initiate the element.

Rule 2. If no `isRepresentedBy` edge belongs to the actual element, expand the element, i.e., search for the part of this element which is not already processed. If all parts are already processed go to the parent element and repeat Rule 2.

Rule 3. If the initialization of a element was successful, limit the ROI of all parts which belong to this element.

Rule 4. If an element is not obligatory, but an initialization is possible, then use Rule 1 for this element.

In our model only the `TwoDRectangles` of the `DominoTileParts` are not obligatory, because we are able to identify a domino tile without these rectangles, but
the knowledge of them gives a additional contribution in the belief that we have
found a domino tile in the image.

Each step in the analysis is encapsulated in one state. The search for the best
association can then be considered as a path search, which can also be performed
if not all states are generated. This search is controled by the A^*-algorithm.

3.4   Belief Functions

With the models and the activity control we are able to instantiate them, but
cannot say which model is plausible and which one is not. Therefore, we need
belief-functions which provide qualitative values for each model.

In this case study we choose the Dempster-Shafer belief function, which allows
to model the functions in a heuristic way without requiring the knowledge of the
statistical distribution of our data. Dempster-Shafer provides also a convenient
combination rule for independent beliefs. Therefore, we need the *basic probability
assignment* (bpa). A bpa must fulfill the conditions:

Given the sample space $\Omega = \{a_k\}, k = 1, \ldots, K, A \subseteq \Omega$, where a_k and A are
arbitrary events.

$$\text{bpa}(\varnothing) = 0 \qquad (1) \qquad\qquad \sum_{A \subseteq \Omega} \text{bpa}(A) = 1 \qquad (2)$$

The combined bpa with Dempster-Shafer is:

$$\text{bpa}_1 \oplus \text{bpa}_2 = \text{bpa}(A) = \begin{cases} 0 & : \; A = \varnothing \\ \frac{\sum_{t \cap u = A} \text{bpa}_1(t)\text{bpa}_2(u)}{1 - \sum_{t \cap u \neq \varnothing} \text{bpa}_1(t)\text{bpa}_2(u)} & : \; \varnothing \neq A \subseteq \Omega \end{cases} \quad (3)$$

The Dempster-Shafer rule is commutative and associative. Accordingly, it is
possible to combine various resources, but the resources have to be independent
of each other because in general $\text{bpa} \oplus \text{bpa} \neq \text{bpa}$ is valid.

We define three general functions which are valid for each `SemanticObject`.
At first we need a function to combine bpa of two events of different sample
spaces which gives both a belief assignment that an accordant element is found
in the image (see eqn. 4). Therefore, the combination rule of DS (eqn. 3) is used
like Quint made it in [2]. Then the belief of a `SemanticObject` is

$$\begin{aligned} \text{bpa}(\texttt{SemanticObject} \mid \text{E}_{parts}, \text{E}_{rep}) = \\ \kappa_1 \, \text{bpa}(\texttt{SemanticObject} \mid \text{E}_{parts}) \oplus \kappa_2 \, \text{bpa}(\texttt{SemanticObject} \mid \text{E}_{rep}) . \end{aligned} \quad (4)$$

With κ_1 and κ_2 you can weight the trust that this event really support the
belief in the `SemanticObject`, where $\kappa_1, \kappa_2 \in [0, 1]$. The information source
E_{parts} describes the observation of the parts of a `SemanticObject` and the
information source E_{rep} specifies the GeometricObject which represents this
`SemanticObject`. A example is given in equation 5 with the belief

$$\text{bpa}(\text{dr}_1 \mid \text{E}_{\text{dr}_i}, \text{E}_\text{R}) = \quad 0.7\text{bpa}(\text{dr}_1 \mid \text{E}_\text{R}) \oplus \text{bpa}(\text{dr}_1 \mid \text{E}_{\text{dr}_i}), i \in \{2,3\} \quad (5)$$

of the `SemanticObject DominoTile` given the information sources E_{dr_i} (observed domino tile parts) and E_R (observed rectangle). The rectangle alone gives a smaller contribution that the `DominoTile` element was found in the image than possibly found domino tile halves, so $\kappa_1 = 0.7 \wedge \kappa_2 = 1$. Also we need to know the belief of a `SemanticObject` given the information source E_{parts} (observed parts). Therefore, we use a function (eqn. 6) equal to the total-probability rule. For any partition B_j, $j = 1, \ldots, N$ of the event space Ω and $\Omega = \{\{fp_1, \ldots, fp_L\}, \{\overline{fp_1}, \ldots, fp_L\}, \ldots, \{\overline{fp_1}, \ldots, \overline{fp_L}\}\}$, where fp equates the event of found a `SemanticObject` part, is

$$\text{bpa}(\texttt{SemanticObject} \mid E_{\text{parts}}) =$$
$$\sum_j \text{bpa}(\texttt{SemanticObject} \mid B_j)\text{bpa}(B_j \mid E_{\text{parts}}) . \tag{6}$$

We apply the belief of a `SemanticObject` given the information source E_{parts} to a `DominoTile` as example (eqn. 7) and calculate the weighted sum over the partition B of the `DominoTileParts`. For this is $\Omega = \{\{dr_2, dr_3\}, \{\overline{dr_2}, dr_3\}, \{dr_2, \overline{dr_3}\}, \{\overline{dr_2}, \overline{dr_3}\}\}$ and

$$\text{bpa}(dr_1 \mid E_{\{dr_2, dr_3\}}) = \sum_j \text{bpa}(dr_1 \mid B_j)\text{bpa}(B_j \mid E_{\{dr_2, dr_3\}}) . \tag{7}$$

Finally, we need the belief of a partition B_j given the information source E_{B_j}:

$$\text{bpa}(B_j \mid E_{B_j}) = \prod_{p_j \in B_j \wedge p_j \text{ isTrue}} \text{bpa}(p_j) . \tag{8}$$

The concrete implementation for the partition B_j of domino tile parts is

$$\text{bpa}(B_j \mid E_{\{dr_2, dr_2\}}) = \prod_{dtp_j \in B_j \wedge dtp_j \text{ isTrue}} \text{bpa}(dtp_j) . \tag{9}$$

An example of a possible partion B_j is $B_j = \{\overline{dr_2}, dr_3\}$.

These three functions are the same for each `SemanticObject`. They have to be supplemented by basic probabilistic assignments bpa for the specific cases. Some important bpa will be presented in the next equations 10 - 13.

The belief of the assignment of a segmented rectangle to a model rectangle is

$$\text{bpa}(dr_1 \mid E_R) = \begin{cases} \frac{\text{ratio}_r}{\text{ratio}_{dr_1}} & : \quad \text{ratio}_{dr_1} > \text{ratio}_r, \quad r \in R \\ \frac{\text{ratio}_{dr_1}}{\text{ratio}_r} & : \quad \text{ratio}_{dr_1} < \text{ratio}_r, \quad r \in R \end{cases} . \tag{10}$$

For the calculation of $\text{bpa}(dr_i \mid E_R)$ we take the already found rectangle dr_1 of the domino tile, divide it in two halves and compare it with the candidates for the domino tile part rectangle dr_i. Therefore, we calculate the intersection area of one of the halves and dr_i and divide the intersection by the entire area of the rectangle half and dr_i.

$$\mathrm{bpa}(\mathrm{dr}_i \mid \mathrm{E_R}) = \frac{\text{intersection area of } \mathrm{dr}_i \text{ and R}}{\text{entire area of } \mathrm{dr}_i \text{ and R}} \text{ with } i \in \{2,3\} \ . \tag{11}$$

The beliefs of the rectangle assignments in (10) and (11) are necessary to distinguish a domino tile from other objects. We also need a belief function which penalize missing assignments of segmentation objects and/or model elements:

$$\mathrm{bpa}(\mathrm{dr}_i \mid \mathrm{P}) = e^{-\frac{1}{2}x^2}$$
$$x = \| \mid C \mid + \mid \{\text{given pips}\} \in P \mid - \mid \{\text{associated pips}\} \in P \| \ . \tag{12}$$

The belief in the assignment of a pip p to a circle c, where (c_x, c_y) and (p_x, p_y) are the center points of the circles, and c_r and p_r are the radiuses, is very important. We choose the exponential form to prevent that circles are assigned to wrong and far away pips:

$$\mathrm{bpa}(p \in P \mid c \in C) = 101 - 200^q - 50 \mid c_r - p_r \mid,$$
$$q = \sqrt{(p_x - c_x)^2 + (p_y - c_y)^2} \ . \tag{13}$$

The choice of the functions (12) and (13) tunes if it is better to drop an assignment or not. As much more missing elements are penalized and as much more the $\mathrm{bpa}(p \in P \mid c \in C)$ forgive differences of pips and circles, the more segmentation objects are assigned and the other way round. For the calculation of the beliefs (11), (12) and (13) we translate and rotate the rectangle and circles in the origin and scale them, so they are comparable with model elements.

With these functions we have now the ability to rate the assignments of model elements to segmentation objects. Furthermore the combination of the functions gives us the total belief that a specific model was detected in the image. With the models, the task-independent activity-control, the belief functions, and a belief propagation we have all parts to find domino tiles in images.

4   Experiments and Results

This section deals with the data acquisition and the conducted experiments.

The data set of images was created with a turn table in a lightbox (JUST Pantone Color Viewing box 1). For the experiments, a data set containing 489 images of single domino tiles on a homogeneous background was used. The images were created with an standard USBcamera in an approximate orthogonal angle to the objects. Furthermore, an adjustment of 22-45 degrees per rotation step (8, 12 or 16 images per light source) was selected for the turn table. In addition to the automatically generated images we also added images with sunlight and ambient light to the data set[2].

We achieved a detection rate of 94.7% and a precision rate of 94.4%. This proves well, that our system works accurately with the given models, and found

---

[2] The dataset is published on er.uni-koblenz.de.

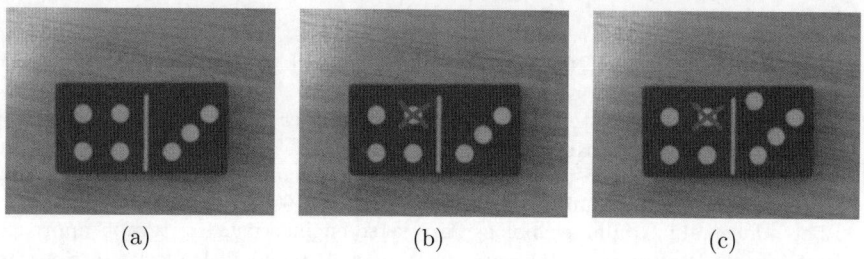

(a)   (b)   (c)

Fig. 2. Image (a) is a possible image with sunlight of the database. This image is additionally distorted to test the classification. Therefore, a circle is masked (b) (c) and a circle is added (c).

rectangles and circles. A recall of 89.4% also seems acceptable and shows that the classification is in balance of precision and recall. The Fig. 2(a) shows one image of the database where our classification correctly recognize the domino tile as a 4-3 domino tile with a belief of 97.3%. We manually distorted this image, where in Fig. 2(b) one circle is not detectable and in Fig. 2(c) a additional circle is added. For Fig. 2(b) the classification delivers as result a 4-3 domino tile with a belief of 84.9%. Hence the classification recognizes the correct domino tile, even though the segmentation is incomplete because we weight the position of a circle more than the number of circles. Whereas for Fig. 2(c) the classification failed. There the classification delivers as result a 4-4 domino tile with a belief of 68,9% because it is more likely that the circle is only at the wrong position than it is a false segmentation, especially where the radius of this circle is correct. As expected, the belief in the result is low. Furthermore, we know the belief of the single assignments. So the belief in the assignment of the wrong circle to the pip is 41.5%, where the belief of a correct circle to a pip is about 98%.

5   Conclusion

We demonstrated that a model-based approach with a task-independent control is able to deliver solid and accurate results for the recognition of domino tiles in images. We achieved a recall of 89.4% and a precision of 94.4%. We showed that we can not only calculate all assignments, but also obtain the knowledge which elements of an image is the best correspondence for an element among the model. To adapt this strategy to another application domain we have to create a new model and implemented the methods for initialization, belief calculation and limitation. Afterwards the activity control is able to classify. In the moment we aply this approach in order to classify poker cards and in the near future the evolved strategies will be adapted to more complex problems, such as the classification of traffic signs and buildings, which will continue the work that we reported on in [20].[3]

---

[3] We thank Kerstin Falkowski and Jrgen Ebert for their fruitful discussions on the component system and the specification in Sect. 3.1.

References

1. Niemann, H., et al.: ERNEST: A Semantic Network System for Pattern Understanding. 12, 883–905 (1990)
2. Quint, F.: Kartengestützte Interpretation monokularer Luftbilder. PhD thesis, Universität Fridericiana zu Karlsruhe, TH (1997)
3. Niemann, H., et al.: Ernest: A semantic network system for pattern understanding. IEEE Trans. Pattern Anal. Mach. Intell. 12(9), 883–905 (1990)
4. Ebert, J., et al.: Graph technology in reverse engineering, the tgraph approach. In: Gimnich, R., Kaiser, U., Quante, J., Winter, A. (eds.) 10th Workshop Software Reengineering (WSR 2008), Bonn. GI Lecture Notes in Informatics, vol. 126, pp. 67–81. GI (2008)
5. Bollmann, M., et al.: Playing Domino: A Case Study for an Active Vision System. In: Christensen, H.I. (ed.) ICVS 1999. LNCS, vol. 1542, pp. 392–411. Springer, Heidelberg (1998)
6. Theodoridis, S., Koutroumbas, K.: Pattern Recognition, 4th edn. Academic Press, London (2009)
7. Cremers, D., Sochen, N., Schnrr, C.: A multiphase dynamic labeling model for variational recognition-driven image segmentation. International Journal of Computer Vision 66(1), 67–81 (2006)
8. Seemann, E., Leibe, B., Schiele, B.: Multi-aspect detection of articulated objects. In: Conference on Computer Vision and Pattern Recognition (CVPR 2006), vol. 2, pp. 1582–1588 (2006)
9. Niemann, H.: Pattern Analysis and Understanding. Springer Series in Information Sciences, vol. 4. Springer, Heidelberg (1990)
10. Hois, J.: Towards Combining Ontologies and Uncertain Knowledge. In: Progic 2007: The Third Workshop on Combining Probability and Logic. University of Kent, Canterbury (2007)
11. Reineking, T., Schult, N., Hois, J.: Evidential Combination of Ontological and Statistical Information for Active Scene Classification. In: KEOD (2009)
12. Beierle, C., Kern-Isberner, G.: Methoden wissensbasierter Systeme - Grundlagen, Algorithmen, Anwendungen. Vieweg, 1. Auflage (2006)
13. Hois, J., Kerstin Schill, J.A.B.: Integrating Uncertain Knowledge in a Domain Ontology for Room Concept Classifications. In: Research and Development in Intelligent Systems XXIII (2007)
14. Neumann, B.: Bayesian compositional hierarchies - a probabilistic structure for scene interpretation. Technical Report FBI-HH-B-282/08, Department of Informatics, Hamburg University (2008)
15. Kummert, F., Sagerer, G., Niemann, H.: A Problem-independent Control Algorithm for Image Understanding. Universität Bielefeld (1992)
16. Sagerer, G.: Darstellung und Nutzung von Expertenwissen fu ein Bildanalysesystem. Springer, Berlin (1985)
17. Niemann, H., et al.: Ernest: A semantic network system for pattern understanding. IEEE Transactions on Pattern Analysis and Machine Intelligence 9, 883–905 (1990), http://www.computer.org/tpami/
18. Crevier, D., Lepage, R.: Knowledge-Based Image Understanding Systems: A Survey. Computer Vision and Image Understanding: CVIU 67, 161–185 (1997)
19. Shafer, G.: A Mathematical Theory of Evidence. Princeton University Press, Princeton (1976)
20. Falkowski, K., et al.: Semi-automatic generation of full citygml models from images. In: Geoinformatik 2009. ifgiPrints, vol. 35, pp. 101–110. Institut für Geoinformatik Westfälische Wilhelms-Universität Münster (April 2009)

Slicing the View:
Occlusion-Aware View-Based Robot Navigation

David Dederscheck, Martin Zahn, Holger Friedrich, and Rudolf Mester

Visual Sensorics and Information Processing Lab
J. W. Goethe University, Frankfurt, Germany
{davidded,zahn,holgerf,mester}@vsi.cs.uni-frankfurt.de
http://www.vsi.cs.uni-frankfurt.de

Abstract. Optical Rails [1] is a purely view-based method for autonomous track following with a mobile robot, based upon compact omnidirectional view descriptors using basis functions on the sphere. We address
the most prominent points of criticism towards holistic methods for robot
navigation: Dealing with occlusions and varying illumination. This is accomplished by slicing the omnidirectional view into segments, enabling
dynamic visual fields capable of masking out occlusions while preserving
proven, efficient paradigms for holistic view comparison and steering.

1 Introduction: Beyond the View-Based Approach

In the field of visual robot navigation, view-based, or 'holistic' approaches have
recently become increasingly popular: They replace the tedious task of matching
prominent points or performing accurate geometric measurements by a comparison of entire images in the spectral domain, utilizing the possibilities of omnidirectional sensors, which provide a large rotation-invariant visual field. The
vulnerability of holistic methods to occlusions of the view, or local changes in
illumination, is commonly considered a major obstacle for their successful deployment. Dederscheck et. al. [1] have shown that illumination-invariant view-based
navigation is possible by using vector-valued image representations. Dynamic
occlusions pose a different challenge: They require *adaptive* visual fields.

In the present paper we propose a simple solution for this task: We slice an
omnidirectional view into multiple segments; while the spatial arrangement of
the slices is known, each segment is represented in the spectral domain, i. e.
by the coefficients of an expansion into low-frequency basis functions on the
sphere. Hence, we denote the proposed hybrid concept as a *semi-spectral* view
representation, extending the track following approach of Dederscheck et. al.
(Optical Rails) towards occlusion-awareness: When comparing views stored in
a database to newly seen images, only those view segments free of occlusions
are regarded. At the same time, handling of illumination changes is facilitated,
enabling segment-wise compensation of lighting conditions.

Semi-spectral views can efficiently be recombined (Sec. 2.1) yielding the coefficients of expansion of a single hemispherical view. Thus, our new approach

M. Goesele et al. (Eds.): DAGM 2010, LNCS 6376, pp. 111–120, 2010.
© Springer-Verlag Berlin Heidelberg 2010

easily connects to existing methods harnessing the traditional virtues of spectral representations, such as efficient rotation estimation.

The Navigation Concept. A path to be followed is represented as a sparse sequence of omnidirectional *reference views* serving as waypoints during track following. Instead of memorizing the shape of the trajectory, steering is purely based on gradient descent in view dissimilarities, which is performed efficiently without any operations in image space. A similar navigation approach has been proposed by Matsumoto et. al. [2] (omnidirectional view sequence). Both approaches can be regarded as topological navigation methods, related to biologically inspired approaches (e. g. Möller and Vardy [3]) based on the *snapshot theory* proposed by Cartwright and Collett [4]. In contrast to the traditional feature-based or landmark-based approaches (e. g. Shah and Aggarwal [5]) we present a *purely view-based* approach not relying on geometry.

2   The Semi-spectral View Representation

Expansion of Spherical Signals and Visual Fields. As in Dederscheck et. al. [1], the representation of omnidirectional views is based upon expansion of image signals on the sphere S^2 into real-valued spherical harmonics, which form an orthonormal basis on the sphere.

We define spherical coordinates $\boldsymbol{\eta} = (\theta, \phi)^T \in S^2$, where $\theta \in [0, \pi]$ denotes the angle of *colatitude* and $\phi \in [0, 2\pi)$ denotes the angle of *longitude*. Image signals on the sphere are denoted as $s(\boldsymbol{\eta})$, and the utilized basis functions as Y_j, $j \in \{1, \ldots, M\}$. A truncated expansion of a spherical signal $s(\boldsymbol{\eta})$ is given by

$$s(\boldsymbol{\eta}) = \sum_{j=0}^{M} a_j \cdot Y_j(\boldsymbol{\eta}). \tag{1}$$

The weights a_j of the expansion form a *coefficient vector* $\boldsymbol{a} := (a_1, \ldots, a_M)^T$.

The *visual field* of an omnidirectional sensor is defined as the subset G of the sphere S^2 where image data can be acquired; in our case of a webcam with a low-cost fisheye lens, an almost hemispherical field of view limited by a maximum angle $\theta_{\max}$ is given by $G := \{(\theta, \phi)^T \in S^2 \mid \theta < \theta_{\max}\}$. The visual field G is then partitioned into segments H_i. Let I be an index set enumerating the segments; we define the partition P of the visual field G by

$$P := \{H_i \subseteq G \mid \bigcup_{i \in I} H_i = G, \forall i \neq j : \ H_i \cap H_j = \emptyset\}. \tag{2}$$

Each of the view segments H_i will be represented by a coefficient vector, forming the *semi-spectral* view representation for Optical Rails. The utilized segmentation scheme (Fig. 1) consists of a central area surrounded by a set of radial slices, corresponding to the characteristics of typical occlusions: each outer slice can consume a person standing close to the robot.

Mask functions. For any visual field $K \subseteq S^2$, we define a mask function $m_K : S^2 \mapsto \{0, 1\}$ which is one within K, zero otherwise. For m_G and m_{H_i} we obtain

$$\sum_{i \in I} m_{H_i}(\theta, \phi) = m_G(\theta, \phi). \tag{3}$$

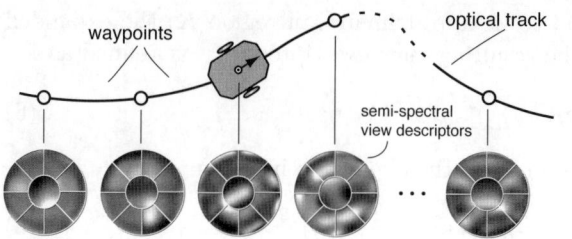

Fig. 1. *Left:* Concept of view-based robot navigation using segmented, semi-spectral views. *Right:* Mobile robot vehicle with upward-facing low-cost omnidirectional camera.

The defined mask functions will be used throughout the following sections to describe areas of interest when comparing visual fields.

Semi-spectral view descriptors. In our approach each segment is treated as an individual signal $s(\boldsymbol{\eta})$ only valid within its respective visual field H_i. Correspondingly, a spherical harmonics expansion is provided for each segment H_i, the resulting coefficient vector is denoted as $\boldsymbol{a}^{(H_i)}$.

A stacked representation of the individual $\boldsymbol{a}^{(H_i)}$ forms the *semi-spectral view descriptor* $\boldsymbol{a}^{\oplus} = (\boldsymbol{a}^{(H_1)}; \ldots; \boldsymbol{a}^{(H_9)})^T$ consisting of all segments: The expansion of a full visual field G into a semi-spectral view descriptor is simply defined as a weighted sum of the expansions of the individual segments

$$\hat{s}(\boldsymbol{\eta}) := \sum_{i \in I} m_{H_i}(\boldsymbol{\eta}) \cdot \sum_{j=1}^{M} a_j^{(H_i)} \cdot Y_j(\boldsymbol{\eta}), \qquad (4)$$

i.e. weighting the individual expansion with the respective mask functions m_{H_i} ensures that each expansion only occupies its respective visual field.

Since spherical harmonics are orthonormal, the coefficients of expansion for a full spherical view are obtained as the inner product of the signal and the basis functions: $a_i = \langle s(\boldsymbol{\eta}), Y_i(\boldsymbol{\eta}) \rangle$. However, for signals defined on only part of the sphere this orthonormality is violated and the above result no longer applies.

In the next section, we derive the optimal expansion of arbitrary visual fields into the same set of basis functions. Finally, the expansion will be performed efficiently, directly using pixel vectors of input images without prior unwrapping.

2.1   Optimized Expansion of Individual Visual Fields

Let $K \subseteq S^2$ and let $\boldsymbol{a}^{(K)}$ be a coefficient vector of the expansion of an image signal $s(\boldsymbol{\eta})$ in the visual field denoted by K. For such $\boldsymbol{a}^{(K)}$ we require that it correctly represents the original signal within K, whereas outside the expansion may assume arbitrary values. The desired view descriptor can be determined using least-squares minimization of the error of approximation within area K. This approach allows optimal expansion of arbitrary visual fields, where the orthogonality of the basis is violated, such as small segments of the sphere.

Let $s(\boldsymbol{\eta})$ be an image signal to be approximated in region K; the expanded image signal represented by the resulting view descriptor $\boldsymbol{a}^{(K)}$ is defined as

$$\hat{s}(\boldsymbol{\eta}) = \sum_{i=1}^{M} a_i^{(K)} \cdot Y_i(\boldsymbol{\eta}). \tag{5}$$

We define the squared residual error of the expansion in region K by

$$R = \int_{\boldsymbol{\eta} \in S^2} m_K(\boldsymbol{\eta}) \cdot \left(\hat{s}(\boldsymbol{\eta}) - s(\boldsymbol{\eta})\right)^2 d\boldsymbol{\eta} \tag{6}$$

where $d\boldsymbol{\eta}$ corresponds to $\sin\theta \, d\theta \, d\phi$. Since m_K is zero outside region K, the residual approximation error is only determined within region K.

Let us now regard the image signals in the cartesian coordinate frame of a planar camera sensor. We define the mapping $\boldsymbol{h}$ between spherical coordinates and the image plane of the sensor by

$$\boldsymbol{h}: S^2 \mapsto \mathbb{R}^2, \ \boldsymbol{x} = \boldsymbol{h}(\boldsymbol{\eta}) \qquad \boldsymbol{h}^{-1}: \mathbb{R}^2 \mapsto S^2, \ \boldsymbol{\eta} = \boldsymbol{h}^{-1}(\boldsymbol{x}). \tag{7}$$

Let the Jacobian of the projection $(\theta, \phi)^T = \boldsymbol{h}^{-1}(\boldsymbol{x})$ be denoted as $\mathbf{J}_{h^{-1}}(\boldsymbol{x})$. We define the weight function $w(\boldsymbol{x}) = \sin\left(\boldsymbol{h}^{-1}(\boldsymbol{x})^T \cdot (1,0)^T\right) \cdot \det(\mathbf{J}_{h^{-1}}(\boldsymbol{x}))$. Now we can directly perform the transition to pixel coordinates of the input image of the omnidirectional camera. Let $\boldsymbol{x}_k$ be the coordinate of the k-th pixel in a continuous planar image signal, where the pixels are numbered in an arbitrary order with indices $k \in \{1, \ldots, N\}$. We define the vectors and matrices

$$\begin{aligned} \mathring{\boldsymbol{y}}_i &= (-Y_i(\boldsymbol{h}^{-1}(\boldsymbol{x}_k))-)^T, & \boldsymbol{w} &= (-(w(\boldsymbol{x}_k) \cdot A_p)-)^T, \\ \boldsymbol{b} &= (-s(\boldsymbol{h}^{-1}(\boldsymbol{x}_k))-)^T, & \mathring{\boldsymbol{m}}_K &= (-m_K(\boldsymbol{h}^{-1}(\boldsymbol{x}_k))-)^T, \end{aligned} \tag{8}$$

$$\mathring{\mathbf{Y}} = (\mathring{\boldsymbol{y}}_1, \cdots, \mathring{\boldsymbol{y}}_M), \quad \mathbf{W}_K = \operatorname{diag}\{\boldsymbol{w}\} \cdot \operatorname{diag}\{\mathring{\boldsymbol{m}}_K\}, \tag{9}$$

where A_p denotes the pixel area and $\mathbf{W}_K$ is a diagonal weight matrix including $\mathring{\boldsymbol{m}}_K$. Using the 'pixel vectors', R simply results in a quadratic form:

$$R = (\mathring{\mathbf{Y}} \cdot \boldsymbol{a}^{(K)} - \boldsymbol{b})^T \cdot \mathbf{W}_K \cdot (\mathring{\mathbf{Y}} \cdot \boldsymbol{a}^{(K)} - \boldsymbol{b}) \tag{10}$$

We minimize R by setting the derivative of R with respect to the expansion coefficients to be zero: $\boldsymbol{0} \overset{!}{=} \partial R / \partial \boldsymbol{a}^{(K)}$. This leads to the normal equation

$$(\mathbf{W}_K \cdot \mathring{\mathbf{Y}})^T \cdot \boldsymbol{b} = \mathbf{G}_K \cdot \boldsymbol{a}^{(K)}, \quad \text{where} \quad \mathbf{G}_K := (\mathring{\mathbf{Y}}^T \cdot \mathbf{W}_K \cdot \mathring{\mathbf{Y}}) \tag{11}$$

is a Gramian matrix. The resulting coefficient vector $\boldsymbol{a}^{(K)}$ is denoted as the *optimal expansion* of an input image (pixel vector) $\boldsymbol{b}$ in K:

$$\boldsymbol{a}^{(K)} = \mathbf{G}_K^{-1} \cdot (\mathbf{W}_K \cdot \mathring{\mathbf{Y}})^T \cdot \boldsymbol{b}. \tag{12}$$

Recombining Slice View Descriptors. The semi-spectral representation consisting of spherical harmonics view expansions of multiple visual fields is not simply a composite form of representing multiple visual fields: The same representation as for a single spherical harmonics expansion of the entire visual field is easily obtained directly from the coefficient vectors.

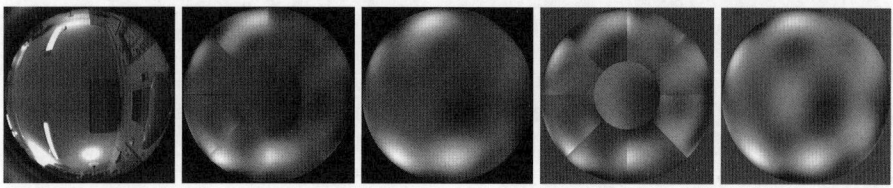

Fig. 2. *Left to right:* Input image, segmented image expansion, recombined view, segmented expansion with normalized illumination (cf. Sec. 3.3), and recombined view. Expansion into spherical harmonics up to order 9 (9×100 resp. 1×100 coefficients).

Replacing K by region H_i in (11) and summarizing both sides leads to

$$\sum_{i \in I} (\mathbf{W}_{H_i} \cdot \mathring{\mathbf{Y}})^T \cdot \boldsymbol{b} = \sum_{i \in I} (\mathring{\mathbf{Y}}^T \cdot \mathbf{W}_{H_i} \cdot \mathring{\mathbf{Y}}) \cdot \boldsymbol{a}^{(H_i)} \tag{13}$$

$$((\sum_{i \in I} \mathbf{W}_{H_i}) \cdot \mathring{\mathbf{Y}})^T \cdot \boldsymbol{b} = \sum_{i \in I} \mathbf{G}_{H_i} \cdot \boldsymbol{a}^{(H_i)}; \tag{14}$$

by equation (3) and $\mathbf{W}_G = \text{diag}\,\{\boldsymbol{w}\} \cdot \text{diag}\,\{\mathring{\boldsymbol{m}}_G\} = \text{diag}\,\{\boldsymbol{w}\} \cdot (\sum_{i \in I} \text{diag}\,\{\mathring{\boldsymbol{m}}_{H_i}\})$ $= \sum_{i \in I} \text{diag}\,\{\boldsymbol{w}\} \cdot \text{diag}\,\{\mathring{\boldsymbol{m}}_{H_i}\} = \sum_{i \in I} \mathbf{W}_{H_i}$ we obtain

$$(\mathbf{W}_G \cdot \mathring{\mathbf{Y}})^T \cdot \boldsymbol{b} = \sum_{i \in I} \mathbf{G}_{H_i} \cdot \boldsymbol{a}^{(H_i)} \tag{15}$$

$$\mathbf{G}_G^{-1} \cdot (\mathbf{W}_G \cdot \mathring{\mathbf{Y}})^T \cdot \boldsymbol{b} = \mathbf{G}_G^{-1} \cdot \sum_{i \in I} \mathbf{G}_{H_i} \cdot \boldsymbol{a}^{(H_i)}, \tag{16}$$

which according to (12) yields the view descriptor for the full visual field

$$\boldsymbol{a}^{(H)} = \mathbf{G}_H^{-1} \cdot \sum_{i \in I} \mathbf{G}_{H_i} \cdot \boldsymbol{a}^{(H_i)}. \tag{17}$$

In general, arbitrary visual fields composed of segments H_i can be recombined if only some of the available $\mathbf{W}_{H_i}$ are summed up on both sides of (13).

3   Occlusion-Aware View Comparison and Steering

In Optical Rails, robot navigation for visual track following is based exclusively on the comparison of views, i.e. the currently observed view and a destination view chosen from a sequence of waypoints. First, a dissimilarity metric Q is defined, which then leads to a gradient of view dissimilarity with respect to robot motions, providing the steering direction towards a waypoint.

For both of these tasks, we introduce the extension to segmented visual fields, yielding figures of dissimilarity and steering vectors for each of the individual 'slices'. Within the comparison result for the full view, each slice can be enabled or disabled individually, considering (both in the current and in the destination view) only those parts of the visual field which are free of occlusions.

We define a *clearance vector* $\boldsymbol{c} = (-\ c_i\ -)^T$ for all i in index set I, where $c_i = 1$ if the visual field H_i is free of occlusions, otherwise $c_i = 0$.

3.1   View Dissimilarities

We compare views using the total squared difference of image signals in the visual field G of the camera. Let $s(\boldsymbol{\eta})$ be the currently observed view, and let $\tilde{s}(\boldsymbol{\eta})$ be a destination view. We define a dissimilarity metric Q_K for an arbitrary visual field K (and analogously Q_G for the full visual field G):

$$Q_K(s(\eta), \tilde{s}(\eta)) := \int_{\boldsymbol{\eta} \in S^2} m_K(\boldsymbol{\eta}) \cdot (s(\boldsymbol{\eta}) - \tilde{s}(\boldsymbol{\eta}))^2 \, d\boldsymbol{\eta}. \tag{18}$$

We now subdivide Q_G into the individual view segments according to (3) and introduce c_i as a weight to each summand to include the i-th segment only if it is free of occlusions. We define the occlusion-aware dissimilarity metric

$$Q = \int_{\boldsymbol{\eta} \in S^2} \sum_{i \in I} c_i \cdot m_{H_i}(\boldsymbol{\eta}) \cdot (s(\boldsymbol{\eta}) - \tilde{s}(\boldsymbol{\eta}))^2 \, d\boldsymbol{\eta} = \sum_{i \in I} c_i \cdot Q_{H_i}(s(\boldsymbol{\eta}), \tilde{s}(\boldsymbol{\eta})). \tag{19}$$

To determine the individual Q_{H_i}, we substitute the two signals with their respective expansions into basis functions according to (5):

$$\begin{aligned} Q_{H_i} &= \int_{\boldsymbol{\eta} \in S^2} m_{H_i}(\boldsymbol{\eta}) \cdot \left[\left(\sum_{k=1}^{M} a_k^{(H_i)} \cdot Y_k(\boldsymbol{\eta}) \right) - \left(\sum_{k=1}^{M} \tilde{a}_k^{(H_i)} \cdot Y_k(\boldsymbol{\eta}) \right) \right]^2 d\boldsymbol{\eta} \\ &= \sum_{k=1}^{M} \sum_{j=1}^{M} (a_k^{(H_i)} - \tilde{a}_k^{(H_i)}) \cdot (a_j^{(H_i)} - \tilde{a}_j^{(H_i)}) \cdot G_{kj}^{(H_i)}, \end{aligned} \tag{20}$$

where the integrals $G^{(H_i)} = \int_{\boldsymbol{\eta} \in S^2} m_{H_i}(\boldsymbol{\eta}) \cdot Y_k(\boldsymbol{\eta}) \cdot Y_j(\boldsymbol{\eta}) \, d\boldsymbol{\eta}$ correspond to the entries of a Gramian matrix $\mathbf{G}_{H_i}$ as defined in Sec. 2.1.

Finally, the dissimilarity Q for segmented semi-spectral views is obtained as

$$Q(\boldsymbol{a}^{\oplus}, \tilde{\boldsymbol{a}}^{\oplus}) = \sum_{i \in I} c_i \cdot (\boldsymbol{a}^{(H_i)} - \tilde{\boldsymbol{a}}^{(H_i)})^T \cdot \mathbf{G}_{H_i} \cdot (\boldsymbol{a}^{(H_i)} - \tilde{\boldsymbol{a}}^{(H_i)}). \tag{21}$$

3.2   The Pose Change Gradient

To determine the steering direction towards a destination waypoint in Optical Rails, gradient descent in dissimilarities Q of two omnidirectional views is performed, with respect to the pose change of the robot. Let $s(\boldsymbol{\eta})$ be the currently acquired view and let $\tilde{s}(\boldsymbol{\eta})$ be the destination view. Let $\boldsymbol{p} = (x_1, x_2, p_{\varphi})^T$ be the local pose (translation, rotation) of the robot, $\boldsymbol{p}_0 = \boldsymbol{0}$ denoting the current pose.

We define the gradient $\boldsymbol{g} = \partial Q / \partial \boldsymbol{p} \big|_{\boldsymbol{p}=\boldsymbol{p}_0}$ which points into the direction of robot pose change leading to the steepest change of the view dissimilarity Q; hence, we denote $\boldsymbol{g}$ as the *pose change gradient*. If the original pose $\boldsymbol{p}_0$ is situated in the vicinity of the destination waypoint, motions in the direction $-\boldsymbol{g}$ lead towards that waypoint.

By predicting the changes of the current view $s(\boldsymbol{\eta})$ upon small motions of the robot, we can determine $\boldsymbol{g}$ analytically. For that purpose the environment is modeled as a hollow semisphere with the robot situated in the center (Fig. 3). This model is closely related to assumptions common also to many landmark-based navigation approaches and view-based visual homing (Möller et al. [3]).

We define a displacement transform $\boldsymbol{f}$ by $\boldsymbol{\eta}' = \boldsymbol{f}(\boldsymbol{\eta}, \boldsymbol{p})$, such that if $s(\boldsymbol{\eta})$ denotes the current view at pose $\boldsymbol{p}_0$, the view predicted after performing a pose change from $\boldsymbol{p}_0$ to $\boldsymbol{p}$ is obtained as $s(\boldsymbol{f}(\boldsymbol{\eta}, \boldsymbol{p}))$. The transform $\boldsymbol{f}$ is obtained by

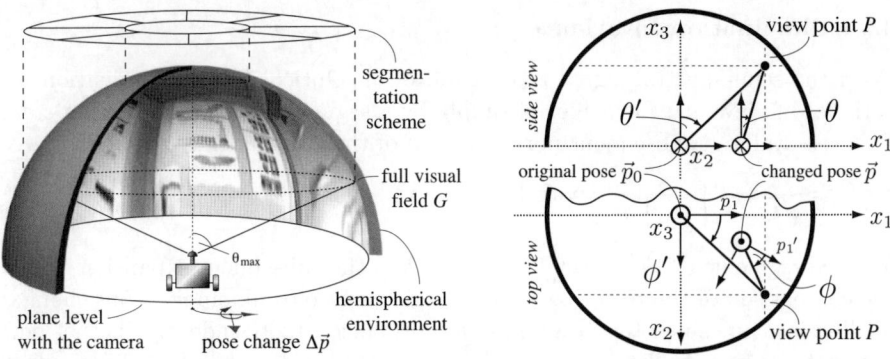

Fig. 3. Predicting view changes due to local robot motions: The hemispherical environment model provides a reasonable depth assumption for a variety of indoor scenarios.

projecting a view point P (3D coordinates of the environment) seen at coordinates $\boldsymbol{\eta} = (\theta, \phi)^T$ from the changed pose $\boldsymbol{p}$ to the camera center at the original pose $\boldsymbol{p}_0$. The resulting view angles yield the spherical coordinates $\boldsymbol{\eta}' = (\theta', \phi')^T$ at which P is seen from $\boldsymbol{p}_0$ (Fig. 3).

Occlusion-aware pose change gradient for semi-spectral view. Corresponding to the definition of Q in (19), the occlusion-aware pose change gradient $\boldsymbol{g}$ is obtained as the sum of pose change gradients $\boldsymbol{g}_{H_i}$ for the individual view segments:

$$\boldsymbol{g} = \frac{\partial Q}{\partial \boldsymbol{p}}\Big|_{\boldsymbol{p}=\boldsymbol{p}_0} = \frac{\partial}{\partial \boldsymbol{p}} \sum_{i \in I} c_i \cdot Q_{H_i}\Big|_{\boldsymbol{p}=\boldsymbol{p}_0} = \sum_{i \in I} c_i \cdot \boldsymbol{g}_{H_i}, \quad \boldsymbol{g}_{H_i} := \frac{\partial Q_{H_i}}{\partial \boldsymbol{p}}\Big|_{\boldsymbol{p}=\boldsymbol{p}_0} \quad (22)$$

Computation of the individual $\boldsymbol{g}_{H_i}$ is performed using the generalized chain rule:

$$\boldsymbol{g}_{H_i} = \frac{\partial Q_{H_i}}{\partial \boldsymbol{p}}\Big|_{\boldsymbol{p}=\boldsymbol{p}_0} = \int_{\boldsymbol{\eta} \in S^2} 2 \cdot m_{H_i}(\boldsymbol{\eta}) \cdot [s(\boldsymbol{f}(\boldsymbol{\eta}, \boldsymbol{p})) - \tilde{s}(\boldsymbol{\eta})] \cdot \left[\frac{\partial s(\boldsymbol{f}(\boldsymbol{\eta}, \boldsymbol{p}))}{\partial \boldsymbol{p}} - \frac{\partial \tilde{s}(\boldsymbol{\eta})}{\partial \boldsymbol{p}}\right]\Big|_{\boldsymbol{p}=\boldsymbol{p}_0} d\boldsymbol{\eta}$$

$$= \int_{\boldsymbol{\eta} \in S^2} 2 \cdot m_{H_i}(\boldsymbol{\eta}) \cdot [s(\boldsymbol{\eta}) - \tilde{s}(\boldsymbol{\eta})] \cdot \frac{\partial \boldsymbol{f}(\boldsymbol{\eta}, \boldsymbol{p})}{\partial \boldsymbol{p}}^T \cdot \frac{\partial s(\boldsymbol{\eta})}{\partial \boldsymbol{\eta}}\Big|_{\boldsymbol{p}=\boldsymbol{p}_0} d\boldsymbol{\eta}. \quad (23)$$

Since views to be compared are represented by view descriptors consisting of spectral coefficients of the original signal for each segment H_i, we replace signals $s(\boldsymbol{\eta}), \tilde{s}(\boldsymbol{\eta})$ by their respective expansions according to (4).

Due to the linearity of integration we can determine a factor which is independent of the signal observed in the respective visual field:

$$\boldsymbol{u}_p^{H_i}(j, k) := 2 \cdot \int_{S^2} m_{H_i}(\boldsymbol{\eta}) \cdot Y_j(\boldsymbol{\eta}) \cdot \frac{\partial \boldsymbol{f}(\boldsymbol{\eta}, \boldsymbol{p})}{\partial \boldsymbol{p}}^T \cdot \frac{\partial Y_k(\boldsymbol{\eta})}{\partial \boldsymbol{\eta}}\Big|_{\boldsymbol{p}=\boldsymbol{p}_0} d\boldsymbol{\eta}. \quad (24)$$

The steering gradient $\boldsymbol{g}_{H_i}$ of the comparison in segment H_i is thus yielded as

$$\boldsymbol{g}_{H_i}(\boldsymbol{a}^{(H_i)}, \tilde{\boldsymbol{a}}^{(H_i)}) = \sum_{j=1}^M \sum_{k=1}^M [a_j^{(H_i)} - \tilde{a}_j^{(H_i)}] \cdot a_k^{(H_i)} \cdot \boldsymbol{u}_p^{H_i}(j, k), \quad (25)$$

where the entries $\boldsymbol{u}_p(j, k)$ are precomputed expressions common to each visual field H_i. For the occlusion-aware pose change gradient $\boldsymbol{g}$ we finally obtain

$$\boldsymbol{g}(\boldsymbol{a}^\circledast, \tilde{\boldsymbol{a}}^\circledast) = \sum_{i \in I} c_i \cdot \sum_{j=1}^M \sum_{k=1}^M [a_j^{(H_i)} - \tilde{a}_j^{(H_i)}] \cdot a_k^{(H_i)} \cdot \boldsymbol{u}_p^{H_i}(j, k). \quad (26)$$

3.3   Illumination Invariance

With the semi-spectral signal representation in Optical Rails, illumination invariance of views can be achieved simply by a segment-wise preprocessing step: Bias removal and subsequent normalization of the image signal results in

$$\boldsymbol{b}_{H_i}^{\text{norm}} = \frac{\boldsymbol{b}_0}{\sqrt{\boldsymbol{b}_0^T \cdot \text{diag}\{\tilde{\boldsymbol{m}}_{H_i}\} \cdot \boldsymbol{b}_0}} \quad \text{with bias removed signal} \quad \boldsymbol{b}_0 := \boldsymbol{b} - \frac{\boldsymbol{b}^T \cdot \tilde{\boldsymbol{m}}_{H_i}}{\tilde{\boldsymbol{m}}_{H_i}^T \cdot \tilde{\boldsymbol{m}}_{H_i}} \quad (27)$$

for each segment $\boldsymbol{a}^{(H_i)}$, and $\boldsymbol{b}_{H_i}^{\text{norm}}$ replaces $\boldsymbol{b}$ in the subsequent expansion. Thus, the comparison of the resulting views is resilient also to inhomogeneous changes in illumination, since the brightness is normalized independently in the view segments. Hence, occlusions in single segments also do not affect illumination compensation in the remaining view segments.

Compared to global illumination compensation with a linear model, our experiments have shown the normalization of individual segments to be favorable, since the magnitude of dissimilarities and the pose change gradient depends less on the distribution of illumination patterns and the large-scale appearance of views: A certain degree of scale invariance of these measures is achieved.

4   Experiments

In our experiments, we show that robust robot navigation with tolerance to occlusions is feasible by selectively masking out the affected visual fields. First, we compare the behavior of the pose change gradient when steering towards an occluded destination view; finally, a comparison of a challenging track following scenario both using full and partially masked out visual fields is shown.

Pose Change Gradient: Effects of Occlusions and Mitigation. Our first experiment provides a systematic comparison of the pose change gradient $\boldsymbol{g}$ used for steering the robot (i) without occlusions, (ii) with occluded views and changed illumination, and (iii) with the affected view segments masked out in the comparison. Fig. 4 shows steering vectors for these three cases, which have been obtained by comparing views from a regularly spaced grid to a destination view.

Results show severe deviations of the steering direction for the occluded case, leading away from the actual destination. Excluding the affected views mitigates this effect, leading to a less pronounced, yet essentially correct pose gradient.

Track Following Experiments. Visual track following in Optical Rails consists of a recording phase, where the robot is manually steered along the desired route while semi-spectral views are acquired in rapid succession, and a driving phase, where the robot autonomously follows the route based upon this view sequence. Both phases have been implemented in real time ($\geq$ 15 frames/sec.) on different mobile robot vehicles running MATLAB for all image processing tasks using the precomputed entities defined in Sec. 2.1 and 3.2.

Prior to track following, a set of distinctive views are automatically selected by filtering the teach-in sequence with a threshold criterion; the visual dissimilarity between adjacent waypoints is required to monotonically decrease in the driving

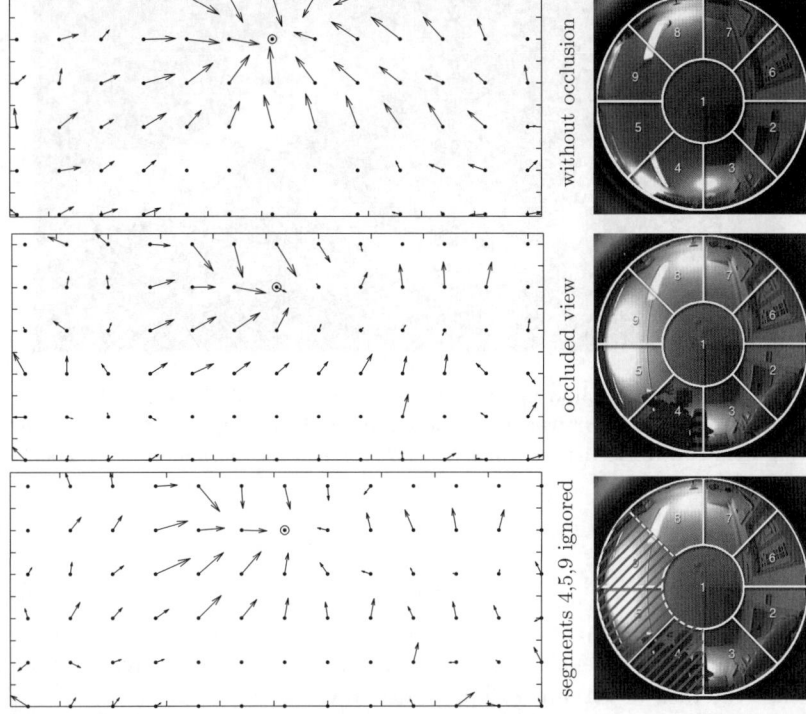

Fig. 4. Results of the pose change gradient using a view grid recorded in our lab, demonstrating the effects of occlusions and severe illumination changes and their mitigation by masking out the affected segments. Arrows show the translation components of the gradient g, which ideally should point towards the true destination (circle mark).

direction, yielding only waypoints within a suitable radius of convergence. While approaching a waypoint by successively computing the pose change gradient, arrival detection (waypoint handover) is performed by comparing the current view to a set of adjacent waypoints from the filtered view sequence.

In Fig. 5, we show a particularly challenging scenario of visual track following in our laboratory environment: An arbitrary path originates in a small closet with a narrow door and ends below a desk, where the complete view of the ceiling has been covered. Despite the resulting dramatic variations in brightness and appearance, the original trajectory could always be reproduced accurately. This specifically includes the part of the route while 'parking' under the desk, where successful navigation was possible only by the introduction of segment-wise normalized illumination.

Finally, to demonstrate that in case of occlusions sufficiently accurate steering would still be possible, two adjacent view segments at the front were masked out, simulating a typical occlusion by a person walking in front: Only slight deterioration of the accuracy of the resulting trajectory occurred.

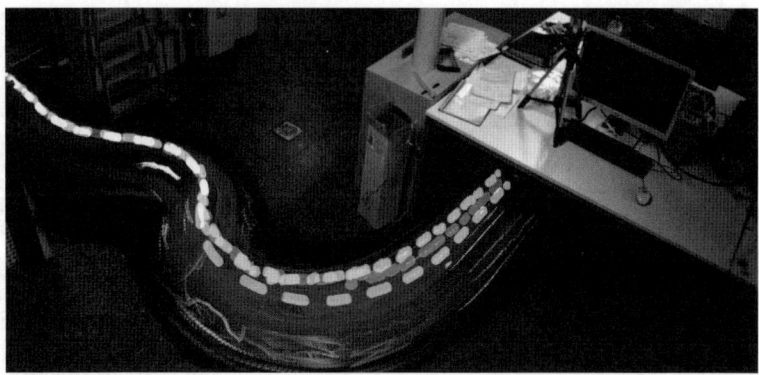

Fig. 5. Results of track following, documented by beacon (blinking at 1 Hz): *Cyan line:* teach in track, *orange line:* reverse track following, full view, *magenta line:* reverse track following with two consecutive segments (at front) masked out, simulating an occlusion.

5   Conclusion

In the present paper we have successfully shown the extension of the traditional view-based navigation paradigm to a segmented hybrid approach with adaptive visual fields. This enables selective masking of occluded areas and largely simplifies the task of attaining illumination invariance.

Obviously, the detection of occlusions and obstacles is a formidable problem in itself; it could be solved by tentatively assuming each segment to be affected by an occlusion, and performing the comparison only with the remaining segments as described in Sec. 3.1, leading to a threshold decision. The presented recombination of views Sec. 2.1 enables application of the method to purely holistic comparisons such as rotation estimation and rotation-invariant matching, which is required for more complex navigation tasks involving self-localization.

In the light of the obtained results and the highly versatile yet simple nature of the approach, view-based navigation appears to us as an attractive field for future challenges.

References

1. Dederscheck, D., Friedrich, H., Lenhart, C., Zahn, M., Mester, R.: 'Featuring' Optical Rails: View-based robot guidance using orientation features on the sphere. In: OMNIVIS workshop, ICCV, Kyoto, Japan. IEEE, Los Alamitos (2009)
2. Matsumoto, Y., Inaba, M., Inoue, H.: View-based navigation using an omniview sequence in a corridor environment. Machine Vision and Applications 14 (2003)
3. Möller, R., Vardy, A.: Local visual homing by matched-filter descent in image distances. Biological Cybernetics 95, 413–430 (2006) ISSN 0340-1200
4. Cartwright, B., Collett, T.: Landmark maps for honeybees. Biological Cybernetics 57, 85–93 (1987)
5. Shah, S., Aggarwal, J.K.: Mobile robot navigation and scene modeling using stereo fish-eye lens system. Machine Vision and Applications 10, 159–173 (1997)

A Contour Matching Algorithm to Reconstruct Ruptured Documents

Anke Stieber, Jan Schneider, Bertram Nickolay, and Jörg Krüger

Fraunhofer IPK, Pascalstr. 8-9, 10587 Berlin, Germany

Abstract. A procedure for reassembling ruptured documents from a large number of fragments is proposed. Such problems often arises in forensic and archiving. Usually, fragments are mixed and take arbitrary shapes. The proposed procedure concentrates on contour information of the fragments and represents it as feature strings to perform a matching based on dynamic programming. Experiments with 500 images of randomly shredded fragments show that the proposed reconstruction procedure is able to compose nearly 98% of the ruptured pages.

1 Introduction

Reassembling ruptured documents and broken two-dimensional objects from a large amount of fragments is a known problem. It often arises in archiving, forensic document examination and archeology. In general the collection of fragments is randomly shredded, that implies no criteria was used performing the rupture process. Additionally, the fragments are randomly mixed and some fragments are missing. Performing a manual reconstruction is a tedious and time consuming task, but reconstructing forensic document and historic objects would be highly important and valuable.

Some methods using digital images to perform this task more efficiently have been proposed in the literature. Most of these methods apply to related problems with specific characteristics. For instance, jigsaw puzzles are special cases of ruptured documents with a fixed number of corners, a predefined and smooth outline of the fragments and a complete outcome.

Those problems have often been addressed in robotics and machine vision [1], [2]. The approaches given in [3] and [4] concentrate on a polygonal approximation of the contour and on geometric feature matching. This method requires a rather coarse contour to be able to extract significant geometric features. The authors of [5] use polygonal approximation combined with dynamic programming. Two curve matching algorithms are given in [6], they are based on a conversion of the outline into shape signature strings. A formal analysis method exploiting the ordering of fragments caused by a common rupturing process is presented in [7]. As a very fast strategy it can be applied to semi-automated reconstruction tasks of large number of fragments. The reassembly of ceramic fragments is addressed in [8] and [9], where the authors used multiscale approaches for outline representation and curve matching.

M. Goesele et al. (Eds.): DAGM 2010, LNCS 6376, pp. 121–130, 2010.

Aim of this work is to benefit from ideas of previous work but to overcome their limitations to solve real world problems. The present approach does not require assumptions to fragment order, fragment shape or completeness. The reassembling method uses a contour representation based on curvature information and performs a partial matching accounting for both curvature information and original contour. According to computed matching scores the reconstruction of a number of fragments is accomplished.

The paper is organized as follows: The matching method to determine if fragments can be paired or not is introduced in section 2 including preprocessing and representing contour information through feature strings, followed by the matching method. In section 3 the reconstruction of a number of fragments is given. Results of conducted experiments are presented in section 4 followed by some conclusions in section 5.

2   Curve Matching

The paper describes a curve matching method that determines a degree of similarity for two outline segments of a pair of fragments. If two fragments share a part of their outline with high similarity they are supposed to be neighbors in the original document and can be merged.

The methodology consists of three steps: Preprocessing, contour representation and matching. In the first step, the outline of any given fragment image is analyzed and segmented. To reduce the complexity of matching only contour segments are matched instead of the entire outlines. In the second step each contour segment is represented by a one-dimensional feature string. The final matching step computes an alignment and a similarity score using original contour segments and their feature representations. Due to partial matching an adaptation of the Smith Waterman Algorithm is applied.

2.1   Preprocessing

Jigsaw puzzles usually include fragments with smooth edges and well defined corners of a fixed number. Considering a randomized rupture process, fragments shredded by hand possess much more complicated outlines. As a result of those arbitrary contours corner detection and outline segmentation is a difficult task.

Contour information is assumed to be noisy. An outline differs from an ideal rupture line due to a number of reasons, for instance physical wear, areas of shear and image quantization. To reduce the noise smoothing is applied to the extracted outline.

Generally, two single fragments, which are supposed to be next to each other in the original document, only share a part of their entire contours. For that reason outlines are divided into contour segments to be used as matching input and the authors of [10] pointed out that even short contour segments contain sufficient information for matching. They analyzed the average information content of an outline segment of a length of $l = 10.8$ mm and inferred that outline matching is

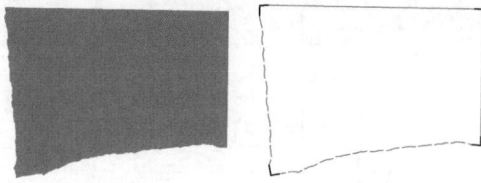

Fig. 1. Fragment and corresponding contour information: corners (black line segments), border segments (gray solid lines) and contour segments (gray broken lines)

suitable for the reassembly of ceramic fragments. A similar behavior is assumed for other materials, thus performing matching on contour segments is sufficient. The closed outlines are segmented with respect to characteristic points such as corners.

At first the outline is extracted counterclockwise from the digital image. Each fragment outline can be regarded as a sequence of discrete points giving a polygonal representation of the real fragment contour. A contour point with a high curvature value considered in an agglomerative polygonal approximation of the local neighborhood is roughly defined to be a candidate for a corner. The decision which candidates become corners depend on the global contour context. Corners separate the outline in contour segments which are located between two consecutive corners as can be seen in Fig. 1. Border segments, depicted by gray solid lines, are disregarded for matching. Hence, matching only requires contour segments, displayed as gray broken lines.

2.2   Contour Representation

The position of a fragment while feeding it into the scanner influences its outline quantization from the digital image. To overcome this drawback any contour segment needs to be assigned appropriate feature values. A well-known approach is the curvature representation. Here, contour points are assigned approximated curvature values, as used in [6] and [9]. These curvature values build up a feature string for any contour segment. The representation through feature strings benefits from its invariance against rotation and translation of the fragment. Thus, similar contour segments provide similar feature strings. Based on this feature representation matching is performed and a similarity score is derived.

The method described by Wolfson in [6] is adopted to approximate the pointwise curvature of the contour segments. A more detailed computation is given below. In the application of reassembling fragments by computer contour information is available as noisy polygonal data. Let P be the polygonal curve of any contour segment, $P = \{p_1, \ldots, p_n\}$ whereby $p_k \in \mathbb{R}^2$ for all $k \in \{1, \ldots, n\}$. Based on Wolfson the first step is to compute the turning function as stated in [11]. More precisely, computing the angle between the counterclockwise tangent and the x-axis at each vertex p_k yield a function of the arc length $\theta(p^{arc})$. p^{arc} is the arc

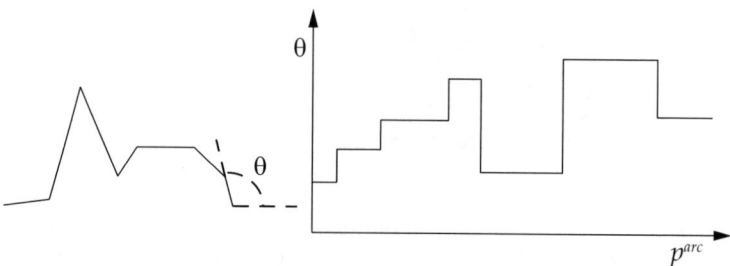

Fig. 2. A polygonal curve and its turning function of the arc length [11]

length function of the polygonal curve P. The turning function $\theta(p^{arc})$ visualized in Fig. 2 is a step function and constant between two consecutive vertices.

Then an equally spaced sampling is applied followed by a linear interpolation on the graph of $\theta(p^{arc})$. The sampling results in the arclength values $p_1^{arc}, \ldots, p_{n_s}^{arc}$ where n_s is the number of equally sampled points on P with a difference of s_e between consecutive points. Wolfson determines values $\Delta\theta(p_k^{arc})$ as described in equation (1) giving an approach to the curvature values for each p_k^{arc}. To provide robust curvature values an average of q consecutive differences is computed in equation (2).

$$\Delta\theta(p_k^{arc}) = \theta(p_k^{arc} + \Delta s) - \theta(p_k^{arc}) \tag{1}$$

$$\phi_k = \frac{1}{q} \sum_{l=0}^{q-1} \Delta\theta(p_k^{arc} + l\delta) \tag{2}$$

s_e, Δs, q, δ are parameters to be adjusted. Δs and δ are bounded by the arc length of the curve P. According to a global scale parameter m, any contour segment is represented by a feature string of averaged curvature values, namely $R = (m\phi_k)_{k=1}^{n_s}$. This feature representation satisfies the following three conditions: it is local, translationally and rotationally invariant and stable in a way that small changes in the contour will only cause small effects in the feature string [6].

Two extracted and smoothed contours of synthetically generated fragments with their determined feature values are visualized in Fig. 3. In general two contours are not equal due to quantization and smoothing, not even concerning synthetically generated fragments. For this reasons the displayed feature strings slightly differ from each other.

The description of all used parameters during contour feature computation are summarized in table 1. These parameters have to be adjusted to get an optimal discrimination between matching and non-matching fragment pairs. Wolfson did not optimize these parameters. The values used in this work have been adjusted to a representative set of fragments using an evolutionary multiobjective optimization. Values are given in section 4.

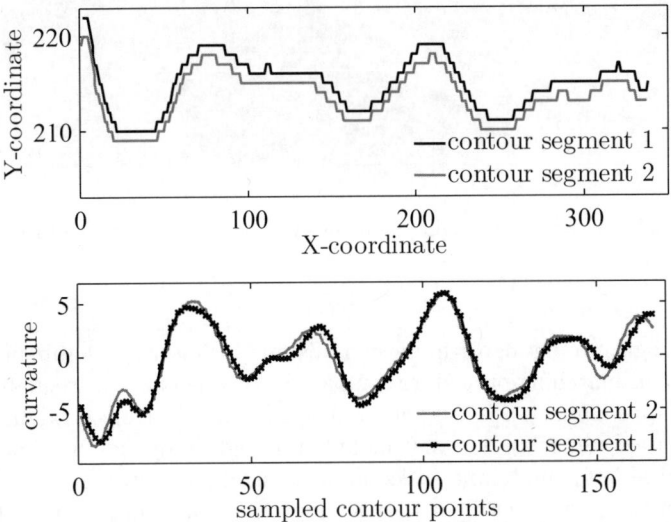

Fig. 3. Smoothed contour segments of synthetically generated matching fragments (top) and their corresponding feature strings (bottom)

Table 1. Collection of the required parameters

name	description
s_e	step size of the equally spaced turning function graph
q	number of differences to be averaged
Δs	distance used to compute the difference in (1)
δ	distance between arclength values whose turning function differences are to be averaged
m	global scale factor

2.3   Matching Method

In this section the matching method based on the principles of dynamic programming is presented. The aim of the method is to compute an alignment in order to put in place the corresponding fragments images. Based on this alignment a similarity score indicating a measurement of accuracy of fit can be derived.

Matching a pair of contour segments, however, is a partial matching. Generally lengths of two contour segments differ from each other, thus both segments do not match from one corner to the other. Two of those contour segments are shown in Fig. 4. This effect is caused by randomly rupturing the original paper document. Additionally, noise, possible punch holes and other effects can reduce the part where both contour segments correspond. As a consequence, a flexible matching procedure is needed to compute the optimal local alignment of two feature strings representing two contour segments. To perform the matching the Smith-Waterman sequence alignment algorithm is applied [12]. It is a well-known

Fig. 4. Partial matching. The right fragment only matches at a part of its left contour segment.

dynamic programming algorithm accomplishing local string alignment. One advantage of this matching procedure compared to geometric feature matching with polygonal approximation is that it even works on relatively straight contours. Polygonal approximation does not include the high-frequency information, thus it is not suitable for matching tasks on fairly straight contours.

The sequence alignment algorithm is adopted to real valued strings. Given two feature strings $f^1 \in \mathbb{R}^m$ and $f^2 \in \mathbb{R}^n$ the problem consists in finding the optimal local alignment of f^1 and f^2 with regard to a scoring scheme. The optimal local alignment can be derived from a matrix M of size $(m+1) \times (n+1)$. M ist created with the following recurrences:

$$M(i,0) = 0, \quad 0 \leqslant i \leqslant m \tag{3}$$

$$M(0,j) = 0, \quad 0 \leqslant j \leqslant n \tag{4}$$

$$M(i,j) = \max \left\{ \begin{array}{l} M(i-1,j-1) + w_{ij} \\ M(i-1,j) + w_{gap} \\ M(i,j-1) + w_{gap} \\ 0 \end{array} \right\}, \quad 1 \leqslant i \leqslant m, \ 1 \leqslant j \leqslant n, \tag{5}$$

where w_{ij} and w_{gap} belong to the following scoring scheme:

$$w_{ij} = \left\{ \begin{array}{ll} 2 & \text{if } |f_i^1 - f_j^2| \leqslant \epsilon_1 \\ -0.1 & \text{if } \epsilon_1 < |f_i^1 - f_j^2| \leqslant \epsilon_2 \\ -2 & \text{if } |f_i^1 - f_j^2| > \epsilon_2 \end{array} \right. \tag{6}$$

$$w_{gap} = -1, \tag{7}$$

with tolerances $\epsilon_1, \epsilon_2 \in \mathbb{R}, 0 < \epsilon_1 < \epsilon_2$. The optimal local alignment is then extracted from M by backtracking from the maximum matrix entry to a zero entry. The proposed scoring scheme was chosen to handle real values of f^1 and f^2. The maximum score of 2 is awarded to f_i^1 and f_j^2 when their difference is equal or less than ϵ_1. If f_i^1 and f_j^2 do not have such a difference but are close enough to each other so that their difference is equal or less than ϵ_2 a penalty score of -0.1 will be assigned. All remaining cases go with a penalty of -2. This scoring scheme is appropriate to handle curvature values of fragment outlines and to cope with small distortions and noise within the feature strings.

According to the optimal local alignment feature substrings can be determined by restricting the feature strings to the computed alignment. Additionally appropriate contour subsegments can also be derived by restricting the contour segments the same way. The obtained alignment is then used to compute a similarity score as a measurement of matching quality.

Similarity Score. The similarity score as a measurement of matching accuracy is constituted as the sum of three component scores: *area score, length score* and *correlation score*. The lower the similarity score $s_{total} > 0$ the likelier both contour segments match.

To compute the area score both contour subsegments are equalized so that the difference of the Euclidean lengths between their start and endpoints is less than one. Then they are transformed in a way that the starting points of the contour subsegments lay on each other and the endpoints are located to each other as close as possible. Thus, both polygonal curves of the contour subsegments combined with each other span an area. Due to regions of overlapping and regions of gap this area might be divided into several subareas. These subareas are summed up to the size of the entire area by a flood fill algorithm. The area score s_{area} is obtained by a weighted ratio of the summed subareas and the arc length of the combined polygonal curves and restricted to the intervall $[0, 1]$. This score is a measurement of gaps and overlapping regions relative to the arc length of contour subsegments when putting two fragments together.

The length score s_{len} measures the length of the matching contour part and is normalized to the shorter arc length of both contour segments. It is defined by the ratio of the arc length of the contour subsegment and the overall arc length of the contour segment. Then s_{len} is mapped to the intervall $[0, 1]$. This score disadvantages fragment pairs sharing only a small part of their contour segments. The feature substrings are used to compute the correlation score s_{cor}. The cross correlation coefficient is determined and also mapped to the intervall $[0, 1]$. The total score using a range of $[0, 3]$ is obtained by the sum of all component scores $s_{total} = s_{area} + s_{len} + s_{cor}$.

3   Reconstruction of Fragments

The previous section described the matching of two fragment images at two contour segments. Performing an iterative reconstruction process of n images of shredded fragments a matching threshold is used to decide which image pairs shall be merged and which shall not. In any iteration matching of all possible pairs of fragment contour segments is performed. Finally, regarding a greedy approach, a sequential merging of fragment pairs with a similarity score lower than a fixed threshold is executed. Any fragment pair is merged at its best matching pair of contour segments. The procedure is given in Algorithm 1.

Given any two fragments i, j the alignment determination is not symmetric to permutation of fragments, thus the algorithm performs the matching of (i, j) and (j, i). In the double-sided case any front side image need to be matched to front

---

Algorithm 1. Reconstruction of n fragments

Require: F: set of n fragments, $\forall f \in F \; \exists C^f$: set of all contour segments of f, *thr*: constant threshold value

1: $P \leftarrow \{(f,g)|f \in F, g \in F, f \neq g\}$
2: $S \leftarrow \emptyset$
3: $flag \leftarrow 0$
4: **repeat**
5:    **for all** $p \in P$ with $p = (f,g)$ **do**
6:      **for all** (c_i, c_j) with $c_i \in C^f$ and $c_j \in C^g$, $i = 1, \ldots, |C^f|$, $j = 1, \ldots, |C^g|$ **do**
7:        **if** $(s_p \leftarrow \min_{i,j}$ match score of $(c_i, c_j))$ exists **then**
8:          $S \leftarrow s_p$
9:    **while** $S \neq \emptyset$ **do**
10:      $s^* \leftarrow \min_{s \in S} s$
11:      **if** $s^* < thr$ **then**
12:        $flag \leftarrow 1$
13:        merge $p^* = (f^*, g^*)$ at (c_{i*}, c_{j*})
14:        delete all $p' \in P$ that contain f^* or g^* and corresponding $s' \in S$
15:      **else**
16:        $S \leftarrow \emptyset$
17: **until** $flag = 0$ or $P = \emptyset$

---

and back sides of all other images but not to its own back side. In case of double-sided merging both front and back sides of a fragment pair are put together.

4   Experiments

To validate the proposed reconstruction procedure 30 documents were ruptured without any constraints. After scanning with a resolution of 300 dpi a randomly mixed set of 500 images was obtained. On average each page decomposed into 8.3 fragments. This reconstruction task is comparable to a medium real world scenario. It can be scaled up but a very high number of fragments might contain similar contours, e.g. due to shredding stacked pages simultaneously. The resulting contours might lead to ambiguous matching results and further features should be used to obtain suitable reconstruction results.

The following parameters were used to conduct the experiments: $s_e = 1.9$, $q = 2$, $\Delta s = 1.8$, $\delta = 3.1$ and $m = 2.6$. Each fragment image is matched with each other except its own back side. The first iteration processed 62,250 image pairs. Since there is no general threshold value working for any application three different threshold values 0.4, 0.45 and 0.5 were considered. In general, a low threshold raises the False Reject Rate (FRR) and a high threshold raises the False Accept Rate (FAR). The experimental results are shown in Table 2. A threshold of 0.45 minimizes the objective function FRR+FAR. Using this threshold a reconstruction rate of nearly 98% could be achieved.

Table 2. Experimental results for three different threshold values are shown. A database of 500 fragment images was used. All fragments need 220 double-sided merging steps built from 105,344 image pairs to compose 60 pages. The database corresponds to 30 documents with 250 physical fragments.

Threshold	0.40	0.45	0.50
Accepts	213	216	213
Correct Accepts CAR	213 96.82%	215 97.73%	210 95.45%
False Accepts FAR	0 0.00%	1 0.46%	3 1.41%
False Rejects FRR	7 3.18%	5 2.27%	10 4.55%

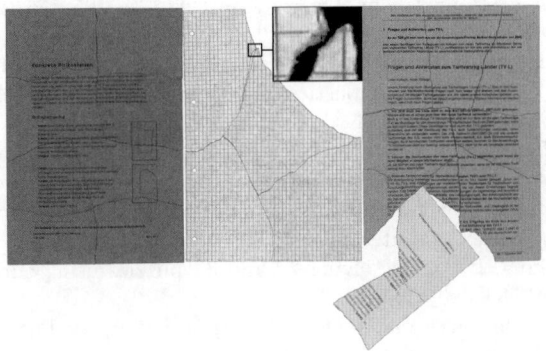

Fig. 5. Reconstruction results: Completely reconstructed page, nearly reconstructed page, falsely reconstructed page

Three different reconstruction results are shown in Fig. 5. Considering the missing merging steps (False Rejects) some pairs could not be merged due to falsely reconstructed pairs in previous steps. Another reason of False Rejects is that some contour segments suffer from gaps as shown in the second reconstruction in Fig. 5. These gaps might result from insufficient mergings of previous steps caused by resolution inaccuracies during the scanning process. Thus, the contour segment containing a gap is obviously longer than the one without gap leading to unsatisfactory contour matching.

Performance. To perform the reconstruction of 500 fragment images with a threshold of 0.45 105,344 pairs needed to be matched, whereas the computation of the matching steps for one pair takes about 100-250 milliseconds using a common PC equipped with an Intel(R) Core(TM) i7 2.80GHz CPU.

5   Conclusion

A matching method was proposed to reconstruct ruptured documents from a large number of fragments based on curvature information and an adapted version of the Smith Waterman algorithm. With a greedy approach 500 fragment images, shredded from 30 documents, could be almost completely reassembled. Even without using obvious features as color, texture and document format a convincing reconstruction rate of nearly 98% could be achieved. Integrating further features could reduce the number of matching steps and improve the reconstruction time.

References

1. Wolfson, H., Schonberg, E., Kalvin, A., Lamdan, Y.: Solving jigsaw puzzles by computer. Ann. Oper. Res. 12(1-4), 51–64 (1988)
2. Goldberg, D., Malon, C., Bern, M.: A global approach to automatic solution of jigsaw puzzles. Comput. Geom. Theory Appl. 28(2-3), 165–174 (2004)
3. Pimenta, A., Justino, E., Oliveira, L.S., Sabourin, R.: Document reconstruction using dynamic programming. In: ICASSP 2009: Proceedings of the 2009 IEEE International Conference on Acoustics, Speech and Signal Processing, Washington, DC, USA, pp. 1393–1396. IEEE Computer Society, Los Alamitos (April 2009)
4. Solana, C., Justino, E., Oliveira, L.S., Bortolozzi, F.: Document reconstruction based on feature matching. In: Rodrigues, M.A.F., Frery, A.C. (eds.) Proceedings of the 18th Brazilian Symposium on Computer Graphics and Image Processing, October 9-12. IEEE Computer Society, Los Alamitos (2005)
5. Kong, W., Kimia, B.B.: On solving 2d and 3d puzzles using curve matching. In: CVPR (2), pp. 583–590 (2001)
6. Wolfson, H.J.: On curve matching. IEEE Transactions on Pattern Analysis and Machine Intelligence 12(5), 483–489 (1990)
7. De Smet, P.: Reconstruction of ripped-up documents using fragment stack analysis procedures. Forensic Science International 176(2-3), 124–136 (2008)
8. McBride, J.C., Kimia, B.B.: Archaeological fragment reconstruction using curve-matching. In: Computer Vision and Pattern Recognition Workshop (CVPRW), vol. 1, p. 3 (2003)
9. Leitão, H.C.d.G., Stolfi, J.: A multiscale method for the reassembly of two-dimensional fragmented objects. IEEE Transactions on Pattern Analysis and Machine Intelligence 24(9), 1239–1251 (2002)
10. Leitão, H.C.d.G., Stolfi, J.: Measuring the information content of fracture lines. International Journal of Computer Vision 65(3), 163–174 (2005)
11. Veltkamp, R.C., Hagedoorn, M.: Shape similarity measures, properties and constructions. In: Laurini, R. (ed.) VISUAL 2000. LNCS, vol. 1929, pp. 467–476. Springer, Heidelberg (2000)
12. Smith, T.F., Waterman, M.S.: Identification of common molecular subsequences. Journal of Molecular Biology 147(1), 195–197 (1981)

Local Structure Analysis by Isotropic Hilbert Transforms

Lennart Wietzke[1], Oliver Fleischmann[2], Anne Sedlazeck[2], and Gerald Sommer[2]

[1] Raytrix GmbH, Germany
[2] Cognitive Systems Group, Department of Computer Science, Kiel University

Abstract. This work presents the isotropic and orthogonal decomposition of 2D signals into local geometrical and structural components. We will present the solution for 2D image signals in four steps: signal modeling in scale space, signal extension by higher order generalized Hilbert transforms, signal representation in classical matrix form, followed by the most important step, in which the matrix-valued signal will be mapped to a so called multivector. We will show that this novel multivector-valued signal representation is an interesting space for complete geometrical and structural signal analysis. In practical computer vision applications lines, edges, corners, and junctions as well as local texture patterns can be analyzed in one unified algebraic framework. Our novel approach will be applied to parameter-free multilayer decomposition.

1 Introduction

Low level image analysis is often the first step of many computer vision tasks. Therefore, local signal features determine the quality of subsequent higher level processing steps. In this work we present a general 2D image analysis theory which is accurate and less time consuming (seven 2D convolutions are required), either because of its rotationally invariance. The first step of low level signal analysis is the designation of a reasonable signal model. Based on the fact that signals $f \in L^2(\Omega) \cap L^1(\Omega)$ with $\Omega \subseteq \mathbb{R}^2$ can be decomposed into their corresponding Fourier series, we assume that each frequency component of the original image signal consists locally of a superposition of intrinsically 1D (i1D) signals $f_\nu(z)$ with $z = (x, y) \in \mathbb{R}^2$, and $\nu \in \{1, 2\}$, see Equation (3). Each of them is determined by its individual amplitude $a_\nu \in \mathbb{R}$, phase $\phi_\nu \in [0, \pi)$ [1,2], and orientation $\theta_\nu \in [0, \pi)$. To access each one of those frequency components, an appropriate filter must be applied to the original signal. Although any scale space concept can be used, in this work we will choose the Poisson low pass filter kernel [3] $p(z; s)$ instead of the Gaussian kernel. The Poisson scale space is naturally related to the generalized Hilbert transform by the Cauchy kernel [4]. In Fourier space $\mathcal{F}\{\cdot\}$ [5] it can be seen that the well known derivative operator of order m

$$\mathcal{F}\{\mathcal{D}^{(m)}\}(u) = [2\pi\, u\, \mathbf{i}]^m \quad \text{with} \quad u \in \mathbb{R}^2 \tag{1}$$

is closely related to the generalized Hilbert transform operator of m concatenations

$$\mathcal{F}\{\mathcal{H}^{(m)}\}(u) = [2\pi\, \bar{u}\, \mathbf{i}]^m \quad \text{with} \quad \bar{u} = \frac{u}{\|u\|} . \tag{2}$$

M. Goesele et al. (Eds.): DAGM 2010, LNCS 6376, pp. 131–140, 2010.
© Springer-Verlag Berlin Heidelberg 2010

2   Local Texture Modeling in Scale Space

Applying the Poisson filter kernel p to the original signal $\mathcal{P}_s\{f\}(z) = (p_s * f)(z)$ results in the smoothed signal model

$$f_p = \underbrace{\sum_{\nu=1}^{n} a_\nu \cos(\langle z, \bar{o}_\nu \rangle + \phi_\nu)}_{f_\nu(z)} \quad \forall z \in \Omega \tag{3}$$

with $\bar{o}_\nu = [\cos\theta_\nu, \sin\theta_\nu]^T$ as the oriented normal, $\langle \cdot, \cdot \rangle$ as the inner product, and $*$ as the convolution operator. This local signal model allows modeling textures and structures such as lines, edges, corners, and junctions in scale space. After having specified the signal model, the mathematical task is the exact retrieval of the signal parameters $(\theta_\nu, \phi_\nu, a_\nu)$ for every position $z \in \Omega$, and for every scale space parameter $s > 0$. In the following f^e will be called the even signal part. Furthermore and without loss of generality, at the origin $(0; s)$ with $\mathbf{0} = (0, 0)$ of the applied local coordinate system, the assumed signal model (3) results in

$$f_p = \mathcal{P}_s\{f\}(\mathbf{0}) = (p_s * f)(\mathbf{0}) = \sum_{\nu=1}^{n} \underbrace{a_\nu \cos\phi_\nu}_{f_\nu^e} . \tag{4}$$

Since the geometrical information θ_ν is not coded in the signal value f_p, an appropriate signal extension is necessary. Normally, this will be done by calculating higher order derivatives of the signal, e.g. the SIFT features [6]. This work generalizes and improves [7] by using higher order Hilbert transforms, and we will compare the results with those of using derivatives.

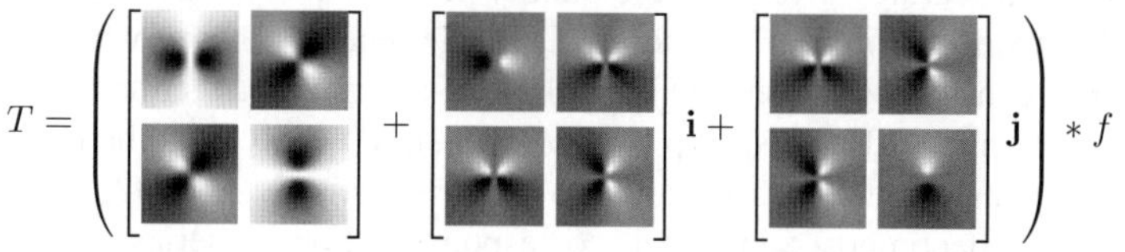

$$T = \left(\begin{bmatrix} \; & \; \\ \; & \; \end{bmatrix} + \begin{bmatrix} \; & \; \\ \; & \; \end{bmatrix} \mathbf{i} + \begin{bmatrix} \; & \; \\ \; & \; \end{bmatrix} \mathbf{j} \right) * f$$

Fig. 1. Illustration of the convolution kernels in the spatial domain of the quaternion-valued matrix signal representation T

3   Signal Extension by Hilbert Transforms

The problem, which has to be solved now, is the search for all unknown structural parameters $a_\nu \in \mathbb{R}$ and $\phi_\nu \in [0, \pi)$ and the unknown geometric parameters $\theta_\nu \in [0, \pi)$. We will restrict the signal model (3) to $n < 3$, since by this restriction most signal structures can be modeled [8]. As the signal parameters are unknown, we have to solve an inverse problem. This can only be done by extending the original signal to result in a system of equations, which includes all unknown signal parameters. This will be done by the generalized Hilbert transforms of higher orders. Our signal model which consists of two superimposed i1D signals results in six degrees of freedom, which require generalized Hilbert transforms of up to order three. The first order Hilbert transform kernels read

$$\begin{bmatrix} h_x \\ h_y \end{bmatrix}(z) = \frac{1}{2\pi\|z\|^3}\begin{bmatrix} x \\ y \end{bmatrix} \tag{5}$$

which are the analogues to the first order partial derivatives. Since we have to analyze the original signal in scale space, it will be of advantage to provide one unified convolution kernel, which consists of the Poisson kernel and the generalized Hilbert transform kernel of order n. The generalized Hilbert transform of order $(i+j)$ in Poisson scale space reads

$$q_{x^i y^j}(z) = (\underbrace{h_x * \ldots * h_x}_{i} * \underbrace{h_y * \ldots * h_y}_{j} * p_s)(z) . \tag{6}$$

The value of the $(i+j)$th order Hilbert transformed signal in Poisson scale space will be derived by convolution in the spatial domain $f_{x^i y^j} = (q_{x^i y^j} * f)(z)$.

3.1 Signal Intelligence in Radon Space

After extending the original signal, the generalized Hilbert transformed signal must be interpreted. This can be done in Radon space by the relation to the Fourier slice theorem. The original signal f transformed into Radon space $f_r = \mathcal{R}\{f\}$ reads

$$f_r(t,\theta;s) = \int_{z\in\mathbb{R}^2} \mathcal{P}_s\{f\}(z)\delta\left(\langle z,\bar{o}\rangle - t\right) \, dz \tag{7}$$

with $\theta \in [0,\pi)$ as the orientation, $t \in \mathbb{R}$ as the minimal distance of the parameterized line to the origin of the local coordinate system of the test point, and δ as the Dirac distribution. The corresponding inverse Radon transform $\mathcal{R}^{-1}$ exists. The $(i+j)$th order generalized Hilbert transformed signal can be expressed in Radon space, which delivers a system of equations of all unknown signal parameters. This system of equations can be solved, which has been done up to now only for $n = 1$ in Equation (3) [8]. The Hilbert transformed signal can be expressed by

$$f_{x^i y^j} = \mathcal{R}^{-1}\left\{\cos^i\theta \sin^j\theta \, h^{(i+j)}(t) * f_r(t;\theta;s)\right\}(z) \tag{8}$$

(Proof: Fourier slice theorem) with the classical one dimensional Hilbert transform kernel [9] of order m

$$h^{(m)}(t) = \begin{cases} \delta(t), & m \bmod 4 = 0 \\ \frac{1}{\pi t}, & m \bmod 4 = 1 \\ -\delta(t), & m \bmod 4 = 2 \\ -\frac{1}{\pi t}, & m \bmod 4 = 3 \end{cases}, t \in \mathbb{R} \tag{9}$$

with δ as the Dirac distribution, which is the algebraic neutral element of the convolution. Finally, the $(i+j)$th Hilbert transformed signal results in

$$f_{x^i y^j} = \sum_{\nu=1}^{n}\left[\cos^i\theta_\nu \sin^j\theta_\nu\right] f_\nu^{(i+j)} \tag{10}$$

(Proof: Linearity of the inverse Radon transform). The odd signal part $f_\nu^o = (h^{(1)} * f_\nu^e)(\phi_\nu) = a_\nu \sin\phi_\nu$ results of the even part by the classical 1D Hilbert transform and

$$f_\nu^{(m)} = \begin{cases} f_\nu^e, & m \bmod 4 = 0 \\ f_\nu^o, & m \bmod 4 = 1 \\ -f_\nu^e, & m \bmod 4 = 2 \\ -f_\nu^o, & m \bmod 4 = 3 \end{cases} \tag{11}$$

In case of the zeroth order Hilbert transform (i.e. $i + j = 0$), this results in the local signal value f_p. According to (10), the first and second order Hilbert transformed signal determines the following system of linear equations

$$\begin{bmatrix} f_x \\ f_y \end{bmatrix} = \sum_{\nu=1}^{n} \begin{bmatrix} \cos \theta_\nu \\ \sin \theta_\nu \end{bmatrix} f_\nu^o \tag{12}$$

and

$$\begin{bmatrix} f_{xx} \\ f_{xy} \\ f_{yy} \end{bmatrix} = \sum_{\nu=1}^{n} \begin{bmatrix} \cos^2 \theta_\nu \\ \cos \theta_\nu \sin \theta_\nu \\ \sin^2 \theta_\nu \end{bmatrix} f_\nu^e \tag{13}$$

from which the signal value can be reconstructed by $f_p = f_{xx} + f_{yy}$. With (10), the third order Hilbert transformed signal determines the following system of linear equations

$$\begin{bmatrix} f_{xxx} \\ f_{xxy} \\ f_{xyy} \\ f_{yyy} \end{bmatrix} = \sum_{\nu=1}^{n} \begin{bmatrix} \cos^3 \theta_\nu \\ \cos^2 \theta_\nu \sin \theta_\nu \\ \cos \theta_\nu \sin^2 \theta_\nu \\ \sin^3 \theta_\nu \end{bmatrix} f_\nu^o \tag{14}$$

from which the first order generalized Hilbert transform can be reconstructed by $f_x = f_{xxx} + f_{xyy}$ and $f_y = f_{xxy} + f_{yyy}$. Due to the relation of the Radon transform to the generalized Hilbert transform of any order, it is possible to result in a system of equations which can be now solved for the unknown signal parameters. Please note that neither the Radon transform nor its inverse are ever applied to the signal in practise. This is a very important advantage compared to the wavelet transforms (e.g. Ridgelet transforms [10]). Those approaches try out only a finite number of directions by the discrete Radon transform [10], which suffers from numerical problems. The resulting disadvantages are inaccuracy, problems resulting from aliasing effects, and higher computational time complexities.

4   Algebraic Signal Representation

Derivative based signal extensions are normally arranged in matrix or tensor form. Since these forms are only hardly suitable for geometric interpretation, we now present a signal representation in the so called multivector form, which comes from the field of geometric algebra [11]. Recent results of the hybrid matrix geometric algebra [12] offer geometric interpretation, which in our case enables the complete signal analysis by mapping tensor structures to multivectors. For the sake of simplicity, we will restrict this paper to the algebra of quaternions, which are solely needed for constructing the signal tensor. Loosely spoken, simply consider the tensor-valued signal extension as a real-valued $2 \times 2 \times 3$ array. According to [12], a mapping from the quaternion-valued tensor

$T \in M(2, \mathbb{H})$ to the quaternion-valued vector $\varphi(T) \in \mathbb{H}^3$ is possible. With the set of basis vectors $\{1, \mathbf{i}, \mathbf{j}, \mathbf{k}\}$ of the quaternions $\mathbb{H}$, the signal tensor for $n < 3$ in Equation (3) can be defined by the generalized Hilbert transforms of second and third order

$$T = \begin{bmatrix} f_{xx} & f_{xy} \\ f_{xy} & f_{yy} \end{bmatrix} + \begin{bmatrix} f_{xxx} & f_{xxy} \\ f_{xxy} & f_{xyy} \end{bmatrix} \mathbf{i} + \begin{bmatrix} f_{xxy} & f_{xyy} \\ f_{xyy} & f_{yyy} \end{bmatrix} \mathbf{j} ,$$

see Figure 1. By introducing the abbreviations $f^- = f_{xx} - f_{yy}$, $f_x^- = f_{xxx} - f_{xyy}$ and $f_y^- = f_{xxy} - f_{yyy}$ the quaternion-valued matrix T can be mapped by the isomorphism φ to a quaternion-valued vector representation

$$\varphi(T) = \begin{bmatrix} \frac{f_p}{2} \\ f_{xy} \\ \frac{f^-}{2} \end{bmatrix} + \begin{bmatrix} \frac{f_x}{2} \\ f_{xxy} \\ \frac{f_x^-}{2} \end{bmatrix} \mathbf{i} + \begin{bmatrix} \frac{f_y}{2} \\ f_{xyy} \\ \frac{f_y^-}{2} \end{bmatrix} \mathbf{j} \tag{15}$$

which will be called signal multivector, see Figure (2). The signal multivector delivers the complete geometrical and structural signal information with respect to both the assumed signal model and the assumed maximal order of Hilbert transforms. In [13] the geometrical signal features have been retrieved by higher order derivatives in the traditional matrix expression. This will be generalized by $\varphi(T)$ in a more natural embedding.

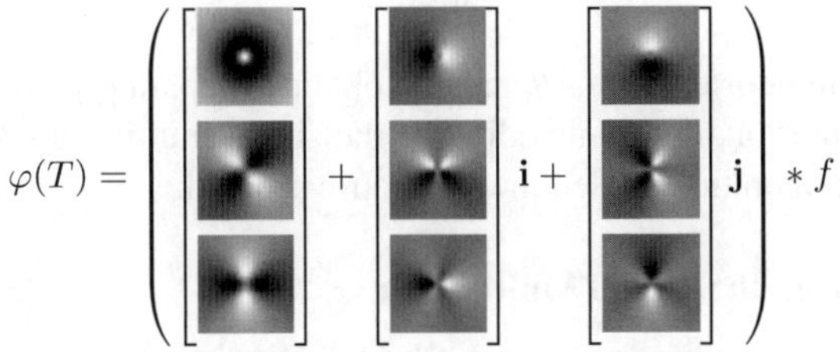

Fig. 2. Illustration of the convolution kernels in the spatial domain of the signal multivector $\varphi(T)$ which is defined in Equation (15)

4.1 Geometry from the Signal Multivector

The hardest challenge of our signal analysis problem is to obtain the exact geometrical signal features such as the orientations θ_ν. The most important relations are

$$\sin(2\theta_{2/1}) = \frac{1}{\det D_{1/2}} \det \begin{bmatrix} f_{xxy} & \cos\theta_{1/2} \\ f_{xyy} & \sin\theta_{1/2} \end{bmatrix} \tag{16}$$

and

$$\cos(2\theta_{2/1}) = \frac{1}{\det D_{1/2}} \det \begin{bmatrix} \frac{f_x^-}{2} & \cos\theta_{1/2} \\ \frac{f_y^-}{2} & \sin\theta_{1/2} \end{bmatrix} \tag{17}$$

with the matrix

$$D_{1/2} = \begin{bmatrix} \frac{f_x}{2} & \cos\theta_{1/2} \\ \frac{f_y}{2} & \sin\theta_{1/2} \end{bmatrix} \tag{18}$$

which follow from Equation (14) of the third order generalized Hilbert transform for $n = 2$. From the fact that $\sin^2(2\theta_{2/1}) + \cos^2(2\theta_{2/1}) = 1$, the nonlinear part of the inverse problem follows in form of a quadratic equation (since two unknown orientations have to hold the equation)

$$\gamma^- \sin^2 \theta_\nu + \alpha \sin(2\theta_\nu) = \beta \tag{19}$$

with

$$\delta = \left[\frac{f_x}{2}\right]^2 - f_{xxy}^2 - \left[\frac{f_x^-}{2}\right]^2 \tag{20}$$

$$\beta = \left[\frac{f_y}{2}\right]^2 - f_{xyy}^2 - \left[\frac{f_y^-}{2}\right]^2 \tag{21}$$

$$\alpha = \frac{f_x}{2}\frac{f_y}{2} - f_{xxy}f_{xyy} - \frac{f_x^-}{2}\frac{f_y^-}{2} \tag{22}$$

$$\gamma^+ = \beta + \delta \tag{23}$$

$$\gamma^- = \beta - \delta \tag{24}$$

The main orientation can be derived by

$$\theta_1 + \theta_2 = \arctan \frac{2\alpha}{\gamma^-} \tag{25}$$

as well as the apex angle

$$\|\theta_1 - \theta_2\| = \arctan \frac{2\sqrt{\alpha^2 - \beta\delta}}{\gamma^+} \tag{26}$$

from which the single orientations θ_ν can be obtained separately. Note, that geometric algebra offers a more natural embedding of the signal multivector and delivers these results by a single operation, called the geometric product.

4.2   Structure from the Signal Multivector

The local phase and amplitude represent the structural signal features, which can be calculated by solving a linear system of equations by the Cramer's rule of 2×2 matrices. The even and odd signal parts can be derived by

$$\begin{bmatrix} f_1^e \\ f_2^e \end{bmatrix} = \frac{1}{\sin(\theta_1 - \theta_2)\cos(\theta_1 + \theta_2)} \begin{bmatrix} \frac{f_p}{2}\sin(2\theta_2) - f_{xy} \\ f_{xy} - \frac{f_p}{2}\sin(2\theta_1) \end{bmatrix} \tag{27}$$

which has been derived by the second order generalized Hilbert transform and

$$\begin{bmatrix} f_1^o \\ f_2^o \end{bmatrix} = \frac{1}{\sin(\theta_1 - \theta_2)} \begin{bmatrix} f_y \cos\theta_2 - f_x \sin\theta_2 \\ f_x \sin\theta_1 - f_y \cos\theta_1 \end{bmatrix} \tag{28}$$

which has been derived by the first order generalized Hilbert transform respectively. By means of the even and odd signal parts, finally the structural signal features such as the phases and the amplitudes can be derived by

$$\phi_\nu = \arctan \frac{f_\nu^o}{f_\nu^e} \tag{29}$$

$$a_\nu = \sqrt{[f_\nu^e]^2 + [f_\nu^o]^2} \tag{30}$$

for $\nu \in \{1, 2\}$. Interestingly, this solution corresponds for each signal component to the classical 1D analytic signal [14].

5   Applications and Experimental Results

The signal multivector is isotropic and therefore needs only seven convolution filters. The signal multivector can be implemented either in Fourier space or in the spatial domain. But the advantage of the spatial domain is the local adaption on the individual scale space parameter which carries the important signal information for each test point. Because of that we favor the convolution in the spatial domain. The implementation of the signal multivector is easy and can be calculated in $O(m)$ with m as the total convolution mask size. In practice the convolution mask size involves 7×7 pixels. Due to the latest developments in graphic controllers, the signal multivector can be also implemented directly using the OpenGL® Shading Language (GLSL). This enables realtime computation of the signal multivector and detecting its optimal scale space parameter by maximizing the local amplitude for each test point individually [8]. Since the signal multivector is a fundamental low-level approach, many applications can be found. In the following we will present the parameter-free decomposition of multilayer textures.

5.1   Multilayer Decomposition

As an application of the signal multivector we will analyze superimposed oriented patterns and compare our results with the derivative based approach presented in [15]. In comparison to [15] our approach does not need any parameter tuning and unifies the case of i1D and i2D signals in one framework.

Derivative based approach. In [15] an i1D signal is assumed at first. An evidence check decides between computation of one single orientation or the double orientation case. The derivative operator for one orientation θ reads

$$\mathcal{D}_\theta = \cos\theta \frac{\partial}{\partial x} + \sin\theta \frac{\partial}{\partial y} \tag{31}$$

In the i1D case, the orientation computation is in essence an eigenspace analysis of the tensor $T = \nabla f \nabla f^T$ computed over a neighborhood Ω. The confidence measure for an i1D structure is determined as $\det(T) \leq \lambda \; \mathrm{trace}^2(T)$ with the tuning parameter $\lambda > 0$ which has to be chosen manually. In the i2D case, the comparison in this paper is restricted to considering overlaid oriented patterns resulting in the model

$$f(z) = \sum_{\nu=1}^{2} f_\nu(z) \quad \text{with } z = (x, y) \in \Omega \tag{32}$$

Using the derivative operator (31) and applying it to the double orientation case, the image signal in Gaussian scale space $\mathcal{G}\{\cdot\}(z; s)$ satisfies the equation

$$\mathcal{D}_{\theta_1} \mathcal{D}_{\theta_2} \mathcal{G}\{f\}(z; s) = c^T \mathcal{D}f = 0 \tag{33}$$

with the so called mixed-orientation vector

$$c = [\cos\theta_1 \cos\theta_2, \sin(\theta_1 + \theta_2), \sin\theta_1 \sin\theta_2]^T \tag{34}$$

and

$$\mathcal{D}f = \left[\frac{\partial^2}{\partial x^2}, \frac{\partial^2}{\partial xy}, \frac{\partial^2}{\partial y^2}\right]^T \mathcal{G}\{f\}(z; s) \tag{35}$$

138   L. Wietzke et al.

Taking into account that real image signals do not satisfy Equation (33) exactly the residual error is defined by

$$\varepsilon(c) = c^T \underbrace{\left[\int_{z \in \Omega} (\mathcal{D}f)(\mathcal{D}f)^T \, dz \right]}_{J} c \qquad (36)$$

which has to be minimized with respect to the vector c under the constraint $c^T c = 1$. The eigenvector analysis of the 3×3 tensor J allows the computation of the mixed-orientation vector c up to an unknown scaling factor $r \in \mathbb{R}$ by using the minors of J. In a second test based on the properties of J, the i2D case is confirmed, otherwise, the i0D case is assumed. In the i2D case, the vector rc has to be solved for the unknown orientations θ_1 and θ_2.

Comparison: signal multivector versus derivatives. Both methods have been tested on a set of synthetic and real images. The experiments on synthetic data have been conducted on patchlets with same size as the convolution kernels. Two overlaid structures have been tested in all possible combinations of angles, see Table (1). In addition, the performance of both methods in case of changing convolution kernel size and changing phase has been determined, see Figure (3). In case of the method [15] applied to real

Table 1. Signal multivector (SMV) average angular error (AAE) of the apex angle θ_a and the main orientation θ_m of junctions and multilayer signals

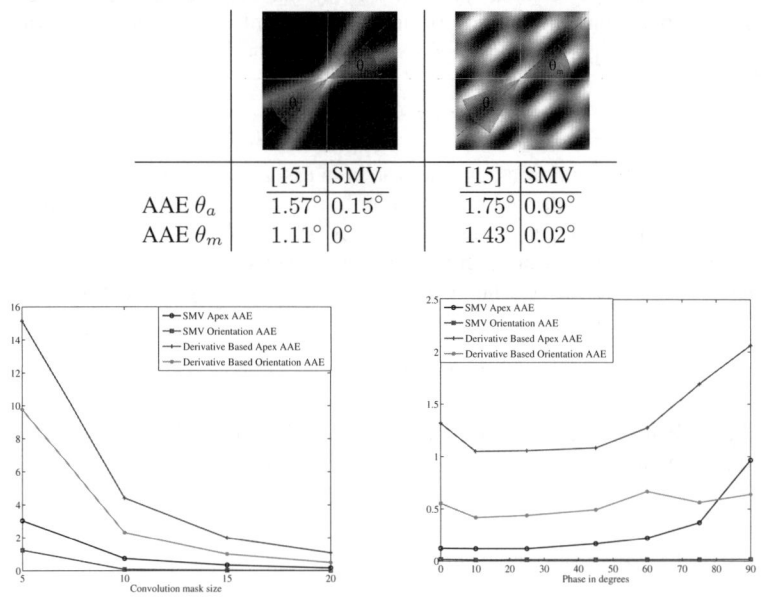

	[15]	SMV	[15]	SMV
AAE θ_a	1.57°	0.15°	1.75°	0.09°
AAE θ_m	1.11°	0°	1.43°	0.02°

Fig. 3. Left figure: Average angular error (AAE) of [15] and the signal multivector (SMV) against varying convolution mask size. The signal multivector performs better with small size which is very important for local feature detection. Right figure: Average angular error (AAE) of [15] and the signal multivector (SMV) against varying signal phase.

images, it was sometimes difficult to adjust the parameter λ deciding between i1D and i2D signals, whereas the signal multivector based method only needs the scale space parameters, which can be adjusted automatically by phase congruency.

6 Conclusion

We have solved a fundamental problem of isotropic signal analysis with applications in parameter-free multilayer decomposition. Our novel approach can be described for arbitrary signal models by the following general steps

1. Signal modeling in scale space and signal extension by the generalized Hilbert transform. The order of the required generalized Hilbert transforms corresponds to the complexity n of the signal model in Equation (3).
2. Retrieving the explicit system of equations including all unknown signal parameters $(\theta_\nu, \phi_\nu, a_\nu)$ by the relation of the generalized Hilbert transform to the Radon transform.
3. Algebraic signal representation in tensor form and subsequent mapping by the isomorphism φ to its corresponding signal multivector.
4. Geometric interpretation of the signal multivector by solving the nonlinear part of the inverse problem.
5. Structural multivector-valued signal interpretation by solving the linear part of the inverse problem.

The message of this contribution is that the signal multivector is isotropic for i1D and two superimposed i1D signals and offers accuracy with less computational time. Future work contains the generalization of the signal multivector to multidimensional signal domains to enable also isotropic motion tracking in computer vision applications.

References

1. Oppenheim, A.V., Lim, J.S.: The importance of phase in signals. Proceedings of the IEEE 69(5), 529–541 (1981)
2. Huang, T., Burnett, J., Deczky, A.: The importance of phase in image processing filters. IEEE Trans. on Acoustics, Speech and Signal Processing 23(6), 529–542 (1975)
3. Felsberg, M., Sommer, G.: The monogenic scale-space: A unifying approach to phase-based image processing in scale-space. Journal of Mathematical Imaging and Vision 21, 5–26 (2004)
4. Delanghe, R.: On some properties of the Hilbert transform in Euclidean space. Bull. Belg. Math. Soc. Simon Stevin 11(2), 163–180 (2004)
5. Köthe, U., Felsberg, M.: Riesz-transforms vs. derivatives: On the relationship between the boundary tensor and the energy tensor. In: Kimmel, R., Sochen, N.A., Weickert, J. (eds.) Scale-Space 2005. LNCS, vol. 3459, pp. 179–191. Springer, Heidelberg (2005)
6. Lowe, D.G.: Distinctive image features from scale-invariant keypoints. International Journal of Computer Vision 60, 91–110 (2004)
7. Wietzke, L., Sommer, G., Fleischmann, O.: The geometry of 2D image signals. In: IEEE Computer Society on Computer Vision and Pattern Recognition, CVPR 2009, pp. 1690–1697 (2009)
8. Felsberg, M.: Low-level image processing with the structure multivector. Technical Report 2016, Kiel University, Department of Computer Science (2002)

9. Hahn, S.L.: Hilbert Transforms in Signal Processing. Artech House Inc., Boston (1996)
10. Pan, W., Bui, T.D., Suen, C.Y.: Rotation invariant texture classification by ridgelet transform and frequency-orientation space decomposition. Signal Process. 88(1), 189–199 (2008)
11. Perwass, C.: Geometric Algebra with Applications in Engineering. Geometry and Computing, vol. 4. Springer, Heidelberg (2009)
12. Sobczyk, G., Erlebacher, G.: Hybrid matrix geometric algebra. In: Li, H., Olver, P.J., Sommer, G. (eds.) IWMM-GIAE 2004. LNCS, vol. 3519, pp. 191–206. Springer, Heidelberg (2005)
13. Danielsson, P.E., Lin, Q., Ye, Q.Z.: Efficient detection of second-degree variations in 2D and 3D images. Journal of Visual Communication and Image Representation 12(3), 255–305 (2001)
14. Gabor, D.: Theory of communication. Journal IEE, London 93(26), 429–457 (1946)
15. Stuke, I., Aach, T., Barth, E., Mota, C.: Analysing superimposed oriented patterns. In: 6th IEEE Southwest Symposium on Image Analysis and Interpretation, pp. 133–137. IEEE Computer Society, Los Alamitos (2004)

Complex Motion Models for Simple Optical Flow Estimation

Claudia Nieuwenhuis[1], Daniel Kondermann[2], and Christoph S. Garbe[2],[*]

[1] Technical University of Munich, Germany
nieuwenhuis@in.tum.de
[2] IWR, University of Heidelberg, Germany

Abstract. The selection of an optical flow method is mostly a choice from among accuracy, efficiency and ease of implementation. While variational approaches tend to be more accurate than local parametric methods, much algorithmic effort and expertise is often required to obtain comparable efficiency with the latter. Through the exploitation of natural motion statistics, the estimation of optical flow from local parametric models yields a good alternative. We show that learned, linear, parametric models capture specific higher order relations between neighboring flow vectors and, thus, allow for complex, spatio-temporal motion patterns despite a simple and efficient implementation. The method comes with an inherent confidence measure, and the motion models can easily be adapted to specific applications with typical motion patterns by choice of training data. The proposed approach can be understood as a generalization of the original structure tensor approach to the incorporation of arbitrary linear motion models. In this way accuracy, specificity, efficiency and ease of implementation can be achieved at the same time.

1 Introduction

1.1 Keeping Optical Flow Estimation Simple

Optical flow refers to the displacement field between subsequent frames of an image sequence. Methods for its computation are in practice usually tradeoffs between speed, accuracy and implementation effort. Local methods such as the Lucas & Kanade approach [1] or the structure tensor approach by Bigün [2] are very fast and easy to implement but not very accurate due to the simplified assumption that neighboring pixels move in the same way. Global methods such as the method by Horn and Schunck [3] and today's state-of-the art approaches are usually more accurate and can sometimes even be applied in realtime, yet with considerable implementation effort and expertise. Knowledge on adequate discretization, multigrid methods [5] and/or GPU implementation, variational calculus or Markov Random Fields, image and gradient filters [6], coarse to fine

[*] This work was funded by the "Heidelberg Graduate School of Mathematical and Computational Methods for the Sciences" (DFG GSC 220) and DFG grants GA1271/2-3 and CR250/6-1.

M. Goesele et al. (Eds.): DAGM 2010, LNCS 6376, pp. 141–150, 2010.

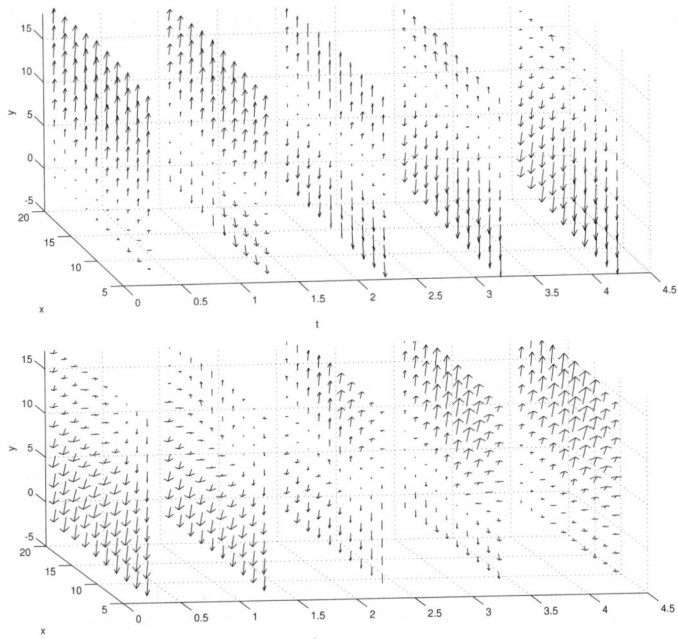

Fig. 1. Examples for learned motion models. The inclusion of temporal information allows for the representation of complex temporal phenomena, e.g. moving motion discontinuities (top) and moving divergences (bottom).

strategies for handling large motion, possibly in combination with image warping [7], as well as different norms and their characteristics for the preservation of motion boundaries is indispensable in order to obtain highly accurate and fast algorithms. Methods from the 1980s such as the Horn-Schunck approach can yield rather good results if a pyramid approach and bicubic interpolation are used to handle large motion combination with a multigrid solver. Yet, for industrial applications such high end knowledge is rare and expensive.

In this paper we reduce the necessary expertise and implementation effort to a minimum by learning statistically optimal (in the Gaussian sense) motion models from training data, which capture complex motion patterns, yet are still simple to compute. The complexity of the estimation task itself can be vastly reduced due to the linearity of the model. At the same time the learning based approach entails a strong adaptability to the specific optical flow estimation problem, e.g. in fluid dynamics or driver assistance systems (see Figure 1). Finally, a confidence measure directly inherent to the flow computation method can be applied to improve the result.

1.2 Motion Models

Because the optical flow problem is underconstrained, all estimation methods involve additional model assumptions on the structure of the motion.

The simplest motion model is a piecewise constant flow, which can be obtained by punishing the l_2 norm of the gradient of the flow vector $\|\nabla u\|^2$ [3] or by assuming constant motion within a small local neighborhood [1,2]. This model is not adequate for most optical flow fields. Other methods assume more general models such as local planar models [8] or affine models [9,10,11]. General affine models have been integrated into a variational framework by Nir et al. [12]. In order to preserve motion boundaries in variational approaches, l_1 regularization in the space of bounded variations, the widely used TV-regularization, was introduced into denoising by Rudin, Osher and Fatemi [13] and was soon applied in optical flow estimation. Recently, a generalized version of the TV-regularizer, the total generalized variation (TGV) regularizer, allowing for piecewise affine motion with sharp boundaries has been introduced into variational approaches [14]. For physics based applications often different conditions apply in flow estimation, e.g. the Navier-Stokes equation for fluid flows [15,16]. In the field of water or heat motion, patterns such as vortices or curls are common and can be handled by means of adequate regularization such as the div-curl regularizers [17] or model based approaches [18]. Flow fields based on such predefined models are often more accurate than those based on assumptions of constant flow. However, there are situations where even more complex and especially application specific models are necessary to compute accurate flow fields.

In these situations learning motion models from given sample motion data is a method to obtain superior results. Roth and Black [19] employed a general learning based approach using fields of experts, which is integrated into a global optical flow method. The approach is rather difficult to implement due to the fields of experts model. Black et al. [20] as well as Yacoob and Davis [21] integrated adapted, learning based models into a local optical flow method. To learn these models, principal component analysis (PCA) is used. This leads to a nonlinear energy functional, which is linearized and minimized by means of a coarse-to-fine strategy and coordinate descent. However, the models employed are either purely spatial [20] or purely temporal [21], or they are used for confidence estimation [22].

Our approach differs in four main aspects from these methods:

1. Instead of formulating a non-linear energy functional and applying gradient descent for its minimization we obtain an overdetermined system of equations which can be easily and globally solved by established least squares methods.
2. We employ spatio-temporal instead of purely spatial or temporal motion models, which can represent complex motion patterns over time.
3. We show results comparable to Farnebäck's (which are the best for local optical flow estimation), but with much less effort.
4. By means of a model-based confidence measure directly inherent to the flow computation method we can sparsify and reconstruct [23] the resulting flow field obtaining significantly lower errors.

Based on learned motion models for complex patterns, we end up with a simple, easily parallelizable and still accurate optical flow method. It is able to incorporate learned prior knowledge on special types of motion patterns and can be adapted to all kinds of specific motion estimation problems. The goal of this paper is not to devise a method more accurate than any other method before, but to point out a simple to implement and efficient alternative to all the state-of-the-art optical flow approaches.

2 Motion Statistics

We use statistical methods to directly learn the motion model from sample motion data. For a given sample flow field $u : \Omega \rightarrow \mathbb{R}^2$ defined on the spatio-temporal image domain $\Omega \subset \mathbb{R}^3$ we randomly choose a specified number of locations (here 5000), where spatio-temporal sample patches of a fixed size $\omega \subset \Omega$ are drawn from. Such sample flow fields can be ground truth flow fields, computed flow fields or any other flow fields containing motion patterns typical for the application. The sample patches are vectorized (horizontal component stacked on top of vertical flow component) and stored as columns in a matrix M. To avoid bias towards any direction, we rotate the training samples four times by 90 degrees in order to obtain a zero sample mean.

We use principal component analysis (PCA) to obtain motion models from the sample data. PCA means that we compute a new orthogonal basis system $B := [b_1, ..., b_p] \in \mathbb{R}^{p \times p}$, $p = 2|\omega|$ (each column represents one eigenvector containing a horizontal and a vertical flow component at each pixel of the patch ω), within which the original sample fields in M are decorrelated. This is simply done by computing the eigenvectors of the matrix M. Examples for such typical motion patterns are presented in Figure 1.

Let the basis components, i.e. the eigenvectors b_j of M, be sorted according to decreasing eigenvalues. Then the first $k \leq p$ eigenvectors with the largest eigenvalues contain most of the variance of the sample data, whereas the eigenvectors with small eigenvalues usually represent noise or errors in the sample flow fields and should be removed from the set. Hence, the first k basis components span a linear k-dimensional subspace of the original sample data space preserving most of the sample data information. In order to select the number of eigenvectors containing the fraction $\delta \in (0, 1)$ of the information of the original dataset we choose the value k based on the eigenvalues λ_i of the eigenvectors $b_i, i \in \mathbb{N}_p$ such that

$$k := \underset{j \in \mathbb{N}_p}{\operatorname{argmin}} \frac{\sum_{i=1}^{j} \lambda_i}{\sum_{i=1}^{p} \lambda_i} \geq \delta \ . \tag{1}$$

Within the resulting k-dimensional subspace a vectorized flow field patch $u(\omega)$ can be approximated by a linear combination of the first k principal components:

$$u(\omega) \approx \sum_{j=1}^{k} \alpha_j b_j \ . \tag{2}$$

The linear subspace restricts possible solutions of the flow estimation problem to the subspace of typical motion patterns statistically learned from sample data.

3   Parameter Estimation

Optical flow computation is based on the assumption that the brightness of a moving pixel remains constant over time. If $x : [0, T] \rightarrow \mathbb{R}^2$ describes the trajectory of a point of an object we can model a constant brightness intensity $I : \Omega \rightarrow \mathbb{R}$ as $I(x(t), t) = \text{const}$. A first order approximation yields the brightness constancy constraint equation (BCCE), $\nabla_{x,y}$ is the spatial gradient operator

$$\frac{\mathrm{d}I}{\mathrm{d}t} = 0 \quad \Leftrightarrow \quad (\nabla_{x,y} I)^T \cdot u + \frac{\partial I}{\partial t} = 0 \ , \tag{3}$$

Instead of estimating the optical flow u itself we want to estimate the coefficients $\alpha_j, j \in \mathbb{N}_k$, in (2) which implicitly define the displacement field for the neighborhood of the current pixel. In this way, the resulting optical flow is restricted to the learned subspace spanned by the k principal components. In the sense of Nir et al. [12] one could speak of an over-parameterized model, since we estimate k coefficients to obtain a two-dimensional flow vector, which is chosen from the center of the reconstructed patch.

To estimate the coefficients α_j we make two assumptions:

1. the current flow field patch can be approximated by a linear combination of principal components (2),
2. each of the flow vectors within the patch fulfills the BCCE (3).

Substituing u in (3) by the linear combination of model vectors in (2), we obtain the following energy to be minimized for a whole patch located at $\omega \subset \Omega$

$$E(\alpha) = \left| \begin{pmatrix} I_{x1} & 0 & \dots & 0 & I_{y1} & 0 & \dots & 0 \\ 0 & I_{x2} & 0 & \dots & 0 & I_{y2} & 0 \dots & 0 \\ \vdots & & \ddots & & & & \ddots & \vdots \\ 0 & \dots & 0 & I_{xn} & 0 & \dots & 0 & I_{yn} \end{pmatrix} \left(\sum_{j=1}^{k} \alpha_j b_j \right) + \frac{\partial I(\omega)}{\partial t} \right|^2 \rightarrow \min,$$

$$\tag{4}$$

where I_{cq} denotes the image derivative with respect to c at patch pixel index q and $I(\omega)$ denotes the vectorized intensities within the image patch ω containing $n := |\omega|$ pixels. Denoting the image gradient matrix in 4 as A, we obtain the following system of equations depending on the parameters α for each patch ω

$$(A \cdot B)^T \cdot \alpha = -I_t, \tag{5}$$

which can be solved by a simple least squares approach (or by the more sophisticated least median of squares, which can handle outliers e.g. at motion boundaries [24]). The resulting parameter vector α represents the estimated flow for the whole patch. To obtain the flow at the central pixel, we compute the linear combination and choose the central flow vector.

The proposed approach can be understood as a generalization of the original structure tensor approach to the incorporation of arbitrary linear motion models. In case we choose only two model vectors, a normalized horizontal and vertical one, we obtain exactly the original structure tensor approach.

4   Confidence Estimation

To improve the resulting optical flow field, we apply the confidence measure proposed in [22], which assigns a reliability value in the interval $[0, 1]$ to each flow vector. Here, 0 stands for no, 1 for full reliability. Based on a confidence map computed flows can be sparsified in order to reduce the average error. In this way the accuracy of further processing steps can be increased or errors can be removed by means of reconstruction algorithms, e.g. inpainting. According to [22] we assume that all correct flow field patches can be described in terms of the learned motion model, i.e. lie in the space of eigenflows. Thus, the inverse of the difference between the projection into the model space spanned by the principal components and the original patch $u(\omega)$ at location $\omega \in \Omega$ centered at x indicates the confidence

$$c(x) = \frac{1}{1 + |u(\omega) - (B \cdot B^T u(\omega))|}. \tag{6}$$

Since the basis system has already been computed, the application of the confidence measure is trivial and effective.

5   Results

In this section we present results on the accuracy, efficiency and adaptability of the proposed optical flow method. For the implementation we use the filters optimized for optical flow by Scharr [6] to estimate image derivatives. We presmoothed all sequences by a Gaussian filter with spatial $\sigma = 0.8$.

Accuracy. Our goal is not to devise an optical flow method yielding accuracy as high as the top ranking state-of-the-art methods on the Middlebury database. Instead, we want to demonstrate that the learned motion models can capture much of the complexity of optical flow fields and allow for an efficient and simple to implement flow computation method. To test our approach we use five different test sequences: the famous Marble sequence, the Yosemite and the Rubber Whale sequence from the Middlebury dataset [4] as well as the Street and Office sequence [25]. Learning is performed on a set of various computed flow fields. Table 1 shows a comparison to results obtained by the original structure tensor approach [2] based on the same patch size. Furthermore, we show error values and chosen parameters for all test sequences for different densities after sparsification based on the confidence measure proposed in section 4. Figure 2 displays the corresponding HSV coded motion fields, which show improvements especially for large moving planes and near motion boundaries. Here oversmoothing due to large patch sizes as in the traditional approach is avoided since the complex relations between neighboring vectors are already contained in the model.

Stability. In the following, we examine the stability of our method for different parameter choices, i.e. patch sizes and numbers of eigenvectors. Table 2 exhibits

Table 1. Comparison of the angular error and standard deviation of the model based approach to the traditional approach. The density refers to the flow field after sparsification based on the confidence measure [22]. ω denotes the spatio-temporal patch size, k the number of eigenvectors.

Results					
Density (%)	Yosemite	Marble	Rubber Whale	Street	Office
100	1.53 ± 1.69	2.55 ± 4.25	7.85 ± 15.95	4.99 ± 13.72	3.83 ± 4.98
90	1.37 ± 1.43	1.87 ± 2.73	5.24 ± 10.43	3.65 ± 8.38	3.35 ± 3.85
80	1.24 ± 1.37	1.49 ± 2.05	4.36 ± 9.45	3.04 ± 6.05	3.01 ± 3.38
70	1.15 ± 1.38	1.27 ± 1.65	4.12 ± 9.75	2.44 ± 4.52	2.75 ± 3.25
traditional	3.42 ± 10.01	5.25 ± 6.49	19.30 ± 17.23	5.75 ± 16.92	5.55 ± 11.82
ω, k	$19 \times 19 \times 3, 10$	$19 \times 19 \times 7, 6$	$19 \times 19 \times 1, 2$	$19 \times 19 \times 3, 2$	$21 \times 21 \times 1, 5$

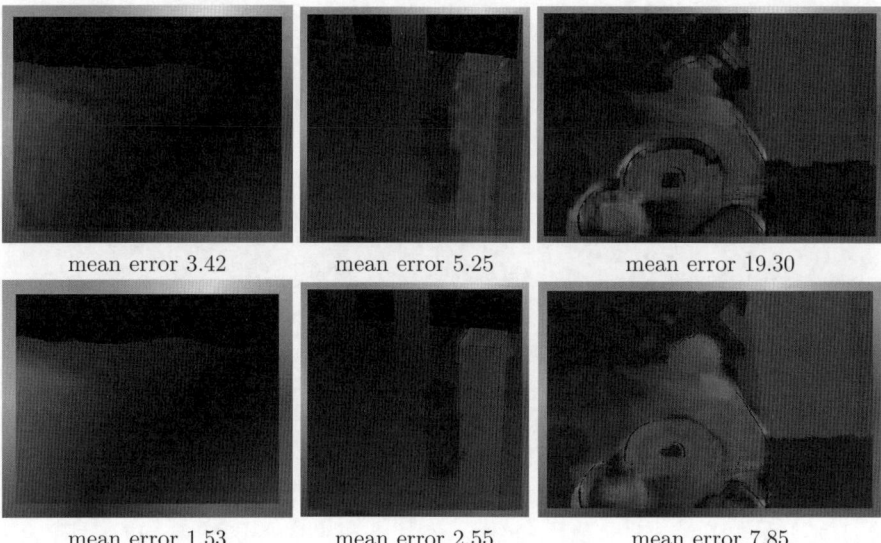

mean error 3.42   mean error 5.25   mean error 19.30

mean error 1.53   mean error 2.55   mean error 7.85

Fig. 2. Comparison of original structure tensor approach (top) and the motion model based structure tensor approach (bottom), HSV-coded flow fields and mean angular error for the Yosemite, Marble and the Rubber Whale sequence.

average error and standard deviation for different patch sizes based on 7 principal components and for different numbers of principal components for fixed patch size $\omega = 21 \times 21 \times 3$. The results suggest that large patch sizes are favorable for lower errors, whereas the number of principal components has less influence.

Adaptability. The proposed algorithm is adaptable to all kinds of scenes where typical, complex motion patterns need to be computed such as in fluid dynamics or driver assistance systems in vehicles. Figure 3 shows spatial principal components computed on particle image velocimetry (PIV) test data, on the Yosemite

Table 2. Left: angular error and standard deviation for different spatio-temporal sizes ω for the Yosemite sequence using 7 principal components. Right: angular error for different numbers of principal components for a fixed patch size of $21 \times 21 \times 3$.

Model Size				Principal components			
space \ time	1	3	7	k	$21 \times 21 \times 3$	k	$21 \times 21 \times 3$
5×5	7.12 ± 12.76	4.72 ± 7.62	3.01 ± 3.55	2	1.93 ± 2.07	6	1.40 ± 1.53
9×9	3.93 ± 6.46	2.69 ± 3.49	2.12 ± 2.27	3	1.86 ± 2.06	7	1.35 ± 1.45
15×15	2.39 ± 3.01	1.81 ± 1.97	1.50 ± 1.70	4	1.53 ± 1.53	8	1.36 ± 1.40
21×21	1.79 ± 1.87	1.66 ± 1.57	1.35 ± 1.45	5	1.44 ± 1.56	9	1.35 ± 1.41

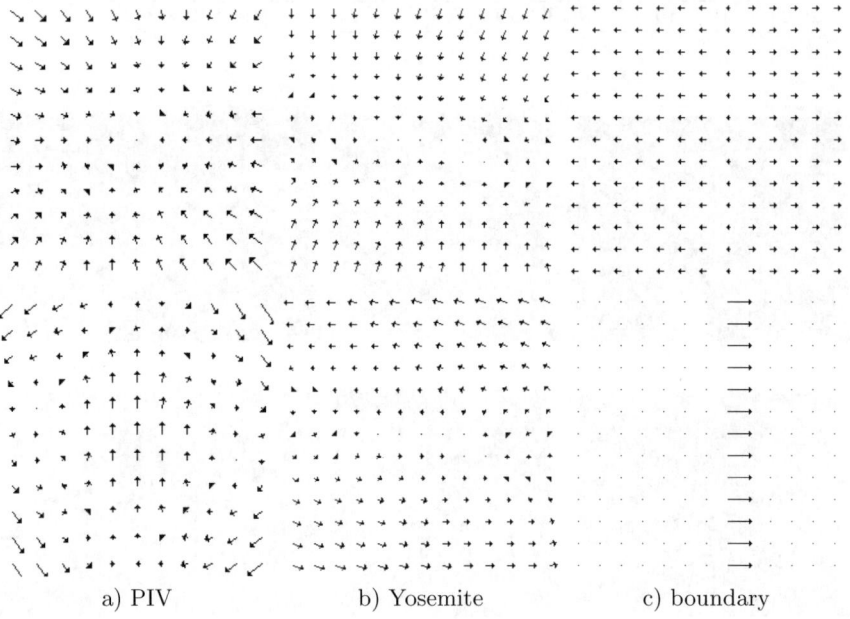

a) PIV   b) Yosemite   c) boundary

Fig. 3. Principal components based on training data from totally different application fields, a) PIV data consisting of fluid motion patterns, b) Yosemite consisting mostly of translations, c) a motion boundary.

sequence and on a motion boundary. The examples show that for very different kinds of flow fields we obtain very different motion models.

Efficiency. The proposed local optical flow method can be implemented efficiently due to several reasons. First, the algorithm only takes into account a limited local image region in order to estimate the displacement vector for each pixel. Hence, it takes only limited space and can be easily parallelized for the computation on graphics hardware. Second, the computation of the PCA model can be carried out once before the estimation of the optical flow and can be used for all kinds of sequences and the confidence estimation later on.

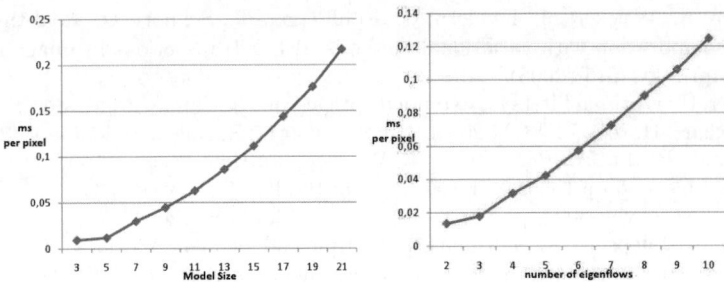

Fig. 4. Computation times per pixel for increasing patch sizes (left) and increasing numbers of eigenvectors (right) on the CPU.

Computation times grow linearly with the number of pixels contained in the patch, and almost linearly with the number of eigenvectors. Figure 4 shows computation times for a single pixel on a standard CPU.

6 Summary and Conclusion

In this paper we proposed a generalization of the traditional algorithm by Bigün for optical flow estimation to the incorporation of complex motion models. This approach has four advantages: 1) The resulting method yields errors approximately half the value of the traditional approach due to the use of motion models, which can capture complex spatio-temporal motion patterns. In this way, we incorporate prior knowledge on regular flow field patches without the need for explicit regularization which would drastically increase computation times and implementation complexity. And the results are improved especially near motion boundaries and for planar motion. 2) The algorithm boils down to the simple task of carrying out principal component analysis on training data and solving an overdetermined linear system of equations at each pixel location by means of least squares. Thus, the implementation effort and necessary expertise are strongly reduced, which makes our approach especially interesting for industrial applications. 3) The learned motion models are adaptable to all kinds of specific applications, where special motion patterns occur, e.g. in the field of fluid dynamics or driver assistance systems. 4) The approach is stable with respect to parameter variations.

References

1. Lucas, B., Kanade, T.: An iterative image registration technique with an application to stereo vision (DARPA). In: Proceedings of the DARPA Image Understanding Workshop, pp. 121–130 (1981)
2. Bigün, J., Granlund, G., Wiklund, J.: Multidimensional orientation estimation with applications to texture analysis and optical flow. IEEE Journal of Pattern Analysis and Machine Intelligence 13(8), 775–790 (1991)
3. Horn, B., Schunck, B.: Determining optical flow. Artificial Intelligence 17, 185–204 (1981)
4. Baker, S., Roth, S., Scharstein, D., Black, M., Lewis, J., Szeliski, R.: A database and evaluation methodology for optical flow. In: Proceedings of ICCV, pp. 1–8 (2007)

5. Bruhn, A., Weickert, J., Feddern, C., Kohlberger, T., Schnörr, C.: Real-time optic flow computation with variational methods. IEEE Transactions in Image Processing 14(5), 608–615 (2005)
6. Scharr, H.: Optimal filters for extended optical flow. In: Jähne, B., Mester, R., Barth, E., Scharr, H. (eds.) IWCM 2004. LNCS, vol. 3417, Springer, Heidelberg (2007)
7. Brox, T., Bruhn, A., Papenberg, N., Weickert, J.: High accuracy optical flow estimation based on a theory for warping. In: Pajdla, T., Matas, J(G.) (eds.) ECCV 2004. LNCS, vol. 3024, pp. 25–36. Springer, Heidelberg (2004)
8. Black, M., Jepson, A.: Estimating multiple independent motions in segmented images using parametric models with local deformations. In: IEEE Workshop on Motion of Non-Rigid and Articulated Objects (1994)
9. Ju, S.X., Black, M.J., Jepson, A.D.: Skin and bones: Multi-layer, locally affine, optical flow and regularization with transparency. In: CVPR (1996)
10. Black, M., Yacoob, Y.: Tracking and recognizing rigid and non-rigid facial motions using local parametric models of image motion. In: Proceedings of the International Conference on Computer Vision, ICCV (1995)
11. Farnebäck, G.: Fast and accurate motion estimation using orientation tensors and parametric motion models. In: ICPR, vol. 1, pp. 135–139 (2000)
12. Nir, T., Bruckstein, A.M., Kimmel, R.: Over-parameterized variational optical flow. International Journal of Computer Vision 76(2), 205–216 (2006)
13. Rudin, L., Osher, S.: Total variation based image restoration with free local constraints. In: ICIP, vol. 1, pp. 31–35 (1994)
14. Bredies, K., Kunish, K., Pock, T.: Total generalized variation, Techn. Rep. (2009)
15. Vlasenko, A., Schnörr, C.: Physically consistent and efficient variational denoising of image fluid flow estimates. IEEE Transact. Image Process. 19(3), 586–595 (2010)
16. Haussecker, H., Fleet, D.: Computing optical flow with physical models of brightness variation. IEEE Transactions on Pattern Analysis and Machine Intelligence (PAMI) 23(6), 661–673 (2001)
17. Gupta, S., Gupta, E.N., Prince, J.L.: Stochastic models for div-curl optical flow methods. IEEE Signal Processing Letters 3, 32–35 (1996)
18. Cuzol, A., Hellier, P., Mémin, E.: A low dimensional fluid motion estimator. Int. J. Comp. Vision 75 (2007)
19. Roth, S., Black, M.: On the spatial statistics of optical flow. In: Proceedings of the International Conference on Computer Vision, vol. 1, pp. 42–49 (2005)
20. Black, M., Yacoob, Y., Jepson, A., Fleet, D.: Learning parameterized models of image motion. In: Proceedings of the International Conference on Computer Vision and Pattern Recognition, CVPR (1997)
21. Yacoob, Y., Davis, L.: Learned temporal models of image motion. In: Proceedings of the International Conference on Computer Vision (1998)
22. Nieuwenhuis, C., Kondermann, D., Jähne, B., Garbe, C.: An adaptive confidence measure for optical flows based on linear subspace projections. In: Hamprecht, F.A., Schnörr, C., Jähne, B. (eds.) DAGM 2007. LNCS, vol. 4713, pp. 132–141. Springer, Heidelberg (2007)
23. Nieuwenhuis, C., Kondermann, D., Garbe, C.: Postprocessing of optical flows via surface measures and motion inpainting. In: Rigoll, G. (ed.) DAGM 2008. LNCS, vol. 5096, pp. 355–364. Springer, Heidelberg (2008)
24. Suter, D.: Motion estimation and vector splines. In: Proceedings of the Conference on Computer Vision and Pattern Recognition, pp. 939–942. IEEE, Los Alamitos (1994)
25. McCane, B., Novins, K., Crannitch, D., Galvin, B.: On benchmarking optical flow. Computer Vision and Image Understanding 84(1), 126–143 (2001)

Tracking People in Broadcast Sports

Angela Yao[1], Dominique Uebersax[1], Juergen Gall[1], and Luc Van Gool[1,2]

[1] ETH Zurich, Switzerland
{yaoa,gall,vangool}@vision.ee.ethz.ch, duebersa@ee.ethz.ch
[2] KU Leuven, Belgium

Abstract. We present a method for tracking people in monocular broadcast sports videos by coupling a particle filter with a vote-based confidence map of athletes, appearance features and optical flow for motion estimation. The confidence map provides a continuous estimate of possible target locations in each frame and outperforms tracking with discrete target detections. We demonstrate the tracker on sports videos, tracking fast and articulated movements of athletes such as divers and gymnasts and on non-sports videos, tracking pedestrians in a PETS2009 sequence.

1   Introduction

Object tracking in video is a long-standing computer vision problem; in particular, tracking people has captured the interest of many researchers due to its potential for applications such as intelligent surveillance, automotive safety and sports analysis. State-of-the-art people trackers have predominantly focused on pedestrians for traffic or surveillance scenarios. For sports analysis, however, standard pedestrian trackers face significant challenges since in many broadcast sports, the camera moves and zooms to follow the movements of the athlete. Furthermore, in some sports, the athlete may perform abrupt movements and have extensive body articulations that result in rapid appearance changes and heavy motion blur. As such, sports tracking to date [1,2,3,4,5,6] has been limited to team sports such as football and hockey, in which there is wide view of the playing field and athletes remain relatively upright. In addition, these works are primarily focused on the data-association problem of multi-target tracking and do not deviate substantially from the pedestrian tracking scenario.

In the current work, we present a method for tracking people in monocular broadcast sports videos by coupling a standard particle filter [7] with a vote-based confidence map of an "athlete"-detector [8]. We target sporting disciplines in which the athletes perform fast and highly articulated movements, e.g. diving and gymnastics. Tracking in these types of sports is particularly difficult since the athletes do not remain in an upright configuration. Our confidence map, built from the Hough accumulator of a generalized Hough transform designed for people detection, is well suited for handling pose and appearance changes and athlete occlusions, as it is generated from a vote-based method. While we focus on tracking in broadcast sports clips, as they provide a challenging testbed,

M. Goesele et al. (Eds.): DAGM 2010, LNCS 6376, pp. 151–161, 2010.

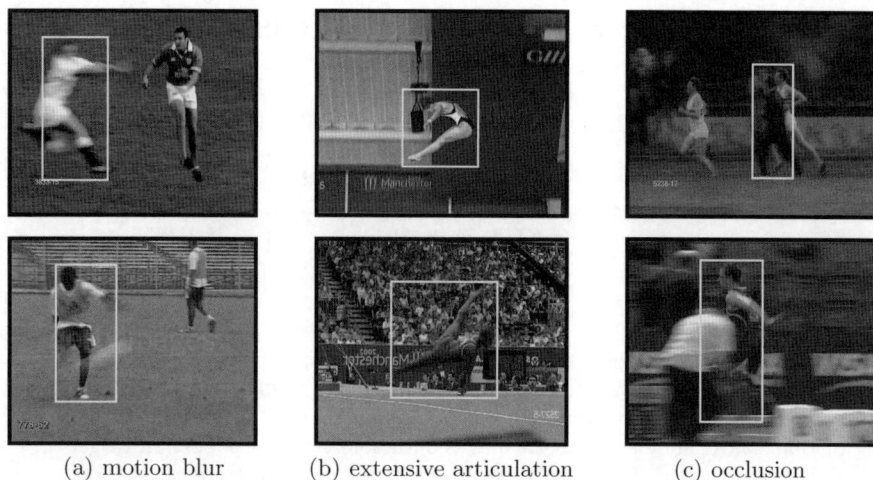

(a) motion blur   (b) extensive articulation   (c) occlusion

Fig. 1. Select frames from the UCF Sports Dataset [9], showing challenges of tracking in sports videos such as *(a)* motion blur, *(b)* extensive body articulation and *(c)* occlusions

our method is applicable to generic people tracking in unconstrained videos. We demonstrate the tracker's effectiveness on the UCF Sports Dataset [9], a collection of footage from the 2008 Olympics and a PETS 2009 sequence [10].

2   Related Works

Early approaches in sports tracking began with background extraction and then morphological operations to isolate foreground areas which may represent the athlete [1,2,11]. Tracking was then performed by enforcing spatial continuity through either Kalman or particle filtering. These approaches, both single- and multi-camera, relied heavily on colour as a cue for separating the athletes from the background as well as for tracking, though shape and motion information of the athletes have also been used [12,4]. Most of the proposed algorithms, however, have been designed for specific sports, such as soccer [1,2], speed-skating [13] or hockey [3] and rely on sport-specific scene-knowledge, such as distances between field lines [14].

Accurate modelling of target observations, be it athletes, pedestrians or generic objects has been the focus of several current tracking works. One line of approach learns and adapts appearance models online [15,16,17]; these methods cope well with appearance changes and are not limited to tracking specific object classes, but are susceptible to drift as tracking errors accumulate. Another line of approach uses pre-trained models of the targets. Tracking-by-detection methods follow this type of paradigm, in which object detectors are first trained offline and detections across the sequence are then associated together to form the track, e.g. by particle filtering. Tracking-by-detection has been used for pedestrians [5,18,19] and in specific sports such as hockey [3,5] and soccer [5,6]. All these approaches, however, assume that the humans remain upright - an assumption that does not hold for broadcast sports videos in general.

The key component of our tracker is the use of a vote-based confidence map to estimate the location of the targets. It is similar in spirit to the Fragment Tracker in [20], which tracks object fragments or patches that vote for an object center. Our work differs from [20] in that we track possible object centres from the accumulated votes in the confidence map rather than the individual patches that vote for a center.

3   Sports Tracker

The sports tracker is a tracking-by-detection approach with three components: *(1)*a continuous vote-based confidence map to estimate the target location (see 3.2), *(2)*appearance matching of the target based on feature templates (see 3.3) and *(3)*motion estimation of the camera and the target from optical flow (see 3.4).

3.1   Tracking Overview

Tracking in the sports videos is done using a particle filter [7]. We model the state $s = \{x, y, c, u, v, d\} \in \mathbb{R}^6$ of a human by the image position and scale (x, y, c) and velocity and change in scale (u, v, d). For particle i, the weight at frame t is assigned as follows:

$$w_t^i = \frac{1}{Z} \exp \Big(-K \cdot \big(\alpha \cdot V_1(s_t^i) + (1 - \alpha) \cdot \sum_f \lambda_f V_2(s_t^i, f) \big) \Big). \tag{1}$$

The term V_1 measures the response in the vote space (Figure 2*(b)*, see 3.2) for particle s_t^i. The term V_2 measures the similarity of particle s_t^i with respect to some template appearance feature f extracted from the associated bounding box of the particle (Figure 2*(f)*, see 3.3). K is a scaling constant and $\alpha \in [0, 1]$ is a weighting parameter for V_1 and V_2. λ_f are weighting parameters between the different features and sum up to 1. Z is the normalization term of the weights.

The tracker is initialized using the ground truth from the first frame of the sequence. Particles are propagated by a dynamical model accounting for camera motion (Figure 2*(c)*) and estimated athlete motion(Figure 2*(d)*, see 3.4).

3.2   Vote-Based Confidence Map

The confidence map is generated from the output of a Hough forest [8] trained for detecting athletes. The Hough forest is a random forest trained to map image feature patches to probabilistic votes in a 3D Hough accumulator H for locations and scales of the athlete. We use cropped and scale-normalized images of the athletes as positive examples, background images as negative examples, and colour and histograms of gradients [21] as features. For a detailed description of the training procedure, we refer to [8]. For detection, feature patches are densely

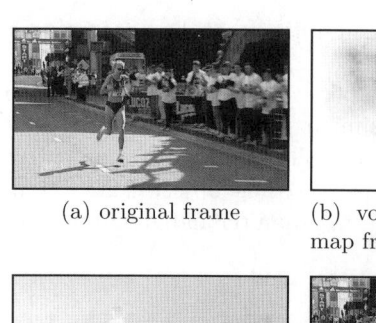
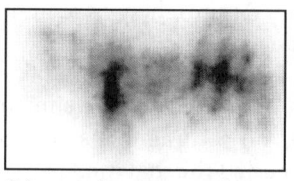

(a) original frame   (b) vote-based confidence map from Hough Forest [8]   (c) camera movement estimation from frame borders

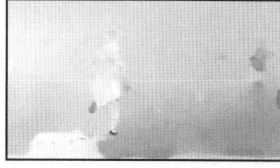

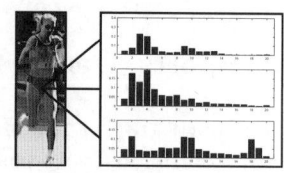

(d) optical flow   (e) particle distribution   (f) colour and texture appearance evaluation

Fig. 2. Components of the sports tracker. From the original frame(a), the vote-based confidence map(b) is computed using a Hough Forest [8]. The dynamical model estimates camera motion from the frame border(c) and motion of the tracked athlete from the frame interior using optical flow(d). Each particle in the particle distribution(e) is weighted according to the confidence map and appearance features such as colour and texture(f).

sampled from the image and passed through the trees of the Hough forest to cast votes in H. While a detector as in [8] thresholds the local maxima in H to obtain a discrete set of object hypotheses, we consider H as a continuous confidence mapping of athlete locations and scales. From H, the vote response $V_1\left(s_t^i\right)$ of particle s_t^i is determined by

$$V_1(s_t^i) = -\log\Big(\sum_{x \in \mathcal{N}(s_t) \cap H} G(s_t^i - x)\Big), \qquad (2)$$

i.e. we sum the votes in the neighborhood $\mathcal{N}$ of s_t weighted by a Gaussian kernel G. Note that the sum is in the range of $[0, 1]$.

3.3 Appearance Model

The appearance of particle s_t^i, denoted as $V_2\left(s_t^i, f\right)$, is a measure of similarity between that particle's feature response $h^f\left(s_t^i\right)$ and some template h_T^f for feature f. To measure similarity, we use the Bhattacharyya coefficient BC:

$$V_2\left(s_t^i, f\right) = 1 - BC(h_T^f, h^f(s_t^i)) \qquad (3)$$

As image features, we use HSV colour histograms and local binary patterns [22] to model colour and texture respectively. For the template, we use a weighted mixture of the particle's feature response in the initial frame at t_0 and the previous frame t–1. Weighting of the individual appearance features in the final particle weight (Equation 1) is determined by λ_f, in our case λ_{colour} and $\lambda_{texture}$.

3.4   Dynamical Model

For the dynamical model, we use an estimated velocity based on optical flow. The reason for this is two-fold. First, constant-velocity models which perform well for tracking walking or running people perform poorly for actions in which the athletes move erratically, i.e. in gymnastics. Secondly, in many broadcast sports, the cinematography already provides some framing and tracking of the athlete, i.e. when the camera pans to follow the athlete across a scene. As such, the position of the athlete changes in an inconsistent manner within the frame and it is necessary to estimate the particle motion while accounting for camera motion. Particles are propagated from frame to frame by

$$(x, y, c)^i_t = (x, y, c)^i_{t-1} + (u, v, d)^i_{t-1} + \mathcal{N}\left(0, \boldsymbol{\sigma}_{tran}\right), \tag{4}$$

where $\boldsymbol{\sigma}_{tran}$ is the variance of added Gaussian noise for the transition. Velocity is estimated as a weighted mixture between camera-compensated optical flow and velocity in the previous frame, while change in scale remains constant.

$$(u, v)^i_t = \eta \cdot \left((u, v)^{of}_{t-1} - \gamma \cdot (u, v)^{cam}_{t-1}\right) + (1 - \eta) \cdot (u, v)^i_{t-1} \tag{5}$$

Optical flow is computed according to [23]; camera motion is estimated as the average optical flow in the border of the frame (Figure 2(b)). η is a weighting parameter between estimated motion versus a constant velocity assumption, while γ serves as a scaling parameter for the estimated camera motion.

4   Experiments

4.1   Datasets

We evaluate our tracker on sports and non-sports videos. For sports, we use the UCF Sports Dataset [9] and our own collection of Olympics footage. The UCF dataset, consisting of 150 sequences (50-100 frames each) from network news videos, was originally intended for action recognition. To supplement the UCF dataset, we annotated 31 sequences (150-2000 frames each) from the 2008 Olympics, featuring sports such as diving, equestrian and various disciplines of gymnastics. The sequences are longer and more challenging than UCF, with significant motion blur and de-interlacing artifacts. For non-sports videos, we track three people from the PETS 2009 [10] sequence *S2.L1, View001*. For the sports datasets, we train on all images of annotated athletes within the dataset other than from the test sequence, in a leave-one-out fashion. For the PETS sequence, we trained on the TUD pedestrian database [18].

4.2   Evaluation

For evaluation, we use the VOC [24] criterion (the intersection over union, IOU, of the tracked bounding box and the ground truth bounding box must be greater than 0.5). We hand annotated select frames of the Olympics data and the PETS sequence and used linear interpolation to generate bounding boxes for the frames in between. For the UCF database, bounding boxes were provided as a part of the ground truth annotation released with the data.

We run three experiments on the Olympics data to test the impact of each component of the tracker. First, the confidence map is compared with discrete detections; for fair comparison, we generate the discrete detections from the confidence maps by thresholding[1] the local maxima of H (see 3.2). Second, the effect of the appearance modelling is tested by removing the colour and texture features from the tracker. In the third experiment, we vary the η and γ parameters and look at the effects of removing camera compensation as well as comparing our current dynamic model to a constant velocity model. We also compare our tracker's performance on the PETS2009 sequence with the Fragment Tracker in [20], using source code provided on the author's website[2]. Run time on all datasets was around 1 second per frame for 50 particles on a standard CPU.

5   Results

Olympics Data. We take the following parameter settings $\{\alpha=0.5, \lambda_{colour}=0.09, \lambda_{texture}=0.91, \eta=0.3, \gamma=1.5\}$ and use these as our default scenario. Parameters are set at these values for all experiments unless otherwise stated. Results for default scenario, split by discipline are shown in Figure 3 *(a)*. Tracking results from the first three experiments are shown in Table 1. From the first experiment, we

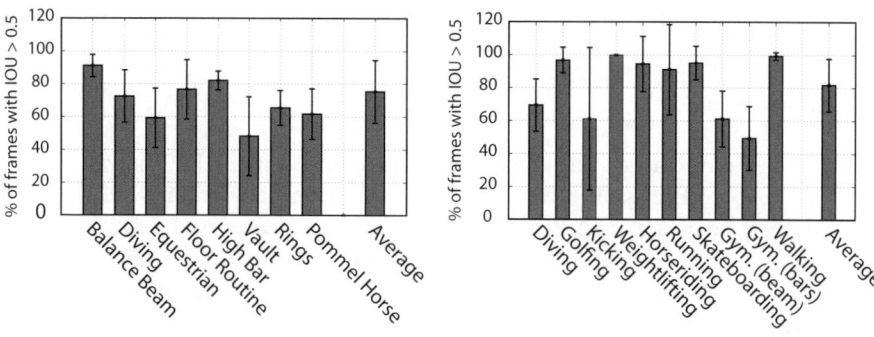

(a) Olympics tracking performance   (b) UCF tracking performance

Fig. 3. Average tracking performance by sport for *(a)*Olympics Dataset and *(b)*UCF Sports Dataset, where a higher % indicates better performance

---

[1] The threshold was set to achieve a high recall.
[2] http://www.cs.technion.ac.il/~amita/fragtrack/fragtrack.htm

Table 1. Average tracking performance on the Olympics sequences, where a higher % indicates better performance. There is a decrease in tracking performance with each removed component of the tracker; the most critical component seems to be the vote map, as using discrete components results in significantly lower performance.

Experimental Variation	Affected Parameter/Variable	% of frames with IOU> 0.5
Default	NA	75.4 ± 13.4
Discrete detections	V_1 from discrete detections	26.1 ± 17.2
No detections	$\alpha = 0$	28.1 ± 17.3
No colour features	$\lambda_{colour} = 0, \lambda_{texture} = 1$	73.9 ± 12.3
No texture features	$\lambda_{colour} = 1, \lambda_{texture} = 0$	71.3 ± 10.3
No appearance features	$\alpha = 1$	70.4 ± 13.1
No camera compensation	$\gamma = 0$	71.8 ± 11.7
Constant velocity	$\eta = 0$	71.8 ± 15.0

see that using the vote-based confidence map in the tracker gives a significant improvement over the use of discrete detections. In fact, for the sports, having discrete detections is comparable to not using any detections ($\alpha = 0$). This can be attributed to the many false-positive detections with high confidences, which have the effect of attracting and clustering the particles to erroneous locations. Our second experiment shows that removing either or both appearance features results only in a slightly decreased performance, again emphasizing the importance of the confidence map in the tracker. In the last experiment, we show that the use of our motion estimate in the dynamical model outperforms a constant velocity model, particularly with having the camera compensation. Varying η and γ had little effect, with performance ranging from 71.6%-74.9%. Select frames from the tracked results are shown in Figure 4.

UCF Sports Dataset. Tracking performance for the UCF Dataset are shown in Figure 3(b); select frames from the tracks are shown in Figure 5. On average, 81.8% ± 16.0% of the frames have tracks with an IOU greater than 0.5. The tracker performs well in sports where people remain upright, i.e. golfing, running, and skateboarding, but faces some difficulty with sports with more extensive articulation such as diving, kicking and gymnastics. Part of the error results from ground truth being tight bounding boxes around the athletes while tracked bounding boxes are of a fixed ratio.

PETS2009. We compare the performance of our Sports Tracker with the Fragment Tracker [20] in Table 2. The Sports Tracker successfully follows two of the three tracks, but breaks down on track 3, most likely due to the lack of multiple target handling. There are two identity switches, first from the target to another person at frame 31 when several people group together and then back to the target after frame 115. Select frames are shown in Figure 6. The Fragment Tracker successfully tracks one of the three tracks, but suffers from drift on the other two tracks and around 100 frames into the tracks, loses the target completely.

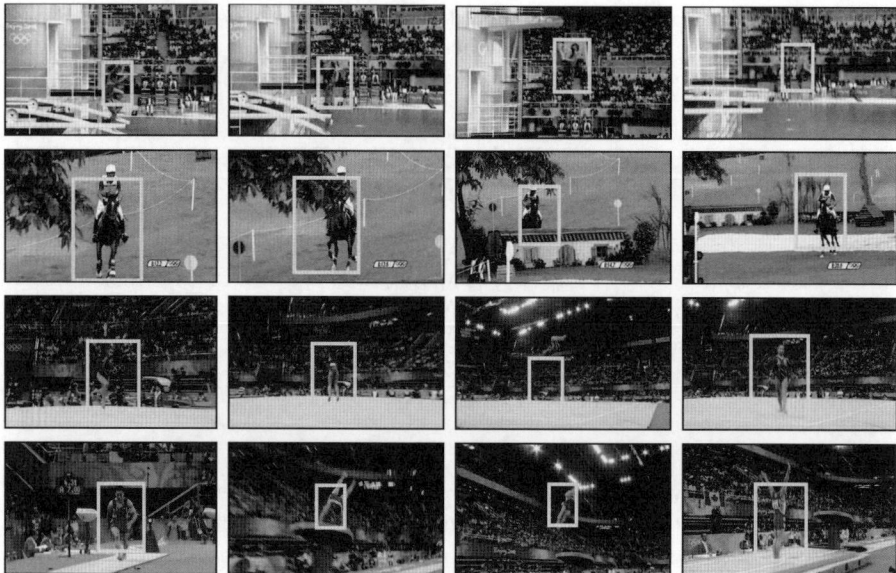

Fig. 4. Tracking on the Olympics sequences: select frames from diving (top), equestrian (second row), floor routine (third row) and vault (bottom). The tracker successfully follows the athletes but has difficulty with very fast motions, e.g. on the floor routine, in the third frame, the tracker fails to track the tumbling sequence through the air.

Fig. 5. Tracking on the UCF Sports Dataset, showing select frames from running (top row), skateboarding (middle row) and gymnastics (bottom row)

Table 2. Comparison of the Sports Tracker with the Fragments Tracker in [20] on the PETS2009 *S2.L1 View001* sequence. Results shown are the % of frames with IOU> 0.5, where a higher % indicates better performance

Track	Frame	Sports Tracker	Fragments Tracker [20]
1	21 - 259	85.4	14.8
2	222 - 794	95.5	12.6
3	0 - 145	13.8	78.6

Fig. 6. Select frames from the PETS2009 sequence. The tracker successfully follows the target in track 1 and 2 (top and middle row). Track 2 is particularly challenging as it is over 500 frames long and several people including the target are all wearing black clothing. In frame 294 of track 2, the tracker handles occlusion of the target by another person wearing similar coloured clothing. In frame 31 of track 3 (bottom row), there is an identity switch (true target is indicated by the white arrow); in frame 115, the tracker switches back onto the correct target. Figure is best viewed in colour.

6   Conclusion

We have presented a method for tracking athletes in broadcast sports videos. Our sports tracker combines a particle filter with the vote-based confidence map of an object detector. The use of feature templates and target motion estimates add to the performance of the tracker, but the strength of the tracker lies in the confidence map. By providing a continuous estimate of possible target locations in each frame, the confidence map greatly outperforms tracking with discrete detections. Possible extensions to the tracker include making voting for the confidence map adaptive and online, so that tracked bounding boxes are of varying ratios to yield tight bounding boxes around the athlete's body, and making a multi-target version of the tracker to better handle team sports.

Acknowledgements. The authors would like to thank Thomas Brox for his optical flow code. This research was funded by the Swiss National Foundation NCCR project IM2 and the EC project IURO; Angela Yao was also funded by NSERC Canada.

References

1. Kang, J., Cohen, I., Medioni, G.: Soccer player tracking across uncalibrated camera streams. In: IEEE International Workshop on Visual Surveillance and Performance Evaluation of Tracking and Surveillance, VS-PETS (2003)
2. Choi, K., Seo, Y., Lee, S.: Probabilistic tracking of soccer players and ball. In: ACCV (2004)
3. Okuma, K., Taleghani, A., de Freitas, N., Little, J., Lowe, D.: A boosted particle filter: Multitarget detection and tracking. In: Pajdla, T., Matas, J(G.) (eds.) ECCV 2004. LNCS, vol. 3021, pp. 28–39. Springer, Heidelberg (2004)
4. Kristan, M., Pers, J., Perse, M., Kovacic, S.: Closed-world tracking of multiple interacting targets for indoor-sports applications. CVIU 113(5), 598–611 (2009)
5. Breitenstein, M., Reichlin, F., Leibe, B., Koller-Meier, E., Gool, L.V.: Robust tracking-by-detection using a detector confidence particle filter. In: ICCV (2009)
6. Hess, R., Fern, A.: Discriminatively trained particle filters for complex multi-object tracking. In: CVPR (2009)
7. Doucet, A., Freitas, N.D., Gordon, N. (eds.): Sequential Monte Carlo Methods in Practice. Springer, New York (2001)
8. Gall, J., Lempitsky, V.: Class-specific hough forests for object detection. In: CVPR (2009)
9. Rodriguez, M.D., Ahmed, J., Shah, M.: Action mach a spatio-temporal maximum average correlation height filter for action recognition. In: CVPR (2008)
10. Ferryman, J., Shahrokni, A.: Pets2009: Dataset and challenge. In: IEEE International Workshop on Performance Evaluation of Tracking and Surveillance (2009)
11. Sullivan, J., Carlsson, S.: Tracking and labelling of interacting multiple targets. In: Leonardis, A., Bischof, H., Pinz, A. (eds.) ECCV 2006. LNCS, vol. 3952, pp. 232–244. Springer, Heidelberg (2006)
12. Lu, W.L., Little, J.J.: Tracking and recognizing actions at a distance. In: Proceedings of the ECCV Workshop on Computer Vision Based Analysis in Sport Environments (CVBASE 2006), Graz, Austria (May 2006)
13. Liu, G., Tang, X., Cheng, H.D., Huang, J., Liu, J.: A novel approach for tracking high speed skaters in sports using a panning camera. Pattern Recogn. 42(11), 2922–2935 (2009)
14. Khatoonabadi, S.H., Rahmati, M.: Automatic soccer players tracking in goal scenes by camera motion elimination. Image Vision Comput. 27(4), 469–479 (2009)
15. Collins, R., Liu, Y., Leordeanu, M.: On-line selection of discriminative tracking features. TPAMI 27(1), 1631 (2005)
16. Grabner, H., Leistner, C., Bischof, H.: Semi-supervised on-line boosting for robust tracking. In: Forsyth, D., Torr, P., Zisserman, A. (eds.) ECCV 2008, Part I. LNCS, vol. 5302, pp. 234–247. Springer, Heidelberg (2008)

17. Babenko, B., Yang, M.H., Belongie, S.: Visual tracking with online multiple instance learning. In: CVPR (2009)
18. Andriluka, M., Roth, S., Schiele, B.: People-tracking-by-detection and people-detection-by-tracking. In: CVPR (2008)
19. Leibe, B., Leonardis, A., Schiele, B.: Robust object detection with interleaved categorization and segmentation. IJCV 77(1-3), 259–289 (2008)
20. Adam, A., Rivlin, E., Shimshoni, I.: Robust fragments-based tracking using the integral histogram. In: CVPR (2006)
21. Dalal, N., Triggs, B.: Histograms of oriented gradients for human detection. In: CVPR (2005)
22. Ojala, T., Pietikainen, M., Maenpaa, T.: Multiresolution gray-scale and rotation invariant texture classification with local binary patterns. TPAMI 24(7), 971–987 (2002)
23. Brox, T., Bruhn, A., Papenberg, N., Weickert, J.: High accuracy optical flow estimation based on a theory for warping. In: Pajdla, T., Matas, J(G.) (eds.) ECCV 2004. LNCS, vol. 3024, pp. 25–36. Springer, Heidelberg (2004)
24. Everingham, M., Van Gool, L., Williams, C.K.I., Winn, J., Zisserman, A.: The PASCAL Visual Object Classes Challenge, VOC 2007 Results (2007), http://www.pascal-network.org/challenges/VOC/voc2007/workshop/index.html

A Template-Based Approach for Real-Time Speed-Limit-Sign Recognition on an Embedded System Using GPU Computing

Pınar Muyan-Özçelik[1], Vladimir Glavtchev[1,2], Jeffrey M. Ota[2], and John D. Owens[1]

[1] University of California, Davis, CA
[2] BMW Group Technology Office, Palo Alto, CA

Abstract. We present a template-based pipeline that performs real-time speed-limit-sign recognition using an embedded system with a low-end GPU as the main processing element. Our pipeline operates in the frequency domain, and uses nonlinear composite filters and a contrast-enhancing preprocessing step to improve its accuracy. Running at interactive rates, our system achieves 90% accuracy over 120 EU speed-limit signs on 45 minutes of video footage, superior to the 75% accuracy of a non-real-time GPU-based SIFT pipeline.

1 Introduction

As object recognition systems continue to increase in accuracy and robustness, we are beginning to see their deployment in real-time applications. In this work we target *real-time embedded systems*: systems that can interact with the real world at interactive rates using embedded processors. The low cost of embedded systems—an order of magnitude below typical CPUs—make them suitable for use in a variety of domains, including the automotive application space that we analyze here. However, meeting real-time performance requirements with the modest computational resources of these embedded processors, particularly with a parallel processing model, presents an important research challenge.

In this study, we aim to address this challenge and perform real-time speed-limit-sign recognition on an embedded platform. To achieve our goal, we leverage the inherent parallelism in the recognition task using Graphics Processing Unit (GPU) computing and construct our pipeline from modular components. The data-parallel nature of recognition tasks is an excellent fit for an embedded, low-power, parallel processor such as the low-end GPU we use in this study. In addition, the GPU offers superior price-performance and power-performance to comparable processors. Hence, in our pipeline we implement template-based recognition techniques that are well-suited to the GPU architecture. In addition, we built our approach from modular parts that can be extended or contracted. We discuss how one can make the best use of the limited resources of underlying hardware by fine-tuning the parameters of these separate components based on the tradeoff between the runtime and success rate in Section 5.

M. Goesele et al. (Eds.): DAGM 2010, LNCS 6376, pp. 162–171, 2010.

As GPUs have become programmable, they have been increasingly used for applications beyond traditional graphics that require general-purpose computation [1]. The computer vision domain is one of the domains GPUs have provided significant performance improvements (e.g. Fung et al.'s OpenVIDIA project [2]). The advent of GPU computing has also allowed researchers to revisit older and simpler, but very effective, data-parallel techniques that have fallen out of favor due to their compute demands. Template-based object recognition in the computer vision literature is one of these techniques. For instance, several other template-based road sign recognition approaches (Section 2) have leveraged template-based techniques. However, to the best of our knowledge, none of these previous studies provided real-time recognition of road signs on an embedded system. They employed commodity computers or optical devices to meet the compute demands of their approaches. Using GPU computing, we parallelize the time-consuming computation of template-based recognition and provide real-time performance on an embedded domain. In addition to being suitable to the GPU architecture, another advantage of using a template-based approach is that our pipeline can be easily modified to recognize other objects, such as US speed-limit signs or other salient road features.

In the computer vision literature, the Scale Invariant Feature Transform (SIFT) [3] is a commonly used method for performing object recognition. Hence, in order to evaluate our template-based approach, we also implement a SIFT-based speed-limit-sign recognition system on the GPU and compare these two approaches. Our results (Section 5) show that the template-based pipeline provides a higher success rate and faster runtime than the SIFT-based pipeline.

2   Previous Work

One of the approaches used for template-based road sign recognition is conventional template matching, in which cross-correlation is calculated between the template and the part of the scene of the same size to measure the match. In the literature, several studies use conventional template matching in the final classification stage of the recognition pipeline, after the candidate road signs are detected [4, 5]. Conventional template matching is not the preferred technique for sign detection because searching the candidate road sign location with this approach needs many cross-correlation computations between the templates and different parts of the scene of the same size. Since this is a convolution-type operation, it requires a long computation time. In order to reduce the search space and thus, the runtime of the conventional template matching, Betke and Makris [6] proposed using simulated annealing.

There are other template-based approaches that also involve a convolution-type operation. To detect the potential road signs, Gavrila [7] proposed matching the template and the scene using distance transforms; Cyganek [8] presented a system that operates on the Gaussian scale-space and does template matching in the log-polar domain.

Several studies in the field of optics have also investigated the template-based recognition of road signs in the frequency space [9,10,11]. They proposed systems that perform FFT correlation between the scene and the filters generated from the templates. Drawing upon this technique, Javidi et al. [12] presented an offline system to perform speed-limit-sign recognition that is most similar in spirit to our implementation.

Some other studies in the literature make use of color information to perform template-based road sign recognition [13,14]. In our approach we cannot utilize these techniques, since we are working with grayscale videos.

3   Approach

With our approach, we have chosen to perform template-based matching in the frequency space, since it provides a faster runtime than the approaches that perform convolution-type operations. FFT correlation involves taking the FFT of both the template and the scene, multiplying the complex conjugate of the FFT of the template with the FFT of the scene, and taking the inverse Fourier transform of the product. Hence, instead of computing many match values using a convolution, we can perform one multiplication in the frequency domain, which is more efficient. Another advantage of working in the frequency space is that it allows us to perform some operations in the Fourier domain to improve the matching performance (e.g. kth-Law, explained below).

FFT-based recognition studies in the optics literature propose correlating the scene with *composite filters* instead of the templates. Composite filters are generated from several templates and can be thought of as "combination templates". The advantage of one composite filter instead of several templates is that it reduces the number of correlations we need to perform and thus, provides faster runtime.

Synthetic discriminant functions (SDF) [15] are one of the popular techniques for generating composite filters. From the several variations of SDF filters, we have chosen to work with the MACE (Minimum Average Correlation Energy) SDF filter [16] due to its low false alarm rate. On the road, several objects may look like a speed-limit sign. The MACE filter provides a high discrimination ability against these impostor objects.

Performing a FFT correlation between the scene and the composite filter produces a correlation plane. The MACE filter minimizes the average correlation energy of the correlation plane and produces a sharp distinct peak where the object is located. We first Fourier-transform the templates we would like to include in the filter and then perform MACE filter synthesis using these transforms.

Although the MACE filter provides good discrimination, it alone does not provide sufficient accuracy. In addition, we needed to improve the *illumination invariance* of our system. To address these challenges, we extend the MACE filter by applying kth-Law nonlinearity [17], which improves the peak sharpness. The nonlinear operation raises the magnitude of the Fourier transform to the power of k, while keeping its original phase. In order to compute a FFT correlation between the scene and a kth-Law MACE filter, we apply a kth-Law nonlinear operation to the FFT of the scene before it is multiplied with the complex conjugate of the kth-Law MACE filter.

Several metrics can evaluate the goodness of the match in correlations. Since the kth-Law MACE filter is designed to suppress the sidelobes adjacent to peaks in the correlation plane, we use PSR (Peak-to-Sidelobe Ratio) [18], which measures the peak sharpness by taking into account the small area around the peak.

Kth-Law nonlinearity produces enhanced illumination invariance, but still misses many cases with low contrast. Hence, we add a *histogram equalization* preprocessing step in our system to improve the contrast of the scene. This technique involves adjusting the intensity values of the scene to equally distribute intensities throughout the whole brightness scale. However, since histogram equalization adjusts the values based on the statistics collected from the entire image, it misses some details. Speed-limit signs usually appear in small regions of the scenes. Hence, it is critical for us to bring out as much image detail as possible: we thus use "Contrast Limited Adaptive Histogram Equalization" (CLAHE) [19] to enhance the contrast of the scene. This algorithm divides the image into small tiles and performs histogram equalization on these small local regions instead of the entire image, thus bringing out more small-scale detail.

4   Implementation

Template-based speed-limit-sign recognition pipeline. The template-based pipeline has four main stages: preprocessing, detection, classification, and temporal integration. Figure 1.a shows the overview of this pipeline. We generate composite filters offline and input them to our system.

The composite filters used in the detection stage are more general than the ones used in the classification stage. They are generated from the templates 00 and 100, which helps with detecting two-digit and three-digit signs, respectively.

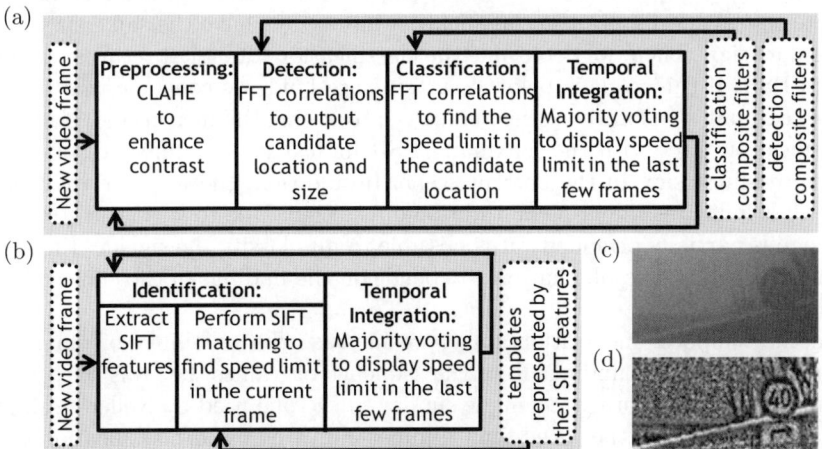

Fig. 1. (a) Template-based pipeline (b) SIFT-based pipeline (c) Before CLAHE (d) After CLAHE

On the other hand, we generate a different set of classification filters for each speed-limit sign we would like to recognize. Both detection and classification filters integrate different out-of-plane rotations of the templates. This allows the system to have rotation invariance along the X and Y axes. In addition, both type of filters have different sizes, which allows the system to have scale invariance. For each size, we have classification filters with different in-plane rotations, which provides the system with rotation invariance along the Z axis. EU speed-limit signs have circular shapes, which are somewhat insensitive to in-plane rotations when the number inside the sign is not considered. To recognize signs with shapes that are more sensitive to in-plane rotations (e.g. triangles), we can also generate in-plane rotations of detection filters to improve accuracy. We set the background of the templates to gray, which helps in recognizing signs of both dark or light backgrounds. We do not include different sizes and in-plane rotations of the templates in the creation of composite filters, because these images typically have higher changes in energy when compared to images that represent different out-of-plane rotations of the templates. Moreover, the number of images we can include in a composite filter is limited.

The effect of the preprocessing stage is shown in Figures 1.c–d. After CLAHE is applied to the scene, the speed-limit sign becomes more visible. Although the "after" scene looks fairly different than the "before" scene due to the noise introduced by CLAHE, the template-based approach we pursue works very well with these kind of preprocessed images.

In the detection stage, we first perform a FFT correlation between the scene and the detection composite filters. Then, we determine the detection filter that returns the maximum PSR. The location of the peak value in the correlation plane generated by this detection filter indicates the location of the candidate sign. Likewise, the size of this composite filter indicates the size of the candidate sign.

We start the classification stage by performing FFT correlations between the classification composite filters and the part of the scene that includes the candidate sign. We only use the classification filters that have the same size as the candidate sign. Then, we determine the classification filter that returns the maximum PSR. If this value is below a certain threshold, we conclude that there is no speed-limit signs in the scene and start processing the next frame. If not, the classification filter with the maximum PSR indicates the number displayed by the speed-limit sign in the current scene. In addition, the in-plane rotation of this filter indicates the in-plane rotation of the sign. Due to various factors (e.g. the sign is partially occluded), it is possible to misclassify the signs in the scene. Hence, providing a result that only depends on the findings of the current frame is not reliable.

In the temporal integration stage, we increase the reliability of our results by accumulating the findings from the sequence of frames. For this purpose, we employ a majority voting technique similar to the one used by Keller et al. [20]. Each frame votes for the speed-limit number indicated by its classification stage. The maximum PSR determined at this stage is used as the base vote value. If the previous frame also voted for the same number, the vote is increased by multiplying the base value with a constant factor when one or both of the following conditions are met: 1) the size of the sign is not decreasing; 2) in-plane rotation of the sign remains the same. After all the frames in the sequence are processed, we display the speed-limit number that collected the most votes over a given threshold as the final result.

Since most operations of our implementation of a template-based approach are data-parallel, this pipeline is suitable to be implemented on the GPU. We use NVIDIA's CUFFT library to take inverse and forward FFTs. We wrote kernels to apply kth-Law nonlinearity to the FFT of the scene, to take the complex conjugate of the composite filter in frequency domain, to multiply these two FFTs, and to normalize the result of this product. In addition, we find the peak in the correlation plane with a GPU kernel that performs a reduction operation. Currently, we use optimized C code to apply CLAHE. However, this operation has several data-parallel parts and could be mapped to the GPU to further improve runtime.

SIFT-based speed-limit-sign recognition pipeline. The SIFT-based pipeline has two main stages: identification and temporal integration. Figure 1.b shows the overview of this pipeline. We extract the SIFT features of the templates offline and input them to our system. The templates we use in this pipeline are the same templates we use in the template-based pipeline to generate the composite filters.

In the identification stage, we first extract SIFT features of the scene. Then, we perform SIFT matching between the features of the scene and templates. We use SiftGPU [21], an open source GPU implementation of SIFT, for feature extraction and matching. To improve the performance, we reject a match if the orientation difference of the matched keys is larger than a certain threshold (as proposed by Kuş et al. [22]). Next, we search for a template that returns the maximum number of matches over a certain threshold to determine whether we have a speed-limit sign in the current frame. Finally, we accumulate findings from a sequence of frames in the temporal integration stage by employing similar techniques we use in the template-based pipeline.

5   Results and Discussion

Template-based versus SIFT-based pipeline. Our EU speed-limit-sign recognition test data is a collection of grayscale videos recorded in different weather (e.g. sunny, foggy, rainy, and snowy) and road (e.g. highway, in the city, and country) conditions in Europe. In total, we use footage captured from 45 minutes of driving that includes 120 EU speed-limit signs. Video size is 640x240. We have run our experiments on a laptop equipped with an Intel Core2 Duo P8600 2.4 GHz CPU and a GeForce 9600M GT, a laptop graphics card comparable in performance to next-generation embedded GPUs.

The runtime of the template-based pipeline is 18.5 fps. Since our video capture rate is slower, we are able to process all frames in real time with template-based approach. Computation time for the SIFT-based pipeline increases with the number of keypoints extracted from an image and for a frame with moderate complexity the runtime is around 120 ms/frame (~8 fps), which is slower than the video capture rate. Hence, the SIFT-based pipeline does not provide real-time performance. The SIFT-based approach has a slower runtime than the template-based one on our resource-constrained GPU, since it consists of different stages that are computationally intensive and require a large GPU memory.

The template-based pipeline returned a 90% success rate with no misclassifi-cations or false positives. An offline run of the SIFT-based pipeline provided a 75% success rate with four misclassifications and nine false positives. The SIFT-based approach has a lower success rate mainly due to two reasons. First, SIFT recognition works best when objects have some complexity. However, speed-limit signs have simple shapes and constant color regions and do not have any texture. In addition, they usually appear small in the videos. Thus, often SIFT cannot extract enough distinct features from these signs and the same number of matches are returned by different templates. Secondly, we could not use CLAHE in the SIFT-based pipeline. Applying CLAHE on the template-based pipeline improved our success rate from 65% to 90% and eliminated all misclassifications and false positives. However, since SIFT cannot handle the noise introduced by CLAHE, we could not utilize this technique in the SIFT-based pipeline.

Both pipelines perform well in simple cases as well as several challenging cases. Both reject signs that have a dominant difference. Because of the thick line that crosses the whole sign, an end-of-50 sign (Figure 2.1) can be distinguished from a speed-limit sign. Both also recognize signs with insignificant modifications. Figure 2.2 depicts a speed-limit sign with a small stain in the digit 0.

We see several cases where the template-based pipeline succeeds and the SIFT-based pipeline fails:

• The template-based approach capably recognizes small signs (e.g. Figure 2.3). As the sign gets closer, we see a larger viewpoint change and thus, recognition becomes harder. As a result, in some cases the SIFT-based pipeline misclassifies the speed-limit sign, since it does not start recognizing the sign when it is far and small. In the SIFT-based pipeline, in order to recognize small signs, we doubled

1) **none**, *none*   2) **60**, *60*   3) **30**, *none* 4) **100**, *none* 5) **30**, *none*

6) **60**, *none*   7) **120**, *none* 8) **none**, *20* 9) **none**, *70* 10) **none**, *none*

Fig. 2. Scene examples: **Template-based** and *SIFT-based* pipeline results shown in **bold** and *italic*, respectively.

the image size and reduced the initial Gaussian blur. Even if these improvements were helpful, they were not effective enough to recognize smaller signs such as the one in Figure 2.3.

• The template-based pipeline is better at handling different kind of noise introduced by effects such as motion blur (Figure 2.4) and partial shade (Figure 2.5). Our template-based approach is resistant to noise, allowing us to use CLAHE. By applying CLAHE, we can recognize hard cases such as when the sun is behind the sign (Figure 2.6) or a light beam effect (Figure 2.7). In order to recognize low contrast cases with a SIFT-based pipeline, we have decreased the threshold used to select potential keypoints. Although this change has provided some improvement, it was not effective enough for recognizing very-low-contrast cases such as Figure 2.6.

• The template-based approach is better at recognizing signs as a whole. Since the SIFT-based pipeline deals with features that are local, it can misclassify signs that look like only part of a sign. For instance, a 2-meter-width-limit sign in Figure 2.8 is misclassified as a 20 km/h speed-limit sign by the SIFT-based approach, since the digit "2" in both signs looks very similar.

We also see cases where the SIFT-based pipeline succeeds and the template-based pipeline fails:

• Although dealing with local features causes the SIFT-based approach to miss the big picture and fail in Figure 2.8, it becomes an advantage for recognizing partially occluded signs. For instance, SIFT-based pipeline performs better than template-based approach in Figure 2.9, where the sign is partially occluded by snow.

• The SIFT-based pipeline is good at recognizing signs with large rotations as well as the ones that initially appear large in the videos. In order to recognize these signs with the template-based pipeline, we need to cover larger rotations and bigger sizes with composite filters, which in turn would increase our runtime.

In some cases, both template-based and SIFT-based approaches fail:

• Although the template-based pipeline succeeds where the SIFT-based approach has problems recognizing small signs (e.g. Figure 2.3), if the signs get even smaller, template-based also starts missing them. Including an additional composite filter with smaller sizes does not help since it introduces misclassifications and false positives.

• Both pipelines perform poorly when a big part of the sign is missing. For instance, in Figure 2.10 a big part of the sign is not visible due to the bright sunshine.

Template-based pipeline parameter study. With additional computational resources, we could perform more computation and achieve higher accuracy. With an embedded system and its limited computational capabilities, however, we instead conducted a parameter study to answer the question "given a fixed amount of compute resources, what is the best way to allocate those resources to achieve maximum accuracy?" We thus varied our base configuration, which consisted of five sizes [25 30 35 40 45], three in-plane rotations $[-6° \ 0° \ 6°] = [0° \ \mp 6°]$, seven out-of-plane rotations along the Y-axis $[0° \ \mp 10° \ \mp 20° \ \mp 30°]$, and three out-of-plane rotations along X-axis $[0° \mp 10°]$, all run on a 4-SM GPU. We found these parameters were well-suited for maximum accuracy on our base hardware platform.

Varying each of these parameters allowed us to extend or contract different modules of our template-based pipeline. Hence, this parameter study also provides insights for making recommendations to achieve optimum performance when we are given less or more compute power. Space prevents us from describing the detailed results, but we draw the following conclusions from these experiments. With less compute power available, we could choose to reduce the number of frames per second that we analyze, but instead a better option is to process only the smaller sizes of signs at a higher frame rate. With more compute power, we can achieve higher accuracy in three principal ways: increase the processing frame rate, add larger sizes of signs, and generate additional composite filters with larger out-of-plane rotations.

6   Conclusion

Our work addresses the main challenge of meeting the real-time performance requirements of speed-limit-sign recognition with limited hardware resources. To achieve this goal, we exploit the inherit parallelism in this task using GPU computing and build our pipeline from parameterized modules. Our template-based pipeline is suitable to be implemented on the GPU and can be easily modified to recognize other salient road features. Our future work includes expanding the breath of detected objects (US signs and other signs of different types), investigating other vision tasks (such as optical flow to detect potential collisions), and developing software support for our data-parallel embedded system that can run multiple tasks simultaneously (such as vision, graphics, and speech recognition) while delivering throughput and/or latency guarantees.

Acknowledgements. Thanks to Szymon Rusinkiewicz, Jan-Michael Frahm, Ali Rahimi, James Davis, Bryan Catanzaro, Justus H. Piater, and Horst Bischof for their helpful suggestions and comments. Also, thanks to our funding agencies: UC MICRO award #08-57 with matching industrial support from BMW, NVIDIA, and Rambus, and the National Science Foundation (Award 0541448).

References

1. Owens, J.D., Luebke, D., Govindaraju, N., Harris, M., Krüger, J., Lefohn, A.E., Purcell, T.: A survey of general-purpose computation on graphics hardware. Computer Graphics Forum 26(1), 80–113 (2007)
2. Fung, J., Mann, S., Aimone, C.: OpenVIDIA: Parallel GPU computer vision. In: ACM Multimedia, pp. 849–852 (2005)
3. Lowe, D.G.: Distinctive image features from scale-invariant keypoints. Int. J. Comput. Vision 60(2), 91–110 (2004)
4. Piccioli, G., De Micheli, E., Parodi, P., Campani, M.: Robust road sign detection and recognition from image sequences. In: IEEE IV, pp. 278–283 (1994)

5. Miura, J., Tsuyoshi, K., Shirai, Y.: An active vision system for real-time traffic sign recognition. In: IEEE ITSC, pp. 52–57 (2000)
6. Betke, M., Makris, N.C.: Fast object recognition in noisy images using simulated annealing. In: IEEE ICCV, pp. 523–530 (1995)
7. Gavrila, D.: Traffic sign recognition revisited. In: DAGM, pp. 86–93 (1999)
8. Cyganek, B.: Road signs recognition by the scale-space template matching in the log-polar domain. In: Martí, J., Benedí, J.M., Mendonça, A.M., Serrat, J. (eds.) IbPRIA. LNCS, vol. 4477, pp. 330–337. Springer, Heidelberg (2007)
9. Guibert, L., Keryer, G., Servel, A., Attia, M., MacKenzie, H., Pellat-Finet, P., de Bourgrenet de la Tocnaye, J.: On-board optical joint transform correlator for real-time road sign recognition. Opt. Eng. 34(1), 135–143 (1995)
10. Taniguchi, M., Mokuno, Y., Kintaka, K., Matsuoka, K.: Correlation filter design for classification of road sign by multiple optical correlators. In: SPIE, vol. 3804, pp. 140–147 (1999)
11. Perez, E., Javidi, B.: Nonlinear distortion-tolerant filters for detection of road signs in background noise. IEEE Transactions on Vehicular Technology 51(3), 567–576 (2002)
12. Javidi, B., Castro, M.A., Kishk, S., Perez, E.: Automated detection and analysis of speed limit signs. Technical Report JHR 02-285, University of Connecticut (2002)
13. Torresen, J., Bakke, W.J., Sekanina, L.: Efficient recognition of speed limit signs. In: IEEE ITSC, pp. 652–656 (2004)
14. Hsu, S.H., Huang, C.L.: Road sign detection and recognition using matching pursuit method. Image and Vision Computing 19(3), 119–129 (2001)
15. Casasent, D.: Unified synthetic discriminant function computational formulation. Appl. Opt. 23(10), 1620–1627 (1984)
16. Mahalanobis, A., Kumar, B.V.K.V., Casasent, D.: Minimum average correlation energy filters. Appl. Opt. 26(17), 3633–3640 (1987)
17. Javidi, B., Painchaud, D.: Distortion-invariant pattern recognition with fourier-plane nonlinear filters. Appl. Opt. 35(2), 318–331 (1996)
18. Savvides, M., Kumar, B.V., Khosla, P.: Face verification using correlation filters. In: IEEE AutoID, pp. 56–61 (2002)
19. Zuiderveld, K.: Contrast limited adaptive histogram equalization. In: Graphics Gems IV, pp. 474–485 (1994)
20. Keller, C.G., Sprunk, C., Bahlmann, C., Giebel, J., Baratoff, G.: Real-time recognition of U.S. speed signs. In: IEEE IV, pp. 518–523 (2008)
21. Wu, C.: SiftGPU: A GPU implementation of scale invariant feature transform, SIFT (2007), http://cs.unc.edu/~ccwu/siftgpu
22. Kuş, M.C., Gökmen, M., Etaner-Uyar, A.S.: Traffic sign recognition using scale invariant feature transform and color classification. In: ISCIS, pp. 1–6 (2008)

Inpainting in Multi-image Stereo

Arnav V. Bhavsar and Ambasamudram N. Rajagopalan

Image Processing and Computer Vision Lab
Dept. of Electrical Engineering
Indian Institute of Technology Madras

Abstract. In spite of numerous works on inpainting, there has been little work addressing both image and structure inpainting. In this work,
we propose a new method for inpainting both image and depth of a
scene using multiple stereo images. The observations contain unwanted
artifacts, which can be possibly caused due to sensor/lens damage or occluders. In such a case, all the observations contain missing regions which
are stationary with respect to the image coordinate system. We exploit
the fact that the information missing in some images may be present in
other images due to the motion cue. This includes the correspondence
information for depth estimation/inpainting as well as the color information for image inpainting. We establish our approaches in the belief
propagation (BP) framework which also uses the segmentation cue for
estimation/inpainting of depth maps.

1 Introduction

Of the computer vision problems recognized and addressed in the last decade,
inpainting has gained a lot of popularity. Arguably, one reason for this may
be its practical utility in fixing damages or removing unwanted occlusions in
images, solely through software. Although earlier works on inpainting mainly
considered only single images, in recent years problems in various domains have
been recognized that may be treated under the aegis of inpainting. These include
fixing damages due to lens/sensor distortions in real-aperture images, filling
missing regions in range images, occlusion removal using stereo images etc.

In this work we address the problem of inpainting depth as well as image
given multiple stereo observations captured from a single moving camera all of
which contain missing regions as a result of artifacts in images. The presence of
such artifacts can be typically attributed to common sensor and lens defects in
cameras. For instance, dust and humidity can enter the camera assembly and
contaminate the sensor [1]. Parts of sensors can also be damaged if exposed to
bright sunlight. Lenses can suffer from local damage due to shocks and climatic
effects. Occlusions due to small unwanted depositions/attachments on the lenses
[2,3] etc can also result in such image defects.

We wish to estimate the image as well as the depth map from a reference view
with such missing regions coherently inpainted. Our approach involves using the
motion cue, present in the stereo images for inpainting. The central idea is that

M. Goesele et al. (Eds.): DAGM 2010, LNCS 6376, pp. 172–181, 2010.

the missing regions which are caused due to corruptions in the camera, have a fixed location in all images while the scene objects undergo an apparent motion depending on their depth. Our approach exploits this phenomena to *discover* pixels, missing in the reference image, in other images and computes the correspondence/color for the missing pixels. We establish our estimation approach within an efficient belief propagation (BP) framework while also accounting for pixel visibility and incorporating the segmentation cue.

1.1   Related Work

Since its inception, the inpainting problem has been mainly addressed for color images [4,5]. Recent works on filling in sensor/lens damage have been reported in [2,3,1]. These approaches operate on single images and compute plausible color values to be filled in the missing regions typically using neighbourhood information in some sense. Unlike, our approach their goal does not encompass depth estimation/inpainting. On the other hand, there exist some works which address the inpainting problem in depth/range maps [6,7] and 3D meshes [8]. However, these approaches work directly with damaged range maps/3D meshes as input and do not involve inpainting color/intensity images.

The dis-occlusion problem in novel view synthesis is similar to inpainting [9]. However, the primary goal of dis-occlusion is to fill in the regions in the novel view where data is not available due to stereo-occlusions, whereas we consider the problem of filling missing regions in the reference image using damaged observations. Although, both problems involve filling in missing data, our inpainting framework is considerably different than that used for dis-occlusion.

Inpainting both images and depth given color/intensity images of the scene with missing data, has received relatively less attention. To our knowledge, only the recent reported works in [10,11] closely relate to ours, which exploit the pixel motion for inpainting. The authors in [11] address the problem in a binocular stereo setting [11]. They consider the case of removing occluders present in the scene. Their approach requires a priori computation of complete depth maps (with the occluders) from both the views. The occluders are then removed as a second step. In contrast to [11], our work inpaints the effects lens/sensor damage, in which case the pixel mapping is quite different. Our method computes the inpainted depth map in a single step and we need to compute the depth map only from the reference view. The work in [10] consider the effects of pixel motion under a shape-from-focus setting. Their approach handles the inpainting problem implicitly as opposed to our approach which explicitly checks for missing pixels. Moreover, unlike in [10] we also consider the occlusion effects and incorporate a cue from image segmentation to improve our estimates. Also, we employ belief propagation as opposed to the inefficient simulated annealing used in [10].

2   Methodology

Given stereo images with marked damaged/occluded regions, we wish to estimate the depth map (from the reference view) where correct/plausible depth values are assigned even in the areas where the observation is missing. Moreover, given this estimated depth map, we also wish to estimate the color information in the missing regions in the (reference) image. Our estimation process employs the efficient-BP algorithm [12], which involves computing messages and beliefs on an image-sized grid where a label is assigned to each node. The messages and beliefs are expressed as data and prior costs. In the subsequent sections, we describe these cost definitions for our problems.

2.1 Depth Inpainting

We begin by marking missing regions in all the observations, since all of them will be affected due to the damage. The locations of the missing pixels do not vary in the image coordinate system since they are a part of the camera and undergo the same motion as the camera. However, pixels locations corresponding to scene points do change in the image. Hence, pixels missing in the reference image may be observed in other images. Thus, even if correspondences cannot be found between the reference image and other images, they may yet be established between other images. We now formalize these ideas in our cost computation. Since the BP algorithm considers computing costs for every label at each node, the costs described below are for a particular label at a particular node (pixel).

2.1.1 Cost Computation

We denote the set of missing pixels as M. We arrange the images in an (arbitrary) order $(g_1, g_2, ..., g_N)$ with g_1 being the reference image. Below we describe the data cost computation in various cases for missing pixels.

Case 1 - Pixel not missing in any of the images: For pixels $\notin M$ for the reference and the ith image, the data cost at a pixel (l_1, l_2) between them is the same as used for the stereo problem.

$$E_{di}(l_1, l_2) = |g_1(l_1, l_2) - g_i(\theta_{1i}, \theta_{2i})| \tag{1}$$

where $(\theta_{1i}, \theta_{2i})$ is the warped location in the ith, which depends on the camera motion and the depth label Z for which the cost is computed.

To consider occlusion we modulate the data cost with a visibility term $V_i(l_1, l_2)$ which switches on/off depending on whether a pixel is visible or occluded in the ith image. The resultant data cost is

$$E_{di}(l_1, l_2) = V_1(l_1, l_2) \cdot |g_1(l_1, l_2) - g_i(\theta_{1i}, \theta_{2i})| \tag{2}$$

For the first iteration, all pixels are considered visible. In subsequent iterations, V_i is computed by warping the current depth estimate to the ith view. We also use geo-consistency to update visibility temporally [13]. The total data cost between the reference image ($i = 1$) and all other images ($i > 1$) is then computed as

$$E_d = \frac{1}{N_i} \sum_i E_{di} \tag{3}$$

where N_i is the total number of images excluding the reference image where the pixel is visible. We note that we select the reference image such that, in a standard stereo scenario (with no missing regions), a pixel will always be visible in at least two observations. Hence, N_i in the above equation can never go to 0.

Case 2 - Pixel missing in reference image but not in the ith image: In the case where $g_1(l_1, l_2) \in M$, we need to *inpaint* the depth value at (l_1, l_2) by searching for the correspondence between images other than the reference. We compute the coordinates $(\theta_{1i}, \theta_{2i})$ and $(\theta_{1j}, \theta_{2j})$ for a depth label. If $g_i(\theta_{1i}, \theta_{2i}) \notin M$ and $g_j(\theta_{1j}, \theta_{2j}) \notin M$, the matching cost between them is defined as

$$E_{di}(l_1, l_2) = V_{ij}^c(l_1, l_2) \cdot |g_i(\theta_{1i}, \theta_{2i}) - g_j(\theta_{1j}, \theta_{2j})| \tag{4}$$

where $1 < i < j$ and the visibility V_{ij}^c is a *compound* visibility term defined as

$$V_{ij}^c(l_1, l_2) = V_i(l_1, l_2)V_j(l_1, l_2) \tag{5}$$

The idea behind defining the *compound* visibility is that the data cost is not computed if a pixel is not observed in either the ith or the jth view.

The corresponding total data cost for $g_1(l_1, l_2)$ involving all images for a depth label is then computed by summing the matching costs as

$$E_d = \frac{1}{N_i} \sum_i E_{di} \tag{6}$$

Here N_i are the number of pairs of images g_i and g_j such that $g_i(\theta_{1i}, \theta_{2i}) \notin M$ and $g_j(\theta_{1j}, \theta_{2j}) \notin M$ and $V_i(l_1, l_2) \neq 0$. Thus, the cost for a pixel missing in the reference image is computed by using those images in which the pixel is visible. In case $N_i = 0$, the pixel is left unlabeled.

Case 3 - Pixels missing in the ith image but not in the reference image: Finally, if a pixel $g_1(l_1, l_2) \notin M$ and $g_i(\theta_{1i}, \theta_{2i}) \in M$ for some $i > 1$ then the data cost between the reference view and the ith view is not computed. In case, $g_j(\theta_{1i}, \theta_{2i}) \in M \; \forall i$, then the pixel is left unlabeled.

To regularize the estimation, the MRF prior enforces smoothness between neighbouring nodes. Moreover, since we also wish to avoid over-smoothing of the prominent discontinuities, we define the smoothness prior cost as a truncated absolute function stated as

$$E_p(n_1, n_2, m_1, m_2) = \min(|Z(n_1, n_2) - Z(m_1, m_2)|, T) \tag{7}$$

where, $Z(n_1, n_2)$ and $Z(m_1, m_2)$ are depth labels for neighbouring nodes and T is the threshold for truncation used for allowing discontinuities.

2.1.2   Segmentation Cue for Depth Inpainting

The estimation process using the cost computation described above, can yield pixels which are not labeled (for which no correspondences can be found). Moreover, as in the depth estimation process, some of the pixels can also be labeled incorrectly. We use the cue from image segmentation to mitigate such errors. The segmentation cue exploits a natural pattern of depth discontinuities coinciding with image discontinuities. Moreover, given a sufficiently over segmented image, each image segment can be assumed to have a planar depth variation.

Initially, we color-segment the reference image using the mean-shift algorithm and classify the pixels as reliable or unreliable. The first BP iteration is run without using the segmentation cue. We then compute a plane-fitted depth map that uses the current estimate, the segmented image and the reliable pixels. The plane-fitting for each segment is carried out via RANSAC. For more details please refer to [14]. We feed the plane-fitted depth back to the iteration process to regularize the data term as

$$E_{ds}(l_1, l_2) = E_d(l_1, l_2) + w(l_1, l_2) \cdot |Z(l_1, l_2) - Z_p(l_1, l_2)| \tag{8}$$

where $E_d(l_1, l_2)$ is the previously defined data cost. Z_p denotes the plane-fitted depth map and the weight w is 0/1 if the pixel is reliable/unreliable. Note that the above energy is also defined at each pixel (l_1, l_2). In fact, it is same energy as described in equations 3 or 6 supplemented with a second term which uses the plane fitted depth map. This term regularizes the unreliable depth estimates such that their labels are close to that of plane-fitted depth map. We use this more general data cost in subsequent iterations after the first.

Note, however, that the color segmentation of damaged observations will yield some segments due to the missing regions. For brevity, we denote a set of such segments by S_m. Each such segment will span across largely different depth values, thus disobeying the very premise for the use of the segmentation cue. Hence, we cannot use such segments to compute the plane-fitted depth map.

To address this issue, we assign the pixels in S_m to the closest segment $\notin S_m$. This essentially extends the segments neighbouring to those in S_m. The *closeness* is determined by searching in eight directions from a pixel. The plane-fitted depth map is then computed using the reliable pixels in these extended segments, (including reliable pixels from segments which were earlier in S_m). The plane-fitted depth map is fed back into the estimation process in the next iteration where the unlabeled pixels are labeled because of the regularizer depending on the plane-fitted depth map. Further iterations help to improve the estimates.

2.2 Image Inpainting

Given the estimated depth map, we now wish to estimate the color labels for the missing pixels in the reference image. We search for pixel color in images other than the reference that map to the missing regions in the reference image. If the pixels at the mapped locations $\notin M$, we use them in our data cost computation.

The data cost for image inpainting compares the intensities of $g_i(\theta_{1i}, \theta_{2i})$ $i > 1$ with an intensity label, if $g_i(\theta_{1i}, \theta_{2i}) \notin M$. This data cost for a particular $g_i(\theta_{1i}, \theta_{2i}) \notin M$ and an intensity label L is defined as

$$E_{di}(l_1, l_2) = V_i(l_1, l_2) \cdot |L - g_i(\theta_{1i}, \theta_{2i})| \tag{9}$$

The total data cost is sum of the N_i data costs similar to that described by equation 6, where N_i is the number of images where $g_i(\theta_{1i}, \theta_{2i}) \notin M \ i > 1$. The smoothness cost for the image is also defined similar to that in equation 7, except that the intensity labels instead of depth labels are used.

Lastly, there may be missing pixels in g_1 for which $g_i(\theta_{1i}, \theta_{2i}) \in M \ \forall i$. Such pixels are left unlabeled. The extent of such unlabeled pixels depends on the original extent of the missing region and pixel motion. We observe in our experiments, that for most of the image the pixel motion is sufficient to leave no missing region unlabeled. The maximum extent of such unlabeled regions, if they exist at all, is up to 2-3 pixels while the original extent of missing regions is about 20 pixels. Such small unlabeled regions can be filled by any inpainting algorithm (for instance, the exemplar-based inpainting method [5]).

3   Experimental Results

We validate our approach via real experiments on the multiple stereo images from the Middlebury datasets. The more recent datasets contain complicated scenes with a variety of shapes, textures and intensity variations. This serves to test our approach quite extensively. We manually synthesized scratched masks and superimposed them on the color images to emulate the damaged observations.

We note that the success of our motion-based inpainting approach essentially depends on the size of the missing regions in the direction of the motion. Since our algorithm considers general camera motion, with a priori knowledge of the damage, one could decide on the camera motion which is suitable for inpainting. Thus, our approach is general enough to handle various magnitudes and direction of missing regions. Since the Middlebury images involve horizontal translation, we typically consider the horizontal extent of the scratches of the order of maximum pixel motion to better demonstrate our approach. Thus, widths of the scratches in our experiment (the minimum horizontal extent) were about 20-25 pixels, while their orientation, shapes, locations etc were arbitrary.

The processing time of our non-optimized Matlab implementation is about 15-20 mins (on a P4 Core 2 Duo processor with 2 GB RAM). The depth estimation part takes most of this time since it involves operating on the complete grid. The image inpainting, on the other hand, takes about a minute since it operates on only the missing pixels.

In each of the following examples we show six sub-figures (a-f), of which (a,b) correspond to two of the four observations used in the experiment, with (a) being the reference image. The sub-figures (d,e) depict the ground-truth and estimated depth map, respectively while sub-figures (c,f) show the ground-truth and the inpainted images from the reference view, respectively. The missing regions are shown by black scratches in the observations.

Our first example shows results for the *teddy* scene (Fig. 1). Note that the scratches span multiple depth labels and some of them cover a considerable distance along the height of the image. However, we note that the estimated depth map contains no traces of the scratches and matches closely with the ground-truth depth map. For instance, the long scratch imposed on a ramp-like

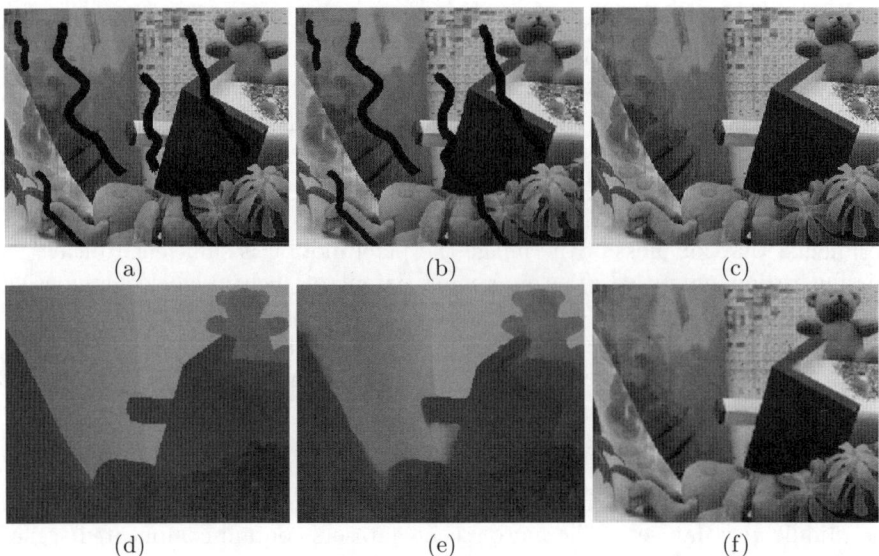

Fig. 1. Teddy scene: (a,b) Two of the four observations used in the experiment. (c) Original Image. (d,e) Ground-truth and estimated depth, respectively. (f) Inpainted image.

surface in the left-half of the image has completely disappeared leaving no artifacts in the estimated smooth depth variation. Also, the depth discontinuities are localized quite well, even when they cross the scratches (e.g. at the chimney in the center and the soft toy at the bottom). The image is also inpainted quite

Fig. 2. Dolls scene: (a,b) Two observations with artifacts. (c) Original Image. (d) Ground-truth depth map. (e) Estimated depth map. (f) Inpainted image.

coherently and is visually very close to the ground-truth image. This can be appreciated by noting the texture preservation at the scratched locations.

Our next example considers the *dolls* scene containing more complicated shapes and more extensive scratches (Fig. 2). Note that in this example, the scratches intersect larger number of depth layers than in the previous example. In spite of such complexities our approach seems to perform quite well. The estimated depth map, again does not contain any apparent signs of the damage. with the shapes well-defined and depth variations estimated close to the ground-truth. The inpainted image is visually identical to the ground-truth reference image with the edges and texture neatly preserved.

We next show results for the *moebius* scene which also contains many complex shapes (Fig. 3). Although one can notice some distortions in the estimated depth, these are quite small when one considers the complexity of the scene. Some of these errors are indeed due to scratches (e.g. the yellow tennis ball at the bottom), but at most places the scratches are successfully inpainted while maintaining the shapes. Note especially objects such as the yellow star at the top right and the green block at the bottom right, which have been localized quite well. The image is also inpainted with good fidelity with the complex edges and texture inpainted quite coherently. Indeed, the inpainted image also compares well with the ground-truth image.

Finally, we show a result on the *rocks* scene which does not contains various types of textures (Fig. 4). To add more variety, we use a different, but equally arbitrary, scratch pattern than the ones used earlier. Although the scene itself does not contain well-defined shapes, the estimated depth map does capture the

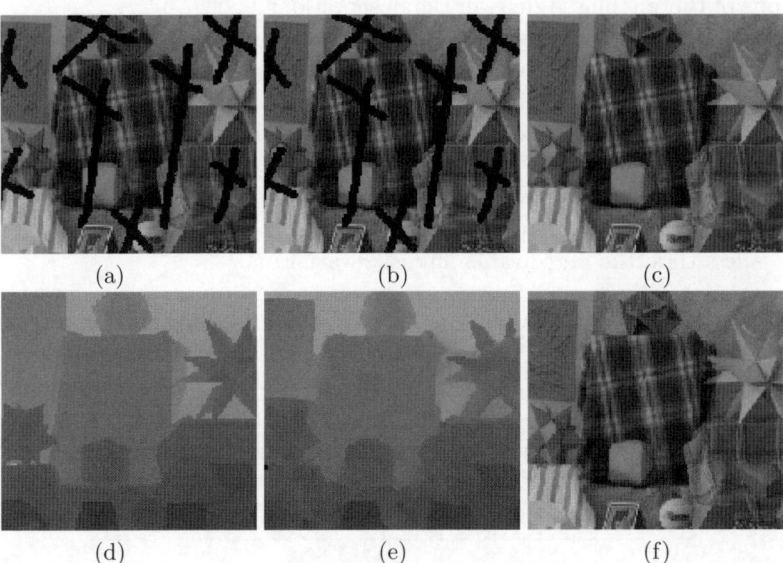

(a)   (b)   (c)

(d)   (e)   (f)

Fig. 3. Moebius scene:(a,b) Damaged observations. (c) Original image. (d,e) Ground-truth and estimated depth, respectively. (f) Inpainted image.

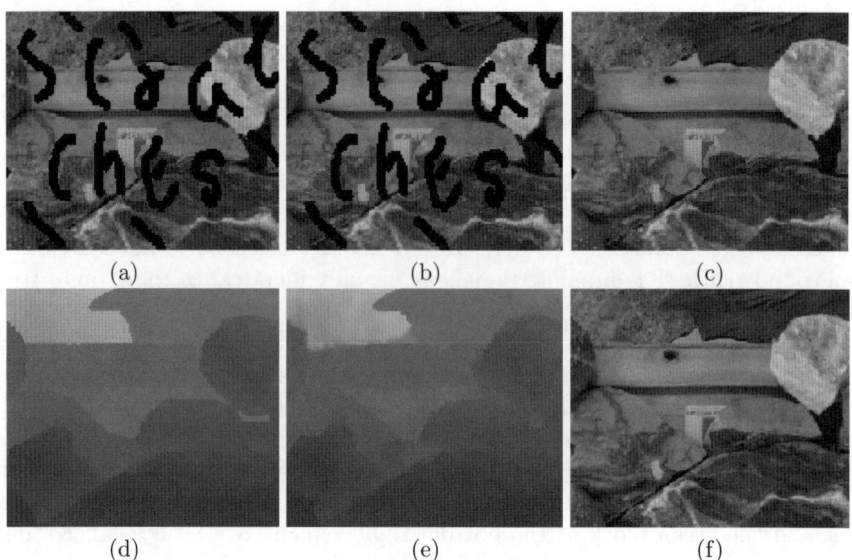

Fig. 4. Rocks scene: (a,b) Two of the four observations. (c) Original Image. (d,e) Ground-truth and estimated depth, respectively. (f) Inpainted image.

prominent shape boundaries and depth variations present in the ground-truth. Moreover our approach is also able to successfully to fill in the scratches. As a consequence, the inpainted image is again virtually no different from the ground-truth reference image, with no apparent distortions in the texture/shapes at the locations of the missing regions in the observations.

In Table 1, we provide the mean absolute error (MAE) with ground-truths, for depth estimation and image inpainting. The image inpainting error is only computed at the missing regions where the inpainting was carried out. For depth estimation, which was carried out on the complete grid, the error is computed at all pixels. The actual depth labels ranged from 15 to 20. Relatively, we observe that the error in depth estimation is very small (less than 5%). Similarly, the image error is also around 10 intensity levels (averaged over all color channels), which is less than the perceivable intensity variation.

Table 1. MAE for estimated depth and inpainted image

Scene	Depth estimation error	Image inpainting error
Teddy	0.68	11.06
Moebius	0.44	10.45
Dolls	0.39	16.71
Rocks	0.30	10.63

4   Conclusion

We proposed an approach to compute an inpainted depth map and image using multiple stereo observations with missing regions. Our approach exploited the motion cue to find correspondences/color information in some images if they are missing in others. We also used the segmentation cue to improve our depth estimates. We establish our inpainting method in the belief-propagation framework. In future, it would be interesting to consider defocus effects in our framework.

References

1. Zhou, C., Lin, S.: Removal of image artifacts due to sensor dust. In: Proc. IEEE Computer Society Conference on Computer Vision and Pattern Recognition (CVPR 2007), pp. 1–8 (2007)
2. Gu, J., Ramamoorthi, R., Belhumeur, P., Nayar, S.: Removing image artifacts due to dirty camera lenses and thin occluders. In: SIGGRAPH Asia 2909: ACM SIGGRAPH Asia 2009 papers, pp. 1–10 (2009)
3. Willson, R., Maimone, M., Johnson, A., Scherr, L.: An optical model for image artifacts produced by dust particles on lenses. In: International Symposium on Artificial Intelligence, Robtics and Automation in Space (2005)
4. Bertalmio, M., Sapiro, G., Caselles, V., Ballester, C.: Image inpainting. In: SIG-GRAPH 2000: Proceedings of the 27th annual conference on Computer graphics and interactive techniques, pp. 417–424 (2000)
5. Criminisi, A., Perez, P., Toyama, K.: Object removal by exemplar-based inpainting. In: Proc. IEEE Computer Society Conference on Computer Vision and Pattern Recognition (CVPR 2003), pp. 721–728 (2003)
6. Bhavsar, A.V., Rajagopalan, A.N.: Range map with missing data - joint resolution enhancement and inpainting. In: Indian Conference on Computer Vision, Graphics and Image Processing (ICVGIP 2008), pp. 359–365 (2008)
7. Mendez, T., Luz, A., Dudek, G.: Inter-image statistics for 3d environment modeling. Int. J. Comput. Vision 79(2) (2008)
8. Davis, J., Marschner, S., Garr, M., Levoy, M.: Filling holes in complex surfaces using volumetric diffusion. In: 3DPVT, pp. 428–438 (2002)
9. Cheng, C., Lin, S., Lai, S., Yang, J.: Improved novel view synthesis from depth image with large baseline. In: International Conference on Pattern Recognition, ICPR 2008 (2008)
10. Sahay, R., Rajagopalan, A.N.: Inpainting in shape from focus: Taking a cue from motion parallax. In: British Machine Vision Conference, BMVC 2009 (2009)
11. Wang, L., Jin, H., Yang, R., Gong, M.: Stereoscopic inpainting: Joint color and depth completion from stereo images. In: Proc. IEEE Computer Society Conference on Computer Vision and Pattern Recognition (CVPR 2008), pp. 1–8 (2008)
12. Felzenszwalb, P., Huttenlocher, D.: Efficient belief propagation for early vision. In: IEEE Computer Society Conference on Computer Vision and Pattern Recognition (CVPR 2004), vol. 1, pp. 261–268 (2004)
13. Drouin, M., Trudeau, M., Roy, S.: Geo-consistency for wide multi-camera stereo. In: IEEE Conference on Computer Vision and Pattern Recognition (CVPR 2005), vol. 1, pp. 351–358 (2005)
14. Bhavsar, A.V., Rajagopalan, A.N.: Depth estimation with a practical camera. In: British Machine Vision Conference, BMVC 2009 (2009)

Analysis of Length and Orientation of Microtubules in Wide-Field Fluorescence Microscopy

Gerlind Herberich[1], Anca Ivanescu[1], Ivonne Gamper[2],
Antonio Sechi[2], and Til Aach[1]

[1] Institute of Imaging and Computer Vision, RWTH Aachen University, Germany
[2] Institute of Biomedical Engineering Dept. of Cell Biology,
RWTH Aachen University, Germany

Abstract. In this paper we present a novel approach for the analysis of microtubules in wide-field fluorescence microscopy. Microtubules are flexible elongated structures and part of the cytoskeleton, a cytoplasmic scaffolding responsible for cell stability and motility. The method allows for precise measurements of microtubule length and orientation under different conditions despite a high variability of image data and in the presence of artefacts. Application of the proposed method to demonstrate the effect of the protein GAR22 on the rate of polymerisation of microtubules illustrates the potential of our approach.

1 Introduction

The movement of cells is essential for several biological processes and it can be altered in pathological conditions such as cancer. It depends on a complex and dynamic cytoplasmic scaffolding called the cytoskeleton, which is composed of three major types of filaments: actin filaments, intermediate filaments and microtubules (MTs). The dynamics of these filament types is regulated by coordinated cycles of assembly and disassembly characterised by the addition or removal of monomeric subunits, respectively.

Many studies have demonstrated that the regulation of actin polymerisation plays a major role in cell motility (see, for instance, [1], [2]). However, early experiments with MT-depolymerising drugs such as nocodazole have shown that the disruption of MTs impairs cell motility [3]. This suggests that actin dynamics per se is not sufficient to support directional cell motility but requires functional coordination with MT dynamics.

The mechanisms by which the actin and MT cytoskeleton influence each other are not completely understood. It has been shown that MTs can affect the adhesive properties of motile cells by inducing the disassembly of focal adhesions [4], [5], discrete subcellular structures that mediate the attachment of the cells' ventral side to the substrate. Other mechanisms involve the physical interaction between actin filaments and MTs. Proteins of the plakin family, in particular MACF1 (MT actin cross-linking factor 1 also known as ACF7), seem to play

M. Goesele et al. (Eds.): DAGM 2010, LNCS 6376, pp. 182–191, 2010.

a major role in this process as suggested by the fact that cells lacking MACF1 have unstable MTs and display deficient motility [6]. Another protein that is capable of actin-MT cross-linking activity is GAR22 (Gas2-related protein on chromosome 22 [7]), whose functions are still unknown.

Many questions concerning the mechanisms that govern the regulation between actin and MT cytoskeleton remain to be answered. For instance, how do they regulate directional cell motility? And, how do they regulate MT dynamics? One possible experimental approach for answering these questions involves the quantification of specific static and dynamic features of actin and MT cytoskeletons under different physiological conditions. Current approaches for studying the cytoskeleton function are based on microscopic techniques (immunofluorescence, etc.) that mostly provide only qualitative and semi-quantitative analyses with few methods tailored towards accurate measurements (e.g. [8], [9]). Semi-automated approaches, however, do not provide entirely objective and reproducible measurements. To the best of our knowledge, only one quantitative and fully automated approach for the analysis of cytoskeletal filaments has been developed so far [10] (slightly modified and extended in [11]). In this approach, the segmentation of cytoskeletal filaments is based on a rotated matched filtering approach using a rod kernel of one-pixel width thereby not accounting for the width of the sought structure.

Therefore it was our goal to develop a more accurate and sophisticated method for the segmentation of cytoskeletal filaments allowing a highly precise analysis. For the segmentation of line-like structures at the supracellular level, numerous approaches have been proposed, tailored towards applications such as vessel or neurite segmentation. Widely used are the Hessian-based vesselness filters. See e.g. [12] for a comparison. Due to the varying width of vessels, filter responses at different scales are typically combined to form a final estimate. In contrast, the problem of MT segmentation can be confined to the problem of ridge detection at a single scale as their width does not vary. Furthermore, it is crucial for our work to not only segment the MTs but also to measure their orientation as the analysis of directed cell motion is one future goal. Therefore, the core of our approach relies on a steerable ridge detector [13] designed from an optimality criterion. This enables us to simultaneously compute segmentation and orientation estimation and to benefit from the advantages of steerable filters [14] over rotated matched filtering. Furthermore, the used steerable ridge detector is shown [13] to have a better orientation selectivity than a popular Hessian-based ridge detector [15].

Our approach will thus allow the accurate quantification of parameters such as MT length and orientation during their re-assembly under various conditions. Hence it establishes the basis for the development of a quantitative analysis of MT dynamics paving the way to better defining the molecular mechanisms that regulate the interplay between actin and MT cytoskeletons and, as a consequence, cell motility.

The remainder of our paper is organized as follows. The experimental setup and image acquisition process are described in section 2. Section 3 explains the image preprocessing applied to enhance the images. The segmentation algorithm is detailed in section 4. The results are illustrated in section 5. Section 6 provides closing remarks and presents prospects for the future.

2   Experimental Procedure and Image Acquisition

To quantify the re-polymerisation of MTs, we acquired images of cells without MTs, and cells in which MT re-polymerization was allowed for 5, 10 and 30 minutes. We acquired such data for cells overexpressing the GAR22 protein as well as for wild type (control) cells. The procedure is detailed in the following for the interested reader but is not crucial for the understanding of our approach.

Briefly, MTs were depolymerised by treatment with nocodazole for 2 h at $37°C$. To induce the re-polymerisation of MTs, cells were washed twice in cell medium and incubated at $37°C$ for 0, 5, 10 or 30 min. At the end of each incubation time, cells were washed twice with pre-warmed ($37°C$) MT-stabilising buffer (MSB) and then extracted using MSB containing 0:5% Triton X-100 for 3 min at $37°C$. Fixation was done using ice-cold methanol ($-20°C$) for 4 min followed by re-hydration with Tris-buffered saline (TBS, a common buffer used in cell biology) containing 0:1% Triton X-100 (3 times/4 min each). Immunofluorescence labelling of the MTs was done according to standard procedures [16], [17] using the anti-tubulin antibody YL1/2 and an Alexa 594-conjugated secondary antibody.

Image acquisition was done using an Axiovert 200 microscope (Carl Zeiss, Germany) equipped with a Plan-Apochromat 100x/1.30 NA oil immersion objective equipped with 2.5x optovar optics. The Alexa 594 fluorophore was illuminated with a 100W HBO mercury lamp using the XF102-2 (Omega Optical) filter set. The excitation time was 500ms. Images were recorded with a cooled, back-illuminated CCD camera (Cascade 512B, Photometrics, USA) with a chip of 512x512 pixels (pixel size: $16\mu m$). Image resolution as measured with a micrometre scale was $15.56 pixel/\mu m$. Greyscale images were acquired as 16-bit, unsigned digital files and cropped to regions containing only a single cell.

3   Image Enhancement

Due to the morphological and functional heterogeneity of the cells, the acquired images inevitably exhibit a high variability with respect to background fluorescence, amount of artefacts and fluorescence intensity of the MTs as illustrated in figure 1.

To cope with the background fluorescence, i.e. to extract the light filaments on a dark slowly changing background, we apply a Top-hat filter. As this filtering operation is not intensity-preserving we apply a linear rescaling to the image afterwards (Fig. 2).

The extremely high dynamic range of the MTs' fluorescence intensity poses a special challenge for the automated analysis of these images: The range of fluorescence intensity values may cover over 90% of the total dynamic range of

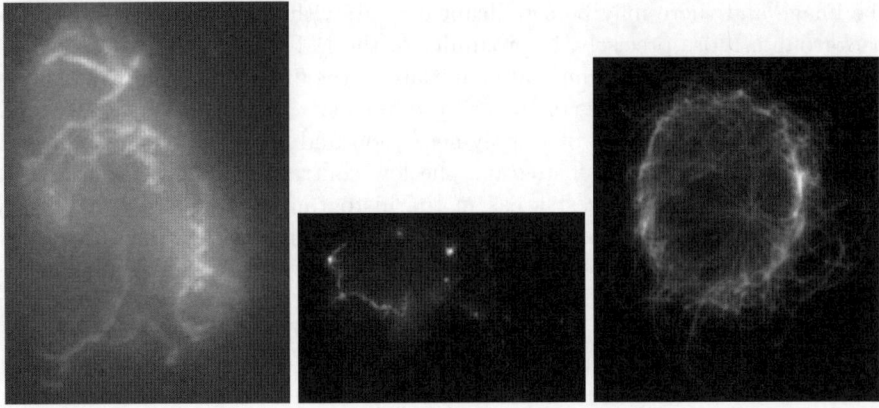

Fig. 1. High variability of image data: Strong background fluorescence (left), artefacts appearing as speckles/dots in the image (middle) and high dynamic range of fluorescence intensity exhibited by microtubules (right)

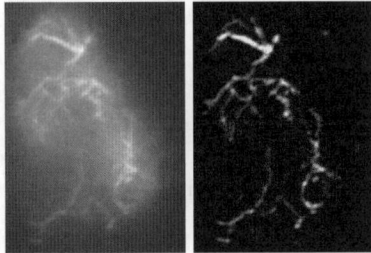

Fig. 2. Original image with strong background fluorescence (left) and result of Top-hat filtering and subsequent linear rescaling (right)

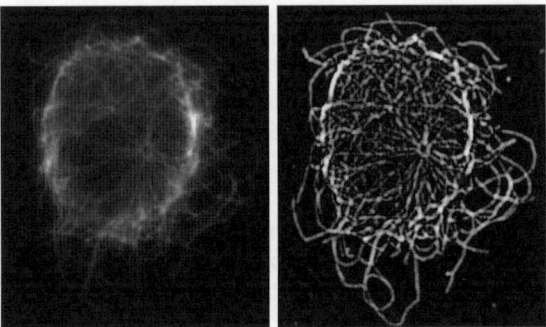

Fig. 3. Original image with high dynamic range of microtubule fluorescence intensity (left) and result of histogram equalization after Top-hat filtering (right)

the image and there may be significant overlap with the dynamic range of the background. More precisely, in proximity of the MT organizing centres (where the MTs polymerisation is nucleated/initiated), the fluorescence intensity is very high whereas in other areas of the cell the MTs are dark as well as quite dense depending on the amount of re-polymerisation and they exhibit low contrast. In the image's grey value histogram, the low contrast MTs form a peak. Due to the fact that the sparsest areas in the histogram correspond to light grey values, a histogram equalization leads to a brightening of these dark and dense MTs and therefore to an enhancement of their contrast (Fig. 3). This enables the segmentation of the MTs despite their highly varying fluorescence intensity.

4   Segmentation

To segment the MTs we follow the well-known methodology of Canny's edge detection algorithm [18] consisting of feature enhancement, thinning and thresholding. The sought feature $f(\mathbf{x})$ in our case is a ridge feature due to the line-like characteristics of filaments. The three steps are detailed in the following.

4.1   Ridge Enhancement

Our task is to design an optimal filter $h_{opt}(\mathbf{x})$ that finds the sought ridge feature $f(\mathbf{x})$ in our image $I(\mathbf{x})$. The optimality criterion is the maximization of signal-to-noise ratio. More generally, we seek to design a filter to find a sought signal in a measured signal. We assume that the measured signal $I(\mathbf{x})$ is composed of the sought signal $f(\mathbf{x})$ and additive white Gaussian noise $\eta(\mathbf{x})$:

$$I(\mathbf{x}) = f(\mathbf{x}) + \eta(\mathbf{x}). \tag{1}$$

The optimal linear filter then is a *matched filter* [19] given by $h_{opt}(\mathbf{x}) = f(-\mathbf{x})$. Filtering the image with this filter is thus equivalent to calculating the cross-correlation between sought feature and image: The result is a feature strength image (Fig. 4 left).

The sought filaments however represent arbitrarily oriented ridges. A simple way to detect these would consist in designing rotated versions of the above filter (*rotated matched filtering*). Each point is then assigned the orientation angle for which the cross-correlation between rotated filter and signal becomes maximal. It is clear that in order to achieve a good orientation selectivity and an accurate estimation of ridge strength and orientation, we need a large number of rotated filters (as many as there are quantization levels of the orientation angle), which makes the filtering procedure very inefficient.

Steerable filtering first introduced by Freeman in [14] is an elegant way to avoid these difficulties: When choosing the detector within the class of steerable filters, the rotated filter $h_{opt}(\mathbf{R}_\theta \mathbf{x}) := h(\mathbf{R}_\theta \mathbf{x})$ can be expressed as linear combination of a small number of basis filters $h_i(\mathbf{x})$ weighted with $b_i(\theta)$:

$$h(\mathbf{R}_\theta \mathbf{x}) = \sum_{i=1}^{M} b_i(\theta) h_i(\mathbf{x}) \tag{2}$$

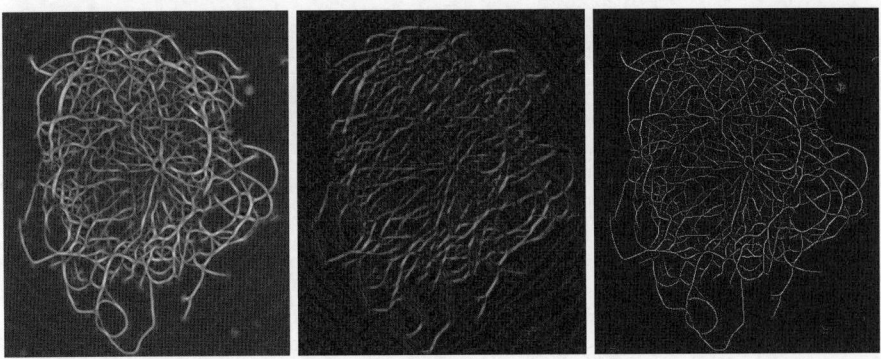

Fig. 4. Steerable filtering applied to enhanced MT image: Ridge strength image (left), orientation image (middle), thinned ridge strength image (right)

where $\mathbf{R}_\theta$ is the rotation matrix $\mathbf{R}_\theta = \begin{bmatrix} \cos(\theta) & \sin(\theta) \\ -\sin(\theta) & \cos(\theta) \end{bmatrix}$. As convolution is a linear operation, the convolution of the image $I(\mathbf{x})$ with a rotated filter $h(\mathbf{R}_\theta \mathbf{x})$ can then be expressed as:

$$h(\mathbf{R}_\theta \mathbf{x}) * I(\mathbf{x}) = \sum_{i=1}^{M} b_i(\theta) s_i(\mathbf{x}), \qquad (3)$$

with $s_i(\mathbf{x}) = h_i(\mathbf{x}) * I(\mathbf{x})$ being the convolution of basis filter $h_i(\mathbf{x})$ with the image. This enables us to analytically determine the filter output as a function of orientation. Maximizing this expression with respect to the orientation angle yields an estimation of the feature orientation (fig. 4 (middle)) which is not restricted anymore to a discrete set of considered orientations and thus becomes more accurate.

The ridge enhancement step of our method relies on a steerable ridge detector proposed by Jacob and Unser [13]. The detector is designed from derivatives of Gaussians such that the resulting filter is separable and they show that the computation of the optimal orientation angle can be solved analytically. Furthermore, in addition to the optimization of signal-to-noise ratio known from matched filtering, two more terms are introduced to design an optimal detector in the style of Canny: First, the localization of the feature is enhanced by maximizing the second derivative of the filter response orthogonal to the feature boundary. Second, false oscillations orthogonal as well as along the feature boundary are minimized by means of a thin-plate-like regularization that enforces the filter response to be smooth.

4.2 Thinning and Thresholding

In the resulting ridge strength image, the location of the filaments now has to be determined. This thinning step is realized by nonmaximum suppression as proposed by [18] such that the thinned ridge strength image contains only one-pixel wide ridges (fig. 4 right). To decide which ridge corresponds to a filament and which one is caused by noise, a thresholding on the ridge strength is necessary. To obtain connected ridges we apply hysteresis thresholding [18]. The lower and upper threshold values are calculated by means of a constant offset from the Otsu threshold [20] maximizing the inter-class variance in order to achieve an optimal classification into fore- and background despite the strong variability of the images.

5   Results

We have applied the proposed method to the image data acquired as described in section 2 to measure the speed of re-polymerisation for cells overexpressing the GAR22 protein in comparison to control cells. For each point in time we have measured between 13 and 20 cells. The segmentation quality has been visually assessed by experts from cell biology. An overview of the segmentation results for both cell types at each point in time is given in figure 5. Examples of the segmentation results are shown in figures 6 - 8. The importance of the contrast enhancing preprocessing for precise ridge detection is exemplarily illustrated in figure 7.

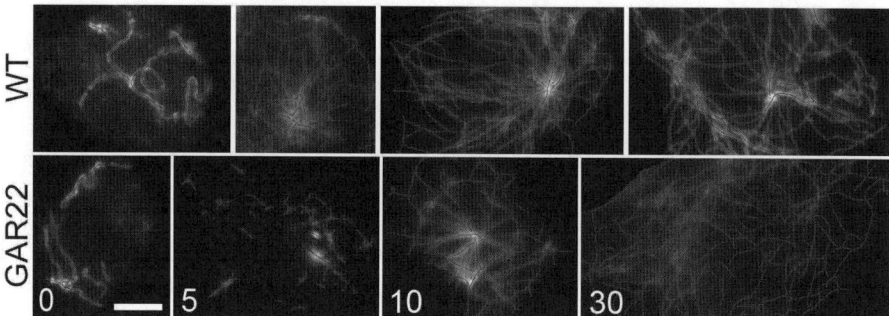

Fig. 5. Overview of the segmentation results for both cell types at each point in time measured (Numbers indicate time in minutes.). Red ridges indicate detected MT locations. Scale bar represents $5\mu m$.

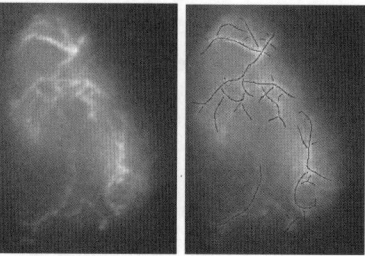

Fig. 6. Example of segmentation result in the presence of strong background fluorescence: Original image (left) and segmentation result (right)

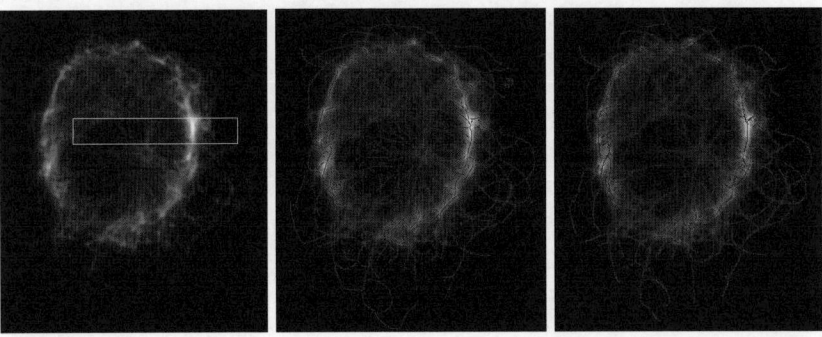

Fig. 7. Example of segmentation result in the case of highly variable MT fluorescence intensity: Original image (left) and segmentation result (middle). The results are shown in detail for the region within the white box in figure 8. The poor segmentation result (right) illustrates the failure of the segmentation step in case the contrast enhancing preprocessing is lacking.

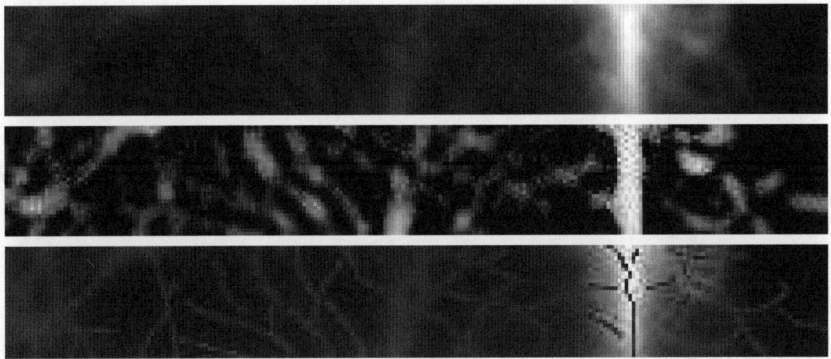

Fig. 8. White box region of segmentation result shown in figure 7. Top: Original image. Middle: Enhanced image. Bottom: Segmentation result.

	WT			GAR22		
Time (min)	Mean	SD	# cells	Mean	SD	# cells
0	530,9412	348,6776	17	555,4615	249,9502	13
5	3639,85	1172,612	20	1425,125	795,9951	16
10	4440,35	1354,821	20	3652,526	882,499	19
30	6960,765	1996,353	17	7544,375	2596,849	16

Fig. 9. Mean total length of MTs in pixels for control cells (left) in comparison with cells overexpressing GAR22 (right) measured at different points of time. The comparison shows that re-polymerisation of MTs is slowed down in cells overexpressing GAR22.

Based on the segmentations we have calculated the mean total MT length in pixels for both cell types for each point in time. The results shown in table 9 clearly demonstrate that the control cells' MTs re-polymerize significantly faster than the MTs of cells overexpressing GAR22 suggesting a relationship between GAR22 and the regulation of MT dynamics. Note that the high standard deviation arises from the high diversity of the cells analyzed and thus should not be interpreted as error measure.

6   Summary and Discussion

In this study, we have developed a method for the segmentation of cytoskeletal filaments in wide-field fluorescence microscopic images based on a contrast enhancing preprocessing and a steerable ridge detector designed from an optimality criterion. Application of the method to image data containing MTs demonstrates its ability to reliably segment MTs despite a high variability of the image data. By applying this novel approach we could precisely analyse MT re-polymerisation under various conditions. Moreover, our data suggest a role for GAR22 in the regulation of MT dynamics. Problems are encountered at locations with crossing MTs as these represent multiply oriented features [21], [22] the ridge detector is not designed for. Future developments will be aimed at the correct segmentation of crossing MTs. Furthermore, we envisage that the simultaneous computation of filament orientation and ridge strength will allow the precise tracking of MTs in live cells during directional cell motility.

References

1. Small, J.V., Stradal, T., Vignal, E., Rottner, K.: The lamellipodium: where motility begins. Trends Cell Biol. 12(3), 112–120 (2002)
2. Sechi, A.S., Wehland, J.: Ena/vasp proteins: multifunctional regulators of actin cytoskeleton dynamics. Front Biosci. 9, 1294–1310 (2004)
3. Goldman, R.D.: The role of three cytoplasmic fibers in bhk-21 cell motility. i. microtubules and the effects of colchicine. J. Cell Biol. 51(3), 752–762 (1971)
4. Kaverina, I., Krylyshkina, O., Small, J.V.: Microtubule targeting of substrate contacts promotes their relaxation and dissociation. J. Cell Biol. 146(5), 1033–1044 (1999)
5. Krylyshkina, O., Kaverina, I., Kranewitter, W., Steffen, W., Alonso, M.C., Cross, R.A., Small, J.V.: Modulation of substrate adhesion dynamics via microtubule targeting requires kinesin-1. J. Cell Biol. 156(2), 349–359 (2002)
6. Kodama, A., Karakesisoglou, I., Wong, E., Vaezi, A., Fuchs, E.: Acf7: an essential integrator of microtubule dynamics. Cell 115(3), 343–354 (2003)
7. Goriounov, D., Leung, C.L., Liem, R.K.H.: Protein products of human gas2-related genes on chromosomes 17 and 22 (hgar17 and hgar22) associate with both microfilaments and microtubules. J. Cell Sci. 116(Pt. 6), 1045–1058 (2003)
8. Kohler, M., Aufderheide, M., Ramm, D.: Method for the description of differences in the filamentous structure of the cytoskeleton in cultured cells. Toxicol Lett. 72(1-3), 33–42 (1994)

9. Rodionov, V., Nadezhdina, E., Peloquin, J., Borisy, G.: Digital fluorescence microscopy of cell cytoplasts with and without the centrosome. Methods Cell Biol. 67, 43–51 (2001)
10. Lichtenstein, N., Geiger, B., Kam, Z.: Quantitative analysis of cytoskeletal organization by digital fluorescent microscopy. Cytometry A 54(1), 8–18 (2003)
11. Shah, S.A., Santago, P., Rubin, B.K.: Quantification of biopolymer filament structure. Ultramicroscopy 104(3-4), 244–254 (2005)
12. Olabarriaga, S., Breeuwer, M., Niessen, W.: Evaluation of Hessian-based filters to enhance the axis of coronary arteries in CT images. In: Lemke, H.U., Vannier, M.W., Inamura, K., Farman, A.G., Doi, K., Reiber, J.H.C. (eds.) Computer Assisted Radiology and Surgery, London. International Congress Series, vol. 1256, pp. 1191–1196. Elsevier, Amsterdam (June 2003)
13. Jacob, M., Unser, M.: Design of steerable filters for feature detection using canny-like criteria. IEEE Transactions on Pattern Analysis and Machine Intelligence 26, 1007–1019 (2004)
14. Freeman, W.T., Adelson, E.H.: The design and use of steerable filters. IEEE Transactions on Pattern Analysis and Machine Intelligence 13, 891–906 (1991)
15. Frangi, A., Niessen, W., Vincken, K., Viergever, M.: Multiscale vessel enhancement filtering. In: Wells, W.M., Colchester, A.C.F., Delp, S.L. (eds.) MICCAI 1998. LNCS, vol. 1496, pp. 130–137. Springer, Heidelberg (1998)
16. Grenklo, S., Geese, M., Lindberg, U., Wehland, J., Karlsson, R., Sechi, A.S.: A crucial role for profilin-actin in the intracellular motility of listeria monocytogenes. EMBO Rep. 4(5), 523–529 (2003)
17. Pust, S., Morrison, H., Wehland, J., Sechi, A.S., Herrlich, P.: Listeria monocytogenes exploits erm protein functions to efficiently spread from cell to cell. EMBO J. 24(6), 1287–1300 (2005)
18. Canny, J.: A computational approach to edge detection. IEEE Transactions on Pattern Analysis and Machine Intelligence 8, 679–698 (1986)
19. Therrien, C.: Decision, Estimation and Classification: Introduction to Pattern Recognition and Related Topics. John Wiley and Sons, Chichester (1989)
20. Otsu, N.: A threshold selection method from gray-level histograms. IEEE Transactions on systems, man, and cybernetics SMC-9, 62–66 (1979)
21. Mühlich, M., Aach, T.: Analysis of multiple orientations. IEEE Transactions on Image Processing 18(7), 1424–1437 (2009)
22. Mühlich, M., Aach, T.: High accuracy feature detection for camera calibration: A multi-steerable approach. In: Hamprecht, F.A., Schnörr, C., Jähne, B. (eds.) DAGM 2007. LNCS, vol. 4713, pp. 284–293. Springer, Heidelberg (2007)

Learning Non-stationary System Dynamics Online Using Gaussian Processes⋆

Axel Rottmann and Wolfram Burgard

Department of Computer Science, University of Freiburg, Germany

Abstract. Gaussian processes are a powerful non-parametric framework for solving various regression problems. In this paper, we address the task of learning a Gaussian process model of non-stationary system dynamics in an online fashion. We propose an extension to previous models that can appropriately handle outdated training samples by decreasing their influence onto the predictive distribution. The resulting model estimates for each sample of the training set an individual noise level and thereby produces a mean shift towards more reliable observations. As a result, our model improves the prediction accuracy in the context of non-stationary function approximation and can furthermore detect outliers based on the resulting noise level. Our approach is easy to implement and is based upon standard Gaussian process techniques. In a real-world application where the task is to learn the system dynamics of a miniature blimp, we demonstrate that our algorithm benefits from individual noise levels and outperforms standard methods.

1 Introduction

Accurately modeling the characteristics of a system is fundamental in a wide range of research and application fields, and it becomes more important as the systems grow more complex and less constrained. A common modeling approach is to use probabilities to represent the dependencies between the system's variables and apply machine learning techniques to learn the parameters of the model from collected data. Consider for example the task of learning the system dynamics of a small blimp. The majority of existing approaches assume stationary systems and equally weight all the training data. The flight characteristics of the blimp, however, are affected by many unconsidered factors that change over time. A common approach to deal with non-stationary systems is to assign higher weights to newer training samples.

In this paper we present a probabilistic regression framework that can accurately describe a system even when its characteristics change over time. More concretely, we extend the Gaussian process (GP) framework to be able to handle training samples with different weights. GPs are a state-of-the-art non-parametric Bayesian regression framework that has been successfully applied

---

⋆ This work has partly been supported by the German Research Foundation (DFG) within the Research Training Group 1103.

M. Goesele et al. (Eds.): DAGM 2010, LNCS 6376, pp. 192–201, 2010.

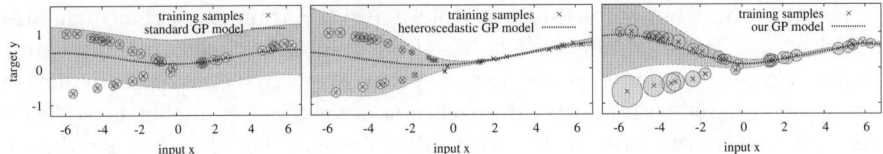

Fig. 1. Different observation noise assumptions in the data lead to different GP models. From left to right: standard approach assuming uniform noise levels, heteroscedastic GP model assuming input-dependent noise levels, and our approach assuming unrestricted noise levels where the samples circled green (the smaller circles) are assigned with higher weights.

for solving various regression problems. One limitation of standard GPs, however, is that the noise in the training data is assumed to be uniform over the whole input domain (homoscedasticity). This assumption is not always valid and different approaches have recently been proposed to deal with varying noise in the data. The main idea behind these approaches is to assume that the noise can be described by a function of the input domain (heteroscedasticity) so that adjacent data is supposed to have similar noise. However, both of these approaches effectively regard all training data as having the same weight. In this paper, we present a general extension of these GP approaches. Our model is able to deal with individual, uncorrelated observation noise levels for each single training sample and thereby is able to weight the samples individually. This flexibility allows us to apply our framework, for example, to an online learning scenario where the underlying function being approximated may change during data collection.

Figure 1 illustrates how different assumptions about the observation noise in the data lead to different predictive distribution of GP models. In the figure, the predicted mean, the 95% confidence interval, and the training samples are shown. The size of the circle around each point corresponds to its estimated noise; the bigger the radius, the larger the noise. The left plot corresponds to the most restrictive, standard GP model where the noise is assumed to be constant. In the plot in the middle, the noise is assumed to depend on the input domain. This corresponds to the more flexible heteroscedastic GP models. This model, however, still has limited flexibility since it does not allow us to deal with unrestricted noise levels. The approach presented in this paper is able to weight the training samples individually by assigning different noise levels. The right plot in Fig. 1 corresponds to a GP learned using our approach. Assuming the samples circled red are outdated information and assigned with lower weights than those in green circles our model selects the noise levels correspondingly. Note that our model as well assigns smaller noise levels to the samples circled red on the right side as there is no newer information available. Finally, the predictive mean function is shifted towards the higher weighted samples and the predictive variance reproduces the distribution of the training samples.

The main contribution of this paper is a novel GP framework that estimates individual, uncorrelated noise levels based on weights assigned to the training samples. Considering unrestricted noise levels allows us to increase the prediction accuracy compared to previous approaches as we can assign higher noise levels to inaccurate observations, so that their influence onto the regression is reduced.

This paper is organized as follows. After reviewing related work in Section 2 we give a short introduction of GP regression in Section 3. Afterward, in Section 4, we introduce our approach of estimating unrestricted noise levels. Finally, in Section 5 we provide several experiments demonstrating the advantages of our method, followed by a conclusion.

2   Related Work

Gaussian process regression has been intensively studied in the past and applied in a wide range of research areas such as statistics and machine learning. A general introduction to GPs and a survey of the enormous approaches of the literature is given in the book of Rasmussen and Kuss [1]. In most GP frameworks a uniform noise distribution throughout the domain is assumed. In contrast to this, a heteroscedastic noise prediction has as well been intensively studied. For instance, the approaches of Goldberg et al. [2] and Kersting et al. [3] deal with input-dependent noise rates. Both use two separate GPs to model the data. One predicts the mean as a regular GP does, whereas the other is used to model the prediction uncertainty. In contrast to our approach, they predict input-dependent noise levels. We extend their approach and additionally estimate for each single training sample an individual noise value. Heteroscedasticity has as well been applied in other regression models. For example, Schölkopf et al. [4] integrated a known variance function into an SVM-based algorithm and Bishop and Quazaz [5] investigated input-dependent noise assumptions for parametric models such as neuronal networks.

GPs have been also successfully applied to different learning tasks. Due to the limited space, we simply refer to some approaches which are closely related to the experiments performed in this paper. Ko et al. [6] presented an approach to improve a motion model of a blimp derived from aeronautic principles by using a GP to model the residual. Furthermore, Rottmann et al. [7] and Deisenroth et al. [8] learned control policies of a completely unknown system in a GP framework. In these approaches stationary underlying functions were assumed. As already discussed above, in real applications this is normally not the case and estimating an individual noise level for each observation can improve the prediction accuracy.

Additionally, alternative regression techniques have been successfully applied to approximate non-stationary functions. D'Souza et al. [9] used Locally Weighted Projection Regression to learn the inverse kinematics of a humanoid robot. The authors include a forgetting factor in their model to improve the influence of newer observations. In contrast to their approach, we obtain an observation noise estimate of each single training sample which, for instance, can be used to remove outdated observations from the data set.

3   Gaussian Process Regression

Gaussian processes (GPs) are a powerful non-parametric framework for regression and provide a general tool to solve various machine learning problems [1]. In the context of regression, we are given a training set $\mathcal{D} = \{(\boldsymbol{x}_i, y_i)\}_{i=1}^N$ of N, d-dimensional states $\boldsymbol{x}_i$ and target values y_i. We aim to learn a GP to model the dependency $y_i = f(\boldsymbol{x}_i) + \epsilon_i$ for the unknown underlying function $f(\boldsymbol{x})$ and, in case of a homoscedastic noise assumption, independent and identically, normally distributed noise terms $\epsilon_i \sim \mathcal{N}(0, \sigma_n^2)$.

A GP is fully specified by its mean $m(\boldsymbol{x})$ and covariance function $k(\boldsymbol{x}_i, \boldsymbol{x}_j)$. Typical choices are a zero mean function and a parametrized covariance function. In this work, we apply $k(\boldsymbol{x}_i, \boldsymbol{x}_j) = \sigma_f^2 \exp\left(-\frac{1}{2}(\boldsymbol{x}_i - \boldsymbol{x}_j)^T \Lambda^{-1}(\boldsymbol{x}_i - \boldsymbol{x}_j)\right)$, where σ_f^2 is the signal variance and $\Lambda = \operatorname{diag}(\ell_1, \ldots, \ell_d)$ is the diagonal matrix of the length-scale parameters.

Given a set of training samples $\mathcal{D}$ for the unknown function and the hyper-parameters $\boldsymbol{\theta} = (\Lambda, \sigma_f^2, \sigma_n^2)$ a predictive distribution $P(f^* \mid \boldsymbol{x}^*, \mathcal{D}, \boldsymbol{\theta})$ for a new input location $\boldsymbol{x}^*$ is again a Gaussian with

$$f_\mu^* = m(\boldsymbol{x}^*) + \boldsymbol{k}(x, \boldsymbol{x}^*)^T (K + R)^{-1} (\boldsymbol{y} - m(x)) \tag{1a}$$

$$f_{\sigma^2}^* = k(\boldsymbol{x}^*, \boldsymbol{x}^*) - \boldsymbol{k}(x, \boldsymbol{x}^*)^T (K + R)^{-1} \boldsymbol{k}(x, \boldsymbol{x}^*). \tag{1b}$$

Here, $K \in \mathbb{R}^{N \times N}$ is the covariance matrix for the training points with $K_{ij} = k(\boldsymbol{x}_i, \boldsymbol{x}_j)$ and $R = \sigma_n^2 I$ is the observation noise.

4   GP Model with Individual Noise Levels

In general, GP regression can be seen as a generalization of weighted nearest neighbor regression and thus can be applied directly to model non-stationary underlying functions. As more and more accurate observations become available the predictive mean function is shifted towards the more densely located training samples. However, assigning lower weights to outdated samples improves the approximation accuracy regarding the actual underlying function. For this purpose, we assign a weighting value $w(\boldsymbol{x}_i), i = 1, \ldots, N$, to each single training sample $\boldsymbol{x}_i$. In case of GPs the weight of a sample and thus the importance on the predictive distribution can be regulated by adapting the observation noise correspondingly. Therefore, given the weights the presented GP framework estimates individual noise levels for each training samples to obtain the most likely prediction of the training samples. Obviously, the prediction accuracy of the actual underlying function highly depends on the progress of the weight values. However, in practical applications such values can easily be established and, even without having knowledge about the optimal values, raising the weights of only a few samples result in a significant improvement of the approximation. In an online learning task, the influence of subsequent observations can be boosted by monotonically increasing values over time. D'Souza *et al.* [9], for instance, apply a constant forgetting factor. Throughout our experiments we set

$$w(\boldsymbol{x}_i) = \begin{cases} 0.1 & \text{if } i < N - \Delta \\ 1.0 & \text{otherwise} \end{cases} \quad, i = 1, \ldots, N\,, \tag{2}$$

where N is the total number of training samples and the parameter Δ specifies how many of the more recent observations are assumed to have higher importance. Although we are only using a simple step function to define the weights, our GP framework is not restricted to any fixed distribution of these values.

To implement individual noise levels the noise matrix R of the GP model is replaced by the diagonal matrix $R_D = \text{diag}(\sigma_1^2, \ldots, \sigma_N^2)$ of the individual noise levels for each training point $x_1, \ldots, x_N$. In general, as the global noise rate σ_n^2 is simply split into individual levels $\sigma_1^2, \ldots, \sigma_N^2$ the GP model remains unaffected and the additional parameters can be added to the set of hyper-parameters $\boldsymbol{\theta}$. Given that, the noise levels can be estimated in the same fashion as the other hyper-parameters. In our current system, we employ leave-one-out cross-validation to adapt the hyper-parameters. Alternative cross-validation approaches in the context of GPs are described by Sundararajan and Keerthi [10]. In general, one seeks to find hyper-parameters that minimize the average loss of all training samples given a predefined optimization criterion. Possible criteria are the negative marginal data likelihood (GPP), the predictive mean squared error (GPE), and the standard mean squared error (CV). The weights $w(\boldsymbol{x}_i)$ can easily be integrated into cross-validation by adding the value of each training sample as an additional factor to the corresponding loss term. This procedure is also known as importance-weighted cross-validation [11].

From (1a) and (1b) we see, that for an arbitrary scaling of the covariance function the predictive mean remains unaffected whereas the predictive variance depends on the scaling. Initial experiments showed that the GPP and GPE criteria scale the covariance function to be zero as they minimize the average loss of all training points. The predictive mean remains unchanged whereas the predictive variance is successively decreased. Therefore, we employ the CV criterion, which is given as

$$CV(\boldsymbol{\theta}) = \frac{1}{w_N} \sum_{i=1}^{N} w(\boldsymbol{x}_i)\,(y_i - \mu_i^*)^2\,. \tag{3}$$

Here, μ_i^* denotes the predicted mean value of $P\left(f_i^* \mid \boldsymbol{x}_i, \mathcal{D}^{(i)}, \boldsymbol{\theta}\right)$, $\mathcal{D}^{(i)}$ is obtained from $\mathcal{D}$ by removing the ith sample, and $w_N = \sum_{i=1}^{N} w(\boldsymbol{x}_i)$ is the normalization term of the importance values.

Using the CV criterion to optimize the hyper-parameters, we obtain individual, uncorrelated noise levels and a mean prediction — we will refer to it as f_μ^{CV} — which is optimal with respect to the squared error. However, an adequate variance prediction of the training samples is not obtained. This is based on the fact that the CV criterion simply takes the predictive mean into account. To achieve this, we employ, in a final step, the obtained mean function as a fixed mean function $m(\boldsymbol{x}) = f_\mu^{CV}$ of a second GP. The predicted mean of the first GP becomes a latent variable for the second one, so the predictive distribution can be written as $P\left(f^* \mid \boldsymbol{x}^*, \mathcal{D}, \boldsymbol{\theta}\right) = \int P\left(f^* \mid \boldsymbol{x}^*, \mathcal{D}, \boldsymbol{\theta}, f_\mu^{CV}\right) \cdot P\left(f_\mu^{CV} \mid \boldsymbol{x}^*, \mathcal{D}, \boldsymbol{\theta}\right)\,df_\mu^{CV}$.

Given the mean f_μ^{CV} the first term is Gaussian with mean and variance as defined by (1a) and (1b), and $m(\boldsymbol{x}) = f_\mu^{CV}$. To simplify the integral, we approximate the expectation of the second term by the most likely predictive mean $\tilde{f}_\mu^{CV} \approx \arg\max_{\tilde{f}_\mu^{CV}} P\left(\tilde{f}_\mu^{CV} \mid \boldsymbol{x}^*, \mathcal{D}, \boldsymbol{\theta}\right)$. This is a proper approximation as most of the probability mass of $P\left(f_\mu^{CV} \mid \boldsymbol{x}^*, \mathcal{D}, \boldsymbol{\theta}\right)$ is concentrated around the mean which minimizes the mean squared error to the training samples.

To adjust the hyper-parameters of the second GP — and to define the final predictive distribution — all we need to do is to apply a state-of-the-art GP approach. The individual noise levels have already been estimated in the first GP and they do not have to be considered in the covariance function of the second GP. Therefore, depending on the noise assumption of the training samples, one can choose a homoscedastic or heteroscedastic GP model. The final predictive variance of our model is defined by the second GP only whereas the individual noise levels $\sigma_1^2, \ldots, \sigma_N^2$ are taken into account in the predictive mean. Still, the hyper-parameters of the second model must be optimized with respect to the weights $w(\boldsymbol{x}_i)$. Therefore, we employ leave-one-out cross-validation based on the GPP criterion with included weights instead of the original technique of the chosen model.

5   Experimental Results

The goal of the experiments is to demonstrate that the approach above outperforms standard GP regression models given a non-stationary underlying function. We consider the task to learn the system dynamics of a miniature indoor blimp [12]. The system is based on a commercial 1.8 m blimp envelope and is steered by three motors. To gather the training data the blimp was flown in a simulation, where the visited states as well as the controls were recorded. To obtain a realistic movement of the system a normal distributed noise term was added to the control commands to simulate outer influence like gust of wind. The system dynamics of the blimp were derived based on standard physical aeronautic principles [13] and the parameters were optimized based on a series of trajectories flown with the real blimp. To evaluate the predictive accuracy, we used 500 randomly sampled points and determined the mean squared error (RMS) of the predictive mean of the corresponding GP model relative to the ground truth prediction calculated by the simulator.

The dynamics obtained from a series of states indexed by time can be written as $\boldsymbol{s}(t+1) = \boldsymbol{s}(t) + \boldsymbol{h}(\boldsymbol{s}(t), \boldsymbol{a}(t))$, where $\boldsymbol{s} \in S$ and $\boldsymbol{a} \in A$ are states and actions, respectively, t is the time index, and $\boldsymbol{h}$ the function which describes the system dynamics given state $\boldsymbol{s}$ and action $\boldsymbol{a}$. Using a GP model to learn the dynamics the input space consists of the state space S and the actions A and the targets represent the difference between two consecutive states $\boldsymbol{s}(t+1) - \boldsymbol{s}(t)$. Then, we learn for each dimension S_c of the state space $S = (S_1, \ldots, S_{|S|})$ a Gaussian process $GP_c : S \times A \rightarrow S_c$. Throughout our experiments, we used a fixed time interval $\Delta t = 1\,\mathrm{s}$ between two consecutive states.

We furthermore carried out multiple experiments on benchmark data sets to evaluate the accuracy of our predictive model given a stationary underlying function. Throughout the experimental section, we use three different GP models: a standard GP model (StdGP) of [1], a heteroscedastic GP model (HetGP) of [3], and our GP model with individual, uncorrelated noise levels (InGP). As mentioned in Section 4, our approach can be combined with a homoscedastic as well as a heteroscedastic variance assumption for the data. In the individual experiments we always specify which specific version of our model was applied. We implemented our approach in `Matlab` using the GP toolbox of [1].

5.1   Learning the System Dynamics

In the first experiment, we analyzed if the integration of individual noise levels for each single training sample yields an improvement of the prediction accuracy. We learned the system dynamics of the blimp using our approach assuming a homoscedastic variance of the data and a standard GP model. To evaluate the performance we carried out several test runs. In each run, we collected 800 observations and calculated the RMS of the final prediction. To simulate a non-stationary behavior, we manually modified the characteristics of the blimp during each run. More precisely, after 320 s we increased the mass of the system to simulate a loss of buoyancy.

We additionally evaluated different distributions of the weights (2) by adjusting the parameter Δ, that specifies how many of the more recent observations have higher importance. Table 1 summarizes the results for different values of Δ. For each dimension of the state vector we plot the residual. The state vector of the blimp contains the forward direction X, the vertical direction Z, and the heading φ as well as the corresponding velocities $\dot{X}$, $\dot{Z}$, and $\dot{\varphi}$. As can be seen from Table 1, the vertical direction is mostly affected by modifying the mass. Also, as expected, increasing Δ raises the importance of more reliable observations (which are the more recent ones in this experiment). Consequently, we obtain a better prediction accuracy. Note that this already happens for values of Δ that are substantially smaller than the optimal one, which would be 480.

Table 1. Prediction accuracy of the system dynamics of the blimp using a standard GP model and our approach with a homoscedastic variance assumption of the data

model	$X_{(mm)}$	$\dot{X}_{(mm/s)}$	$Z_{(mm)}$	$\dot{Z}_{(mm/s)}$	$\varphi_{(deg)}$	$\dot{\varphi}_{(deg/s)}$
StdGP	53.7	40.7	128.4	18.4	3.3	1.2
LWPR	43.4	33.9	27.9	9.1	3.7	1.1
InGP, $\Delta = 200$	51.1	35.4	30.4	10.1	3.3	1.3
InGP, $\Delta = 300$	42.7	38.4	27.5	10.1	3.6	1.3
InGP, $\Delta = 400$	44.3	33.7	26.2	8.8	3.3	1.2
optimal prediction	50.4	32.1	12.5	7.1	3.0	1.3

For comparison, we trained a standard GP model based on stationary dynamics. The accuracy of this model, which corresponds to the optimum, is given in the bottom of Table 1. Furthermore, we applied the Locally Weighted Projection Regression (LWPR) algorithm [9] to the data set and obtained equivalent results compared to our approach with $\Delta = 400$. LWPR is a powerful method to learn non-stationary functions. In contrast to their approach, however, we obtain for each input value a Gaussian distribution over the output values. Thus, the prediction variance reproduce the distribution of the trained samples. Further outputs of our model are individual, uncorrelated noise levels which are estimated based on the location and the weights of the training samples. These levels are a meaningful rating for the training samples. The higher the noise level the less informative is the target to reproduce the underlying function. We analyze this additional information in the following experiment.

5.2   Identifying Outliers

This experiment is designed to illustrate the advantage of having an individual noise estimate for each observation. A useful property of our approach is that it automatically increases this level if a point is not reflecting the underlying function. Depending on the estimated noise value, we can determine whether the corresponding point should be removed from the training set. The goal of this experiment is to show that this way of identifying and removing outliers can significantly improve the prediction accuracy.

To perform this experiment, we learned the dynamics of the blimp online and manually modified the behavior of the blimp after 50 s by increasing the mass. As soon as 10 new observations were received, we add them to the existing training set. To increase the importance of the subsequent observations, we used (2) with $\Delta = 10$. Then, according to the estimated noise levels $\sigma_1^2, \ldots, \sigma_N^2$ we labeled observations with a value exceeding a given threshold ν as an outlier and removed it from the data set. Throughout this experiment, we used the standard deviation of the noise levels: $\nu = \xi \cdot \sqrt{\sum_{i=1}^{N} \sigma_i^2}$. After that, we learned a standard GP model on the remaining points.

Figure 2 shows the learning rate of the vertical direction Z averaged over multiple runs. Regarding the prediction accuracy, the learning progress based on removing outliers is significantly improvement ($p = 0.05$) compared to the standard GP model which uses the complete data set. Additionally, we evaluated our InGP model with rejected outliers for the second GP and this model performs like the standard GP model with removed outliers. This may be based on the fact that we only took the predictive mean function into account. To have a baseline, we additionally trained a GP model based only on observations that correspond to the currently correct model. The prediction of this model can be regarded as optimal. In a second experiment, we evaluated final prediction accuracies after 200 s for different values of ξ. The results are shown in Table 2. As can be seen, the improvement is robust against variations of ξ. In our experiment, keeping 95% of the points on average lead to the best behavior.

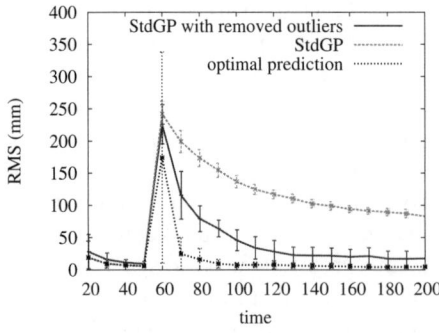

Fig. 2. Prediction accuracies plotted over time using $\xi = 2.0$

Table 2. Prediction accuracies of the system dynamics using different thresholds ξ to identify outliers

model	RMS$_{(mm)}$
StdGP	83.6 ± 5.6
removing outliers, $\xi = 1.5$	22.4 ± 12.2
removing outliers, $\xi = 2.0$	18.7 ± 12.1
removing outliers, $\xi = 2.5$	20.4 ± 12.4
removing outliers, $\xi = 3.0$	21.6 ± 12.3
optimal prediction	5.7 ± 2.7

5.3   Benchmark Test

We also evaluated the performance of our approach based on different data sets frequently used in the literature. We trained our GP model with a homoscedastic as well as a heteroscedastic noise assumption of the data and compared the prediction accuracy to the corresponding state-of-the-art approaches. We assigned uniform weights to our model as the underlying function of each data set is stationary. For each data set, we performed 20 independent runs. In each run, we separated the data into 90% for training and 10% for testing and calculated the negative log predictive density $NLPD = \frac{1}{N}\sum_{i=1}^{N} -logP(y_i \mid \boldsymbol{x}_i, \mathcal{D}, \boldsymbol{\theta})$. Table 3 shows typical results for two synthetic data sets $\mathcal{A}$ and $\mathcal{B}$; and a data set of a simulated motor-cycle crash $\mathcal{C}$, which are introduced in detail in [2], [14], and [15], respectively. As can be seen, our model with individual noise levels achieves an equivalent prediction accuracy compared to the alternative approaches.

Table 3. Evaluation of GP models with different noise assumptions

data set	homoscedastic noise		heteroscedastic noise	
	StdGP	InGP	HetGP	InGP
$\mathcal{A}$	1.506 ± 0.263	1.491 ± 0.255	1.455 ± 0.317	1.445 ± 0.276
$\mathcal{B}$	1.834 ± 0.245	1.827 ± 0.262	1.496 ± 0.279	1.512 ± 0.269
$\mathcal{C}$	4.528 ± 0.189	4.515 ± 0.233	4.315 ± 0.474	4.277 ± 0.530

6   Conclusions

In this paper we presented a novel approach to increase the accuracy of the predicted Gaussian process model based on a non-stationary underlying function. Using individual, uncorrelated noise levels the uncertainty of outdated observation is increased. Our approach is an extension of previous models and easy to implement. In several experiments, in which we learned the system dynamics of a miniature blimp robot, we show that the prediction accuracy is improved significantly. Furthermore, we showed that our approach, when applied to data sets coming from stationary underlying functions, performs as good as standard Gaussian process models.

References

1. Rasmussen, C.E., Williams, C.: Gaussian Processes for Machine Learning. MIT Press, Cambridge (2006)
2. Goldberg, P., Williams, C., Bishop, C.: Regression with input-dependent noise: A Gaussian process treatment. In: Proc. of the Advances in Neural Information Processing Systems, vol. 10, pp. 493–499. MIT Press, Cambridge (1998)
3. Kersting, K., Plagemann, C., Pfaff, P., Burgard, W.: Most likely heteroscedastic Gaussian process regression. In: Proc. of the Int. Conf. on Machine Learning, pp. 393–400 (2007)
4. Schölkopf, B., Smola, A., Williamson, R., Bartlett, P.: New support vector algorithms. Neural Computation 12, 1207–1245 (2000)
5. Bishop, C., Quazaz, C.: Regression with input-dependent noise: A bayesian treatment. In: Proc. of the Advances in Neural Information Processing Systems, vol. 9, pp. 347–353. MIT Press, Cambridge (1997)
6. Ko, J., Klein, D., Fox, D., Hähnel, D.: Gaussian processes and reinforcement learning for identification and control of an autonomous blimp. In: Proc. of the IEEE Int. Conf. on Robotics & Automation, pp. 742–747 (2007)
7. Rottmann, A., Plagemann, C., Hilgers, P., Burgard, W.: Autonomous blimp control using model-free reinforcement learning in a continuous state and action space. In: Proc. of the IEEE Int. Conf. on Intelligent Robots and Systems, pp. 1895–1900 (2007)
8. Deisenroth, M., Rasmussen, C., Peters, J.: Gaussian process dynamic programming. Neurocomputing 72(7-9), 1508–1524 (2009)
9. D'Souza, A., Vijayakumar, S., Schaal, S.: Learning inverse kinematics. In: Proc. of the IEEE/RSJ Int. Conf. on Intelligent Robots and Systems, pp. 298–303 (2001)
10. Sundararajan, S., Keerthi, S.: Predictive approaches for choosing hyperparameters in Gaussian processes. Neural Computation 13(5), 1103–1118 (2001)
11. Sugiyama, M., Krauledat, M., Müller, K.R.: Covariate shift adaptation by importance weighted cross validation. J. Mach. Learn. Res. 8, 985–1005 (2007)
12. Rottmann, A., Sippel, M., Zitterell, T., Burgard, W., Reindl, L., Scholl, C.: Towards an experimental autonomous blimp platform. In: Proc. of the 3rd Europ. Conf. on Mobile Robots, pp. 19–24 (2007)
13. Zufferey, J., Guanella, A., Beyeler, A., Floreano, D.: Flying over the reality gap: From simulated to real indoor airships. Autonomous Robots 21(3), 243–254 (2006)
14. Yuan, M., Wahba, G.: Doubly penalized likelihood estimator in heteroscedastic regression. Statistics and Probability Letter 69(1), 11–20 (2004)
15. Silverman, B.: Some aspects of the spline smoothing approach to non-parametric regression curve fitting. Journal of the Royal Statistical Society 47(1), 1–52 (1985)

Computational TMA Analysis and Cell Nucleus Classification of Renal Cell Carcinoma

Peter J. Schüffler, Thomas J. Fuchs, Cheng Soon Ong,
Volker Roth, and Joachim M. Buhmann

Department of Computer Science, ETH Zurich, Switzerland

Abstract. We consider an automated processing pipeline for tissue micro array analysis (TMA) of renal cell carcinoma. It consists of several consecutive tasks, which can be mapped to machine learning challenges. We investigate three of these tasks, namely nuclei segmentation, nuclei classification and staining estimation. We argue for a holistic view of the processing pipeline, as it is not obvious whether performance improvements at individual steps improve overall accuracy. The experimental results show that classification accuracy, which is comparable to trained human experts, can be achieved by using support vector machines (SVM) with appropriate kernels. Furthermore, we provide evidence that the shape of cell nuclei increases the classification performance. Most importantly, these improvements in classification accuracy result in corresponding improvements for the medically relevant estimation of immunohistochemical staining.

1 Introduction

Cancer tissue analysis consists of several consecutive estimation and classification steps which are currently highly labour intensive. The tissue microarray (TMA) technology promises to significantly accelerate studies seeking for associations between molecular changes and clinical endpoints [10]. In this technology, $0.6mm$ tissue cylinders are extracted from primary tumor blocks of hundreds of different patients and these cylinders are subsequently embedded into a recipient tissue block. Sections from such array blocks can then be used for simultaneous in situ analysis of hundreds or thousands of primary tumors on DNA, RNA, and protein level. Although the production of tissue microarrays is an almost routine task for most laboratories, the evaluation of stained tissue microarray slides remains tedious, time consuming and prone to error. The high speed of arraying, the lack of a significant damage to donor blocks, and the regular arrangement of arrayed specimens substantially facilitates automated analysis.

This paper investigates an automated system to model such a workflow for renal cell carcinoma (RCC). Current image analysis software requires extensive user interaction to properly identify cell populations, to select regions of interest for scoring, to optimize analysis parameters and to organize the resulting raw data. Due to these drawbacks in current software, pathologists typically collect tissue microarray data by manually assigning a composite staining score for

M. Goesele et al. (Eds.): DAGM 2010, LNCS 6376, pp. 202–211, 2010.

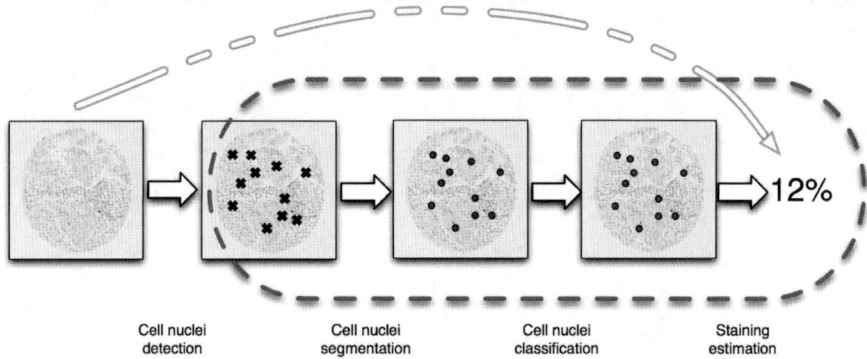

Fig. 1. TMA processing pipeline, consisting of the following stages: (1) Detection of cell nuclei within a high resolution TMA image, (2) nuclei segmentation, (3) nuclei classification into malignant and benign, and (4) calculation of the percentage of tumor cells and protein expressing tumor cells. The pathologists directly assign a staining score (pale dashed arrow). We consider the subset of tasks indicated by the boxed region.

each spot - often during multiple microscopy sessions over a period of days. Such manual scoring can result in serious inconsistencies between data collected during different microscopy sessions. Manual scoring also introduces a significant bottleneck that limits the use of tissue microarrays in high-throughput analysis.

The manual rating and assessment of TMAs under the microscope by pathologists is quite error prone due to the subjective perception of humans. In fact, one pathologist might differ in the detection and classification of the same cell nuclei within the same image in a second annotation round [7]. Reasons for such a discrepancy may relate to the partial destruction of a cell nucleus during the preparation of a TMA; the slow and often gradual transformation of a healthy cell to a tumor cell, and the subjective experiences of the pathologist. Therefore, decisions for grading and/or cancer therapy might be inconsistent among pathologists.

In this paper, we follow the workflow in [7] which consists of cell nuclei detection, segmentation and classification, followed by estimation of the proportion of nuclei stained by the antibody under investigation (Figure 1). In particular, we investigate the effect of different image features and kernels on the accuracy of classifying whether a cell nucleus is cancerous or not (Section 3.1). By considering the different types of features, we show in Section 3.2 the importance of using shape features. The effect of classification accuracy on staining estimation is shown in Section 3.3. Our contribution in this paper includes a comprehensive investigation of various image features and associated kernels on the performance of a support vector machine classifier for cancerous cells. Since the classifier is only a part of a larger pipeline, we show that the observed improvements in classification results in improvements in staining estimation. The estimation of staining of various antibodies forms the basis for localized biomarker assessment.

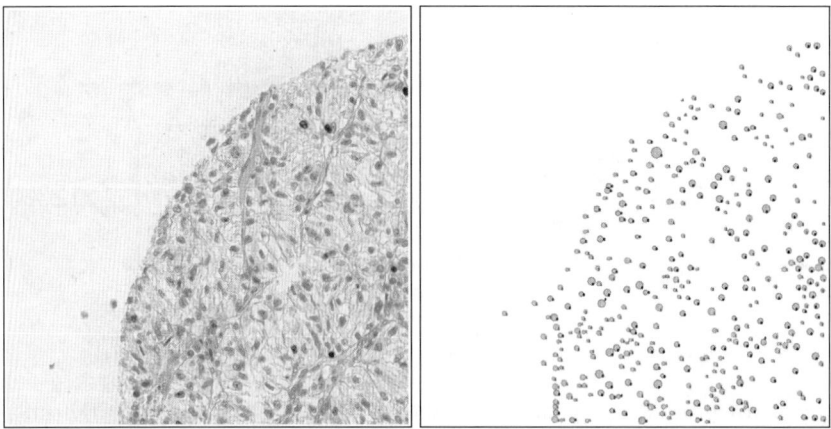

Fig. 2. Left: Top left quadrant of a TMA spot from a RCC patient. **Right:** A pathologist labeled all cell nuclei and classified them into malignant (black) and benign (red).

1.1   Tissue Micro Arrays

Tissue micro arrays (TMA) are an important preparation technique for the quantitative analysis of various types of cancer, like clear cell renal carcinoma (ccRCC). The TMA glass plates carry small round tissue spots of prospective cancerous tissue samples with a thickness of one cell layer for each spot. Our TMAs are immunohistochemically stained for the proliferation indicator protein MIB-1. Positive cell nuclei indicate cell division and appear brown in the image. Additionally, eosin counter-staining is used for discovering the morphological structure of the tissue and the nuclei on the TMA. Hence, MIB-1 negative nuclei are visualized as blue spots in the image.

In this study, we used the top left quarter of eight tissue spots from eight patients. Therefore, each image shows a quarter of the whole spot, i.e. 100-200 cells per image (see Figure 2). The TMA slides were immunohistochemically stained with the MIB-1 (Ki-67) antigen and scanned on a Nanozoomer C9600 virtual slide light microscope scanner from HAMAMATSU Photonics K.K.. The magnification of 40x resulted in a per pixel resolution of $0.23\mu m$. Finally the spots of single patients were extracted as separate three channel color images of 3000 x 3000 pixels size.

1.2   Support Vector Machines and Kernels

Support vector machines (SVM, e.g. [11,2]) are in widespread and highly successful use for bioinformatics tasks. SVMs exhibit very competitive classification performance, and they can conveniently be adapted to the problem at hand. This adaptation is achieved by designing appropriate kernel functions, which can be seen as problem-specific similarity functions between examples. The kernel function implicitly maps examples from their input space $\mathcal{X}$ to a space $\mathcal{H}$

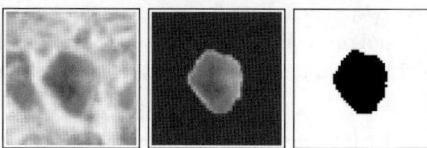

Fig. 3. Example of nucleus segmentation. **Left:** The original 80x80 pixel patch. **Middle:** The segmentation via graphcut. **Right:** The resulting shape of the nucleus.

of real-valued features (e.g. $\mathcal{H} = \mathbb{R}^d, d \in \mathbb{N} \cup \{\infty\}$) via an associated function $\Phi : \mathcal{X} \rightarrow \mathcal{H}$. The kernel function k provides an efficient method for implicitly computing dot products in the feature space $\mathcal{H}$ via $k(x_i, x_j) = \langle \Phi(x_i), \Phi(x_j) \rangle$.

The resulting optimization problem is convex and the global optimum can be found efficiently. Furthermore, there are many freely available software packages which can be used. One remaining question is the choice of features to use for a particular image x and how to compare them via the kernel $k(x_i, x_j)$. Our approach is described in detail in Section 2.4.

2   Methods

2.1   Nuclei Extraction from Labeled TMA Images

TMA images of renal cell carcinoma were independently labeled by two pathologists [7]. From eight exhaustively labeled TMA images, we extracted 1633 patches of size 80x80 pixels centered at labeled cell nuclei (see Figure 3). For 1272 (78 %), the two pathologists agree on the label: 890 (70 %) benign and 382 (30 %) malignant nulcei.

We further labeled the nuclei according to their staining status. For each patch, a color histogram was calculated for a 30x30 pixel size center square. A higher mean of the red histogram than of the blue histogram indicated a stained nucleus.

2.2   Segmentation

Segmentation of cell nuclei was performed with graphcut [1,4,5,9]. The gray intensities were used as unary potentials. A circular shape prior was used to prefer roundish objects (see Figure 3). To this end, the binary potentials were weighted based on their distance to the center. The contour of the segmented object was used to calculate several shape features as described in the following section.

2.3   Feature Extraction

One computationally beneficial aspect of RCC is the fact that the classification of cancerous cells can be performed locally (i.e. patch-wise). This advantage is

Table 1. Guidelines used by pathologists for renal nuclei classification. In addition to the depicted benign and malignant RCC nuclei the tissue consist of a large number of benign non-renal cells like lymphocytes and endothelial cells which were all labeled as non-cancerous.

	Benign nucleus	Malignant nucleus
Shape	roundish	irregular
Membrane	regular	thick/thin irregular
Size	smaller	bigger
Nucleolus	none	dark spot in the nucleus
Texture	smooth	irregular

absent for example in prostate cancer, where the morphology of whole glands is crucial for the classification. Pathologists use several intuitive guidelines to classify nuclei as described in Table 1. One aim of this study was to design features, which are able to capture these guidelines. The following list summarizes the extracted shape and histogram features:

- Histogram of **foreground intensity, FG** (nucleus, 32 bins)
- Histogram of **background intensity, BG** (surrounding tissue, 32 bins)
- **Freeman Chain Code, FCC:** FCC describes the nucleus' boundary as a string of numbers from 1 to 8, representing the direction of the boundary line at that point ([8]). The boundary is discretized by subsampling with grid size 8. For rotational invariance, the first difference of the FCC with minimum magnitude is used. The FCC is represented in a 8-bin histogram.
- **1D-signature, SIG:** Lines are considered from the object center to each boundary pixel. The angles between these lines form the signature of the shape ([8]). As feature, a 16-bin histogram of the signature is generated.
- **Pyramid histograms of oriented gradients, PHOG:** PHOGs are calculated over a level 3 pyramid on the gray-scaled patches ([3]).
- Shape descriptors derived from MATLAB's `regionprops` function (**PROP**) Area `BoundingBox(3:4)`, `MajorAxisLength`, `MinorAxisLength`, `ConvexArea`, `Eccentricity`, `EquivDiameter`, `Solidity`, `Extent`, `Perimeter`, `MeanIntensity`, `MinIntensity`, `MaxIntensity`;

2.4   Kernel Calculation

The feature vectors extracted from the patches were used to calculate a set of kernel matrices. All histograms are normalized. For the histogram features, ten kernel functions and eight distance measures for histograms have been investigated, whereas for the PROP features, only the linear, polynomial and Gaussian kernels were calculated (see Table 2).

Table 2. Commonly used kernels and distances for two scalar feature vectors u and v of the length p. For the histogram features all kernels and distances were employed, while for the PROP feature only the top most three kernels were used.

Kernel	Definition
Linear	$u' * v$
Polynomial (degree d=(3,5,7,10))	$((1/p)(u' * v))^d$
Gaussian	$e^{-(1/p)\sum_i (u_i - v_i)^2}$
Hellinger	$\sum_i \sqrt{u_i * v_i}$
Jensen Shanon	$\dfrac{-1}{\log 2}\sum_i u_i \log \dfrac{u_i}{u_i + v_i} + v_i \log \dfrac{v_i}{u_i + v_i}$
Total variation	$\sum_i \min u_i, v_i$
χ^2	$\sum_i \dfrac{u_i * v_i}{u_i + v_i}$

Distance	Definition
Euclidean	$\sqrt{\sum_i (u_i - v_i)^2}$
Intersection	$\min\left(\sum_i u_i, \sum_i v_i\right) * \left(1 - \dfrac{\sum_i \min(u_i, v_i)}{\min\left(\sum u, \sum v\right)}\right)$
Bhattacharya	$-\log \sum_i \sqrt{u_i * v_i}$
χ^2	$\sum_i \dfrac{(u_i - v_i)^2}{u_i + v_i}$
Kullback Leibler	$\sum_i u_i * \log \dfrac{u_i}{v_i} + \sum_i v_i * \log \dfrac{v_i}{u_i}$
Earth Mover	$\sum_{i=1}^{p} \lvert \sum_{j=1}^{i} u_j - v_j \rvert$
ℓ_1	$\sum_i \lvert u_i - v_i \rvert$

Resulting dissimilarity matrices D were centered to have zero mean and checked for being positive semidefinite, to serve as kernel matrices K. Where needed, negative Eigenvalues were mirrored:

$$D_{centered} = -0.5 * Q * D * Q \ where \ Q = \begin{pmatrix} 1 - \frac{1}{n} & & -\frac{1}{n} \\ & \ddots & \\ -\frac{1}{n} & & 1 - \frac{1}{n} \end{pmatrix}$$

$$K = V * |\Lambda| * V' \ where \ V = Eigenvectormatrix(K)$$

2.5   SVM Training

Training of the SVMs was preformed using the libSVM package for Matlab ([6]). To generate a more reliable gold standard, we selected the patches with consistent labels from both pathologists for training and testing. To combine different kernels, a normalization by their traces was performed. Normalization is especially crucial for the addition of kernels from different scales. Parameter optimization for capacity C was performed with exhaustive search, combining different parameter values with the SVM classifiers.

3   Results

We focus on three main questions in our experiments: (i) Can we at all classify the cell nuclei into a cancerous and a benign group? (ii) Which features are important for such a classification? Is shape important? (iii) Does superior classification rates lead to improved staining estimation by the complete analysis pipeline?

3.1   Cell Nuclei Classification

We investigated the performance of the classification task using 10-fold cross-validation over all patches. The results clearly demonstrate that the data support to automatically classify cell nuclei into benign and malignant at a comparable performance level of pathologists (see Figure 4). The best performing kernels utilize all features: foreground and background histograms, shape descriptors and PHOG. The median misclassification error is 17%. The best kernels showed a capacity of $C = 1000$. To confirm that we did not overfit the data, we chose the best kernel using a further cross validation level on the training data. The found best kernel was then tested on a separate test subset of samples that was not used for training. This classifier achieved a median misclassification error of 18%. In 6 out of 10 of the splits, the diffusion distance (with all histogram features) combined with a linear kernel for the PROP features was identified as best performing SVM kernel.

3.2   Importance of Different Image Features

The features that we consider can be grouped into intensity features (foreground and background), shape features (FCC, SIG and PROP) and PHOG, which combines intensity gradients with a region of interest, i.e. the nucleus shape. To see how the different classes of features affect the performance of classifiers, we again performed a double CV over all kernels, separating the kernels into these three groups. Two conclusions can be drawn from Figure 5: (i) shape information improves classification performance, and (ii) the above mentioned feature classes measure different properties of the data; combining them improves the classifiers.

3.3   Effect of Classifier Performance on Staining Estimation

Recall from Figure 1 that we are ultimately interested in estimating the fraction of cancerous cell nuclei which are stained. In Figure 6, we show the absolute

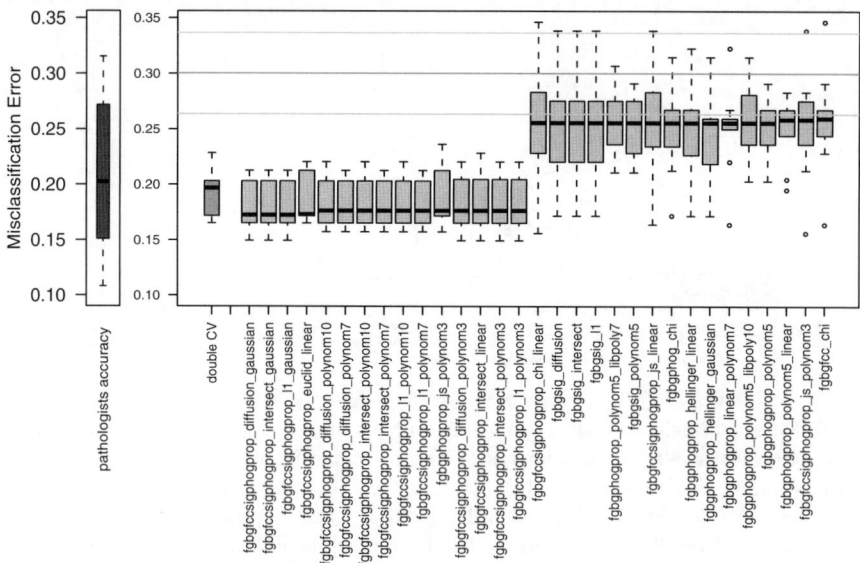

Fig. 4. Left: The "performance" of the pathologist is computed from the confusion matrix between the labels of the two pathologists. **Right:** Performance of kernels in nucleus classification. 15 best performing and 15 worse performing kernels (blue) are shown. Performance measure is the misclassification error in a 10-fold CV. The kernels' names consists of the used features (see Section 2.3) and the kernel function (for histogram and non-histogram features, if needed). The orange bar represents the double CV result, indicating non-overfitting and the ability to classify new samples (see text). The horizontal line shows the mean (and standard deviation) of 100 permutation tests, indicating chance level of prediction.

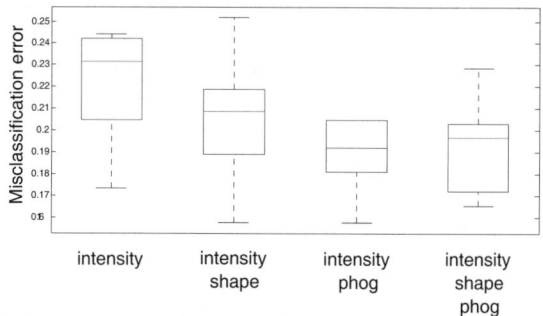

Fig. 5. Misclassification error of best kernels within a certain feature class (intensity: kernels using FG, BG; shape: kernels using FCC, SIG, PROP; phog: kernels using PHOG). Each bar shows the performance of the best kernel using a validation set and a double CV: in the inner CV, the best kernel in a feature class is chosen based on 90% the samples. In the outer CV, this kernel is tested on the remaining 10%. The plot shows that each image feature class carries information for classification.

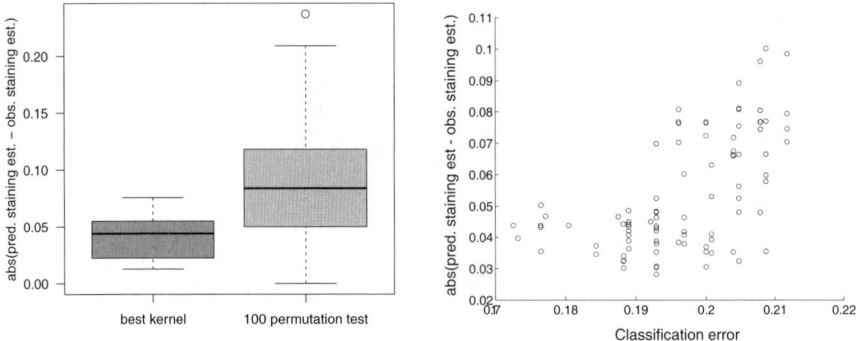

Fig. 6. Effect of nucleus classification performance on staining estimation. **Left:** Comparison between the best classifier and a random classifier with 100 permutation tests on the staining estimation task. In a 10-fold CV, the classifier was trained and used to predict the fraction of stained vs. all cancerous nuclei in the test set. The absolute difference of the predicted fractions to the fractions calculated from the labeled nuclei is shown in the plot. **Right:** Relation between the classifiers' classification performance and staining estimation error (shown for the best 100 kernels). The staining error (absolute difference) of a classifier is calculated in the same way as in the left plot. The better the classification of a kernel is (more left), the better its staining estimation is (more down). The correlation coefficient 0.48.

difference in error between the predicted fraction of staining and the fraction of staining indicated by the pathologists' labels. Note that we used a simple histogram method to estimate the colour. First, we compared the best classifier in Figure 4 to a random classifier. Our results show that a good classifier is able to estimate the staining of the cancerous nuclei with higher accuracy than a random classifier (see Figure 6 (left)). Since the fraction of stained cancerous nuclei is roughly 7% in the data, a classifier that results in an estimate of no staining will have an error of 7% on this plot. In Figure 6 (right) we show the relationship between different classification error rates with the staining estimation error.

4   Conclusion and Outlook

With this study, we contributed in several aspects: (i) We demonstrated that graph cuts can be employed in conjunction with a circular shape prior to segment cell nuclei in a robust fashion. (ii) The classification of nuclei into malignant and benign is not only feasible but additional shape features boost the classification performance. (iii) We investigated and validated a large number of kernels, distance function and combination thereof (Figure 4). The lesson learned is that all extracted features are necessary for optimal performance and the best kernels perform significantly better than chance and comparable to human domain experts. (iv) Finally we demonstrated the influence of the classification task on the subsequent staining estimation problem.

Future goals of our research are going to be the incorporation of the proposed system into a general purpose TMA analysis framework. Part of that is building a robust nuclei detector and analyzing the resulting estimates in the scope of survival statistics. We are convinced that an automated and objective analysis pipeline will significantly further biomarker detection and cancer research.

Acknowledgements. This work was supported by the FET-Open Programme within the 7th Framework Programme for Research of the European Commission, under project SIMBAD grant no. 213250.

References

1. Bagon, S.: Matlab wrapper for graph cut (December 2006), http://www.wisdom.weizmann.ac.il/~bagon
2. Ben-Hur, A., Ong, C.S., Sonnenburg, S., Schölkopf, B., Rätsch, G.: Support vector machines and kernels for computational biology. PLoS Computational Biology 4(10), e1000173 (2008)
3. Bosch, A., Zisserman, A., Munoz, X.: Representing shape with a spatial pyramid kernel. In: CIVR 2007: Proceedings of the 6th ACM international conference on Image and video retrieval, pp. 401–408. ACM, New York (2007)
4. Boykov, Y., Kolmogorov, V.: An experimental comparison of min-cut/max-flow algorithms for energy minimization in vision. IEEE transactions on Pattern Analysis and Machine Intelligence 26(9), 1124–1137 (2004)
5. Boykov, Y., Veksler, O., Zabih, R.: Efficient approximate energy minimization via graph cuts. IEEE transactions on Pattern Analysis and Machine Intelligence 20(12), 1222–1239 (2001)
6. Fan, R.E., Chen, P.H., Lin, C.J.: Working set selection using second order information for training support vector machines. J. Mach. Learn. Res. 6, 1889–1918 (2005)
7. Fuchs, T.J., Wild, P.J., Moch, H., Buhmann, J.M.: Computational pathology analysis of tissue microarrays predicts survival of renal clear cell carcinoma patients. In: Metaxas, D., Axel, L., Fichtinger, G., Székely, G. (eds.) MICCAI 2008, Part II. LNCS, vol. 5242, pp. 1–8. Springer, Heidelberg (2008)
8. Gonzalez, R.C., Woods, R.E., Eddins, S.L.: Digital image processing using matlab (2003), 993475
9. Kolmogorov, V., Zabih, R.: What energy functions can be minimized via graph cuts? IEEE transactions on Pattern Analysis and Machine Intelligence 26(2), 147–159 (2004)
10. Kononen, J., Bubendorf, L., et al.: Tissue microarrays for high-throughput molecular profiling of tumor specimens. Nat. Med. 4(7), 844–847 (1998)
11. Schölkopf, B., Smola, A.J.: Learning with Kernels. MIT Press, Cambridge (2002)

Efficient Object Detection Using Orthogonal NMF Descriptor Hierarchies*

Thomas Mauthner, Stefan Kluckner, Peter M. Roth, and Horst Bischof

Institute for Computer Graphics and Vision
Graz University of Technology, Austria
{mauthner,kluckner,pmroth,bischof}@icg.tugraz.at

Abstract. Recently descriptors based on Histograms of Oriented Gradients (HOG) and Local Binary Patterns (LBP) have shown excellent results in object detection considering the precision as well as the recall. However, since these descriptors are based on high dimensional representations such approaches suffer from enormous memory and runtime requirements. The goal of this paper is to overcome these problems by introducing hierarchies of orthogonal Non-negative Matrix Factorizations (NMF). In fact, in this way a lower dimensional feature representation can be obtained without loosing the discriminative power of the original features. Moreover, the hierarchical structure allows to represent parts of patches on different scales allowing for a more robust classification. We show the effectiveness of our approach for two publicly available datasets and compare it to existing state-of-the-art methods. In addition, we demonstrate it in context of aerial imagery, where high dimensional images have to be processed requiring efficient methods.

1 Introduction

Object detection is an important task in computer vision and thus still of high scientific interest. Most successful approaches are either based on extracting and describing key-points [1,2] or use a sliding window technique [3,4]. Recently, for the later one the usage of Histograms of Oriented Gradients (HOG) [3] and Local Binary Patterns (LBP) [5] in combination with support vector machines (SVM) have been of considerable interest. Since these descriptors are quite general, can be applied for different kind of objects, and are, to some extent, robust to many distortions such approaches become quite popular and were widely applied (e.g., [3,5,6]). However, they are based on high-dimensional feature vectors resulting in an increased computational effort. In particular, at evaluation time each patch of an image, in most cases at multiple scales, has to be tested if it is consistent with the previously learned model or not.

---

* This work was supported by the Austrian Research Promotion Agency (FFG) within the project APAFA (813397) and the project SECRET (821690) under the Austrian Security Research Programme KIRAS.

M. Goesele et al. (Eds.): DAGM 2010, LNCS 6376, pp. 212–221, 2010.

Thus, there has been a considerable interest in speeding up the the classification process [7,8,9]. Zhu et al. [7] proposed to use a cascade of HOGs with variable cell distributions. Rejecting samples in early cascades significantly speeds up the classification while preserving the given accuracy. Maji et al. [8] introduced intersection kernel SVMs (IKSVM) and applied multi-scale histograms of oriented edge energies. Compared to linear SVMs [3] the runtime is constant in terms of the number of required support vectors. Hence, they showed competitive classification results on significantly reduced run-time. Other approaches to reduce the evaluation costs are based on fast pre-searching [9,10,11]. The hough voting schemes by Ommer and Malik [10] or Maji and Malik [11] generate candidate hypotheses which are finally verified with a HOG based classifier. Especially, in [11] it was shown that sliding window classifiers can clearly be outperformed. In contrast to these voting schemes, Lampert et al. [9] proposed a branch-and-bound algorithm for efficient hypothesis generation.

A totally different way to accelerate the classification is to apply a dimensionality reduction technique such as Principal Component Analysis (PCA), Independent Component Analysis (ICA), or Non-negative Matrix Factorization (NMF) to the original feature vectors. Especially, NMF [12] has recently drawn a lot of attention. Since the method does not allow negative entries, neither in the basis nor in the encoding, additive basis vectors are obtained, which mostly represent local structures and are highly suitable for sparse encoding. This is of particular interest if the data can be described by distinctive local information (such as HOGs or LBPs) resulting in a very sparse representation. Moreover, in contrast to the original representation local parts and multi-modalities can be described very well. Thus, an NMF dimension reduction step has been applied in a variety of applications including human pose representation [13], action recognition [14,15], or motion segmentation [16].

NMF, however, has two main disadvantages. First, there exists no closed form solution for the underlying optimization problem - an iterative procedure is required (for training as well as for evaluation). Second, the random initialization and the non-convex optimization problem result in non-unique solutions. To overcome these two problems, we propose to use an orthogonal NMF (ONMF) hierarchy, which has several benefits: (a) The orthogonal basis vectors describe the local information (parts) considerable better than a non-orthonormal basis; in particular, if the data is characterized by a larger variability. (b) The evaluation time is drastically reduced, since the representation can be estimated by a direct projection and no iterative procedure is required. (c) The controlled hierarchical initialization scheme allows us to find reliable basis vectors with different spatial resolutions. We confirm these benefits in an experimental evaluation by applying the approach to different detection tasks.

The reminder of the paper is organized as follows. First, in Section 2 we review the main ideas of NMF and ONMF. Then, in Section 3 we present the novel hierarchical ONMF descriptor tree. Experimental results on different data sets are given in Section 4. Finally, we summarize and conclude the paper in Section 5.

2   Orthogonal NMF

In this section, we review the main concepts of NMF and orthogonal NMF and summarize the required numerical steps[1] which are required for the computation of the hierarchical descriptor tree in Section 3.

2.1   NMF

Given a non-negative matrix $\mathbf{V} \in \mathbb{R}^{m \times n}$, the goal of NMF is to find non-negative matrices $\mathbf{W} \in \mathbb{R}^{m \times r}$ and $\mathbf{H} \in \mathbb{R}^{r \times n}$ that approximate the original data by $\mathbf{V} \approx \mathbf{WH}$. Since there exists no closed-form solution, both matrices $\mathbf{W}$ and $\mathbf{H}$ have to be estimated in an iterative way. Therefore, we consider the optimization problem

$$\min ||\mathbf{V} - \mathbf{WH}||^2$$
$$\text{s.t. } \mathbf{W}, \mathbf{H} \geq 0 \, , \tag{1}$$

where $||.||^2$ denotes the Euclidean distance. Using a gradient formulation we get an iterative solution for the optimization problem (1) by the multiplicative update rules [12]:

$$\mathbf{H} \leftarrow \mathbf{H} \odot \frac{\left[\mathbf{W}^\top \mathbf{V}\right]}{\left[\mathbf{W}^\top \mathbf{WH}\right]} \qquad \mathbf{W} \leftarrow \mathbf{W} \odot \frac{\left[\mathbf{VH}^\top\right]}{\left[\mathbf{WHH}^\top\right]} \, , \tag{2}$$

where $\odot$ denotes the Hadamard product and $[.]/[.]$ an element-wise division.

2.2   Orthogonal NMF

Considering the formulations (1) and (2), two major problems arise: First, an iterative procedure is required for training and evaluation and, second, since the optimization problem (1) is not convex, non-unique solutions are estimated. Thus, the estimation of the coefficients is too slow for many practical applications and the non-unique solutions model the object class only to some extent. In order to overcome these problems, as proposed in [18,17], we introduce an additional orthogonality constraint. Hence, we can re-write the optimization problem (1) to

$$\min ||\mathbf{V} - \mathbf{WH}||^2$$
$$\text{s.t.} \mathbf{W}, \mathbf{H} \geq 0 \ and \ \mathbf{W}^\top \mathbf{W} = \mathbf{I} \, , \tag{3}$$

where the following multiplicative update rules can be derived [17]:

$$\mathbf{H} \leftarrow \mathbf{H} \odot \frac{\left[\mathbf{W}^\top \mathbf{V}\right]}{\left[\mathbf{W}^\top \mathbf{WH}\right]} \qquad \mathbf{W} \leftarrow \mathbf{W} \odot \left(\frac{\left[\mathbf{VH}^\top\right]}{\left[\mathbf{WW}^\top \mathbf{VW}^\top\right]}\right)^{\frac{1}{2}} \, . \tag{4}$$

---

[1] For detailed discussions and the derivation of the given update rules we would refer to [12,17,18].

Compared to the update rules defined in (2), the estimated basis matrix $\mathbf{W}$ is orthogonal. Thus, even requiring an iterative procedure during training, given the data $\mathbf{V}$ during evaluation the computation of the coefficient matrix $\mathbf{H}$ can be reduced to a linear transformation: $\mathbf{H} = \mathbf{W}^\top \mathbf{V}$.

Alternatively, a more efficient update scheme can be obtained if the structure of the constraint surface is considered. Since $\mathbf{W}^\top \mathbf{W} = \mathbf{I}$, i.e., $\mathbf{W}$ is an orthogonal matrix, the vectors $\mathbf{w}_i$, $\mathbf{W} = [\mathbf{w}_1, \ldots, \mathbf{w}_r]$, describe a Stiefel manifold [19]. Thus, the required operations can be performed based on the canonical metric of the Stiefel manifold, yielding the following multiplicative update rules [18]:

$$\mathbf{H} \leftarrow \mathbf{H} \odot \frac{\left[\mathbf{W}^\top \mathbf{V}\right]}{\left[\mathbf{W}^\top \mathbf{W} \mathbf{H}\right]} \qquad \mathbf{W} \leftarrow \mathbf{W} \odot \frac{\left[\mathbf{V} \mathbf{H}^\top\right]}{\left[\mathbf{W} \mathbf{H} \mathbf{V}^\top \mathbf{W}\right]} . \tag{5}$$

From (2), (4), and (5) it can be seen that for all three methods the update rule for $\mathbf{H}$ has the same formulation and only the update rules for $\mathbf{W}$ differ. However, since the Stiefel manifold formulation provides a computationally more efficient update rule in the following we perform the updates according to (5).

3 Hierarchical ONMF

In this section we introduce our new hierarchical ONMF descriptor, which is illustrated in Fig. 1. The main idea is to describe a flat cell structure (e.g., [8]) by an ONMF hierarchy, which can then be used as input for, e.g., an SVM. In contrast to similar approaches such as Pyramid of Histograms of Orientation Gradients (PHOG) [20] or multi-level oriented edge energy features [8] the granularity is not pre-defined. In fact, it can be derived from the data and the bases are not restricted to be geometrically connected. In the following, we first give an overview of the applied low level features, i.e., HOG and LBP, and then we introduce our new ONMF descriptor hierarchy.

3.1 Features

HOG. HOGs are locally normalized gradient histograms, which are estimated as follows. Given an image $\mathbf{I}$ the gradient components $g_x(x, y)$ and $g_y(x, y)$ for every position (x, y) the image is filtered by 1-dimensional masks $[-1, 0, 1]$ in x and y direction [3]. Then, to create the HOG descriptor, the image is divided into non-overlapping 10×10 cells. For each cell, the orientations are quantized into 9 bins and weighted by their magnitude. Overlapping blocks are formed by grouping 2×2 cells, where each cell is normalized using the L^1-norm. The final descriptor is built by concatenation of all normalized cells. In contrast to [8], we do not build a pyramid of different cell sizes, but keep the flat 10×10 pixels cell structure as the input of our ONMF hierarchies. In our case, the spatial grouping known from PHOG [20] or multi-level features [8] is accomplished by the proposed hierarchies.

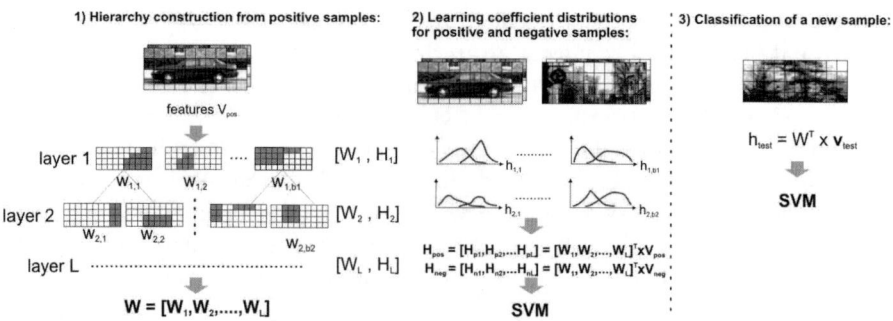

Fig. 1. Concept of hierarchical ONMF for training (left) and testing (right). During the construction of the hierarchy starting from a flat cell-based representation local data-dependent modes are generated. Note that the basis vectors **w** can also be spatially unconnected. The estimated descriptors are then used as input for an SVM.

LBP. An LBP pattern p is constructed by binarization of intensity differences between a center pixel and a number of n sampling points with radius r. The pattern p is assigned 1 if the intensity of a sampling point has a higher intensity than the center pixel and 0 otherwise. The final pattern is formed by the $0 - 1$ transitions of the sampling points in a given rotation order. To avoid ambiguities due to rotation and noise we restrict the number of allowed $0 - 1$ transitions to a maximum u, hence, defining uniform patterns $LBP_{n,r}^u$. For our final description for each cell we build $LBP_{8,1}^4$ pattern histograms and sum up the nonuniform patterns to one bin. To finally estimate the LBP descriptors, we keep the cell-based splitting of the HOGs and extract pattern histograms as described before for each cell.

3.2   Training ONMF Hierarchies

Given the (positive) training data $\mathbf{V} \in \mathbb{R}^{d \times n}$, to build the ONMF hierarchy with L levels, we first have to estimate a root node. For that purpose, we estimate a full ONMF model of size b_1, where the basis matrix $\mathbf{W}_1 \in \mathbb{R}^{d \times b_1}$ and the coefficient matrix $\mathbf{H}_1 \in \mathbb{R}^{b_1 \times n}$ are initialized randomly. Later on, these are updated according to (5). In the subsequent levels $l \in \{2, ..., L\}$ the granularity of the representation is refined by introducing bases of higher dimensions. In fact, given a splitting parameter s and the number of bases b_{l-1}, in level l we get a basis of size $b_l = s \cdot b_{l-1}$, which is initialized by using the basis from level $l - 1$. In particular, to increase the numerical stability, the basis $\mathbf{W}_{l-1}$ is independently augmented with noise obtaining $\widetilde{\mathbf{W}}_{l-1}$, which is then copied s times: $\widehat{\mathbf{W}}_l = \left[\widetilde{\mathbf{W}}_{l-1}, \dots, \widetilde{\mathbf{W}}_{l-1} \right]$. Using $\widehat{\mathbf{W}}_l$ and a randomly initialized encoding $\mathbf{H}_l$ both matrices are again updated according to (5), finally obtaining a basis $\mathbf{W}_l \in \mathbb{R}^{d \times b_l}$ and an encoding $\mathbf{H}_l \in \mathbb{R}^{b_l \times n}$.

This scheme guarantees overlaps between successive hierarchy levels. This is of particular interest for describing spatially important parts of objects. Moreover, since better initial solutions for the bases are given the convergence of the multiplicative update scheme (5) is speeded up. Finally, when the last level L in the hierarchy is reached the final representation $\mathbf{W}$ is estimated by $\mathbf{W} = [\mathbf{W}_1, \ldots, \mathbf{W}_L]$. The overall representation $\mathbf{H}$ is then computed by $\mathbf{H} = \mathbf{W}^\top \mathbf{V}$. The overall number of basis vectors in a hierarchy is given by $b = b_1 \cdot \frac{s^L - 1}{s - 1}$, thus, $\mathbf{W} \in \mathbb{R}^{d \times b}$ and $\mathbf{H} \in \mathbb{R}^{b \times n}$. If several feature types are used in parallel, independent hierarchies are built for each feature cue.

3.3   Classification

Given positive $\mathbf{V}_{pos}$ and negative $\mathbf{V}_{neg}$ training samples in any higher dimensional representation. To train a binary classifier, we first project the data onto the estimated ONFM hierarchy, obtaining the new feature representations $\mathbf{H}_{pos} = \mathbf{W}^\top \mathbf{V}_{pos}$ and $\mathbf{H}_{neg} = \mathbf{W}^\top \mathbf{V}_{neg}$. Then using this new representation we train an SVM classifier, where due to the significant dimensionality reduction the training time can be decreased. To classify a unlabeled sample $\mathbf{v}$, it is first projected onto $\mathbf{W}$ with $\mathbf{h} = \mathbf{W}^\top \mathbf{v}$ and then $\mathbf{h}$ is used as input for the SVM classification step. Again, since the thus encoded feature vector is much smaller than the original descriptor dimension the classification step is computational much more efficient.

4   Experimental Results

To demonstrate the efficiency of our approach, we applied it on two publicly available standard benchmark data sets, i.e., UIUC Cars and TUD Pedestrian and compared it to state-of-the-art methods. In particular, we show the performance gain in terms of precision and recall whereas the computational costs are decreased due to the hierarchical structure. To increase the readability, in the following we refer to the proposed method to as *NMF*, where, e.g., *NMF300* indicates that in the last level 300 basis vectors were used. We additionally quote the results obtained with raw HOG/LBP features. Both representations were trained using a linear SVM. In addition, we applied the proposed approach for car detection in aerial images. Since high dimensional images have to be handled, especially for this application an efficient method is required.

4.1   UIUC Cars

The UIUC dataset [21] includes a collection of single- and multi-scaled cars from the side-view, which represents several real world problems such as varying background, changing illumination conditions, low contrast, and partial occlusions. For the experiments we use the provided evaluation script and the original ground truth annotations. There are two test sets, one for single scales images (approximately 100×40 pixels), which consists of 170 images including 210 cars, which we will refer as to as *UIUC-S*; the second test set representing cars of different scales consists of 108 images showing 139 cars with scales, which we will refer as to as *UIUC-MS*. In addition, we use the given training set consisting of 550 positive samples 500 negative samples.

For evaluation purposes, we trained different classifiers using SVM using different feature representation: raw features - *HOG* and combined HOG and LBP (*HOGLBP*) and corresponding ONMF hierarchies of different sizes. These classifiers were then applied in a sliding window manner to the test images. For the multi-scales test set, we additionally generated an image pyramid taking into account scaling factors of $2^{0.125}$. To compare these results to existing methods, as typical for the UIUC dataset, we estimated recall-precision curves (RPC) and the equal error rate (EER). These results are given in Table 1 and Fig. 2. It can be seen that we achieve state-of-the-art or even slightly better performance, even though in contrast to other methods a pure patch-based representation is applied. Moreover, Fig. 2 reveals that ONMF hierarchies outperform raw feature representation although they are trained on a limited amount of training data.

Table 1. Comparison of the UIUC results using the EER

Method	UIUI-S	UIUC-MS
[8]	97.5 %	n.a %
[2]	97.5 %	95.0 %
[9]	98.5 %	98.6 %
[1]	98.5 %	98.6 %
HOGLBP	97.0 %	95.3 %
NMF300	98.8 %	95.6 %

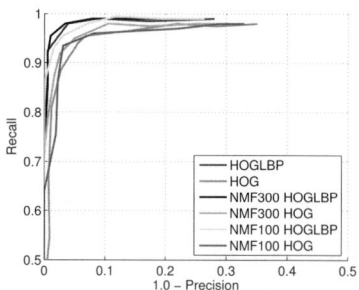

Fig. 2. RPCs for UIUC single scale for different feature combinations

4.2 TUD Pedestrian

Since the UIUC dataset includes only rigid objects, i.e., cars, we also demonstrate our approach for detecting more challenging (articulated) objects, i.e., pedestrians. In particular, we use the TU Darmstadt data set [22] consisting of 400 training images, which include articulated persons from side views, and 250 test images with scale-varying pedestrians. In a first step, we collected positive samples and simultaneously generated an initial negative training set using randomly selected background patches from the INRIA dataset. The experimental setup is the same as described in Section 4.1.

The results are summarized in Fig. 3, where it can be seen that existing methods can be outperformed. This can be explained by the fact that articulated objects such as walking pedestrians can be modeled considerably better by the ONMF hierarchy, which captures sparse local modes on different scales. Therefore, the gap between raw features and their ONMF representation is more distinctive than recognized from the UIUC dataset. This effect is also reflected by the detection results shown in Fig. 4, where it can be seen that raw features often prefer simple vertical structures. Moreover, Fig. 3 shows that the proposed feature combination i.e., HOG and LBP (as also shown in [5]), clearly improves the classification results. Moreover, compared to the underlying features, the runtime during testing can be reduced by a factor of two to four, which is directly related to the reduced dimensionality.

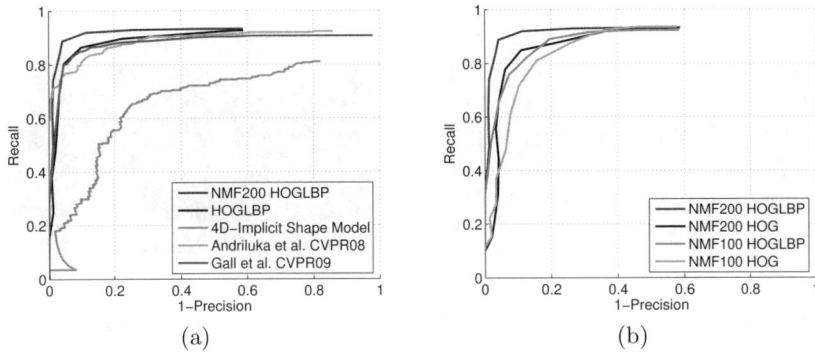

(a)   (b)

Fig. 3. Detection results obtained for the TU Darmstadt dataset: (a) comparison to state-of-the-art methods and (b) a comparison of different feature types and different representation dimensionalities within the ONMF hierarchy

Fig. 4. Illustrative detection results on the TUD data set: the detection results for raw features (green) and NMF (red) are compared to the ground-truth (blue)

4.3   Car Detection in Aerial Images

Finally, we demonstrate our approach for car detection in aerial imagery. In particular for this task an efficient method is required, since we have to cope with high-resolution images. In order to train the classifier, we manually labeled 2873 cars and 4668 background patches of a size of size of 35×70 pixels. Additionally, we synthetically increased the training set by augmenting the images with flipped ones. We separately trained a linear SVM classifier directly on HOG/LBP as well as for the corresponding the NMF feature representations with reduced dimension of 200. At evaluation time we performed car detection on full aerial images with a dimension of 10000×6700 pixels. In order to capture all orientations, the images are rotated in steps of $\pi/8$. For a hand-labeled region (including 1260 cars) we yield an overall detection rate of 72.82 % (at the EER point). A small part of such an aerial image is shown in Fig. 5(b). In addition, for this experiment we carried out a more detailed runtime analysis (on a comparable classification level), which is summarized in Fig. 5(a). Even though, the training time is slightly increased (i.e., a large amount of high dimensional data has to be processed during the ONMF step), the evaluation time can be reduced by a factor of 5.

timings	train	test
HOGLBP	889.0	725.6
HOG	601.0	513.6
HOGLBP NMF200	1024.3	177.3
HOG NMF200	701.4	107.8
HOGLBP NMF400	2174.3	319.3
HOG NMF400	1413.7	197.2

(a)   (b)

Fig. 5. Experimental results for the aerial image data set: (a) timings for training and testing and (b) illustrative detection results (red points indicate the ground-truth, blue points detections obtained with NMF200)

5   Conclusion

In this work we have presented an approach for training efficient hierarchical descriptor-based classifiers. In particular, we build on HOG and LBP features which are then represented by an orthogonal NMF hierarchy. In contrast to similar approaches like the Pyramid of Histograms of Orientation Gradients or multi-level oriented edge energy features the main advantage is the self defining granularity of the ONMF step in each hierarchy level. Thus, we are not limited to a fixed cell size or a fragmentation at each level. In our case the underlying cell size is fixed, but ONMF instantiates the grouping data-dependent. We have demonstrated the benefits of our feature description on competitive data sets in terms of improved detection results and reduced run-time at the same time. Possible extensions and future work would investigate the applicability of direct occlusion and/or defect handling. Orthogonal NMF representation could also increase applicability of existing methods by replacing the general iterative projection with the proposed hierarchies. Moreover, a sophisticated combination of several hierarchies with different parametrization should yield further robustness.

References

1. Gall, J., Lempitsky, V.: Class-specific hough forests for object detection. In: Proc. CVPR (2009)
2. Leibe, B., Leonardis, A., Schiele, B.: Robust object detection with interleaved categorization and segmentation. Int'l. Journal of Computer Vision 77(1-3), 259–289 (2008)

3. Dalal, N., Triggs, B.: Histograms of oriented gradients for human detection. In: Proc. CVPR (2005)
4. Viola, P., Jones, M.J., Snow, D.: Detecting pedestrians using patterns of motion and appearance. In: Proc. ICCV (2003)
5. Wang, X., Han, T.X., Yan, S.: An HOG-LBP human detector with partial occlusion handling. In: Proc. ICCV (2009)
6. Felzenszwalb, P., McAllester, D., Ramanan, D.: A discriminatively trained, multi-scale, deformable part model. In: Proc. CVPR (2008)
7. Zhu, Q., Yeh, M.C., Cheng, K.T., Avidan, S.: Fast human detection using a cascade of histograms of oriented gradients. In: Proc. CVPR (2006)
8. Maji, S., Berg, A.C., Malik, J.: Classification using intersection kernel support vector machines is efficient. In: Proc. CVPR (2008)
9. Lampert, C., Blaschko, M., Hofmann, T.: Beyond sliding windows: Object localization by efficient subwindow search. In: Proc. CVPR (2008)
10. Ommer, B., Malik, J.: Multi-scale detection by clustering lines. In: Proc. ICCV (2009)
11. Maji, S., Malik, J.: Object detection using a max-margin hough transform. In: Proc. CVPR (2009)
12. Lee, D.D., Seung, H.S.: Algorithms for non-negative matrix factorization. In: Advances in NIPS, pp. 556–562 (2001)
13. Agarwal, A., Triggs, B.: A local basis representation for estimating human pose from cluttered images. In: Narayanan, P.J., Nayar, S.K., Shum, H.-Y. (eds.) ACCV 2006. LNCS, vol. 3851, pp. 50–59. Springer, Heidelberg (2006)
14. Thurau, C., Hlaváč, V.: Pose primitive based human action recognition in videos or still images. In: Proc. CVPR (2008)
15. Ikizler-Cinbis, N., Cinbis, R.G., Sclaroff, S.: Learning actions from the web. In: Proc. ICCV (2009)
16. Cheriyadat, A.M., Radke, R.J.: Non-negative matrix factorization of partial track data for motion segmentation. In: Proc. ICCV (2009)
17. Ding, C., Li, T., Peng, W., Park, H.: Orthogonal nonnegative matrix tri-factorizations for clustering. In: Proc. Int'l. Conf. on Knowledge Discovery and Data Mining, pp. 126–135 (2006)
18. Yoo, J., Choi, S.: Orthogonal nonnegative matrix factorization: Multiplicative updates on stiefel manifolds. In: Fyfe, C., Kim, D., Lee, S.-Y., Yin, H. (eds.) IDEAL 2008. LNCS, vol. 5326, pp. 140–147. Springer, Heidelberg (2008)
19. Stiefel, E.: Richtungsfelder und Fernparallelismus in n-dimensionalen Mannigfaltigkeiten. Commentarii Mathematici Helvetici 9(1), 305–353 (1935)
20. Bosch, A., Zisserman, A., Munoz, X.: Image classification using random forests and ferns. In: Proc. ICCV (2007)
21. Agarwal, S., Awan, A., Roth, D.: Learning to detect objects in images via a sparse, part-based representation. IEEE Trans. PAMI 26(11), 1475–1490 (2004)
22. Andriluka, M., Roth, S., Schiele, B.: People-tracking-by-detection and people-detection-by-tracking. In: Proc. CVPR (2008)

VF-SIFT: Very Fast SIFT Feature Matching

Faraj Alhwarin, Danijela Ristić–Durrant, and Axel Gräser

Institute of Automation, University of Bremen, Otto-Hahn-Alle NW1,
D-28359 Bremen, Germany
{alhwarin,ristic,ag}@iat.uni-bremen.de

Abstract. Feature-based image matching is one of the most fundamental issues in computer vision tasks. As the number of features increases, the matching process rapidly becomes a bottleneck. This paper presents a novel method to speed up SIFT feature matching. The main idea is to extend SIFT feature by a few pairwise independent angles, which are invariant to rotation, scale and illumination changes. During feature extraction, SIFT features are classified based on their introduced angles into different clusters and stored in multidimensional table. Thus, in feature matching, only SIFT features that belong to clusters, where correct matches may be expected are compared. The performance of the proposed methods was tested on two groups of images, real-world stereo images and standard dataset images, through comparison with the performances of two state of the arte algorithms for ANN searching, hierarchical k-means and randomized kd-trees. The presented experimental results show that the performance of the proposed method extremely outperforms the two other considered algorithms. The experimental results show that the feature matching can be accelerated about 1250 times with respect to exhaustive search without losing a noticeable amount of correct matches.

Keywords: Very Fast SIFT, VF-SIFT, Fast features matching, Fast image matching.

1 Introduction

Feature-based image matching is a key task in many computer vision applications, such as object recognition, images stitching, structure-from-motion and 3D stereo reconstruction. These applications require often real-time performance.

The SIFT algorithm, proposed in [1], is currently the most widely used in computer vision applications due to the fact that SIFT features are highly distinctive, and invariant to scale, rotation and illumination changes. However, the main drawback of SIFT is that the computational complexity of the algorithm increases rapidly with the number of keypoints, especially at the matching step due to the high dimensionality of the SIFT feature descriptor. In order to overcome this drawback, various modifications of SIFT algorithm have been proposed. Ke and Sukthankar [2] applied Principal Components Analysis (PCA) to the SIFT descriptor. The PCA-SIFT reduces the SIFT feature descriptor dimensionality from 128 to 36, so that the PCA-SIFT is size of the SIFT feature descriptor length, which speeds up feature matching by a factor 3 compared to the original SIFT method.

M. Goesele et al. (Eds.): DAGM 2010, LNCS 6376, pp. 222–231, 2010.

Recently, several papers [5, 6] were published addressing the use of modern graphics hardware (GPU) to accelerate some parts of the SIFT algorithm, focused on features detection and description steps. In [7] GPU was exploited to accelerate features matching. These GPU-SIFT approaches provide 10 to 20 times faster processing. Other papers such as [8] addressed implementation of SIFT on a Field Programmable Gate Array (FPGA) achieving about 10 times faster processing.

The matching step can be speeded up by searching for the Approximate Nearest Neighbor (ANN) instead of the exact one. The most widely used algorithm for ANN search is the kd-tree [9], which successfully works in low dimensional search space, but performs poorly when feature dimensionality increases. In [1] Lowe used the Best-Bin-First (BBF) method, which is expanded from kd-tree by modification of the search ordering so that bins in feature space are searched in the order of their closest distance from the query feature and stopping search after checking the first 200 nearest-neighbors. The BBF provides a speedup factor of 2 times faster than exhaustive search while losing about 5% of correct matches. In [10] Muja and Lowe compared many different algorithms for approximate nearest neighbor search on datasets with a wide range of dimensionality and they found that two algorithms obtained the best performance, depending on the dataset and the desired precision. These algorithms used either the hierarchical k-means tree or randomized kd-trees.

In [11] a novel strategy to accelerate SIFT feature matching as a result of extending a SIFT feature by two new attributes (feature type and feature angle) was introduced. When these attributes are used together with SIFT descriptor for matching purposes so that only features having the same or very similar attribute are compared, the execution of the SIFT feature matching can be speeded up with respect to exhaustive search by a factor of 18 without a noticeable loss of accuracy.

In this paper, a SIFT feature is extended by 4 new pairwise independent angles. These angles are computed from SIFT descriptor. In the SIFT feature extraction phase, the features are stored in 4 dimensional table without extra computational cost. Then, in the matching phase only SIFT features belonging to cells where correct matches may be expected are compared. By exploiting this idea, the execution of the SIFT feature matching can be speeded up by a factor of 1250 with respect to exhaustive search without a noticeable loss of accuracy.

2 Original SIFT Method

The Scale Invariant Feature Transform (SIFT) method takes an image and transforms it into a set of local features extracted through the following three stages, explained here shortly. The more details can be found in [1]:

1. Feature detection and localization: The locations of potential interest points in the image are determined by selecting the extrema of DoG scale space. For searching scale space extrema, each pixel in the DoG images is compared with its 26 neighbors in 3×3 regions of scale-space. If the pixel is lower/larger than all its neighbors, then it is labeled as a candidate keypoint. Each of these keypoints is exactly localized by fitting a 3 dimensional quadratic function computed using a second order Taylor expansion around keypoint. Then keypoints are filtered by discarding points of low contrast and points that belong to edges.

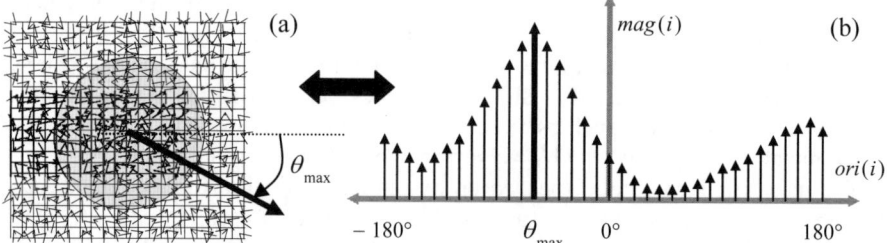

Fig. 1. (a) Gradient image patch around a keypoint. (b) A 36 bins OH constructed from gradient image patch.

2. Feature orientation assignment: An orientation is assigned to each key point based on local image gradient data. For each pixel in a certain image region around the keypoint, the first order gradient is calculated (gradient magnitude and orientation). The gradient data are weighted by scale dependent Gaussian window (illustrated by a circular window on Fig 1a) and then used to build a 36-bin orientation histogram (OH) covering the range of orientations [-180°, 180°] as shown in Fig. 1b. The orientation of the SIFT feature θ_{max} is defined as the orientation corresponding to the maximum bin of the OH as shown in Fig. 1.

3. Feature descriptor: The gradient image patch around keypoint is weighted by a Gaussian window with σ equal to one half the width of the descriptor window (illustrated with a circular window on Fig. 2a) and rotated by θ_{max} to align the feature orientation with the horizontal direction in order to provide rotation invariance (see Fig. 2a). After this rotation, the region around the keypoint is subdivided into 4x4 square sub-regions. From each sub-region, an 8 bin sub-orientation histogram (SOH) is built as shown in Fig. 2b. In order to avoid boundary affects, trilinear interpolation is used to distribute the value of each gradient sample into adjacent histogram bins. Finally, the 16 resulting SOHs are transformed into 128-D vector. The vector is normalized

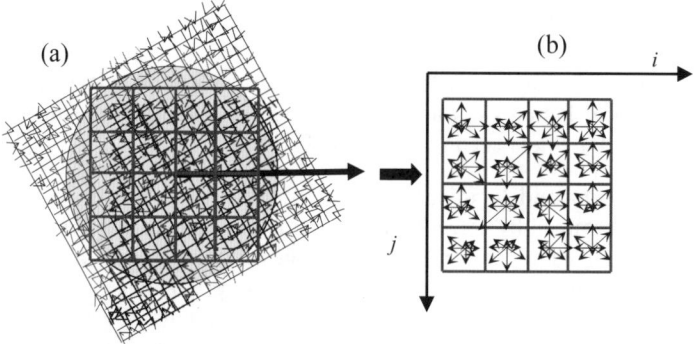

Fig. 2. (a) Rotated gradient image patch with a 4x4 rectangular grid. (b) 16 8-bins SOHs used to build SIFT-descriptor.

to unit length to achieve the invariance against illumination changes. This vector is called SIFT descriptor (SIFT-D) and is used for similarity measuring between two SIFT features.

3   Very Fast SIFT Feature

Generally, if a scene is captured by two cameras or by one camera but from two different viewpoints, the corresponding points in two resulted images will have different image coordinates, different scales, and different orientations. Nevertheless, they must have almost similar descriptors which are used to match the images using a similarity measure [1]. The high dimensionality of descriptor makes the feature matching very time-consuming.

In order to speed up the features matching, it is assumed that 4 pairwise independent angles can be assigned to each feature. These angles are invariant to viewing geometry and illumination changes. When these angles are used for feature matching together with SIFT-D, we can avoid the comparison of a great portion of features that can not be matched in any way. This leads to a significant speed up of the matching step as will be shown below.

3.1   SIFT Feature Angles

In [11], a speeding up of SIFT feature matching by 18 times compared to exhaustive search was achieved by extending SIFT feature with one uniformly-distributed angle computed from the OH and by splitting features into Maxima and Minima SIFT features. In this paper the attempts are made to extend SIFT feature by few angles, which are computed from SIFT-D. As described in section 2, for computation of SIFT-D, the interest region around keypoint is subdivided in sub-regions in a rectangular grid. From each sub-region a SOH is built. Theoretically, it is possible to extend a SIFT feature by a number of angles equal to the number of SOHs as these angles are to be calculated from SOHs. In case of 4x4 grid, the number of angles is then 16. However, to reach the very high speed of SIFT matching, these angles should be components of a multivariate random variable that is uniformly distributed in the 16-dimensional space$[-180°, 180°]^{16}$. In order to meet this requirement, the following two conditions must be verified [15]:

- Each angle has to be uniformly distributed in $[-180°, 180°]$ (equally likely condition).
- The angles have to be pairwise independent (pairwise independence condition).

In this section, the goal is to find a number of angles that are invariant to geometrical and photometrical transformations and that meet the above mentioned conditions. First, the angles between the orientations corresponding to the vector sum of all bins of each SOH and the horizontal orientation are suggested as the SIFT feature angles. Fig. 3b presents geometrically the vector sum of a SOH. Mathematically, the proposed angles $\{\theta_{ij}; i, j = 1,...,4\}$ are calculated as follows:

$$\theta_{ij} = \tan^{-1}\left(\sum_{k=0}^{7} mag_{ij}(k) \cdot \sin\left(ori_{ij}(k)\right) \middle/ \sum_{k=0}^{7} mag_{ij}(k) \cdot \cos\left(ori_{ij}(k)\right)\right) \qquad (1)$$

where $mag_{ij}(k)$ and $ori_{ij}(k)$ are the magnitude and the orientation of the kth bin of the ij^{th} SOH respectively. Since the angles θ_{ij} are computed from SOHs, from which the SIFT-D is built, they are invariant to geometrical and photometrical transformations. However, these angles must be examined, whether they meet the equally likely and pairwise independence conditions.

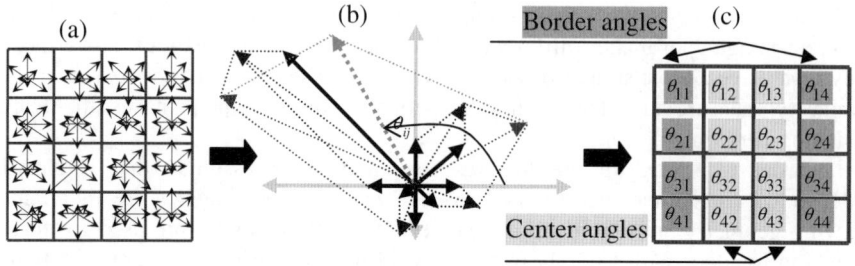

Fig. 3. (a) SOHs, (b):Vector sum of the bins of a SOH, (c) angles computed from SOHs

The equally likely condition: To examine whether the angles θ_{ij} meet the equally likely condition, they are considered as random variables Θ_{ij}. The probability density functions (PDFs) of each angle are estimated from 10^6 SIFT features extracted from 700 test images (500 standard data set images and 200 stereo images from a real-world robotic application). Some examples of used test images are given in Fig 6.

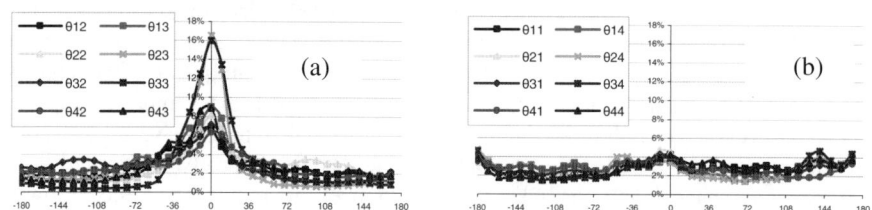

Fig. 4. The PDFs of (a) center and (b) border angles estimated from 10^6 SIFT features extracted from 700 images

The PDFs of Θ_{ij} was computed by dividing the angle space [-180°, 180°] into 36 sub-ranges, where each sub-range cover 10°, and by counting the numbers of SIFT features whose angle θ_{ij} belong to each sub-range. As can be seen from Fig. 4, the angles that are calculated from SOHs around the center of SIFT feature (called center angles), have distributions concerned about 0°, whereas the angles that are calculated from SOHs of the grid border (called border angles), tend to be equally likely distributed over the angle range. The reason of this outcome can be interpreted as follows: On the one hand, the SOHs are computed from the interest region (where OH is computed) after its rotation as shown in Fig. 2a. Therefore the orientations of the maximum bin of each center SOH tend to be equal 0°. On the other hand, for each SOH, the orientation of the maximum bin and the orientation of the vector sum of all bins are strongly dependent since the vector sum includes the maximum bin that has the dominant influence to the vector sum [11]. In the contrary, the border SOHs and the OH do not share the same gradient data, therefore only border angles meet the equally likely condition. Fig. 3c presents the border and center angles.

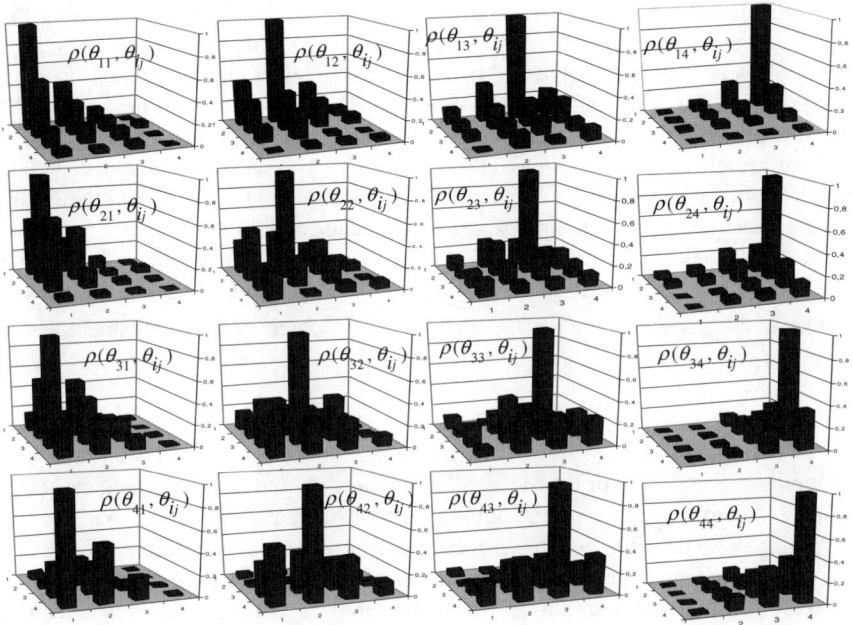

Fig. 5. The correlation coefficients between angles of SIFT features. For example the top left diagram presents correlation coefficients between θ_{11} and all θ_{ij}. The x and y axes present indices i and j respectively while z axis present correlation factor.

The pairwise independence condition: In order to examine whether suggested angles θ_{ij} meet the pairwise independence condition, it is needed to measure the dependence between each two angles. The most familiar measure of dependence between two quantities is the Pearson product-moment correlation coefficient. It is obtained by dividing the covariance of the two variables by the product of their standard deviations. Assuming that two random variables are given X and Y with expected values μ_x and μ_y and standard deviations σ_x and σ_y then the Pearson product-moment correlation coefficient ρ_{xy} between them is defined as:

$$\rho_{xy} = E\left[\left(X - \mu_x\right)\left(Y - \mu_y\right)\right]/\sigma_x\sigma_y \tag{2}$$

where $E[\bullet]$ is the expected value operator.

The correlation coefficients between each two angles α and β are computed using 10^6 SIFT features extracted from the considered test images.

$$\rho_{\alpha\beta} = 10^6 \cdot \sum_{i=1}^{10^6} \left(\alpha_i - \mu_\alpha \right)\left(\beta_i - \mu_\beta \right) \Bigg/ \left(\sqrt{\sum_{i=1}^{10^6} \left(\alpha_i - \mu_\alpha \right)^2} \cdot \sqrt{\sum_{i=1}^{10^6} \left(\beta_i - \mu_\beta \right)^2} \right) \tag{3}$$

The estimated correlation coefficients are explained in Fig. 5. As evident from Fig. 5, angles that are computed from contiguous SOHs, are highly correlated, whereas there is no or very weak correlations between two angles that computed from non-contiguous SOHs. The reason of this outcome is caused by the trilinear interpolation that distributes the gradient samples over contiguous SOHs. In other words, each gradient sample is added to each SOH weighted by 1-d, where d is the distance of the sample from the center of the corresponding sub-region [1]. Hence from the 16 angles at most 4 angles can meet the pairwise independence condition.

As mentioned above, four angles can be pairwise independent and only border angles can meet the equally likely condition, therefore the best choice are the corner angles: $\phi_1 = \theta_{11}$, $\phi_2 = \theta_{14}$, $\phi_3 = \theta_{41}$, and $\phi_4 = \theta_{44}$ which can be considered as new attributes of the SIFT feature.

3.2 Very Fast SIFT Features Matching

Assuming that two sets of extended SIFT features R and L, containing respectively r and l features, are given,. The number of possible matches is equal to $r \cdot l$.

Among these possible matches a small number of correct matches may exist.

To avoid the check of all possible matches, the introduced angles are exploited.

Assuming that the four angles are considered as components of 4-dimensional random vector of angles $\vec{\Phi} = \Phi_1, \Phi_2, \Phi_3, \Phi_4$. This vector is uniformly distributed in the 4-dimensional range $[-180°, 180°]^4$ due to its components meet the equally likely and pairwise independence conditions. For possible SIFT matches, a random vector difference can be constructed.

$$\Delta\vec{\Phi} = \vec{\Phi}_r - \vec{\Phi}_l \tag{4}$$

Generally, the difference between two independent uniformly-distributed random angles is uniformly distributed in $[-180°, 180°]$ [12]. Hence, if $\vec{\Phi}_r$ and $\vec{\Phi}_l$ are independent, then $\Delta\vec{\Phi}$ is uniformly distributed in the 4-dimensional range $[-180°, 180°]^4$.

The behavior of $\Delta\vec{\Phi}$ varies differently according to the type of matches (correct and false matches): For false matches, each two corresponding angles are independent. Hence $\Delta\vec{\Phi}$ is uniformly-distributed. On the other hand, for correct matches, each two corresponding angles tend to be equal, since the features of correct matches tend to have the same SIFT-Ds. Therefore the $\Delta\vec{\Phi}$ tends to have PDF which is concentrated in narrow range around $\Delta\vec{\Phi} = \vec{0}$ (called range of correct matches w_{corr}).

Practically, 95% of correct matches have angle differences in the range $[-36°, 36°]^4$.

Consider that one of the sets of features R or L (for example R) is stored in a 4-dimensional table of size b^4, so that the $ijfg^{th}$ cell contains only SIFT features whose angles meet the following criteria: $\phi_1 \in [-\pi + (i-1) \cdot 2\pi/b, -\pi + i \cdot 2\pi/b)$, $\phi_2 \in [-\pi + (j-1) \cdot 2\pi/b, -\pi + j \cdot 2\pi/b)$, $\phi_3 \in [-\pi + (f-1) \cdot 2\pi/b, -\pi + f \cdot 2\pi/b)$ and $\phi_4 \in [-\pi + (g-1) \cdot 2\pi/b, -\pi + g \cdot 2\pi/b)$.

The number of features of the set R can be expressed as:

$$r = \sum_{i=1}^{b} \sum_{j=1}^{b} \sum_{f=1}^{b} \sum_{g=1}^{b} r_{ijfg} \tag{5}$$

Because of the uniformly distribution of $\bar{\Phi}_r$ in the 4-dimensional range $[-180°, 180°]$, the features are almost equally distributed into b^4 cells. Therefore, it can be asserted that the feature numbers of each cell are almost equal to each other.

$$\forall i, j, f, g \in \{1, 2, \ldots b\}: r_{ijfg} \cong r/b^4 \tag{6}$$

To exclude matching of features that have angle differences outside the range $[-a°, a°]^4$, each SIFT feature of the set L is matched to its corresponding cell and to n neighbour cells to the left and n neighbour cells to the right side for each dimension. In this case the matching time is proportional to the term:

$$T = l \cdot \sum_{o=i-n}^{i+n} \sum_{p=j-n}^{j+n} \sum_{s=f-n}^{f+n} \sum_{t=g-n}^{g+n} r_{opst} = l \cdot r \cdot \left(2n + 1/b\right)^4 \tag{7}$$

Therefore, the achieved speedup factor with respect to exhaustive search is equal to:

$$SF = \left(b/2n + 1\right)^4 \tag{8}$$

The relation between n, a and b is as follows:

$$(2n + 1) \cdot 360°/b = 2a \tag{9}$$

Substituting of (9) into (8) yields:

$$SF = \left(360/2a\right)^4 \tag{10}$$

To exclude matching of features that have angle differences outside the range $[-36°, 36°]^4$ we chose n=1 and b=15, then the matching is speeded up by a factor of 625. When this modification of original SIFT feature matching is combined with the split SIFT features matching explained in [11], the obtained speedup factor reaches 1250 without losing a noticeable portion of correct matches.

4   Experimental Results

The proposed method (VF-SIFT) was tested using a standard image dataset [13] and real-world stereo images. The used image dataset consists of about 500 images of 34 different scenes (some examples are shown in Fig. 6a and 6b). Real-world stereo

a   b   c

Fig. 6. Examples of the standard dataset (a,b) and real world stereo images (c)

images was captured using robotic vision system (A Bumblebee 2 stereo camera with the resolution of. 1024X768 pixels), an example is shown in Fig. 6c.

In order to evaluate the effectiveness of the proposed method, its performance was compared with the performances of two algorithms for ANN (Hierarchical K-Means Tree (HKMT) and Randomized KD-Trees (RKDTs)) [10]. Comparisons were performed using the Fast Library for Approximate Nearest Neighbors (FLANN) [14]. For all algorithms, the matching process is run under different precision degrees making trade off between matching speedup and matching accuracy. The precision degree is defined as the ratio between the number of correct matches returned using the considered algorithm and using the exhaustive search, whereas the speedup factor is defined as the ratio between the exhaustive matching time and the matching time for the corresponding algorithm.

For both ANN algorithms, the precision is adjusted by the number of nodes to be examined, whereas for the proposed VF-SIFT method, the precision is determined by adjusting the width of the range of correct matches w_{corr}.

To evaluate the proposed method two experiments were run. In the first experiment image to image matching was studied. SIFT features were extracted from 100 stereo image pairs and then each two corresponding images were matched using HKMT, RKDTs and VF-SIFT, under different degrees of precision. The experimental results are shown in Figure 7a. The second experiment was carried out on the images of the dataset [13] to study matching image against a database of images. SIFT features extracted from 10 query images are matched against database of 100000 SIFT features using all three considered algorithms, with different degrees of precision. The experimental results are shown in Figure 7b. As can be seen from Figure 7, VF-SIFT extremely outperforms the two other considered algorithms in speeding up of feature matching for all precision degrees. For precision around 95%, VF-SIFT gets a speedup factor of about 1250. For the lower precision degree speedup factor is much higher. Through comparison between Fig. 7a and Fig. 7b, it can be seen that the

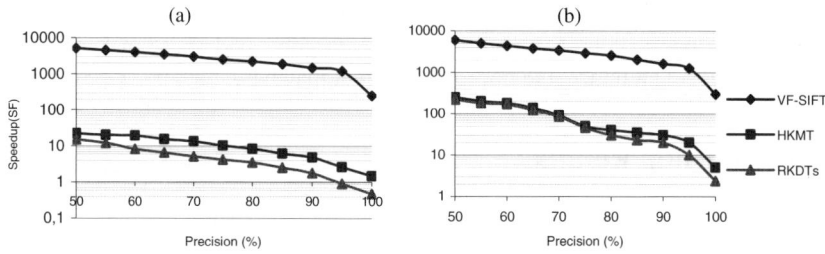

Fig. 7. Trade-off between matching speedup (SF) and matching precision

proposed method performs similarly for both cases of image matching (image to image and image against database of images), whereas ANN algorithms are more suitable for matching image against database of images.

6 Conclusion

In this paper, a new method for fast SIFT feature matching is proposed. The idea behind is to extend a SIFT feature by 4 pairwise independent angles, which are invariant to rotation, scale and illumination changes. During extraction phase, SIFT features are classified based on their angles into different clusters. Thus in matching phase, only SIFT features that belong to clusters where correct matches may be expected are compared. The proposed method was tested on real-world stereo images from a robotic application and standard dataset images. The experimental results show that the feature matching can be speeded up by 1250 times with respect to exhaustive search without lose of accuracy.

References

1. Lowe, D.G.: Distinctive image features from scale-invariant keypoints. Int. Journal of Computer Vision 60(2), 91–110 (2004)
2. Ke, Y., Sukthankar, R.: PCA-sift: A more distinctive representation for local image descriptors. In: Int. Conf. on Computer Vision and Pattern Recognition, pp. 506–513 (2004)
3. Mikolajczyk, K., Schmid, C.: A performance evaluation of local descriptors. IEEE Transactions on pattern analysis and machine intelligence 27(10) (2005)
4. Bay, H., Tuytelaars, T., Van Gool, L.: SURF: Speeded Up Robust Features. Computer Vision and Image Understanding 110(3), 346–359 (2008)
5. Sinha, S.N., Frahm, J.-M., Pollefeys, M., Genc, Y.: GPU-based video feature tracking and matching. Technical report, Department of Computer Science, UNC Chapel Hill (2006)
6. Heymann, S., Miller, K., Smolic, A., Froehlich, B., Wiegand, T.: SIFT implementation and optimization for general-purpose gpu. In: WSCG 2007 (January 2007)
7. Chariot, A., Keriven, R.: GPU-boosted online image matching. In: 19th Int. Conf. on Pattern Recognition, Tampa, Florida, USA (2008)
8. Se, S., Ng, H., Jasiobedzki, P., Moyung, T.: Vision based modeling and localization for planetary exploration rovers. In: Proceedings of International Astronautical Congress (2004)
9. Firedman, J.H., Bentley, J.L., Finkel, R.A.: An algorithm for finding best matches in logarithmic expected time. ACM Transactions Mathematical Software, 209–226 (1977)
10. Muja, M., Lowe, D.G.: Fast Approximate Nearest Neighbors with Automatic Algorithm Configuration. In: Int. Conf. on Computer Vision Theory and Applications (2009)
11. Alhwarin, F., Ristic Durant, D., Gräser, A.: Speeded up image matching using split and extended SIFT features. In: Conf. on Computer Vision Theory and Applications (2010)
12. Simon, M.K., Shihabi, M.M., Moon, T.: Optimum Detection of Tones Transmitted by a Spacecrft, TDA PR 42-123, pp.69–98 (1995)
13. Image database: http://lear.inrialpes.fr/people/Mikolajczyk/Database/index.html
14. FLANN: http://people.cs.ubc.ca/~mariusm/index.php/FLANN/FLANN
15. Fleischer, K.: Two tests of pseudo random number generators for independence and uniform distribution. Journal of statistical computation and simulation 52, 311–322 (1995)

One-Shot Learning of Object Categories Using Dependent Gaussian Processes

Erik Rodner and Joachim Denzler

Chair for Computer Vision
Friedrich Schiller University of Jena
{Erik.Rodner,Joachim.Denzler}@uni-jena.de
http://www.inf-cv.uni-jena.de

Abstract. Knowledge transfer from related object categories is a key
concept to allow learning with few training examples. We present how
to use dependent Gaussian processes for transferring knowledge from
a related category in a non-parametric Bayesian way. Our method is
able to select this category automatically using efficient model selection
techniques. We show how to optionally incorporate semantic similarities obtained from the hierarchical lexical database WordNet [1] into
the selection process. The framework is applied to image categorization
tasks using state-of-the-art image-based kernel functions. A large scale
evaluation shows the benefits of our approach compared to independent
learning and a SVM based approach.

1 Introduction

Learning an object category with a single example image seems to be a difficult
task for a machine learning algorithm, but an easy everyday task for the human
visual recognition system. A common hypothesis to justify the ability of the human cognition system to generalize quickly from few training examples is our use
of prior knowledge from previously learned object categories [2]. This concept
is known as *interclass* or *knowledge* transfer. In general, machine learning problems with few training examples are often highly ill-posed. Knowledge transfer
from related categories allows to use prior knowledge automatically, which can
be utilized to regularize such problems or enrich the training data set indirectly.

In the following we concentrate on knowledge transfer between binary classification tasks, which is also termed one-shot learning for the special case of a
single training example. Given a target task with few positive training examples, one tries to select a support classification task from a heterogenous set
of tasks with each having a relatively large number of training examples. These
additional examples are then used to transfer prior knowledge to the target task.

Knowledge transfer techniques for image categorization were introduced by
Fei-Fei et al. [3], who model knowledge as a prior distribution of the parameters of an object part constellation model. This prior distribution is used in a
maximum-a-posteriori estimation of the target task model parameters. Tommasi
and Caputo [4] present an extension to least-squares SVM which allows to adapt

M. Goesele et al. (Eds.): DAGM 2010, LNCS 6376, pp. 232–241, 2010.

the SVM solution of the target task to the decision boundary of a related object category. Our approach is based on classification and regression with Gaussian processes (GP), which has recently developed to a widely applied and studied machine learning technique [5] and is also used for image categorization [6]. One of the first papers investigating knowledge transfer with GP is the work of Lawrence et al. [7]. They show that the joint optimization of hyper-parameters using all tasks can be highly beneficial. Urtasun et al. [8] assume a shared latent feature space across tasks which can be also modeled in a GP framework.

We use dependent Gaussian process priors, as studied in [9,10] and show how to utilize them for image categorization. Dependent GP priors allow us to efficiently transfer the information contained in the training data of a support classification task in a non-parametric way by using a combined (kernel) covariance matrix. The amount of information transferred is controlled by a single parameter estimated automatically which allows to move gradually from independent to complete combined learning. Parallel to our work, Cao et al. [11] used the same framework for machine learning problems, such as WiFi localization.

Additionally we handle the case of heterogenous tasks, where the set of available support tasks also includes unrelated categories, which do not contain any valuable information for the target task. Similar to [4], we utilize efficient leave-one-out estimates available for GP regression to select a single support classification task. We also show how to use similarities estimated with WordNet [1] to improve this selection. The basic steps of our approach are illustrated in Fig. 1.

The remainder of the paper is organized as follows. We will briefly review classification and regression with Gaussian processes, which is followed by describing transfer learning with dependent Gaussian processes. The question how to choose a valuable support task is answered in Sect. 3.1. Our choice of image-based kernel

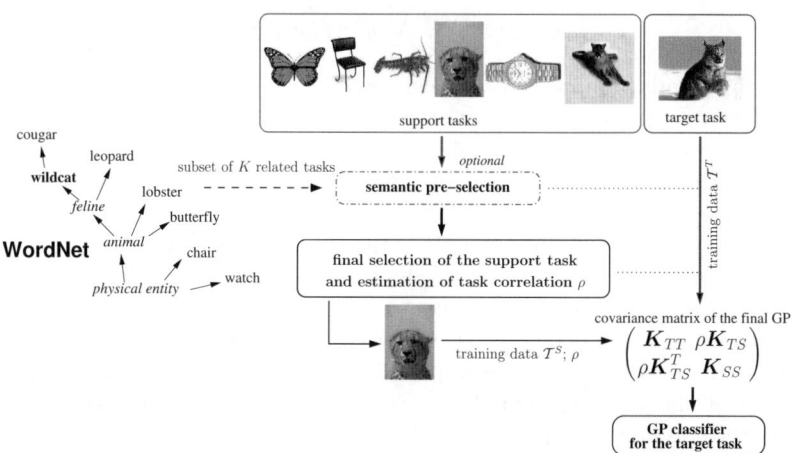

Fig. 1. Basic outline of the proposed transfer learning approach: Semantic similarities between categories and leave-one-out estimates are utilized to select a support task, which is used to transfer knowledge to a target task with dependent Gaussian processes

functions is presented in Sect. 4. Experiments in Sect. 5 show the benefits of our approach in an image categorization application. A summary of our findings and a discussion of future research directions conclude the paper.

2   Classification with Gaussian Process Priors

In the following we will briefly review Gaussian process regression and classification. Due to the lack of space, we concentrate only on the main model assumptions and the resulting prediction equation. For a presentation of the full Bayesian treatment we refer to Rasmussen and Williams [5].

Given training examples $\boldsymbol{x}_i \in \mathcal{T}$, which denote feature vectors or images, and corresponding labels $y_i \in \{-1, 1\}$ we would like to predict the label y_* of an unseen example $\boldsymbol{x}_*$. The two main assumptions of Gaussian processes for regression or classification are:

1. There is an underlying latent function $\boldsymbol{f}$, so that labels y_i are conditionally independent given $\boldsymbol{f}(\boldsymbol{x}_i)$ and described using the so called noise model $p(y_i \mid \boldsymbol{f}(\boldsymbol{x}_i))$.
2. The function $\boldsymbol{f}$ is a sample of a Gaussian process (GP) prior $\boldsymbol{f} \sim \mathcal{GP}(\boldsymbol{0}, \mathcal{K}(\cdot, \cdot))$ with zero mean and covariance or kernel function $\mathcal{K}$.

The Gaussian process prior enables us e.g. to model the covariance of outputs $\boldsymbol{f}(\boldsymbol{x})$ as a function of inputs $\boldsymbol{x}$. With $\mathcal{K}$ being a kernel function describing the similarity of two inputs, one can model the common smoothness assumption that similar inputs should lead to similar function values and thus similar labels. The noise model can be quite general, and for classification tasks one often uses cumulative Gaussian or sigmoid functions [5]. In contrast, we will follow Kapoor et al. [6] and use a Gaussian noise model with variance σ^2

$$p(y_i \mid f(\boldsymbol{x}_i)) = \mathcal{N}(y_i \mid f(\boldsymbol{x}_i), \sigma^2) \tag{1}$$

which is the standard model for GP regression. The advantage is that we do not have to rely on approximated inference methods, such as Laplace approximation or Expectation Propagation. As we will show in Sect. 3.1, this also allows us to compute efficient leave-one-out estimates, which can be used for model selection. The treatment of the classification problem as a regression problem, which regards y_i as real-valued function values instead of discrete labels, can be seen as a clear disadvantage. Nevertheless, as shown in Nickisch et al. [12] the performance of this method is often comparable with Laplace approximation for classification tasks and is computationally much more efficient.

The GP regression model assumptions lead to analytical solutions for the prediction of the label y_*. Let $\boldsymbol{K}$ be the kernel matrix with pairwise kernel values of the training examples $\boldsymbol{K}_{ij} = \mathcal{K}(\boldsymbol{x}_i, \boldsymbol{x}_j)$ and $\boldsymbol{k}_*$ be kernel values $(\boldsymbol{k}_*)_i = \mathcal{K}(\boldsymbol{x}_i, \boldsymbol{x}_*)$ corresponding to a test example $\boldsymbol{x}_*$. The GP model for regression leads to the following equation for the prediction $\bar{y}_*$:

$$\bar{y}_*(\boldsymbol{x}_*) = \boldsymbol{k}_*^T (\boldsymbol{K} + \sigma^2 \boldsymbol{I})^{-1} \boldsymbol{y} \ . \tag{2}$$

3   Transfer Learning with Dependent Gaussian Processes

We now consider the case that two binary classification tasks are given: a so called support task with a large amount of training data $\mathcal{T}^S$ and a target task with only few training examples $\mathcal{T}^T$. This setting is different from the scenario of multi-task learning in which one wants to train classifiers for multiple binary classification tasks in combination. In our case, we do not want to improve the classifier for the support task. This scenario for knowledge transfer is known as the concept of domain adaptation [4] or one-shot learning [3].

Our use of dependent Gaussian processes for transfer learning is based on the model proposed by Chai et al. [9]. For each task j we now have a latent function f_j which is assumed to be sampled from a GP prior. The key idea is that these functions are not assumed to be independent samples which allows us to transfer knowledge between latent functions. Thus, we use a combined latent function $f((j, x)) = f_j(x)$ which is a single sample of a GP prior with a suitable kernel function modeled by:

$$\mathcal{K}((j, x), (j', x')) = \begin{cases} \mathcal{K}^x(x, x') & j = j' \\ \rho\,\mathcal{K}^x(x, x') & j \neq j' \end{cases} , \tag{3}$$

with $\mathcal{K}^x$ being a base kernel function measuring the similarities of input examples. The hyper-parameter ρ of the extended kernel function with $0 \leq \rho \leq 1$ controls the correlation of the tasks: $\rho = 0$ corresponds to the case of independent learning whereas $\rho = 1$ assumes that the tasks are highly related. It should be noted that this type of knowledge transfer can also be motivated theoretically with a decomposition of the latent function into an average latent function shared by all tasks and an independent latent function [13].

We use only one single support classification task which is automatically selected using the techniques described in Sect. 3.1. In comparison to the single task GP model in equation (2), only the kernel function changes. Therefore, the label prediction of an unseen example x_* can be calculated as follows:

$$\bar{y}_*(x_*) = k_*^T (K(\rho) + \sigma^2 I)^{-1} y$$
$$= \begin{pmatrix} k_{T*} \\ \rho k_{S*} \end{pmatrix}^T \left(\begin{pmatrix} K_{TT} & \rho K_{TS} \\ \rho K_{TS}^T & K_{SS} \end{pmatrix} + \sigma^2 I \right)^{-1} \begin{pmatrix} y_T \\ y_S \end{pmatrix} , \tag{4}$$

with y_T and y_S denoting the binary labels for the target and the support task respectively. The matrix K_{TS} contains the pairwise kernel values of the target task and the support task. The same type of notational convention is used for K_{SS}, K_{TT}, k_{S*} and k_{T*}.

Shared Background Category. In the context of image categorization, one often has one single background and multiple object categories [14]. Thus, binary classification tasks share the background category. In this case $\mathcal{T}^S$ and $\mathcal{T}^T$ are not disjoint, which leads to an ill-conditioned kernel matrix $K(\rho)$. We solve this problem by restricting the support training set only to examples of the object category. Therefore the label vector $\boldsymbol{y}_S$ is always a vector of ones. Please note that due to our zero mean assumption of the GP prior this leads to a valid classifier model and for the case of independent learning ($\rho = 0$) to an one-class GP classifier for the support task.

3.1   Selection of a Support Task Using Leave-One-Out Estimates

The optimization of the hyper-parameter ρ and the selection of an appropriate support task can be handled as a combined model selection problem. To solve this problem, we use leave-one-out estimates similar to [4]. In the context of Gaussian process regression, the posterior of the label of a training example $\boldsymbol{x}_i$ conditioned on all other training examples can be computed in closed form [5]

$$\log p(y \mid (\mathcal{T}^T \cup \mathcal{T}^S) \setminus \{\boldsymbol{x}_i\}, \boldsymbol{y}, \rho) = -\frac{1}{2} \log \eta_i^2 - \frac{(y - \mu_i)^2}{2\eta_i^2} - \frac{1}{2} \log 2\pi , \quad (5)$$

with η_i^2 being the variance of the leave-one-out estimate μ_i:

$$\eta_i^2 = 1/\left(\boldsymbol{K}(\rho)^{-1}\right)_{ii} \quad \text{and} \quad \mu_i = y_i - \left(\boldsymbol{K}(\rho)^{-1}\boldsymbol{y}\right)_i \eta_i^2 . \quad (6)$$

The estimates μ_i offer to use a wide range of model selection criteria, such as leave-one-out log predictive probability [5] or squashed and weighted variants [4]. A common measure to assess the performance of a binary classification task is average precision [15]. Therefore, we use the calculation of the average precision directly using the estimates μ_i and ground truth labels y_i. This decision is additionally justified by experiments in the last paragraph of Sect. 5.2, which compares average precision to multiple model selection criteria embedded in our approach. Those experiments will also show that the conditional likelihood $p(\boldsymbol{y}^T \mid \boldsymbol{y}^S, \mathcal{T}^S, \mathcal{T}^T)$ is a non-appropriate model selection criterion in our setting.

We optimize the average precision with respect to ρ, which is a simple one-dimensional optimization, with golden section search [16] for each task of the set of given support tasks. The task and corresponding ρ value which yield the best average precision are chosen to build the final classifier according to equation (4).

3.2   Automatic Pre-selection Using WordNet

Selecting a support classification task among a large set of available tasks using only a single example is itself a very difficult problem, and the selection method described above, might not be able to transfer beneficial information. A solution is the use of prior knowledge from other information sources to pre-select tasks which are likely to be related.

We optionally use WordNet, which is a hierarchical lexical database of the English language, and the textual label of each object category. The usefulness of this information source has been demonstrated recently in the context of attribute based knowledge transfer [17] and hierarchical classification [18]. A possible assumption would be that semantically related object categories are also visual similar. Thus the support task could be selected by semantic similarity measures such as the Reznik measure [1]. Whereas this assumption might hold for e.g. animal hierarchies, it might not hold in all cases and prevents important knowledge transfer from only visual similar tasks. Therefore we use WordNet in advance to leave-one-out selection and pre-select the K most related tasks among all available tasks based on their semantic similarity. For $K = 1$, WordNet selects the support task using the semantic of the category name and the leave-one-out method only optimizes ρ. If K equals the number of available support tasks, WordNet pre-selection does not influence transfer learning and the selection is based on visual similarity only. The importance of the combination of visual and semantic similarities for the selection will be analyzed empirically in Sect. 5.2.

4   Categorization Using Image-Based Kernels

One of the state-of-the-art feature extraction approaches for image categorization is the bag-of-features (BoF) idea. A quantization of local features which is often called a codebook, is computed at the time of training. We use OpponentSIFT [15] descriptors calculated on a dense grid and the method of Moosmann et al. [19] as the clustering method. For each image a histogram is calculated which counts for each codebook entry the number of matching local features. A standard way to apply the BoF idea to kernel-based classifiers is to use the calculated histograms as feature vectors and apply a traditional kernel function such as the radial basis function kernel.

In contrast, we define the kernel function directly on images. The spatial pyramid matching kernel as proposed by Lazebnik et al. [20] extends the BoF idea and divides the image recursively into cells (e.g. 2×2). In each cell the BoF histogram is calculated and the kernel value is computed using a weighted combination of histogram intersection kernels corresponding to each cell. In addition we use the gray-value based PHoG (pyramid histogram of oriented gradients) kernel [21] to compare our results directly to [4] in Sect. 5.1.

5   Experiments

Experiments are performed using all 101 object categories of Caltech 101 and a subset of the Caltech 256 database [3]. Both databases contain a large number of challenging object categories and a suitable background category. In each experiment a target task and corresponding few training images are selected. Training and testing is done for each target task 100 times with a random split of the data, which yields mean performance measure values. In our experiments we empirically support the following *hypotheses*:

1. Our transfer learning approach improves the mean performance compared to independent learning even with a large heterogenous set of available support classification tasks.
2. By using WordNet pre-selection, one can achieve a performance gain for nearly all classification tasks.

3. With a given set of related classification tasks, our method achieves higher recognition rates than Adapted LS-SVM [4].
4. Using the average precision of leave-one-out estimates as described in Sect. 3.1 yields the best performance among several other model selection criteria.

In contrast to multi-task learning with a shared training set [10], a non-zero noise variance σ is not essential to transfer knowledge. For this reason, we choose the noise variance σ^2 adaptively. We iteratively increase the value of σ^2 $(0, 10^{-8}, 10^{-7}, 10^{-6}, \dots)$ until the Cholesky decomposition of the kernel matrix can be calculated ensuring its positive-definiteness.

5.1 Experiments with Caltech 256

We compare our approach to Adapted LS-SVM as proposed by [4] and tried to use an equivalent experimental setting. Two sets of classification tasks are chosen to study the cases of transferring knowledge using only related support classification tasks (car, fire-truck and motorbike) and using a heterogenous set of classification tasks (school-bus, dog and duck). Training and testing is done with a variable number of training images for the target object category and 18 training images for the background and support categories. It is important to note that in contrast to [4] we did not perform a manual selection of images, where the object is clearly visible without occlusion. To compare our results to [4] (values were extracted from Fig 1(a) and Fig 2(a) in the paper) we used the mean recognition rate of all tasks as a performance measure. A pre-selection of classification tasks using WordNet is not applied in this experiment.

Evaluation. The results are shown in Fig. 2. First of all, it is clearly visible that learning benefits from knowledge transfer using our approach even in the "unrelated case" (*Hypothesis 1, page 6*). The same plots also validate that we are able to improve the results of [4] in the "related case" even by using images with occluded objects and different view points (*Hypothesis 3*). In the "unrelated

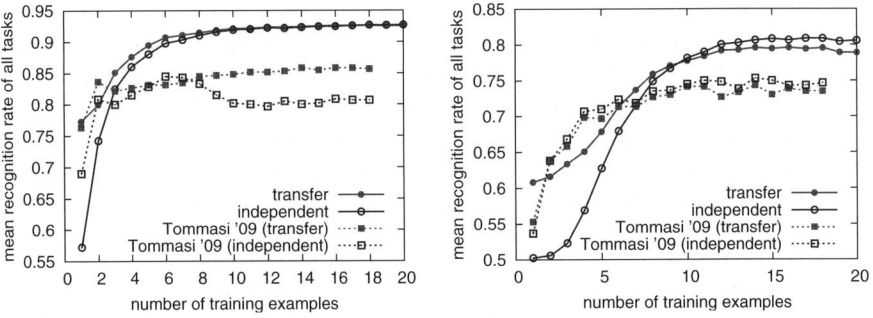

Fig. 2. Caltech 256 results for our transfer learning approach, independent learning and Adapted LS-SVM [4] (which performs a manual selection of adequate object images in advance): (Left) using *related* classification tasks, (Right) using *unrelated* tasks

case" this unconstrained setting yields to lower results for independent learning, which makes transfer learning more important and leads to a significant performance gain even by using unrelated tasks. Our approach also improves [4] for the case of one-shot learning and when more than 7 training images are used.

5.2   Experiments with Caltech 101

In these experiments we use all 101 object categories as available support tasks and a subset of possible target tasks (listed in Fig. 4). As a performance measure for each binary classification task we use average precision as used in the Pascal VOC challenges [15]. Training and testing is done with a variable number of training images for the target object category, 30 training images for the support object categories and 200 background images.

Evaluation. As to be seen in the left plot of Fig. 3 our transfer learning approach without WordNet pre-selection improves the mean average precision compared to independent learning when using few training examples and converges to it with more than 10 training examples (*Hypothesis 1*).

The detailed results for each task using a single training example are included in the left plot of Fig. 4 and deliver additional insight into the methods behavior: Transfer learning improves the average precision for some tasks significantly, e.g. task "gerenuk" with a performance gain of more than 11%, but also fails for some tasks like "okapi". This is due to a wrong selection of the support task using leave-one-out estimates and can be handled in almost all cases by using the WordNet pre-selection method (*Hypothesis 2*). Our transfer learning method fails for the task "watch", because there seems to be no related task in general. The right plot in Fig. 3 shows the benefit of WordNet for those cases by varying the number K of pre-selected support tasks. The same plot also highlights that

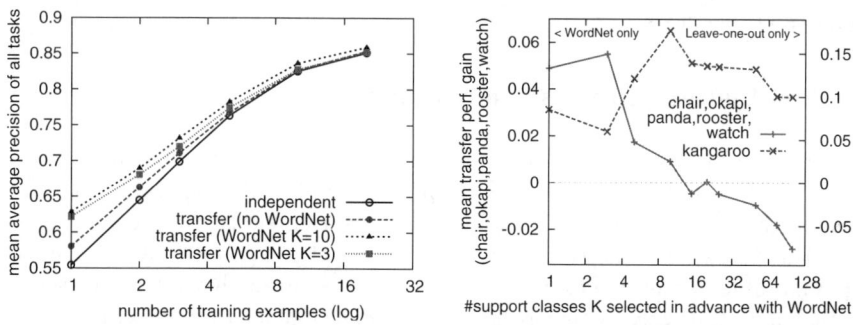

Fig. 3. (Left) Mean average precision of all tasks with a varying number of training examples. (Right) Different peaks of the one-shot learning performance for a varying number of support classes K pre-selected using WordNet: Mean average precision of tasks, which did not benefit from knowledge transfer without WordNet, and performance values of the kangaroo task for different values of K. The results of the kangaroo task highlights the importance of the combination of WordNet and our model-selection.

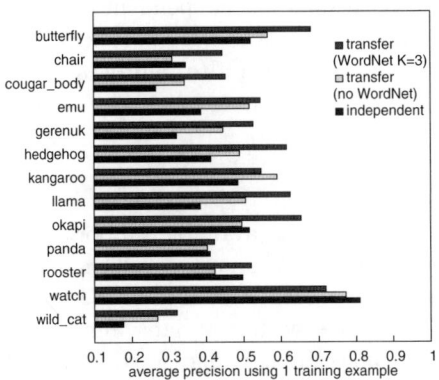

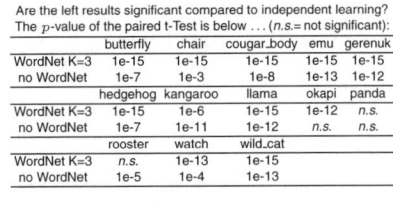

Are the left results significant compared to independent learning?
The p-value of the paired t-Test is below ... ($n.s.$= not significant):

	butterfly	chair	cougar_body	emu	gerenuk
WordNet K=3	1e-15	1e-15	1e-15	1e-15	1e-15
no WordNet	1e-7	1e-3	1e-8	1e-13	1e-12
	hedgehog	kangaroo	llama	okapi	panda
WordNet K=3	1e-15	1e-6	1e-15	1e-12	n.s.
no WordNet	1e-7	1e-11	1e-12	n.s.	n.s.
	rooster	watch	wild_cat		
WordNet K=3	n.s.	1e-13	1e-15		
no WordNet	1e-5	1e-4	1e-13		

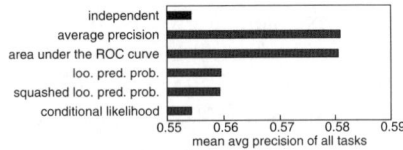

Fig. 4. (Left) Caltech 101 results for our transfer learning approach with and without pre-selection of support classification tasks using WordNet and for independent learning using a single training example. (Right) Mean average precision of all tasks using a single training example without pre-selection and different model selection criteria.

severe pre-filtering with WordNet ($K < 10$) leads to worse results for the task "kangaroo". The same holds for the mean average precision of all tasks which is lower for a strict pre-selection (with $K = 3$) compared to a pre-selection of only 10 support tasks (cf. left plot of Fig. 3). Therefore, only a combination of WordNet pre-selection with a selection based on leave-one-out estimates is reasonable when confronted with a new task.

We additionally evaluated our approach with different model selection criteria: average precision and area under the ROC curve using leave-one-out estimates, leave-one-out predictive probability [5] with squashed variants [4] and the conditional likelihood of the target task training set [11]. The results are shown in the right plot of Fig. 4, justifying our choice of average precision using leave-one-out estimates (*Hypothesis 4*).

6   Conclusions and Further Work

We presented an approach to transfer learning using dependent Gaussian processes, which is able to significantly improve the classification performance of one-shot learning and learning with few examples. Dependent Gaussian processes allowed us to express transfer learning in terms of a combined latent function with a suitable kernel function. Our method chooses a highly related classification task automatically by using the average precision achieved by leave-one-out estimates. We also studied the influence of the number of available tasks on the performance of the selection and demonstrated that an optional pre-selection of tasks using semantic similarities obtained from WordNet can be beneficial.

Further research has to be done to develop a more efficient model selection method to robustly estimate multiple hyper-parameters of the combined covariance function. For example, a combination of performance measures based on leave-one-out estimates and standard maximum likelihood estimation might be suitable. Additionally, dependent Gaussian processes can also be used in conjunction with approximation methods for GP classification rather than regression.

References

1. Pedersen, T., Patwardhan, S., Michelizzi, J.: Wordnet: Similarity - measuring the relatedness of concepts. In: Fifth Annual Meeting of the North American Chapter of the Association for Computational Linguistics (NAACL 2004), pp. 38–41 (2004)
2. Ahn, W., Brewer, W.F., Mooney, R.J.: Schema acquisition from a single example. J. of Experim. Psychology: Learning, Memory, and Cognition 18, 391–412 (1992)
3. Fei-Fei, L., Fergus, R., Perona, P.: One-shot learning of object categories. PAMI 28(4), 594–611 (2006)
4. Tommasi, T., Caputo, B.: The more you know, the less you learn: from knowledge transfer to one-shot learning of object categories. In: BMVC (2009)
5. Rasmussen, C.E., Williams, C.K.I.: Gaussian Processes for Machine Learning. Adaptive Computation and Machine Learning. The MIT Press, Cambridge (2005)
6. Kapoor, A., Grauman, K., Urtasun, R., Darrell, T.: Gaussian processes for object categorization. IJCV 88(2), 169–188 (2009)
7. Lawrence, N.D., Platt, J.C., Jordan, M.I.: Extensions of the informative vector machine. In: Deterministic and Statist. Methods in Machine Learn., pp. 56–87 (2004)
8. Urtasun, R., Quattoni, A., Lawrence, N.D., Darrell, T.: Transfering nonlinear representations using gaussian processes with a shared latent space. In: Proceedings of the Learning Workshop (Snowbird) (2008), MIT-CSAIL-TR-2008-020
9. Chai, K.M.: Generalization errors and learning curves for regression with multi-task gaussian processes. In: NIPS, pp. 279–287 (2009)
10. Bonilla, E., Chai, K.M., Williams, C.: Multi-task gaussian process prediction. In: NIPS, pp. 153–160. MIT Press, Cambridge (2008)
11. Cao, B., Pan, S.J., Zhang, Y., Yeung, D.Y., Yang, Q.: Adaptive transfer learning. In: Proceedings of the 24th AAAI Conference on Artificial Intelligence (2010)
12. Nickisch, H., Rasmussen, C.E.: Approximations for binary gaussian process classification. Journal of Machine Learning Research 9, 2035–2078 (2008)
13. Pillonetto, G., Dinuzzo, F., Nicolao, G.D.: Bayesian online multitask learning of gaussian processes. PAMI 2, 193–205 (2010)
14. Torralba, A., Murphy, K.P., Freeman, W.T.: Sharing visual features for multiclass and multiview object detection. PAMI 29(5), 854–869 (2007)
15. van de Sande, K.E.A., Gevers, T., Snoek, C.G.M.: Evaluating color descriptors for object and scene recognition. PAMI (2010) (in press)
16. Kiefer, J.: Sequential minimax search for a maximum. Proceedings of the American Mathematical Society 4(3), 502–506 (1953)
17. Rohrbach, M., Stark, M., Szarvas, G., Schiele, B., Gurevych, I.: What helps where - and why? semantic relatedness for knowledge transfer. In: CVPR (2010)
18. Marszalek, M., Schmid, C.: Semantic hierarchies for visual object recognition. In: CVPR, pp. 1–7 (2007)
19. Moosmann, F., Triggs, B., Jurie, F.: Fast discriminative visual codebooks using randomized clustering forests. In: NIPS, pp. 985–992 (2006)
20. Lazebnik, S., Schmid, C., Ponce, J.: Beyond bags of features: Spatial pyramid matching for recognizing natural scene categories. In: CVPR, pp. 2169–2178 (2006)
21. Bosch, A., Zisserman, A., Munoz, X.: Representing shape with a spatial pyramid kernel. In: CIVR: Conference on Image and Video Retrieval, pp. 401–408 (2007)

Uncertainty Driven Multi-scale Optimization

Pushmeet Kohli[1], Victor Lempitsky[2], and Carsten Rother[1]

[1] Microsoft Research Cambridge
[2] University of Oxford

Abstract. This paper proposes a new multi-scale energy minimization algorithm which can be used to efficiently solve large scale labelling problems in computer vision. The basic modus operandi of any multi-scale method involves the construction of a smaller problem which can be solved efficiently. The solution of this problem is used to obtain a partial labelling of the original energy function, which in turn allows us to minimize it by solving its (much smaller) projection. We propose the use of new techniques for both the construction of the smaller problem, and the extraction of a partial solution. Experiments on image segmentation show that our techniques give solutions with low pixel labelling error and in the same or less amount of computation time, compared to traditional multi-scale techniques.

1 Introduction

Energy minimization and discrete optimization have become a cornerstone of computer vision. This has primarily been driven by their ability to efficiently compute the Maximum a Posteriori (MAP) solutions in models such as Markov and Conditional random fields (MRFs and CRFs), e.g. [1,3].

In recent years, advances in image acquisition technologies have significantly increased the size of images and 3D volumes. For instance, the latest commercially available cameras can capture images with almost 20 million pixels. In fact it is now possible to capture giga-pixel images of complete cities [7]. Similarly, latest medical imaging systems can acquire 3D volumes with billions of voxels. This type of data gives rise to large scale optimization problems which are very computationally expensive to solve and require large amounts of memory.

Multi-scale processing has long been a popular approach to reduce the memory and computational requirements of optimization algorithms (see [11,4,10] for a review). The basic structure of these methods is quite simple. In order to label a large image (or 3D volume) they first solve the problem at low resolution, obtaining a coarse labelling of the original high resolution problem. This labelling is refined by solving another optimization on a small subset of the pixels. A classic example of such a multi-scale method is the boundary band algorithm [9] for segmenting large images and 3D volumes. Given a solution on a coarse scale (fig. 1c), a partial solution (narrow band around segmentation) is extracted (fig. 1d) which is optimized again on high resolution (fig.1b). This algorithm suffers form the problem that it cannot efficiently recover from large errors present in the coarse labelling. For instance, if a thin foreground structure is missed in

M. Goesele et al. (Eds.): DAGM 2010, LNCS 6376, pp. 242–251, 2010.
© Springer-Verlag Berlin Heidelberg 2010

the coarse labelling, a large band of pixels will need to be analyzed at the fine scale. This would make the size of the resulting higher resolution problem large and reduce the computational benefits. An interesting method to resolve this problem was proposed by Sinop and Grady [13]. Motivated by the problem of segmenting thin structured objects they used the information from a Laplacian pyramid to isolate pixels which might not have attained their correct labelling at the low resolution image. Recently, Lempitsky and Boykov [8] presented an interesting *touch-expand* algorithm that is able to minimize pseudo-boolean energy functions using a narrow band, while retaining the global optimality guarantees. On the downside, it has no bounds on the size of the band it may need to consider, and in the worst case the band can progressively grow to encompass the whole image. While for highly structured unary terms, concerned with the shape fitting task considered in [8], the bands are reasonably small, they are highly likely not to be so for the less structured unary terms in e.g. segmentation problems.

Our Contributions. The goal of this paper is to develop a multi-scale algorithm which can be used to minimize energy functions with a large number of variables. To do this, we need to answer the following questions: **(1)** How to construct the energy for the small scale problem? **(2)** After minimizing this energy, how do we then isolate variables which need to be solved at the finer resolution? As we will explain later in the paper, the answers to these two important questions are not independent. We will now provide a brief overview of our strategy. For ease of explanation, we will use the two-label interactive image segmentation problem as an example. However, our method is general and can be used for any labelling problem such as 3D reconstruction, stereo, object segmentation and optical flow.

Constructing the Low Resolution Energy. Ideally, we would want to construct the energy function in such a manner that its optimal solution, when projected to the full grid, matches the optimal solution of the original energy as closely as possible. Recent band-based methods for image segmentation such as [9] and [13] construct the small scale energy from a low-resolution version of the image to be segmented. In contrast, our approach constructs the small scale energy directly from the energy of the full resolution image. Experiments show that this strategy results in substantial improvements in running time and accuracy.

Uncertainty Driven Bands. The band-based multi-scale segmentation methods use the MAP solution of the small scale problem to isolate which pixels need to be solved at the fine scale. They ignore the confidence or uncertainty associated with the MAP solution. Intuitively, if a variable has low confidence in the MAP label assignment, the labels for its corresponding variables at the fine grid should be inferred by minimizing the original energy. Our method computes uncertainty estimates (fig. 1e) and uses them to choose which regions (fig. 1f) of the image should be included in the optimization at the finer level. Experimental results show that this technique enables us to identify thin structures of the object which had been misclassified in the solution of the coarse energy.

2   Multi-scale Energy Minimization

Most of the our ideas can be applied to any pairwise MRF and CRF. Since we use interactive image segmentation as the example application, we introduce the energy

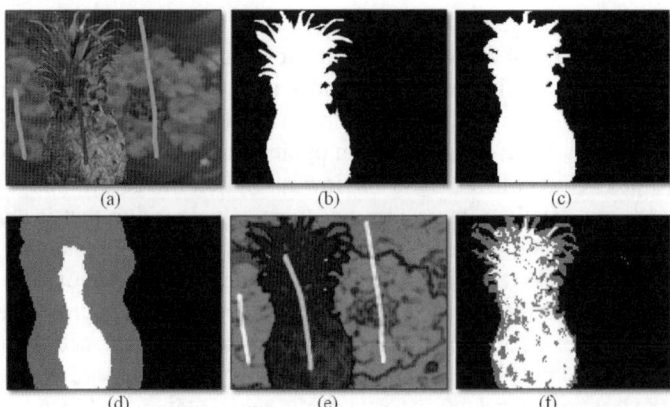

Fig. 1. Uncertainty driven multi-scale image segmentation. (a) Image with user marked brush strokes for different segments. (b) Segmentation obtained by minimizing a conventional segmentation energy (1) defined over the image grid. (c) Segmentation obtained by minimizing an energy defined over a coarse level gird which is constructed using our method (see section 3). Observe that many pixels take labels different from the MAP labels shown in (b). To correct such errors we need to mark such pixels as unlabelled, and find their labels at the fine scale. (d) Partial segmentation obtained by marking pixels in the band around the segmentation boundary of (c) as unlabelled (marked gray). The size of the band is chosen to include all incorrectly labelled pixels. (e) Min-marginal based confidence values for pixels taking the MAP label (bright pixels are more confident) — see section 4 for more details. (f) Partial labelling obtained by marking pixels below a confidence score as unlabelled. As for (d) the confidence threshold is chosen to include all incorrect pixels. For this example, with the uncertainty based scheme 3 times less number of pixels need to be marked as unlabelled compared to the number marked with the boundary band. As less number of variable need to be solved at the fine resolution, we get a larger speed-up.

model only for this application. The energy $E : \mathcal{L}^n \to \mathbb{R}$ can be written as a sum of unary and pairwise functions:

$$E(\mathbf{x}) = \sum_{i \in \mathcal{V}} \phi_i(x_i) + \sum_{(i,j) \in \mathcal{E}} \phi_{ij}(x_i, x_j). \tag{1}$$

The set $\mathcal{V}$ corresponds to the set of all image pixels, $\mathcal{E}$ is set of all edges between pixels in a 4 or 8 neighborhood. The random variable X_i denotes the labelling of pixel i of the image. The label set $\mathcal{L}$ consists of two labels: foreground (fg) and background (bg). Every possible assignment of the random variables $\mathbf{x}$ defines a segmentation. The unary potential is given as $\phi(x_i = \mathcal{S}) = -\log \Pr(I_i | x_i = \mathcal{S})$ where $\mathcal{S} \in \{fg, bg\}$, and initialized using a standard GMM model [12]. The pairwise terms ϕ_{ij} of the CRF take the form of a contrast sensitive Ising model, i.e. $\phi(x_i, x_j) = g(i, j)[x_i \neq x_j]$, where $[arg]$ is 1 if "arg" is true and 0 otherwise. The function $g(i, j)$ is an edge feature based on the difference in colors of neighboring pixels [1]. It is typically defined as:

$$g(i, j) = \theta_p + \theta_v \exp(-\theta_\beta ||I_i - I_j||^2), \tag{2}$$

where I_i and I_j are the colour vectors of pixel i and j respectively. The energy (1) is submodular, hence the global optimum can be computed efficiently with min-cut/maxflow, also known as graph cut, [1].

We now provide an overview of multi-scale methods for energy minimization. These algorithms have the following basic steps:

Construction the smaller problem. A new energy function $E^l : \mathcal{L}^{n\omega_s} \to \mathbb{R}$ is constructed over a smaller grid $(\mathcal{V}^l, \mathcal{E}^l)$ where $\mathcal{V}^l$ denotes the set of lattice points, and $\mathcal{E}^l$ denotes the corresponding edge set. This grid has $|\mathcal{V}^l| = n\omega_s$ variables (original energy E had n variables), where ω_s is the scaling parameter ($0 \leq \omega_s \leq 1$). Let $\mathbf{X}^l = \{X_i^l, i \in \mathcal{V}^l\}$ denote the vector of variables defined on $\mathcal{V}^l$. We will denote their labelling by $\mathbf{x}^l = \{x_1^l, x_2^l, ..., x_{n\omega_s}^l\}$.

Computation of a partial labelling. The coarse energy E^l is minimized to extract a partial labelling $\mathbf{x}^*$ for the original random variables $\mathbf{X}$. Formally, each variable X_i is assigned one label from the extended label set $\mathcal{L} \cup \{\epsilon\}$. The assignment $x_i^* = \epsilon$ indicates that variable X_i has not been assigned any label.

Solving the Partial Labelling induced Projection. The final solution of the original problem is obtained by minimizing a projection of the original energy function E. This energy projection $E' : \mathcal{L}^{n_\epsilon} \to \mathbb{R}$ is constructed from $E(\cdot)$ by fixing the values of the labelled variables as: $E'(\mathbf{x}) = E(\mathbf{x}_p)$ where n_ϵ is the number of unlabelled variables i.e. those assigned label ϵ.

2.1 Partial Labelling Quality

We will now discuss the question of *what is a good partial labelling?* If all variables in the partial solution $\mathbf{x}^*$ are labelled, then the projection E' of the energy will take no variables as argument (a constant function) and would be trivially minimized. On the other hand, if all variables are unlabelled, the projection of the energy will be the same as the original energy ($E' = E$) and we would not obtain any speed-up. While constructing the partial labelling $\mathbf{x}^*$, we also want to make sure that all labelled variable are assigned the MAP label i.e. $\mathbf{x}_i^* \neq \epsilon \Rightarrow \mathbf{x}_i^* = \mathbf{x}_i^{\text{opt}}$. This will ensure that $\min E'(\mathbf{x}) = \min E(\mathbf{x})$.

We will measure the quality of a partial labelling using two measures: (1) Percentage of unlabelled variables (P_u) (lower the better), and (2) Percentage of correct label assignments (P_c). Formally, these are defined as:

$$P_u = \frac{100}{|\mathcal{V}|} \sum_{i \in \mathcal{V}} [x_i^p \neq \epsilon], \text{ and } P_c = \frac{100 \sum_{i \in \mathcal{V}} [x_i^p = x_i^{\text{opt}}]}{\sum_{i \in \mathcal{V}} [x_i^p \neq \epsilon]}, \tag{3}$$

where $[arg]$ is as defined above.

Computation Complexity. Let us denote the complexity of the algorithm we are using to minimize the original energy E by $O(\mathcal{T}(n))$, where $\mathcal{T}(n)$ is any function of n. For instance, the complexity of max-flow based algorithms for minimizing submodular functions of the form (1) is $O(n^3)$, so $\mathcal{T}(n) = n^3$. The computation time for the multi-scale algorithm can be divided into two parts. **(1)** The time taken for computing the partial solution by minimizing the coarse energy E^l. More specifically, $\mathcal{T}(n\omega)$ for minimizing the energy over $n\omega$ variables and a linear term (n) for extracting the partial solution, thus resulting in the complexity $O(\mathcal{T}(n\omega) + n)$. **(2)** Time taken for minimizing the projection of the energy which is $O(\mathcal{T}(P_u))$. The final complexity is: $O(\mathcal{T}(n\omega) + n + \mathcal{T}(P_u))$.

3   Constructing the Low Resolution Problem

We now explain how a smaller energy minimization problem over the coarse grid $\mathcal{V}^l$ is constructed from the original large scale problem, defined over $\mathcal{V}$.

There is a many-one mapping between points in $\mathcal{V}$ and $\mathcal{V}^l$. We denote the set of indices of nodes in $\mathcal{V}$ which map to the node $i \in \mathcal{V}^l$ by $\mathcal{V}(i)$ which we will call the child set of i. We also define the function $k : \mathcal{V} \to \mathcal{V}^l$ which given a node i in the original grid, returns the index of its parent node in the reduced grid $\mathcal{V}^l$. For image labelling problems, the traditional approach is to map a square $\theta_s \times \theta_s$ grid of nodes in $\mathcal{V}$ to a single node in the small scale grid $\mathcal{V}^l$, where $\theta_s^2 = \frac{1}{\omega_s}$. We also use this, however, we can extend to other mappings using e.g. super-pixels.

The energy E^l defined over $\mathcal{V}^l$ has the same form as the original energy E (1), with new unary ϕ_i^l and pairwise ϕ_{ij}^l potentials, as defined next.

Scale Dependent Parameter Selection. Traditional band-based multi-scale methods for image segmentation (e.g. [9,13]) define the energy potentials using a low-resolution version $\mathcal{I}^l$ of the original image $\mathcal{I}$. These methods typically over-look the fact the energy should be adjusted and simple use the original energy, i.e. $\phi_i^l = \phi_i$ and pairwise $\phi_{ij}^l = \phi_{ij}$. Figure 2b shows a result, and we refer to the solution with the symbol $\mathbf{I}^1$.

Using the work of Boykov and Kolmogorov [2] it is clear that the strength of the pairwise potentials has to be adjusted when changing resolution. This is due to the fact that the length of the segmentation boundary, in pixel terms, is reduced when we move from the original image $\mathcal{I}$ to the low-resolution image $\mathcal{I}^l$. This reduction is inversely proportional to $\theta_s = \frac{1}{\sqrt{\omega_s}}$. Thus, we need to reduce the strength of the pairwise potentials by the same amount, hence the terms in eqn. (2) are chosen as $\{\theta_p^l, \theta_v^l, \theta_\beta^l\} = \{\sqrt{\omega_s}\theta_p, \sqrt{\omega_s}\theta_v, \theta_\beta\}^2$. Figure 2c shows an example, which we denote by the symbol $\mathbf{I}^c$.

Construction from the Original Energy. A simple method to compute the unary potential for a variable X_i^l is to sum the unary potentials of all the variables in its child set $\mathcal{V}(i)$. Similarly, the pairwise potential for an edge $(u, v) \in \mathcal{E}^l$ is computed by summing the pairwise potentials defined between their children. The segmentation result is shown in fig. 2(d), and denoted solution $\mathbf{E}$.

At first glance this strategy seems reasonable, however, it ignores the definition of the pairwise potentials defined on variables X_i and X_j $(i, j \in \mathcal{V})$ which have the same parent i.e. $k(i) = k(j)$. In fact, it can be verified that this approximation is correct only if we assume that Ising model pairwise potentials with infinite cost are defined over every pair of variables X_i and X_j $(i, j \in \mathcal{V})$ which share the same parent.

This situation can be more easily understood by considering the maxflow problem corresponding to the original energy minimization problem. As an example, consider a multi-scale decomposition where variables in a 2×2 square on the original grid share the same parent. The pairwise potential definition would translate into a capacity in the max-flow graph that would allow flow coming into any child node to pass through to any other child node and flow out from it. Obviously, this is a very bad assumption

---

[1] It indicates that the coarse scale energy was constructed from the low-res image.

[2] Note that the parameter values depend on the topology of the graph, and this equation would be different for the 3D voxel segmentation problem.

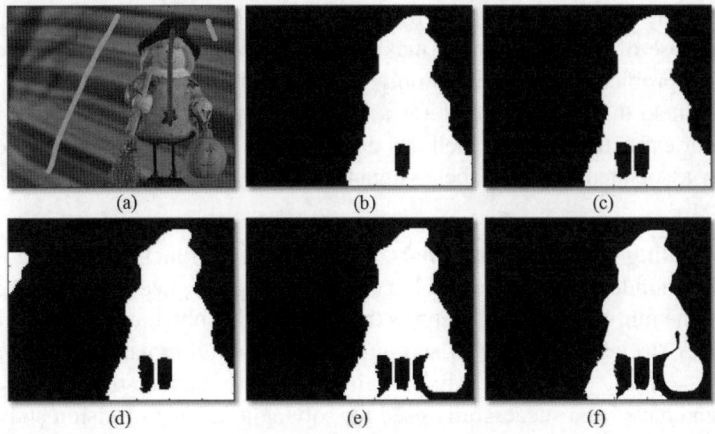

(a)   (b)   (c)

(d)   (e)   (f)

Fig. 2. Constructing the coarse energy. The figure shows the results of using different methods for constructing the coarse energy function. (a) The original image with user marked brush strokes for the different segments (here $\omega_s = 0.04; \theta_s = 5$). (b) The solution $\mathbf{I}$ obtained by constructing the energy using a low resolution version of the original image. (c) Solution $\mathbf{I^c}$ of the energy with the scale-corrected parameter values for the pairwise potentials. (d) Solution $\mathbf{E}$ obtained by using the energy constructed from the original energy. (e) Solution $\mathbf{E^c}$ obtained by using the pairwise potential definition in eqn. (4). (f) The solution obtained by minimizing the energy function (1) defined over the full-resolution image grid.

since in reality the child nodes in the graph corresponding to the original energy may be disconnected from each other[3]. This added phantom capacity would make the pairwise potentials very strong and result in over-smooth segmentations (as seen in fig. 2d). We resolve the problem of excess flow capacity by computing a lower bound on the flow that can be passed between child nodes constituting any two sides of the child-set square of a coarse variable $X_i^l (i \in \mathcal{V}^l)$. This capacity is used as the upper bound on the capacity of the edges which connect a particular parent node to other parent nodes. We estimate the lower bound by finding the minimum capacity edge in the child set.

Coming back to the energy formulation, instead of eqn. (2) we use

$$g_e^l(i,j) = \mathcal{R}(i,j) \min_{\substack{k \in \{i,j\},(u,v) \in \mathcal{E} \\ u \in \mathcal{V}(k), v \in \mathcal{V}}} \theta_p + \theta_v \exp(-\theta_\beta \|I_u - I_v\|^2), \qquad (4)$$

where $\mathcal{R}(i,j)$ is the number of edges between child-sets of the two coarse level variables X_i and X_j $(i,j \in \mathcal{V}^l)$, i.e. $\mathcal{R}(i,j) = \sum_{(u,v) \in \mathcal{E}:u \in \mathcal{V}(i),v \in \mathcal{V}(j)} 1$. A result is shown in fig. 2e, marked with the symbol $\mathbf{E^c}$.

4   Computing Partial Labellings

Conventional multi-scale methods use the lowest cost solution $\mathbf{x}^{l*}$ of the coarse energy E^l for defining the partial labelling. For instance, the method proposed in [9] first defined a full labelling of the original variables $\mathbf{x}^e$ as: $x_i^e = x_{k(i)}^{l*}$, where recall $k(i)$ returns

---

[3] This is true if the Ising model penalty for taking different labels is zero.

the parent of any variable $X_i, i \in \mathcal{V}$. From the solution $\mathbf{x}^e$, a new set $\mathcal{P}_B(\delta_B)$ is derived, which comprise of pixels that are a maximum distance δ_B away from the boundary. The original problem is then solved only for pixels in $\mathcal{P}_B(\delta_B)$. This band has to be large enough, so that no thin structures are lost, example in fig. 1d. This band-based approach for extracting partial labellings does not take into account the confidence or uncertainty associated with the label assignment for any variable $x_i^l, \ i \in \mathcal{V}^l$, which we will do next.

Partial Labelling from Min-marginals. Given an energy function, the min-marginal encodes the confidence associated with a variable being assigned the MAP label. More concretely, the min-marginal $\psi_{i;a}$ returns the energy value obtained by fixing the value of variable X_i to label a ($x_i = a$) and minimizing over all remaining variables. Formally, $\psi_{i;a} = \min_{\mathbf{x}, x_i = a} E(\mathbf{x})$. Min-marginals naturally encode the uncertainty of a labelling and have been successfully used for solving a number of vision and learning problems, e.g. [5]. The exact min-marginals associated with graph cut solutions can be efficiently computed using dynamic graph cuts in roughly 3-4 times the time taken for minimizing the energy itself [6].

We use the absolute difference between the min-marginals corresponding to the fg and bg labels as our confidence score function $\mu : \mathcal{V} \rightarrow \mathbb{R}$. Formally, $\mu(i) = ||\psi_{i;fg} - \psi_{i;bg}||$. If the difference between min-marginals of any variable X_i corresponding to taking the MAP label and any other label is large, then the variable is assigned a high confidence

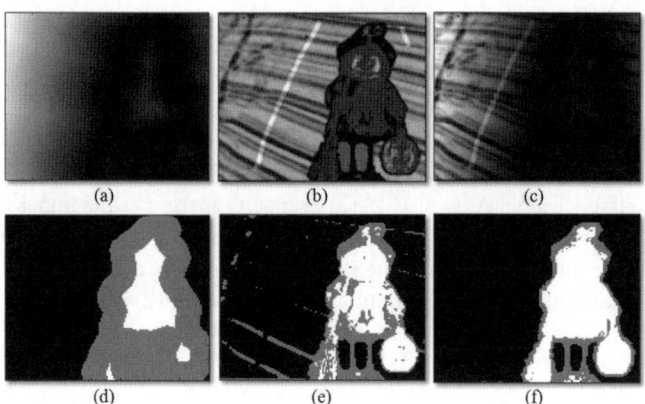

Fig. 3. Computing the partial labelling. The figure shows the results of using different techniques for computing the partial labelling. For this experiment, we used the image shown in figure (2a). We constructed an energy on a coarse level grid with scaling parameter $\omega_s = 0.04$ ($\theta_s = 5$) using the method explained in sec. 3, with the result in fig. (2e). Images (a), (b) and (c) depict the response of a boundary distance function, confidence score $\mu(\cdot)$, and hybrid score $\mathcal{H}(\cdot)$ respectively. These functions were used to obtain the partial solutions shown in images (d), (e) and (f) is the same order. The thresholds for marking pixels as unlabelled was chosen to ensure all marked pixels took the MAP label of the original energy. It can be seen that the hybrid approach requires less number of unlabelled pixels compared to the confidence function which in turn requires less pixels compared to the boundary band approach.

score. The set of variables assigned the label ϵ in the partial solution is now computed by finding the set of nodes $\mathcal{P}_M(\delta)$ whose confidence scores are less than some constant δ_μ i.e. $x_i^e = \epsilon, \forall i \in \mathcal{V}, \mu(i) \leq \delta_\mu$. Formally, the set is defined as $\mathcal{P}_M(\delta_\mu) = \{ i : i \in \mathcal{V}, \mu(i) \leq \delta_\mu \}$. Similar to the boundary band-width parameter δ_B, the value of the confidence threshold δ_μ can be used to the change the number of unlabelled variables (see fig. 3e).

Although, the min-marginals based confidence function is able to obtain good partial labellings, we observed that it sometimes selects variables which are spatially distant from the main foreground segment. This motivated us to test a new hybrid measure which combines the boundary and uncertainty based techniques described above. We construct the new function $\mathcal{H} : \mathcal{V} \rightarrow \mathbb{R}$ which is defined as:$\mathcal{H}(i) = \mu(i)\mathcal{D}(i)$, where $\mathcal{D}$ is the boundary distance function. As before, the set of variables assigned the label ϵ is now computed by finding the set of nodes $\mathcal{P}_H(\delta) = \{ i : i \in \mathcal{V}, \mathcal{H}(i) \leq \delta_H \}$. Formally, the partial solution is defined as: $x_i^e = \epsilon, \forall i \in \mathcal{V}, \mathcal{H}(i) \leq \delta_H$. (see fig. 3f)

5   Experiments

Relating Speed with Accuracy. The speed and accuracy of a multi-scale method are inversely proportional to each other. The correctness of the partial labellings can be easily changed by changing the threshold parameters δ_B, δ_μ, and δ_H.[4] The key matter we want to investigate is, how the percentage of variables (P_u) unlabelled in the partial solutions produced by the different multi-scale minimization techniques affect correctness P_c of the solution. We divide our experiments into two parts to investigate how the performance is affected by the use of different: **(1)** Methods for constructing the smaller energy minimization problem (section 3), **(2)** Methods for extracting the partial labelling from the smaller energy (section 4).

Comparing Energy Construction Methods. We compared the quality of partial labellings generated from different coarse energy constructions using the boundary band method. The results for the images shown in fig. 1(a) and 2(a) are shown in graphs in fig. 4(a) and (b). It can be seen from the results that using scale dependent parameters is better than the traditional approach. Further, the method for constructing coarse energy directly from the original energy function outperforms other methods. It is able to achieve a correctness of $P_c = 99.5\%$ with less than 10% of unlabelled variables.

Comparing Methods for Partial Solution Extraction. The relative performance of different techniques for extracting the partial solution is now analyzed. Consider the problem of segmenting the image in fig. 2(a). Figure 3 shows the different partial labellings extracted from the coarse energy. The size of the sets $\mathcal{P}_B$, $\mathcal{P}_M$, and $\mathcal{P}_H$ was chosen to ensure that the partial labelling were fully correct ($P_c = 100\%$), i.e. this gives the optimal solution of the original problem. The percentage of unlabelled variables required for the boundary band, uncertainty, and hybrid approaches were 35.29%, 17.36%, and 9.03% respectively. The results on the image shown in fig. 1(a) are shown in fig. 5(a).

---

[4] For instance, setting $\delta_B = \sqrt{I_{width}^2 + I_{height}^2}$ will make sure that all variables in the partial solution are unlabelled. Here I_{width} and I_{height} are the width and height of the image I to be segmented respectively.

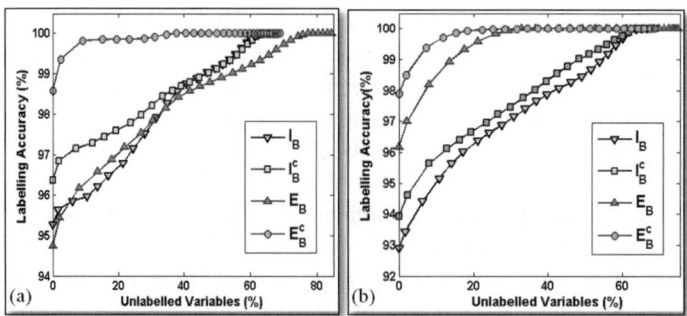

Fig. 4. Results of different multi-scale energy constructions. The graphs show how the accuracy P_c of a partial solution changes as we increase the percentage of unlabelled variables (P_u). Graphs (a) and (b) show the results of using the band based approach on the solutions generated from different energy construction methods. **Key:** $\mathbf{I_B}$: result of energy constructed from the low resolution image, $\mathbf{I_B^c}$: same energy with scale dependent parameters, $\mathbf{E_B}$: smaller problem constructed from the original energy, $\mathbf{E_B^c}$: smaller problem constructed using the lower bound on pairwise potentials.

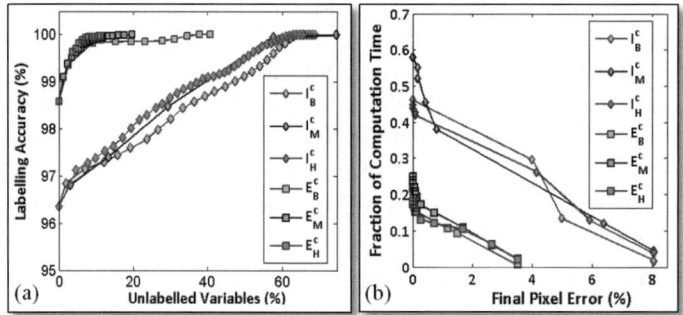

Fig. 5. Computation time and accuracy of different multi-scale methods. Graph (a) shows how the accuracies P_c of partial solutions extracted using different methods change as we increase the percentage of unlabelled variables (P_u). It depicts the results of using different partial solution extraction methods. They key is the same as the one used in graph 4. Subscripts B, M and H denote that the partial solutions were extracted using boundary distance, min-marginal based uncertainty, and the hybrid uncertainty boundary bands respectively. Graph (b) shows the fraction of computation required to achieve a particular pixel labelling accuracy in the final segmentation solution.

Due to space, we only show the better performing methods for constructing the energy, i.e. I^c and E^c. It can be seen that the hybrid partial labelling technique results in a much smaller problem to be solved while still obtaining the exact global minimum.

Relating Computational Speedup and Accuracy. We now discuss the speed-up obtained by our multi-scale methods. As explained in section 2, the total computation time T of a multi-scale method has two primary components: time for partial solution computation t_s, and that for solving the resulting projection (t_p). The size of the projection (and thus t_p) is dependent on the level of accuracy required by the user, while t_s is independent.

For the boundary band method, t_s is equal to the time needed to minimize the coarse energy. For the min-marginal based confidence and hybrid extraction methods, t_s is the time needed to find the min-marginals, which is a much more expensive operation. For instance, for the image shown in figure 1(a), it takes only 1 msec to minimize the coarse energy, while it takes 10 msec to compute all the min-marginals. However, for any given solution accuracy, the min-marginal based methods produce a smaller partial solution compared to the boundary band method. For high levels of accuracy, the size of the projection is large and thus t_p is the dominant time. Thus, min-marginals based methods are able to out-perform band based methods. However, for low levels of accuracy, the size of the projection is very small, which makes t_s to dominate. In such cases, the boundary band based approach outperforms the min-marginals based approach. The performance of all the methods can be seen in the graph shown in fig. 5(b).

6   Discussion and Conclusions

In this paper, we presented a uncertainty driven approach for multi-scale energy minimization. We showed that this strategy allows us to compute solutions close to the globally optimal in a fraction of the time required by a conventional energy minimization algorithm. The method proposed in this paper is general and can be applied to any labelling problem. In future work we would like to investigate how general energies defined over variables with large label sets can be minimized in a multi-scale fashion.

References

1. Boykov, Y., Jolly, M.: Interactive graph cuts for optimal boundary and region segmentation of objects in N-D images. In: ICCV, pp. I: 105–112 (2001)
2. Boykov, Y., Kolmogorov, V.: Computing geodesics and minimal surfaces via graph cuts. In: ICCV, pp. 26–33 (2003)
3. Boykov, Y., Veksler, O., Zabih, R.: Fast approximate energy minimization via graph cuts. PAMI (2001)
4. Gidas, B.: A renormalization group approach to image processing problems. PAMI (1989)
5. Glocker, B., Paragios, N., Komodakis, N., Tziritas, G., Navab, N.: Optical flow estimation with uncertainties through dynamic mrfs. In: CVPR (2008)
6. Kohli, P., Torr, P.: Efficiently solving dynamic markov random fields using graph cuts. In: ICCV, vol. II, pp. 922–929 (2005)
7. Kopf, J., Uyttendaele, M., Deussen, O., Cohen, M.F.: Capturing and viewing gigapixel images. ACM Trans. Graph. (2007)
8. Lempitsky, V.S., Boykov, Y.: Global optimization for shape fitting. In: CVPR (2007)
9. Lombaert, H., Sun, Y., Grady, L., Xu, C.: A multilevel banded graph cuts method for fast image segmentation. In: ICCV (2005)
10. Pérez, P., Heitz, F.: Restriction of a markov random field on a graph and multiresolution statistical image modeling. IEEE Trans. on Inf. Theory (1996)
11. Puzicha, J., Buhmann, J.: Multiscale annealing for grouping and unsupervised texture segmentation. In: CVIU (1999)
12. Rother, C., Kolmogorov, V., Blake, A.: Grabcut: interactive foreground extraction using iterated graph cuts. In: SIGGRAPH, pp. 309–314 (2004)
13. Sinop, A.K., Grady, L.: Accurate banded graph cut segmentation of thin structures using laplacian pyramids. In: Larsen, R., Nielsen, M., Sporring, J. (eds.) MICCAI 2006. LNCS, vol. 4191, pp. 896–903. Springer, Heidelberg (2006)

The Group-Lasso:
$\ell_{1,\infty}$ Regularization versus $\ell_{1,2}$ Regularization

Julia E. Vogt and Volker Roth

Department of Computer Science, University of Basel,
Bernoullistr. 16, CH-4056 Basel, Switzerland
{julia.vogt,volker.roth}@unibas.ch

Abstract. The $\ell_{1,\infty}$ norm and the $\ell_{1,2}$ norm are well known tools for joint regularization in Group-Lasso methods. While the $\ell_{1,2}$ version has been studied in detail, there are still open questions regarding the uniqueness of solutions and the efficiency of algorithms for the $\ell_{1,\infty}$ variant. For the latter, we characterize the conditions for uniqueness of solutions, we present a simple test for uniqueness, and we derive a highly efficient active set algorithm that can deal with input dimensions in the millions. We compare both variants of the Group-Lasso for the two most common application scenarios of the Group-Lasso, one is to obtain sparsity on the level of groups in "standard" prediction problems, the second one is *multi-task* learning where the aim is to solve many learning problems in parallel which are coupled via the Group-Lasso constraint. We show that both version perform quite similar in "standard" applications. However, a very clear distinction between the variants occurs in multi-task settings where the $\ell_{1,2}$ version consistently outperforms the $\ell_{1,\infty}$ counterpart in terms of prediction accuracy.

1 Introduction

In 1996, Tibshirani [1] introduced the Lasso, an ℓ_1-constrained method for sparse variable selection. This well known method in machine learning was extended by Yuan and Lin [2] and by Turlach et. al. [3] to the problem, where explanatory factors are represented as *groups* of variables, leading to solutions that are sparse on the group level. In recent years, mainly two variants of the Group-Lasso have been proposed: one uses the $\ell_{1,2}$ norm and the other one the $\ell_{1,\infty}$ norm as regularization. The $\ell_{1,2}$ norm penalizes the sum of the group-wise ℓ_2-norms of the regression weight, whereas the $\ell_{1,\infty}$ norm penalizes the sum of maximum absolute values per group. Both regularizer induce sparsity on the group level. For $\ell_{1,2}$-constrained problems, extensive research was done, for example in [2], [4], [5] or [6]. The solution was characterized by analyzing the optimality conditions by way of subgradient calculus, and conditions for the uniqueness of the solution were formulated. There exist efficient algorithms that can handle large scale problems with input dimension in the millions, see for instance [7].

Algorithms for the second variant of the Group-Lasso utilizing the $\ell_{1,\infty}$ norm were studied in [3,8,9]. However, questions about the uniqueness of solutions were not addressed in detail, and the method still suffers from high computational costs.

M. Goesele et al. (Eds.): DAGM 2010, LNCS 6376, pp. 252–261, 2010.
© Springer-Verlag Berlin Heidelberg 2010

Existing algorithms can handle input dimensions up to thousands [9] or even up to several thousands [10], but in practical applications these limits are easily exceeded. Interestingly, it seems that no direct comparisons between these two methods have been conducted. In this paper, we address these problems by deriving conditions for the the uniqueness of solutions when using the $\ell_{1,\infty}$ constraint. Such a characterization of solutions is particularly important, because non-uniqueness may severely hamper the interpretation of sparse solutions. As a "by-product" we derive a highly efficient active set algorithm which makes it possible to directly compare the different Group-Lasso variants on large real-world datasets.

For the comparison, we consider two common application scenarios of the Group-Lasso. On the one hand, the Group-Lasso is used as a generalization of the standard Lasso for prediction problems in which single explanatory factors are encoded by a group of variables. Samples of this kind include dummy coding for categorical measurements or polynomial expansions of input features. In these cases, the focus is on *interpretation*, since it may be difficult to interpret a solution which is sparse on the level of single variables.

On the other hand, the Group-Lasso is often used in *multi-task* learning problems, where the likelihood *factorizes* over the individual tasks. The motivation for using the Group-Lasso is to *couple* the individual tasks via the group-structure of the constraint term. Multi-task learning is based on the assumption that multiple tasks share some features or structures. Each task should benefit from the richness of data of all the other tasks, so that many learning problems can be solved in parallel, as was shown in [5]. It should be noticed that in this case the Group-Lasso cannot be interpreted as a direct generalization of the standard Lasso, since the latter is unable to couple the individual tasks.

Large-scale experiments for both types of applications show a clear over-all advantage of the $\ell_{1,2}$ constraint over the $\ell_{1,\infty}$ version: in application scenarios of the first kind, there are no pronounced differences in terms of prediction accuracy, but the $\ell_{1,2}$ seems to have slight advantages regarding the uniqueness of solutions and the computational complexity. For multi-task learning, the distinction between the variants is highly significant, since in this case the $\ell_{1,2}$ version has consistently better predictive performance.

The remainder of this paper is organized as follows: In section 2, conditions for the completeness and uniqueness of Group-Lasso estimates are given, where we adapt the notation in [7] which characterizes a solution as being *complete* if it includes all groups that might be relevant in other solutions. A simple procedure for testing for uniqueness is proposed. In section 3, an active set algorithm is derived that is able to deal with input dimensions in the millions so that large-scale problems can be handled efficiently. In section 4, we report experiments on simulated and real data sets which demonstrate the advantages of the $\ell_{1,2}$ variant of the Group-Lasso.

2   Characterization of Solutions for the $\ell_{1,\infty}$ Group-Lasso

In this section we basically lean on [11], with the difference that we deal with the $\ell_{1,\infty}$ Group-Lasso and with a more general class of likelihood functions. We consider the following setting of a generalized linear model (see [12] for more details): Given an i.i.d. data sample $\{x_1, ..., x_n\}$, $x_i \in \mathbb{R}^d$, arranged as rows of the data matrix X, and a corresponding vector of responses $y = (y_1, ..., y_n)^\top$, we will consider the problem of minimizing a negative log-likelihood function $l(y, \nu, \theta) = - \sum_i \log f(y_i; \nu_i, \theta)$ where f is an exponential family distribution $f(y; \nu, \theta) = \exp(\theta^{-1}(y\nu - b(\nu)) + c(y, \theta))$. Thereby c is a known function and we assume that the scale parameter θ is known, for the sake of simplicity we assume $\theta = 1$. With $\nu = x^\top \beta$ and $b'(\nu) = \eta^{-1}(\nu)$, the gradient can be seen as a function in either ν or β:

$$\nabla_\nu l(\nu) = -(y - \eta^{-1}(\nu)) \quad \text{or} \quad \nabla_\beta l(\beta) = -X^\top \nabla_\nu l(\nu) = -X^\top(y - \eta^{-1}(X\beta)),$$

where $\eta^{-1}(\nu) := (\eta^{-1}(\nu_1), ..., \eta^{-1}(\nu_n))^\top$ and η denotes a link function.

For the following analysis, we partition X, β and $h := \nabla_\beta l$ into J subgroups: $X = (X_1, ..., X_J)$, $\beta = (\beta_1, ..., \beta_J)^\top$ with $\beta_j = (\beta_{j1}, ..., \beta_{jk})^\top$ for $j = 1, ..., J$ and $h = (h_1, ..., h_J)^\top = (X_1^\top \nabla_\nu l, ..., X_J^\top \nabla_\nu l)^\top$. Thereby $l(\beta)$ is a convex objective function and the constrained optimization problem has the following form

$$l(\beta) \to \min \quad \text{s.t} \quad g(\beta) \geq 0 \qquad \text{where} \quad g(\beta) = \kappa - \sum_{j=1}^{J} \|\beta_j\|_\infty. \qquad (1)$$

For the *unconstrained* problem, the solution is *not* unique if the dimensionality exceeds n: Let β^0 be a solution to problem (1) and $\xi \in \mathcal{N}(X)$ where $\mathcal{N}(X)$ is the null space of X, then every $\beta^* := \beta^0 + \xi$ is also a solution. We will require the constraint to be active by defining $\kappa_0 := \min_{\xi \in \mathcal{N}(X)} \sum_{j=1}^{J} \|\beta_j^0 + \xi_j\|_\infty$ and then assume that $\kappa < \kappa_0$. Note that even if there may exist several vectors $\xi \in \mathcal{N}(X)$, the minimum κ_0 is unique.

We restrict our further analysis to finite likelihood functions. Under this assumption, we have $l > -\infty$, and as l is continuous and and the feasible set compact, there exists a solution $\widehat{\beta}$ to (1). Further, as $\kappa < \kappa_0$, any solution $\widehat{\beta}$ to (1) will lie on the boundary of the feasible set, i.e $\sum_{j=1}^{J} \|\widehat{\beta}_j\|_\infty = \kappa$. The solution set of (1) is convex, as l is a convex function, g is a concave function and hence the region of feasible values defined by $g(\beta) \geq 0$ is convex. If additionally X has full rank and $d \leq n$, then it holds that the solution $\widehat{\beta}$ is unique.

Now we consider the Lagrangian function to (1):

$$\mathcal{L}(\beta, \lambda) = l(\beta) - \lambda g(\beta) \qquad (2)$$

For a given $\lambda > 0$, $\mathcal{L}(\beta, \lambda)$ is a convex function in β. As we assume $l > -\infty$, a minimum to (2) exists, because $\mathcal{L}(\beta, \lambda) \to \infty$ for $\|\beta\|_\infty \to \infty$. Hence, there exists at least one $\widehat{\beta}$ that minimizes $\mathcal{L}(\beta, \lambda)$ and $\widehat{\beta}$ is a minimizer iff the d-dimensional null-vector 0_d is an element of the subdifferential $\partial_\beta \mathcal{L}(\beta, \lambda)$. Let d_j denote the dimension of the j-th sub vector β_j. The subdifferential has the following form

$$\partial_\beta \mathcal{L}(\beta, \lambda) = \nabla_\beta l(\beta) + \lambda v = X^\top \nabla_\nu l(\nu) + \lambda v \qquad (3)$$

with $v = (v_1, ... v_J)^\top$ defined by:

$$\|v_j\|_1 \leq 1 \quad \text{if} \quad \|\beta_j\|_\infty = 0, \quad \|v_j\|_1 = 1 \quad \text{if} \quad \|\beta_j\|_\infty > 0 \qquad (4)$$

and in the case $\|\beta_j\|_\infty > 0$ we differentiate between the following three cases:

$$v_{ji} \geq 0 \text{ if } \beta_{ji} = \|\beta_j\|_\infty, \quad v_{ji} \leq 0 \text{ if } \beta_{ji} = -\|\beta_j\|_\infty, \quad v_{ji} = 0 \text{ if } |\beta_{ji}| \neq \|\beta_j\|_\infty \quad (5)$$

Thus, $\widehat{\beta}$ is a minimizer for fixed λ iff

$$0_d = X^T \nabla_\nu l(\nu)|_{\nu=\widehat{\nu}} + \lambda v, \quad (\text{with } \widehat{\nu} = X\widehat{\beta}). \qquad (6)$$

Hence, for all j with $\widehat{\beta}_j = 0_{d_j}$ it holds that $\lambda \geq \|X_j^T \nabla_\nu l(\nu)|_{\nu=\widehat{\nu}}\|_1$. This yields:

$$\lambda = \max_j \|X_j^T \nabla_\nu l(\nu)|_{\nu=\widehat{\nu}}\|_1 \qquad (7)$$

For all j with $\beta_j \neq 0_{d_j}$ it holds that

$$\lambda = \|X_j^T \nabla_\nu l(\nu)|_{\nu=\widehat{\nu}}\|_1 . \qquad (8)$$

With these properties we can state the following theorem:

Theorem 1. *Let $\widehat{\beta}$ be a solution of (1) and $\lambda = \lambda(\widehat{\beta})$ the associated Lagrangian multiplier. Then the following holds:*

(i) λ and $\widehat{h} = \nabla_\beta l(\beta)_{|\beta=\widehat{\beta}}$ are constant across all solutions $\widehat{\beta}_{(i)}$ of (1).

(ii) Let $\widehat{h}$ be the gradient vector from (i) and $\mathcal{B} = \{j_1, ..., j_p\}$ the unique set for which $\|\widehat{h}_j\|_1 = \lambda$. Then $\widehat{\beta}_j = 0_{d_j}\ \forall j \notin \mathcal{B}$ across all solutions $\widehat{\beta}_{(i)}$ of (1).

Proof. (i): Since the value of the objective function $l(\nu_{(i)}) = l_*$ is constant across all solutions and l is strictly convex in $\nu = X\beta$ and convex in β, it follows that $\widehat{\nu}$ must be constant across all solutions $\widehat{\beta}_{(i)}$, hence $\nabla_\beta l(\beta)|_{\beta=\widehat{\beta}} = X^T \nabla_\nu l(\nu)|_{\nu=\widehat{\nu}}$ is constant across all solutions. Uniqueness of λ follows from (7).
(ii) A solution with $\widehat{\beta}_j \neq 0_{d_j}$ for at least one $j \notin \mathcal{B}$ would contradict (8). □

Completeness of Solutions. Assume we have found a solution $\widehat{\beta}$ of (1) with the set of "active" groups $\mathcal{A} := \{j : \widehat{\beta}_j \neq 0\}$. If $\mathcal{A} = \mathcal{B} = \{j : \|\widehat{h}_j\| = \lambda\}$, then there cannot exist any other solution with an active set $\mathcal{A}'$ with $|\mathcal{A}'| > |\mathcal{A}|$. Thus, $\mathcal{A} = \mathcal{B}$ implies that all relevant groups are contained in the solution $\widehat{\beta}$, i.e we cannot have overlooked other relevant groups. Hence the solution is complete, according to [7]. If $\mathcal{A} \neq \mathcal{B}$, then the additional elements in $\mathcal{B} \setminus \mathcal{A}$ define all possible groups that could become active in alternative solutions.

Uniqueness of Solutions. Note that even if $\mathcal{A}$ is complete, it might still contain redundant groups. The question if we have found a *unique* set $\mathcal{A}$ is not answered yet. The following theorem characterizes a simple test for uniqueness under a further rank assumption of the data matrix X. With $X_\mathcal{A}$ we denote the $n \times s$ submatrix of X composed of all active groups, where $\mathcal{A}$ is the active set corresponding to some solution $\widehat{\beta}$ of (1). Then the following theorem holds:

Theorem 2. *Assume that every $n \times n$ submatrix of X has full rank and that $\mathcal{A}$ is complete, i.e. $\mathcal{A} = \mathcal{B}$. Then, if $s \leq n$, $\widehat{\beta}$ is the unique solution of (1).*

Proof. Since the set $\mathcal{B}$ is unique, the assumption $\mathcal{A} = \mathcal{B}$ implies that the search for the optimal solution can be restricted to the space $\mathbb{S} = \mathbb{R}^s$. If $s \leq n$, $X_{\mathcal{A}}$ must have full rank by assumption. Thus, $l(\beta_{\mathbb{S}})$ is a strictly convex function on $\mathbb{S}$ which is minimized over the convex constraint set. Thus, $\widehat{\beta}_{\mathbb{S}}$ is the unique minimizer on $\mathbb{S}$. Since all other $\widehat{\beta}_{j:j \notin \mathcal{A}}$ must be zero, $\widehat{\beta}$ is unique on the whole space. $\square$

3   An Efficient Active-Set Algorithm

With the characterization of the optimal solution presented in section 2 we can now build a highly efficient active set algorithm. The algorithm starts with only one active group. In every iteration, further active groups are selected or removed, dependent on the violation of the Lagrangian condition. At the end we test for completeness of the active set and therewith are able to identify all groups that could be relevant in alternative solutions. The algorithm is a straight-forward generalization of the subset algorithm for the standard Lasso problem presented in [11].

Algorithm 1. Active Set Algorithm

A : Initialize set $\mathcal{A} = j_0$, β_{j_0} arbitrary with $\|\beta_{j_0}\|_\infty = \kappa$.
begin

    B : Optimize over the current active set $\mathcal{A}$.
    Define set $\mathcal{A}^+ = \{ j \in \mathcal{A} : \|\beta_{j_0}\|_\infty > 0 \}$.
    Define $\lambda = \max_{j \in \mathcal{A}^+} \|h_j\|_1$. Adjust the active set $\mathcal{A} = \mathcal{A}^+$.
    C : Lagrangian violation: $\forall j \notin \mathcal{A}$, check if $\|h_j\|_1 \leq \lambda$. If this is the case, we have found a global solution. Otherwise, include the group with the largest violation to $\mathcal{A}$ and go to **B**.
    D : Completness and uniqueness: $\forall j \notin \mathcal{A}$, check if $\|h_j\|_1 = \lambda$. If so, there might exist other solutions with identical cost that include these groups in the active set. Otherwise, the active set is complete. If $X_{\mathcal{A}}$ has full rank $s \leq n$, uniqueness can be checked additionally via theorem 2.

end

The optimization in step **B** can be performed efficiently by the projected gradient method introduced in [9]. The main challenge typically is to compute efficient projections to the $\ell_{1,\infty}$ ball. In [9] an efficient algorithm for the projection to the $\ell_{1,\infty}$ ball was presented where the cost of the algorithm is dominated by sorting and merging vectors. We refer to [9] for details. During the whole algorithm, access to the full set of variables is only necessary in steps **C** and **D**, which are outside the core optimization routine. Step **D** requires almost no additional computations, since it is a by-product of step **C**.

Computing the Solution Path. The Group-Lasso does not exhibit a piecewise linear solution path. But we can still approximate the solution path by starting with a very small κ^0 and then iteratively relaxing the constraint. This results in

---

Algorithm 2. Optimization Step **B**

---

begin

> **B1** : **Gradient**: At time $t-1$, set $b^* := \beta^{t-1} - s\nabla_\beta l(\beta^{t-1})$ where s is the step size parameter, $\mathcal{A}^+ = \mathcal{A}$ and $b_{ji} := |b_{ji}^*|$ for $i = 1, ..., k$.
> **B2** : **Projection**: Calculate vector $\mu = (\mu_1, ..., \mu_J)$ according to [9].
> **B3** : **New solution** :
> if $b_{ji} \geq \mu_j$ then $\beta_{ji}^t = \mu_j$; if $b_{ji} \leq \mu_j$ then $\beta_{ji}^t = b_{ji}$; if $\mu_j = 0$ then $\beta_{ji}^t = 0$.
> **B4** : **Recover sign**: $\mathrm{sgn}(\beta_{ji}^t) := \mathrm{sgn}(b_{ji}^*)$

end

---

a series of increasing values of κ^i with $\kappa^i > \kappa^{i-1}$. Completeness and uniqueness can be tested at every step i.

4 Applications

4.1 Multi-task Experiments

Synthetic Experiments. We address the problem of learning classifiers for a large number of tasks. In multi-task learning, we want to solve many classification problems in parallel and come to a good generalization across tasks. Each task should benefit from the amount of data that is given by all tasks together and hence yield to better results than examining every task by oneself. In all cases we use an active set algorithm, the only difference lies in the projection step.

The synthetic data was created in a similar way as in [9]: We consider a multi-task setting with m tasks and d features with a $d \times m$ parameter matrix $W = [w_1, ..., w_m]$, where $w_i \in \mathbb{R}^d$ is a parameter vector for the i-th task. Further, assume we have a dataset $D = (z_1, ..., z_n)$ with points z belonging to some set Z, where Z is the set of tuples (x_i, y_i, l_i) for $i = 1, ..., n$ where each $x_i \in \mathbb{R}^d$ is a feature vector, $l_i \in 1, ..., m$ is a label that specifies to which of the m tasks the example belongs to and $y_i \in \{-1, 1\}$ is the corresponding label for the example. First we generated the parameter matrix W by sampling each entry from a normal distribution $\mathcal{N}(0, 1)$. We selected 2% of the features to be the set V of relevant features. For each task, a subset $v \subseteq V$ was sampled uniformly at random from the set $\{\#V/2, ..., \#V\}$. All parameters outside v were zeroed. This yields the sparse matrix W. For the training set, we sampled n-times a $d \times m$ matrix, where each entry of the matrix was sampled from the normal distribution $\mathcal{N}(0, 1)$. The corresponding labels $y \in \mathbb{R}^{nm}$ are computed by $y_k = (\mathrm{sgn}(w_k^\top x_k^1), ..., \mathrm{sgn}(w_k^\top x_k^n))^\top \in \mathbb{R}^n$ for $k = 1, ..., m$. The test data was obtained by splitting the training data in three parts and keeping $1/3$ as an "out-of-bag" set. We ran two rounds of experiments where we fixed the number of tasks K to 50 and the number of features d to 500, but changed the number of examples from $N = 20$ to $N = 500$. We evaluated three different approaches: the $\ell_{1,\infty}$ regularization, the $\ell_{1,2}$ regularization and the ℓ_1 regularization. In Figure 1 one can clearly see that the

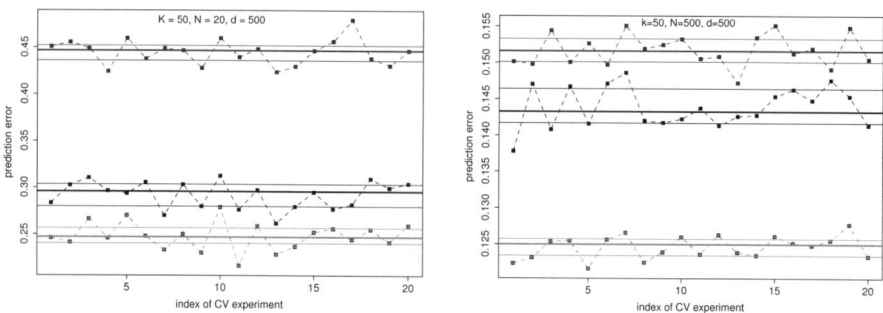

Fig. 1. Prediction error of the different regularizers: red curve: single ℓ_1, blue curve: $\ell_{1,\infty}$, green curve: $\ell_{1,2}$. Left: 20 examples. Right: 500 examples

$\ell_{1,2}$ norm yields the best prediction for every data set. The left picture shows the experiment with only few examples. $\ell_{1,2}$ performs best, followed by $\ell_{1,\infty}$ and single ℓ_1 shows definitely the worst performance. For the experiment with more examples, the order of performance stays the same, but the gap to the single ℓ_1 norm is notably reduced. There is not one single case where the $\ell_{1,\infty}$ norm performs better than the $\ell_{1,2}$ regularization. There exists a convincing explanation for the better performance of the $\ell_{1,2}$ variant: The different tasks are only connected with each other over the constraint term. The $\ell_{1,\infty}$ norm just penalizes the maximum absolute entry of a group, whereas the $\ell_{1,2}$ norm penalizes the average of a group. That means, the $\ell_{1,2}$ norm connects the different tasks a lot stronger than the $\ell_{1,\infty}$ norm and hence leads to better results in multi-task learning, where one wants to profit from the wealth of the data of all the tasks. For only few examples the single ℓ_1 norm yields very bad results as there exists no coupling between the different tasks. Concerning the run-time of the algorithm, there was no advantage seen for the $\ell_{1,\infty}$ case. Both algorithms use the same active set algorithm, the only difference lies in the projection step. Projection to the $\ell_{1,2}$ ball is slightly faster, as one can avoid the merging and sorting steps that are necessary for the projection to the $\ell_{1,\infty}$ ball.

Cross-Platform siRNA efficacy prediction. Gene silencing using small interfering RNA (siRNA) is a molecular tool for drug target identification. The aim in this problem is the joint analysis of different RNAi experiments to predict the siRNA efficacy. See [13] for details. In this data set we consider 14 cross-platforms, i.e 14 tasks, 19 features and 5 - 179 examples [1]. We obtain the test set in the same way as in the artificial experiment. This experiment shows the same tendency as in the synthetic data, see Figure 2. We tested the statistical significance with the Kruskal-Wallis rank-sum test and the Dunn post test with Bonferroni correction for pairwise analysis. These tests show that both Group-Lasso methods perform significantly better than the single ℓ_1 norm and $\ell_{1,2}$ shows slightly better prediction than $\ell_{1,\infty}$.

---

[1] The data is available at http://lifecenter.sgst.cn/RNAi/.

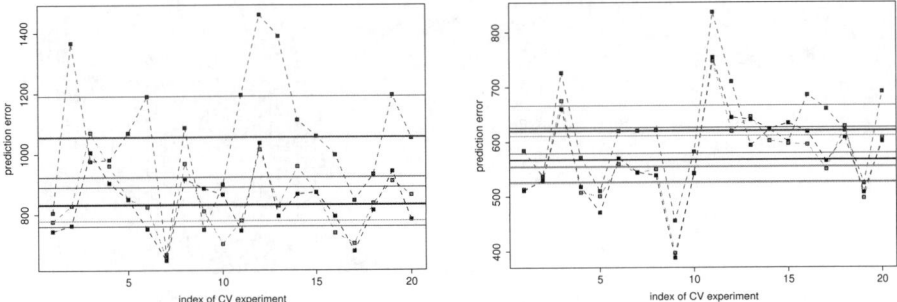

Fig. 2. Prediction error of the different regularizers: red curve: single ℓ_1, blue curve: $\ell_{1,\infty}$, green curve: $\ell_{1,2}$. Left: trained with 10% of the data from each task. Right: trained with 50% of the data from each task.

4.2 Standard Prediction Problems

Splice Site Detection. As a real world experiment, we considered the splice site detection problem as it was discussed in [7] for the $\ell_{1,2}$ Group-Lasso. The prediction of splice sites plays an important role in gene finding algorithms. Splice sites are the regions between coding (exons) and non-coding (introns) DNA segments. The *MEMset Donor* dataset [2] consists of a training set of 8415 true and 179438 false human donor sites. An additional test set contains 4208 true and 89717 "false" (or *decoy*) donor sites. A sequence of a real splice site is modeled within a window that consists of the last 3 bases of the exon and the first 6 bases of the intron. Decoy splice sites also match the consensus sequence at position zero and one. Removing this consensus "GT" results in sequences of length 7, i.e. sequences of 7 factors with 4 levels $\{A, C, G, T\}$, see [14] for details.

The goal of this experiment is to overcome the restriction to marginal probabilities (main effects) in the widely used *Sequence-Logo* approach by exploring all possible interactions up to order 4. Every interaction is encoded using dummy variables and treated as a group. [7] considered one experiment with a small window size and one with a bigger window size, resulting in a huge number of dimensions. We accomplished exactly the same experiments and obtained almost the same results. There is no advantage in using the $\ell_{1,\infty}$ Group-Lasso, neither in terms of prediction nor in interpretation.

Here we elaborate the results for the problem with the larger window size where the experiment shows that the interpretation of the Group-Lasso might be complicated. We accomplished exactly the same experiment as in [7], i.e. we look at all interactions up to order 4, use windows of length 21 and have in total 27896 groups which span a 22,458,100-dimensional feature space. Figure 3 shows our results, that are very similar to the results obtained in [7] for the $\ell_{1,2}$ Group-Lasso. For the $\ell_{1,\infty}$ norm, the optimal model at $\kappa = 60$ has correlation coefficient 0.625 (left picture of figure 3), compared with $\kappa = 66$ and correlation coefficient 0.631 for the $\ell_{1,2}$ norm. Hence, in terms of prediction, there is no

---

[2] Available at http://genes.mit.edu/burgelab/maxent/ssdata/.

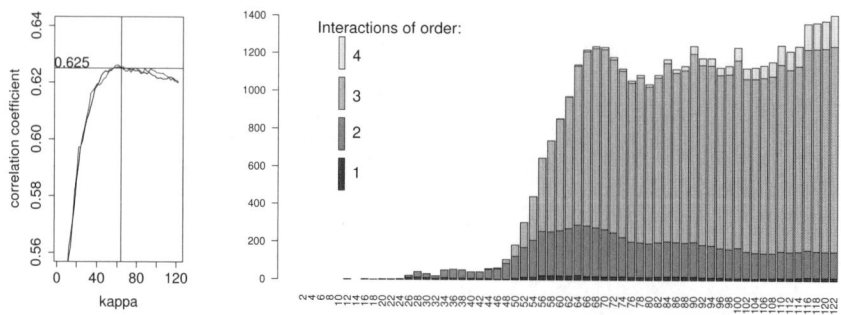

Fig. 3. Left: Correlation coefficient as a function of κ. Red curve: correlation on the separate test set. Black curve: correlation on the validation set. Right: Acceptor splice site prediction: groups that must be included in the Group-Lasso estimates to obtain complete models (gray values stand for different orders of interactions).

advantage in using the $\ell_{1,\infty}$ Group-Lasso. Among the 10 highest-scoring groups the main effects are at positions -3, -5 and 0, i.e we obtain exactly the same results as in [7]. In terms of interpretation of the solution, the $\ell_{1,\infty}$ case brings no advantage as well. The right picture in Figure 3 shows the results of the completeness tests. All solutions with $\kappa > 46$ are difficult to interpret, since an increasing number of groups must be added to obtain complete models. This is again almost the same result as in [7]. The number of groups that must be included in the optimal model ($\kappa = 60$) to obtain a complete models is 900, in the $\ell_{1,2}$ norm experiment the number of groups to include is 300 for the optimal $\kappa = 66$. Hence one can conclude that using the $\ell_{1,\infty}$ Group-Lasso brings no advantage, neither in prediction, nor in interpretability.

5   Conclusion

We give a complete analysis of the $\ell_{1,\infty}$ regularization, including results about uniqueness and completeness of solutions and a very efficient active set algorithm. With these results, we successfully compare two types of Group-Lasso methods by applying them to the two most common problem settings, multi-task learning and the "standard" prediction problems. In the multi-task setting, where a strong coupling between the different tasks is desirable, we can show that the $\ell_{1,2}$ method outperforms the $\ell_{1,\infty}$ method both in terms of prediction and run-time. There was not one single example in the synthetic experiments where the $\ell_{1,\infty}$ performed better than the $\ell_{1,2}$ norm. Both Group-Lasso methods show better results than the standard Lasso. The cross-platform siRNA efficacy prediction example confirmed this tendency in a real-world context. In the $\ell_{1,2}$ case the average over groups is considered and not only the maximum absolute value of each group as in the $\ell_{1,\infty}$ case, hence the coupling in the $\ell_{1,\infty}$ norm regularization is not as strong as the coupling in the $\ell_{1,2}$ norm regularization. This property leads to better prediction for the $\ell_{1,2}$ Group-Lasso. In the standard splice-site prediction problem we could show that using the $\ell_{1,\infty}$ norm regularization yields no advantage, neither in terms of prediction nor in terms of interpretability of the solution. In all experiments, the $\ell_{1,2}$ Group-Lasso performed best in all tested properties, i.e. in terms of prediction, complexity and interpretability. In summary one can conclude that there is no advantage in using the $\ell_{1,\infty}$ Group-Lasso.

References

1. Tibshirani, R.: Regression shrinkage and selection via the Lasso. J. Roy. Stat. Soc. B 58(1), 267–288 (1996)
2. Yuan, M., Lin, Y.: Model selection and estimation in regression with grouped variables. J. Roy. Stat. Soc. B, 49–67 (2006)
3. Turlach, B.A., Venables, W.N., Wright, S.J.: Simultaneous variable selection. Technometrics 47, 349–363 (2005)
4. Meier, L., van de Geer, S., Bühlmann, P.: The Group Lasso for Logistic Regression. J. Roy. Stat. Soc. B 70(1), 53–71 (2008)
5. Argyriou, A., Evgeniou, T., Pontil, M.: Multi-task feature learning. In: Advances in Neural Information Processing Systems, vol. 19. MIT Press, Cambridge (2007)
6. Kim, Y., Kim, J., Kim, Y.: Blockwise sparse regression. Statistica Sinica 16, 375–390 (2006)
7. Roth, V., Fischer, B.: The Group-Lasso for generalized linear models: uniqueness of solutions and efficient algorithms. In: ICML 2008, pp. 848–855. ACM, New York (2008)
8. Schmidt, M., Murphy, K., Fung, G., Rosales, R.: Structure learning in random fields for heart motion abnormality detection. In: CVPR (2008)
9. Quattoni, A., Carreras, X., Collins, M., Darrell, T.: An efficient projection for $l_{1\infty}$ regularization. In: 26th Intern. Conference on Machine Learning (2009)
10. Liu, H., Palatucci, M., Zhang, J.: Blockwise coordinate descent procedures for the multi-task lasso, with applications to neural semantic basis discovery. In: 26th Intern. Conference on Machine Learning (2009)
11. Osborne, M., Presnell, B., Turlach, B.: On the LASSO and its dual. J. Comp. and Graphical Statistics 9(2), 319–337 (2000)
12. McCullaghand, P., Nelder, J.: Generalized Linear Models. Chapman & Hall, Boca Raton (1983)
13. Liu, Q., Xu, Q., Zheng, V.W., Xue, H., Cao, Z., Yang, Q.: Multi-task learning for cross-platform sirna efficacy prediction: an in-silico study. BMC Bioinformatics 11(1), 181 (2010)
14. Yeo, G., Burge, C.: Maximum entropy modeling of short sequence motifs with applications to RNA splicing signals. J. Comp. Biology 11, 377–394 (2004)

Random Fourier Approximations for Skewed Multiplicative Histogram Kernels

Fuxin Li, Catalin Ionescu, and Cristian Sminchisescu

Institute für Numerische Simulation, University of Bonn

Abstract. Approximations based on random Fourier features have recently emerged as an efficient and elegant methodology for designing large-scale kernel machines [4]. By expressing the kernel as a Fourier expansion, features are generated based on a finite set of random basis projections with inner products that are Monte Carlo approximations to the original kernel. However, the original Fourier features are only applicable to translation-invariant kernels and are not suitable for histograms that are always non-negative. This paper extends the concept of translation-invariance and the random Fourier feature methodology to arbitrary, locally compact Abelian groups. Based on empirical observations drawn from the exponentiated χ^2 kernel, the state-of-the-art for histogram descriptors, we propose a new group called the *skewed-multiplicative group* and design translation-invariant kernels on it. Experiments show that the proposed kernels outperform other kernels that can be similarly approximated. In a semantic segmentation experiment on the PASCAL VOC 2009 dataset, the approximation allows us to train large-scale learning machines more than two orders of magnitude faster than previous nonlinear SVMs.

1 Introduction

In recent years, datasets containing large amounts of labeled data are increasingly common in learning problems, such as text classification [1], spam filtering [2] and visual object recognition [3]. It is however difficult to apply high-performance kernel methods to these tasks, as the constraint to operate with the kernel matrix makes such methods scale more than quadratically in the size of the dataset. A number of recent algorithms perform explicit feature transforms [4,5,6], so that nonlinear kernels can be approximated by linear kernels in the transformed space. This makes possible to use efficient linear methods that depend only linearly on the size of the training set [7,8]. If the approximations are accurate, complex nonlinear functions can be learned using linear algorithms, thus allowing to solve large-scale learning problems efficiently.

Random Fourier approximations (RF) provides an elegant and efficient methodology to create explicit feature transforms. By applying Bochner's theorem, translation-invariant kernels are computed as inner products in the frequency domain (after a Fourier transform). Then m-dimensional feature vectors are created for examples so that their inner products are Monte Carlo approximations of the original kernel. The method has the convergence rate of Monte

M. Goesele et al. (Eds.): DAGM 2010, LNCS 6376, pp. 262–271, 2010.

Carlo: $O(m^{-\frac{1}{2}})$ independent of the input dimension. One usually needs only a few hundred dimensions to approximate the original kernel accurately.

Previously, RF were developed for translation-invariant kernels on $\mathbb{R}^n$. In this paper we study the applicability of RF for histogram features where it is known that kernels defined on $\mathbb{R}^n$ do not usually produce good results [9]. The best performing kernel to-date on histogram features [9] is the exponentiated χ^2 kernel [10]. However, this kernel cannot be approximated with RF. Our aim is to design a kernel that has similar performance, but fits within the RF framework.

We first extend the random Fourier feature methodology to translation-invariant kernels on general locally compact Abelian groups. It is hypothesized that two factors are important for the performance of the χ^2 kernel: the sensitivity to the scale of the features and the multiplicative decomposition as a product of components along each dimension, instead of a sum. Therefore we design a new group called the *skewed multiplicative group*, which has built-in sensitivity to feature scale. We propose multiplicative kernels on this group and apply the RF framework on it.

In experiments, we show that our designed kernels are easy to approximate, have better performance than other kernels usable within the RF framework, and offer a substantial speed-up over previous nonlinear SVM approaches.

2   Fourier Transform and Random Features on Groups

We use n to denote the number of training examples, d the input dimensionality and m the dimensionality of the extracted random features. $\mathcal{F}[f]$ denotes the Fourier transform of f, and $\mathrm{U}[a,b]$ is the uniform distribution on $[a,b]$. $\mathbf{E}_\mu[x]$ takes the expectation of x w.r.t to the measure μ.

2.1   Fourier Transform on Groups

Let $(G,+)$ be any locally compact abelian (LCA) group, with 0 the identity. There exists a non-negative regular measure m called the *Haar measure* of G, which is translation-invariant: $m(E+x) = m(E)$ for every $x \in G$ and every Borel set E in G. The Haar measure is provably unique up to a multiplicative positive constant, and is required in the *Haar integral*: $\int_G f(x)dm$, essentially a Lebesgue integral on the Haar measure [11].

Now we establish the character and (Pontryagin) dual group of G [11]. A complex function γ on G is called a *character* if $|\gamma(x)| = 1$ for all $x \in G$ and if

$$\gamma(x+y) = \gamma(x)\gamma(y), \forall x,y \in G \tag{1}$$

All complex $\gamma(x)$ with $|\gamma(x)| = 1$ can be represented as $\gamma(x) = e^{ig(x)}$. Therefore to make a unique character, only a real-valued $g(x)$ needs to be decided. The set of all continuous characters of G forms the *dual group* Γ, where addition is defined by $(\gamma_1 + \gamma_2)(x) = \gamma_1(x)\gamma_2(x)$. It follows that Γ is also an LCA group. To emphasize duality, we write $(x,\gamma) = \gamma(x)$.

For all f that are integrable on G, the function $\mathcal{F}$ defined on Γ by

$$\mathcal{F}[f](\gamma) = \int_G f(x)(-x, \gamma)dm \qquad (2)$$

is called the *Fourier transform* of f.

The simplest example is $\mathbb{R}$, $\gamma_\eta(x) = e^{2\pi\eta x i}$, where η is an arbitrary number. Eq. (1) could easily be verified, and (2) becomes the conventional Fourier transform $\mathcal{F}[f](\gamma_\eta) = \int_\mathbb{R} f(x)e^{-2\pi\eta x i}dx$.

2.2 Random Features on Groups

Now we introduce Bochner's theorem which is the main result we need [11]:

Theorem 1. *A continuous function f on G is positive-definite if and only if there is a non-negative measure μ on Γ such that $f(x) = \int_\Gamma (x, \gamma)d\mu(\gamma)$.*

Usually one is able to verify if a translation-invariant kernel $k(x, y) = f(x - y)$ is positive-definite. For such kernels, we can use Bochner's theorem for the explicit feature transform [4]:

$$k(x - y) = \int_G (y - x, \gamma)d\mu(\gamma) = \mathbf{E}_\mu[\zeta_\gamma(x)\zeta_\gamma(y)^*], \qquad (3)$$

where $\zeta_\gamma(x) = (-x, \gamma)$ and $*$ is the conjugate. To construct ζ_γ explicitly, note that $(-x, \gamma) = e^{-ig_\gamma(x)} = \cos(g_\gamma(x)) - i\sin(g_\gamma(x))$. Then, $k(x - y) = \mathbf{E}_\mu[\cos(g_\gamma(x) - g_\gamma(y))] + i\mathbf{E}_\mu[\sin(g_\gamma(x) - g_\gamma(y))]$. For the real kernels we work with, the imaginary part must be zero. Therefore we only need to approximate the real part $\mathbf{E}_\mu[\cos(g_\gamma(x) - g_\gamma(y))]$. Define

$$z_\gamma(x) = \cos(g_\gamma(x) + b), \qquad (4)$$

where $b \sim \mathrm{U}[0, 2\pi]$. It follows that $\mathbf{E}_\mu[\cos(g_\gamma(x) - g_\gamma(y))] = \mathbf{E}_\mu[z_\gamma(x)z_\gamma(y)]$, thus (4) is the explicit transform we seek. To approximate the expectation $\mathbf{E}_\mu[\zeta_\gamma(x)\zeta_\gamma(y)^*]$, we sample from the distribution μ. In principle, the expectation can be approximated by linear functions on explicit features:

$$Z_x = \left[\cos(g_{\gamma_1}(x) + b_1), \cos(g_{\gamma_2}(x) + b_2), \ldots, \cos(g_{\gamma_k}(x) + b_k)\right] \qquad (5)$$

Basically, the algorithm has the following steps: 1) Generate k random samples $\gamma_1, \ldots, \gamma_k$ from the distribution μ; 2) Compute Z_x as the RF feature for all training examples and use linear methods to perform the learning task. In practice, g_γ uniquely decides γ, and the group G defines the form of g_γ. In $\mathbb{R}^d$ for example, the form is $g_\gamma(x) = r_\gamma^T x$ (dropping the constant scaling factor 2π), where r_γ is a real vector with the same length as x [4]. Therefore, sampling only needs to be done on r_γ. The distribution is decided by the Fourier transform of the kernel. For example, in the case of a Gaussian kernel, the distribution is still Gaussian. See [4] for details on other kernels.

3   The Skewed Multiplicative Group

3.1   Fourier Transform of the Skewed Multiplicative Group

We make use of a group operation that combines multiplication and addition, The inclusion of an additive part makes the group sensitive to scaling:

$$x \otimes y = (x + c)(y + c) - c \qquad (6)$$

The group is defined on $(-c, \infty)$ with $c \geq 0$. Here $1 - c$ is the identity element, since $(1 - c) \otimes y = y$. Then x^{-1} could be solved from $x \otimes x^{-1} = 1 - c$, to obtain $x^{-1} = \frac{1}{x+c} - c$. Therefore, the translation-invariant kernel on this group is

$$k(x, y) = f(x \otimes y^{-1}) = f\left(\frac{x + c}{y + c} - c\right), \qquad (7)$$

The Haar measure and the Fourier transform are given next.

Proposition 1. *On the skewed multiplicative group* $((-c, \infty), \otimes)$*, the following results hold:*

1) The Haar measure is given by $\mu(S) = \int_S \frac{1}{t+c} dt$.
2) The characters are $\gamma_\eta(x) = e^{2\pi\eta \log(x+c)i}$*, with* $\eta \in \mathbb{R}$.
3) The Fourier transform is given by $\mathcal{F}[f](\eta) = \int_{-\infty}^{\infty} f(e^x - c)e^{-2\pi\eta x i} dx$.

Proof. 1) Since $m([d \otimes a, d \otimes b]) = \int_{(d+c)(a+c)-c}^{(d+c)(b+c)-c} \frac{1}{t+c} dt = \log(d + c)(b + c) - \log(d + c)(a + c) = \log(b + c) - \log(a + c) = \int_a^b \frac{1}{t+c} dt = m([a, b])$, the measure is translation-invariant. Since the Haar measure is unique, we conclude that $\mu(S) = \int_S \frac{1}{t+c} dt$ is the Haar measure on the group.
2) We only need to verify (1): $\gamma_\eta(x \otimes y) = e^{2\pi\eta \log((x+c)(y+c))i}$
$= e^{2\pi\eta \log(x+c)i} e^{2\pi\eta \log(y+c)i} = \gamma_\eta(x)\gamma_\eta(y)$.
3) From (2), $\mathcal{F}[f](\eta) = \int_{-c}^{\infty} \frac{f(x)}{x+c} e^{2\pi\eta \log(x+c)i} dx = \int_{-c}^{\infty} f(x)e^{2\pi\eta \log(x+c)i} d(\log(x + c)) = \int_{-\infty}^{\infty} f(e^x - c)e^{-2\pi\eta x i} dx$.

When $c = 0$, we obtain the regular multiplicative group on $\mathbb{R}^+$, denoted as $(\mathbb{R}^+, \times)$. The identity on this group is 1. The translation-invariance property in this group is scale invariance, since translation-invariant kernels have $k(x, y) = f(x \times y^{-1}) = f(\frac{x}{y}) = f(\frac{d \times x}{d \times y})$. For this group, the Fourier transform is known to be $\mathcal{F}[f](e^x)$ in $\mathbb{R}$ [19] which is equivalent to Proposition 1.

3.2   Kernels

Only a few functions have explicit Fourier transforms. Here we consider two functions

$$f_1(x) = \frac{2}{\sqrt{x + c} + \sqrt{\frac{1}{x+c}}}, f_2(x) = \min\left(\sqrt{x + c}, \frac{1}{\sqrt{x + c}}\right) \qquad (8)$$

which correspond to kernels that we refer as the *skewed* χ^2 and the *skewed intersection* kernels, respectively:

$$k_1(x, y) = \frac{2\sqrt{x+c}\sqrt{y+c}}{x+y+2c}, k_2(x, y) = \min\left(\sqrt{\frac{x+c}{y+c}}, \sqrt{\frac{y+c}{x+c}}\right) \qquad (9)$$

From Proposition 1, the corresponding Fourier transforms can be computed. In this case, they are the hyperbolic secant and Cauchy distributions, respectively:

$$\mathcal{F}_1(\omega) = \text{sech}(\pi\omega), \mathcal{F}_2(\omega) = \frac{2}{\pi(1 + 4\omega_i^2)} \qquad (10)$$

The multidimensional kernels are defined as a product of one-dimensional kernels: $k(\mathbf{x}, \mathbf{y}) = \prod_{i=1}^{d} k(x_i, y_i)$, where d is the dimensionality of the data. The multi-dimensional Fourier transform is just the product of the transform on each dimension, $\mathcal{F}(\omega) = \prod_{i=1}^{d} \mathcal{F}(\omega_i)$. In the case of $\mathcal{F}_1(\omega)$ and $\mathcal{F}_2(\omega)$, this just means that the Fourier transform of the kernel is a joint distribution on ω, where each dimension is independent of others.

In the skewed multiplicative group, the form of g_γ is $g_\gamma(x) = r_\gamma^{\text{T}} \log(x + c)$. To apply the RF methodology, one would need to sample from (10), in order to obtain r_γ to compute the random features (5). We use the inverse transformation method: sampling uniformly from $U[0, 1]$ and transforming the samples by multiplying with the inverse CDF of the distribution.

4   Motivation for the Skewed Approximations

The exponentiated χ^2 kernel $k(x, y) = \exp(-\sum_i \frac{(x_i - y_i)^2}{x_i + y_i})$ has achieved the best performance to-date on histogram features for visual object detection and recognition [9]. However, for the multiplicative group of $\mathbb{R}^+$, we would need to compute the equivalent Fourier transform of $f(\exp(\frac{x}{y}))$ in $\mathbb{R}$. In the case of any exponentiated kernel, we might need to compute the Fourier transform of a function represented as $\exp(-\gamma g(\exp(\frac{x}{y})))$, for some $g(x)$. With two exponentials, it is difficult to find analytical forms for the transform.

Our motivation is to design a kernel within the RF framework that preserves some properties of the χ^2 kernel, while being at the same time tractable to approximate. To do this, we develop some intuition on why the χ^2 kernel works better than others. First, we conjecture that the exponentiated χ^2 kernel works well because *it adapts to different scales* in the input features. Secondly, we conjecture that its *multiplicative* properties might be an advantage over additive kernels. We will explain these two conjectures in the sequel.

The scale in a histogram feature is proportional to the number of occurrences of a random variable (its frequency). The χ^2 kernel is based on the Pearson χ^2 test, designed to favor variables that are observed more frequently. The gist is that higher frequencies are more stable finite-sample estimators of probabilities. Hence, kernel dimensions with higher frequency should be emphasized when two histograms are compared. The translation-invariant Gaussian kernel does not

Table 1. A list of kernels used in visual recognition. Previous work empirically showed that the exponentiated χ^2 kernel performs best among the kernels listed.

Name	$k(x,y)$	Group	Mult. or Add.	RF proved in
Gaussian	$\exp(-\gamma\|\|x-y\|\|^2)$	$(\mathbb{R}^d, +)$	Multiplicative	[4]
$1-\chi^2$	$\sum_i \left(1 - \frac{(x_i-y_i)^2}{x_i+y_i}\right)$	$(\mathbb{R}^d_+, \times)$	Additive	[12]
Exponentiated χ^2	$\exp\left(-\gamma\sum_i \frac{(x_i-y_i)^2}{x_i+y_i}\right)$	N/A	Multiplicative	N/A
Intersection	$\sum_i \min(x_i, y_i)$	$(\mathbb{R}^d_+, \times)$	Additive	[12]
Linear Kernel	$\sum_i x_i y_i$	N/A	Additive	N/A
Skewed-χ^2	$\prod_i \frac{2\sqrt{x_i+c}\sqrt{y_i+c}}{x_i+y_i+2c}$	$((-c,\infty), \otimes)$	Multiplicative	This paper
Skewed-Intersection	$\prod_i \min\left(\sqrt{\frac{x_i+c}{y_i+c}}, \sqrt{\frac{y_i+c}{x_i+c}}\right)$	$((-c,\infty), \otimes)$	Multiplicative	This paper

have this property. This may explain why the χ^2 kernel significantly outperforms the Gaussian in visual learning problems.

In Table 1, several other kernels that adapt to the scale of the features are shown. E. g., the $1-\chi^2$ kernel is based on exactly the same χ^2 statistic as the exponentiated one. We conjecture that one difference is important: the $1-\chi^2$ kernel and the other kernels are additive, i.e. the kernel value on multiple dimensions is a sum of the kernel value on each dimension. In contrast, the exponentiated kernel is multiplicative: $\exp\left(-\gamma\sum_i \frac{(x_i-y_i)^2}{x_i+y_i}\right) = \prod_i \exp\left(-\gamma\frac{(x_i-y_i)^2}{x_i+y_i}\right)$.

Moreover, we argue that a multiplicative kernel is more sensitive to large deviations between x and y in one or a few dimensions. Assuming $\chi^2(x_i, y_i) \leq \chi^2(x_u, y_u)$ for all i, we have $\exp(-\gamma\chi^2(x,y)) \leq \exp(-\gamma\chi^2(x_u, y_u))$. Therefore, one extremely noisy dimension may negatively impact the exponentiated kernel severely. Otherwise said, to make $k(x,y)$ large (i.e., x, y similar), the two histograms must be similar in almost all dimensions. For an additive kernel, this effect is much less obvious. $k(x,y)$ is high if x and y match on some important bins, but not necessarily all.

Why is matching all bins important? Intuitively, in localization tasks, under relatively weak models, the number of negative object hypotheses one must go over is usually huge. Therefore, if the similarity between two object hypotheses is large when they are only partially matched, there might be simply too many hypotheses with good similarity to the ground truth. In such circumstances the false positive rate may increase significantly.

5   Related Work

RF belongs to the class of methods that replace the kernel with a low-rank approximation. In [13,14], the authors proposed incomplete Cholesky decomposition methods that compute a low-rank approximation to the kernel matrix while simultaneously solving the SVM optimization. These methods are computationally powerful but to predict new data, kernel values still have to be computed between all test and training examples, which is slow for large-scale problems. Alternatively, one can use Nyström methods [15] to subsample the training set and operate on a reduced kernel matrix. However the convergence rate of this approximation is slow, $(O(m^{-\frac{1}{4}}))$ [16], where m is the number of samples used.

In computer vision, the exponentiated χ^2 kernel was known to be both the best-performing and the most expensive to compute. A cheaper variant is the histogram intersection kernel [17], for which a computational trick for fast testing is available [18]. However, training time remains a severe problem in this approach since the speedup does not apply. Therefore, many systems directly use linear kernels. Vedaldi et al. proposed a 3-step approach starting with 2 fast linear filtering steps, followed by a non-linear SVM on the exponentiated χ^2 kernel [9]. Bo and Sminchisescu proposed EMK to learn low-dimensional kernel approximations and showed comparable performances with RF for the Gaussian kernel [6].

The work of [12] complements ours, in that it also seeks a low-dimensional linear approximation based on the Fourier theory. However, their development is based on the result of [19], which only applies to scale-invariant kernels in $\mathbb{R}^+$. To adapt to scale, one has to use a kernel that is *additive*, so that the scale of the data $\sqrt{x}$ is multiplied to the kernel on each dimension. Using this approach one could approximate the $1 - \chi^2$ and the intersection kernels (Table 1). However, the technique does not immediately extend to the important case of multiplicative kernels. When one has null components in some dimensions, multiplying by $\sqrt{x}$ sets the entire kernel to 0. Although one may palliate such effects e.g., by multiplying with $\exp(-x)$ instead of $\sqrt{x}$, it may be difficult to identify the form of the kernel after such transformations.

6   Experiments

We conduct experiments in a semantic image segmentation task within the PASCAL VOC 2009 Challenge, widely acknowledged as one of the most difficult benchmarks for the problem [20]. In this task, we need to both recognize objects in an image correctly, and generate pixel-wise segmentations for these objects. Ground truth segments of objects paired with their category labels are available for training. A recent approach that achieves state-of-the-art results train a scoring function for each class on many putative figure-ground segmentation hypotheses, obtained using a parametric min-cut method [21]. This creates a large-scale learning task even if the original image database has moderate size: with 90 segments in each image, training on 5000 images creates a learning problem with $450,000$ training examples.

We test a number of kernels on the VOC 2009 dataset. training on the VOC train and test on the validation, which has approximately 750 images and 1600 objects each. Using the methodology in [21,22], we select up to 90 putative segments in each image for training and testing. Altogether, there are $62,747$ training segments and $60,522$ test segments. Four types of descriptors are used: a bag of words of dense gray-level SIFT, and three pyramid HOGs, as in [22]. The total number of dimensions is 3270. The final kernel is a weighted sum of

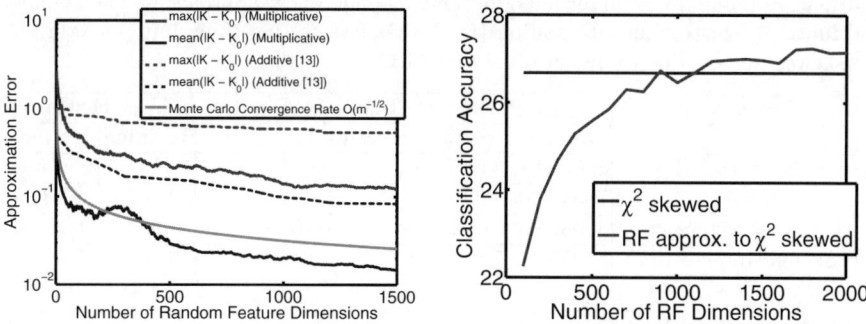

Fig. 1. (*left*) Approximation quality when a linear kernel $K = z_\mu z_\mu^T$ is used to estimate the original kernel matrix K_0. Both the L_∞ error (maximal error) and the average L_1 error are shown. It could be seen that the convergence rate of the multiplicative kernel is consistent with the theoretical $O(m^{-1/2})$ rate for Monte Carlo methods. The rate of the additive kernel is dependent on the input dimension, hence much slower. (*right*) The accuracy as a function of the number of dimensions needed to approximate the kernel.

kernels on each individual descriptor. The kernel parameters are estimated using the approach in [22]. Other parameters, such as c in the skewed kernel and the regularization parameter are chosen by cross-validation on the training set.

In the first experiment we test the quality of the RF approximation for the skewed-χ^2 kernel. Computing the full kernel matrix would require a prohibitive amount of memory. Therefore, testing is done on a 3202×3202 kernel matrix by selecting only the ground truth segment and the best-overlapping putative segment for each object. We plot the result for one HOG descriptor with 1700 dimensions (fig. 1(a)). Notice that the convergence rate of the RF is quite consistent with the theoretical $O(m^{-1/2})$. We also compare with the approximation of the additive χ^2 kernel given in [12]. It can be clearly seen that a skewed multiplicative kernel needs fewer dimensions for good approximation accuracy.

Speed of Training and Testing: Next we compare the speed of the RF approach with a previous nonlinear SVM regression approach [22]. For RF features, we use 2000 dimensions for each type of descriptor, for a total of 8000 dimensions. For RF features on additive kernels, 3 dimensions are used for each input dimension, to make the dimensionality of the RF feature comparable to our multiplicative ones. The results are obtained on an 8-core Pentium Xeon 3.0GHz computer. Since no fast linear SVM regression algorithms are available, we use ridge regression in conjunction with RF features.

Training and testing times for different methods are given in Table 2. One could see that RF offer a substantial speed-up over previous approaches, and is able to scale to much larger datasets[1].

---

[1] The code for the nonlinear χ^2 kernel is more heavily optimized (using Christoph Lampert's SIMD-optimized χ^2 code) than the skewed kernels, hence Table 2 should not be used to compare speeds among the nonlinear versions of those kernels.

Table 2. Running times (in seconds) for nonlinear and linear approaches. The nonlinear and linear RF histogram intersection [18,12] has fast testing time, but is slower than the skewed kernels due to higher dimensionality.

Kernel Name	Nonlinear		Linear by Random Fourier Features		
	training	testing	Feature Generation	Training	Testing
Exponentiated χ^2	20647.82	34027.86	N/A	N/A	N/A
Skewed χ^2	70548.20	102277.78	519.22	914.70	57.39
Histogram Intersection	30082.08	742.36	3716.07	1498.05	69.91
Skewed Intersection	53235.17	79821.94	505.37	913.87	56.81

Table 3. Segment classification accuracies (for the best segments in our pool, as determined by ground truth data) for both original non-linear kernels and their approximation using RF.

Kernel	Accuracy		Kernel	Accuracy	
	Nonlinear	Fourier Approx.		Nonlinear	Fourier Approx.
Gaussian	21.31%	24.71%	Exponentiated χ^2	29.54%	N/A
$1 - \chi^2$	20.63%	23.75%	Skewed χ^2	26.68%	27.16%
Intersection	22.08%	23.65%	Skewed Intersection	26.34%	26.73%

Results on Different Kernels: Having established that random features offer a substantial speed-up, the question is how good the prediction accuracy of the proposed skewed kernels is. In Table 3 we compare the classification accuracy on all the segments and skip the post-processing step in [22]. Usually this result correlates linearly to the VOC criteria. For the skewed χ^2 kernel, we plot the performance against the number of RF dimensions in fig. 1 (b). One can see that approximations based on random Fourier features can even improve performance of the original kernel. This might be caused by the difference in learning algorithms used (squared loss vs. hinge loss) or the fact that the RF function class is richer than the kernel method: the kernel can be represented by the inner product on RF, but some other functions may also be represented by weighted inner products on RF. Our skewed χ^2 kernel outperforms all the other kernels, but there is still a 2% performance lag with respect to the exponentiated kernel.

7   Conclusion

In this paper, we extend the random Fourier feature methodology to locally compact abelian groups, where kernels on histogram features are considered. Based on empirical observations on the exponentiated χ^2 kernel, we propose a new group on which we build kernels that are not scale-invariant, yet can be approximated linearly using random Fourier features. The experiments show that our kernels are much faster to compute than many nonlinear kernels, and outperform kernels for which approximations are previously known. However, the performance of the proposed kernels is still inferior to that of the exponentiated χ^2 kernel. Designing better kernels to close the gap is an interesting avenue for future work.

Acknowledgments. This work was supported, in part, by the European Commission, under a Marie Curie Excellence Grant MCEXT-025481.

References

1. Lewis, D.D., Yang, Y., Rose, T.G., Li, F.: Rcv1: A new benchmark collection for text categorization research. JMLR 5, 361–397 (2004)
2. Attenberg, J., Dasgupta, A., Langford, J., Smola, A., Weinberger, K.: Feature hashing for large scale multitask learning. In: ICML (2009)
3. Russell, B.C., Torralba, A., Murphy, K.P., Freeman, W.T.: Labelme: A database and web-based tool for image annotation. IJCV 77(1-3), 157–173 (2008)
4. Rahimi, A., Recht, B.: Random features for large-scale kernel machines. In: NIPS (2007)
5. Shi, Q., Patterson, J., Dror, G., Langford, J., Smola, A., Strehl, A., Vishwanathan, V.: Hash kernels. In: AISTATS (2009)
6. Bo, L., Sminchisescu, C.: Efficient match kernels between sets of features for visual recognition. In: NIPS (2009)
7. Fan, R.E., Chang, K.W., Hsieh, C.J., Wang, X.R., Lin, C.J.: Liblinear: A library for large linear classification. Journal of Machine Learning Research, 1871–1874 (2008)
8. Shalev-Shwartz, S., Singer, Y., Srebro, N.: Pegasos: Primal estimated sub-gradient solver for svm. In: ICML (2007)
9. Vedaldi, A., Gulshan, V., Varma, M., Zisserman, A.: Multiple kernels for object detection. In: ICCV (2009)
10. Chapelle, O., Haffner, P., Vapnik, V.: Support vector machines for histogram-based image classification. IEEE Transactions on Neural Networks 10 (1999)
11. Rudin, W.: Fourier Analysis on Groups (1962)
12. Vedaldi, A., Zisserman, A.: Efficient additive kernels via explicit feature maps. In: CVPR (2010)
13. Fine, S., Scheinberg, K.: Efficient svm training using low-rank kernel representation. JMLR 2, 243–264 (2001)
14. Bach, F., Jordan, M.I.: Predictive low-rank decomposition for kernel methods. In: ICML (2005)
15. Williams, C.K.I., Seeger, M.: Using the nyström method to speed up kernel machines. In: NIPS (2001)
16. Drineas, P., Mahoney, M.: On the nyström method for approximating a gram matrix for improved kernel-based learning. JMLR 6, 2153–2175 (2005)
17. Grauman, K., Darrell, T.: The pyramid match kernel: Efficient learning with sets of features. JMLR 8, 725–760 (2007)
18. Maji, S., Berg, A.C., Malik, J.: Classification using intersection kernel support vector machines is efficient. In: CVPR (2008)
19. Hein, M., Bousquet, O.: Hilbertian metrics and positive definite kernels on probability measures. In: AISTATS (2005)
20. Everingham, M., Van Gool, L., Williams, C.K.I., Winn, J., Zisserman, A.: The PASCAL Visual Object Classes Challenge, VOC 2009 Results (2009), http://www.pascal-network.org/challenges/VOC/voc2009/workshop/index.html
21. Carreira, J., Sminchisescu, C.: Constrained parametric min cuts for automatic object segmentation. In: CVPR (2010)
22. Li, F., Carreira, J., Sminchisescu, C.: Object recognition as ranking holistic figure-ground hypotheses. In: CVPR (2010)

Gaussian Mixture Modeling with Gaussian Process Latent Variable Models

Hannes Nickisch[1] and Carl Edward Rasmussen[2,1]

[1] MPI for Biological Cybernetics, Tübingen, Germany
hn@tue.mpg.de
[2] Department of Engineering, University of Cambridge, UK
cer54@cam.ac.uk

Abstract. Density modeling is notoriously difficult for high dimensional data. One approach to the problem is to search for a lower dimensional manifold which captures the main characteristics of the data. Recently, the Gaussian Process Latent Variable Model (GPLVM) has successfully been used to find low dimensional manifolds in a variety of complex data. The GPLVM consists of a set of points in a low dimensional latent space, and a stochastic map to the observed space. We show how it can be interpreted as a density model in the observed space. However, the GPLVM is not trained as a density model and therefore yields bad density estimates. We propose a new training strategy and obtain improved generalisation performance and better density estimates in comparative evaluations on several benchmark data sets.

Modeling of densities, aka unsupervised learning, is one of the central problems in machine learning. Despite its long history [1], density modeling remains a challenging task especially in high dimensional spaces. For example, the generative approach to classification requires density models for each class, and training such models well is generally considered more difficult than the alternative discriminative approach. Classical approaches to density modeling include both parametric and non parametric methods. In general, simple parametric approaches have limited utility, as the assumptions might be too restrictive. Mixture models, typically trained using the EM algorithm, are more flexible, but e.g. Gaussian mixture models are hard to fit in high dimensions, as each component is either diagonal or has in the order of D^2 parameters, although the mixtures of Factor Analyzers algorithm [2] may be able to strike a good balance. Methods based on kernel density estimation [3,4] are another approach, where bandwidths may be set using cross validation [5].

The methods mentioned so far have two main shortcomings: 1) they typically do not perform well in high dimensions, and 2) they do not provide an intuitive or generative understanding of the data. Generally, we can only succeed if the data has some regular structure, the model can discover and exploit. One attempt to do this is to assume that the data points in the high dimensional space lie on – or close to – some smooth underlying lower dimensional manifold. Models based on this idea can be divided into models based on *implicit* or *explicit*

M. Goesele et al. (Eds.): DAGM 2010, LNCS 6376, pp. 272–282, 2010.

representations of the manifold. An implicit representation is used by [6] in a non-parametric Gaussian mixture with adaptive covariance to every data point. Explicit representations are used in the Generative Topographic Map [7] and by [8]. Within the explicit camp, models contain two separate parts, a lower dimensional latent space equipped with a density, and a function which maps points from the low dimensional latent space to the high dimensional space where the observations lie. Advantages of this type of model include the ability to understand the structure of the data in a more intuitive way using the latent representation, as well as the technical advantage that the density in the observed space is automatically properly normalised by construction.

The Gaussian Process Latent Variable Model (GPLVM) [9] uses a Gaussian process (GP) [10] to define a (stochastic) map between a lower dimensional latent space and the observation space. However, the GPLVM does not include a density in the latent space. In this paper, we explore extensions to the GPLVM based on densities in the latent space. One might assume that this can trivially be done, by thinking of the latent points learnt by the GPLVM as representing a mixture of delta functions in the latent space. Since the GP based map is stochastic, it induces a proper mixture in the observed space. However, this formulation is unsatisfactory, because the resulting model is not trained as a density model. Consequently, our experiments show poor density estimation performance.

Mixtures of Gaussians form the basis of the vast majority of density estimation algorithms. Whereas kernel smoothing techniques can be seen as introducing a mixture component for each data point, infinite mixture models [11] explore the limit as the number of components increases and mixtures of factor analysers impose constraints on the covariance of individual components. The algorithm presented in this paper can be understood as a method for stitching together Gaussian mixture components in a way reminiscent of [8] using the GPLVM map from the lower dimensional manifold to induce factor analysis like constraints in the observation space. In a nutshell, we propose a density model in high dimensions by transforming a set of low-dimensional Gaussians with a GP.

We begin by a short introduction to the GPLVM and show how it can be used to define density models. In section 2, we introduce a principled learning algorithm, and experimentally evaluate our approach in section 3.

1   The GPLVM as a Density Model

A GP f is a probabilistic map parametrised by a covariance $k(\mathbf{x}, \mathbf{x}')$ and a mean $m(\mathbf{x})$. We use $m(\mathbf{x}) \equiv 0$ and automatic relevance determination (ARD) $k(\mathbf{x}^i, \mathbf{x}^j) = \sigma_f^2 \exp\left(-\frac{1}{2}(\mathbf{x}^i - \mathbf{x}^j)^\top \mathbf{W}^{-1}(\mathbf{x}^i - \mathbf{x}^j)\right) + \delta_{ij}\sigma_\eta^2$ in the following. Here, σ_f^2 and σ_η^2 denote the signal and noise variance, respectively and the diagonal matrix $\mathbf{W}$ contains the squared length scales. Since a GP is a distribution over functions $f : \mathcal{X} \to \mathcal{Z}$, the output $\mathbf{z} = f(\mathbf{x})$ is random even though the input $\mathbf{x}$ is deterministic. In GP regression, a GP prior is combined with training data $\{\mathbf{x}^i, z^i\}_{i \in \mathcal{I} = \{1..N\}}$ into a GP posterior conditioned on the training data with mean $\mu_*(\mathbf{x}_*) = \boldsymbol{\alpha}^\top \mathbf{k}_*$ and covariance $\bar{k}(\mathbf{x}_*, \mathbf{x}'_*) = k(\mathbf{x}_*, \mathbf{x}'_*) - \mathbf{k}_*^\top \mathbf{K}^{-1} \mathbf{k}'_*$ where

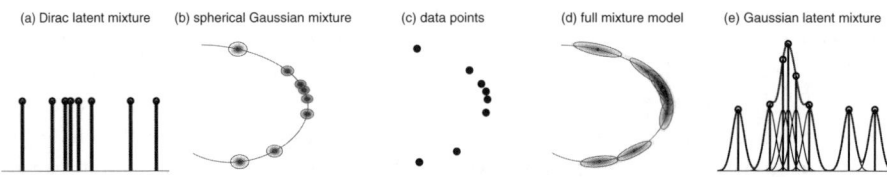

Fig. 1. The high dimensional ($D = 2$) density of the data points $\mathbf{z}^i$ in panel (c) is modelled by a mixture of Gaussians $\mathbb{P}(\mathbf{z}) = \frac{1}{N} \sum_i \mathcal{N}(\mathbf{z}|\boldsymbol{\mu}_{\mathbf{x}^i}, \boldsymbol{\Sigma}_{\mathbf{x}^i})$ shown in panel (b,d) where the means $\boldsymbol{\mu}_{\mathbf{x}^i}$ and variances $\boldsymbol{\Sigma}_{\mathbf{x}^i}$ are given by the predictive means and covariances of a set of independent Gaussian processes $f_j : \mathcal{X} \to \mathcal{Z}$ conditioned on low-dimensional ($d = 1$) latent locations $\mathbf{x}^i$. A latent Dirac mixture (a) yields a spherical Gaussian mixture with varying widths (b) and a latent Gaussian mixture (e) results in a fully coupled mixture model (d) smoothly sharing covariances across mixture components.

$\mathbf{k}_* = [k(\mathbf{x}^1, \mathbf{x}_*), .., k(\mathbf{x}^N, \mathbf{x}_*)]^\top$, $\mathbf{K} = [k(\mathbf{x}^i, \mathbf{x}^j)]_{ij=1..N}$, $\boldsymbol{\Sigma}_* = [\bar{k}(\mathbf{x}^i, \mathbf{x}^j)]_{ij=1..N}$ and $\boldsymbol{\alpha}^\top = [z^1, .., z^N]\mathbf{K}^{-1}$. Deterministic inputs $\mathbf{x}$ lead to Gaussian outputs and Gaussian inputs lead to non-Gaussian outputs whose first two moments can be computed analytically [12] for ARD covariance. Multivariate deterministic inputs $\mathbf{x}$ lead to spherical Gaussian outputs $\mathbf{z}$ and Gaussian inputs $\mathbf{x}$ lead to non-Gaussian outputs $\mathbf{z}$ whose moments $(\boldsymbol{\mu}_*, \boldsymbol{\Sigma}_*)$ are given by:

$\mathbf{x} \sim \delta(\mathbf{x}_*) \xrightarrow{f \sim \mathcal{GP}} \mathbf{z} \sim \mathcal{N}(\boldsymbol{\mu}_*, \sigma_*^2 \mathbf{I})$	$\mathbf{x} \sim \mathcal{N}(\mathbf{x}_*, \mathbf{V}_\mathbf{x}) \xrightarrow{f \sim \mathcal{GP}} \mathbf{z} \overset{(\approx)}{\sim} \mathcal{N}(\boldsymbol{\mu}_*, \boldsymbol{\Sigma}_*)$
$\boldsymbol{\mu}_* = \mathbf{A}^\top \mathbf{k}_*$ $\sigma_*^2 = k_{**} - \mathbf{k}_*^\top \mathbf{K}^{-1} \mathbf{k}_* \in [\sigma_\eta^2, \sigma_\eta^2 + \sigma_f^2]$	$\boldsymbol{\mu}_* = \mathbf{A}^\top \tilde{\mathbf{k}}_*$ $\boldsymbol{\Sigma}_* = \left(k_{**} - \text{tr}(\mathbf{K}^{-1}\hat{\mathbf{K}}_*)\right)\mathbf{I} + \mathbf{A}^\top (\hat{\mathbf{K}}_* - \tilde{\mathbf{k}}_* \tilde{\mathbf{k}}_*^\top)\mathbf{A}$

Here, $\mathbf{A}^\top = [\boldsymbol{\alpha}_1, .., \boldsymbol{\alpha}_D]^\top = [\mathbf{z}^1, .., \mathbf{z}^N]\mathbf{K}^{-1}$ and the quantities $\tilde{\mathbf{k}}_* = \mathbb{E}[\mathbf{k}]$ and $\hat{\mathbf{K}}_* = \mathbb{E}[\mathbf{k}\mathbf{k}^\top]$ denote expectations of $\mathbf{k} = \mathbf{k}(\mathbf{x}) = [k(\mathbf{x}^1, \mathbf{x}), .., k(\mathbf{x}^N, \mathbf{x})]^\top$ w.r.t. the Gaussian input distribution $\mathcal{N}(\mathbf{x}|\mathbf{x}_*, \mathbf{V}_\mathbf{x})$ that can readily be evaluated in closed form [12] as detailed in the Appendix. In the limit of $\mathbf{V}_\mathbf{x} \to \mathbf{0}$ we recover the deterministic case as $\tilde{\mathbf{k}}_* \to \mathbf{k}_*$, $\hat{\mathbf{K}}_* \to \mathbf{k}_* \mathbf{k}_*^\top$ and $\boldsymbol{\Sigma}_* \to \sigma_*^2 \mathbf{I}$. Non-zero input variance $\mathbf{V}_\mathbf{x}$ results in full non-spherical output covariance $\boldsymbol{\Sigma}_*$, even for independent GPs because all the GPs are driven by the same (uncertain) input.

A GPLVM [9] is a successful and popular non-parametric Bayesian tool for high dimensional nonlinear data modeling taking into account the data's manifold structure based on a low-dimensional representation. High dimensional data points $\mathbf{z}^i \in \mathcal{Z} \subset \mathbb{R}^D$, $\mathbf{Z} = [\mathbf{z}^1, \ldots, \mathbf{z}^N]$, are represented by corresponding latent points $\mathbf{X} = [\mathbf{x}^1, \ldots, \mathbf{x}^N]$ from a low-dimensional latent space $\mathcal{X} \subset \mathbb{R}^d$ mapped into $\mathcal{Z}$ by D independent GPs f_j – one for each component z_j of the data. All the GPs f_j are conditioned on $\mathbf{X}$ and share the same covariance and mean functions. The model is trained by maximising the sum of the log marginal likelihoods over the D independent regression problems with respect to the latent points $\mathbf{X}$.

While most often applied to nonlinear dimensionality reduction, the GPLVM can also be used as a tractable and flexible density model in high dimensional spaces as illustrated in Figure 1. The basic idea is to interpret the latent points $\mathbf{X}$ as centres of a mixture of either Dirac (Figure 1a) or Gaussian (Figure 1e) distributions in the latent space $\mathcal{X}$ that are *projected forward* by the GP to produce a high dimensional Gaussian mixture $\mathbb{P}(\mathbf{z}) = \frac{1}{N} \sum_i \mathcal{N}(\mathbf{z}|\boldsymbol{\mu}_{\mathbf{x}^i}, \boldsymbol{\Sigma}_{\mathbf{x}^i})$ in the observed space $\mathcal{Z}$. Depending on the kind of latent mixture, the density model $\mathbb{P}(\mathbf{z})$ will either be a mixture of spherical (Figure 1b) or full-covariance Gaussians (Figure 1d). By that mechanism, we get a tractable high dimensional density model $\mathbb{P}(\mathbf{z})$: A set of low-dimensional coordinates in conjunction with a probabilistic map f yield a mixture of high dimensional Gaussians whose covariance matrices are smoothly shared between components. As shown in Figure 1(d), the model is able to capture high dimensional covariance structure along the data manifold by relatively few parameters (compared to D^2), namely the latent coordinates $\mathbf{X} \in \mathbb{R}^{d \times N}$ and the hyperparameters $\boldsymbol{\theta} = [\mathbf{W}, \sigma_f, \sigma_\eta, \mathbf{V}_{\mathbf{x}}] \in \mathbb{R}_+^{2d+2}$ of the GP.

The role of the latent coordinates $\mathbf{X}$ is twofold: they both *define the GP*, mapping the latent points into the observed space, and they *serve as centres* of the mixture density in the latent space. If the latent density is a mixture of Gaussians, the centres of these Gaussians are used to define the GP map, but the full Gaussians (with covariance $\mathbf{V}_{\mathbf{x}}$) are projected forward by the GP map.

2   Learning Algorithm

Learning or model fitting is done by minimising a loss function L w.r.t. the latent coordinates $\mathbf{X}$ and the hyperparameters $\boldsymbol{\theta}$. In the following, we will discuss the usual GPLVM objective function, make clear that it is not suited for density estimation and use leave-out estimation to avoid overfitting.

2.1   GPLVM Likelihood

A GPLVM [9] is trained by setting the latent coordinates $\mathbf{X}$ and the hyperparameters $\boldsymbol{\theta}$ to maximise the probability of the data

$$\mathbb{P}(\mathbf{Z}|\mathbf{X}, \boldsymbol{\theta}) = \prod_{j=1}^{D} \mathbb{P}(\mathbf{z}_j|\mathbf{X}, \boldsymbol{\theta}) = -\frac{DN}{2}\ln 2\pi - \frac{D}{2}\ln|\mathbf{K}| - \frac{1}{2}\mathrm{tr}\left(\mathbf{K}^{-1}\mathbf{Z}^\top\mathbf{Z}\right) \quad (1)$$

that is the product of the marginal likelihoods of D independent regression problems. Using $\frac{\partial L}{\partial \mathbf{K}} = \frac{1}{2}\mathbf{K}^{-1}(\mathbf{Z}^\top\mathbf{Z} - D\mathbf{K})\mathbf{K}^{-1}$, conjugate gradients optimisation at a cost of $\mathcal{O}(DN^3)$ per step is straightforward but suffers from local optima.

However, optimisation of $L_Z(\mathbf{X}, \boldsymbol{\theta})$ does not encourage the GPLVM to be a good density model. Only indirectly, we expect the predictive variance to be small (implying high density) in regions supported by many data points. The main focus of $L_Z(\mathbf{X}, \boldsymbol{\theta})$ is on faithfully predicting $\mathbf{Z}$ from $\mathbf{X}$ (as implemented by the fidelity trace term) while using a relatively smooth function (as favoured by the log determinant term). Therefore, we propose a different cost function.

2.2   General Leave-Out Estimators

Density estimation [13] constructs parametrised estimators $\hat{\mathbb{P}}_{\boldsymbol{\theta}}(\mathbf{z})$ from iid data $\mathbf{z}^i \sim \mathbb{P}(\mathbf{z})$. We use the Kullback-Leibler divergence $J(\boldsymbol{\theta}) \overset{c}{=} -\int \mathbb{P}(\mathbf{z}) \ln \hat{\mathbb{P}}_{\boldsymbol{\theta}}(\mathbf{z})d\mathbf{z}$

to the underlying density and its empirical estimate $\hat{J}_e(\boldsymbol{\theta}) = -\sum_{i \in I} \ln \hat{\mathbb{P}}_{\boldsymbol{\theta},I}(\mathbf{z}^i)$ as quality measure where I emphasises that the full dataset has been used for training. This estimator, is prone to overfitting if used to adjust the parameters via $\boldsymbol{\theta}^* = \arg\min_{\boldsymbol{\theta}} \hat{J}_e(\boldsymbol{\theta})$. Therefore, estimators based on K subsets of the data $\hat{J}_v(\boldsymbol{\theta}) = -\frac{1}{K} \sum_{k=1}^{K} \sum_{i \notin I_k} \ln \hat{\mathbb{P}}_{\boldsymbol{\theta},I_k}(\mathbf{z}^i)$, $I_k \subset I$ are used. Two well known instances are K-fold cross-validation (CV) and leave-one-out (LOO) estimation. The subsets for CV are $I_k \cap I_{k'} = \emptyset, I = \bigcup_{k=1}^{K} I_k, |I_k| \approx |I_{k'}|$ and $K = N, I_k = I \backslash \{k\}$ for LOO. Both of them can be used to optimise $\boldsymbol{\theta}$.

2.3   GPLVM Leave-One-Out Density

There are two reasons why training a GPLVM with the log likelihood of the data $L_Z(\mathbf{X}, \boldsymbol{\theta})$ (Eq. 1) is not optimal in the setting of density estimation: Firstly, it treats the task as regression, and doesn't explicitly worry about how the density is spread in the observation space. Secondly, our empirical results (see Section 3) indicate, that the test set performance is simply not good. Therefore, we propose to train the model using the leave-one-out density

$$-L_{LOO}(\mathbf{X}, \boldsymbol{\theta}) = \ln \prod_{i=1}^{N} \mathbb{P}_{\neg i}(\mathbf{z}^i) = \sum_{i=1}^{N} \ln \frac{1}{N-1} \sum_{j \neq i} \mathcal{N}\left(\mathbf{z}^i | \boldsymbol{\mu}_{\mathbf{x}^j}, \boldsymbol{\Sigma}_{\mathbf{x}^j}\right). \quad (2)$$

This objective is very different from the GPLVM criterion as it measures how well a data point is explained under the mixture models resulting from projecting each of the latent mixture components forward; the leave-out aspect enforces that the point $\mathbf{z}^i$ gets assigned a high density even though the mixture component $\mathcal{N}\left(\mathbf{z}^i | \boldsymbol{\mu}_{\mathbf{x}^i}, \boldsymbol{\Sigma}_{\mathbf{x}^i}\right)$ has been removed from the mixture. The leave-one-out idea is trivial to apply in a mixture setting by just removing the contribution in the sum over components, and is motivated by the desire to avoid overfitting. Evaluation of $L_{LOO}(\mathbf{X}, \boldsymbol{\theta})$ requires $\mathcal{O}(DN^3)$ assuming $N > D > d$.

However, removing the mixture component is not enough since the latent point $\mathbf{x}^i$ is still present in the GP. Using rank one updates to compute inverses and determinants of covariance matrices $\mathbf{K}_{\neg i}$ with row and column i removed, it is possible to evaluate Eq. 3 for mixture components $\mathcal{N}\left(\mathbf{z}^i | \boldsymbol{\mu}_{\mathbf{x}^j}^{\neg i}, \boldsymbol{\Sigma}_{\mathbf{x}^j}\right)$ with latent point $\mathbf{x}^i$ removed from the mean prediction $\boldsymbol{\mu}_{\mathbf{x}^j}^{\neg i}$ – which is what we do in the experiments. Unfortunately, going further by removing $\mathbf{x}^i$ also from the covariance $\boldsymbol{\Sigma}_{\mathbf{x}^j}$ increases the computational burden to $\mathcal{O}(DN^4)$ because we need to compute rank one corrections to all matrices $\hat{\mathbf{K}}_\ell, \ell = 1..N$. Since $\boldsymbol{\Sigma}_{\mathbf{x}^j}^{\neg i}$ is only slightly smaller than $\boldsymbol{\Sigma}_{\mathbf{x}^j}$, we refrain from computing it in the experiments.

In the original GPLVM, there is a clear one-to-one relationship between latent points $\mathbf{x}^i$ and data points $\mathbf{z}^i$ – they are inextricably tied together. However, the leave-one-out (LOO) density $L_{LOO}(\mathbf{X}, \boldsymbol{\theta})$ does not impose any constraint of that sort. The number of mixture components does not need to be N, in fact we can choose any number we like. Only the data visible to the GP $\{\mathbf{x}^j, \bar{\mathbf{z}}^j\}$ is tied together. The actual latent mixture centres $\mathbf{X}$ are not necessarily in correspondence with any actual data point $\mathbf{z}^i$. However, we can choose $\bar{\mathbf{Z}}$ to be a subset of $\mathbf{Z}$. This is reasonable because any mixture centre $\boldsymbol{\mu}_{\mathbf{x}^j} = \bar{\mathbf{Z}} \mathbf{K}^{-1} \mathbf{k}(\mathbf{x}^j)$

(corresponding to the latent centre $\mathbf{x}^j$) lies in the span of $\bar{\mathbf{Z}}$, hence $\bar{\mathbf{Z}}$ should approximately span $\mathbf{Z}$. In our experiments, we enforce $\bar{\mathbf{Z}} = \mathbf{Z}$.

2.4 Overfitting Avoidance

Overfitting in density estimation means that very high densities are assigned to training points, whereas very low densities remain for the test points. Despite its success in parametric models, the leave-one-out idea alone, is not sufficient to prevent overfitting in our model. When optimising $L_{LOO}(\mathbf{X}, \boldsymbol{\theta})$ w.r.t. $(\mathbf{X}, \boldsymbol{\theta})$ using conjugate gradients, we observe the following behaviour: The model circumvents the LOO objective by arranging the latent centres in pairs that take care of each other. More generally, the model partitions the data $\mathbf{Z} \subset \mathbb{R}^D$ into groups of points lying in a subspace of dimension $\leq D - 1$ and adjusts $(\mathbf{X}, \boldsymbol{\theta})$ such that it produces a Gaussian with very small variance $\sigma_\perp^2$ in the orthogonal complement of that subspace. By scaling $\sigma_\perp^2$ to tiny values, $L_{LOO}(\mathbf{X}, \boldsymbol{\theta})$ can be made almost arbitrarily large. It is understood that the hyperparameters of the underlying GP take very extreme values: the noise variance σ_η^2 and some length scales w_i become tiny. In $L_Z(\mathbf{X}, \boldsymbol{\theta})$, this is penalised by the $\ln|\mathbf{K}|$ term, but $L_{LOO}(\mathbf{X}, \boldsymbol{\theta})$ is happy with very improbable GPs. In our initial experiments, we observed this "cheating behaviour" on several of datasets.

We conclude that even though the LOO objective (Eq. 3) is the standard tool to set KDE kernel widths [13], it breaks down for too complex models. We counterbalance this behaviour by leaving out not only one point but rather P points at a time. This renders cheating tremendously difficult. In our experiments we use the leave-P-out (LPO) objective

$$L_{LPO}(\mathbf{X}, \boldsymbol{\theta}) = -\sum_{k=1}^{K} \sum_{i \notin I_k} \ln \frac{1}{N-P} \sum_{j \in I_k} \mathcal{N}\left(\mathbf{z}^i | \boldsymbol{\mu}_{\mathbf{x}^j}^{-i}, \boldsymbol{\Sigma}_{\mathbf{x}^j}\right). \tag{3}$$

Ideally, one would sum over all $K = \binom{N}{P}$ subsets $I_k \in I$ of size $|I_k| = N - P$. However, the number of terms K soon becomes huge: $K \approx N^P$ for $P \ll N$. Therefore, we use an approximation where we set $K = N$ and I_k contains the indices j that currently have the smallest value $\mathcal{N}\left(\mathbf{z}^k | \boldsymbol{\mu}_{\mathbf{x}^j}^{-i}, \boldsymbol{\Sigma}_{\mathbf{x}^j}\right)$.

All gradients $\frac{\partial L_{LPO}}{\partial \mathbf{X}}$ and $\frac{\partial L_{LPO}}{\partial \boldsymbol{\theta}}$ can be computed in $\mathcal{O}(DN^3)$ when using $\boldsymbol{\mu}_{\mathbf{x}^j}^{-i}$. Since the expressions take several pages, we will only include them in the documentation of the code once the paper is accepted. We use a conjugate gradient optimiser to find the best parameters $\mathbf{X}$ and $\boldsymbol{\theta}$.

3 Experiments

In the experimental section, we show that the GPLVM trained with $L_Z(\mathbf{X}, \boldsymbol{\theta})$ (Eq. 1) does not lead to a good density model in general. Using our L_{LPO} training procedure (Section 2.4, Eq. 3), we can turn it into a competitive density model. We demonstrate that a latent variance $\mathbf{V_x} \succ \mathbf{0}$ improves the results even further in some cases and that on some datasets, our density model training procedure performs better than all the baselines.

3.1   Datasets and Baselines

We consider 9 data sets[1], frequently used in machine learning. The data sets differ in their domain of application, their dimension D, their number of instances N and come from regression and classification. In our experiments, we do not use the labels.

dataset	breast	crabs	diabetes	ionosphere	sonar	usps	abalone	bodyfat	housing
N,D	449,9	200,6	768,8	351,33	208,60	9298,256	4177,8	252,14	506,13

We do not only want to demonstrate that our training procedure yields better test densities for the GPLVM. We are rather interested in a fair assessment of how competitive the GPLVM is in density estimation compared to other techniques. As baseline methods, we concentrate on three standard algorithms: penalised fitting of a mixture of full Gaussians (gm), kernel density estimation (kde) and manifold Parzen windows [6] (mp). We run these algorithms for three different type of preprocessing: raw data (r), data scaled to unit variance (s) and whitened data (w). We explored a large number of parameter settings and report the best results in Table 1.

Penalised Gaussian mixtures. In order to speed up EM computations, we partition the dataset into K disjoint subsets using the K-means algorithm[2]. We fitted a penalised Gaussian to each subset and combined them using the relative cluster size as weight $\mathbb{P}(\mathbf{z}) = \frac{1}{N}\sum_k N_k\mathbb{P}_k(\mathbf{z})$. Every single Gaussian $\mathbb{P}_k(\mathbf{z})$ has the form $\mathbb{P}_k(\mathbf{z}) = \mathcal{N}(\mathbf{z}|\mathbf{m}^k, \mathbf{C}^k + w\mathbf{I})$ where $\mathbf{m}^k$ and $\mathbf{C}^k$ equal the sample mean and covariance of the particular cluster, respectively. The global ridge parameter w prevents singular covariances and is chosen to maximise the LOO log density $-L(w) = \ln\prod_j \mathbb{P}_{\neg j}(\mathbf{z}^j) = \ln\prod_j \sum_k N_k\mathcal{N}(\mathbf{z}^j|\mathbf{m}^k_{\neg j}, \mathbf{C}^k_{\neg j} + w\mathbf{I})$. We use simple gradient descent to find the best parameter $w \in \mathbb{R}_+$.

Diagonal Gaussian KDE. The kernel density estimation procedure fits a mixture model by centring one mixture component at each data point $\mathbf{z}^i$. We use independent multi-variate Gaussians: $\mathbb{P}(\mathbf{z}) = \frac{1}{N}\sum_i \mathcal{N}(\mathbf{z}|\mathbf{z}^i, \mathbf{W})$, where the diagonal widths $\mathbf{W} = \mathrm{Dg}(w_1, .., w_D)$ are chosen to maximise the LOO density $-L(\mathbf{W}) = \ln\prod_j \mathbb{P}_{\neg j}(\mathbf{z}^j) = \ln\prod_j \frac{1}{N}\sum_{i\neq j} \mathcal{N}(\mathbf{z}^j|\mathbf{z}^i, \mathbf{W})$. We employ a Newton-scheme to find the best parameters $\mathbf{W} \in \mathbb{R}^D_+$.

Manifold Parzen windows. The manifold Parzen window estimator [6] tries to capture locality by means of a kernel k. It is a mixture of N full Gaussians where the covariance $\boldsymbol{\Sigma}^i = w\mathbf{I} + (\sum_{j\neq i} k(\mathbf{z}^i, \mathbf{z}^j)(\mathbf{z}^i - \mathbf{z}^j)(\mathbf{z}^i - \mathbf{z}^j)^\top)/(\sum_{j\neq i} k(\mathbf{z}^i, \mathbf{z}^j))$ of each mixture component is only computed based on neighbouring data points.

As proposed by the authors, we use the r-nearest neighbour kernel and do not store full covariance matrices $\boldsymbol{\Sigma}^i$ but a low rank approximation $\boldsymbol{\Sigma}^i \approx w\mathbf{I} + \mathbf{V}\mathbf{V}^\top$ with $\mathbf{V} \in \mathbb{R}^{D\times d}$. As in the other baselines, the ridge parameter w is set to maximise the LOO density.

Baseline results. The results of the baseline density estimators can be found in Table 1. They clearly show three things: (i) More data yields better performance,

---

[1] http://www.csie.ntu.edu.tw/~cjlin/libsvmtools/datasets/
[2] http://cseweb.ucsd.edu/~elkan/fastkmeans.html

Table 1. Average log test densities over 10 random splits of the data. We did not allow N_{tr} to exceeded $N/2$. We only show the method yielding the highest test density among the three baseline candidates penalised full Gaussian mixture $gm(K,\rho)$, diagonal Gaussian kernel density estimation $kde(\rho)$ and manifold Parzen windows $mp(d,r,\rho)$. The parameter $K = \{1,..,13\}$ is the number of cluster centers used for gm, $d = \lceil D \cdot \{5,12,19,26,33,40\}/100\rceil$ is the number of latent dimensions and $r = \lceil N \cdot \{5,10,15,20,25,30\}/100\rceil$ the neighbourhood size for mp and ρ is saying which preprocessing has been used (raw r, scaled to unit variance s, whitened w). The Gaussian mixture model yields in all cases the highest test density except for one case where the Parzen window estimator performs better.

dataset	breast	crabs	diabetes	ionosphere	sonar	usps	abalone	bodyfat	housing
$N_{tr}=50$	−9.1 gm(10,s)	0.9 gm(5,r)	−11.0 gm(4,r)	−34.1 gm(10,r)	−67.7 gm(1,r)	18.4 gm(1,r)	12.5 gm(8,r)	−36.0 gm(1,w)	−33.4 gm(6,s)
$N_{tr}=100$	−8.6 gm(4,r)	1.9 gm(7,r)	−10.0 gm(3,w)	−30.5 gm(13,r)	−62.0 gm(1,r)	124.8 gm(1,r)	13.9 gm(5,r)	−35.2 gm(2,w)	−30.6 mp(6,21,s)
$N_{tr}=150$	−8.4 gm(9,s)		−9.6 gm(3,w)	−33.9 gm(6,s)	−61.5 gm(4,w)	185.4 gm(1,r)	14.3 gm(10,r)	−34.7 gm(5,w)	−29.1 mp(6,32,s)
$N_{tr}=200$	−8.2 gm(9,r)		−8.3 gm(4,w)	−31.8 gm(6,w)		232.6 gm(3,w)	14.2 gm(13,r)		−23.5 gm(4,s)
$N_{tr}=250$	−8.1 gm(11,r)		−8.2 gm(5,w)			261.6 gm(6,w)	14.3 gm(13,r)		−16.0 gm(3,w)

(ii) penalised mixture of Gaussians is clearly and consistently the best method and (iii) manifold Parzen windows [6] offer only little benefit. The absolute values can only be compared within datasets since linearly transforming the data $\mathbf{Z}$ by $\mathbf{P}$ results in a constant offset $\ln|\mathbf{P}|$ in the log test probabilities.

3.2   Experimental Setting and Results

We keep the experimental schedule and setting of the previous Section in terms of the 9 datasets, the 10 fold averaging procedure and the maximal training set size $N_{tr} = N/2$. We use the GPLVM log likelihood of the data $L_Z(\mathbf{X},\boldsymbol{\theta})$, the LPO log density with deterministic latent centres (L_{LPO}-$det(\mathbf{X},\boldsymbol{\theta})$, $\mathbf{V_x} = \mathbf{0}$) and the LPO log density using a Gaussian latent centres L_{LPO}-$rd(\mathbf{X},\boldsymbol{\theta})$ to optimise the latent centres $\mathbf{X}$ and the hyperparameters $\boldsymbol{\theta}$. Our numerical results include 3 different latent dimensions d, 3 preprocessing procedures and 5 different numbers of leave-out points P. Optimisation is done using 600 conjugate gradient steps alternating between $\mathbf{X}$ and $\boldsymbol{\theta}$. In order to compress the big amount of numbers, we report the method with highest test density as shown in Figure 2, only.

The most obvious conclusion, we can draw from the numerical experiments, is the bad performance of $L_Z(\mathbf{X},\boldsymbol{\theta})$ as a training procedure for GPLVM in the context of density modeling. This finding is consistent over all datasets and numbers of training points. We get another conclusive result in terms of how the latent variance $\mathbf{V_x}$ influences the final test densities[3]. Only in the bodyfat data set it is not beneficial to allow for latent variance. It is clear that this is an intrinsic property of the dataset itself, whether it prefers to be modelled by a spherical Gaussian mixture or by a full Gaussian mixture.

An important issue, namely how well a fancy density model performs compared to very simple models, has in the literature either been ignored [7,8] or only done in a very limited way [6]. Experimentally, we can conclude that on some datasets e.g. diabetes, sonar, abalone our procedure cannot compete

---

[3] In principle, $\mathbf{V_x}$ could be fixed to $\mathbf{I}$ because its scale can be modelled by $\mathbf{X}$.

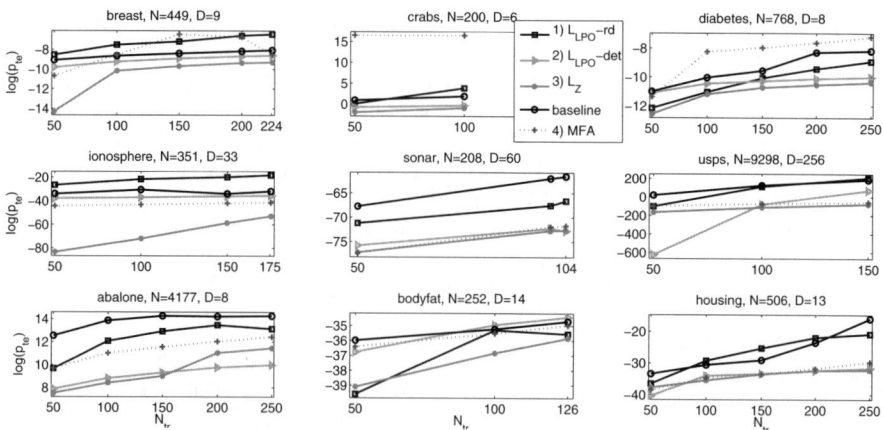

Fig. 2. Each panel displays the log test density averaged over 10 random splits for three different GPLVM training procedures and the *best* out of 41 baselines (penalised mixture $k = 1..13$, diag.+isotropic KDE, manifold Parzen windows with 36 different parameter settings) as well as various mixture of factor analysers (MFA) settings as a function of the number of training data points N_{tr}. We report the maximum value across latent dimension $d = \{1, 2, 3\}$, three preprocessing methods (raw, scaled to unit variance, whitened) and $P = \{1, 2, 5, 10, 15\}$ leave-out points . The GPLVM training procedures are the following: L_{LPO}-rd: stochastic leave-P-out density (Eq. 3 with latent Gaussians, $\mathbf{V_x} \succ \mathbf{0}$), L_{LPO}-det: deterministic leave-P-out density (Eq. 3 with latent Diracs, $\mathbf{V_x} = \mathbf{0}$) and L_Z: marginal likelihood (Eq. 1).

with a plain gm model. However note, that the baseline numbers were obtained as the maximum over a wide (41 in total) range of parameters and methods.

For example, in the usps case, our elaborate density estimation procedure outperforms a single penalised Gaussian only for training set sizes $N_{tr} > 100$. However, the margin in terms of density is quite big: On $N_{tr} = 150$ prewhitened data points $L_{LPO}(\mathbf{X}, \boldsymbol{\theta})$ with deterministic latents yields 70.47 at $d = 2$, whereas full $L_{LPO}(\mathbf{X}, \boldsymbol{\theta})$ reaches 207 at $d = 4$ which is significantly above 185.4 as obtained by the gm method – since we work on a logarithmic scale, this corresponds to factor of $2.4 \cdot 10^9$ in terms of density.

3.3   Running Times

While the baseline methods such as gm, kde and mp run in a couple of minutes for the usps dataset, training a GPLVM with either $L_{LPO}(\mathbf{X}, \boldsymbol{\theta})$, $\mathbf{V_x} = \mathbf{0}$ or $L_Z(\mathbf{X}, \boldsymbol{\theta})$ takes considerably longer since a lot of cubic covariance matrix operations need to be computed during the joint optimisation of $(\mathbf{X}, \boldsymbol{\theta})$. The GPLVM computations scale cubically in the number of data points N_{tr} used by the GP forward map and quadratically in the dimension of the observed space D. The major computational gap is the transition from $\mathbf{V_x} = \mathbf{0}$ to $\mathbf{V_x} \succ \mathbf{0}$ because in the latter case, covariance matrices of size D^2 have to be evaluated which cause the optimisation to last in the order of a couple of hours. To provide concrete

timing results, we picked $N_{tr} = 150$, $d = 2$, averaged over the 9 datasets and
show times relative to L_Z.

alg	gm(1)	gm(10)	kde	mp	mfa	L_Z	L_{LPO}-det	L_{LPO}-rd
t_{rel}	0.27	0.87	0.93	1.38	0.30	1.00	35.39	343.37

Note that the methods L_{LPO} are run in a conservative fail-proof black box
mode with 600 gradient steps. We observe good densities after considerably less
gradient steps already. Another straightforward speedup can be obtained by
carefully pruning the number of inputs to the L_{LPO} models.

4   Conclusion and Discussion

We have discussed how the basic GPLVM is not in itself a good density model,
and results on several datasets have shown, that it does not generalise well. We
have discussed two alternatives based on explicitly projecting forward a mixture
model from the latent space. Experiments show that such density models are
generally superior to the simple GPLVM.

Among the two alternative ways of defining the latent densities, the simplest
is a mixture of delta functions, which – due to the stochasticity of the GP map
– results in a smooth predictive distribution. However, the resulting mixture of
Gaussians, has only axis aligned components. If instead the latent distribution
is a mixture of Gaussians, the dimensions of the observations become correlated.
This allows the learnt densities to faithfully follow the underlying manifold.

Although the presented model has attractive properties, some problems remain: The learning algorithm needs a good initialisation and the computational
demand of the method is considerable. However, we have pointed out that in
contrast to the GPLVM, the number of latent points need not match the number
of observations allowing for alternative sparse methods.

We have detailed how to adapt ideas based on the GPLVM to density modeling
in high dimensions and have shown that such models are feasible to train. Code
can be obtained from `http://www.kyb.mpg.de/~hn`.

References

1. Izenman, A.J.: Recent developments in nonparametric density estimation. Journal
   of the American Statistical Association 86, 205–224 (1991)
2. Ghahramani, Z., Beal, M.J.: Variational inference for Bayesian mixtures of factor
   analysers. In: NIPS, vol. 12 (2000)
3. Rosenblatt, M.: Remarks on some nonparametric estimates of a density function.
   Annals of Mathematical Statistics 27(3), 832–837 (1956)
4. Parzen, E.: On estimation of a probability density function and mode. Annals of
   Mathematical Statistics 33(3), 1065–1076 (1962)
5. Rudemo, M.: Empirical choice of histograms and kernel density estimators. Scandinavian Journal of Statistics 9, 65–78 (1982)
6. Vincent, P., Bengio, Y.: Manifold parzen windows. In: NIPS, vol. 15 (2003)
7. Bishop, C.M., Svensén, M., Williams, C.K.I.: The generative topographic mapping.
   Neural Computation 1, 215–234 (1998)
8. Roweis, S., Saul, L.K., Hinton, G.E.: Global coordination of local linear models.
   In: NIPS, vol. 14 (2002)

9. Lawrence, N.: Probabilistic non-linear principal component analysis with Gaussian process latent variable models. JMLR 6, 1783–1816 (2005)
10. Rasmussen, C.E., Williams, C.K.I.: Gaussian Processes for Machine Learning. The MIT Press, Cambridge (2006)
11. Rasmussen, C.E.: The infinite Gaussian mixture model. In: NIPS, vol. 12 (2000)
12. Quiñonero-Candela, J., Girard, A., Rasmussen, C.E.: Prediction at an uncertain input for GPs and RVMs. Technical Report IMM-2003-18, TU Denmark (2003)
13. Wasserman, L.: All of Nonparametric Statistics. Springer, Heidelberg (2006)

Appendix

Both $\hat{\mathbf{K}}_* = \mathbb{E}[\mathbf{k}\mathbf{k}^\top] = [\hat{k}_*(\mathbf{x}^i, \mathbf{x}^j)]_{ij}$ and $\tilde{\mathbf{k}}_* = \mathbb{E}[\mathbf{k}] = [\tilde{k}_*(\mathbf{x}^j)]_j$ are the following expectations of $\mathbf{k} = [k(\mathbf{x}, \mathbf{x}^1), .., k(\mathbf{x}, \mathbf{x}^N)]^\top$ w.r.t. $\mathcal{N}(\mathbf{x}|\mathbf{x}_*, \mathbf{V_x})$:

$$\tilde{k}_*(\mathbf{x}^i) = \sigma_f^2 \left|\mathbf{V_x}\mathbf{W}^{-1} + \mathbf{I}\right|^{-\frac{1}{2}} \rho\left(\mathbf{V_x} + \mathbf{W}, \mathbf{x}^i - \mathbf{x}_*\right), \ \rho(\mathbf{D}, \mathbf{y}) = e^{-\frac{1}{2}\mathbf{y}^\top \mathbf{D}^{-1}\mathbf{y}}, \text{ and}$$

$$\hat{k}_*(\mathbf{x}^i, \mathbf{x}^j) = \frac{k(\mathbf{x}^i, \mathbf{x}_*)k(\mathbf{x}^j, \mathbf{x}_*)}{\sqrt{|2\mathbf{V_x}\mathbf{W}^{-1} + \mathbf{I}|}} \rho\left(\frac{1}{2}\mathbf{W}\mathbf{V_x}^{-1}\mathbf{W} + \mathbf{W}, \frac{\mathbf{x}^i + \mathbf{x}^j}{2} - \mathbf{x}_*\right).$$

Classification of Swimming Microorganisms Motion Patterns in 4D Digital In-Line Holography Data

Laura Leal-Taixé[1,*], Matthias Heydt, Sebastian Weiße[2], Axel Rosenhahn[2,3], and Bodo Rosenhahn[1]

[1] Leibniz Universität Hannover, Appelstr. 9A, Hannover, Germany
[2] Applied Physical Chemistry, University of Heidelberg, INF 253, Heidelberg, Germany
[3] Institute of Toxicology and Genetics (ITG), Forschungszentrum Karlsruhe, Germany
leal@tnt.uni-hannover.de

Abstract. Digital in-line holography is a 3D microscopy technique which has gotten an increasing amount of attention over the last few years in the fields of microbiology, medicine and physics. In this paper we present an approach for automatically classifying complex microorganism motions observed with this microscopy technique. Our main contribution is the use of Hidden Markov Models (HMMs) to classify four different motion patterns of a microorganism and to separate multiple patterns occurring within a trajectory. We perform leave-one-out experiments with the training data to prove the accuracy of our method and to analyze the importance of each trajectory feature for classification. We further present results obtained on four full sequences, a total of 2500 frames. The obtained classification rates range between 83.5% and 100%.

1 Introduction

Many fields of interest in biology and other scientific research areas deal with intrinsically three-dimensional problems. The motility of swimming microorganisms such as bacteria or algae is of fundamental importance for topics like pathogen-host interactions [1], biofilm-formation [2], or biofouling by marine microorganisms [3].

Understanding the motility and behavioral patterns of microorganisms allows us to understand their interaction with the environment and thus to control environmental parameters to avoid unwanted consequences such as infections or biofouling. To study these effects in 3D several attempts have been made: tracking light microscopy, capable of tracking one bacterium at a time [4], stereoscopy [5] or confocal microscopy [6].

Fully automated analyzing tools are becoming necessary given the huge amount of data that can be obtained with these imaging techniques. Besides generating motion trajectories from microscopic data, a classification afterwards allows the biologists to get in a compact and compressed fashion the desired information from the large image sets. Indeed, the classification of motion patterns in biology is a well-studied topic [7] but identifying these patterns manually is a complicated task. Recently, machine learning and pattern recognition techniques have been introduced to analyze in detail such complex movements. These techniques include: Principal Component Analysis (PCA) [8],

---

* Corresponding author.

M. Goesele et al. (Eds.): DAGM 2010, LNCS 6376, pp. 283–292, 2010.
© Springer-Verlag Berlin Heidelberg 2010

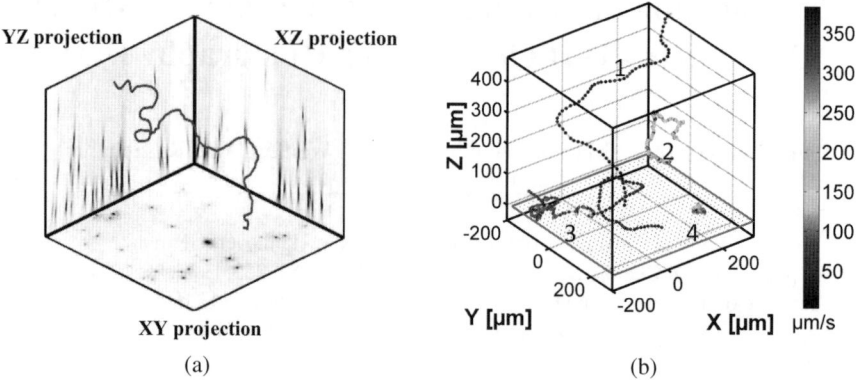

Fig. 1. (a) Projections obtained with digital in-line holography (inverted colors for better visualization). Sample trajectory in red. (b) Four patterns colored according to speed: orientation (1), wobbling (2), gyration (3) and intensive surface probing (4)

a linear transformation used to analyze high dimensional data; Bayesian models [9] which use a graph model and the rules of probability theory to select among different hypotheses; or Support Vector Machines (SVM) [10], which use training data to find the optimum parameters of the model representing each class. A comparison of machine learning approaches applied to biology can be found in [11].

In order to classify biological patterns, we need to use an approach able to handle time-varying signals. Hidden Markov Models [12] are statistical models especially known for their application in temporal pattern recognition. They were first used in speech recognition and since then, HMMs have been extensively applied to vision. Applications vary from handwritten word recognition [13], face recognition [14] or human action recognition [15, 16].

In this paper, we focus on the classification of four motion patterns of the green alga *Ulva linza* with the use of Hidden Markov Models. Furthermore, our system is able to find and separate different patterns within a single sequence. Besides classification of motion patterns, a key issue is the choice of features used to classify and distinguish the involved patterns. For this reason we perfom an extensive analysis of the importance of typical motion parameters, such as velocity, curvature, orientation, etc. Our developed system is highly flexible and can easily be extended. Especially for forthcoming work on cells, microorganisms or human behavior, such automated algorithms are of pivotal importance for high throughput analysis of individual segments in motion data.

2   Digital in-line Holography (DIH)

An alternative to conventional optical microscopy is provided by digital in-line holography, a lensless microscopy technique which intrinsically contains three-dimensional information about the volume under investigation.

The important requirements are a sample of sufficient transparency and a divergent, coherent wave. The holographic microscope setup follows directly Gabors initial idea [17] and has been implemented for laser radiation by Xu et al. [18]. A divergent wavefront is generated by diffraction of a laser beam at a pinhole. A so-called *hologram* is then recorded by a CCD- or CMOS-chip. This hologram is then reconstructed back into real space by a Kirchhoff-Helmholtz transformation [18]:

$$K(\mathbf{r}) = \int_S I(\xi) \exp\left[\frac{ik\mathbf{r}\xi}{|\xi|}\right] d\xi \tag{1}$$

The integration extends over the 2D surface of the screen with coordinates $\xi = (X, Y, L)$, where L is the distance from the source (pinhole) to the center of the detector (CCD chip), $I(\xi)$ is the contrast image (hologram) on the screen obtained by subtracting the images with and without the object present and k the wave number: $k = 2\pi/\lambda$.

From the reconstruction 3 projections XY, XZ and YZ are obtained (see Figure 1(a)) as described in [19]. These projections contain the image information of the complete observation volume, i.e. from every object located in the light cone between pinhole and detector. The extraction of the particle coordinates in combination with a time series of holograms enables one to track multiple objects in 3D over time [3, 20].

Determining 3D trajectories is a complex task which still presents some major challenges. We make use of the system described in [21], which uses the multi-level Hungarian to obtain the full 3D trajectories from 3 projections. Trajectories are then manually verified by specialists and tagged according to their motion pattern.

3   Hidden Markov Models

Hidden Markov Models [12] are statistical models of sequential data widely used in many applications in artificial intelligence, speech and pattern recognition and modeling of biological sequences.

In an HMM it is assumed that the system being modeled is a Markov process with unobserved states. This hidden stochastic process can only be observed through another set of stochastic processes that produce the sequence of symbols $O = o_1, o_2, ..., o_M$. An HMM consists of a number N of states $S_1, S_2, ..., S_N$. The system is at one of the states at any given time. Every HMM can be defined by the triple $\lambda = (\Pi, A, B)$. $\Pi = \{\pi_i\}$ is the vector of initial state probabilities. Each transition from S_i to S_j can occur with a probability of a_{ij}, where $\sum_j a_{ij} = 1$. $A = \{a_{ij}\}$ is the state transition matrix. In addition, each state S_i generates an output o_k with a probability distribution $b_{ik} = P(o_k|S_i)$. $B = \{b_{ik}\}$ is the emission matrix.

A detailed introduction to HMM theory can be found in [12].

4   HMMs for Motion Pattern Classification

In this section we describe the different types of motion patterns to classify, as well as the design of the complete HMM and the features used for classification.

4.1   Types of Patterns

In our experimental setup we are interested in the four patterns depicted in Figure 1(b): Orientation(1), Wobbling(2), Gyration(3) and intensive surface probing or Spinning(4).

They show a high similarity with the patterns observed before in [22] for the brown algae *Hincksia Irregularis*.

Orientation. Pattern 1 in Figure 1(b) is an example for the Orientation pattern. This pattern typically occurs in solution and far away from surfaces. The most important characteristics of the pattern are the high swimming speed (a mean of $150\mu m/s$) and a straight swimming motion with moderate turning angles.

Wobbling. Pattern 2 is called the Wobbling pattern and its main characteristic is a much slower mean velocity of around $50\mu m/s$. The spores assigned to the pattern often change their direction of movement and only swim in straight lines for very short distances. Compared to the orientation pattern this leads to less smooth trajectories.

Gyration. Pattern 3 is called the Gyration pattern. This pattern is extremely important for the exploration of surfaces as occasional surface contacts are observable. The behavior in solution is similar to the Orientation pattern. Since in this pattern spores often switch between swimming towards and away from the surfaces, it can be interpreted as a pre-stage to surface probing.

Intensive surface probing and Spinning. Pattern 4 involves a swimming in circles close to the surface within a very limited region. After a certain exploration time, the spores leave the surface to the next position and start swimming in circular patterns again. This motion is characterized by decreased mean velocities of about $30\mu m/s$ in combination with a higher tendency to change direction (see Figure 1(b), case 4).

4.2   Features Used for Classification

An analysis of the features used for classification is presented in this section. Many of the features are typical and can be used in any motion analysis problem. An intrinsic characteristic of digital in-line holography is the lower resolution of the z position compared to the x, y resolution [23]. Since many of the following features depend on the depth value, we compute the average measurements within 5 frames in order to reduce the noise of such features. The four characteristic features used are:

- v, *velocity*: the speed of the particles is an important descriptive feature as we can see in Figure 1(b). We use only the magnitude of the speed vector, since the direction is described by the next two parameters. Range is $[0, maxSpeed]$. $maxSpeed$ is the maximum speed of the particles as found experimentally in [19].
- α, *angle between velocities*: it measures the change in direction, distinguishing stable patterns from random ones. Range is $[0, 180]$.
- β, *angle to normal of the surface*: it measures how the particles approaches the surface or how it swims above it. Range is $[0, 180]$.
- D, *distance to surface*: this can be a key feature to differentiate surface-induced movements from general movements. Range is $(m_z, M_z]$, where m_z and M_z are the z limits of the volume under study.

In order to work with Hidden Markov Models, we need to represent the features for each pattern with a fixed set of symbols. The number of total symbols will depend on the number of symbols used to represent each feature $N_{symbols} = N_v N_\alpha N_\beta N_D$.

In order to convert every symbol for each feature into a unique symbol for the HMM, we use Equation (2), where Y is the final symbol we are looking for, $Y_{1..4}$ are the symbols for each of the features, ranged $[1..N_{Y_{1..4}}]$, where $N_{Y_{1..4}}$ are the number of symbols per feature.

$$ Y = Y_1 + (Y_2 - 1)N_{Y_1} + (Y_3 - 1)N_{Y_1}N_{Y_2} + (Y_4 - 1)N_{Y_1}N_{Y_2}N_{Y_3} \qquad (2) $$

In the next sections we present how to use the resulting symbols to train the HMMs. The symbols are the observations of the HMM, therefore, the training process gives us the probability of emitting each symbol for each of the states.

4.3 Building and Training the HMMs

In speech recognition, an HMM is trained for each of the phonemes of a language. Later, words are constructed by concatenating several HMMs of the phonemes that form the word. HMMs for sentences can even be created by concatenating HMMs of words, etc. We take a similar hierarchical approach in this paper. We train one HMM for each of the patterns and then we combine them into a unique Markov chain with a simple yet effective design that will be able to describe any pattern or combination of patterns. This approach can be used in any problem where multiple motion patterns are present.

Individual HMM per pattern. In order to represent each pattern, we build a Markov chain with N states and we only allow the model to stay in the same state or move one state forward. Finally, from state N we can also go back to state 1. The number of states N is found empirically using the training data. The HMM is trained using the Baum-Welch algorithm to obtain the transition and emission matrices.

Complete HMM. The idea of having a complete HMM that represents all the patterns is that we can not only classify sequences where there is one pattern present, but sequences where the particle makes transitions between different patterns. In Figure 2(a) we can see a representation of the complete model while the design of the transition matrix is depicted in Figure 2(b). The four individual HMMs for each of the patterns are placed in parallel (blue). In order to deal with the transitions we create two special states: the START and the SWITCH state.

The START state is just created to allow the system to begin at any pattern (orange). We define $P_{start} = P_{SwitchToModel} = \frac{1-P_{switch}}{N_P}$ where N_P is the number of patterns. As START does not contain any information of the pattern, it does not emit any symbol.

The purpose of the new state SWITCH is to make transitions easier. Imagine a given trajectory which makes a transition from Pattern 1 to Pattern 2. While transitioning, the features create a symbol that neither belongs to Pattern 1 nor 2. The system can then go to state SWITCH to emit that symbol and continue to Pattern 2. Therefore, all SWITCH emission probabilities are $\frac{1}{N_{symbols}}$. Since SWITCH is such a convenient state, we need to impose restrictive conditions so that the system does not go or stay in SWITCH too often. This is controlled by the parameter P_{switch}, set at the minimum

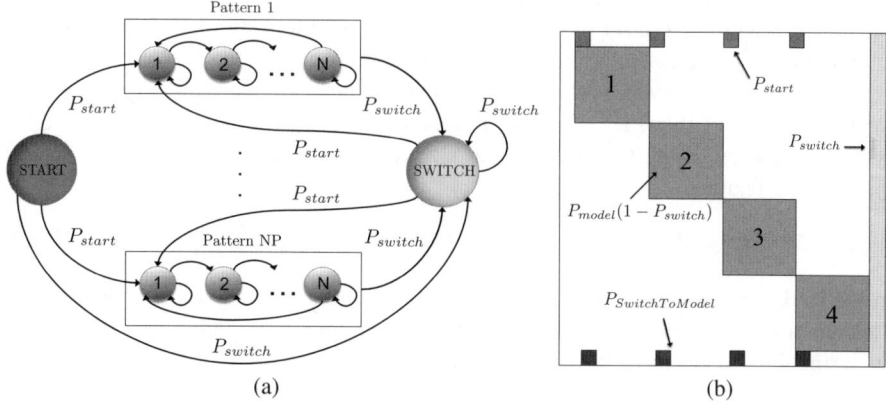

Fig. 2. (a) Complete HMM created to include changes between patterns within one trajectory. (b) Transition matrix of the complete HMM

value of all the P_{model} minus a small ϵ. This way, we ensure that P_{switch} is the lowest transition probability in the system.

Finally, the sequence of states given by the Viterbi algorithm determines the motion pattern observed. Our implementation uses the standard MatLab HMM functions.

5 Experimental Results

In this section we present several experimental results to prove the use of Hidden Markov Models to classify biological patterns.

5.1 Evaluation of the Features Used for Classification

The experiments in this section have the purpose of determining the impact of each feature for the correct classification of each pattern. We perform leave-one-out tests on our training data which consists of 525 trajectories: 78 for wobbling, 181 for gyration, 202 for orientation and 64 for intensive surface probing. The trajectories are obtained automatically with the method in [21] and verified and classified manually by experts.

The first experiment that we conduct (see Figure 3) is to determine the effect of each parameter for the classification of all the patterns. The number of symbols and states can only be determined empirically since they depend heavily on the amount of training data. In our experiments, we found the best set of parameters to be $N = 4$, $N_v = 4$, $N_\alpha = 3$, $N_\beta = 3$ and $N_D = 3$, for which we obtain a classification rate of 83.86%.

For each test, we set one parameter to 1, which means that the corresponding feature has no effect in the classification process. For example, the first bar in blue labeled "No Depth" is done with $N_D = 1$. The classification rate for each pattern (labeled from 1 to 4) as well as the mean for all the patterns (labeled Total) is recorded.

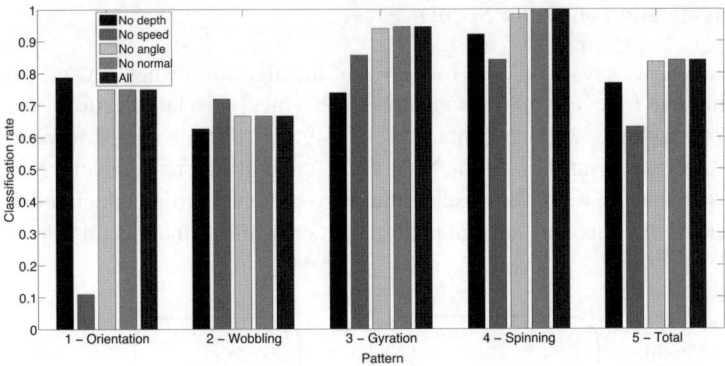

Fig. 3. Classification rate for parameters $N = 4$, $N_v = 4$, $N_\alpha = 3$, $N_\beta = 3$ and $N_D = 3$. On each experiment, one of the features is not used. In the last experiment all features are used.

As we can see, the angle α and the normal β information are the less relevant features, since the classification rate with and without these features is almost the same. The angle information depends on the z component and, as explained in section 4.2, the lower resolution in z can result in noisy measurements. In this case, the trade-off is between having a noisy angle data which can be unreliable, or an average measure which is less discriminative for classification. The most distinguishing feature according to Figure 3 is the speed. Without it, the total classification rate decreases to 55.51% and down to just 11.05% for the orientation pattern.

Based on the previous results, we could think of just using the depth and speed information for classification. But if $N_\alpha = N_\beta = 1$, the rate goes down to 79.69%. That means that we need one of the two measures for correct classification. The parameters used are: $N = 4$, $N_v = 4$, $N_\alpha = 1$, $N_\beta = 3$ and $N_D = 3$, for which we obtain a classification rate of 83.5%. This rate is very close to the result with $N_\alpha = 3$, with the advantage that we now use less symbols to represent the same information. Several tests lead us to choose $N = 4$ number of states.

The confusion matrix for these parameters is shown in Figure 4. As we can see, patterns 3 and 4 are correctly classified. The common misclassifications occur when Orientation (1) is classified as Gyration (3), or when Wobbling (2) is classified as Spinning (4). In the next section we discuss these misclassifications in detail.

	1 - Ori	2 - Wob	3 - Gyr	4 - Spin
1 - Ori	0.75	0.09	0.16	
2 - Wob	0.07	0.68	0.01	0.24
3 - Gyr	0.01		0.94	0.05
4 - Spin			0.02	0.98

Fig. 4. Confusion matrix with parameters $N = 4$, $N_v = 4$, $N_\alpha = 1$, $N_\beta = 3$ and $N_D = 3$

5.2   Classification on Other Sequences

In this section, we present the performance of the algorithm when several patterns appear within one trajectory and also analyze the typical misclassifications. As test data we use four sequences which contain 27, 40, 49 and 11 trajectories, respectively. We obtain classification rates of 100%, 85%, 89.8% and 100%, respectively. Note that for the third sequence, 60% of the misclassifications are only partial, which means that the model detects that there are several patterns but only one of them is misclassified.

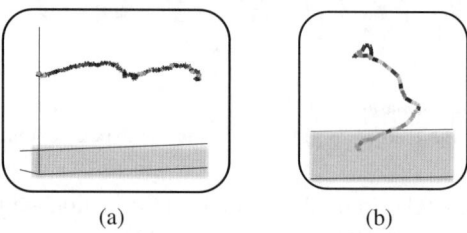

(a)   (b)

Fig. 5. (a) Wobbling (pattern 2) misclassified as Spinning (4). (b) Gyration (3) misclassified as Orientation (1). Color coded according to speed as in Figure 1(b)

One of the misclassifications that can occur is that Wobbling (2) is classified as Spinning (4). Both motion patterns have similar speed values and the only truly differentiating characteristics are the depth and the angle α. Since we use 3 symbols for depth, the fact that the microorganism touches the surface or swims near the surface leads to the same classification. That is the case of Figure 5(a), in which the model chooses pattern Spinning (4) because the speed is very low (dark blue) and sometimes the speed in the Wobbling pattern can be a little higher (light blue).

As commented in section 4.1, Gyration (3) and Orientation (1) are two linked patterns. The behavior of gyration in solution is similar to the orientation pattern, that is why the misclassification shown in Figure 5(b) can happen. In this case, since the microorganism does not interact with the surface and the speed of the pattern is high (red color), the model detects it as an orientation pattern. We note that this pattern is difficult to classify, even for a trained expert.

On the other hand, the model has been proven to handle changes between patterns extremely well. In Figure 6(a), we see the transition between Gyration (3) and Spinning (4). In Figure 6(b), color coded according to classification, we can see how the model detects the Orientation part (red) and the Gyration part (yellow) perfectly well. The model performs a quick transition (marked in blue) and during this period the model stays in the SWITCH state. We have verified that all the transition periods detected by the model lie within the manually annotated transition boundaries marked by experts, even when there is more than one transition present in a trajectory.

The classification results on a full sequence are shown in Figure 7.

Finally, we can obtain the probability of each transition (e.g. from Orientation to Spinning) for a given dataset under study. This is extremely useful for experts to understand the behavior of a certain microorganism under varying conditions.

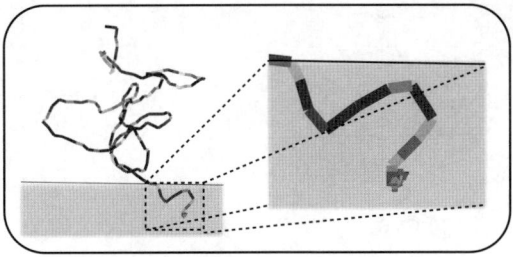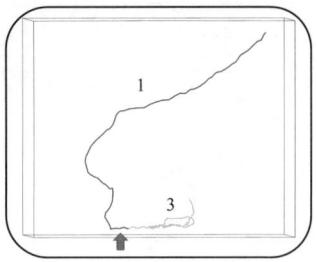

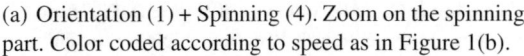

(a) Orientation (1) + Spinning (4). Zoom on the spinning part. Color coded according to speed as in Figure 1(b).

(b) Orientation (1, red) + Gyration (3, yellow). Transition marked in blue and pointed by an arrow.

Fig. 6. Sequences containing two patterns within one trajectory

6   Conclusions

We presented a fully automatic method to classify four different motion patterns of a microorganism observed with digital in-line holography. We used Hidden Markov Models for classification, since it allows us to encode the dynamic information of each pattern. We presented a simple yet effective hierarchical design which combines multiple trained HMMs (one for each of the patterns), which has proved successful to identify different patterns within one single trajectory. The changes between one pattern and another are correctly detected by the complete HMM. The experiments performed on four full sequences result in a total classification rate between 83.5% and 100%. Furthermore, we presented a detailed analysis of the impact of each of the features used for classification. The proper use of a powerful machine learning tool, such as Hidden Markov Models, can be extremely useful to study microorganism motility, providing a vast amount of analyzed data to the experts.

Acknowledgements. This work is partially funded by the German Research Foundation, DFG projects RO 2497/7-1 and RO 2524/2-1 and the EU project AMBIO.

References

1. Ginger, M., Portman, N., McKean, P.: Swimming with protists: perception, motility and flagellum assembly. Nature Reviews Microbiology 6(11), 838–850 (2008)
2. Stoodley, P., Sauer, K., Davies, D., Costerton, J.: Biofilms as complex differentiated communities. Annual Review of Microbiology 56, 187–209 (2002)
3. Heydt, M., Rosenhahn, A., Grunze, M., Pettitt, M., Callow, M.E., Callow, J.A.: Digital inline holography as a 3d tool to study motile marine organisms during their exploration of surfaces. The Journal of Adhesion 83(5), 417–430 (2007)
4. Frymier, P., Ford, R., Berg, H., Cummings, P.: 3d tracking of motile bacteria near a solid planar surface. Proc. Natl. Acad. Sci. U.S.A. 92(13), 6195–6199 (1995)
5. Baba, S., Inomata, S., Ooya, M., Mogami, Y., Izumikurotani, A.: 3d recording and measurement of swimming paths of microorganisms with 2 synchronized monochrome cameras. Rev. of Sci. Instruments 62(2), 540–541 (1991)

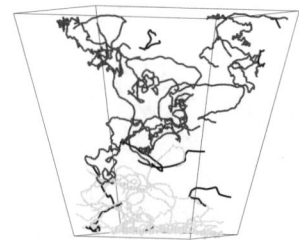

Fig. 7. Complete volume with patterns: Orientation (1, red), Wobbling (2, green), Gyration (3, yellow). The Spinning (4) pattern is not present in this sequence. Patterns which are too short to be classified are plotted in black. See Sequence 1 in the video included as supplemental material.

6. Weeks, E., Crocker, J., Levitt, A., Schofield, A., Weitz, D.: 3d direct imaging of structural relaxation near the colloidal glass transition. Science 287(5452), 627–631 (2000)
7. Berg, H.: Random walks in biology. Princeton University Press, Princeton (1993)
8. Hoyle, D., Rattay, M.: Pca learning for sparse high-dimensional data. Europhysics Letters 62(1) (2003)
9. Wang, X., Grimson, E.: Trajectory analysis and semantic region modeling using a nonparametric bayesian model. In: CVPR (2008)
10. Guyon, I., Weston, J., Barnhill, S., Vapnik, V.: Gene selection for cancer classification using support vector machines. Machine Learning 46(1-3), 389–442 (2004)
11. Sbalzariniy, I., Theriot, J., Koumoutsakos, P.: Machine learning for biological trajectory classification applications. Center for Turbulence Research, 305–316 (2002)
12. Rabiner, L.: A tutorial on hidden markov models and selected applications in speech recognition. Proc. IEEE 77(2) (1989)
13. Chen, M., Kundu, A., Zhou, J.: Off-line handwritten word recognition using a hidden markov model type stochastic network. IEEE Trans. Pattern Anal. Mach. Intell. (TPAMI) 16 (1994)
14. Nefian, A., Hayes, M.H.: Hidden markov models for face recognition. In: ICASSP (1998)
15. Yamato, J., Ohya, J., Ishii, K.: Recognizing human action in time-sequential images using hidden markov model. In: CVPR (1992)
16. Brand, M., Kettnaker, V.: Discovery and segmentation of activities in video. IEEE Trans. Pattern Anal. Mach. Intell (TPAMI) 22(8), 844–851 (2000)
17. Gabor, D.: A new microscopic principle. Nature 161(8), 777 (1948)
18. Xu, W., Jericho, M., Meinertzhagen, I., Kreuzer, H.: Digital in-line holography for biological applications. Proc. Natl. Acad. Sci. U.S.A. 98(20), 11301–11305 (2001)
19. Heydt, M., Divós, P., Grunze, M., Rosenhahn, A.: Analysis of holographic microscopy data to quantitatively investigate three dimensional settlement dynamics of algal zoospores in the vicinity of surfaces. Eur. Phys. J. E (2009)
20. Lu, J., Fugal, J., Nordsiek, H., Saw, E., Shaw, R., Yang, W.: Lagrangian particle tracking in 3d via single-camera in-line digital holography. New Journal of Physics 10 (2008)
21. Leal-Taixé, L., Heydt, M., Rosenhahn, A., Rosenhahn, B.: Automatic tracking of swimming microorganisms in 4d digital in-line holography data. In: IEEE WMVC (2009)
22. Iken, K., Amsler, C., Greer, S., McClintock, J.: Qualitative and quantitative studies of the swimming behaviour of hincksia irregularis (phaeophyceae) spores: ecological implications and parameters for quantitative swimming assays. Phycologia 40, 359–366 (2001)
23. Fugal, J., Schulz, T., Shaw, R.: Practical methods for automated reconstruction and characterization of particles in digital in-line holograms. Meas. Sci. Technol. 20, 075501 (2009)

Catheter Tracking:
Filter-Based vs. Learning-Based

Alexander Brost[1], Andreas Wimmer[1], Rui Liao[2],
Joachim Hornegger[1], and Norbert Strobel[3]

[1] Pattern Recognition Lab, Department of Computer Science,
Friedrich-Alexander-University of Erlangen-Nuremberg, Erlangen, Germany
[2] Siemens Corporate Research, Princeton, NJ, USA
[3] Siemens AG, Forchheim, Germany

Abstract. Atrial fibrillation is the most common sustained arrhythmia. One important treatment option is radio-frequency catheter ablation (RFCA) of the pulmonary veins attached to the left atrium. RFCA is usually performed under fluoroscopic (X-ray) image guidance. Overlay images computed from pre-operative 3-D volumetric data can be used to add anatomical detail otherwise not visible under X-ray. Unfortunately, current fluoro overlay images are static, i.e., they do not move synchronously with respiratory and cardiac motion. A filter-based catheter tracking approach using simultaneous biplane fluoroscopy was previously presented. It requires localization of a circumferential tracking catheter, though. Unfortunately, the initially proposed method may fail to accommodate catheters of different size. It may also detect wrong structures in the presence of high background clutter. We developed a new learning-based approach to overcome both problems. First, a 3-D model of the catheter is reconstructed. A cascade of boosted classifiers is then used to segment the circumferential mapping catheter. Finally, the 3-D motion at the site of ablation is estimated by tracking the reconstructed model in 3-D from biplane fluoroscopy. We compared our method to the previous approach using 13 clinical data sets and found that the 2-D tracking error improved from 1.0 mm to 0.8 mm. The 3-D tracking error was reduced from 0.8 mm to 0.7 mm.

1 Motivation

Recent research in the area of X-ray guidance for electrophysiology (EP) procedures found that augmented fluoroscopy using overlay images rendered from 3-D images (CT, MRI, C-Arm CT) facilitates more precise catheter navigation and a reduction in fluoroscopy time [1,2,3]. Critical structures like the esophagus and the left atrial appendage are invisible under regular fluoroscopy unless contrast agent is applied. Thus, rendering overlays of such structures for visual procedure guidance further improves safety. Unfortunately, current image overlay methods still lack motion compensation. A first approach tracking a commonly used mapping catheter has been proposed in [4]. This circumferential mapping catheter measures the electrical potentials at the ostium of the pulmonary vein (PV) considered for

M. Goesele et al. (Eds.): DAGM 2010, LNCS 6376, pp. 293–302, 2010.

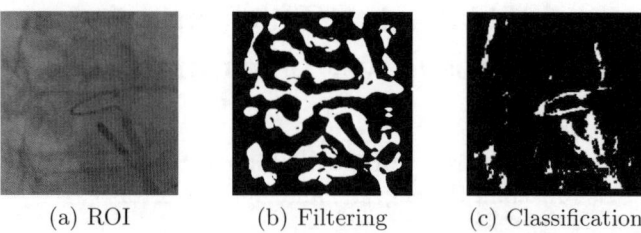

(a) ROI   (b) Filtering   (c) Classification

Fig. 1. (a) A region-of-interest around the catheter is presented on the left. (b) The result of the segmentation by filter methods [4,7,8]. (c) Segmentation using a boosted classifier cascade.

ablation. Catheter tracking was accomplished by calculating a 3-D model of the catheter, a filter-based segmentation and 2-D/3-D registration of the catheter model to biplane fluoroscopic images. Various methods for catheter tracking have been proposed. They involve filter-based techniques [5] as well as template-matching and learning-based approaches [6]. For electrophysiology procedures, different types of catheters are available. They differ in width, number of electrodes and electrode spacing. These parameters have to be considered explicitly for a filter-based catheter tracking approach. This adds additional complexity often reduces the robustness of filter-based approaches. This is why learning-based methods are often preferable for more complicated pattern recognition problems. They can reach a better performance if the training set is sufficiently comprehensive to capture all relevant catheter features encountered in clinical practice. Learning-based algorithms are usually superior with respect to suppressing interfering structures that are not of interest. This is demonstrated in Fig. 1 presenting a comparison between segmentation results obtained using filtering [4,7,8] and by classification. We used a boosted classifier cascade to segment the circumferential mapping catheter. In the next step, the 3-D catheter model is generated as proposed in [4,7,8]. Tracking itself is performed by a 2-D/3-D registration. These steps are explained in more detail below.

2   Catheter Model Generation

Our method requires the generation of a 3-D catheter model, which is based on the assumption that the perspective projection of the circumferential mapping catheter, when fit to the pulmonary veins, can be approximated as a 3-D ellipse. The circumferential mapping catheter can also be approximated as an ellipse in 2-D, because a 3-D elliptical object remains elliptical when perspectively projected onto a 2-D imaging plane. The ellipses on the 2-D fluoroscopic images are denoted as $C_{A/B} \in \mathbb{R}^{3 \times 3}$, with the index A or B indicating the corresponding imaging plane of the C-arm. A 3-D elliptical cone can then be spanned with the projection matrix $P_{A/B} \in \mathbb{R}^{3 \times 4}$ and the ellipse within the imaging plane. The base of the elliptical cone is the ellipse in the imaging plane and the vertex is the optical center. It can be shown that the elliptical cone can be represented as

$$Q_{A/B} = P_{A/B}^T C_{A/B} P_{A/B} \tag{1}$$

in matrix presentation [9]. The 3-D ellipse representing the 3-D mapping catheter is reconstructed by intersecting the two elliptical cones Q_A and Q_B corresponding to plane A and plane B of a biplane system respectively. The solution is found by calculating η such that the quadric

$$Q(\eta) = Q_A + \eta Q_B \tag{2}$$

is of rank 2 [9]. As pointed out in [4,7,8], there are two possible solutions. Prior knowledge about the pseudo-circular shape of the mapping catheter is used and the result that is more circular is chosen.

3   Classifier Cascade

The catheter segmentation method not only has to be reliable, but it needs to be fast as well. Speed is necessary to ensure that the catheter can be tracked in real-time at the frame rate set at the X-ray acquisition system. We found that a combination of Haar-like features and a cascade of boosted classifiers met both requirements to differentiate the live fluoroscopic images into *catheter* and *background*. Haar-like features [10] calculate various patterns of intensity differences. Several feature prototypes are listed in Fig. 2(a). Some features detect edges, whereas others focus on line structures. Especially the latter are useful for detecting the circumferential mapping catheter, which often appears as a thin, elongated object with a loop at its end, see Fig. 1(a). Actual features are obtained by shifting and scaling the prototypes within a predefined window. In our case, a window size of 15×15 was found to be sufficient for good results. Thereby, contextual information around the center pixel is considered, which is

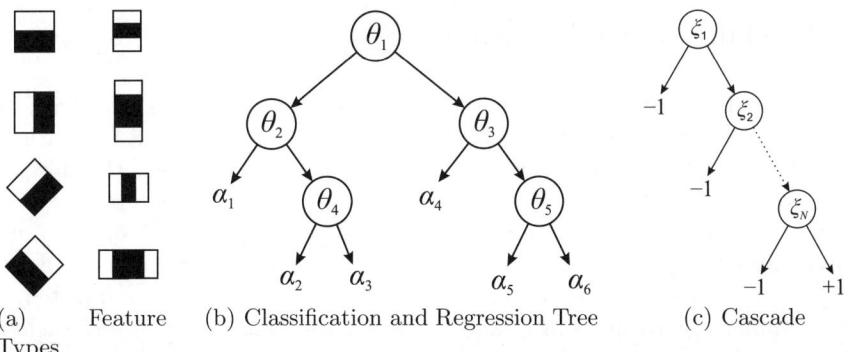

(a)   Feature   (b) Classification and Regression Tree   (c) Cascade
Types

Fig. 2.   Features types and classifier structure for catheter segmentation. (a) Several prototypes of Haar-like features. (b) Exemplary classification and regression tree (CART) with five feature nodes $\theta_1, \ldots, \theta_5$ and six leaves $\alpha_1, \ldots, \alpha_6$. (c) Classifier cascade consisting of N stages with strong classifiers $\xi_1, \ldots \xi_N$; each strong classifier ξ_i consists of a linear combination of weak classifiers, here CARTs.

important to differentiate between catheter and background structures. However, even for moderate window sizes, the resulting number of features is large and easily amounts to several hundreds of thousands. Features are calculated efficiently through integral images [10]. To achieve reliable and fast segmentation, the most suitable features for discriminating between catheter and background have to be chosen and integrated into a classifier in a suitable manner. This is carried out by the AdaBoost algorithm [11]. The idea is to combine several weak classifiers, to form a strong classifier. The classifier minimizing the classification error is added to a linear combination of weak classifiers until the overall error is below the desired threshold. After each training iteration, the importance of individual samples is re-weighted to put more emphasis on misclassifications for the next evaluation. Instead of single features and intensity thresholds, we use classification and regression trees (CARTs) [12] as weak classifiers. A CART is a small tree of fixed size. At each node, a threshold θ_j associated with a feature partitions the feature space. This way, flexibility is increased and objects with complex feature distributions can be handled. The result of a CART is the value α_k of the classifier reached as leave node. An exemplary CART is shown in Fig. 2(b). We organize N strong classifiers $\xi_i, \ldots, \xi_N$ composed of weighted combinations of CARTs into a cascade, which is illustrated in Fig. 2(c). In our case, four strong classifiers ($N = 4$) yielded good results. At each stage, a sample is either rejected (-1) or passed on to the next stage. Only if the sample is accepted ($+1$) at the final stage, it is accepted as part of the object. Thus during training, the focus is on maintaining a high true positive rate while successively reducing the false positive rate, either by adding more weak classifiers to a stage or by adding an entirely new stage. The training data set consisted of 13 clinical data sets with a total of 938 monoplane frames. For evaluation, the classifier cascade was trained on a leave-one-out basis, i.e., 12 sequences were used for training and the remaining sequence was used for segmentation and tracking.

4   Tracking by Registration

The elliptical shape of the circumferential mapping catheter is used for tracking. Catheter tracking itself is performed by rigid registration [13] of the catheter model to the segmentation result derived from the previous step. To this end, the same ROI as for the classification is used. As the size of the mapping catheter may not be available beforehand, the previous approach in [4,7,8] used normals to the ellipse to simulate the width of the catheter. As the length and the sampling of the normals depends on further parameters that need to be adjusted, we use a thinning algorithm as proposed in [14]. By thinning, we generate a skeleton of the catheter, which involves far fewer parameters than needed otherwise. A distance map $I_{\text{DT,A/B}}$ is calculated from the skeleton as proposed in [15] for each imaging plane. It encodes the absolute distance from a pixel to its closest segmented catheter pixel. It also provides a smooth representation of the fluoroscopic image with a pronounced minimum around the shape of the mapping catheter to increase the capture range. Model-based catheter tracking in 3-D is

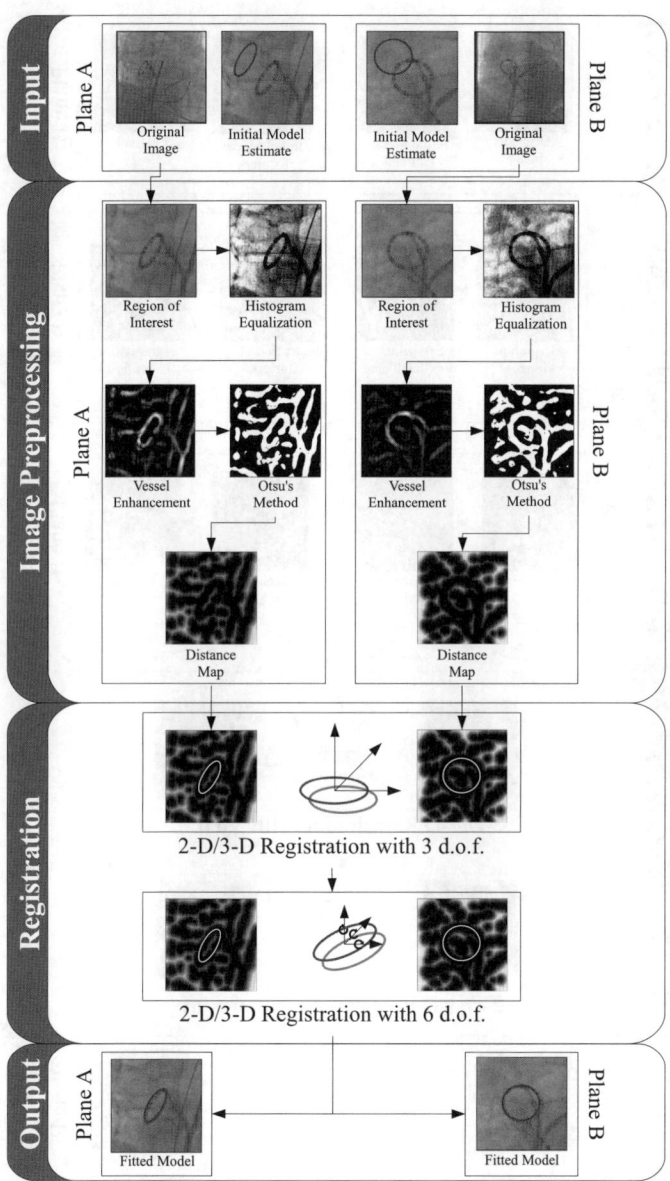

Fig. 3. Flow diagram of the filter-based catheter tracking approach for motion compensation [8]. The objective is to obtain a dynamic fluoroscopic overlay image for improved catheter navigation.

298   A. Brost et al.

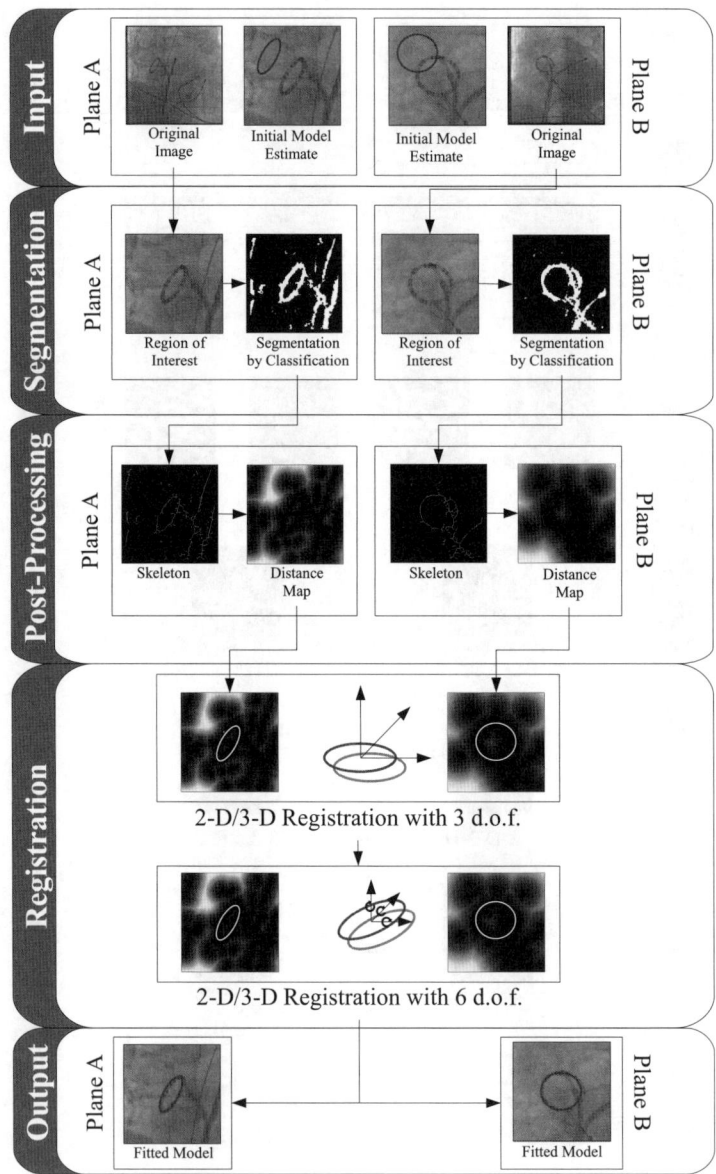

Fig. 4. Flow diagram of our learning-based motion compensation approach. Image pre-processing has been replaced by classification-based segmentation followed by a post-processing step. The goal is to obtain a distance map.

achieved by performing 2-D/3-D registration. Hence, the reconstructed catheter model is rotated by $\boldsymbol{R} \in \mathbb{R}^{4\times4}$ and translated by $\boldsymbol{T} \in \mathbb{R}^{4\times4}$ first. It is then projected onto the two imaging planes of the bi-plane C-arm system. The average distance between the projected points and the closest feature point (i.e. the circumferential mapping catheter) in fluoroscopic images is efficiently calculated using the distance map introduced above. A suitable rotation and translation is found by optimizing

$$\hat{\boldsymbol{R}}, \hat{\boldsymbol{T}} = \arg\min_{R,T} \sum_i \boldsymbol{I}_{\mathrm{DT}}(\boldsymbol{P}_A \cdot \boldsymbol{T} \cdot \boldsymbol{R} \cdot \boldsymbol{w}_i) + \sum_i \boldsymbol{I}_{\boldsymbol{DT}}(\boldsymbol{P}_B \cdot \boldsymbol{T} \cdot \boldsymbol{R} \cdot \boldsymbol{w}_i) \qquad (3)$$

with the 3-D catheter model points $\boldsymbol{w}_i \in \mathbb{R}^4$ in homogeneous coordinates. The projection matrices $\boldsymbol{P}_A$ and $\boldsymbol{P}_B$ do not need to be identical to the ones in Eq. 1. The parameters used for optimizing are three rotation angles around the main axes in 3-D, combined in $\boldsymbol{R}$, as well as a three-dimensional translation, represented in $\boldsymbol{T}$. As optimization strategy, a nearest neighbor search [16] is used, i.e., the position of the local optimum on a large scale is taken as starting point for the optimization on a smaller scale. The estimated 3-D rotation and translation can be directly applied to the 2-D overlay to move it in sync with the tracked device. An overview of the reference method [4,7,8] is presented in Fig. 3 and an overview of our proposed algorithm is given in Fig. 4.

5   Evaluation and Results

Our approach was evaluated on 13 clinical data sets, collected from 6 different patients at one clinical site. Three different circumferential mapping catheters were used. For evaluation, we calculate the 2-D tracking error as the average 2-D distance between the projection of the 3-D catheter model and a 2-D gold-standard segmentation of the circumferential mapping catheter provided by a cardiologist. We compare our results with those in [4,7,8], see Fig. 5. Clinical data

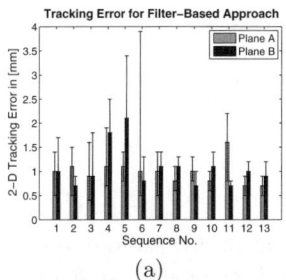
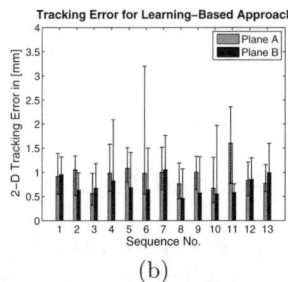

(a)   (b)

Fig. 5. Comparison of the different catheter tracking approaches. (a) The result of the reference method presented in [4,7,8]. This method yielded an average 2-D tracking error of 1.0 mm ± 0.4 mm. (b) Our improved algorithm using a boosted classifier cascade to segment the circumferential mapping catheter yielded a 2-D error of 0.8 mm ± 0.4 mm.

set No. 6 contains a barium swallow of the patient to outline the esophagus, a critical structure during ablation. Unfortunately, in one frame of this sequence, the barium hides the mapping catheter, resulting in a rather high maximum error. This single frame was not excluded. Since catheter tracking is performed in 3-D, we follow the evaluation in [7,8] to estimate the 3-D motion correction. Therefore, the tip of the mapping catheter was manually localized throughout all sequences by triangulating its 3-D position from bi-plane frames to get a reference point. In the next step, we applied our motion estimation approach to the catheter tip to move it from its 3-D position in the previous frame to the next frame. Because of that, we can compare the 3-D position reached by applying the estimated motion to the actual 3-D reference point obtained by triangulation [17]. Finally, the error was calculated as the Euclidean distance in 3-D space. Moreover, an error without performing motion compensation can be calculated was well. To this end, the 3-D distance between the first frame to all remaining frames is used to estimate the observed 3-D motion. A comparison of the observed 3-D motion to both motion correction approaches is shown in Fig. 6(a). A direct comparison of the filter-based approach versus the learning-based method is given in Fig. 6(b).

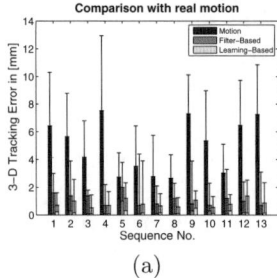 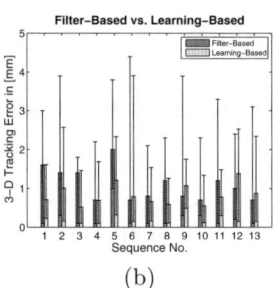

(a)   (b)

Fig. 6. Comparison of the different catheter tracking approaches. (a) The result of the filter-based method [4,7,8] and the learning-based method compared to the actual 3-D motion. An average 3-D motion of 4.5 mm ± 2.4 mm has been observed in our clinical data. (b) Direct comparison of the 3-D tracking error of the filter-based and the learning-based method. The filter-based method yielded an average 3-D tracking error of 0.8 mm ± 0.5 mm, whereas the learning-based approach yielded an average error of 0.7 mm ± 0.4 mm.

6   Discussion and Conclusions

We presented a method for 3-D motion estimation for radio-frequency catheter ablation of atrial fibrillation. It is based on tracking of a circumferential mapping catheter in biplane fluoroscopy imaging. Catheter tracking is performed by 2-D/3-D registration of a 3-D elliptical catheter model to 2-D biplane images. The method assumes that the circumferential mapping catheter remains anchored at the pulmonary vein during ablation. Our clinical data suggests that the circumferential mapping catheter indeed moves very little with respect to the PV

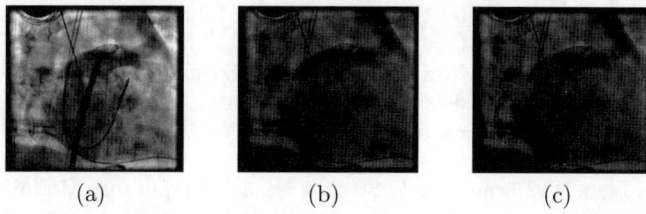

| (a) | (b) | (c) |

Fig. 7. Motion compensation can be visually assessed by contrast injection into a pulmonary vein. (a) One image of a fluoroscopic sequence showing the administration of contrast agent. (b) Misfit of a static overlay due to motion. (c) Visual overlay with improved positioning of the (red) fluoroscopic overlay image thanks to motion compensation.

ostia when used to measure the electrical signals at the pulmonary ostia. When comparing the two tracking approaches, it can be seen, that the learning-based approach performs better than the filter-based approach overall. The 2-D tracking error could be reduced from 1.0 mm ± 0.4 mm to 0.8 mm ± 0.4 mm and the 3-D error from 0.8 mm ± 0.5 mm to 0.7 mm ± 0.4 mm. This has been displayed in Fig. 1 showing one frame of Seq. 5. Here, the learning-based method reduced the average 3-D tracking error from 2.0 mm to 1.2 mm. The benefit of motion compensation for X-ray fluoroscopy guidance can be appreciated by looking at contrast-enhanced anatomical structures. An example is presented in Fig. 7. The main advantage of the proposed learning-based approach is its robustness. In particular, it generates fewer false positives as obtained when using the filter-based approach. The advantage of 2-D/3-D registration with biplane images is that it provides a more robust 3-D tracking compared to a monoplane situation. The quality of the segmentation could be further improved by using either more cascades or an increased number of features, but this goes hand in hand with higher computational time. Our current implementation reaches a processing speed of one frame-per-second (fps), as this frame rate is used at our clinical partner for simultaneously biplane fluoroscopy. The presented method has not yet been optimized for multi-core CPUs or GPUs. Further speed improvements can be expected by taking advantage of parallel processing options. Moreover, a classifier cascade was used to segment the catheter, but other segmentation approaches could be applied as well. Beyond improving the technology, future work will also focus on clinical evaluation of this method.

References

1. Ector, J., De Buck, S., Huybrechts, W., Nuyens, D., Dymarkowski, S., Bogaert, J., Maes, F., Heidbüchel, H.: Biplane three-dimensional augmented fluoroscopy as single navigation tool for ablation of atrial fibrillation: Accuracy and clinical value. Heart Rhythm 5(7), 957–964 (2008)
2. Sra, J., Narayan, G., Krum, D., Malloy, A., Cooley, R., Bhatia, A., Dhala, A., Blanck, Z., Nangia, V., Akhtar, M.: Computed Tomography-Fluoroscopy Image

Integration-Guided Catheter Ablation of Atrial Fibrillation. J. Cardiovasc. Electrophysiol 18(4), 409–414 (2007)

3. De Buck, S., Maes, F., Ector, J., Bogaert, J., Dymarkowski, S., Heidbüchel, H., Suetens, P.: An augmented reality system for patient-specific guidance of cardiac catheter ablation procedures. IEEE Transactions on Medical Imaging 24(11), 1512–1524 (2005)

4. Brost, A., Liao, R., Hornegger, J., Strobel, N.: 3-D Respiratory Motion Compensation during EP Procedures by Image-Based 3-D Lasso Catheter Model Generation and Tracking. In: Yang, G.-Z., Hawkes, D., Rueckert, D., Noble, A., Taylor, C. (eds.) MICCAI 2009. LNCS, vol. 5761, pp. 394–401. Springer, Heidelberg (2009)

5. Palti-Wassermann, D., Brukstein, A., Beyar, R.: Identifying and Tracking a Guide Wire in the Coronary Arteries During Angioplasty from X-Ray Images. IEEE Transactions on Biomedical Engineering 44(2), 152–164 (1997)

6. Barbu, A., Athitsos, V., Georgescu, B., Boehm, S., Durlak, P., Comaniciu, D.: Hierarchical Learning of Curves: Application to Guidewire Localization in Fluoroscopy. In: IEEE Conference on Computer Vision and Pattern Recognition (CVPR 2007), pp. 1–8 (2007)

7. Brost, A., Liao, R., Hornegger, J., Strobel, N.: 3D model-based catheter tracking for motion compensation in EP procedures. In: Medical Imaging 2010: Visualization, Image-Guided Procedures, and Modeling, vol. 7625, p. 762507. SPIE, San Jose (2010)

8. Brost, A., Liao, R., Strobel, N., Hornegger, J.: Respiratory motion compensation by model-based catheter tracking during EP procedures. In: Medical Image Analysis (2010) (in press) (Corrected Proof)

9. Quan, L.: Conic Reconstruction and Correspondence From Two Views. IEEE Trans Pattern Anal Mach Intell 18(2), 151–160 (1996)

10. Viola, P., Jones, M.: Robust real-time face detection. Int. J. Comput. Vision 57(2), 137–154 (2004)

11. Freund, Y., Schapire, R.: A decision-theoretic generalization of on-line learning and an application to boosting. JCSS 55(1), 119–139 (1997)

12. Breiman, L., Friedman, J., Olshen, R., Stone, C.: Classification and Regression Trees. Chapman & Hall, New York (1984)

13. Hill, D., Batchelor, P., Holden, M., Hawkes, D.: Medical image registration. Phys. Med. Biol. 46(3), R1–R45 (2001)

14. Cychosz, J.: Efficient Binary Image Thinning using Neighborhood Maps. In: Graphics Gems IV, pp. 465–473 (1994)

15. Breu, H., Gil, J., Kirkpatrick, D., Werman, M.: Linear time Euclidean distance transform algorithms. IEEE Trans. Pattern Anal. Mach. Intell. 17, 529–533 (1995)

16. Duda, R., Hart, P.: Pattern Classification, 2nd edn. John Wiley & Sons, Inc., Chichester (August 2000)

17. Brost, A., Strobel, N., Yatziv, L., Gilson, W., Meyer, B., Hornegger, J., Lewin, J., Wacker, F.: Geometric Accuracy of 3-D X-Ray Image-Based Localization from Two C-Arm Views. In: Workshop on Geometric Accuracy In Image Guided Interventions - Medical Image Computing and Computer Assisted Interventions, MICCAI 2009, London UK, pp. 12–19 (September 2009)

Exploiting Redundancy for Aerial Image Fusion Using Convex Optimization*

Stefan Kluckner, Thomas Pock, and Horst Bischof

Institute for Computer Graphics and Vision
Graz University of Technology, Austria
{kluckner,pock,bischof}@icg.tugraz.at

Abstract. Image fusion in high-resolution aerial imagery poses a challenging problem due to fine details and complex textures. In particular, color image fusion by using virtual orthographic cameras offers a common representation of overlapping yet perspective aerial images. This paper proposes a variational formulation for a tight integration of redundant image data showing urban environments. We introduce an efficient wavelet regularization which enables a natural-appearing recovery of fine details in the images by performing joint inpainting and denoising from a given set of input observations. Our framework is first evaluated on a setting with synthetic noise. Then, we apply our proposed approach to orthographic image generation in aerial imagery. In addition, we discuss an exemplar-based inpainting technique for an integrated removal of non-stationary objects like cars.

1 Introduction

In general, image fusion integrates information of multiple images, taken from the same scene, in order to obtain an improved result with respect to noise, outliers, illumination changes etc. Fusion from multiple observations is a hot topic in computer vision and photogrammetry since scene information can be taken from different view points without additional costs. In particular, modern aerial imaging technology provides multi-spectral images, which map every visible spot of urban environments from many overlapping camera viewpoints. Typically, a point on ground is at least visible in ten cameras. The provided, highly redundant data enables efficient techniques for height field generation [1], but also methods for resolution and quality enhancement [2,3,4,5,6]. On one hand, taking into account redundant observations of corresponding points in a common 3D world, the localization accuracy can be significantly improved using an integration of range data e.g. for 3D reconstruction [7]. On the other hand, accurate height fields can also be exploited to align data, such as the corresponding color information, within a common coordinate system. In our approach we exploit derived range data to compute geometric transformations between the original images

---

* This work was financed by the Austrian Research Promotion Agency within the projects vdQA (No. 816003) and APAFA (No. 813397).

M. Goesele et al. (Eds.): DAGM 2010, LNCS 6376, pp. 303–312, 2010.

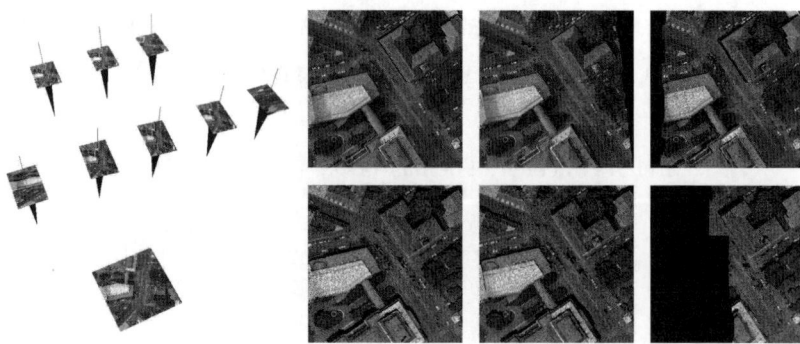

Fig. 1. An observed scene with overlapping camera positions. The scene is taken from different viewpoints. We exploit computed range images to transform the point cloud into a common orthographic aerial view. Our joint inpainting and denoising approach takes redundant observations as input data and generates an improved fused image. Note that some observations include many undefined areas (black pixels) caused by occlusions and non-stationary objects.

and an orthographic view, which is related to novel view synthesis [2,3,4,8]. Due to missing data in the individual height fields (e.g. caused by non-stationary objects or occlusions) the initial alignment causes undefined areas, artifacts or outliers in the novel view. Figure 1 depicts an urban scene taken from different camera positions and a set of redundant images, geometrically transformed to a common view. Some image tiles show large areas of missing information and erroneous pixel values. Our task can also be interpreted as an image fusion from multiple input observations of the same scene by joint inpainting and denoising. While inpainting fills undefined areas, the denoising removes strong outliers and noise by exploiting the high redundancy in the input data.

This paper has several contributions: First, we present a novel variational framework for gray and color image fusion, which provides a smooth solution over the image domain by exploiting redundant input images. In order to compute natural appearing images we further introduce a wavelet transform [9], providing an improved texture prior for regularization, in our convex optimization framework (Section 3). In the experimental section we show that our framework can be successfully applied to image recovery and orthographic image generation in high-resolution aerial imagery (Section 4). In addition, we present results for exemplar-based inpainting, which enables an integrated removal of undesired, non-stationary objects like cars. Finally, Section 5 concludes our work and gives an outlook on future work.

2 Related Work

The challenging task of reconstructing an original image from given (noisy) observations is known to be ill-posed. Although fast mean or median computation over multiple pixel observations will suppress noisy or undefined areas, each pixel in the result is treated independently. A variety of proposed algorithms for a fusion of redundant information is based on image priors [2,8], image transforms [10], *Markov* random field optimization procedures [3] and generative models [4]. Variational formulations are well-suited for finding smooth and consistent solutions of the inverse problem by exploiting different types of regularizations [7,11,12,13,14]. The quadratic model [11] uses the L^2 norm for regularization, which causes smoothed edges. Introducing a total variation (TV) norm instead leads to the edge preserving denoising model proposed by Rudin, Osher and Fatemi (ROF) [12]. The authors in [13] proposed to also use a L^1 norm in the data term to estimate the deviation between sought solution and input observation. Thus the resulting TV-L^1 model is more effective in removing impulse noise containing strong outliers than the ROF model. Zach et al. [7] applied the TV-L^1 to robust range image integration from multiple views. Although TV-based methods are well suited for tasks like range data integration, in texture inpainting the regularization produces results that look unnatural near recovered edges (too much contrast). To overcome the problem of synthetic appearance, natural image priors based on multi-level transforms like wavelets [9,15,16] or curvelets [17] can be used within the inpainting and fusion model [14,18]. These transforms provide a compact yet sparse image representation obtained with low computational costs. Similar to [14], we exploit a wavelet transform for natural regularization within our proposed variational fusion framework capable to handle multiple input observations.

3   Convex Fusion Model

In this section we describe our generic fusion model which takes into account multiple observations of the same scene. For clarity, we derive our model for gray-valued images, however the formulation can be easily extended to vector-valued data like color images.

3.1   The Proposed Model

We consider a discrete image domain Ω as a regular grid of size $W \times H$ pixels with $\Omega = \{(i,j) : 1 \leq i \leq W, 1 \leq j \leq H\}$, where the tupel (i,j) denotes a pixel position in the domain Ω.

Our fusion model, which takes into account multiple observations and a wavelet-based regularization, can be seen as an extension of the TV-L^1 denoising model proposed by Nikolova [13]. In the discrete setting the minimization problem of the common TV-L^1 model for an image domain Ω is formulated as

$$\min_{u \in X} \left\{ \|\nabla u\|_1 + \lambda \sum_{i,j \in \Omega} |u_{i,j} - f_{i,j}| \right\}, \tag{1}$$

where $X = \mathbb{R}^{WH}$ is a finite-dimensional vector space provided with a scalar product $\langle u, v \rangle_X = \sum_{i,j} u_{i,j} v_{i,j}$, $u, v \in X$. The first term denotes the TV of the sought solution u and reflects the regularization in terms of a smooth solution. The second term accounts for the summed errors between u and the (noisy) input data f. The scalar λ controls the fidelity between data fitting and regularization. In following we derive our model for the task of image fusion from multiple observations.

As a first modification of the TV-L^1 model defined in (1), we extend the convex minimization problem to handle a set of K scene observations $(f^1, \ldots, f^K)$. Introducing multiple input images can be accomplished by summing the deviations between the sought solution u and available observations f^k, $k = 1 \ldots K$ according to

$$\min_{u \in X} \left\{ \|\nabla u\|_1 + \lambda \sum_{k=1}^{K} \sum_{i,j \in \Omega} |u_{i,j} - f_{i,j}^k| \right\}. \tag{2}$$

Since orthographic image generation from gray or color information with sampling distances of approximately 10 cm requires an accurate recovery of fine details and complex textures, we replace the TV-based regularization with a dual-tree complex wavelet transform (DTCWT) [9,16]. The DTCWT is nearly invariant to rotation, which is important for regularization, but also to translations and can be efficiently computed by using separable filter banks. The transform is based on analyzing the signal with two separate wavelet decompositions, where one provides the real-valued part and the other one yields the complex part. Due to the redundancy in the proposed decomposition, the directionality can be improved, compared to standard discrete wavelets [9]. In order to include the linear wavelet-based regularization into our generic formulation we replace the gradient operator ∇ by the linear transform $\Psi : X \to C$. The space $C \subseteq \mathbb{C}^D$ denotes the real- and complex-valued transform coefficients $c \in C$. The dimensionality of $\mathbb{C}^D$ directly depends on parameters like the image dimensions, the number of levels and orientations. The adjoint operator of the transform Ψ, required for the signal reconstruction, is denoted as Ψ^* and is defined through the identity $\langle \Psi u, c \rangle_C = \langle u, \Psi^* c \rangle_X$.

As the L^1 norm in the data term is known to be sensitive to Gaussian noise (we expect a small amount), we use the robust *Huber* norm [19] to estimate the error between sought solution and observations instead. The *Huber* norm is quadratic for small values, which is appropriate for handling Gaussian noise, and linear for larger errors, which amounts to median like behavior. The *Huber* norm is defined as

$$|t|_\epsilon = \begin{cases} \frac{t^2}{2\epsilon} & : 0 \le t \le \epsilon \\ t - \frac{\epsilon}{2} & : \epsilon < t \end{cases}. \tag{3}$$

Because of the height field driven alignment of the appearance information, undefined areas can be simply determined in advance for a geometrically transformed image f^k. Therefore, we support our formulation with a spatially varying term $w_{i,j}^k \in \{0,1\}^{WH}$, which encodes the inpainting domain. The choice $w_{i,j}^k = 0$ corresponds to pure inpainting at a pixel location (i,j).

Considering the wavelet-based regularization, the encoded inpainting domain and the *Huber* norm, our extended energy minimization problem for redundant observations can now be formulated for the image domain Ω as

$$\min_{u \in X} \left\{ \|\Psi u\|_1 + \lambda \sum_{k=1}^{K} \sum_{i,j \in \Omega} w_{i,j}^k |u_{i,j} - f_{i,j}^k|_\epsilon \right\}. \tag{4}$$

In the following we highlight an iterative strategy, based on an optimal first-order primal-dual algorithm, to minimize the non-smooth problem defined in (4).

3.2 Primal-Dual Formulation

Note that the minimization problem given in (4) poses a large-scale (the dimensionality directly depends on the number of image pixels e.g. for a small color image tile: 3×1600^2 pixels) and non-smooth optimization problem. Following recent trends in convex optimization [20,21], we use an optimal first-order primal-dual scheme [22,23] to minimize the energy. Thus we first need to convert the formulation defined in (4) into a classical convex-concave saddle-point problem. The general minimization problem is written as

$$\min_{x \in X} \max_{y \in Y} \langle Kx, y \rangle + G(x) - F^*(y), \tag{5}$$

where K is a linear operator, G and F^* are convex functions and the term F^* denotes the convex conjugate of the function F. The finite-dimensional vector spaces X and Y provide a scalar product $\langle \cdot, \cdot \rangle$ and a norm $\|\cdot\| = \langle \cdot, \cdot \rangle^{\frac{1}{2}}$. By applying the Legendre-Fenchel transform to (4), we obtain an energy minimization problem as follows

$$\min_u \max_{c,q} \left\{ \langle \Psi u, c \rangle - \delta_C(c) + \sum_{k=1}^{K} \left(\langle u - f^k, q^k \rangle - \delta_{Q^k}(q^k) - \frac{\epsilon}{2} \|q^k\|^2 \right) \right\}. \tag{6}$$

In our case, the convex sets Q and C are defined as follows

$$Q^k = \left\{ q^k \in \mathbb{R}^{WH} : |q_{i,j}^k| \le \lambda w_{i,j}^k, (i,j) \in \Omega \right\}, \quad k = 1 \dots K, \tag{7}$$

$$C = \left\{ c \in \mathbb{C}^D : \|c\|_\infty \le 1 \right\}, \tag{8}$$

where the norm of the coefficient vector space C is defined as

$$\|c\|_\infty = \max_{i,j} |c_{i,j}|, \quad |c_{i,j}| = \sqrt{(c_{i,j}^1)^2 + (c_{i,j}^2)^2}. \tag{9}$$

Considering (6), we can first identify $F^* = \delta_C(c) + \sum_{k=1}^{K} \left(\delta_{Q^k}(q^k) + \frac{\epsilon}{2} \|q^k\|^2 \right)$. The functions δ_C and δ_{Q^k} are simple indicator functions of the convex sets and are given with

$$\delta_C(c) = \begin{cases} 0 & \text{if} \quad c \in C \\ +\infty & \text{if} \quad c \notin C \end{cases} \quad \delta_{Q^k}(q^k) = \begin{cases} 0 & \text{if} \quad q^k \in Q^k \\ +\infty & \text{if} \quad q^k \notin Q^k \end{cases}. \tag{10}$$

Since a closed form solution for the sum over multiple L^1 norms cannot be implemented efficiently, we additionally introduce a dualization of the data term with respect to G, which yields an extended linear term with $\langle Kx, y \rangle = \langle \Psi u, c \rangle + \sum_{k=1}^{K} \langle u - f^k, q^k \rangle$. According to [22,23], the primal-dual algorithm can be summarized as follows: First, we set the primal and dual time steps with $\tau > 0$, $\sigma > 0$. Additionally, we construct the required structures with $u_0 \in \mathbb{R}^{WH}$, $\bar{u}_0 = u_0$, $c_0 \in C$ and $q_0^k \in Q^k$. Based on the iterations proposed in [22], the iterative scheme is then given by

$$
\begin{cases}
c_{n+1} &= \operatorname{proj}_C \left(c_n + \sigma \Psi \bar{u}_n \right) \\
q_{n+1}^k &= \operatorname{proj}_{Q^k} \left(\frac{q_n^k + \sigma(\bar{u}_n - f^k)}{1 + \sigma\epsilon} \right), \ k = 1 \ldots K \\
u_{n+1} &= u_n - \tau \left(\Psi^* c_{n+1} + \sum_{k=1}^{K} q_{n+1}^k \right) \\
\bar{u}_{n+1} &= 2u_{n+1} - u_n .
\end{cases}
\tag{11}
$$

In order to iteratively compute the solution of (6) by using the primal-dual scheme, point-wise Euclidean projections of the dual variables q and c onto the convex sets C and Q are required. The projection of the wavelet coefficients c is defined as

$$
\operatorname{proj}_C(\tilde{c}_{i,j}) = \frac{\tilde{c}_{i,j}}{\max(1, |\tilde{c}_{i,j}|)} .
\tag{12}
$$

The corresponding projections for the dual variables q^k with $k = 1 \ldots K$ are given by

$$
\operatorname{proj}_{Q^k}(\tilde{q}_{i,j}^k) = \frac{\tilde{q}_{i,j}^k}{\min(+\lambda w_{i,j}^k, \max(-\lambda w_{i,j}^k, |\tilde{q}_{i,j}^k|))} .
\tag{13}
$$

Note that the iterative minimization scheme mainly consists of simple point-wise operations, therefore it can be considerably accelerated by exploiting multi-core systems such as graphics processing units. In the next section we use our model to perform image fusion of synthetic and real image data.

4   Experimental Evaluation

In this section we first demonstrate our convex fusion model on synthetic data, then we apply it to real world aerial images.

4.1   Synthetic Experiments

To show the performance with respect to recovered fine details, our first experiment investigates the fusion and inpainting capability of our proposed model using images with synthetically added noise. We therefore take the *Barbara* gray-valued image (512×512 pixels), which contains fine structures and highly textured areas. In order to imitate the expected noise model, we add a small amount of Gaussian noise ($\mu = 0$, $\sigma = 0.01$) and replace a specified percentage of pixels with undefined areas (we use 10% and 50%), which can be seen as simulation of occluded regions caused by perspective views. An evaluation in terms of peak signal-to-noise ratios (PSNR) for different amounts of undefined pixels

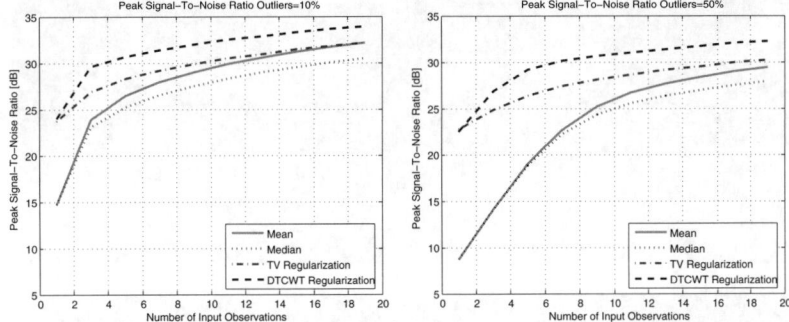

Fig. 2. Quantitative results for the *Barbara* image: PSNR depending on synthetically added noise (averaged noise values: 10%: 14.63 dB and 50%: 8.73 dB) and a varying number of input observations. Our proposed model using the wavelet-based regularization yields the best noise suppression.

and quantities of observations is shown in Figure 2. We compare our model to the TV-L^1 formulation, the mean and the median computation. For the TV-L^1 and our model we present the plots computed for the optimal parameters determined by cross validation. One can see that our joint inpainting and denoising model, using the parameter setting $\tau = 0.05$, $\sigma = 1/8/\tau$, $\epsilon = 0.1$, $\lambda = 1.2$ and 3 levels of wavelet decomposition (we use 13,19-tap and Q-shift 14-tap filter kernels, respectively), performs best in both noise settings. Moreover, it is obvious that an increasing number of input observations improves the result significantly. Compared to the TV-L^1 model, the wavelet-based regularization improves the PSNR by an averaged value of 2 dB.

4.2 Fusion of Real Images

Our second experiment focuses on orthographic color image fusion in aerial imagery. The images are taken with the *Microsoft UltraCam* out of an aircraft in overlapping strips, where each image has a resolution of 11500×7500 pixels with a ground sampling distance of approximately 10 cm. Depending on the overlap in the imagery, the mapped area provides up to ten redundant observations for the same scene. To obtain the required range data for each input image we use a dense matching algorithm similar to the method proposed in [1]. By taking into account the ranges and available camera data, each pixel in the images can be transformed to common 3D world coordinates forming a large cloud of points, which are then defined by location and color information. Introducing virtual orthographic cameras, together with a defined pixel resolution (we use the same sampling distance provided by the original images), enables a projection of the point cloud of each scence observation to the ground plane (we simply set the height coordinate to a fixed value). Computed fusion results for different

Fig. 3. Some fusion results. The first column shows results obtained with the TV-L^1 model (three input observations). The second column depicts corresponding images computed with our fusion model using a DTCWT regularization, which yields images with an improved natural appearance ($\lambda = 1.0$). Larger fusion results are given in the third column, where we exploit a redundancy of ten input images. The color fusion (1600×1600 pixels) can be obtained within two minutes. Best viewed in color.

dimensions are shown in Figure 3. The obtained results show an improved natural appearance, resulting from the wavelet-based regularization in our fusion model.

4.3   Removal of Non-stationary Objects

Non-stationary objects such as cars disturb in orthographic image generation. We therefore use our model to remove cars by simultaneous inpainting. Car detection masks can be efficiently obtained by an approach as described in [24]. In order to fill the detected car areas, our strategy is inspired by the work of Hays and Efros [25]. We perform scene completion with respect to the detection mask by using a pool of potential exemplars. To do so, we randomly collect image patches (the dimension is adapted for a common car length) and apply image transformations like rotation and translation in order to synthetically increase the pool. To find the best matching candidate for each detected car we compute a sum of weighted color distances between a masked detection and each exemplar. The weighting additionally prefers pixel locations near the mask boundary and is derived by using a distance transform. The detection mask with overlaid exemplars is then used as an additional input observation within the fusion model. Obtained removal results are shown in Figure 4.

Fig. 4. Inpainting results using a car detection mask. From left to right: The car detection mask, the fusion result computed without using a car detection mask, the result obtained by pure inpainting and the inpainting with supporting exemplars. The car areas are successfully removed in both cases, however the exemplar-based fill-in appears more naturally. Best viewed in color.

5   Conclusion

We have presented a novel variational method to fuse redundant gray and color images by using wavelet-based priors for regularization. To compute the solution of our large-scale optimization problem we exploit an optimal first-order primal-dual algorithm, which can be accelerated using parallel computation techniques. We have shown that our fusion method is well suited for orthographic image generation in high-resolution aerial imagery, but also for an integrated exemplar-based fill-in to remove e.g. non-stationary objects like cars. Future work will concentrate on synthetic view generation in ground-level imagery, similar to the idea of [3], and on computing super-resolution from many redundant observations.

References

1. Hirschmüller, H.: Stereo vision in structured environments by consistent semi-global matching. In: Proc. Conf. on Comp. Vision and Pattern Recognition (2006)
2. Fitzgibbon, A., Wexler, Y., Zisserman, A.: Image-based rendering using image-based priors. In: Proc. Int. Conf. on Comp. Vision (2003)

3. Agarwala, A., Agrawala, M., Cohen, M., Salesin, D., Szeliski, R.: Photograph-
   ing long scenes with multi-viewpoint panoramas. ACM Trans. on Graphics (SIG-
   GRAPH) 25(3) (2006)
4. Strecha, C., Gool, L.V., Fua, P.: A generative model for true orthorectification.
   Int. Archives of Photogrammetry and Remote Sensing 37, 303–308 (2008)
5. Goldluecke, B., Cremers, D.: A superresolution framework for high-accuracy multi-
   view reconstruction. In: Denzler, J., Notni, G., Süße, H. (eds.) DAGM 2009. LNCS,
   vol. 5748, pp. 342–351. Springer, Heidelberg (2009)
6. Unger, M., Pock, T., Werlberger, M., Bischof, H.: A convex approach for variational
   super-resolution. In: Proc. Pattern Recognition DAGM (2010)
7. Zach, C., Pock, T., Bischof, H.: A globally optimal algorithm for robust TV-L^1
   range image integration. In: Proc. Int. Conf. on Comp. Vision (2007)
8. Woodford, O.J., Reid, I.D., Torr, P.H.S., Fitzgibbon, A.W.: On new view synthesis
   using multiview stereo. In: Proc. British Machine Vision Conf. (2007)
9. Selesnick, I.W., Baraniuk, R.G., Kingsbury, N.G.: The dual-tree complex wavelet
   transform. Signal Processing Magazine 22(6), 123–151 (2005)
10. Pajares, G., de la Cruz, J.M.: A wavelet-based image fusion tutorial. Pattern Recog-
    nition 37(9), 1855–1872 (2004)
11. Tikhonov, A.N.: On the stability of inverse problems. Doklady Akademii Nauk
    SSSR 39(5), 195–198 (1943)
12. Rudin, L., Osher, S.J., Fatemi, E.: Nonlinear total variation based noise removal
    algorithms. Physica D. 60, 259–268 (1992)
13. Nikolova, M.: A variational approach to remove outliers and impulse noise. Journal
    of Mathematical Imaging and Vision 20(1-2), 99–120 (2004)
14. Carlavan, M., Weiss, P., Blanc-Féraud, L., Zerubia, J.: Complex wavelet regular-
    ization for solving inverse problems in remote sensing. In: Proc. Geoscience and
    Remote Sensing Society (2009)
15. Portilla, J., Simoncelli, E.P.: A parametric texture model based on joint statistics
    of complex wavelet coefficients. Int. Journal of Comp. Vision 40, 49–71 (2000)
16. Fadili, M., Starck, J.L., Murtagh, F.: Inpainting and zooming using sparse repre-
    sentations. Computer Journal 52(1) (2009)
17. Candés, E., Laurent, D., Donoho, D., Ying, L.: Fast discrete curvelet transforms.
    Multiscale Modeling and Simulation 5(3), 861–899 (2006)
18. Starck, J.-L., Elad, M., Donoho, D.: Image decomposition via the combination of
    sparse representations and a variational approach. Trans. on Image Processing 14,
    1570–1582 (2004)
19. Huber, P.: Robust Statistics. Wiley, New York (1981)
20. Nesterov, Y.: Smooth minimization of nonsmooth functions. Mathematical pro-
    gramming Series A 103, 127–152 (2005)
21. Nemirovski, A.: Prox-method with rate of convergence $O(1/t)$ for variational
    inequalities with Lipschitz continuous monotone operators and smooth convex-
    concave saddle point problems. Journal on Optimization 15(1), 229–251 (2004)
22. Chambolle, A., Pock, T.: A first-order primal-dual algorithm for convex problems
    with applications to imaging. Technical report, TU Graz (2010)
23. Esser, E., Zhang, X., Chan, T.: A general framework for a class of first order
    primal-dual algorithms for tv minimization. Technical Report 67, UCLA (2009)
24. Grabner, H., Nguyen, T.T., Grabner, B., Bischof, H.: On-line boosting-based car
    detection from aerial images. J. of Photogr. and R. Sensing 63(3), 382–396 (2008)
25. Hays, J., Efros, A.A.: Scene completion using millions of photographs. ACM Trans.
    on Graphics (SIGGRAPH) 26(3) (2007)

A Convex Approach for Variational Super-Resolution

Markus Unger, Thomas Pock, Manuel Werlberger, and Horst Bischof

Institute for Computer Graphics and Vision, Graz University of Technology, Austria

Abstract. We propose a convex variational framework to compute high resolution images from a low resolution video. The image formation process is analyzed to provide to a well designed model for warping, blurring, downsampling and regularization. We provide a comprehensive investigation of the single model components. The super-resolution problem is modeled as a minimization problem in an unified convex framework, which is solved by a fast primal dual algorithm. A comprehensive evaluation on the influence of different kinds of noise is carried out. The proposed algorithm shows excellent recovery of information for various real and synthetic datasets.

1   Introduction

The reconstruction of highly resolved images out of multiple smaller images is an important problem that occurs in surveillance, remote sensing, medical imaging, video restoration, up sampling and still image extraction. Video frames are representations of a scene that undergo arbitrary motion from frame to frame, degradation by the optical system and the digitization process. Although motion might seem to be a problem, exactly these sub-pixel shifts caused by moving objects or the camera, provide the necessary information utilized in super-resolution reconstruction. The super-resolution problem is difficult to solve because one has to deal with two kinds of image degradation: First, the camera system, that adds blur (eg. by the optical system like lenses and filters) and performs spatial integration on the sensor (often these are not square pixels). With exact knowledge of the Point Spread Function (PSF) of the camera system and sufficiently enough samples by shifted images this degradation is invertible up to the limits posed by Shannon [1]. Unfortunately the second group of degradation, namely noise, cannot be undone [2], making super-resolution an ill-posed problem. Noise occurs in different forms: Gaussian type of noise (eg. caused by sensor heating and analog processing), Outlier noise (eg. occlusions) and systematic noise (eg. quantization and compression).

The limitations of super-resolution were already studied by Kosarev [2] who stated a logarithmic dependence of quality on the signal-to-noise ratio of the input. Later, the limits on image super-resolution were analyzed by Baker and Kanade [3]. They provided experimental results using 8bit images, showing a degradation of image quality with increasing magnification. This experiments

M. Goesele et al. (Eds.): DAGM 2010, LNCS 6376, pp. 313–322, 2010.
© Springer-Verlag Berlin Heidelberg 2010

already demonstrated that the limited dynamic range causes a dramatic loss of information. In Section 5, we will provide a deeper analysis of various types of noise. To overcome the limitations of noise some prior information might be used in the reconstruction process. Baker and Kanade [3] proposed a learning based recognition approach (called 'hallucination') to improve super-resolution on a limited class of images. More general approaches try to utilize redundant structures in images. Potter et al. [4] use a Non-local-Means algorithm for super-resolution reconstruction. A similar approach is taken by Glasner et al. in [5], where patch redundancy over various scales of a single image is used to significantly improve zooming for pictures with redundant structures.

There is also a great number of super-resolution approaches that rely on a more general prior [6]. Some of these approaches use Total Variation (TV) regularization as eg. the approach by Mitzel et al. [7]. Farsiu et al. [8], use bilateral TV (that is closely related to Non-local TV) to overcome stair-casing artifacts usually induced by TV regularization. Our approach is closely related to the variational approach of Mitzel et al. [7]. While Mitzel et al. used L^1-norms for regularization and in the data term, we replace them in our model (see Section 3) with Huber-Norms [9]. The Huber-Norm has the advantage of smooth gray values while preserving strong edges. Another improvement over [7] is the used first-order primal dual algorithm in Section 4. Additionally we provide a comprehensive investigation of the crucial super-resolution operators used for warping, blurring and downsampling. Another energy minimization based approach is investigated by Schoenemann [10] that combines motion layer decomposition with super-resolution. He introduces an additional term that imposes regularity on the geometry of the layers.

As the input images are related by some arbitrary unknown motion, the accurate estimation of this motion is obviously very important. For small motions this can be done implicitly eg. by Non-local methods [4] or by performing joint space-time super-resolution as done by Shechtman [11]. There are also semi-implicit methods eg. using steering kernels as done by Takeda et al. [12]. For large arbitrary motion an explicit optical flow calculation is required. Fortunately dense optical flow algorithms have become very accurate and sufficiently fast [13]. We will do motion estimation by the variational optical flow proposed by Werlberger et al. [14], for which GPU-binaries are available.

Contribution: The contribution of this paper is threefold: First, we extend the variational model by Mitzel et al. [7] by the usage of the Huber-Norm and an exact choice of the crucial linear operators (Section 3). The choice and implementation of these operators as well as the discretization are described in sufficient detail that the proposed method can easily be reimplemented. Second, we provide a fast minimization procedure in Section 4. Therefore we adapt the first-order primal-dual algorithm from Pock et al. [15]. Finally, we investigate the effects of different kinds of noise on super-resolution reconstruction in Section 5. We also compare the algorithm to [7,10], and show superior results obtained with the proposed algorithm, demonstrating its robustness for arbitrary motion and occlusions.

2   Discretization

Before describing the super-resolution model we have to make some thoughts on discretization. An image is given on a two dimensional regular Cartesian grid of the size $M \times N$:

$$\{(ih, jh) : 1 \le i \le M, 1 \le j \le N\}, \tag{1}$$

with the indices of the discrete locations given by (i, j) and the pixel size (or spacing) h. We define a finite dimensional vector space $X = \mathbb{R}^{MN}$ with a scalar product

$$\langle v, w \rangle_X^h = h^2 \sum_{i,j} v_{i,j} w_{i,j}, \quad v, w \in X . \tag{2}$$

Furthermore, we define a vector space $Y = \mathbb{R}^{MN} \times \mathbb{R}^{MN}$, with the gradient operator as a linear mapping $\nabla^h : X \to Y$ using finite differences and Neumann boundary conditions:

$$(\nabla^h v)_{i,j} = \left((\delta_x^{h+} v)_{i,j}, (\delta_y^{h+} v)_{i,j} \right)^T , \tag{3}$$

where

$$(\delta_x^{h+} v)_{i,j} = \begin{cases} \frac{v_{i+1,j} - v_{i,j}}{h} & \text{if } i < M \\ 0 & \text{if } i = M \end{cases} , \quad (\delta_y^{h+} v)_{i,j} = \begin{cases} \frac{v_{i,j+1} - v_{i,j}}{h} & \text{if } j < N \\ 0 & \text{if } j = N \end{cases} . \tag{4}$$

Given two vectors $\boldsymbol{p} = (p^x, p^y)^T, \boldsymbol{q} = (q^x, q^y)^T \in Y$ we define the scalar product as following:

$$\langle \boldsymbol{p}, \boldsymbol{q} \rangle_Y^h = h^2 \sum_{i,j} p_{i,j}^x q_{i,j}^x + p_{i,j}^y q_{i,j}^y . \tag{5}$$

Additionally we have to define a divergence operator $\text{div}^h : Y \to X$ by choosing it to be adjoint to the gradient operator in (3), and thus fulfilling the equality $\langle \nabla^h u, \boldsymbol{p} \rangle_Y^h = -\left\langle u, \text{div}^h \boldsymbol{p} \right\rangle_X^h$. Therefore, the discrete divergence operator is given as:

$$(\text{div}^h \boldsymbol{p})_{i,j} = (\delta_x^{h-} p^x)_{i,j} + (\delta_y^{h-} p^y)_{i,j} , \tag{6}$$

with

$$(\delta_x^{h-} p^x)_{i,j} = \begin{cases} 0 & \text{if } i = 0 \\ \frac{p_{i,j}^x - p_{i-1,j}^x}{h} & \text{if } 0 < i < M \\ -\frac{p_{i-1,j}^x}{h} & \text{if } i = M \end{cases} , \quad (\delta_y^{h-} p^y)_{i,j} = \begin{cases} 0 & \text{if } j = 0 \\ \frac{p_{i,j}^y - p_{i,j-1}^y}{h} & \text{if } 0 < j < N \\ -\frac{p_{i,j-1}^y}{h} & \text{if } j = N \end{cases} \tag{7}$$

3   The Super-Resolution Model

In this section the super-resolution model is defined as a convex minimization problem, and we discuss the operators in detail. The exact minimization procedure follows in Section 4.

As input for the super-resolution algorithm, n input images $\check{f}_i \in \check{X}$ of size $\check{M} \times \check{N}$ and pixel size ξh are given. We denote the scale factor as $\xi \in \mathbb{R}^+$. The input images are warped, blurred and noisy samples of some continuous image $g : \Omega \to \mathbb{R}$. Based on the redundancy of the input images we aim to find one higher resolved super-resolution image $\hat{u} \in \hat{X}$ of size $\hat{M} \times \hat{N}$ with pixel size h. Note that we use the $\check{}$ accent to indicate that a variable belongs to the coarse (input) level with pixel size ξh and the $\hat{}$ accent to indicate everything that is related to the fine (super-resolution) level with pixel size h.

A Convex Minimization Problem: We define the super-resolution model as the following convex minimization problem:

$$\min_{\hat{u}} \left\{ \lambda \left|\left| \nabla^h \hat{u} \right|\right|_{\varepsilon_u}^{h} + \sum_{i=1}^{n} \left|\left| \mathbf{DBW}_i \hat{u} - \check{f}_i \right|\right|_{\varepsilon_d}^{\xi h} \right\}, \tag{8}$$

with regularization using the Huber-Norm [9] that is defined as:

$$||x||_\varepsilon^h = \sum_{0 \le i,j \le MN} |x_{i,j}|_\varepsilon \, h^2 \quad \text{and} \quad |x|_\varepsilon = \begin{cases} \frac{|x|^2}{2\varepsilon} & \text{if } |x| \le \varepsilon \\ |x| - \frac{\varepsilon}{2} & \text{if } |x| > \varepsilon \end{cases} . \tag{9}$$

While Total Variation based approaches [16] favor flat gray value regions causing staircase artifacts, the Huber-Norm has the advantage of smoothing small gradients while preserving strong edges. The linear operators $\mathbf{D}$, $\mathbf{B}$ and $\mathbf{W}$ denote downsampling, blurring and warping operators and will be explained in detail in the following. The free parameter λ models the tradeoff between regularization and data term.

Warping Operator W: An exact warping to align the input images is a crucial factor for super-resolution. To allow for arbitrary motion, sub-pixel accurate optical flow is required. There are already various dense approaches with very high accuracy available [13]. Throughout this paper we used the GPU-based implementation from Werlberger et al. [14]. This approach utilizes a variational minimization problem using Huber-Norm regularization and an L^1 based data term to model the optical flow constraint. For optical flow calculation we used bicubic upsamplings $\hat{f}_i$ of the input images $\check{f}_i$. We denote the reference image that is used for super-resolution as $\hat{f}_k$ with $1 \le k \le n$. From the image $\hat{f}_k$ we calculate the optical flow to all input images. As a result we get n flow vector fields $\hat{w}_i : \Omega \to \mathbb{R}^2$. In the super-resolution model (8) we denoted the optical flow as a linear operator $\mathbf{W}_i : \mathbb{R}^{\hat{M}\hat{N}} \to \mathbb{R}^{\hat{M}\hat{N}}$. As $\mathbf{W}_i$ has a size of $(\hat{M}\hat{N})^2$, direct storage and computation is not feasible. Therefore, we directly utilize the flow fields $\hat{w}_i$ to warp the super-resolution image to the input images using bicubic interpolation. For the proposed minimization algorithm we also need the transposed operator $\mathbf{W}_i^T$ such that $\langle \mathbf{W}_i a, b \rangle_X = \langle a, \mathbf{W}_i^T b \rangle_X$, as detailed in Section 4. This inverse warping can again be realized using the flow fields $\hat{w}_i$, but this time the input images are warped to the reference image. Therefore, in each pixel of the reference, the flow is used to find the corresponding position in the input image. The pixel values in the input image are weighted by the coefficients of the bicubic interpolation and added up in an accumulator image.

Blurring Operator B: To account for blurring introduced by atmospheric effects, the optical system and the sensor with preceding filters can get very complex. More specifically one has to measure the point spread function for one specific configuration. As the aim of this paper is to present a general super-resolution algorithm one has to provide a generic model. Therefore the blurring operator $\mathbf{B}$ is modeled by a simple Gaussian kernel. We chose the standard deviation $\sigma = \frac{1}{4}\sqrt{\xi^2 - 1}$ and 3σ for the kernel size. Again the transposed blurring operator $\mathbf{B}^T$ is not the same as a simple Gaussian blur as which $\mathbf{B}$ is implemented. In turn, one has to perform the operation using an accumulator to obtain correct results.

Downsampling Operator D: We first define the formation of a pixel value $f_{i,j}$ at position (ih, jh) and size h^2 by calculating the mean of the continuous image $g : \Omega \to \mathbb{R}$ in the region of the pixel $f_{i,j} = \frac{1}{h^2}\int_{\Delta_{i,j}^h} g(\boldsymbol{x})d\boldsymbol{x}$, with the pixel region $\Delta_{i,j}^h = (ih, jh) + \left[-\frac{h}{2}, \frac{h}{2}\right]^2$. The input images and the super-resolution image are just samplings with different pixel size h. Since we only know the discretized input images we have to model the downsampling process in the discrete setting. This is done using a weighted area

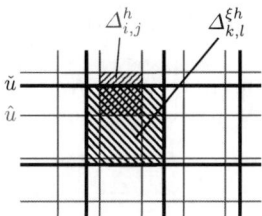

Fig. 1. Illustration of the downsampling process that is modeled as an area integral

integral over the region of the low resolution pixel (see Fig. 1 for an illustration):

$$\check{u}_{k,l} = \frac{1}{\mu(\Delta_{k,l}^{\xi h})} \sum_{0 \leq i,j \leq \hat{M}\hat{N}} \mu(\Delta_{i,j}^h \cap \Delta_{k,l}^{\xi h})\hat{u}_{i,j} \,, \tag{10}$$

with the Lebesgue measure $\mu(\Delta)$ denotes the area of the pixel region. The proposed definition of the downsampling operator $\mathbf{D}$ has the advantage that the scale $\xi \in \mathbb{R}^+$ and is not restricted to integer values. Again, an accumulator is used to calculate $\mathbf{D}^T$.

4   A First Order Primal-Dual Algorithm

Recently, in [15] and [17], a first order primal-dual algorithm was proposed to solve convex-concave saddle-point problems of the type:

$$\min_{x \in X} \max_{y \in Y} \left\{ \langle K\boldsymbol{x}, \boldsymbol{y} \rangle + G(\boldsymbol{x}) - F^*(\boldsymbol{y}) \right\} \,, \tag{11}$$

with a continuous linear operator $K : X \to Y$, and $G : X \to [0, \infty)$ and $F^* : Y \to [0, \infty)$ being convex functions. Basically, the algorithm consists of taking simple gradient steps in the primal variables $\boldsymbol{x}$ and dual variables $\boldsymbol{y}$. In addition a leading point $\bar{\boldsymbol{x}}$ is computed to ensure convergence of the algorithm [15]. The basic iterations of the algorithm are defined as

$$y^{n+1} = (1 + \sigma \partial F^*)^{-1}(y^n + \sigma K \bar{x}^n)$$
$$x^{n+1} = (1 + \tau \partial G)^{-1}(x^n - \tau K^* y^{n+1}) \tag{12}$$
$$\bar{x}^{n+1} = 2x^{n+1} - x^n ,$$

with ∂F^* and ∂G the subgradients of F^* and G. The operators $(1 + \sigma \partial F^*)^{-1}$ and $(1 + \tau \partial G)^{-1}$ denote the usual resolvent operators. The primal and dual step sizes $\tau > 0$ and $\sigma > 0$ are chosen such that $\tau \sigma L^2 \leq 1$, where $L = \|K\|$ is the norm of the linear operator K.

In order to apply the primal-dual algorithm to the proposed super-resolution model, we have to transform the minimization problem (8) into the form of (11). Using duality principles (in particular the Legendre-Fenchel transform), we arrive at the following primal-dual formulation of the super-resolution model:

$$\min_{\hat{u}} \sup_{\hat{p}, \check{q}} \left\{ \langle \nabla^h \hat{u}, \hat{p} \rangle_Y^h - \frac{\varepsilon_u}{2\lambda h^2} \|\hat{p}\|^2 - \delta_{\{|\hat{p}| \leq \lambda h^2\}} \right.$$
$$\left. + \sum_{i=1}^n \left(\langle \check{q}_i, \mathbf{DBW}_i \hat{u} - \check{f}_i \rangle_X^{\xi h} - \frac{\varepsilon_d}{2(\xi h)^2} \|\check{q}_i\|^2 - \delta_{\{|\check{q}_i| \leq (\xi h)^2\}} \right) \right\} , \tag{13}$$

with $\hat{p} \in \hat{Y}$ and $\check{q} \in \check{X}$ denoting the dual variables. The indicator function δ_Σ for the set Σ given as $\delta_\Sigma(x) = \begin{cases} 0 & \text{if } x \in \Sigma , \\ \infty & \text{else .} \end{cases}$

Now, applying the basic iterations (12) to our saddle-point problem (13), we obtain the following iterative algorithm:

$$\hat{p}^{n+1} = \Pi_{B_0^{\lambda h^2}} \left(\frac{\hat{p}^n + \sigma h^2 \nabla^h \overline{u}^n}{1 + \frac{\sigma \varepsilon_u}{\lambda h^2}} \right) ,$$
$$\check{q}_i^{n+1} = \Pi_{B_0^{(\xi h)^2}} \left(\frac{\check{q}_i^n + \sigma (\xi h)^2 (\mathbf{DBW}_i \overline{u}^n - f_i)}{1 + \frac{\sigma \varepsilon_d}{(\xi h)^2}} \right) ,$$
$$\hat{u}^{n+1} = \hat{u}^n - \tau \left(-\text{div}^h \hat{p}^{n+1} + (\xi h)^2 \sum_{i=1}^n \left(\mathbf{W}_i^T \mathbf{B}^T \mathbf{D}^T \check{q}_i^{n+1} \right) \right) , \tag{14}$$
$$\overline{u}^{n+1} = 2\hat{u}^{n+1} - \hat{u}^n .$$

The projector $\Pi_{B_0^r}$ denotes the orthogonal projection to a L^2 ball with radius r. In the 2D-case this can be computed as $\Pi_{B_0^{\lambda h^2}} = \hat{p}/\max\{1, \frac{|\hat{p}|}{\lambda h^2}\}$. While the 1D-case $\Pi_{B_0^{(\xi h)^2}}$ results in a simple clamping to the interval $[-(\xi h)^2, (\xi h)^2]$. Based on experiments, we are using the step sizes $\tau = \frac{\xi}{\sqrt{L^2 \lambda}}$ and $\sigma = \frac{1}{\sqrt{\tau L^2}}$.

5   Experimental Results

The proposed algorithm (14) was implemented on the GPU using the CUDA framework. We will prove that the chosen model genaralizes very well by using different input sources for all experiments. First we evaluated the influence

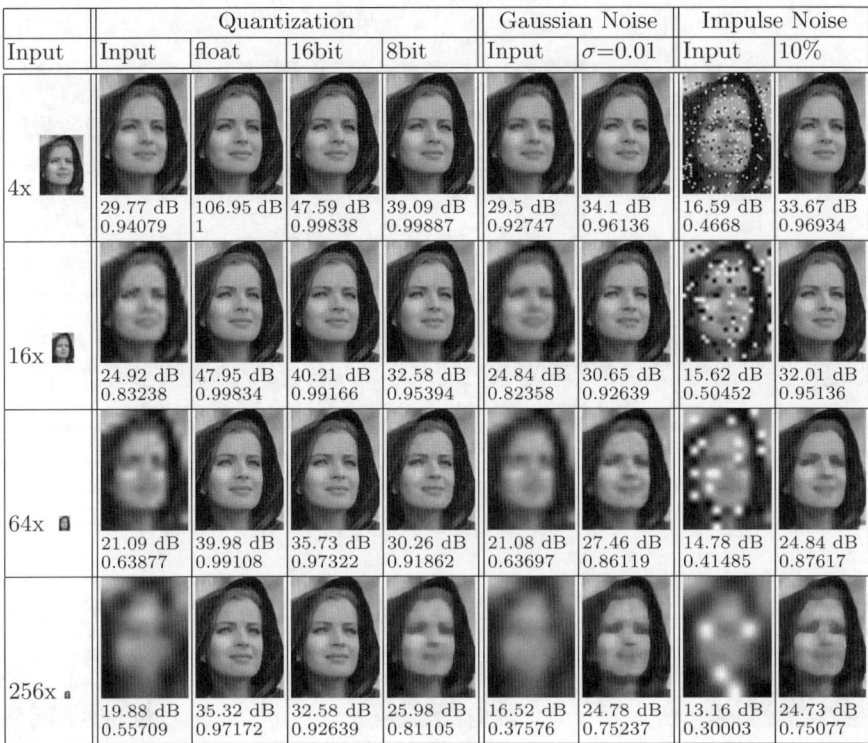

Input	Quantization				Gaussian Noise		Impulse Noise	
	Input	float	16bit	8bit	Input	σ=0.01	Input	10%
4x	29.77 dB 0.94079	106.95 dB 1	47.59 dB 0.99838	39.09 dB 0.99887	29.5 dB 0.92747	34.1 dB 0.96136	16.59 dB 0.4668	33.67 dB 0.96934
16x	24.92 dB 0.83238	47.95 dB 0.99834	40.21 dB 0.99166	32.58 dB 0.95394	24.84 dB 0.82358	30.65 dB 0.92639	15.62 dB 0.50452	32.01 dB 0.95136
64x	21.09 dB 0.63877	39.98 dB 0.99108	35.73 dB 0.97322	30.26 dB 0.91862	21.08 dB 0.63697	27.46 dB 0.86119	14.78 dB 0.41485	24.84 dB 0.87617
256x	19.88 dB 0.55709	35.32 dB 0.97172	32.58 dB 0.92639	25.98 dB 0.81105	16.52 dB 0.37576	24.78 dB 0.75237	13.16 dB 0.30003	24.73 dB 0.75077

Fig. 2. Comparison of the influence of different noise on the superresolution reconstruction for the scales 2, 4, 8 and 16 using synthetic data. The input columns always depict the input image that was chosen as reference image (using bicubic upsampling).

of different types of noise, namely quantization noise, Gaussian noise and salt and pepper noise. In Fig. 2 the results are depicted for different scale factors. The input data was generated artificially such that the exact warping, blur and downsampling operators are known. The results are compared to the original image, and the Signal-to-noise ratio (SNR) and the Structural Similarity (SSIM) [18] were calculated. Fig. 2 demonstrates that quantization noise using an 8bit representation causes a dramatic loss of information for large scale factors, while using 16bit quantization the visual appearance for $\xi = 16$ still recovers most of the fine details. Unfortunately even weak Gaussian noise causes strong degeneration. It also shows that the proposed super-resolution model can handle a reasonable amount of outliers due to the robust Huber-Norm in the data term.

The effect of quantization noise is also investigated for real data in Fig. 3. We used a Prosilica GC1600 together with a Pentax 4.8mm 1:1.8 lens to capture a 8bit and a 12bit video. Unfortunately, in this case no notable visual gain can be seen when comparing the super-resolution results. A thorough evaluation of different cameras is left for future investigations.

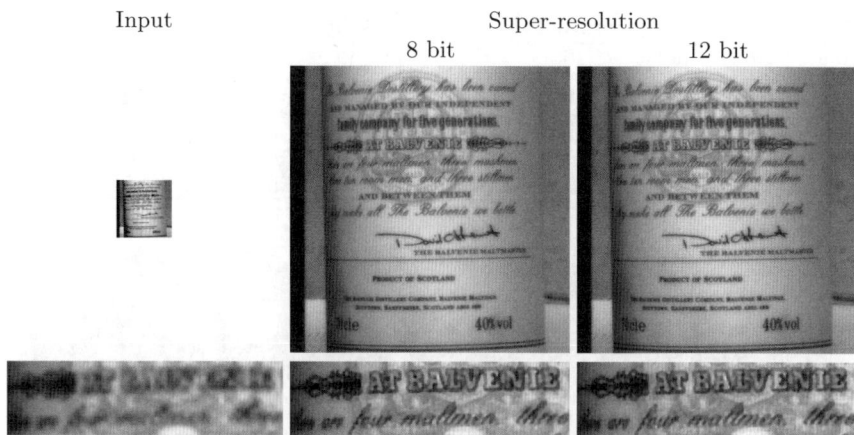

Fig. 3. Comparison of the influence of quantization using a real dataset. The bottom row depicts contrast adapted crops of the top images.

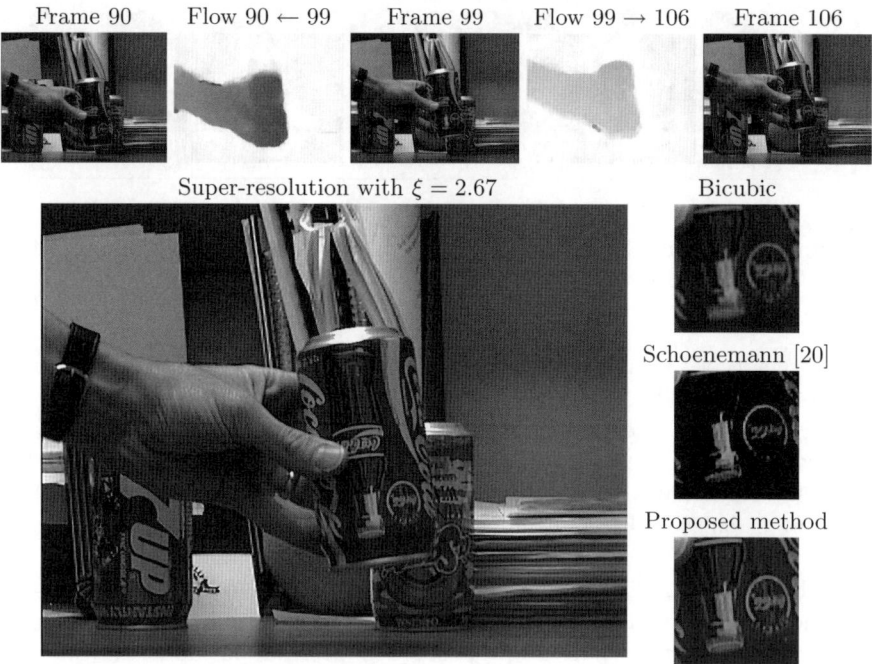

Fig. 4. Demonstration of superresolution on real data with heavy occlusions. The flow images in the first row use Middlebury color coding.

In Fig. 4, a scene with strong motion is used as input. Optical Flow was calculated using [14]. To demonstrate the capability of using arbitrary scale factors, we chose $\xi = 2.67$ as scale factor. The results demonstrate that the proposed algorithm can easily handle strong occlusions due to the robust Huber-Norm. It shows that we obtain good results that are comparable to the more complex super-resolution motion layer decomposition approach of Schoenemann [10].

Finally, we compare our algorithm to the closely related work of Mitzel et al. [7]. In Fig. 5, super-resolution was done on a public car sequence [1]. Note that we clearly improve the sharpness and detail recovery in the super-resolution image. Using the proposed algorithm on can easily read the cars license plate which is not the case for the other algorithm.

16 input images   Super-resolution $\xi = 3$ Bicubic

Mitzel et al. [7]

Proposed method

Fig. 5. Comparison to the closely related work of Mitzel et al. [7] using super-resolution to recover a license plate. (Contrast adapted for crops)

6   Conclusion

We presented a variational super-resolution approach that uses a robust Huber-Norm for regularization as well as in the data term. A fast primal-dual algorithm was used to solve a convex saddle-point problem. We put particular emphasis to the accurate design of the model, the used operators and discretization. The exact choice of warping, blurring and downsampling operators was discussed, and results demonstrate that we obtain state of the art results even for very difficult scenes. The proposed approach can handle large occlusions as well as arbitrary scale factors. An extensive evaluation of the influence of noise was carried out. It showed that in theory a higher dynamic range can significantly improve the recovered results. Though for real data, sensor noise is the limiting factor. We hope this will trigger further research on the practical implications of bit depth on superresolution. In future work we will also study more powerful regularization terms (e.g. wavelets).

---

[1] http://users.soe.ucsc.edu/~milanfar/software/sr-datasets.html

Acknowledgement

This work was supported by the Austrian Research Promotion Agency within the vdQA project (no. 816003).

References

1. Shannon, C.E.: A mathematical theory of communication. SIGMOBILE Mob. Comput. Commun. Rev. **5**(1) (2001) 3–55
2. Kosarev, E.L.: Shannon's superresolution limit for signal recovery. Inverse Problems **6**(1) (1990) 55
3. Baker, S., Kanade, T.: Limits on super-resolution and how to break them. IEEE Transactions on Pattern Analysis and Machine Intelligence **24** (2002) 1167–1183
4. Protter, M., Elad, M., Takeda, H., Milanfar, P.: Generalizing the non-local-means to super-resolution reconstruction. In: IEEE Transactions on Image Processing. (2009) 36
5. Glasner, D., Bagon, S., Irani, M.: Super-resolution from a single image. In: ICCV. (2009)
6. van Ouwerkerk, J.: Image super-resolution survey. Image and Vision Computing **24**(10) (2006) 1039 – 1052
7. Mitzel, D., Pock, T., Schoenemann, T., Cremers, D.: Video super resolution using duality based TV-L1 optical flow. In: Denzler, J., Notni, G., Süße, H. (eds.) DAGM 2009. LNCS, vol. 5748, pp. 432–441. Springer, Heidelberg (2009)
8. Farsiu, S., Robinson, D., Elad, M., Milanfar, P.: Fast and robust multi-frame super-resolution. IEEE Transactions on Image Processing **13** (2003) 1327–1344
9. Huber, P.: Robust Statistics. Wiley, New York (1981)
10. Schoenemann, T.: Combinatorial Solutions for Shape Optimization in Computer Vision. PhD thesis, Department of Computer Science, University of Bonn, Germany (2008)
11. Shechtman, E., Caspi, Y., Irani, M.: Space-time super-resolution. IEEE Transactions on Pattern Analysis and Machine Intelligence **27** (2005) 531–545
12. Takeda, H., Milanfar, P., Protter, M., Elad, M.: Super-resolution without explicit subpixel motion estimation. Trans. Img. Proc. **18**(9) (2009) 1958–1975
13. Middlebury: http://vision.middlebury.edu/flow/ (2010) accessed 06-May-2010.
14. Werlberger, M., Trobin, W., Pock, T., Wedel, A., Cremers, D., Bischof, H.: Anisotropic Huber-L1 optical flow. In: BMVC, London, UK (September 2009)
15. Pock, T., Cremers, D., Bischof, H., Chambolle, A.: An algorithm for minimizing the mumford-shah functional. In: ICCV. (2009)
16. Rudin, L.I., Osher, S., Fatemi, E.: Nonlinear total variation based noise removal algorithms. Phys. D **60**(1-4) (1992) 259–268
17. Esser, E., Zhang, X., Chan, T.F.: A general framework for a class of first order primal-dual algorithms for tv minimization. UCLA CAM Report [09-67] (August 2009)
18. Wang, Z., Bovik, A.C., Sheikh, H.R., Simoncelli, E.P.: Image quality assessment: From error visibility to structural similarity. IEEE Transactions on Image Processing **13** (2004) 600–612

Incremental Learning in the Energy Minimisation Framework for Interactive Segmentation

Denis Kirmizigül and Dmitrij Schlesinger*

Dresden University of Technology

Abstract. In this article we propose a method for parameter learning within the energy minimisation framework for segmentation. We do this in an incremental way where user input is required for resolving segmentation ambiguities. Whereas most other interactive learning approaches focus on learning appearance characteristics only, our approach is able to cope with learning prior terms; in particular the Potts terms in binary image segmentation. The artificial as well as real examples illustrate the applicability of the approach.

1 Introduction

Energy minimisation techniques are proven to be a powerful tool for image segmentation. However, one of the most important questions – how to learn unknown model parameters – still remains on the agenda. There are many approaches addressing this problem. One possible way is to exploit the probabilistic nature of commonly used energy minimisation functions – they are Maximum A-posteriori decisions for corresponding Markov Random Fields. Consequently, the task of parameter learning can be formulated using established statistical methods, like e.g. Maximum Likelihood principle [1]. Although this approach has many advantages (it is well grounded, the learning can be sometimes done in a fully unsupervised manner etc.), it has also certain drawbacks. First of all, it is often computationally infeasible (the corresponding tasks are NP-complete). There are many approximate solutions, but in most cases there is no estimation for the approximation quality. Second, these methods attempt to find parameters of the underlying probability distributions, rather than the parameters of the corresponding classifiers/algorithms. It is known that e.g. the Maximum A-posteriori decision is biased in a certain sense – it does not reflect the model statistics (see e.g. [2]). Consequently, the parameters of the probability distribution are not necessarily optimal for a classifier, if the latter is rated according to an arbitrary measure (e.g. the number of misclassified pixels).

Another way is to consider classifiers "as is" without probabilistic background. A rather straightforward approach is to use cross-validation on test images with

---

* This work was supported by Grant 13487 of the Sächsische Aufbaubank (SAB) and DFG Grant FL307/2-1.

M. Goesele et al. (Eds.): DAGM 2010, LNCS 6376, pp. 323–332, 2010.

ground truth. Usually, the parameter under consideration is resampled within some reasonable range. For each value the inference is performed and a rating score is computed. It can be for instance the one, which minimises the number of misclassified pixels. More elaborated techniques (see e.g. [3]) can be used as well. The parameter value with optimal score is chosen as the optimal one. The main drawback of this method is, that its direct extension to more than one parameter leads to computational explosion. Another disadvantage is the following. The dependency of the chosen rating score from the parameter value needs not necessarily be smooth – i.e. the resampling (substitution of a continuous range by a discrete set) may lead to a parameter, that is far from optimal.

There is a group of methods based on Parametric Flow [4]. They allow (for certain models) to compute all solutions for a predefined continuous parameter range, rather than for a discrete set as in the previous case. The optimal parameter value is then chosen according to a given quality measure. A comprehensive review of such methods can be found in [5].

It is worth mentioning that all non-probabilistic methods described above need classified data in order to work at all – i.e. ground truth segmentation. This fact motivated development of interactive segmentation schemes. Prominent representatives are e.g. [6,7]. In these schemes there is no ground truth in advance. A non-complete ground truth (in some pixels only) is produced by user during the segmentation. Usually, the overall scheme consists of a loop. In each iteration there is a set of actual parameters, according to which the actual segmentation is performed. The user has the possibility either to accept the segmentation (to break the loop and finish the work) or to correct it manually. In the latter case parameters are re-estimated according to the user interaction and the whole procedure is repeated again. One important characteristic feature of almost all recent interactive segmentations is that only appearance characteristics are learned by user interactions. Prior terms are specified in advance and remain unchanged.

In this work we propose a novel approach for parameter learning, which is based on the idea of incremental learning. In contrast to other methods there is no single parameter in each iteration of the algorithm, but a set of feasible ones, i.e. those, which do not contradict to the user inputs. If this set is ambiguous – more than one optimal segmentation is possible for different parameter values from the set – the user is asked to resolve this situation. His feedback is used to restrict the set of feasible parameters. The difference from known approaches is twofold. First, the proposed scheme produces a range of feasible unambiguous parameters, rather than a single "optimal" one. Second, interactions between the algorithm and the user are initiated not by the user but by the algorithm – i.e. unlike other interactive methods (e.g. [8,6]) there is a clear stopping criterion. Finally, the approach can be used for learning of prior parameters. In particular, we consider in this work in detail how to learn the strength of Potts interaction for binary segmentation.

The rest of the paper is organised as follows. In the next section we present the model and formulate the task we are interested in. We also recall the Parametric

Flow approach, which our method is based on. In Section 3 we present the idea of the incremental learning and show how to apply this idea to the task introduced before. In the next section we present experiments and finalize with conclusions and open questions.

2   Model

In this article we are concerned with binary segmentation of images. Let R be a set of pixels. The image $x : R \rightarrow C$ is a mapping that assigns a colour value $c \in C$ to each pixel $r \in R$. The colour value in a pixel r is denoted by x_r. In binary segmentation a label $l \in \{0, 1\}$ (background/foreground) should be assigned to each position r forming a labelling $s : R \rightarrow \{0, 1\}$ (a label chosen by the segmentation in a pixel r is denoted by s_r). A common way is to formulate the segmentation task as an Energy minimisation problem as follows. The pixels are considered as vertices of a graph $G = (R, E)$, where the edges $\{r, r'\} \in E$ connect neighbouring pixels (usually the 4-neighbourhood structure is used). The task is to find the labelling of the minimal energy, i.e

$$s^* = \arg\min_s E(x, s) = \arg\min_s \left[\sum_{r \in R} q(x_r, s_r) + \sum_{\{r, r'\} \in E} g(s_r, s_{r'}) \right] . \quad (1)$$

The functions $q : C \times \{0, 1\} \rightarrow \mathbb{R}$ (usually called data terms) are penalties for assigning the label s_r to the colour value x_r in the pixel r. In the simplest case they are negated logarithms of corresponding conditional probability distributions $p(c|l)$ to observe the colour value $c \in C$ given the label l. The second summation in (1) (usually called model term) captures prior assumptions about the labellings. In many applications one favours compact segments. This corresponds to the Potts model $g(l, l') = \lambda \cdot \mathbf{1}(l \neq l')$, where λ is the strength of the Potts interactions. Summarizing the energy of a labelling s is[1]

$$E(\lambda, s) = \sum_{r \in R} q_r(s_r) + \lambda \sum_{\{r, r'\} \in E} \mathbf{1}(s_r \neq s_{r'}) . \quad (2)$$

The parameter $\lambda \in \mathbb{R}_0^+$ weights the relative importance of the prior assumptions about the labellings against the observation penalties. Of course, the segmentation heavily depends on its choice. For example $\lambda = 0$ leads to the segmentation that purely depends on the observation – the assignment of a label in one pixel is not influenced by the label assignments of its neighbours. On the other hand, if $\lambda > \lambda^{max} = \min_{l \in \{0,1\}} [\sum_r q_r(l)]$ is used, the optimal labelling is constant: $s_r = \arg\min_{l \in \{0,1\}} [\sum_r q_r(l)]$ for all r. Therefore it is possible to restrict the range of λ to the interval $\Lambda = [0, \lambda^{max}] \subset \mathbb{R}_0^+$. The main issue of this article is the investigation of the set Λ of possible λ values. Informally said, the goal is to chose an "optimal" subinterval of Λ that coincides with user inputs.

---

[1] Since the image x is given, we sometimes omit it for readability. For data terms we use the notation $q_r(s_r)$ instead.

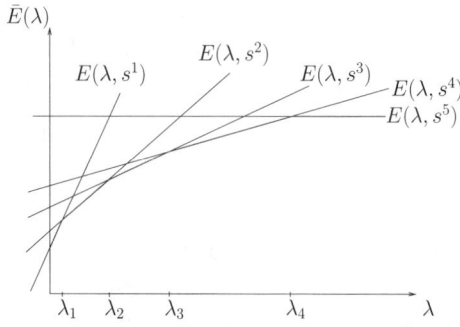

Fig. 1. The graph of $\bar{E}(\lambda)$

At this point we would like to recall the basic idea of Parametric Flow, which is used in our method. Denoting by $\bar{E}(\lambda) = \min_s E(\lambda, s)$, the graph of $\bar{E}(\lambda)$ is illustrated in Fig. 1. The graph of $\bar{E}(\lambda)$ is the lower envelope of piecewise linear (with respect to λ) functions $E(\lambda, s)$. The points where $\bar{E}(\lambda)$ changes its slope are referred as breakpoints. These breakpoints correspond to values of λ where transitions from one minimizing segmentation s of (2) to another minimizing segmentation s' take place. The slope of each linear part of the graph is the number of edges $\{r, r'\}$, for which different labels are assigned by the corresponding minimizer s to r and r'. Consequently, the number of breakpoints in $\bar{E}(\lambda)$ is bounded by the number of edges.

The aim of the Parametric Flow algorithm is to find all breakpoints $\lambda_0 = 0, \lambda_1, \ldots, \lambda_m = \lambda^{max}$. This is done recursively by subdividing the initial interval Λ. In [5] a subdividing-scheme is given, which we adapted to our case. The idea is as follows. Starting with an initial interval $[\lambda_i, \lambda_j]$ the labellings $s_i = \arg\min_s E(\lambda_i, s)$ and $s_j = \arg\min_s E(\lambda_j, s)$ are calculated. This can be done exactly e.g. via MinCut/MaxFlow algorithms. We used the implementations presented in [9,10,11] for this. If s_i and s_j are equal, then the interval cannot be further subdivided and the labelling associated to this interval is s_i. If s_i and s_j are different, then a new breakpoint $\lambda_k \in [\lambda_i, \lambda_j]$ is calculated as the intersection of the linear functions $E(\lambda, s_i)$ and $E(\lambda, s_j)$, i.e. solving $E(\lambda, s_i) = E(\lambda, s_j)$ with respect to λ. With λ_k the initial interval is subdivided into $[\lambda_i, \lambda_k] \cup [\lambda_k, \lambda_j]$ and the procedure is separately applied to these two subintervals. Applying this scheme until all the occurring intervals cannot be further subdivided gives all intermediate breakpoints λ_i and the minimizers s_i which correspond to the intervals $[\lambda_i, \lambda_{i+1}]$.

3 Incremental Learning

The general idea of incremental learning is as follows (see [12] for details). Let $\mathcal{X}$ be a set of observations and K be a set of hidden classes. A classifier $f : \mathcal{X} \to K$ is a mapping that assigns a class $k \in K$ to each observation $x \in \mathcal{X}$. Usually, a classifier is known up to an unknown parameter (we denote it by Θ).

The conventional learning task is to find a parameter Θ^* that classifies a given training set $L = ((x^i, k^i)|i = 1 \ldots l)$ correctly, i.e. $f(x^i; \Theta^*) = k^i$ holds for all i. After the learning phase is performed, the recognition phase (classification) consists of the application of the learned parameter, i.e. $k = f(x; \Theta^*)$ to each unknown x.

In contrast to the conventional scheme, in the incremental learning there is no separation between the learning and the recognition phases. The idea is to estimate at a time not only a single parameter, but the set of all feasible ones, which do not contradict to the training set. The latter may be thereby incomplete. The procedure is as follows. Starting from a "full set" θ of classifiers repeat:

(1) Observe current x;
(2) Perform recognition for all $\Theta \in \theta$ – calculate the subset $K' \subset K$ of classes that can be obtained using current parameter set:

$$k \in K' \Leftrightarrow \exists \Theta \in \theta | f(x; \Theta) = k$$

(3) If the recognition is not unique, i.e. $|K'| > 1$:
   (a) Ask teacher for the correct $k^* \in K'$,
   (b) Restrict θ in order to satisfy teacher input:

$$\theta^{new} = \{\Theta | \Theta \in \theta, f(x; \Theta) = k^*\}.$$

Our approach is based on the observation that the Energy Minimisation formulation is in fact a classifier, where: a) the set of observations $\mathcal{X}$ is the set of all images; b) the set of classes K is the set of all labellings; c) unknown parameter Θ is the strength of the Potts interaction λ, i.e. $f(x; \Theta) = f(x; \lambda) = \min_s E(x, s; \lambda)$.[2] Let us consider this in more detail. Step (2) of the above scheme can be done by Parametric Flow as considered in the previous section. The speciality of our case is a huge set of classes. Fortunately it is not the set of all labellings because the number of optimal ones for the full range of λ is bounded by the number of edges as mentioned previously. However, it is still to large to be convenient for the user. To avoid this problem, we need to modify the step (3a) to meet our needs. It can be noticed that it is not necessary to decide for a particular labelling in order to restrict the set of feasible λ-s. For example, the user can just assign manually the right label in a single pixel. Obviously, such an action is profitable only for those pixels, where different labels are possible according to the actual set of minimizing labellings. Summarizing, the algorithm should ask the user to fix a label in such a pixel, that after the user's assignment the set of feasible λ is restricted as much as possible. We refer to this activity – i.e. proposition for a pixel – as "user request". In particular, we use the following very simple request strategy. For each pixel a label histogram $h_r(l)$ is computed, i.e. for each label how many minimizing labellings assign label l to the pixel r. The pixel with lowest difference $|h_r(0) - h_r(1)|$ is proposed the user for evaluation. Summarizing, the learning schema for one image x looks as follows:

---

[2] Moreover, the Energy Minimisation is a Fisher classifier, because the energy $E(x, s; \lambda)$ can be written as a scalar product (see e.g. [13] for detail).

(1) Compute the set of minimizers $S = \{s_1, s_2, \ldots, s_m\}$ by Parametric Flow;
(2) Repeat:
  (a) Formulate the user request: compute the label histograms

$$h_r(l) = \sum_{s \in S | s_r = l} 1$$

  for all pixels and ask user to fix the label l^* in the pixel

$$r^* = \arg\min_r |h_r(0) - h_r(1)|.$$

  (b) Restrict S (and therefore also the set of feasible λ values): keep only those labellings, where the assigned label coincide with the user input:

$$S^{new} = \{s | s \in S, s_{r^*} = l^*\}$$

The loop (2) is repeated as long as the set S consists of more than one labelling.

4   Experiments

Since we wanted to evaluate our interactive segmentation scheme not only on "isolated" image examples, we automated the user interaction by replacing the real user with a "RoboUser" [14]. In cases that the above segmentation scheme requests user input for resolving ambiguous label assignments in one pixel, the RoboUser assigns this pixel according to the ground truth label. First, we evaluated our method on artificially generated images. They were created by sampling ground truth labellings according to the prior model with different generating Potts weights denoted by λ_{gen}. The sampling was done by Gibbs Sampler with about 2000 sampling iterations. To obtain the final image samples the segments were filled in with different grey-values (96 and 160) and disturbed by Gaussian noise of a variance σ. For λ_{gen} we used 9 different values ranging from 1.0 to 3.0 in steps of 0.25. The parameter σ was set to the values 10, 20, 30 and 50. The experiments were carried out on two image samples for each combination of (λ_{gen}, σ) values.

In order to evaluate the method we chose a labelling (and the corresponding λ interval), that can be understood as "the best possible in the scope of the used model". It was chosen as follows: we applied the Parametric Flow algorithm as described in section 2 to get the set of all minimizing labellings S within the interval Λ. Thereby the negative logarithms of the generating Gaussian noise distributions served as the q functions in (1). Among all minimizers from S the one having minimal Hamming distance from the real ground truth and the corresponding λ interval is chosen. We denote the minimal Hamming distance (averaged over the two image samples) as H^* and the mean of the corresponding λ interval as λ^*. The aim of the experiments is to compare H^* and λ^* with the values reached by the interactive learning scheme.

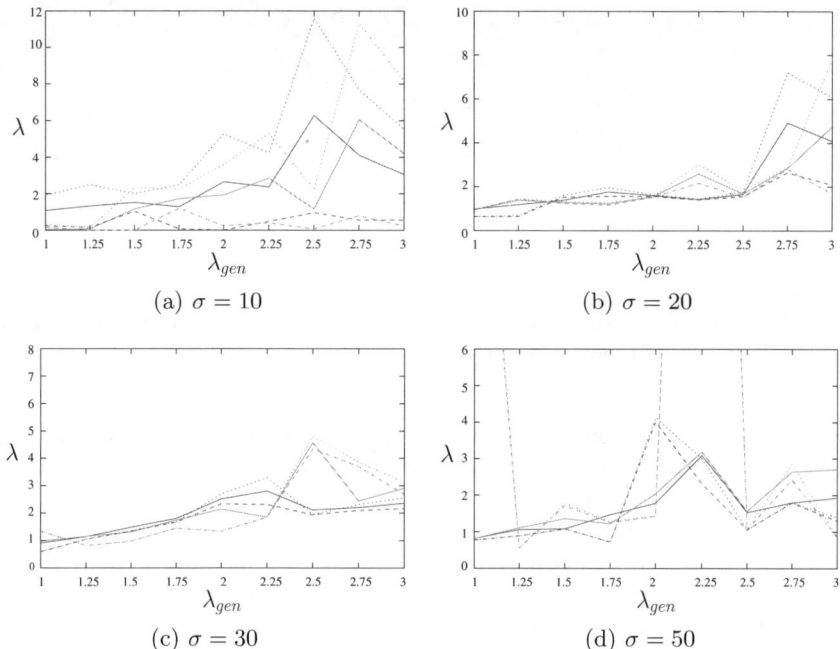

Fig. 2. Optimal λ^* (solid lines) and found λ intervals (dashed and dotted lines) with respect to λ_{gen} for different σ values

The results of the method – the minimal and maximal values of the subintervals the interactive learning algorithm led to – are shown in Fig. 2 as dashed and dotted lines respectively, whereas λ^* is plotted as a solid line. In Fig. 3 the Hamming distances of the labelling corresponding to the found subintervals are depicted as dashed lines and the minimal Hamming distances H^* as solid lines. In the latter figure we omitted plotting the Hamming distances for $\sigma = 10$ and 20 because of their small values. Note that in Fig. 2 different colours represent different image samples and in Fig. 3 different colours represent different values for σ.

The following effects can be observed. In most of the experiments the interactive learning scheme found the same λ value as the Parametric Flow did (in the corresponding points of the plots in Fig. 2 solid line lies between dashed and dotted ones). In some seldom cases they do not correspond exactly (see e.g. $\lambda_{gen} = 2.75$ in Fig. 2(c)). However, the corresponding Hamming distances are almost equal (see the same λ value in Fig. 3) – i.e. different Potts parameters lead to the same recognition result. These effect becomes more distinctive with increasing of σ and λ_{gen}. Finally, there are "outliers" – experiments, in which the found λ interval (as well as the reached Hamming distance) has nothing in common with the true one. The presence of these cases can be explained by the very simple request strategy used in the experiments. Not surprisingly, such cases are observed much more often for big σ values. In these situations even

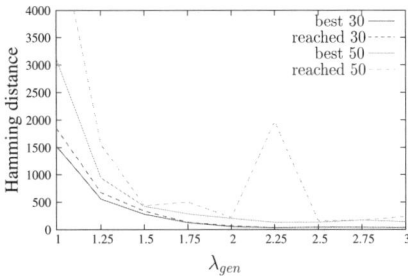

Fig. 3. Optimal Hamming distances H^* (solid lines) and reached Hamming distances (dashed lines) for artificially generated images with $\sigma = 30$ and $\sigma = 50$

the best possible Hamming distance is still very big, because the Gaussians for different segments heavily overlap. Consequently, there are many pixels, having the following property. The label which corresponds to the best possible segmentation and the label in the ground truth are different. If in an early stage of the algorithm such a pixel is proposed for evaluation, the best (according to the Hamming distance) labelling is removed from the set of feasible labellings, that leads to the wrong learning result.

An interesting effect can be observed especially for small σ-s. In these cases the data terms in (2) are very distinctive, i.e. they practically determine the labelling even for "wrong" λ values. Consequently, the found range of λ becomes larger. According to this, the length of the reached λ range can serve as a quality measure for the "goodness" of data terms in practice.

For the experiments on real images (see Fig. 4) we used the database [15] and segmentation results of the GrabCut [6] algorithm as ground truth. Furthermore we also used the data terms GrabCut had learnt during its segmentation for our q functions. The image in Fig. 4(b) shows the corresponding confidence values

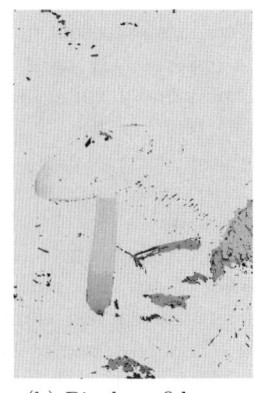

(a) Original image   (b) Pixel confidences   (c) Segmentation

Fig. 4. A real example

$|h_r(0)-h_r(1)|$ based on the initial minimizing labelling set S (scaled for visibility). In Fig. 4(c) the final segmentation is presented, which was obtained by our scheme after 11 RoboUser iterations. This example just demonstrates the applicability of our approach for real images as well.

5   Conclusions

In this work we presented a novel learning approach for the Energy Minimisation framework, which is based on incremental learning. We applied it to binary segmentation problem for interactive learning of the strength of Potts interactions between neighbouring pixels. The main differences from the known methods are the following:

- The method is able to learn prior parameters.
- The method produces a *range* of parameters, rather than a single one. It makes possible to combine the method with other ones, using it e.g. as an additional constraint.
- The interactions between the algorithm and the user is initiated by the algorithm, but not by the user. First of all it leads to the clear stopping criterion. Second, this situation is in a certain sense more user friendly, because often it is much more easier for the user to answer a simple question as to control the system – i.e. to decide, whether to accept the actual segmentation, which pixels to mark otherwise etc.

The presented work is the first trial at most. Consequently, there are many direction for further development. The most intriguing question is how to extend the approach to the case of more then one parameter. This problem is common for almost all learning schemes, mentioned in the paper (cross-validation, pure Parametric Flow, our approach etc.). Therefore, its reasonable (may be approximate) solution would essentially extend the capabilities of all approaches. Interestingly, in the case of incremental learning the task can be formulated in a slightly another way, because here it is not necessary in general to enumerate all feasible solutions – it is enough only to answer, whether the current parameter set is ambiguous, in order to initiate request to the user.

In the proposed interactive scheme we used a very simple request strategy – the user should fix label just in one pixel, this pixel is chosen by the system in a very simple manner. Of course, other strategies are possible as well, which formulate more elaborated requests. Obviously, they would lead to the reduction of the number of user interactions, demanding at the same time more elaborated user feedback. A related question is how to combine incremental learning with other interactive learning techniques, e.g. to learn strength λ and appearance characteristics q simultaneously.

Last but not least, a very interesting question is, how to adapt our scheme (as well as for example Parametric Flow) to the situation, that the task is not exactly solvable for a fixed parameter value.

References

1. Schlesinger, D., Flach, B.: A probabilistic segmentation scheme. In: Rigoll, G. (ed.) DAGM 2008. LNCS, vol. 5096, pp. 183–192. Springer, Heidelberg (2008)
2. Woodford, O.J., Rother, C., Kolmogorov, V.: A global perspective on map inference for low-level vision. In: IEEE International Conference on Computer Vision (ICCV) (October 2009)
3. Peng, B., Veksler, O.: Parameter selection for graph cut based image segmentation. In: British Machine Vision Conference (BMVC) (September 2008)
4. Gallo, G., Grigoriadis, M.D., Tarjan, R.E.: A fast parametric maximum flow algorithm and applications. SIAM J. Comput. 18(1), 30–55 (1989)
5. Kolmogorov, V., Boykov, Y., Rother, C.: Applications of parametric maxflow in computer vision. In: IEEE 11th International Conference on Computer Vision, ICCV 2007, pp. 1–8 (October 2007)
6. Rother, C., Kolmogorov, V., Blake, A.: "grabcut": interactive foreground extraction using iterated graph cuts. ACM Trans. Graph. 23(3), 309–314 (2004)
7. Boykov, Y.Y., Jolly, M.P.: Interactive graph cuts for optimal boundary and region segmentation of objects in n-d images (2001)
8. Blake, A., Rother, C., Brown, M., Pérez, P., Torr, P.H.S.: Interactive image segmentation using an adaptive gmmrf model. In: Pajdla, T., Matas, J(G.) (eds.) ECCV 2004, Part I. LNCS, vol. 3021, pp. 428–441. Springer, Heidelberg (2004)
9. Boykov, Y., Olga Veksler, R.Z.: Efficient approximate energy minimization via graph cuts. IEEE transactions on PAMI 20, 1222–1239 (2001)
10. Kolmogorov, V., Zabin, R.: What energy functions can be minimized via graph cuts? IEEE Transactions on Pattern Analysis and Machine Intelligence 26(2), 147–159 (2004)
11. Boykov, Y., Kolmogorov, V.: An experimental comparison of min-cut/max- flow algorithms for energy minimization in vision. IEEE Transactions on Pattern Analysis and Machine Intelligence 26(9), 1124–1137 (2004)
12. Schlesinger, M.I., Hlaváč, V.: Ten lectures on statistical and structural pattern recognition. Computational Imaging and Vision, vol. 24. Kluwer Academic Publishers, Dordrecht (2002)
13. Franc, V., Savchynskyy, B.: Discriminative learning of max-sum classifiers. Journal of Machine Learning Research 9, 67–104 (2008)
14. Nickisch, H., Kohli, P., Rother, C.: Learning an interactive segmentation system (December 2009), http://arxiv.org/abs/0912.2492
15. Martin, D., Fowlkes, C., Tal, D., Malik, J.: A database of human segmented natural images and its application to evaluating segmentation algorithms and measuring ecological statistics. In: Proc. 8th Int'l. Conf. Computer Vision, vol. 2, pp. 416–423 (July 2001)

A Model-Based Approach to the Segmentation of Nasal Cavity and Paranasal Sinus Boundaries

Carsten Last[1], Simon Winkelbach[1], Friedrich M. Wahl[1],
Klaus W.G. Eichhorn[2], and Friedrich Bootz[2]

[1] Institut fuer Robotik und Prozessinformatik, TU Braunschweig,
Muehlenpfordtstr. 23, 38106 Braunschweig, Germany
{c.last,s.winkelbach,f.wahl}@tu-bs.de
[2] Klinik und Poliklinik fuer HNO-Heilkunde/Chirurgie, Universitaetsklinikum Bonn,
Sigmund-Freud-Str. 25, 53105 Bonn, Germany
{klaus.eichhorn,friedrich.bootz}@ukb.uni-bonn.de

Abstract. We present a model-driven approach to the segmentation of nasal cavity and paranasal sinus boundaries. Based on computed tomography data of a patients head, our approach aims to extract the border that separates the structures of interest from the rest of the head. This three-dimensional region information is useful in many clinical applications, e.g. diagnosis, surgical simulation, surgical planning and robot assisted surgery. The desired boundary can be made up of bone, mucosa or air what makes the segmentation process very difficult and brings traditional segmentation approaches, like e.g. region growing, to their limits. Motivated by the work of Tsai *et al.* [1] and Leventon *et al.* [2], we therefore show how a parametric level-set model can be generated from hand-segmented nasal cavity and paranasal sinus data that gives us the ability to transform the complex segmentation problem into a finite-dimensional one. On this basis, we propose a processing chain for the automated segmentation of the endonasal structures that incorporates the model information and operates without any user interaction. Promising results are obtained by evaluating our approach on two-dimensional data slices of 50 patients with very diverse paranasal sinuses.

1 Introduction and Related Work

Three-dimensional model data of nasal cavity and paranasal sinuses is useful in many clinical applications. It can be used for e.g. diagnosis of sinus pathologies, simulation of endonasal surgeries, surgical planning and robot assisted surgery. In the last few years, *Functional Endoscopic Sinus Surgery* (FESS) has been established as the state of the art technique for the treatment of endonasal pathologies. One important disadvantage of this approach is that the surgeon has to keep the endoscope in his one hand during the whole surgery and consequently has only one hand left for the other surgical instruments. *Robot Assisted FESS* (RAFESS) may help to overcome this problem by passing the tedious job of endoscope guidance to a robot [3].

M. Goesele et al. (Eds.): DAGM 2010, LNCS 6376, pp. 333–342, 2010.

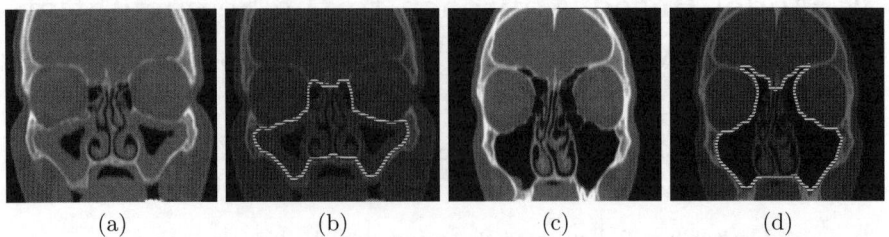

(a)   (b)   (c)   (d)

Fig. 1. Example slices in coronal view from two different CT datasets, showing (a,c) the great inter-patient variability and (b,d) the overlaid desired segmentation boundaries

To exactly define the workspace of the robot, the three-dimensional model data is needed. In order to quickly generate such a model from computed tomography (CT) data, segmentation of the structures of interest is unavoidable. Manual segmentation takes about 900 minutes [4] what is infeasible for daily surgical workflow. Consequently, automatic segmentation approaches are required. From our knowledge, no fully-automatic approach to the segmentation of paranasal sinuses exists so far. This is because of the anatomical complexity and the high inter-patient variability of the endonasal structures (see Fig. 1).

In 2004, Apelt *et al.* [5] published a semi-automatic framework for segmentation of the paranasal sinus boundaries. In each second to tenth slice of the CT dataset, the user has to define a *Volume of Interest* (VOI) around every object that should be segmented. Afterwards, an interactive watershed transform is applied inside the user-defined regions. They reported segmentation times of about 1 hour for a complete segmentation of the paranasal sinuses what is still not feasible for daily surgical workflow. Thereby, most time is spent for the manual selection of the different VOIs.

To further speed up the segmentation process, Salah *et al.* [6] proposed another semi-automatic approach based on 3D region-growing with an intensity threshold criterion that does not require per-slice user-interaction. Nevertheless, post-processing is required because the region-growing approach usually leaks into unwanted parts. They reported segmentation times of about five to ten minutes. However, it seems that they concentrated on segmenting the air-filled parts of the paranasal sinuses. As reported in [5] and [7], even more user action is required when the goal is to segment the outer border of the paranasal sinuses, including the mucosa, which is especially necessary in case of pathological sinuses like modified mucosa or sinusitis.

In summary, it is apparent that the segmentation of the paranasal sinuses is a complicated task. Even medical experts interpret CT data in different ways [8]. For a non-expert it is practically impossible to produce a correct segmentation because high anatomical knowledge is required to identify the boundaries of the paranasal sinuses. Due to this, we believe that a fully-automatic segmentation is only possible with approaches that include model information of the endonasal structures into the segmentation process.

A first attempt in this direction was made by Cootes *et al.* [9] by introducing the *Active Shape Models*. They manually labeled a set of training shapes and built a point distribution model by applying *Principal Component Analysis* (PCA) on the covariance matrix of vectors describing the training shapes. Following this idea, Leventon *et al.* [2] published an approach for incorporating model information into the evolution process of geodesic active contours [10]. They enhanced the shape model of [9] by representing a set of training shapes through their signed distance functions and computing the inter-shape variation by performing PCA on the covariance matrix of these signed distance functions. This helped to overcome the problem of manual labeling the training shapes. The resulting distribution was used to guide the curve evolution to more-likely solutions that are in correspondence with the prior shape model. Other approaches that tried to incorporate model information into the level-set segmentation approach were published by e.g. Chen *et al.* [11], Cremers *et al.* [12], Bresson *et al.* [13] and Rousson *et al.* [14]. The large amount of publications shows the importance of model-based segmentation in medical-imaging.

In 2003, Tsai *et al.* [1] tried an approach different from the curve evolution framework. They adopted the implicit representation of [2] and extended it by calculating the model-parameters to minimize the region-based Mumford-Shah functional [15] directly in the subspace spanned by the training shapes. This reduced the optimization problem to a finite-dimensional one and showed great potential in 2D as well as 3D medical-image segmentation. They evaluated their approach by segmenting the left ventricle in two-dimensional and the prostate in three-dimensional image data.

Inspired by this attempt, our contribution in this work is to transfer the approach of [1] to the segmentation of the nasal cavity and paranasal sinuses. According to [5], our goal is to segment the outer paranasal sinus boundaries because these are the critical structures in RAFESS.

2   Data-Based Shape Model

Training Data. To construct our deformable model, we build up on a database of hand-segmented CT datasets [7] in which the nasal cavity and paranasal sinuses are separated from the other anatomical structures inside the head (as depicted in Fig. 1(b,d)). Using five anatomical landmarks (right styloid process, left styloid process, crista galli, anterior nasal spine and posterior nasal spine), a similarity transformation is computed that scales the datasets to equal size and aligns them with regard to rotation and translation (see e.g. [16] for a detailed description). Afterwards, a corresponding slice is extracted from each aligned dataset which is used for further processing. Up to now, we concentrated on segmenting the nasal structures from a single two-dimensional slice of each complete CT dataset only. Nevertheless, the following approach can be easily applied to three-dimensional data as well.

Model Representation. From the training data described in section 2, we obtain a set $\{C_1, C_2, ..., C_n\}$ of closed shapes, one for each of the n CT datasets.

Every single shape describes the outer border of the endonasal structures for the chosen CT data. In conformity with [2] and [1], we use an Eulerian level-set representation, as introduced by Osher and Sethian [17], to describe the shapes: Each paranasal boundary $C_i \subset \Omega$, with $\Omega \subset \mathbb{N}^d$ representing the CT data domain, is defined as the zero level-set of a higher-dimensional function $\Phi_i : \Omega \to \mathbb{R}$ so that

$$C_i = \{\boldsymbol{x} \mid \Phi_i(\boldsymbol{x}) = 0\} \ . \tag{1}$$

These level-set functions Φ_i are given by signed distance transforms [18] yielding

$$\Phi_i(\boldsymbol{x}) = \mathrm{sign}(\boldsymbol{x}) \min_{\boldsymbol{u} \in C_i} \|\boldsymbol{x} - \boldsymbol{u}\| \ . \tag{2}$$

In (2), $\mathrm{sign}(\boldsymbol{x})$ takes the value -1 if the point $\boldsymbol{x}$ lies inside the closed shape C_i and $+1$ otherwise. The mean level-set function Φ_{mean} is calculated by averaging over all training shapes. The result is subtracted from all of the signed-distance functions $\{\Phi_1, \Phi_2, ..., \Phi_n\}$ to obtain a new set of zero-mean functions $\{\bar{\Phi}_1, \bar{\Phi}_2, \ldots, \bar{\Phi}_n\}$ with

$$\bar{\Phi}_i(\boldsymbol{x}) = \Phi_i(\boldsymbol{x}) - \Phi_{\mathrm{mean}}(\boldsymbol{x}) \ . \tag{3}$$

Each of these functions $\bar{\Phi}_i$ contains information about the offset of the corresponding training shape from the mean signed-distance function Φ_{mean}.

To better identify the variances in shape, a PCA is performed on the set of zero-mean functions. Therefore, each function $\bar{\Phi}_i$ is rearranged as a row-vector to form the $(n \times |\Omega|)$-dimensional shape-variability matrix S. The $n-1$ nonzero eigenvalues and eigenvectors of the covariance matrix $\frac{1}{n-1}SS^T$ are computed using *Singular Value Decomposition*. For further usage, the eigenvectors must be arranged back in the d-dimensional space Ω to obtain the $n-1$ eigenshapes $\{\tilde{\Phi}_1, \tilde{\Phi}_2, \ldots, \tilde{\Phi}_{n-1}\}$. They agree with the (orthogonal) principal modes of shape variation and the eigenvalues $\{\sigma_1^2, \ldots, \sigma_{n-1}^2\}$ represent the variance of data on each of these main axes.

The level-set function $\Phi_{\boldsymbol{w}}$ of our deformable shape model is finally obtained by combining the mean level-set function Φ_{mean} with linear combinations of the $m \leq (n-1)$ eigenshapes $\tilde{\Phi}_i$ that have most influence on shape variation. So, we get

$$\Phi_{\boldsymbol{w}}(\boldsymbol{x}) = \Phi_{\mathrm{mean}}(\boldsymbol{x}) + \sum_{i=1}^{m} w_i \tilde{\Phi}_i(\boldsymbol{x}) \tag{4}$$

with $\boldsymbol{w} = (w_1, w_2, \ldots, w_m)^T$ being a vector of weighting factors for the incorporated eigenshapes. The corresponding segmentation shape is then given as

$$C = \{\boldsymbol{x} \mid \Phi_{\boldsymbol{w}}(\boldsymbol{x}) = 0\} \ . \tag{5}$$

3   Contour Extraction

Problem Definition. Given any CT data I that is rigidly aligned with the average shape model, we want to find the outer nasal cavity and paranasal sinus border. With the help of our deformable shape model Φ_w, defined in eq. (4), the goal is to find a vector w of weighting parameters that minimizes a given objective function on the data I with regard to the segmentation shape C defined in eq. (5).

In contrast to [1], we do not try to minimize the region-based Chan-Vese energy functional [15] on the whole data domain Ω. This is because the assumption made in [15], that the CT data consists of two regions of approximately constant intensities, does not hold for our segmentation problem. As clearly visible in Fig. 1(b,d), the region inside the desired segmentation shape consists of bone, mucosa and air with the corresponding intensities being completely different from one another. Also the approach proposed in [1], to transform the data into a bimodal set by calculating the magnitude of the gradient, is not applicable. There exist large intensity changes not only on the desired segmentation shape but also inside and outside the segmented region.

Instead, we follow the lead by [2] and try to minimize a gradient-based objective function along our segmentation shape C. This choice was made because the desired segmentation border is mostly located in areas that contain high gradient values. As explained in detail in section 3, we use the objective function

$$O_w = -\frac{\oint_C (G_\sigma * E)(x)\, dx}{\oint_C 1\, dx} \tag{6}$$

where G_σ defines a Gaussian smoothing kernel with variance σ^2 and E is an intensity-weighted gradient volume. For the energy defined in eq. (6), only the properties on the current shape are of interest so that high gradient values in other regions do not effect the result.

Processing chain. Our processing chain for extracting the outer border of nasal cavity and paranasal sinuses is depicted in Fig. 2.

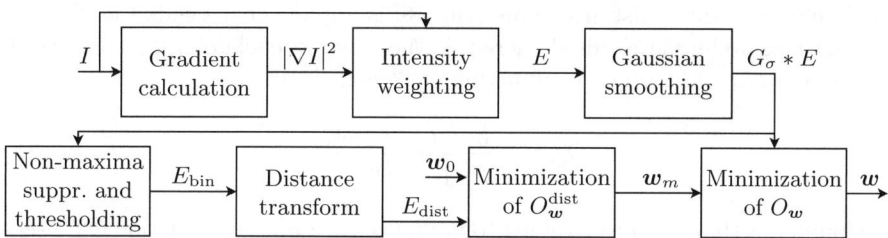

Fig. 2. Processing chain of our presented approach to the segmentation of nasal cavity and paranasal sinuses: Based on the given CT data I and the initial weights $w_0 = (\sigma_1^2, \ldots, \sigma_{n-1}^2)^T$, the final weights w of our deformable model Φ_w are estimated

At first, we take the given CT data I and approximate the squared magnitude of the gradient $|\nabla I|^2$ by using central differences. To suppress edges in dark regions and emphasize the ones in regions being more likely to contain the desired boundary, we calculate the intensity-weighted gradient volume E with

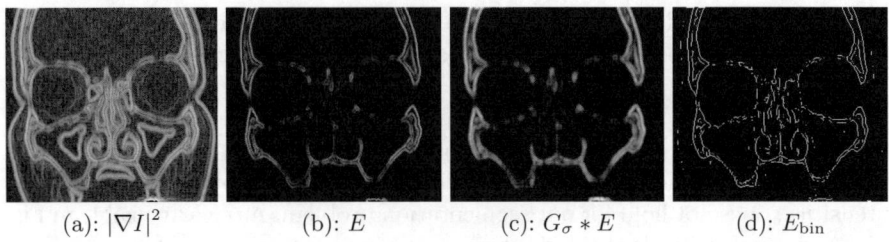

(a): $|\nabla I|^2$ (b): E (c): $G_\sigma * E$ (d): E_{bin}

Fig. 3. Intermediate steps of our approach applied to the CT data in Fig. 1(a)

$$E(\boldsymbol{x}) = |\nabla I(\boldsymbol{x})|^2 \cdot \frac{1}{\sqrt{2\pi}\sigma_e} \exp\left(-\frac{1}{2}\left(\frac{I(\boldsymbol{x}) - \mu_e}{\sigma_e}\right)^2\right) . \tag{7}$$

This volume is subsequently smoothed with a Gaussian convolution kernel G_σ so that we arrive at our objective function $O_{\boldsymbol{w}}$ defined in eq. (6). Besides noise reduction, the reason for the smoothing step is to get a smoother objective function so that our segmentation shape is not so likely to get trapped in local minima.

Now that we have specified our objective function, we can use the well established Nelder-Mead simplex method [19] for minimization of $O_{\boldsymbol{w}}$. However, informal tests showed that $O_{\boldsymbol{w}}$ tends to be very sensitive to the initial values of the weights $\boldsymbol{w}$. To circumvent this drawback, we introduce an intermediate step to define good start values for $\boldsymbol{w}$ by minimizing a second objective function $O_{\boldsymbol{w}}^{\text{dist}}$ that contains a distance transform of the smoothed gradient volume $G_\sigma * E$. By this means, $O_{\boldsymbol{w}}^{\text{dist}}$ has a wider capture range than $O_{\boldsymbol{w}}$ but is not as accurate.

For the calculation of the distance volume E_{dist}, we take the smoothed gradient volume $G_\sigma * E$ from eq. (6) and perform non-maxima suppression followed by thresholding with threshold t to generate a binary edge volume E_{bin}. On this binary volume a distance transform [18] is applied that yields the distance volume E_{dist}. The metric used therein is the squared euclidean distance. With the help of E_{dist}, the objective function $O_{\boldsymbol{w}}^{\text{dist}}$ is defined as

$$O_{\boldsymbol{w}}^{\text{dist}} = \frac{\oint_C E_{dist}(\boldsymbol{x}) \, d\boldsymbol{x}}{\oint_C 1 \, d\boldsymbol{x}} . \tag{8}$$

We found out that it is more robust to minimize the objective function $O_{\boldsymbol{w}}^{\text{dist}}$ separately on each of the m principal axes used in our shape model (eq. (4)) to get sufficient initial values for the final optimization of $O_{\boldsymbol{w}}$. So, the task is to solve m one-dimensional optimization problems. Employing again the simplex method, we begin optimizing the weight w_1 to get its optimal value w_1^{opt}. Based on the initial weights $\boldsymbol{w}_0 = (\sigma_1^2, \ldots, \sigma_{n-1}^2)^T$, the resulting vector $\boldsymbol{w}_1$, after optimization of w_1, differs only in σ_1^2 being replaced by w_1^{opt} giving $\boldsymbol{w}_1 = (w_1^{\text{opt}}, \sigma_2^2, \ldots, \sigma_{n-1}^2)^T$. Continuing from the vector $\boldsymbol{w}_1$, we then optimize w_2 to obtain the vector $\boldsymbol{w}_2 = (w_1^{\text{opt}}, w_1^{\text{opt}}, \sigma_3^2, \ldots, \sigma_{n-1}^2)^T$. This procedure is kept on for all m dimensions of our shape model so that the final output after separate minimization in all dimensions is represented by the vector $\boldsymbol{w}_m = (w_1^{\text{opt}}, \ldots, w_m^{\text{opt}})^T$. This vector can be used as a good initial value for the optimization of the energy function $O_{\boldsymbol{w}}$ defined in eq. (6). In contrast to optimizing $O_{\boldsymbol{w}}^{\text{dist}}$, the optimization of $O_{\boldsymbol{w}}$ is treated as one m-dimensional problem in the subspace spanned by the principal shapes so that potential mutual dependencies are also considered.

4   Evaluation

Experimental Setup. To evaluate our contribution, we use a leave-one-out approach. From our 50 hand-segmented datasets, we incorporate $n = 49$ datasets in the generation of our model (as explained in section 2). The remaining CT data is used to compare the result of our approach with the hand-segmentation. Leaving out each dataset in turn, we thereby get an automatic segmentation result for each dataset. Please note that each deformable model is based solely on the data of the remaining datasets and not on the CT data being currently evaluated.

As already mentioned in section 2, we evaluate our approach in $d = 2$ dimensions. Each slice I has a resolution of 512×366 pixels and a pixel spacing of $0.46\,\text{mm}$. In our deformable shape model, we use the $m = 10$ most influent eigenshapes. The gradient data $|\nabla I|^2$ is weighted by a Gaussian distribution with $\mu_e = 650$ and $\sigma_e = 250$. It is subsequently smoothed by means of a Gaussian kernel with zero mean and $\sigma = 1$. Thresholding is performed with $t = 0.35$.

We calculate two error measures to evaluate the accuracy of our approach. The first one is the maximal root mean squared (euclidean) distance e_{rms} between our resulting shape C_{res} and the reference shape C_{ref}. It is defined as

$$e_{\text{rms}} = \sqrt{\max\left\{\frac{\oint_{C_{\text{res}}} \inf_{\boldsymbol{y} \in C_{\text{ref}}} \|\boldsymbol{x} - \boldsymbol{y}\|^2 \, d\boldsymbol{x}}{\oint_{C_{\text{res}}} 1 \, d\boldsymbol{x}}, \frac{\oint_{C_{\text{ref}}} \inf_{\boldsymbol{x} \in C_{\text{res}}} \|\boldsymbol{x} - \boldsymbol{y}\|^2 \, d\boldsymbol{y}}{\oint_{C_{\text{ref}}} 1 \, d\boldsymbol{y}}\right\}} . \quad (9)$$

Second, we use the Hausdorff distance e_{h} that measures the maximal absolute (euclidean) distance between our resulting shape and the reference shape:

$$e_{\text{h}} = \max\left\{\sup_{\boldsymbol{x} \in C_{\text{res}}} \inf_{\boldsymbol{y} \in C_{\text{ref}}} \|\boldsymbol{x} - \boldsymbol{y}\|, \sup_{\boldsymbol{y} \in C_{\text{ref}}} \inf_{\boldsymbol{x} \in C_{\text{res}}} \|\boldsymbol{x} - \boldsymbol{y}\|\right\} . \quad (10)$$

Experimental Results. The outcomes of both error measures are depicted in Fig. 4. Using unoptimized Matlab code, the calculation takes about 40 seconds for each dataset. The average root mean squared distance $\bar{e}_{\text{rms}}$ for all 50 datasets is $3.74\,\text{mm}$ with a standard deviation of $2.42\,\text{mm}$. There are only 5 datasets which exceed a distance of $6\,\text{mm}$. These datasets all have in common that the frontal sinuses are very distinctive (compare Fig. 5(i-l)). The average Hausdorff distance $\bar{e}_{\text{h}}$ is $12.39\,\text{mm}$ with a standard deviation of $7.66\,\text{mm}$. The maximum peaks are also due to distinctive frontal sinuses so that they occur for the same datasets as those in the mean squared distance (e.g. $40.83\,\text{mm}$ for dataset 21).

340   C. Last et al.

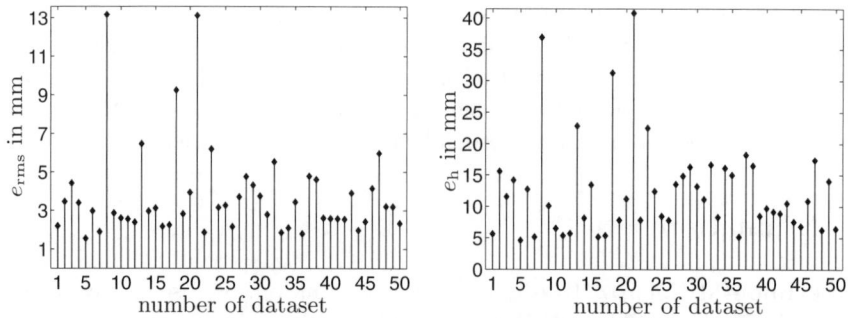

Fig. 4. Results of the error measures (eq. (9) and (10)) plotted against each dataset

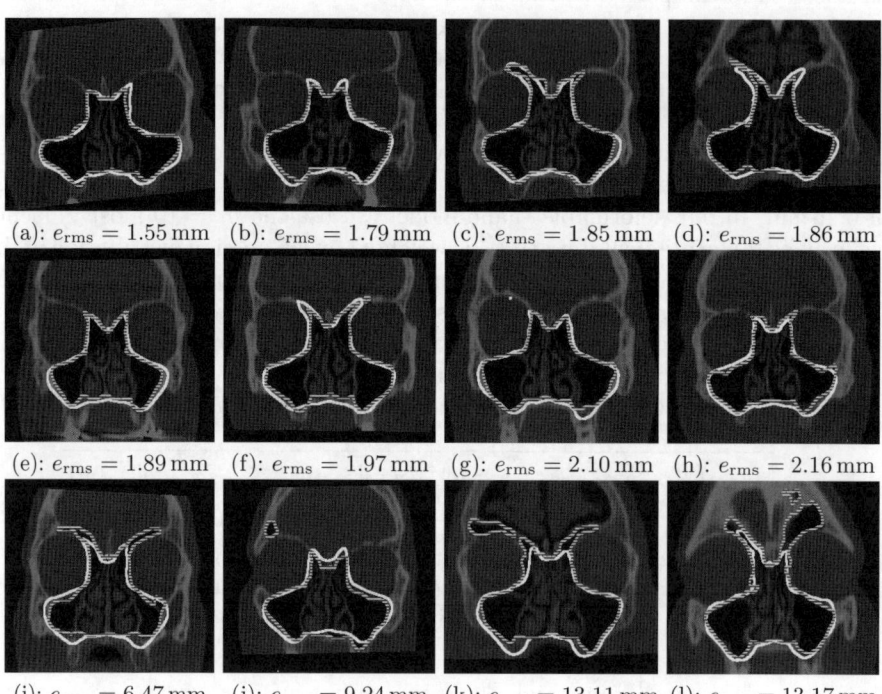

(a): $e_{rms} = 1.55$ mm (b): $e_{rms} = 1.79$ mm (c): $e_{rms} = 1.85$ mm (d): $e_{rms} = 1.86$ mm

(e): $e_{rms} = 1.89$ mm (f): $e_{rms} = 1.97$ mm (g): $e_{rms} = 2.10$ mm (h): $e_{rms} = 2.16$ mm

(i): $e_{rms} = 6.47$ mm (j): $e_{rms} = 9.24$ mm (k): $e_{rms} = 13.11$ mm (l): $e_{rms} = 13.17$ mm

Fig. 5. Chosen CT slices, showing the segmentation result C_{res} (solid line) and the hand-segmented reference C_{ref} (dashed line). They depict in descending order the eight best results (a - h) and the four worst results (i - l) according to the outcomes of e_{rms}.

In Fig. 5(a-h) the eight best segmentation results, according to the outcomes of e_{rms}, are depicted and in Fig. 5(i-l) the four worst segmentation results are depicted, respectively. It can be clearly seen that the overall shape of the nasal cavity, ethmoidal cells and maxillary sinuses is well approximated in all these datasets. However, it is also visible that our approach comes to its limits when the task is to adapt to local deviations that are not represented in our global shape model. This is especially the case for the frontal sinuses in Fig. 5(i-l). Each closer adaptation would implicitly force the model to depart from the remaining para-nasal boundaries because of the strong coupling of the various paranasal sinuses in our proposed model. Nevertheless, the results obtained from our model-based approach represent a very good initial solution that, in most cases, can easily be adapted to the desired paranasal boundaries with a traditional level-set approach like the one presented in [10].

5   Conclusion and Future Work

We have presented a model-driven approach to the segmentation of the outer nasal cavity and paranasal sinus boundaries. Based on a set of hand-segmented training data, we built up a deformable model that can be used for finding the structures of interest. The key contribution was the integration of this deformable model into a processing chain for the automated segmentation of the complex endonasal structures.

Although showing already great performance in the segmentation of the over-all shape of nasal cavity, ethmoidal cells and maxillary sinuses, our model is cur-rently not able to properly capture individual differences of the various datasets (e.g. diverse frontal sinuses). This is because the optimization is performed in a global manner. We are currently trying to extend our model so that the weighting parameters can be optimized separately for local data regions.

We think that this can give us great performance improvements because of the possibility to focus on the mutual variations of the individual datasets. Ap-proaches that try to identify local attributes in the parameter space of the de-formable model, like the ones presented by Blanz and Vetter [20] and Hasler *et al.* [21], could be the key to the solution of this problem.

References

1. Tsai, A., Yezzi Jr., A., Wells, W., Tempany, C., Tucker, D., Fan, A., Grimson, W., Willsky, A.: A shape-based approach to the segmentation of medical imagery using level sets. IEEE Transactions on Medical Imaging 22(2), 137–154 (2003)
2. Leventon, M., Grimson, W., Faugeras, O.: Statistical shape influence in geodesic active contours. In: Proc. of IEEE Conference on Computer Vision and Pattern Recognition, pp. 316–323 (2000)
3. Rilk, M., Wahl, F., Eichhorn, K., Wagner, I., Bootz, F.: Path planning for robot-guided endoscopes in deformable environments. In: Kröger, T., Wahl, F. (eds.) Advances in Robotics Research, pp. 263–274. Springer, Heidelberg (2009)
4. Tingelhoff, K., Moral, A., Kunkel, M., Rilk, M., Wagner, I., Eichhorn, K., Wahl, F., Bootz, F.: Comparison between manual and semi-automatic segmentation of nasal cavity and paranasal sinuses from ct images. In: Proc. of 29th Annual International Conference of the IEEE EMBS, pp. 5505–5508 (2007)
5. Apelt, D., Preim, B., Hahn, H., Strauß, G.: Bildanalyse und Visualisierung für die Planung von Nasennebenhöhlen-Operationen. In: Tolxdorff, T., Braun, J., Handels, H., Horsch, A., Meinzer, H.P. (eds.) Bildverarbeitung für die Medizin 2004, pp. 194–198. Springer, Heidelberg (2004)

6. Salah, Z., Bartz, D., Dammann, F., Schwaderer, E., Maassen, M., Straßer, W.: A fast and accurate approach for the segmentation of the paranasal sinus. In: Meinzer, H.P., Handels, H., Horsch, A., Tolxdorff, T. (eds.) Bildverarbeitung für die Medizin 2005, pp. 93–97. Springer, Heidelberg (2005)
7. Pirner, S., Tingelhoff, K., Wagner, I., Westphal, R., Rilk, M., Wahl, F., Bootz, F., Eichhorn, K.: CT-based manual segmentation and evaluation of paranasal sinuses. European Archives of Oto-Rhino-Laryngology 266(4), 507–518 (2009)
8. Tingelhoff, K., Eichhorn, K., Wagner, I., Kunkel, M., Moral, A., Rilk, M., Wahl, F., Bootz, F.: Analysis of manual segmentation in paranasal ct images. European Archives of Oto-Rhino-Laryngology 265(9), 1061–1070 (2008)
9. Cootes, T., Taylor, C., Cooper, D., Graham, J.: Active shape models - their training and application. Computer Vision and Image Understanding 61(1), 38–59 (1995)
10. Caselles, V., Kimmel, R., Sapiro, G.: Geodesic active contours. International Journal of Computer Vision 22(1), 61–79 (1997)
11. Chen, Y., Thiruvenkadam, S., Huang, F., Wilson, D., Geiser, E.: On the incorporation of shape priors into geometric active contours. In: Proc. of IEEE Workshop on Variational and Level Set Methods, pp. 145–152 (2001)
12. Cremers, D., Tischhäuser, F., Weickert, J., Schnörr, C.: Diffusion snakes: Introducing statistical shape knowledge into the mumford-shah functional. International Journal of Computer Vision 50(3), 295–313 (2002)
13. Bresson, X., Vandergheynst, P., Thiran, J.: A priori information in image segmentation: Energy functional based on shape statistical model and image information. In: Proc. of IEEE International Conference on Image Processing, pp. 428–431 (2003)
14. Rousson, M., Paragios, N., Deriche, R.: Implicit active shape models for 3d segmentation in mr imaging. In: Barillot, C., Haynor, D.R., Hellier, P. (eds.) MICCAI 2004. LNCS, vol. 3216, pp. 209–216. Springer, Heidelberg (2004)
15. Chan, T., Vese, L.: Active contours without edges. IEEE Transactions on Image Processing 10(2), 266–277 (2001)
16. Dhawan, A.: Medical Image Analysis. Wiley-IEEE Press (2003)
17. Osher, S., Sethian, J.: Fronts propagating with curvature-dependent speed: Algorithms based on hamilton-jacobi formulations. Journal of Computational Physics 79(1), 12–49 (1988)
18. Breu, H., Gil, J., Kirkpatrick, D., Werman, M.: Linear time euclidean distance transform algorithms. IEEE Transactions on Pattern Analysis and Machine Intelligence 17(5), 529–533 (1995)
19. Lagarias, J., Reeds, J., Wright, M., Wright, P.: Convergence properties of the nelder–mead simplex method in low dimensions. SIAM Journal on Optimization 9(1), 112–147 (1998)
20. Blanz, V., Vetter, T.: A morphable model for the synthesis of 3d faces. In: Proc. of 26th ACM International Conference on Computer Graphics and Interactive Techniques, pp. 187–194 (1999)
21. Hasler, N., Stoll, C., Sunkel, M., Rosenhahn, B., Seidel, H.P.: A statistical model of human pose and body shape. Computer Graphics Forum (Proceedings of Eurographics 2009) 28(2), 337–346 (2009)

Wavelet-Based Inpainting for Object Removal from Image Series

Sebastian Vetter, Marcin Grzegorzek, and Dietrich Paulus

Active Vision Group
Institute for Computational Visualistics
University of Koblenz-Landau
Universitätsstr. 1, 56070 Koblenz, Germany

Abstract. We propose several algorithmic extensions to inpainting that have been proposed to the spatial domain by other authors and apply them to an inpainting technique in the wavelet domain. We also introduce a new merging stage. We show how these techniques can be used to remove large objects in complex outdoor scenes automatically. We evaluate our approach quantitatively against the aforementioned inpainting methods and show that our extensions measurably increase the inpainting quality.

1 Introduction

The digital nature of most images that are used today, make it fairly easy to alter the image content using image processing tools. The removal of entire objects from images, however, is a very complicated task that usually requires the expertise of professionals to achieve sufficient results in the altered image. It is, therefore, an even greater challenge to automate this process such that the results are perceived as un-altered.

Our need for inpainting came from a project that required removal of objects, a colour checker in particular, from a series of highly structured images. Fig. 1 shows an example from the test set. In an initial processing step, the colour checker is located in the image and a binary mask is generated identifying the pixels belonging to this object. It is then removed using image inpainting.

We propose a modified approach for image inpainting based on an approach described by Ignácio et al. [1] using wavelet coefficients to determine the order in which the unknown region is filled. Their idea is adapted from Criminisi et al. [2] where the authors apply the same technique in the spatial domain. Our approach defines extensions to improve the wavelet-based inpainting approach by Ignácio et al. [1]. These extensions are similar to those proposed by Cheng et al. [3] to improve [2].

We outline related work in section 2, briefly introduce the idea of the wavelet-based inpainting approaches in section 3, describe our extensions to Ignácio et al. [1] in section 4 and provide the corresponding experimental results in section 5. We conclude in section 6.

M. Goesele et al. (Eds.): DAGM 2010, LNCS 6376, pp. 343–352, 2010.

Fig. 1. Images from our test set showing the original (left) and the inpainted image using our approach with the colour checker removed (right)

Fig. 2. Some original scenes used in the test

2   Related Work

The removal of objects from still images has been the subject of many research projects. Initially, approaches only had to deal with missing data in the size of a few pixels. These damages could be repaired by using well-known interpolation techniques which are incorporated into almost any image processing application available.

Reconstructing larger regions of missing data, as they occur when removing objects from images is much more difficult. This task usually requires the expertise of professionals to provide a sufficient quality of results. Even more difficult is the development of automated algorithms that allow inpainting of such regions. Approaches in this field have slowly emerged from two fields of research, namely *texture synthesis* and *structure inpainting*. Research concerned with texture synthesis expects a small texture sample and tries to create a much larger texture image automatically. In contrast, structure inpainting initially focusses on the removal of small damages by reproducing intensities based on neighbouring pixels.

A popular attempt has been described by Harrison [4] who removes an object using exemplar-based texture synthesis, sampling from a given texture to fill the unknown intensities. This is closely related to the ideas of Garber and Sawchuk [5] as well as Efros and Leung [6] who proposed algorithms to create new intensity values by sampling their best-matching neighbouring pixels. Wei and Levoy [7] extended the latter approach by combining a texture- and example-based technique working through different levels of coarseness in a pyramid scheme to circumvent the size restrictions of sample pixels that apply to [6].

Structure inpainting, in contrast, looks at the problem of filling in missing data from an artistic point of view. As part of their work, Bertalmio et al. [8] consolidated inpainting artists to examine their method of operation restoring a painting; they tried to replicate manual inpainting by propagating the known intensities into the unknown region along so called *isophotes*, representing the smallest spatial change of intensities, i.e. structure. The authors continued working on that problem and discovered that "different techniques work better for different parts" [9] and started to develop a new approach based on the decomposition of an image into two parts. One part represents the structure, the other part the texture of the damaged image and structure inpainting and texture synthesis are applied to the separated components. In a similar approach, Drori et al. [10] used adaptive circular fragments operating on different scales capturing both, global and local structures and approximating the missing region.

Criminisi et al. [2] proposed an approach employing rectangular patches that are iteratively filled depending on calculated priorities along the boundary of known and unknown region. Due to its intuitive principle, it was applied not only to object removal but also to remove rifts in puzzles of archaeological fragments as described in Sagiroglu and Ercil [11]. Cheng et al. [3] extended the priority equation of Criminisi et al. [2] and made it adjustable to the structural and textural characteristics specific to an individual image.

The simplicity of the concept in Criminisi et al [2] was taken up by Ignácio et al. [1] who applied it in the wavelet domain. They transform the image and binary mask and then use wavelet coefficients to determining the fill-order guided by a similarly defined priority.

3   Wavelet-Based Image Inpainting

Applying the approaches [2,3,1] to our images revealed that they all struggle with images of highly structured content such as buildings, pavements, etc. The extension described by Cheng et al. [3], however, shows an improvement compared to [2]. Further experiments revealed that results produced by [1] are of similar quality to those obtained by [3]. An example is shown in Fig. 3.

We observed that the results for [2] and [1] are largely dependent on the content of each individual image which is described Cheng et al. [3] as the ratio of structural and textural content. Their proposed extension to [2] incorporates these observations and provides an adjustable algorithm for inpainting images. In accordance with their observations, we decided to develop a similar extension to [1] to make it adjustable while exploiting its high-frequency coefficients. They provide the edge-related information suitable for correctly inpainting structures in highly complex images.

We expect an input image I and a binary mask specifying the object to be removed resulting in a region of unknown intensities Ω. Samples to fill Ω are

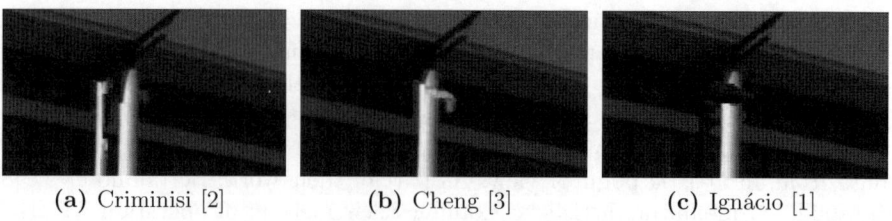

(a) Criminisi [2]   (b) Cheng [3]   (c) Ignácio [1]

Fig. 3. The images show the improvement achieved by Cheng et al. [3] towards the approach by Criminisi et al. [2] and Ignácio et al. [1].

taken from Φ holding $I = \Omega \cup \Phi$. The filling algorithm operates on small image regions called *patches* where a patch is defined as a set of pixel locations $\Psi(\boldsymbol{p})$ centred at location $\boldsymbol{p}$. Each patch has a square size of $M \times M$ pixels.

In accordance to [1], we transform both, input image and binary mask, into the wavelet domain using a *Haar* wavelet and apply an iterative process of three consecutive steps in the wavelet domain: *determine the fill-order (A), find the best match (B)* and *fill the search patch (C)*.

In step (A) we calculate a priority value for each patch $\Psi(\boldsymbol{p})$ that is centred on the boundary $\delta\Omega_W$ between the target region Ω_W and source region Φ_W in the transformed image. This is called the *fill-order*. In step (B) we use the search patch $\Psi(\hat{\boldsymbol{p}})$ with the highest priority and search for the most similar sample patch $\Psi(\hat{\boldsymbol{q}})$ in Φ_W providing the coefficients unknown in $\Psi(\hat{\boldsymbol{p}})$. In step (C) we fill $\Psi(\hat{\boldsymbol{p}})$ by simply copying the corresponding coefficients from $\Psi(\hat{\boldsymbol{q}})$.

After the entire target region Ω_W is filled with sampled coefficients we transform the result back into the spatial domain and obtain an image where Ω has been reconstructed by sampling from Φ.

4   Modified Wavelet Inpainting

In accordance to the original approach, the key concept of our approach remains its fill-order. The priority value determining the fill-order of Ω_W is calculated for each search patch $\Psi(\boldsymbol{p})$ centred on $\delta\Omega_W$. Ignácio et al. [1] define the priority value $P(\boldsymbol{p})$ as

$$P(\boldsymbol{p}) = K(\boldsymbol{p})\, S_S(\boldsymbol{p})\, S_O(\boldsymbol{p}) \quad , \tag{1}$$

where $K(\boldsymbol{p})$ denotes the confidence, $S_S(\boldsymbol{p})$ the structure significance, and $S_O(\boldsymbol{p})$ is the structure orientation at the pixel location $\boldsymbol{p}$.

The last two terms correspond to those named *edge strength* and *edge orientation* in [1]. We refrain from using these terms because the high frequencies in the wavelet domain are different from edge strength and edge orientation in the spatial domain as used in [2].

As in [1], we use the concept of a fill-order determined by priorities calculated for each search patch $\Psi(\boldsymbol{p})$ centred on $\delta\Omega_W$. We, however, introduce several modifications to the priority equations based on modifications to [2] proposed in [3]. We observed that corresponding modifications to equation 1 resulted in

Criminisi [2]   Ignácio [1]   Additive method   Mixed method   Blending

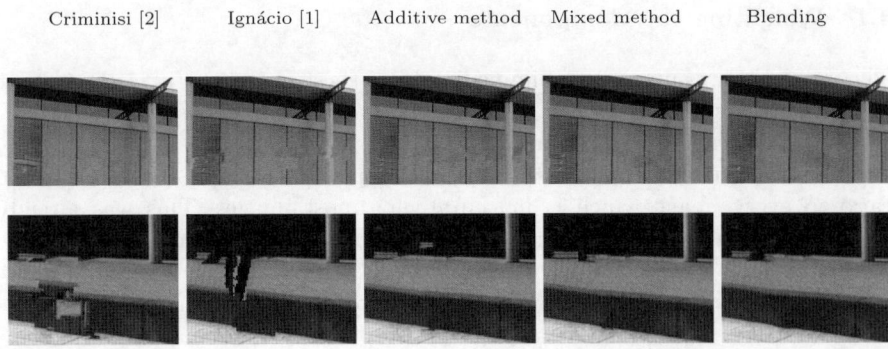

Fig. 4. Excerpts showing the inpainting results generated by [2] and [1] compared to our modifications. Each of our modifications show an increase in quality. Added blending produces the best results.

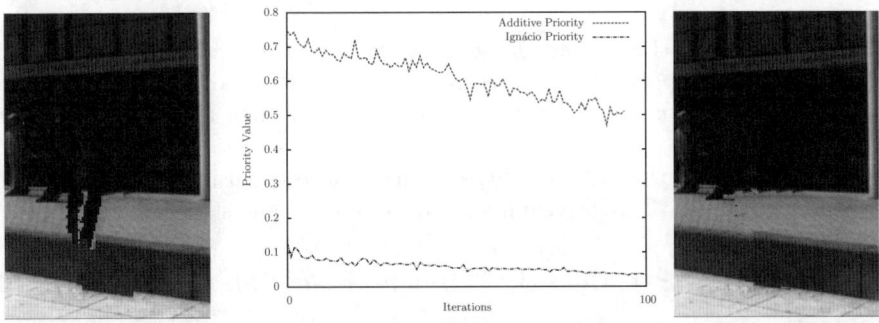

Fig. 5. The plot shows that priorities calculated using (2) vary more then priorities used in [1] which reduces the influence of noise and outliers. The difference in results is illustrated for Ignácio [1] (left) and our Additive approach (right)

higher inpainting quality and, as a side effect, allowed adjusting the fill-order to the relative occurrence of structure and texture in an image. This allows us to counterbalance the high impact of $K(\boldsymbol{p})$ on $P(\boldsymbol{p})$ in [1] which resulted in a fill-order mainly driven by high reliability instead of structural properties, reducing the inpainting quality as shown in Fig. 4 where $K(\boldsymbol{p})$ outweighs the structural components and mainly inpaints the textures.

To evade this negative influence of $K(\boldsymbol{p})$, we propose to change the equation for $P(\boldsymbol{p})$ used in [1] to equation (2). This modification corresponds to the proposal of Cheng et al. in [3] to modify the priority equation in [2]. Fig. 5 illustrates the increase in variation of priorities. This makes the equation more resilient to noise and outliers in either component. We apply the same strategy to reduce the impact of the other components on $P(\boldsymbol{p})$. This leaves us with a modified equation for the priority obtained by adding the respective components. We define it as

$$P(\boldsymbol{p}) = K(\boldsymbol{p}) + S_S(\boldsymbol{p}) + S_O(\boldsymbol{p}) \qquad (2)$$

4.1 Weighting the Components

The inpainting results respond immediately to these changes. Fig. 4 shows that inpainting the same image using the *Additive* approach increases the continuation of isophotes and reduces artefacts.

This modified equation, as the original, applies the same structure-texture ratio to every image which is inaccurate for most images. This was already observed in [3] and inspired our next modification making equation (2) adjustable to the different characteristics of images.

We introduce the concept of adapting equation (2) by introducing two weighting parameters ω_S and ω_C to adjust the proportional dominance of the components. We name ω_S the *structure weight* and use it to control the relative importance of structure orientation and significance resulting in a weighted structure value $S(\boldsymbol{p})$ defined as

$$S(\boldsymbol{p}) = (1 - \omega_S)\, S_O(\boldsymbol{p}) \;+\; \omega_S\, S_S(\boldsymbol{p}) \tag{3}$$

with $0 \leq \omega_S \leq 1$. Increasing ω_S stresses the structure significance S_S which resembles the strength of isophotes in a patch $\Psi(\boldsymbol{p})$. Reducing it boosts the orientation-related characteristic of isophotes disregarding their possible difference in significance.

We then weight the obtained $S(\boldsymbol{p})$ against the $K(\boldsymbol{p})$ using weight ω_C. This parameter controls the relative influence of confidence and structure components on the priority:

$$P_A(\boldsymbol{p}) = (1 - \omega_C)\, K(\boldsymbol{p}) \;+\; \omega_C\, S(\boldsymbol{p}) \tag{4}$$

where $S(\boldsymbol{p})$ is the weighted structure value in equation 3 and ω_C holds $0 \leq \omega_C \leq 1$. In case the settings hold $\omega_S = \omega_C = 0.5$, the calculated priority corresponds to an unweighted Additive priority using a separate normalisation. Altering the fill-order by using a higher ω_C results in a dominance of the structural component where inpainting is mainly isophote-driven.

4.2 Reducing Adjustable Parameters

Experiments with this extension showed that finding suitable parameters ω_S and ω_C for equation (4) can be difficult and time consuming. This motivated the reduction to a single weight ω_C combining the structure orientation and significance into a single component making ω_S obsolete. We call this new priority value *mixed priority* and define it as

$$P_M(\boldsymbol{p}) = (1 - \omega_C)K(\boldsymbol{p}) \;+\; \omega_C\, (S_O(\boldsymbol{p}) \cdot S_S(\boldsymbol{p})) \tag{5}$$

with $0 \leq \omega_C \leq 1$. Fig. 4 shows that results produced by *Mixed* priorities approach are similar to those produced using the Additive priorities. The most important isophotes are continued correctly and the remaining artefacts are very similar with the improvement of one parameter less.

4.3   Alpha Blending

So far we modified the fill-order by making it adjustable to image properties. Several visible artefacts remain: displaced isophotes, patch-shaped artefacts caused by adjoining textures and repetitive patterns in the background texture. To reduce these artefacts we intervene in the step of filling $\Psi(\hat{p})$ at the end of each iteration and introduce a blending of coefficients into the filling process.

Manual inpainting tools in image processing applications, e.g. the *healing brush*, use a blending mask for the brush to provide a smooth transition between added intensities and the background. We adapted this concept and added a blending method to the filling of $\Psi(\hat{p})$.

We use coefficients from $\Psi(\hat{q})$ to fill $\Psi(\hat{p})$ by copying corresponding values to Ω_W equivalent to [1]. Source coefficients in $\Psi(\hat{q})$ however are now blended with corresponding coefficients from $\Psi(\hat{p})$. We consider each pixel in the source region of $\Psi(\hat{p})$ in the blending process weighting it against its corresponding coefficient in $\Psi(\hat{q})$.

Let r_i be a pixel in $\Psi(\hat{p})$ holding $r_i \in \Phi_W \cap \Psi(\hat{p})$ and its correspondence $s_i \in \Psi(\hat{q})$. The new coefficient r_i is calculated by weighting the current coefficient r_i with the one corresponding to s_i. The weight is

$$\omega_G = \frac{1}{2\pi\sigma^2} \, \exp\left(-\frac{d_x^2 + d_y^2}{2\sigma^2} \right) \tag{6}$$

where d_x and d_y denote the distance of s_i to its patch centre in horizontal and vertical direction respectively. The weight ω_G is determined by a Gaussian distribution weighting each pair of coefficients. The blending is carried out accordingly for each subband which is defined as

$$W_n(\hat{r}_i) = (1 - \omega_G) \cdot W_n(r_i) \, + \, \omega_G \cdot W_n(s_i) \tag{7}$$

where $n = a, v, h, d$ correspond to the four wavelet subbands. ω_G holds $0 \leq \omega_G \leq 1$ to ensure that it does not exceed 1, hence, retaining its original energy.

5   Experiments

We applied these modifications to our campus images (Fig. 2) and examined the inpainting results. As the example in Fig. 4 shows, our first modification proposing two parameters to adjust the fill-order to the image-specific properties performs much better then the original approach which introduces visible artefacts. Our adjustable approach adapts to the characteristics of the image and increases perceived quality.

As an alternative, we proposed the *Mixed* approach in section 4.2 reducing the complexity of finding the correct set of parameters producing results equivalent

BibFront   ColourChecker

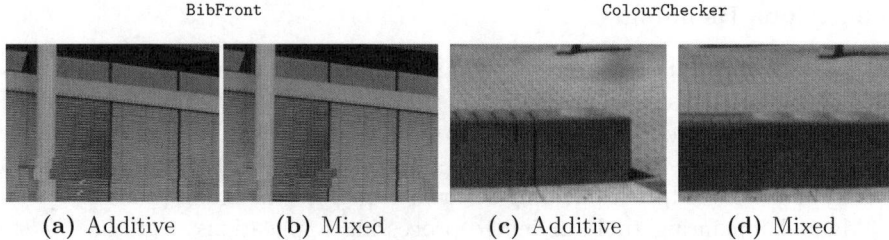

(a) Additive   (b) Mixed   (c) Additive   (d) Mixed

Fig. 6. Samples inpainted with the Mixed approach, shown in (b) and (d), yield better results compared to the Additive modifications, shown in (a) and (c)

to those of the Additive approach. Fig. 6 illustrates this with slight improvements using the Mixed approach.

We also introduced a blended filling process at the end of each iteration. The results in Fig. 4 show that using our blended approach reduces the amount of artefacts introduced by patches, improves the fill-order and smooths the transition of different textures.

Hence, the most reliable modification providing the best quality of results is the Mixed approach extended by our blending method. Its reduced parametric complexity with similar or even improved results, compared to the other approaches, makes it the favoured combination of our extensions. Table 1 shows that our extensions provide improved results compare to Ignácio et al. [1] and Criminisi et al. [2] and provides similar to better results when compared to Cheng et al. [3]. In addition, these result show that our extension provides a more consistent quality for all images whereas they can vary extensibly for the other approaches.

Table 1. PSNR for selected images from the series inpainted with [2], [3], [1] and our modifications

Image	PSNR (dB)					
	Criminisi [2]	Cheng [3]	Ignácio [1]	Additive	Mixed	Blended
Entrance	44.62	49.17	46.45	46.73	46.67	47.37
G_Entrance_Top	44.61	48.72	47.45	47.34	46.79	48.11
Drain	44.26	44.52	43.89	44.15	43.97	44.52
LibFront_HorizLong	40.93	39.82	39.99	39.53	40.30	41.60
Shutter	31.23	40.55	40.25	42.28	42.56	42.74
Gravel	35.30	34.74	35.50	35.85	35.85	36.32
Menseria	42.55	43.76	41.91	42.39	42.56	43.04
Menseria_Top	36.48	28.90	33.60	35.61	35.97	36.80
Obelisk	29.66	29.38	33.74	34.01	34.03	34.17
CampusWater	31.889	37.05	35.06	34.61	34.88	36.31

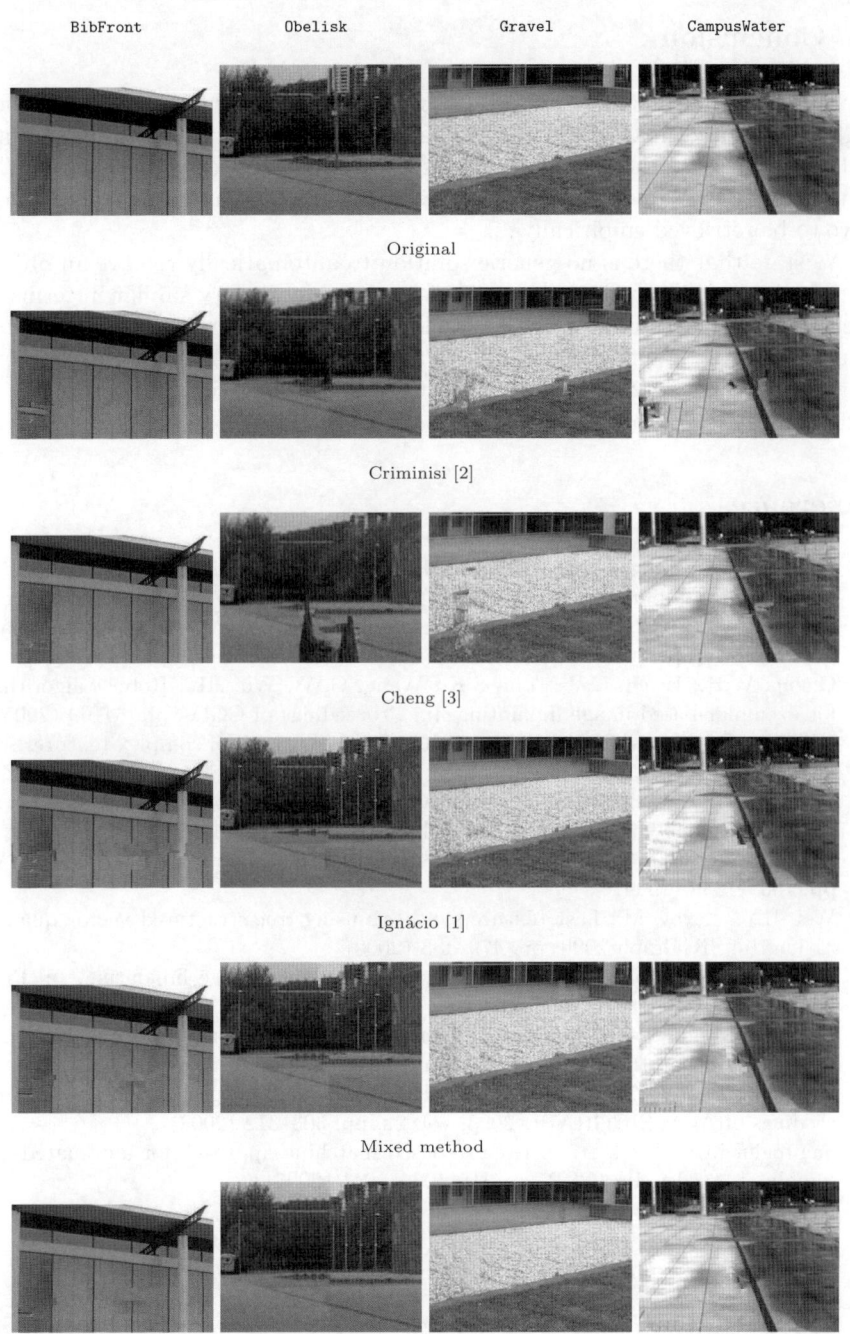

Fig. 7. Excerpts showing the inpainting results generated by [2] and [1] compared to our modifications. Each of our modifications show an increase in quality. Added blending produces the best results.

6   Conclusion

We conclude that our Mixed approach with blended filling increases quality for highly structured images. We achieved a higher stability with an improved fill-order and increase the inpainting quality adjusting the weight in equation (5) to the characteristics of each image individually. The optimal weights, however, have to be retrieved empirically.

We state that there is no generic solution to automatically remove an object from an image. Although the content of our images are very similar in terms of their texture-structure ratio, the remaining differences still require an adjustable solution to provide sufficient results. An approach proposing an automated solution, therefore, depends on the identification and classification of different image properties for an automated adjustment of the described parameters.

References

1. Ignacio, U.A., Jung, C.R.: Block-based image inpainting in the wavelet domain. The Visual Computer 23(9-11) (2007)
2. Criminisi, A., Perez, P., Toyama, K.: Region filling and object removal by exemplar-based image inpainting. IEEE Transactions on Image Processing 13(9) (2004)
3. Cheng, W.H., Hsieh, C.W., Lin, S.K., Wang, C.W., Wu, J.L.: Robust algorithm for exemplar-based image inpainting. In: Proceedings of CGIV, pp. 64–69 (2005)
4. Harrison, P.: A non-hierarchical procedure for re-synthesis of complex textures. In: WSCG, pp. 190–197 (2001)
5. Garber, D.D., Sawchuk, A.A.: Computational models for texture analysis and synthesis. In: Image Understanding Workshop, pp. 69–88 (1981)
6. Efros, A.A., Leung, T.K.: Texture synthesis by non-parametric sampling. In: ICCV, pp. 1033–1038 (1999)
7. Wei, L.Y., Levoy, M.: Fast texture synthesis using tree-structured vector quantization. In: SIGGraph 2000, pp. 479–488 (2000)
8. Bertalmio, M., Sapiro, G., Caselles, V., Ballester, C.: Image inpainting. In: Proceedings of SIGGRAPH (2000)
9. Bertalmio, M., Vese, L., Sapiro, G., Osher, S.: Simultaneous structure and texture image inpainting. IEEE Transactions on Image Processing 12, 882–889 (2003)
10. Drori, I., Cohen-Or, D., Yeshurum, H.: Fragment-based image completion. In: Proceedings of ACM SIGGRAPH 2003, vol. 22, pp. 303–312 (2003)
11. Sagiroglu, M.S., Ercil, A.: A texture based matching approach for automated assembly of puzzles. In: ICPR, pp. III: 1036–1041 (2006)

An Empirical Comparison of Inference Algorithms for Graphical Models with Higher Order Factors Using OpenGM

Björn Andres, Jörg H. Kappes, Ullrich Köthe,
Christoph Schnörr, and Fred A. Hamprecht

HCI, IWR, University of Heidelberg

Abstract. Graphical models with higher order factors are an important tool for pattern recognition that has recently attracted considerable attention. Inference based on such models is challenging both from the view point of software design and optimization theory. In this article, we use the new C++ template library OpenGM to empirically compare inference algorithms on a set of synthetic and real-world graphical models with higher order factors that are used in computer vision. While inference algorithms have been studied intensively for graphical models with second order factors, an empirical comparison for higher order models has so far been missing. This article presents a first set of experiments that intends to fill this gap.

1 Introduction and Related Work

Graphical models have been used very successfully in pattern analysis, usually as probabilistic models in which the graph expresses conditional independence relations on a set of random variables [1,2]. Graphical models are not restricted to probabilistic modeling and have also been used more generally to represent the factorization of arbitrary multivariate functions (w.r.t. a given operation) into factors that depend on subsets of all variables [3]. Factor graphs [3,4] are a common way of representing this factorization. In this article, we focus on functions which depend on discrete variables that can attain only finitely many values.

The optimization of such functions is important to perform MAP estimation (inference) under the assumption of a probabilistic model as well as to find configurations with minimal energy in non-probabilistic models. In several special cases the optimization problem can be solved in polynomial time (in the number of variables), in particular if the graphical model is acyclic [1] or if the energy function is (permutation) submodular [5,6,7]. However, if the model does not belong to either of these classes, exact optimization is NP-hard in the general [6].

For several years, research efforts focused mainly on functions which decompose into factors that depend on at most two variables. However, in order to model more complex problems, higher order factors have recently become an active field of research [8,9,10,11]. While second order factors are conceptually simple, higher order factors are challenging from the view point of optimization theory and implementation.

M. Goesele et al. (Eds.): DAGM 2010, LNCS 6376, pp. 353–362, 2010.

At least two types of algorithms exist : *message passing algorithms* (e.g. Loopy Belief Propagation (LBP) [1,12,13] and Tree-Reweighted Belief Propagation (TRBP) [14,15]) and *search-based algorithms* (e.g. A* search [16], Iterated Conditional Modes (ICM) [17], and a generalization if ICM called the Lazy Flipper [18]). While message passing algorithms implicitly approximate the objective function, search-based algorithms either restrict the search space or else have a runtime that is in the worst case exponentially large in the number of variables. All these algorithms output upper bounds on the global minimum (when used for minimization). TRBP in addition affords a lower bound on the global minimum.

For the sake of comparability, it is essential that these different algorithms are used with the same underlying data structures. While data structures for factors that depend only on binary variables are simple, consisting mostly of low-level functions close to machine code, similar data structures which allow the variables to have different domains are non-trivial and require unavoidable overhead. To quantify the effect from using different data structures on the absolute runtime of a particular algorithm, the same algorithm needs to be run with different underlying data structures.

We developed the extendible C++ template library OpenGM for this comparison. OpenGM allows the programmer to use different inference algorithms and different factor data structures interchangeably. While the experiments in this article are restricted to graphical models with discrete variables (binary and non-binary), OpenGM is general enough to also work with parameterized factors that depend on continuous variables. In contrast to Infer.NET [19] which has been published without source code under a fairly restrictive licence and libDAI [20] which is open source and published under a General Public Licence that forces the user to publish derived code under the same licence (so-called copyleft terms), the OpenGM source code will be published under the MIT licence that imposes almost no restrictions and does not contain copyleft terms.

We show in this article that the examined algorithms perform very differently, depending on the structure of the graphical model, both in terms of the upper bound on the global minimum as well as in terms of absolute runtime. Moreover, we show that the absolute runtime crucially depends on the data structures that are used to represent factors. In contrast to the Middleburry MRF Benchmark [21] and the quantitative comparison in [22], our comparison includes graphical models with higher order factors, different topologies, and different variable domains.

2   Optimization Problem and Algorithms

The models considered in this article are given in factor graph notation. A factor graph $G = (V, F, E)$ is a bipartite graph that consists of three sets: a set of variable nodes V, a set of factor nodes F, and a set of edges $E \subseteq V \times F$ that connect variables to factors. For each factor node, $\mathrm{ne}(f) := \{a \in V : (a, f) \in E\}$ denotes the set of all variable nodes that are connected to the factor.

With each variable node $a \in V$, a variable $x_a \in \mathcal{X}_a$ is associated. For a set of variable nodes $A \subseteq V$, $\mathcal{X}_A = \bigotimes_{a \in A} \mathcal{X}_a$ denotes the Cartesian product of the respective variable domains. Corresponding sequences of variables are written as $x_A = (x_a)_{a \in A}$. Moreover, with each factor node $f \in F$, a function $\varphi_f : \mathcal{X}_{\mathrm{ne}(f)} \to \mathbb{R}$ is associated. Together with some commutative and associative operation (addition throughout this article), the factor graph describes a function over $\mathcal{X} := \mathcal{X}_V$:

$$J(x) = \sum_{f \in F} \varphi_f(x_{\mathrm{ne}(f)}) \ . \tag{1}$$

We will consider the following discrete optimization problem:

$$x^* = \arg\min_{x \in \mathcal{X}} \sum_{f \in F} \varphi_f(x_{\mathrm{ne}(f)}) \tag{2}$$

where, for all $a \in V$, $\mathcal{X}_a = \{1, \ldots, L\}$.

Five algorithms to tackle this problem are compared in this article, the message passing algorithms LBP and TRBP as well as the search-based algorithm A* search, ICM, and the Lazy Flipper.

Motivated by Pearl's Belief Propagation algorithm [1] which is exact for tree structured models, LBP [12,13] is one of the toady's standard methods. It applies the message passing rules for acyclic graphs to graphs with cycles, without providing any convergence guarantees. Even if this method is rather heuristic, it shows quite good performance in real-world applications.

The more mathematically sound message passing algorithm TRBP was presented by Wainwright [14] who considers a convex relaxation of the problem by a tree-decomposition. The resulting message passing algorithm can be seen as a fixed point iteration on this convex outer relaxation. In subsequent work [15], Kolmogorov proposed a sequential version (TRW-S) which is guaranteed to converge to fix-points satisfying the so-called week tree agreement.

Very recently, several methods [16,23] have been suggested which solve discrete minimization problems in computer vision by branch and bound search. We implemented the methods presented in [16] which transform the optimization problem (2) into a shortest path problem on a graph whose size is exponential in the size of the graphical model. The shortest path problem is then solved by A* search using a tree-based approximation of the original graph to approximate the further cost while searching. This algorithm is guaranteed to converge to global optima and performs well on some classes of models. However, the worst-case runtime is exponential in the number of variables.

ICM [17] is a simple algorithm that keeps all variables except one fixed in each step and adjusts the free variable such that the objective function is minimized. The variables are visited repeatedly in a certain order until no alteration of a single variable can further reduce the value of the objective function.

The Lazy Flipper [18] is a generalization of ICM for models with binary variables. It extends the ICM search to subsets that contain more than one variable. The Lazy Flipper is more efficient than exhaustive search (by an amount that can be exponential in the number of variables) because the search space is restricted to a set of variables which are connected via factors in the graphical model and which have not been visited in previous iterations. The maximum size of subsets can be supplied as a parameter to the algorithm. When set to infinity, the Lazy Flipper is guaranteed to converge to a global optimum. Its runtime is exponential in the worst case.

3   Empirical Comparison of Inference Algorithms

For a comparison of the algorithms, we consider both synthetic and real-world graphical models with discrete variables that appear in computer vision applications. Synthetic models have the advantage that several instances of the same model can be generated which allows us to decide whether differences in performance and runtime are significant.

3.1   Synthetic Models

We characterize models by their *graph structure*, the *number of variables*, the *number of values each variable can attain*, the *order of factors*, and the *distribution of factor values*. For simplicity, we let the number of values be equal for all variables and let each model contain only factors of the orders 1 and M. Two different graph structures are considered, each with two different orders:

1. Fully connected models with second and third order factors, respectively, consisting of 8 variables each of which can attain 20 different values. These models are often used in part based object detection [16].
2. Grid graph models with first order factors as well as second and fourth order factors, respectively, which are frequently used in image segmentation. A grid with 40 times 40 (1600) variables is used, each variable attaining 2 and 5 different values, respectively. For the grid-based models, the additional parameter $\lambda \in [0,1]$ controls the coupling strength between first and higher order factors according to

$$J(x) \;=\; (1-\lambda) \sum_{f\in F, |\mathrm{ne}(f)|=1} \varphi_f(x_{\mathrm{ne}(f)}) \;+\; \lambda \sum_{f\in F, |\mathrm{ne}(f)|>1} \varphi_f(x_{\mathrm{ne}(f)}) \qquad (3)$$

The four different graph structures for the synthetic models are depicted in Fig. 3.1 for a small number of variables. The factors of all models are sampled independently, an assumption which may not hold in real data. Two different types of factors are considered: The values of *uniform factors* are sampled uniformly from the interval $[0,1]$. For *log-uniform factors*, values v are sampled uniformly from the interval $(0,1]$, and the values of factors set to $-\log(v)$. This results in very selective factors which in this form often appear within part based models [16,23]. For each model, an ensemble of 10 instances is generated.

3.2   Real-World Models

In addition, we consider 100 graphical models obtained from the 100 natural test images in the Berkeley Segmentation Dataset [24] that are used to remove

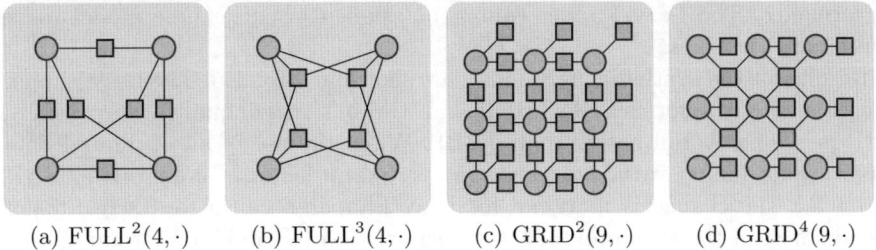

(a) FULL^2(4, ·)   (b) FULL^3(4, ·)   (c) GRID^2(9, ·)   (d) GRID^4(9, ·)

Fig. 1. Graph structures of the synthetic models with less variables

excessive boundaries from image over-segmentations. These real-world models have on average 8800 binary variables, 5700 third order and 100 fourth order factors. Each variable corresponds to a boundary between segments, indicating whether this boundary is to be removed (0) or preserved (1). Unary factors relate these variables to the image content while non-submodular third and fourth order factors connect adjacent boundaries, supporting the closedness and smooth continuation of preserved boundaries.

3.3   Results

In the tables below, the mean upper bounds $\mathbb{E}(J)$ on the minimum energy and the mean runtimes $\mathbb{E}(t)$ (in seconds) over these ensembles are shown. Runtimes are measured on one core of an Intel Pentium Dual Core at 2.00 GHz. In addition, we note in the tables how often each algorithm outputs the smallest upper bound on the minimum energy among the compared algorithms. When algorithms use a data structure that is specialized for binary variables, this is marked with a 2 at the end of the algorithm name.

Results for the fully connected synthetic models are shown in Tab. 1. While A* search guarantees global optimality, LBP, TRBP, and ICM show inferior

Table 1. Results for fully connected models with 8 variables and 20 labels: On the 2nd order model FULL^2(8, 20) A* search outperforms LBP and TRBP in terms of energy and runtime. LBP sometimes also ends up in a global optimum for 2nd order models. On the 3rd order model FULL^3(8, 20), A* search still calculates the global optima, contrary to all other algorithms

| | 2nd order | | | | | | 3rd order | | | | | |
| | uniform | | | log | | | uniform | | | log | | |
	$\mathbb{E}\{J\}$	$\mathbb{E}\{t\}$	best	$\mathbb{E}\{J\}$	$\mathbb{E}\{t\}$	best	$\mathbb{E}\{J\}$	$\mathbb{E}\{t\}$	best	$\mathbb{E}\{J\}$	$\mathbb{E}\{t\}$	best
LBP	8.21	0.88	40%	12.70	1.06	20%	24.14	197.69	0%	51.69	197.38	0%
TRBP	10.19	1.54	0%	21.36	1.58	0%	25.55	99.00	0%	55.52	76.63	0%
ASTAR	4.82	0.82	**100%**	6.12	0.55	**100%**	14.19	20693	**100%**	20.05	16881	**100%**
ICM	10.37	0.00	0%	20.29	0.00	0%	22.58	0.00	0%	40.45	0.00	0%

performance. The Lazy Flipper cannot be applied because these models have non-binary variables.

Results for the synthetic grid models are shown in Tab. 2–5. The Lazy Flipper consistently outperforms LBP, TRBP, and ICM in terms of quality. Surprisingly, LBP performs overall better than TRBP. While the use of an optimized data structure for binary variables results in a speed-up factor of 2 for LBP, TRBP, and ICM, the change is marginal for Lazy Flipper because the Lazy Flipper spends most of the time on graph traversal, while LBP and TRBP sum up and minimize multi-dimensional factors during message passing and ICM mostly evaluates factors for certain assignments of values to the variables. It is hard to make any general claims on the runtime of LBP and TRBP since they do not convergence, and so the runtime usually depends linearly on the maximal number of iterations.

Table 2. Results for the binary second order grid model $\mathrm{GRID}^2(1600, 2)$ consisting of 40 times 40 variables. For smaller coupling strength $\lambda = 0.25$, LBP and TRBP perform comparable with the Lazy Flipper. For larger coupling strength, the Lazy Flipper consistently outperforms LBP and TRBP in comparable runtime.

| | uniform | | | | | |
| | $\lambda = 0.25$ | | | $\lambda = 0.75$ | | |
	$\mathbb{E}\{J\}$	$\mathbb{E}\{t\}$	best	$\mathbb{E}\{J\}$	$\mathbb{E}\{t\}$	best
LBP	754.76	7.30	**90%**	995.65	31.60	0%
TRBP	754.78	18.44	**80%**	995.62	39.65	0%
LF	754.76	10.36	**90%**	993.68	10.77	**100%**
ICM	790.51	2.67	0%	1303.53	2.77	0%
LBP2	754.76	3.40	**90%**	995.65	14.58	0%
TRBP2	754.78	8.24	**80%**	995.62	17.66	0%
LF2	754.76	10.00	**90%**	993.68	10.56	**100%**
ICM2	790.51	1.37	0%	1303.53	1.42	0%

| | log | | | | | |
| | $\lambda = 0.25$ | | | $\lambda = 0.75$ | | |
	$\mathbb{E}\{J\}$	$\mathbb{E}\{t\}$	best	$\mathbb{E}\{J\}$	$\mathbb{E}\{t\}$	best
LBP	1229.87	17.04	30%	1599.70	31.35	0%
TRBP	1229.89	23.58	20%	1594.76	39.74	0%
LF	1229.60	10.31	**90%**	1588.69	10.87	**100%**
ICM	1379.28	2.70	0%	2542.86	2.82	0%
LBP2	1229.87	7.90	30%	1599.70	14.48	0%
TRBP2	1229.89	10.47	20%	1594.76	17.54	0%
LF2	1229.60	10.03	**90%**	1588.69	10.61	**100%**
ICM2	1379.28	1.38	0%	2542.86	1.46	0%

Table 3. Results for the binary 4th order grid model $\mathrm{GRID}^4(1600, 2)$ consisting of 40 times 40 variables. Compared to the 2nd order model, the energy functions are much more challenging which results in a 17-times longer runtime for the Lazy Flipper. Similar to the 2nd order model, the Lazy Flipper outperforms LBP and TRBP, even for the weakly coupled models.

| | uniform | | | | | |
| | $\lambda = 0.25$ | | | $\lambda = 0.75$ | | |
	$\mathbb{E}\{J\}$	$\mathbb{E}\{t\}$	best	$\mathbb{E}\{J\}$	$\mathbb{E}\{t\}$	best
LBP	562.19	142.68	0%	497.22	142.90	0%
TRBP	570.41	161.19	0%	555.47	142.37	0%
LF	558.44	170.07	**100%**	449.93	222.45	**100%**
ICM	589.86	1.85	0%	700.53	1.85	0%
LBP2	562.19	64.55	0%	497.22	64.68	0%
TRBP2	570.41	71.60	0%	555.47	62.63	0%
LF2	558.44	167.28	**100%**	449.93	217.22	**100%**
ICM2	589.86	1.01	0%	700.53	1.03	0%

| | log | | | | | |
| | $\lambda = 0.25$ | | | $\lambda = 0.75$ | | |
	$\mathbb{E}\{J\}$	$\mathbb{E}\{t\}$	best	$\mathbb{E}\{J\}$	$\mathbb{E}\{t\}$	best
LBP	874.94	142.77	0%	786.36	142.00	0%
TRBP	891.07	161.69	0%	888.04	163.44	0%
LF	863.72	170.50	**100%**	683.87	238.41	**100%**
ICM	975.74	1.88	0%	1339.57	1.93	0%
LBP2	874.94	64.68	0%	786.36	64.08	0%
TRBP2	891.07	71.77	0%	888.04	71.98	0%
LF2	863.72	164.88	**100%**	683.87	231.82	**100%**
ICM2	975.74	1.01	0%	1339.57	1.05	0%

Table 4. Results for the 2nd order grid models with 5 labels, $\mathrm{GRID}^2(1600, 5)$. For this non-binary problem, we compare LBP, TRBP and ICM. For small coupling strength, LBP and TRBP perform comparable; LBP shows significantly better performance for larger coupling strength

| | uniform | | | | | | —log— | | | | | |
| | $\lambda = 0.25$ | | | $\lambda = 0.75$ | | | $\lambda = 0.25$ | | | $\lambda = 0.75$ | | |
	$\mathbb{E}\{J\}$	$\mathbb{E}\{t\}$	best	$\mathbb{E}\{J\}$	$\mathbb{E}\{t\}$	best	$\mathbb{E}\{J\}$	$\mathbb{E}\{t\}$	best	$\mathbb{E}\{J\}$	$\mathbb{E}\{t\}$	best
LBP	514.55	10.71	10%	706.35	10.75	**100%**	710.62	10.70	60%	1035.78	10.87	**100%**
TRBP	514.22	13.70	90%	772.77	13.71	0%	711.08	13.73	40%	1164.19	13.67	0%
ICM	591.13	8.27	0%	1235.02	8.30	0%	1024.98	8.22	0%	2426.99	8.58	0%

Table 5. Results for the 4th order grid models with 5 labels, $\text{GRID}^4(1600, 5)$. LBP outperforms TRBP when both run the same number of iterations.

	uniform					
	$\lambda = 0.25$			$\lambda = 0.75$		
	$\mathbb{E}\{J\}$	$\mathbb{E}\{t\}$	best	$\mathbb{E}\{J\}$	$\mathbb{E}\{t\}$	best
LBP	344.87	271.34	**100%**	354.92	271.24	**90%**
TRBP	414.42	284.81	0%	368.98	284.87	10%
ICM	390.75	5.96	0%	636.23	5.96	0%

	log					
	$\lambda = 0.25$			$\lambda = 0.75$		
	$\mathbb{E}\{J\}$	$\mathbb{E}\{t\}$	best	$\mathbb{E}\{J\}$	$\mathbb{E}\{t\}$	best
LBP	452.70	271.48	**100%**	467.57	271.61	**100%**
TRBP	547.41	285.03	0%	527.51	284.66	0%
ICM	622.89	5.98	0%	1226.44	6.06	0%

Table 6. Results for the irregular 4th order segmentation models with binary variables. The Lazy Flipper consistently outperforms LBP and ICM in terms of energy and runtime. Due to the irregularity, the construction of a meaningful set of spanning trees is non-trivial. TRBP is therefore not applied.

	$\mathbb{E}\{J\}$	$\mathbb{E}\{t\}$	best
LBP	1053.16	99.67	0%
LF	870.52	26.12	**100%**
ICM	2360.76	79.23	0%
LBP2	1053.16	48.51	0%
LF2	870.52	25.34	**100%**
ICM2	2360.76	55.48	0%

Results for the real-world segmentation models are shown in Tab. 6. The Lazy Flipper consistently outperforms LBP and ICM in terms of energy and runtime. Due to the irregularity of the model, the construction of a meaningful set of spanning trees is non-trivial. TRBP is therefore not applied.

We run 400 LBP and TRBP iterations on the fully connected models and on $\text{GRID}^2(1600, 2)$, 1000 iterations on $\text{GRID}^4(1600, 2)$, 300 iterations on the irregular segmentation models, and 100 iterations, otherwise, with a message damping of 0.3 for all models. Message passing is terminated when the maximal change in all messages is less than 10^{-6}. For the fully connected models, all spanning trees are considered for TRBP. For the grid graphs, we set the probability that a factor appears in a sub-tree to the reciprocal of its order. The heuristic for A* search is based on a fan-graph rooted in the last node. The Lazy Flipper is run with a maximal subgraph size of 6.

4   Conclusion

This article presents an empirical comparison of inference algorithms on graphical models with higher order factors. The experiments show that search-based algorithms such as A* search and the Lazy Flipper are powerful tools which can outperform message passing algorithms in these settings. While the set of experiments is far from being exhaustive, it demonstrates the flexibility and modularity of the OpenGM library, in particular the exchangeability of data structures and inference algorithms. More inference algorithms as well as specialized data structures can therefore be examined in the future.

Acknowledgement. This work is connected to the Heidelberg Research Training Group (GRK 1653) on Probabilistic Graphical Models (`http://graphmod.iwr.uni-heidelberg.de/`). Authors acknowledge corresponding support by the German Research Foundation (DFG).

References

1. Pearl, J.: Probabilistic reasoning in intelligent systems: networks of plausible inference. Morgan Kaufmann, San Francisco (1988)
2. Koller, D., Friedman, N.: Probabilistic Graphical Models. MIT Press, Cambridge (2009)
3. Aji, S., McEliece, R.: The generalized distributive law. IEEE Transactions on Information Theory 46(2), 325–343 (2000)
4. Kschischang, F., Member, S., Frey, B.J., Andrea Loeliger, H.: Factor graphs and the sum-product algorithm. IEEE Transactions on Information Theory 47, 498–519 (2001)
5. Boykov, Y., Veksler, O., Zabih, R.: Fast approximate energy minimization via graph cuts. IEEE TPAMI 23(11), 1222–1239 (2001)
6. Kolmogorov, V., Zabih, R.: What energy functions can be minimized via graph cuts? In: Heyden, A., Sparr, G., Nielsen, M., Johansen, P. (eds.) ECCV 2002. LNCS, vol. 2352, pp. 65–81. Springer, Heidelberg (2002)
7. Schlesinger, D.: Exact solution of permuted submodular minsum problems. In: Yuille, A.L., Zhu, S.-C., Cremers, D., Wang, Y. (eds.) EMMCVPR 2007. LNCS, vol. 4679, pp. 28–38. Springer, Heidelberg (2007)
8. Komodakis, N., Paragios, N.: Beyond Pairwise Energies: Efficient Optimization for Higher-order MRFs (June 2009)
9. Kohli, P., Kumar, M.P., Torr, P.H.: P3 & beyond: Move making algorithms for solving higher order functions. IEEE Transactions on Pattern Analysis and Machine Intelligence 31(9), 1645–1656 (2009)
10. Rother, C., Kohli, P., Feng, W., Jia, J.: Minimizing sparse higher order energy functions of discrete variables. In: CVPR, pp. 1382–1389 (2009)
11. Kohli, P., Ladický, L., Torr, P.H.: Robust higher order potentials for enforcing label consistency. Int. J. Comput. Vision 82(3), 302–324 (2009)
12. Murphy, K.P., Weiss, Y., Jordan, M.I.: Loopy belief propagation for approximate inference: An empirical study. In: Foo, N.Y. (ed.) AI 1999. LNCS, vol. 1747, pp. 467–475. Springer, Heidelberg (1999)

13. Weiss, Y., Freeman, W.T.: On the optimality of solutions of the max-product belief-propagation algorithm in arbitrary graphs. IEEE Transactions on Information Theory 47(2), 736–744 (2001)
14. Wainwright, M.J., Jordan, M.I.: Graphical Models, Exponential Families, and Variational Inference. Now Publishers Inc., Hanover (2008)
15. Kolmogorov, V.: Convergent tree-reweighted message passing for energy minimization. IEEE Trans. Patt. Anal. Mach. Intell. 28(10), 1568–1583 (2006)
16. Bergtholdt, M., Kappes, J., Schmidt, S., Schnörr, C.: A study of parts-based object class detection using complete graphs. Int. J. Comp. Vision 87(1-2), 93–117 (2010)
17. Besag, J.: On the statisical analysis of dirty pictures. Journal of the Royal Statistical Society B 48, 259–302 (1986)
18. Andres, B., Kappes, J.H., Koethe, U., Hamprecht, F.A.: The Lazy Flipper: A minimal exhaustive search algorithm for higher order graphical models (2010) (forthcoming)
19. Minka, T., Winn, J., Guiver, J., Kannan, A.: Infer.NET 2.3, Microsoft Research Cambridge (2009), http://research.microsoft.com/infernet
20. Mooij, J.M., et al.: libDAI 0.2.4: A free/open source C++ library for Discrete Approximate Inference (2010), http://www.libdai.org/
21. Szeliski, R., Zabih, R., Scharstein, D., Veksler, O., Kolmogorov, V., Agarwala, A., Tappen, M., Rother, C.: A comparative study of energy minimization methods for markov random fields with smoothness-based priors. IEEE Trans. Pattern Anal. Mach. Intell. 30(6), 1068–1080 (2008)
22. Kolmogorov, V., Rother, C.: Comparison of energy minimization algorithms for highly connected graphs. In: Leonardis, A., Bischof, H., Pinz, A. (eds.) ECCV 2006. LNCS, vol. 3952, pp. 1–15. Springer, Heidelberg (2006)
23. Tian, T.P., Sclaroff, S.: Fast Globally Optimal 2D Human Detection with Loopy Graph Models. In: CVPR (2010)
24. Martin, D., Fowlkes, C., Tal, D., Malik, J.: A database of human segmented natural images and its application to evaluating segmentation algorithms and measuring ecological statistics. In: Proc. 8th Int'l. Conf. Computer Vision, vol. 2, pp. 416–423 (July 2001)

N-View Human Silhouette Segmentation in Cluttered, Partially Changing Environments *,**

Tobias Feldmann[1], Björn Scheuermann[2],
Bodo Rosenhahn[2], and Annika Wörner[1]

[1] Karlsruhe Institute of Technology (KIT), Germany
{feldmann,woerner}@kit.edu
[2] Leibniz Universität Hannover, Germany
{scheuermann,rosenhahn}@tnt.uni-hannover.de

Abstract. The segmentation of foreground silhouettes of humans in camera images is a fundamental step in many computer vision and pattern recognition tasks. We present an approach which, based on color distributions, estimates the foreground by automatically integrating data driven 3d scene knowledge from multiple static views. These estimates are integrated into a level set approach to provide the final segmentation results. The advantage of the presented approach is that ambiguities based on color distributions of the fore- and background can be resolved in many cases utilizing the integration of implicitly extracted 3d scene knowledge and 2d boundary constraints. The presented approach is thereby able to automatically handle cluttered scenes as well as scenes with partially changing backgrounds and changing light conditions.

1 Introduction

The problem of segmenting foreground silhouettes of humans in camera images is a fundamental problem in computer vision. High quality silhouettes are an essential prerequisite for dense camera based 3d reconstruction or image based human pose estimation. Camera based dense 3d reconstruction of humans can, hence, be partitioned into three main blocks: Modality of image acquisition, foreground estimation and -separation and finally, dense 3d reconstruction.

Regarding the modality, image based human motion capture has been done monocular [1], with stereo [2], multi view [3,4,5] or multi view stereo setups [6].

The estimation of foreground from the image data can be realized by image differencing over time [7], by using color model coherence by integrating appropriate a priori knowledge of fore- and background [8,9] or by integrating 3d knowledge from stereo [2] or n-view reconstructions [4,5]. If colors are used for foreground segmentation, the approaches can be separated in simple per channel differencing approaches, codebooks models [10] and mixture models [11].

---

* This work was partially supported by a grant from the *Ministry of Science, Research and the Arts of Baden-Württemberg.*

** This work is partially funded by the German Research Foundation(RO 2497/6-1).

M. Goesele et al. (Eds.): DAGM 2010, LNCS 6376, pp. 363–372, 2010.

Based on the color models, the segmentation is usually performed based on probabilities [5] or energy minimization, e.g. level set approaches [12,13] or graph cuts [14]. The 2d information of multiple cameras can be fused by the voxel carving approach [3], by probabilistic data based fusion [15], probabilistic fusion with integration of a priori knowledge about the appearance of human silhouettes [1] or energy based formulations [4,6].

Most of the mentioned approaches for detailed 3d reconstruction focus on the segmentation and 3d reconstruction in artificial or laboratory like scenarios with homogenous but mostly disjunct colors of fore- and background. The approaches, which take into account clutter and occlusions, often need a manual initialization step [6,9,16]. We, thus, present an approach, which conjoins probabilistic 3d fusion and energy based level set approaches, which enables auto initialization and adaptivity to scenes with cluttered, moderately changing backgrounds. Based on our recordings with a calibrated multi camera setup in realistic, cluttered and partially changing environments, we can show that our approach is able to produce high quality foreground segmentation results of human silhouettes. Utilizing these silhouettes for dense 3d reconstructions gains convincing results in these difficult scenarios.

2   Segmentation by Probabilistic 3d Fusion

The segmentation via probabilistic 3d fusion proposed in [5] is based on two ideas: First, a probabilistic 2d segmentation of fore- and background in all camera images of a static, calibrated multi camera setup is performed based on color distribution models. To make this segmentation more robust and adaptive, the second part integrates 3d scene information reconstructed from all cameras. The 3d information is used as a feedback mechanism to the segmentation task. Hereby the color distributions are adapted automatically to achieve better segmentation results. The basic assumption is that observed objects are surrounded by multiple cameras to obtain complete 3d reconstructions of the foreground.

The steps of the approach are depicted in Fig. 1. First, coarse fore- and background models are generated. They are used with the current camera images to create a probabilistic 3d voxel reconstruction of the scene. Probabilistic in this context means that each reconstructed voxel has a specific occupation probability derived from the probabilities of the corresponding pixels in all views to be foreground. The 3d reconstruction is projected into the camera images, thresholded and in this way provides a masked area of foreground in the images. Image areas which are not covered by this mask are used to update the background model. By utilizing this updated model a segmentation is performed to precisely determine the foreground silhouettes. The silhouettes are used to update the foreground model accurately in a succeeding step. The fore- and background models are then used to create a probabilistic 3d reconstruction of the foreground by using the next camera frame and the loop restarts.

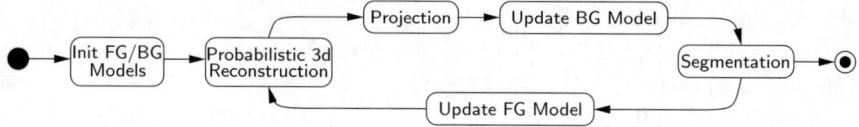

Fig. 1. Segmentation loop utilizing probabilistic 3d fusion as data driven feedback mechanism to enhance the segmentation by automatically adapted color distributions.

2.1 Fore- and Background Model

To model fore- and background, the random variable $\mathcal{F} \in \{0, 1\}$ decides whether a pixel at a given time t is fore- or background ($\mathcal{F} = 1$ respectively $\mathcal{F} = 0$). Based on a given color vector $\boldsymbol{c}$ the color distribution $p(\boldsymbol{c}|\mathcal{F} = 1)$ models the foreground and is used to infer the conditional probability $P(\mathcal{F} = 1|\boldsymbol{c})$. The foreground model is generated based on the foreground segment for each frame separately and consists of two parts A and B:

$$p(\boldsymbol{c}|\mathcal{F} = 1) = \underbrace{(1 - P_{\mathrm{NF}}) \sum_{k=1}^{K_{\mathrm{fg}}} \omega^k \eta(\boldsymbol{c}, \boldsymbol{\mu}^k, \boldsymbol{\Sigma}^k)}_{A} + P_{\mathrm{NF}} \underbrace{\mathcal{U}(\boldsymbol{c})}_{B} \ . \tag{1}$$

The first part A models known foreground in terms of a Gaussian Mixture Model (GMM) with the density function $\eta(\boldsymbol{c}, \boldsymbol{\mu}, \boldsymbol{\Sigma})$ where $\boldsymbol{\mu}^k$ and $\boldsymbol{\Sigma}^k$ are mean and variance of the kth of K_{fg} components of the mixture and ω^k is the component's weight. B models a uniform color distribution which is necessary to integrate suddenly arising new foreground. Both parts are coupled by the probability $P_{\mathrm{NF}} = \frac{1}{2}$ of new foreground. The model is generated continuously by utilizing k-means clustering of the colors of the foreground silhouette during consecutive frames. The background model consists of two parts as well:

$$p(\boldsymbol{c}_t|\mathcal{F}_t = 0) = \underbrace{(1 - P_{\mathrm{S}}) \sum_{k=1}^{K_{\mathrm{bg}}} \omega_t^k \eta(\boldsymbol{c}_t, \boldsymbol{\mu}_t^k, \boldsymbol{\Sigma}_t^k)}_{C} + P_{\mathrm{S}} \underbrace{\sum_{k=1}^{K_{\mathrm{bg}}} \omega_t^k p(\boldsymbol{c}_t|\mathcal{S}_t^k = 1)}_{D} \ . \tag{2}$$

Part C models the color distribution of the background similar to the model in eq. 1 with K_{bg} components. In contrast to eq. 1, the model is updated over the whole observation time t. The second part D models the occurrence of shadows and highlights. Both parts are again coupled with an additionally probability of shadows $P_{\mathrm{S}} = \frac{1}{2}$. The shadow and highlight model D is modeled in analogy to the background color model C, i.e. the weightings of C are reused. To determine shaded areas or areas of highlights, the colors are examined in the YUV color space. A luminance ratio λ is calculated in the Y channel: $\lambda = \frac{Y_t}{Y_B} = \frac{c_t^1}{\mu_t^{k,1}}$. Two thresholds are introduced to detect shadows, if $\tau_S < 1$, and highlights, if $\tau_H > 1$. The resulting shadow model is:

$$p(c_t|S_t^k = 1) = \begin{cases} \frac{1}{(\tau_H - \tau_S)\mu_t^{k,1}} \prod_{d=2,3} \eta(c_t^d, {\mu'}_t^{k,d}, \Sigma_t^{k,d}) & \text{if } \tau_S \le \lambda_t^k \le \tau_H \\ 0 & \text{else} \end{cases} . \quad (3)$$

The scale factor $\frac{1}{(\tau_H - \tau_S)\mu_t^{k,1}}$ is needed to achieve the density's integration to result in 1. The background model in eq. 2 is updated continuously by integration of all previous frames over time by utilizing an online Expectation Maximization (EM) approach as presented in [5].

2.2 Probabilistic 3d Fusion

To update fore- and background models, a method is needed to reliably identify foreground in the camera images. In case of multi camera setups it is feasible to exploit the strong prior of geometric coherence of the scene observed from multiple views by using the approach of a bayesian probabilistic 3d reconstruction [15]. The volume seen by the cameras is discretized into voxels $\mathcal{V} \in \{0, 1\}$. For each voxel the probability of being foreground is derived from the foreground probabilities of the corresponding pixels in all cameras according to the model definition in [5]. Four a priori probabilities are introduced into the reconstruction model. First, the probability of voxel occupation: $P(\mathcal{V}) = \frac{1}{2}$. Additionally, three error probabilities P_{DF}, P_{FA} and P_O. P_{DF} means a *detection failure*, i.e. a voxel should be occupied but is not due to e.g. camera noise. P_{FA} means a *false alarm*, i.e. a voxel should not be occupied but erroneously is, e.g. due to shadows. Finally, P_O means an *obstruction*, i.e. a voxel should not be occupied but is on the same line of sight as another voxel which is occupied and, hence, classified incorrectly. The conditional probability of foreground of an unoccupied voxel is, thus, $\mathcal{V}$: $P(\mathcal{F}_n = 1|\mathcal{V} = 0) = P_O(1 - P_{DF}) + (1 - P_O)P_{FA}$. The conditional probability of background of an unoccupied voxel is $\mathcal{V}$: $P(\mathcal{F}_n = 0|\mathcal{V} = 0) = 1 - [P_O(1 - P_{DF}) + (1 - P_O)P_{FA}]$. Values of 5% for P_{DF}, P_{FA} and P_O provide reasonable results. We use the joint probability distribution defined in [5], and marginalize over the unknown variables $\mathcal{F}_n$ by observing the colors $c_1, \dots, c_N$ at the corresponding pixels in the images of the cameras $1, \dots, N$ by eq. 4:

$$P(\mathcal{V} = 1|c_1, \dots, c_N) = \frac{\prod_{n=1}^N \sum_{f \in \{0,1\}} P(\mathcal{F}_n = f|\mathcal{V} = 1)p(c_n|\mathcal{F}_n = f)}{\sum_{v \in \{0,1\}} \prod_{n=1}^N \sum_{f \in \{0,1\}} P(\mathcal{F}_n = f|\mathcal{V} = v)p(c_n|\mathcal{F}_n = f)} . \quad (4)$$

The resulting probabilistic 3d reconstruction is backprojected into the camera images and then used to identify fore- and background segments (cf. sec. 2).

2.3 Probabilistic Foreground Detection

By using the probability densities $p(c|\mathcal{F} = 1)$ and $p(c|\mathcal{F} = 0)$ (sec. 2.1) the conditional probability $P(\mathcal{F} = 1|c)$ that a pixel belongs to the foreground based on an observed color value c can be calculated using Bayes' rule which under assumption of no a priori knowledge about the unconditional probabilities $P(\mathcal{F} = f)$ and a resulting uniform distribution cancels out to:

$$P(\mathcal{F} = 1|\boldsymbol{c}) = \frac{p(\boldsymbol{c}|\mathcal{F} = 1)}{\sum\limits_{f \in \{0,1\}} p(\boldsymbol{c}|\mathcal{F} = f)} \ . \tag{5}$$

3   Variational Segmentation

The problem of segmentation has been formalized by Mumford and Shah as the minimization of a functional [17]. The level set method was introduced by Osher and Sethian [18] to implicitly propagate hypersurfaces by evolving an appropriate embedding function to find minimizers to such a functional. The variational approach used in our segmentation framework is based on the works of [12,13]. In this section we will shortly review this variational framework and the way the different information is fused. The basis of our segmentation framework is a variation of the very well known energy functional for image segmentation:

$$E(\varphi) = -\int_{\Omega} H(\varphi) \sum_{j=1}^{k} \log p_{1,j}(\boldsymbol{c}) \, d\Omega - \int_{\Omega} (1 - H(\varphi)) \sum_{j=1}^{k} \log p_{2,j}(\boldsymbol{c}) \, d\Omega$$
$$+ \nu_1 \int_{\Omega} |\nabla H(\varphi)| \, d\Omega \ , \tag{6}$$

where $\boldsymbol{c} \in \mathbb{R}^k$ is the image feature vector, $H(\varphi)$ is a regularized Heaviside function and $p_{i,j}$ are specific, independent object $(i = 1)$ and background $(i = 2)$ distributions for the different image feature channels j. These distributions can be inferred from the respective regions (divided by $\varphi(x)$) by fitting parametric distributions or by performing the nonparametric Parzen density estimates [19] to histograms of the feature channels.

Instead of multiplying the different probabilities arising from the feature channels, which leads to the above formulation of the segmentation energy, we generalized this approach and use Dempster-Shafer theory of evidence [20] to fuse information arising from different feature channels. The key idea, which makes it different from other Bayesian frameworks, is the use of Dempster's rule of combination to fuse different information [20]. This allows to favor feature channels that support a specific region instead of favor channels with low support for a region. We will make use of this property to fuse the image data of traditional segmentation frameworks and the information arising from segmentation by probabilistic foreground detection.

The energy functional, which uses evidence theory can be expressed as follows:

$$E(\varphi) = -\int_{\Omega} H(\varphi) \log m(\Omega_1) \, d\Omega - \int_{\Omega} (1 - H(\varphi)) \log m(\Omega_2) \, d\Omega$$
$$+ \nu_1 \int_{\Omega} |\nabla H(\varphi)| \, d\Omega \ , \tag{7}$$

where $m = m_1 \otimes m_2 \otimes \ldots \otimes m_k$ is the mass function, fusing k feature channels with Dempster's rule of combination. The single mass functions m_j are defined by the object and background distributions $p_{i,j}$:

$$m_j(\emptyset) = 0 \,, \qquad m_j(\Omega) = 1 - (p_{1,j}(\boldsymbol{c}) + p_{2,j}(\boldsymbol{c})) \,,$$
$$m_j(\Omega_1) = p_{1,j}(\boldsymbol{c}), \quad m_j(\Omega_2) = p_{2,j}\boldsymbol{c} \,, \tag{8}$$

for $j \in \{1, \ldots, k\}$. The mass $m_j(\Omega) = m_j(\{\Omega_1, \Omega_2\})$ introduces a way to represent inaccuracy and uncertainty of the feature channels, while the mass $m_j(\Omega_i)$ can be interpreted as the belief strictly placed on foreground- (Ω_1) and background (Ω_2) regions. Dempster's rule of combination is defined by:

$$m(\rho_1) = m_1(\rho_1) \otimes m_2(\rho_1) = \frac{\displaystyle\sum_{\rho_2 \cap \rho_3 = \rho_1} m_1(\rho_2) m_2(\rho_3)}{1 - \displaystyle\sum_{\rho_2 \cap \rho_3 = \emptyset} m_1(\rho_2) m_2(\rho_3)} \,, \tag{9}$$

where $\rho_1, \rho_2, \rho_3 \in \wp\{\Omega_1, \Omega_2\} = \{\emptyset, \Omega_1, \Omega_2, \{\Omega_1, \Omega_2\}\}$.

The minimization of the energy (7) with respect to φ can be performed using variational methods and a gradient descent [16]. Thus, the segmentation process works according to the EM principle with an initial partitioning.

4   Integrating Probabilistic 3d Fusion into Variational Segmentation

Given the probabilities $P(\mathcal{F} = 1|\boldsymbol{c})$ for each feature vector $\boldsymbol{c}$ arising from the probabilistic foreground detection (5) we build the following mass function:

$$m_{\text{fg}}(\emptyset) = 0 \,, \qquad m_{\text{fg}}(\Omega) = 1 - \nu_2 \,,$$
$$m_{\text{fg}}(\Omega_1) = \nu_2 \cdot P(\mathcal{F} = 1|\boldsymbol{c}), \quad m_{\text{fg}}(\Omega_2) = \nu_2 \cdot (1 - P(\mathcal{F} = 1|\boldsymbol{c})) \,, \tag{10}$$

with a weighting parameter $\nu_2 \in [0, 1]$. This parameter can be interpreted as the belief we put on the probabilistic foreground detection. With a parameter $\nu_2 < 1$ we integrate inaccuracy. As a consequence, the evolving boundary is directly driven by the intensity information of the image and the result of the probabilistic 3d fusion.

The mass function m_{fg} is now integrated into the variational approach for image segmentation (7) using Dempster's rule of combination:

$$m_{\text{new}} = m \otimes m_{\text{fg}} = m_1 \otimes m_2 \otimes \ldots \otimes m_k \otimes m_{\text{fg}} \,. \tag{11}$$

The energy functional for segmentation fusing image features and probabilistic foreground detection can be written as:

$$E(\varphi) = \underbrace{- \int_\Omega H(\varphi) \log m_{\text{new}}(\Omega_1) \, d\Omega - \int_\Omega (1 - H(\varphi)) \log m_{\text{new}}(\Omega_2) \, d\Omega}_{\text{fusion of image features and probabilistic foreground detection}} \tag{12}$$
$$+ \nu_1 \int_\Omega |\nabla H(\varphi)| \, d\Omega \,.$$

Compared to the Bayesian approach the proposed framework is able to correct wrong classifications coming from the probabilistic foreground detection and vice versa, because channels with a strong support are favored.

5 Evaluation

We present a qualitative and a quantitative analysis of our algorithm based on the images of the *Dancer Sequence* in [5] and our own recordings of gymnasts with seven Prosilica GE680C cameras in a circular setup. The quantitative analysis is performed based on hand labeled data.

In a qualitative analysis we compare the results of the approach of [5] with the results of a variational segmentation, with GrabCut [14] and the results of the proposed combined approach. The probabilistic segmentation of [5] is initialized with a priori recorded background images. These images varied in lighting and details which was automatically compensated by the presented approach. In case of the variational segmentation and GrabCut, the result of the probabilistic 3d fusion is used as the initial boundary. In the combined approach the information from the probabilistic 3d fusion is used as the initial boundary and integrated into the variational segmentation framework as proposed in eq. (12).

In Fig. 2 we present exemplary results of all four approaches performed on a difficult scene with very similar color distributions of fore- and background. It is clearly observable that neither the variational approach nor the segmentation by probabilistic fusion are able to fully cope with that ambiguity. The variational approach integrates large parts of the wooden background into the foreground silhouette while the approach of [5] leads to very low probabilities of foreground in the ambiguous areas. Solely, the proposed approach leads to satisfying results in such difficult scenarios. As an alternative to variational segmentation, the results of the probabilistic segmentation could also be used as initialization for GrabCut. But we found that only the combination of initialization by probabilistic segmentation and fusing this information utilizing the Dempster-Shafer approach can close erroneous holes and, thus, recover from false classifications.

Due to the convincing results of Fig. 2 we performed a quantitative analysis of the three approaches and measured the error compared to hand labeled data. Exemplary results of the cameras 6 and 7 are presented in Fig. 3. Camera 6 has been chosen because this view contains background motion and we want to demonstrate that the adaptivity of [5] is not compromised by the presented approach. The results of Camera 7 are selected to link the qualitative results in Fig. 2 with quantitative results to clarify the benefits of the presented approach. In all cases the proposed approach provides better results over the full sequence.

Finally, we performed a qualitative analysis of the proposed approach on the dancer from [5]. We were able to show, that again, our approach gains better segmentation results (cf. Fig. 4) than the probabilistic segmentation. We could also additionally demonstrate that the proposed approach is applicable in these kinds of difficult scenarios with occluding noise and, thus, unites the benefits of robust segmentation and robust dense 3d reconstruction results.

370   T. Feldmann et al.

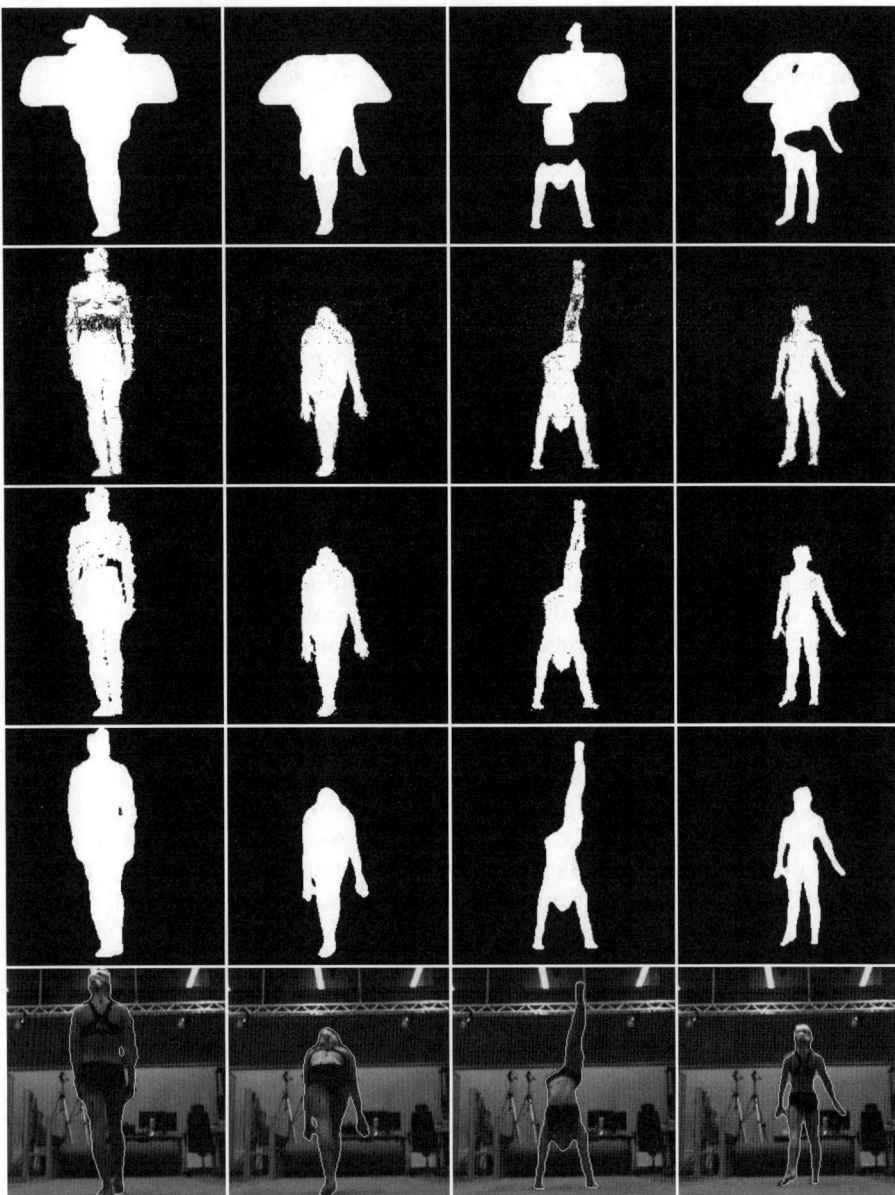

Fig. 2. Frames 100, 300, 500 and 700 of camera 7. First row: Variational segmentation only. Second row: Segmentation by probabilistic fusion only without post processing. Third row: Combined approach with GrabCut segmentation. Fourth row: Proposed combined approach with variational segmentation. Fifth row: Input image and detected contour of combined approach. All single approaches have difficulties in areas with nearly identical color distributions of fore-/background. Only the proposed combined approach is able to cope with these kinds of ambiguities.

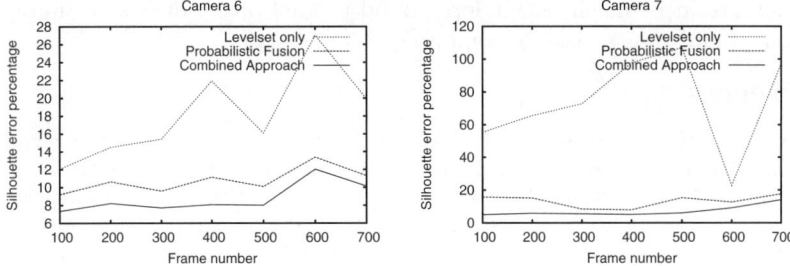

Fig. 3. Silhouette error percentage in steps of 100 frames in cameras 6 and 7 of the gymnast sequence. The proposed approach generates the best results with the fewest errors compared to the variational approach and the approach of [5].

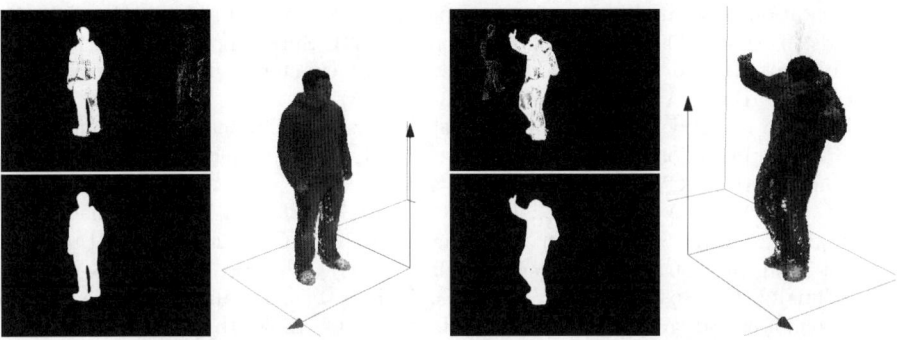

Fig. 4. Column 1, top: Probabilistic segmentation of the second frame (after first model update) of camera 6 of the dancer sequence; Bottom: Segmentation of proposed approach. Column 2: Resulting 3d reconstruction of proposed approach. Column 3, top: Probabilistic segmentation of frame 645; Bottom: Segmentation of the proposed approach. Column 4: Resulting 3d reconstruction.

6   Conclusion

In the presented work we developed a new approach for color based foreground segmentation with multi camera setups which implicitly integrates geometric priors of the used camera setup and energy based constraints to allow an adaptive, purely data driven high quality segmentation of foreground in cluttered, changing and, thus, realistic scenarios. The new approach combines the segmentation by probabilistic 3d fusion and the variational approach of level set segmentation based on Dempster-Shafer theory of evidence. We revealed that both algorithms on their own have massive difficulties in scenarios with very similar color distributions of fore- and background. However, we were able to show, that with our specific approach the integration of both methods allows tremendous improvements of the segmentation results in these kinds of scenarios. To attest the impact of our method, we performed qualitative as well as quantitative evaluations on natural image sequences. We showed that the combination of probabilistic 3d fusion and the level set segmentation based on Dempster-Shafer theory of evidence produces much better foreground extractions, which is an important prerequisite for many tasks in computer vision.

References

1. Grauman, K., Shakhnarovich, G., Darrell, T.: A bayesian approach to image-based visual hull reconstruction. In: IEEE CVPR, vol. 1, pp. 187–194 (2003)
2. Gordon, G., Darrell, T., Harville, M., Woodfill, J.: Background estimation and removal based on range and color. In: IEEE CVPR, vol. 2, pp. 24–59 (1999)
3. Cheung, G.K., Kanade, T., Bouguet, J.Y., Holler, M.: A real time system for robust 3d voxel reconstruction of human motions. In: IEEE CVPR, vol. 2, pp. 714–720 (2000)
4. Kolev, K., Brox, T., Cremers, D.: Robust variational segmentation of 3d objects from multiple views. In: Franke, K., Müller, K.-R., Nickolay, B., Schäfer, R. (eds.) DAGM 2006. LNCS, vol. 4174, pp. 688–697. Springer, Heidelberg (2006)
5. Feldmann, T., Dießelberg, L., Wörner, A.: Adaptive foreground/background segmentation using multiview silhouette fusion. In: Denzler, J., Notni, G., Süße, H. (eds.) DAGM 2009. LNCS, vol. 5748, pp. 522–531. Springer, Heidelberg (2009)
6. Vogiatzis, G., Torr, P.H.S., Cipolla, R.: Multi-view stereo via volumetric graph-cuts. In: IEEE CVPR, vol. 2, pp. 391–398 (2005)
7. Lim, S.N., Mittal, A., Davis, L.S., Paragios, N.: Fast illumination-invariant background subtraction using two views: Error analysis, sensor placement and applications. In: IEEE CVPR, pp. 1071–1078 (2005)
8. Lee, W., Woo, W., Boyer, E.: Identifying foreground from multiple images. In: Yagi, Y., Kang, S.B., Kweon, I.S., Zha, H. (eds.) ACCV 2007, Part II. LNCS, vol. 4844, pp. 580–589. Springer, Heidelberg (2007)
9. Schmaltz, C., Rosenhahn, B., Brox, T., Weickert, J.: Localised mixture models in region-based tracking. In: Denzler, J., Notni, G., Süße, H. (eds.) DAGM 2009. LNCS, vol. 5748, pp. 21–30. Springer, Heidelberg (2009)
10. Kim, K., Chalidabhongse, T., Harwood, D., Davis, L.: Background modeling and subtraction by codebook construction. In: ICIP, vol. 5, pp. 3061–3064 (October 2004)
11. Stauffer, C., Grimson, W.: Adaptive background mixture models for real-time tracking. In: IEEE CVPR, vol. 2, pp. 2246–2252 (1999)
12. Chan, T., Vese, L.: Active contours without edges. IEEE TIP 10(2), 266–277 (2001)
13. Zhu, S.C., Yuille, A.: Region competition: unifying snakes, region growing, and bayes/mdl for multiband image segmentation. IEEE TPAMI 18(9), 884–900 (1996)
14. Rother, C., Kolmogorov, V., Blake, A.: "grabcut": interactive foreground extraction using iterated graph cuts. ACM Trans. Graph. 23(3), 309–314 (2004)
15. Franco, J.S., Boyer, E.: Fusion of multi-view silhouette cues using a space occupancy grid. Technical Report 5551, INRIA (April 2005)
16. Scheuermann, B., Rosenhahn, B.: Analysis of numerical methods for level set based image segmentation. In: Bebis, G., Boyle, R., Parvin, B., Koracin, D., Kuno, Y., Wang, J., Pajarola, R., Lindstrom, P., Hinkenjann, A., Encarnação, M.L., Silva, C.T., Coming, D. (eds.) ISVC 2009, Part II. LNCS, vol. 5876, pp. 196–207. Springer, Heidelberg (2009)
17. Mumford, D., Shah, J.: Boundary detection by minimizing functionals. In: IEEE CVPR, San Francisco, CA, pp. 22–26 (1985)
18. Osher, S., Sethian, J.: Fronts propagating with curvature dependent speed: Algorithm based on hamilton-jacobi formulation. J. Comput. Phys. 79, 12–49 (1988)
19. Kim, J., Fisher III, J., Yezzi Jr., A., Cetin, M., Willsky, A.: Nonparametric methods for image segmentation using information theory and curve evolution. In: ICIP, pp. 797–800 (2002)
20. Dempster, A.P.: A generalization of bayesian inference. Journal of the Royal Statistical Society, Series B (Methodological) 30(2), 205–247 (1968)

Nugget-Cut: A Segmentation Scheme for Spherically- and Elliptically-Shaped 3D Objects

Jan Egger[1,2], Miriam H.A. Bauer[1,2], Daniela Kuhnt[1], Barbara Carl[1],
Christoph Kappus[1], Bernd Freisleben[2], and Christopher Nimsky[1]

[1] Dept. of Neurosurgery, University of Marburg, Baldingerstraße, 35043 Marburg, Germany
[2] Dept. of Math. and Computer Science, University of Marburg, Hans-Meerwein-Str. 3,
35032 Marburg, Germany
{egger,bauermi,kuhntd,carlb,kappus,nimsky}@med.uni-marburg.de
freisleb@informatik.uni-marburg.de

Abstract. In this paper, a segmentation method for spherically- and elliptically-shaped objects is presented. It utilizes a user-defined seed point to set up a directed 3D graph. The nodes of the 3D graph are obtained by sampling along rays that are sent through the surface points of a polyhedron. Additionally, several arcs and a parameter constrain the set of possible segmentations and enforce smoothness. After the graph has been constructed, the minimal cost closed set on the graph is computed via a polynomial time s-t cut, creating an optimal segmentation of the object. The presented method has been evaluated on 50 Magnetic Resonance Imaging (MRI) data sets with World Health Organization (WHO) grade IV gliomas (glioblastoma multiforme). The ground truth of the tumor boundaries were manually extracted by three clinical experts (neurological surgeons) with several years (> 6) of experience in resection of gliomas and afterwards compared with the automatic segmentation results of the proposed scheme yielding an average Dice Similarity Coefficient (DSC) of 80.37±8.93%. However, no segmentation method provides a perfect result, so additional editing on some slices was required, but these edits could be achieved quickly because the automatic segmentation provides a border that fits mostly to the desired contour. Furthermore, the manual segmentation by neurological surgeons took 2-32 minutes (mean: 8 minutes), in contrast to the automatic segmentation with our implementation that took less than 5 seconds.

Keywords: glioma, segmentation, polyhedra, graph, minimal s-t cut.

1 Introduction

Gliomas are the most common primary brain tumors, evolving from the cerebral supportive cells. The histological type is determined by the cells they arise of, most frequently astrocytomas (astrocytes), oligodendrogliomas (oligodendrocytes) or ependymomas (ependymal) cells. Furthermore, there are mixed forms containing different cell types, such as oligoastrocytomas. With over 60%, astrocytic tumors are the most common tumors. The grading system for astrocytomas according to the World Health Organization (WHO) subdivides grades I-IV, whereas grade I tumors

M. Goesele et al. (Eds.): DAGM 2010, LNCS 6376, pp. 373–382, 2010.
© Springer-Verlag Berlin Heidelberg 2010

tend to be least aggressive [1]. 70% count to the group of malignant gliomas (anaplastic astrocytoma WHO grade III, glioblastoma multiforme WHO grade IV). According to its histopathological appearance, the grade IV tumor is given the name glioblastoma multiforme (GBM).

The glioblastoma multiforme is the most frequent malignant primary tumor and is one of the highest malignant human neoplasms. The interdisciplinary therapeutical management today contains maximum safe resection, percutaneus radiation and most frequently chemotherapy. Still, despite new radiation strategies and the development of oral alcylating substances, the survival rate is still only approximately 15 months [2].

Although in former years the surgical role was controversial, several studies have been able to prove maximum surgical resection as a positive predictor for patient survival [3]. Microsurgical resection is today optimized with the technical development of neuronavigation containing functional data sets such as diffusion tensor imaging (DTI), functional MRI (fMRI), magnetoencephalography (MEG), magnetic resonance spectroscopy (MRS), or positron-emission-computed-tomography (PET).

For clinical follow-up, the evaluation of the tumor volume in the course of disease is essential. The volumetric assessment of a tumor applying manual segmentation is a time-consuming process.

In this paper, a graph-based segmentation method for spherical and elliptical objects is presented. The approach utilizes a user-defined seed point inside the object to create a directed graph. Then, the minimal cost closed set on the graph is computed via a polynomial time s-t cut, providing an optimal segmentation. To evaluate the new scheme, gliomas in Magnetic Resonance Imaging (MRI) data sets have been segmented. The results of the automatic segmentation have been compared with manual segmentations of three neurological surgeons that are experts in their fields and have several years of experience in resection of gliomas. The outcomes were evaluated by calculating the Dice Similarity Coefficient (DSC).

The paper is organized as follows. Section 2 reviews related work. Section 3 presents the details of the proposed approach. In Section 4, experimental results are discussed. Section 5 concludes the paper and outlines areas for future work.

2   Related Work

Several algorithms for glioma segmentation based on MRI data have been proposed. A good overview of different deterministic and statistical approaches is given by Angelini et al. [4]. Most of them are region-based, more recent ones are based on deformable models and include edge information.

Gibbs et al. [5] have introduced a combination of region growing and morphological edge detection for segmenting enhancing tumors in T1 weighted MRI data. Based on a manually provided initial sample of tumor signal and surrounding tissue, an initial segmentation is performed using pixel thresholding, morphological opening and closing and fitting to an edge map. The authors have evaluated their method with one phantom data set and ten clinical data sets. However, the average segmentation time for a tumor was ten minutes and they did not exactly classify the tumors they used.

An interactive method for segmentation of full-enhancing, ring-enhancing and non-enhancing tumors has been proposed by Letteboer et al. [6] and evaluated with twenty clinical cases. Depending on a manual tracing of an initial slice, several morphological filter operations were applied to the MRI volume to separate the data in homogenous areas.

Depending on intensity-based pixel probabilities for tumor tissue, Droske et al. [7] have presented a deformable model, using a level set formulation, to divide the MRI data into regions of similar image properties for tumor segmentation. This model-based segmentation was performed on the imaging data of twelve patients.

Clark et al. [8] have introduced a knowledge-based automated segmentation on multispectral data in order to partition glioblastomas. After a training phase with fuzzy C-means classification and clustering analysis and a brain mask computation, initial tumor segmentation from vectorial histogram thresholding has been postprocessed to eliminate non-tumor pixels. The presented system has been trained on three volume data sets and then tested on thirteen unseen volume data sets.

Segmentation based on outlier detection in T2 weighted MR data has been proposed by Prastawa et al. [9]. The image data is registered on a normal brain atlas to detect the abnormal tumor region. The tumor and the edema are then isolated by statistical clustering of the differing voxels and a deformable model. However, the authors have applied the method only to three real data sets. For each case, the time required for the automatic segmentation method was about 90 minutes.

Sieg et al. [10] have introduced an approach to segment contrast-enhanced, intracranial tumors and anatomical structures of registered, multispectral MR data. Multilayer feedforward neural networks with backpropagation have been trained and a pixel-oriented classification has been applied for segmentation. The approach has been tested on twenty-two data sets, but no computation times were provided.

3   Methods

Our overall method starts by setting up a directed 3D graph from a user-defined seed point that is located inside the object. For setting up the graph, the method samples along rays that are sent through the surface points of a polyhedron with the seed point as center. The sampled points are the nodes $n \in V$ of the graph $G(V, E)$ and $e \in E$ is the corresponding set of edges. There are edges between the nodes and edges that connect the nodes to a source s and a sink t to allow the computation of a s-t cut (the source and the sink $s, t \in V$ are virtual nodes). The idea of setting up the graph with a polyhedron goes back to a catheter simulation algorithm where several polyhedra were used to align the catheter inside the vessel [11]. In the segmentation scheme, this idea is combined with a graph-based method that has been introduced for the semi-automatic segmentation of the aorta [12], [13], [14] and diffusion tensor imaging (DTI) fiber bundle segmentation [15]. However, in this case, setting up the graph was performed by sampling the nodes in several 2D planes and therefore is not useful for the segmentation of spherical or elliptical 3D objects. Other publications that introduce approaches for segmenting objects in 2D images with graph-cuts are those of Veksler [16] and Ishikawa et al. [17]. Additionally the publication of Grady et al. [18] presents a method that finds partitions with a small isoperimetric constant in an image graph.

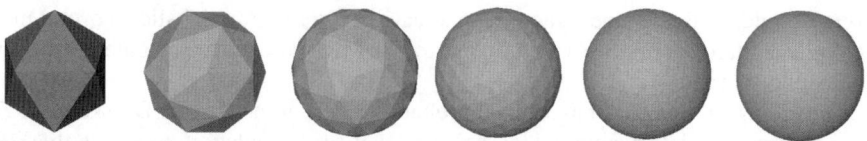

Fig. 1. Polyhedra with 12, 32, 92, 272, 812 and 2432 surface points (recursively refined) [11]

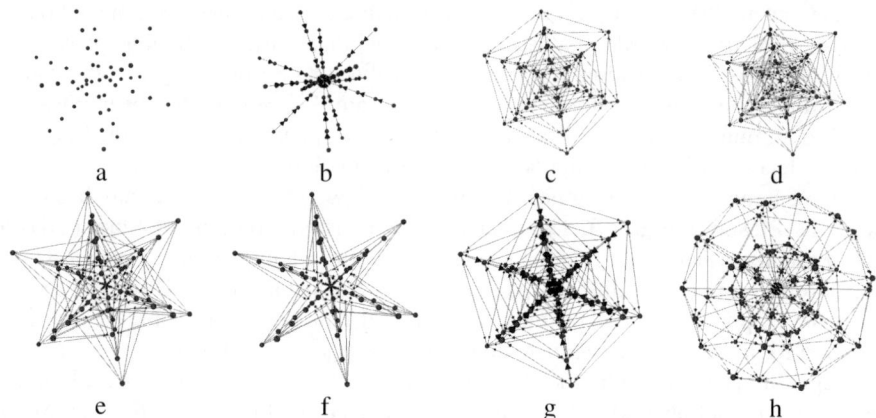

Fig. 2. Principle of graph construction: a) five sampled points (red) along each of the 12 rays that provide the nodes for the graph. b) edges between the nodes belonging to the same ray. c) edges between nodes of different rays for Δ_r=0, d) Δ_r=1, e) Δ_r=2 and f) Δ_r=3. g) complete graph for Δ_r=0. h) complete graph with 32 surface points, 3 nodes per ray and Δ_r=0.

Polyhedra with different numbers of surface points are shown in Figure 1. These polyhedra are just for illustration and should give an idea were the sampled points in Figure 2 are coming from. For a later segmentation, even more surface points (e.g. 7292) are used, depending on the size of the object that has to be segmented.

The principle of the graph construction is shown in Figure 2 (a-h). In (a), five points (red) are sampled along 12 rays that are sent to a polyhedron with 12 surface points. These points plus the source and the sink define the whole set of nodes for the graph when a polyhedron with 12 surface points is used.

The arcs $<v_i, v_j> \in E$ of the graph G connect two nodes v_i, v_j. There are two types of ∞-weighted arcs: z-arcs A_z and r-arcs A_r (Z is the number of sampled points along one ray $z=(0,...,Z-1)$ and R is the number of rays sent out to the surface points of a polyhedron $r=(0,...,R-1)$), where $V(x_n,y_n,z_n)$ is one neighbor of $V(x,y,z)$ – in other words $V(x_n,y_n,z_n)$ and $V(x,y,z)$ belong to the same triangle in case of a triangulation of the polyhedron (see also Figure 1):

$$A_z = \{\langle V(x, y, z), V(x, y, z-1)\rangle \mid z > 0\}$$

$$A_r = \{\langle V(x, y, z), V(x_n, y_n, \max(0, z - \Delta_r))\rangle\}$$

(1)

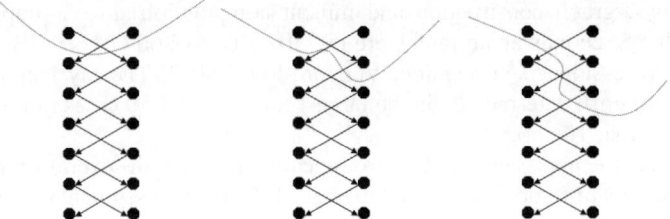

Fig. 3. Principle of a cut of edges between two rays for $\Delta_r=1$. Left and middle: Same cost for a cut (2·∞). Right: Higher cost for a cut (4·∞).

The arcs between two nodes along a ray A_z ensure that all nodes below the polyhedron surface in the graph are included to form a closed set (correspondingly, the interior of the object is separated from the exterior in the data). The arcs A_r between the nodes of different rays constrain the set of possible segmentations and enforce smoothness via the parameter Δ_r. The larger this parameter is, the larger is the number of possible segmentations (see Figure 3).

After graph construction, the minimal cost closed set on the graph is computed via a polynomial time s-t cut [19]. A Markov Random Field (MRF) approach where each voxel of the image is a node is definitely too time-consuming for the data we used (512x512xX). A MRF approach in a recent publication needed already several minutes for the cut of one small 2D image [20]. We also considered an Active Contour Approach (ACM) [21] where the initial contour is a polyhedron with an initial radius definitely smaller than the object (tumor). However, ACMs can get stuck in local minima during the iterative segmentation (expansion) process. In contrast, a graph cut approach provides an optimal segmentation for the constructed graph.

The s-t cut creates an optimal segmentation of the object under influence of the parameter Δ_r that controls the stiffness of the surface. A delta value of 0 ensures that the segmentation result is a sphere. The weights $w(x, y, z)$ for every edge between $v \in V$ and the sink or source are assigned in the following manner: weights are set to $c(x,y,z)$ when z is zero and otherwise to $c(x,y,z)$-$c(x,y,z$-$1)$, where $c(x,y,z)$ is the absolute value of the intensity difference between an average grey value of the desired object and the grey value of the voxel at position (x,y,z) – for a detailed description, see [13] and [14].

The average grey value that is needed for the calculation of the costs and the graphs weights is essential for the segmentation result. Based on the assumption that the user-defined seed point is inside the object, the average grey value can be estimated automatically. Therefore, we integrate over a small cube of dimension d centered on the user-defined seed-point (s_x, s_y, s_z):

$$\int_{-d/2}^{d/2} \int_{-d/2}^{d/2} \int_{-d/2}^{d/2} T(s_x + x, s_y + y, s_z + z) dx dy dz \qquad (2)$$

4   Results

The presented methods were implemented in C++ within the MeVisLab platform [22]. Using 2432 and 7292 polyhedra surface points, the overall segmentation (sending rays, graph construction and mincut computation) in our implementation took less that 5 seconds on an Intel Core i5-750 CPU, 4x2.66 GHz, 8 GB RAM, Windows XP Professional x64 Version, Version 2003, SP 2. The ray length is a fixed parameter (10 cm), determined via the largest tumor of the 50 cases (all tumors had a diameter less that 10 cm).

To evaluate the approach, three neurological surgeons with several years of experience in resection of tumors performed manual slice-by-slice segmentation of 50 WHO grade IV gliomas. The tumor outlines for the segmentation were displayed by the contrast-enhancing areas in T1 weighted MRI data sets. Afterwards, the manual segmentations were compared with the one click segmentation results of the proposed method via the Dice Similarity Coefficient (DSC) [23], calculated as follows:

$$DSC = \frac{2 \cdot V(A \cap R)}{V(A) + V(R)} \qquad (3)$$

The Dice Similarity Coefficient is the relative volume overlap between A and R, where A and R are the binary masks from the automatic (A) and the reference (R) segmentation. $V(\cdot)$ is the volume (in cm^3) of voxels inside the binary mask, by means of counting the number of voxels, then multiplying with the voxel size. The average Dice Similarity Coefficient for all data sets is $80.37 \pm 8.93\%$ (see Table 1).

Table 1. Summary of results: min., max., mean μ and standard deviation σ for 50 gliomas

	Volume of tumor (cm^3)		Number of voxels		DSC (%)
	Manual	automatic	manual	automatic	
Min	0.47	0.46	524	783	46.33
Max	119.28	102.98	1024615	884553	93.82
$\mu \pm \sigma$	23.66 ± 24.89	21.02 ± 22.90	145305.54	137687.24	80.37 ± 8.93

However, additional editing on some slices was required, but these edits were achieved quite quickly (in about one minute) because the automatic segmentation provides a border that at least fits partially to the desired contour. The pure manual segmentation by neurological surgeons took about 2-32 minutes (μ=8 minutes, σ =5.7), compared with an automatic segmentation of a data set with our implementation that took less than 5 seconds plus about one minute to review the result and correct some parts of the recovered tumor border. Compared with existing methods for (semi-) automatic brain tumor segmentation (see Section 2), we used much more data sets (50) for evaluation (in contrast: existing methods $\leq$ 22 cases). Additionally, the existing methods have a much higher computing time (if specified) than our method.

Figure 4 and Figure 5 show different 3D views of two automatically segmented tumors (red). Additionally, the voxelized tumor masks are shown (rightmost images for Figure 4 and Figure 5). The presented tumors of Figure 4 and Figure 5 belong to the slices of Figure 6 and Figure 7, respectively. Figure 6 and Figure 7 show parts of the results of the automatic segmentation of the two gliomas (the whole tumors are located over 60 slices for Figure 6 and 38 slices for Figure 7).

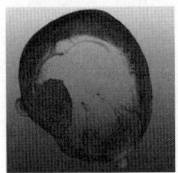 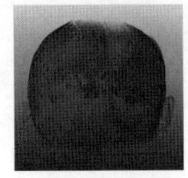 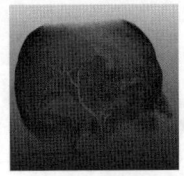 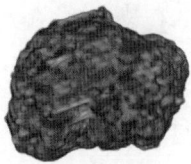

Fig. 4. Different 3D views of the automatically segmented tumor (red) of Figure 6 and the voxelized tumor mask (rightmost image).

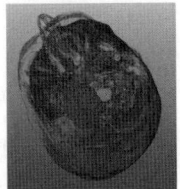 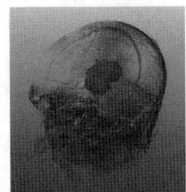 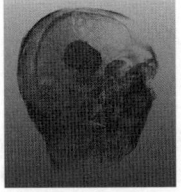 

Fig. 5. Different 3D views of the automatically segmented tumor (red) of Figure 7 and the voxelized tumor mask (rightmost image).

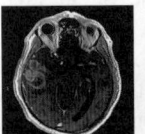 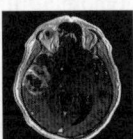 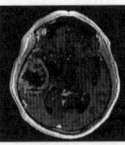 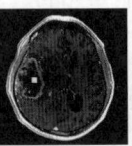 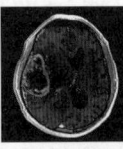 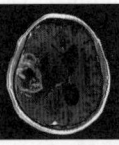

Fig. 6. Result of automatic tumor segmentation (DSC=81.33%). The yellow point (inside the tumor) in the fourth image from the left side is the user-defined seed point. Manual segmentation performed by a neurological surgeon took 16 minutes for this data set.

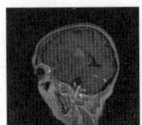 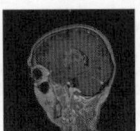 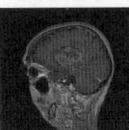 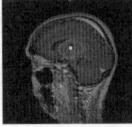 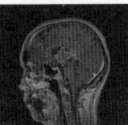 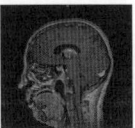

Fig. 7. Result of automatic tumor segmentation (DSC=76.19%). The yellow point (inside the tumor) in the fourth image from the left side is the user-defined seed point. Manual segmentation performed by a neurological surgeon took 9 minutes for this data set.

As shown in Figure 6 and Figure 7, the segmentation works also with more elliptically shaped tumors. The algorithm only assumes that the object of interest is not extremely tubular, like vessels or the spinal cord. Also, the user defined seed point does not have to be exactly in the center of the tumor, as shown in Figure 6 (yellow). Even with a seed point that was located far from the center, the border of the tumor in Figure 6 (red) could be still recovered with a DSC of over 80%.

In the meantime, we already enhanced our segmentation scheme [24]: the user can improve the results by specifying an arbitrary number of additional seed points to support the algorithm with grey value information and geometrical constraints. Using

 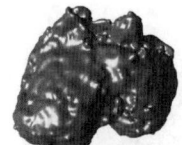  

Fig. 8. Four 3D models of (semi-) automatically segmented tumors.

this enhanced scheme for 12 selected MRI datasets, the DSC could be improved from 77.72% to 83.91% (Figure 8).

5 Conclusions

In this paper, a graph-based segmentation scheme for spherically- and elliptically-shaped objects was presented. The introduced method uses only one user-defined seed point inside the object to set up a 3D graph and to perform the segmentation. Therefore, rays are sent out radially from the seed point through the surface points of a polyhedron to generate the directed graph. After the graph has been constructed, the minimal cost closed set on the graph is computed via a polynomial time s-t cut, creating an optimal segmentation of the object.

The presented method has been tested on 50 MRI data sets with World Health Organization grade IV gliomas (glioblastoma multiforme). The ground truth of the tumor boundaries were manually extracted by three neurological surgeons with several years of experience in resection of gliomas and was compared with the automatic segmentation results, yielding an average Dice Similarity Coefficient of 80.37± 8.93%. However, additional editing on some slices was required for every case, but these edits could be achieved quickly because the automatic segmentation provides a border that at least fits partially to the desired contour.

There are several areas of future work. For example, some parameter specifications (e.g. Δ_r) of the proposed algorithm can be automated. Additionally, the method can be enhanced with statistical information about the shape and the texture of the desired object [25]. Furthermore, we plan to evaluate the method on MRI data sets with World Health Organization grade I, II and III gliomas. As compared to high-grade gliomas, low-grade tumors lack gadolinium enhancement. Thus, for these tumors, outlines cannot be expressed by contrast-enhancing T1 weighted images, but by surrounding edema in T2 weighted images. Moreover, we want to apply the scheme to segment other spherically- and elliptically-shaped organs and pathologies, e.g. pituitary adenoma [26] and cerebral aneurysms [27].

Furthermore, we considered increasing the sampling rate (for the nodes) near the tumor border, because with an equidistant sampling rate, there are more nodes near the center of the polyhedron, and less nodes going farther out. However, for objects like the brain tumors we segmented and with a few thousand surface points, this is not an issue. But for (larger) objects (e.g. the whole brain or the liver), the segmentation quality is probably going to be poorer near the boundaries, and there it can make sense to increase the sampling rate near the object border.

The user-defined seed point position that is located inside the object is also an issue that can be analyzed in a next step. The method can be improved by performing the whole segmentation iteratively: After the segmentation is performed, the center of gravity of the segmentation can be used as a new seed point for a new segmentation and so on. This might result in more robustness w.r.t. the initialization. However, for our evaluation tests, we needed no more than five attempts to achieve a satisfying segmentation result and for the automatic segmentation time of less than 5 seconds this is not time critical at all – especially if it is compared with the average manual segmentation time of 8 minutes.

Acknowledgments. The authors would like to thank Fraunhofer MeVis in Bremen, Germany, for their collaboration and especially Horst K. Hahn for his support.

References

1. Kleihues, P., et al.: The WHO classification of tumors of the nervous system. Journal of Neuropathology & Experimental Neurology 61(3), 215–229 (2002)
2. Kortmann, R.D., et al.: Radiochemotherapy of malignant gliom in adults. Clinical experiences. Strahlenther Onkol. 179(4), 219–232 (2003)
3. Lacroix, M., Abi-Said, D., Fourney, D.R., et al.: A multivariate analysis of 416 patients with glioblastoma multiforme: Prognosis, extent of resection and survival. Journal of Neurosurgery 95, 190–198 (2001)
4. Angelini, E.D., Clatz, O., Mandonnet, E., Konukoglu, E., Capelle, L., Duffau, H.: Glioma Dynamics and Computational Models: A Review of Segmentation, Registration, and In Silico Growth Algorithms and their Clinical Applications. Current Medical Imaging Reviews 3, 262–276 (2007)
5. Gibbs, P., Buckley, D.L., Blackband, S.J., et al.: Tumour volume determination from MR images by morphological segmentation. Physics in Med. & Biology 41(11), 2437–2446 (1996)
6. Letteboer, M.M.J., Olsen, O.F., Dam, E.B., et al.: Segmentation of tumors in magnetic resonance brain images using an interactive multiscale watershed algorithm. Academic Radiology 11, 1125–1138 (2004)
7. Droske, M., Meyer, B., Rumpf, M., et al.: An adaptive level set method for interactive segmentation of intracranial tumors. Neurol. Res. 27(4), 363–370 (2005)
8. Clark, M., Hall, L.O., Goldgof, D.B., et al.: Automatic tumor segmentation using knowledge-based techniques. IEEE TMI 17(2), 187–201 (1998)
9. Prastawa, M., Bullitt, E., Ho, S., et al.: A brain tumor segmentation framework based on outlier detection. Medical Image Analysis 8, 275–283 (2004)
10. Sieg, C., Handels, H., Pöppl, S.J.: Automatic Segmentation of Contrast-Enhanced Brain Tumors in Multispectral MR-Images with Backpropagation-Networks. In: Bildverarbeitung für die Medizin (BVM), pp. 347–351. Springer Press, Heidelberg (2001) (in German)
11. Egger, J., Mostarkic, Z., Großkopf, S., Freisleben, B.: A Fast Vessel Centerline Extraction Algorithm for Catheter Simulation. In: 20th IEEE International Symposium on Computer-Based Medical Systems, Maribor, Slovenia, pp. 177–182. IEEE Press, Los Alamitos (2007)
12. Egger, J., O'Donnell, T., Hopfgartner, C., Freisleben, B.: Graph-Based Tracking Method for Aortic Thrombus Segmentation. In: Proceedings of 4th European Congress for Medical and Biomedical Engineering, Engineering for Health, Antwerp, Belgium (2008)

13. Egger, J., Freisleben, B., Setser, R., Renapuraar, R., Biermann, C., O'Donnell, T.: Aorta Segmentation for Stent Simulation. In: 12th International Conference on Medical Image Computing and Computer Assisted Intervention (MICCAI), Cardiovascular Interventional Imaging and Biophysical Modelling Workshop, London, United Kingdom, 10pages (2009)

14. Li, K., Wu, X., Chen, D.Z., Sonka, M.: Optimal Surface Segmentation in Volumetric Images – A Graph-Theoretic Approach. IEEE Transactions on Pattern Analysis and Machine Intelligence 28(1), 119–134 (2006)

15. Bauer, M.H.A., Egger, J., O'Donnell, T., Freisleben, B., Barbieri, S., Klein, J., Hahn, H.K., Nimsky, C.: A Fast and Robust Graph-based Approach for Boundary Estimation of Fiber Bundles Relying on Fractional Anisotropy Maps. In: 20th International Conference on Pattern Recognition (ICPR), Istanbul, Turkey. IEEE Computer Society, Los Alamitos (2010)

16. Veksler, O.: Star Shape Prior for Graph-Cut Image Segmentation. In: Forsyth, D., Torr, P., Zisserman, A. (eds.) ECCV 2008, Part III. LNCS, vol. 5304, pp. 454–467. Springer, Heidelberg (2008)

17. Ishikawa, H., Geiger, D.: Segmentation by Grouping Junctions. In: IEEE Computer Society Conference on Computer Vision and Pattern Recognition, pp. 125–131 (1998)

18. Grady, L., Schwartz, E.L.: Isoperimetric Graph Partitioning for Image Segmentation. IEEE Trans. on Pattern Analysis and Machine Intelligence 28(3), 469–475 (2006)

19. Boykov, Y., Kolmogorov, V.: An Experimental Comparison of Min-Cut/Max-Flow Algorithms for Energy Minimization in Vision. IEEE Transactions on Pattern Analysis and Machine Intelligence 26(9), 1124–1137 (2004)

20. Shabou, A., et al.: A graph-cut based algorithm for approximate MRF optimization. In: International Conference on Image Processing (ICIP), pp. 2413–2416 (2009)

21. Kass, M., Witkin, A., Terzopoulos, D.: Constraints on Deformable Models: Recovering 3D Shape and Nongrid Motion. Artificial Intelligence 36, 91–123 (1988)

22. MeVisLab – development environment for medical image processing and visualization. MeVis Medical Solutions AG and Fraunhofer MEVIS, Bremen, Germany, http://www.mevislab.de

23. Zou, K.H., Warfield, S.K., Bharatha, A., et al.: Statistical Validation of Image Segmentation Quality Based on a Spatial Overlap Index: Scientific Reports. Academic Radiology 11(2), 178–189 (2004)

24. Egger, J., Bauer, M.H.A., Kuhnt, D., Kappus, C., Carl, B., Freisleben, B., Nimsky, C.: A Flexible Semi-Automatic Approach for Glioblastoma multiforme Segmentation. In: Biosignal Processing Conference, DGBMT, IEEE, Charité, Berlin, Germany (2010)

25. Greiner, K., et al.: Segmentation of Aortic Aneurysms in CTA-images with the Statistic Method of the Active Appearance Models. In: Bildverarbeitung für die Medizin (BVM), pp. 51–55. Springer Press, Heidelberg (2008) (in German)

26. Egger, J., Bauer, M.H.A., Kuhnt, D., Freisleben, B., Nimsky, C.: Pituitary Adenoma Segmentation. In: Proceedings of International Biosignal Processing Conference, DGBMT, IEEE, Charité, Berlin, Germany (2010)

27. Ma, B., Harbaugh, R.E., Raghavan, M.L.: Three-Dimensional Geometrical Characterization of Cerebral Aneurysms. Ann. of Biomed. Eng. 32(2), 264–273 (2004)

Benchmarking Stereo Data
(Not the Matching Algorithms)

Ralf Haeusler and Reinhard Klette

The University of Auckland

Abstract. Current research in stereo image analysis focuses on improving matching algorithms in terms of accuracy, computational costs, and robustness towards real-time applicability for complex image data and 3D scenes. Interestingly, performance testing takes place for a huge number of algorithms, but, typically, on very small sets of image data only. Even worse, there is little reasoning whether data as commonly applied is actually suitable to prove robustness or even correctness of a particular algorithm. We argue for the need of testing stereo algorithms on a much broader variety of image data then done so far by proposing a simple measure for putting image stereo data of different quality into relation to each other. Potential applications include purpose-directed decisions for the selection of image stereo data for testing the applicability of matching techniques under particular situations, or for realtime estimation of stereo performance (without any need for providing ground truth) in cases where techniques should be selected depending on the given situation.

1 Introduction

Performance evaluation of stereo algorithms became increasingly popular since the availability of various test sites such as [17] at Middlebury University. Such evaluations were speeding up progress in the design of stereo matching algorithms. Ranking is typically done by comparing a few error measures, calculated with respect to given ground truth and a relatively small number of images. Evaluations lead to particular insights, for example about the role of used cost functions [7], or of image preprocessing methods.

Necessity and limitation of such evaluations have been extensively discussed in the literature. Issues often treated are missing ground truth for real-world scenes [4] and a lack in theoretical understanding that prevents from making intelligent predictions of stereo performance on yet unseen imagery [18].

Stereo image data, depending on recorded scenes, sensor quality and so forth, can be of very different characteristics and origin (e.g., synthetic, controlled indoor, real-world outdoor). The question arises: Given a stereo image pair, what is the minimum error we may expect? This question should be answered for a wide range of different types of stereo image data, ultimately allowing to quantify this material in terms of quality. However, for the most interesting scenarios – outdoor real-world, highly dynamic and complex scenes with potentially very

M. Goesele et al. (Eds.): DAGM 2010, LNCS 6376, pp. 383–392, 2010.
© Springer-Verlag Berlin Heidelberg 2010

poor image quality – the common evaluation approach of stereo matching techniques is not feasible due to the lack of ground truth. Previous work [10,13] that does not require ground truth needs at least three time-synchronous views of a scene. We propose an alternative approach that only needs binocular imagery.

The objective of the paper is to demonstrate that it might be possible to quantify the quality of recorded stereo images with respect to some measures. We also suggest that those measures may be used to indicate domains of relevant imaging scenarios when performing evaluations for some particular test data.

The proposed approach is based on Lowe's SIFT-descriptor [11], which in general outperforms other descriptors in terms of discriminative power [12]. SIFT-matching supports the definition of similarity measures that allow us to derive spatial relations between (e.g.) millions of images [14]. Such results suggest that SIFT-matching can be used to define a measure for establishing some relationships between different sets of stereo image data. There is space for more advanced proposals in future, but a simple SIFT-based measure of matching counts

Fig. 1. Illustration of sparse stereo matching with SIFT-features (not constrained by epipolar geometry, but on rectified images) applied to stereo pairs of different characteristics (top row: Tsukuba and synthetic EISATS stereo pairs; bottom row: real-world scenes of poor quality). Straight connectors of locations of matched features are overlaid to the left image of the used image pair. Synthetic or engineered images generally show a majority of same-row matches.

(Figure 1 illustrates SIFT matches in four stereo pairs) is sufficient to initiate a discussion about this type of data evaluation.

We envision four major benefits of assessing stereo image data independently from geometric ground truth. First, it can guide the selection of applied methods as already mentioned above. Second, it may make processing of real-world stereo images more tractable by providing an additional measure of confidence. Third, we can identify "problematic" situations in real-time; this gives a chance to identify unexpected problems when doing an on-line stereo analysis of real-world stereo image sequences, and to be aware of those when further improving stereo matching. Fourth, it may advance theoretical knowledge about stereo matching by implementing performance evaluation on sophisticated synthetic scenes (i.e., using progress in physics-based rendering) and showing its conclusiveness regarding relevance to real-world scenarios.

The paper is structured as follows. Section 2 introduces two measures based on SIFT matching counts. Section 3 provides details of data used in this study and presents results from experiments to point out the feasibility of the approach. Section 4 explains potential applications in more detail and concludes.

2   Our Method

SIFT features are defined by extrema in a difference-of-Gaussians scale-space, also applying sub-pixel accuracy and rejection of poorly defined locations. Together with a well-constructed descriptor, these are called *distinctive features.*

Our hypothesis is that sparse matching of distinctive features provides measures strongly correlated to the outcome of a dense stereo matching process. The chosen implementation [19] together with the method outlined below seems to be sufficient to illustrate this correlation according to our experiments.

For a rectified stereo pair and known ground truth, a match between a feature location (i_l, j_l) in the left image and a feature location (i_r, j_r) in the right image is *correct up to known constraints* if

$$(i_r - \varepsilon_i < i_l < i_r + \varepsilon_i) \wedge (j_l + d_{ij} - \varepsilon_j \le j_r \le j_l + d_{ij} + \varepsilon_j) \qquad (1)$$

for small $\varepsilon_i, \varepsilon_j > 0$ with known disparity values d_{ij} (i.e., the ground truth). If ground truth is not available, then we evaluate by testing for

$$(i_r - \varepsilon_i < i_l < i_r + \varepsilon_i) \wedge (j_l \le j_r \le j_l + d_{max}) , \qquad (2)$$

where d_{max} is the maximum disparity between both stereo views. We choose $\varepsilon_i = \varepsilon_j = 1$.

Equation (2) appears to be very much "forgiving". However, note that in this case of modeled unavailable ground truth, the probability of the event that "a mismatch is wrongly classified as being correct up to known constraints" has a very small probability of at most $(2\varepsilon_i d_{max} - 1)/(I \cdot J)$ in an image of size $I \times J$. This assumption can be violated, for example, for images with repetitive textures in some areas.

We analyze the counts of correct matches (up to known constraints) and the ratio between detected and matched features for given stereo pairs. Assume that the feature detector identifies n features in the base image that lead to m matches in the match image, and that from those m matches, o are classified as being incorrect. In this case, we define that

$$x = n/m \qquad \text{and} \qquad y = 100 \times o/m \,, \qquad (3)$$

where x is the *matching rate* and y the *mismatch rate*. Thus, $x \geq 1$ and $y \leq 100\%$.

The matching rate x expresses how many features on average lead to one match (no matter whether correct or not), while the mismatch rate y identifies the percentage of incorrect matches.

3   Experiments

Our experiments are designed to demonstrate that the information provided by a selective stereo matching process of distinctive features may be suitable to label stereo image data with an expected quality of disparity calculations, without requiring any ground truth except the value of d_{max}.

Comparison of SIFT-matches on various data sets. In particular, we compare recorded stereo pairs, both "engineered" and real-world, to synthetic pairs, and we attempt to modify the synthetic stereo pairs in a way such that they quantify similar to the recorded pairs for the proposed measures. We compare values of our measures with values of the normalized cross correlation (NCC) derived from prediction errors following [13], on stereo sequences showing "problematic" situations. We use the following stereo image data:

(1) Synthetic data:
- EISATS 2, Sequence 1, see [2]: a sequence of 100 frames with low object complexity showing views from a simulated moving vehicle.
- EISATS 2, Sequence 2, same source: a more complex sequence of 300 frames, containing vegetation modelled with L-Systems.
- Synthetic stereo data of high complexity, rendered by the authors with physically correct simulation of the light distribution, using path-tracing [16]. Different image sensor distortion effects are applied to study their effect, including blooming and chromatic aberration.
(2) Engineered test images (i.e., photos taken under controlled lighting):
- Middlebury 2001 and 2003, see [17], in particular the stereo sets named Tsukuba, Venus, Cones, and Teddy.
- Middlebury 2006, see [7], a more extensive stereo test set, containing 21 images; each image is available for three different illuminations and three different exposures (normal, two f-stops under- and overexposed).
(3) Real-world sequences (150 - 200 stereo frames per sequence) of public road scenarios captured with industrial b/w cameras from a moving vehicle:
- EISATS 1, "Construction site", see [2]: a 10-bit stereo recording.
- NZ Road 1-3, traffic scenes on New Zealand roads, 8-bit trinocular recordings as made available by [13]; these sequences support an error estimation without ground truth based on calculating the third view.

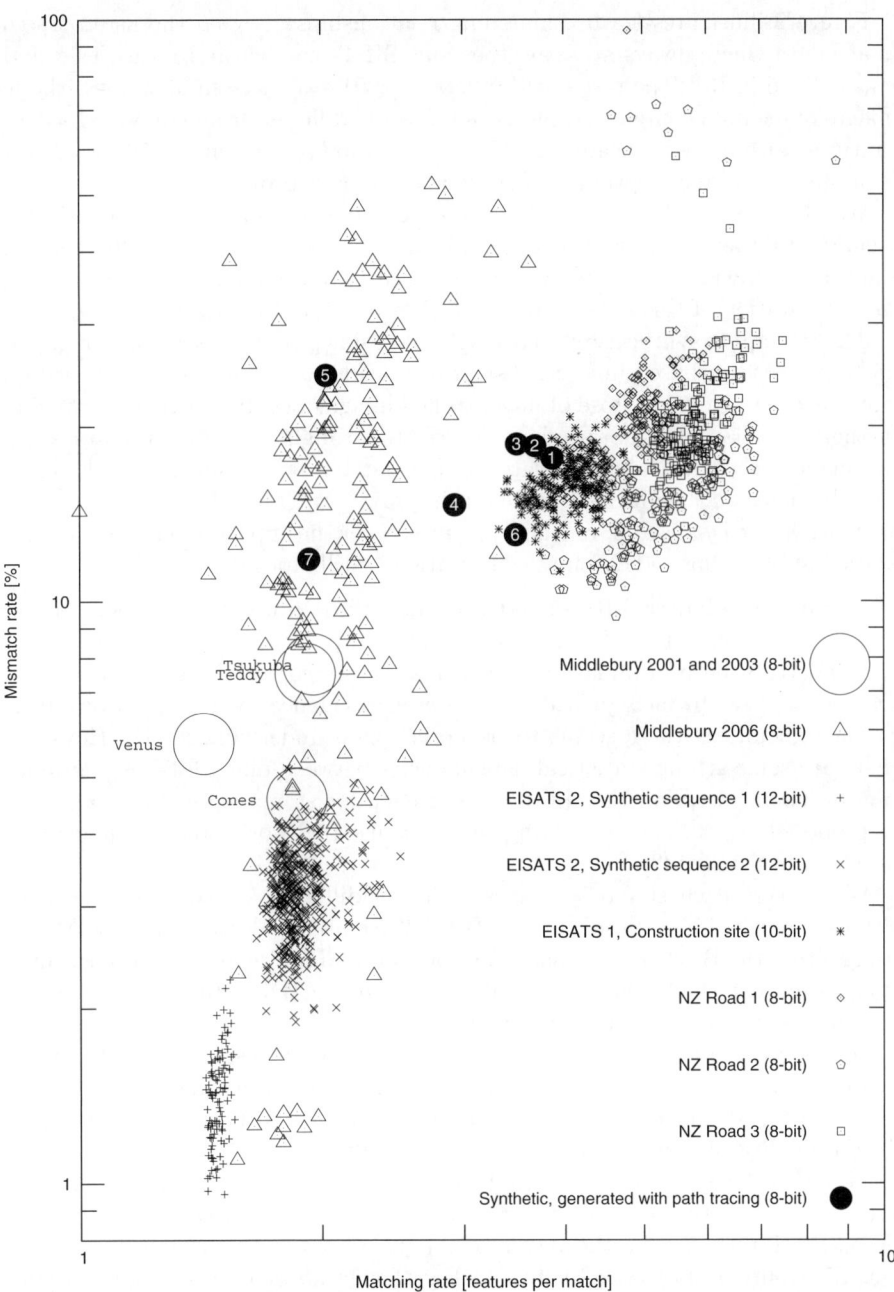

Fig. 2. Mismatch rate y (in percent) and matching rate x in logarithmic scales. Symbols show how stereo data of different origin and quality is discriminated by the proposed measures. Filled black disks for physics-based synthetic data are numbered as follows: 1 (original), 2,3,5 (low, moderate, or severe blooming), 4,6 (moderate or strong chromatic aberration), and 7 (comparison to ordinary raytracing).

Figure 2 illustrates feature matching relationships between the listed stereo image data when always applying the same SIFT matcher and measures x and y as defined in (3). The test set Middlebury 2001 evaluates similar to synthetic images of medium complexity, but is significantly different from real world scenes captured with industrial cameras. The quantization resolution (8-, 10- or 12-bit) is of minor relevance, optimal exposure and contrast provided.

We also see that the more extensive (and somehow "closer" to uncontrolled scenarios) dataset Middlebury 2006, which is not yet widely used for testing, spans a much wider region in our xy-space. However, our xy-space still shows a clear separation of this dataset from real-world outdoor scenes.

The attempt to synthesize stereo image data using physics-based rendering, also including physics-based imaging distortions, leads to distributions of xy-values which are very close to those of uncontrolled image data. Interestingly, applying further distortions does not produce the results we might expect: Chromatic aberration increases both, matching rate and mismatch rate. Adding sensor blooming slightly increases the mismatch rate but improves matching. This indicates to us that either our xy-space is somehow incomplete, or the applied model for the simulation of blooming and chromatic aberration is still "too simple".

Comparison with results based on third-view analysis. This subsection discusses how our simple SIFT-based evaluation relates to a particular kind of "ground truth-based evaluation" when testing stereo matching techniques on real-world data. In fact, providing theoretical evidence for this relationship is rather difficult, as there seems to be no common underlying model. However, there are some strong statistical dependencies between our SIFT-based evaluation on two views, and the third-eye approach for stereo algorithm evaluation as proposed in [13]. For illustrating those, we use real-world stereo sequences as provided in Set 5 of [2].

We process each stereo sequence with five different stereo matching algorithms, namely belief propagation (BP) [3], semi-global matching (SGM) [6] using either the Birchfield-Tomasi (BT) or a mutual information (MI) cost function, graph cut (GC) [9], or dynamic programming (DP) [15].[1] Each of those algorithms run either on the original stereo sequence, a Sobel operator preprocessed stereo sequence, or on residual images [1] with respect to 40-times repeated 3×3 mean filtering (or one run of a comparable large smoothing kernel). In uncontrolled image data, suitable preprocessing often has a dramatic effect on the quality of stereo results. We compare altogether 15 different matching results, used for generating a virtual third view, compared by normalized cross correlation with the recorded third view. For a simple comparison to the proposed SIFT test, we use the mean $(x + y)/2$ of matching and mismatch rate. The distribution of observed values in Fig. 2 suggests that this even more simplified measure is sufficiently discriminative. See Fig. 3 and Fig. 4 for results on real-world stereo sequences with 150 stereo frames. For this visual comparison, all these error measures are normalized as follows: if T is the number of frames and $\mathrm{NCC}(t)$ is the error measure for a particular frame t with

---

[1] Sources of used matching programs are as acknowledged in [13].

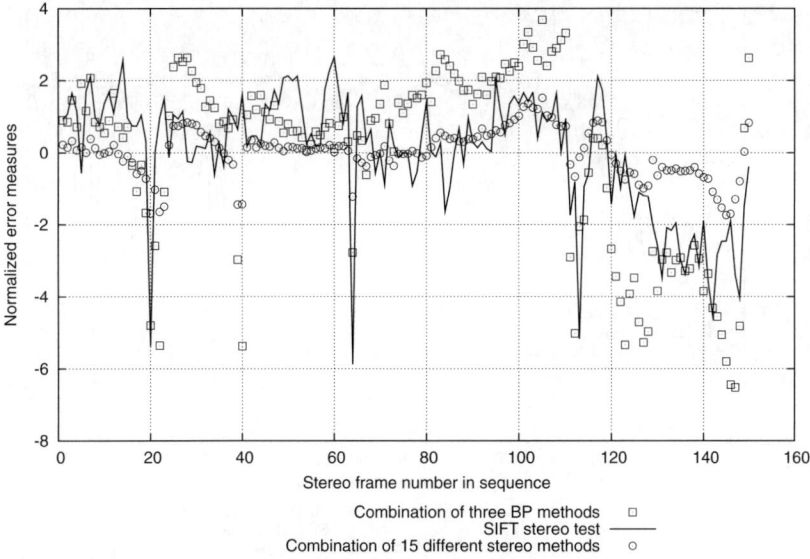

Combination of three BP methods   □
SIFT stereo test   ———
Combination of 15 different stereo methods   ○

Fig. 3. Normalized error measures for stereo frames 1 to 150 of a day-light highway sequence. We compare results of the proposed SIFT-measure with prediction error based on third-view-synthesis using 15 different stereo matching schemes. For clarity of presentation, only the mean of selected values is displayed.

$1 \leq t \leq T$, we display $(\mathrm{NCC}(t) - \mu_T)/\sigma_T$, where $\mu_T = 1/T \sum_{t=1}^{T} \mathrm{NCC}(t)$ and $\sigma_T^2 = 1/(T-1) \sum_{t=1}^{T} (\mathrm{NCC}(t) - \mu_T)^2$. The same normalization is applied to the results of SIFT matching.

Statistical relation between error measures. Normalized cross correlation was used again to examine the relationship between error measures of all stereo matching algorithms and between stereo and SIFT-matching counts, for long sequences as illustrated by the previous two figures. The correlation coefficients and p-values were computed. Table 1 summarizes the correlation between those stereo algorithms. Due to space limitations, we only display results for the mean of NCC values for the three different preprocessing options of the two sequences already illustrated in Figs. 3 and 4.

Table 1 indicates a moderate correlation between errors of the SIFT-measure and all stereo algorithms except DP. Strongest correlations are mostly found between global algorithms, but all measures in the highway sequence are significantly correlated ($p < 0.001$) except the combinations SIFT – DP ($p = 0.59$), and SGM(MI) – DP ($p = 0.17$). In the night-time sequence, all measures are significantly correlated($p < 0.001$). Reasons for outliers in particular frames leading to weaker correlation between BP and SIFT based measures are as follows:

In the highway sequence, the most obvious deviation is in Frames 39 and 40. In these images, a large area (a big truck on the highway) is coming close (less than ten times the baseline) to the camera, resulting in semi-occluded areas at the

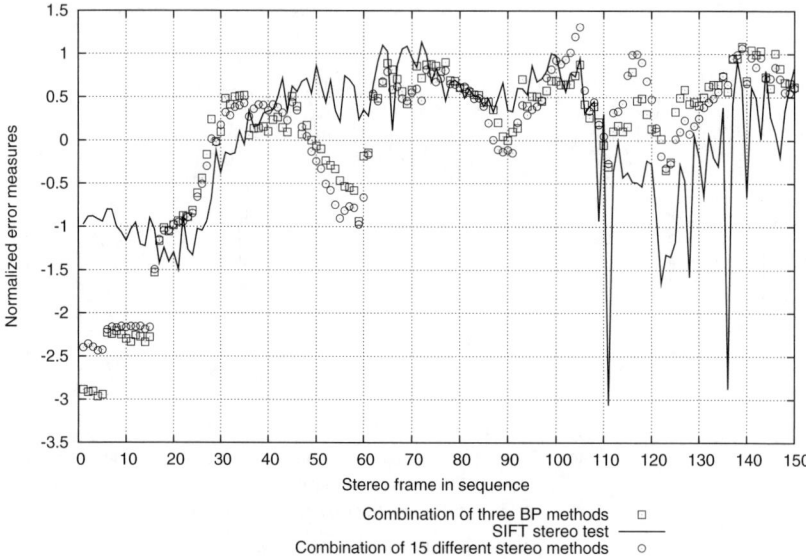

Fig. 4. Same measures as in Fig. 3 but on a night-time sequence of 150 stereo frames

image border. Many stereo algorithms do not cope with this situation. However, for the method described above this simply results in no matches being found in this area, thus no mismatches can occur. Frames 120 to 150 are subject to major brightness differences, where belief propagation stereo performs poorly.

For the night-time sequence, significant deviations occur in Frames 1 to 16, and 50 to 60. Outliers in Frames 111, 128 and 136 are caused by time-synchronization problems. Frames 50 to 60 are big objects coming closer and becoming increasingly semi-occluded by the image border. Of interest are Frames 1 to 16, where strong blooming (caused by strong light sources nearby) is present. This is not very well detected by counting matches.

Table 1. Pearson correlation between error measures

Algorithm	Sequence	BP	SGM(BT)	DP	GC	SGM(MI)	SIFT
Belief propagation	Highway	1	0·95	0·30	0·81	0·69	0·63
	Night	1	0·97	0·85	0·97	0·96	0·57
Semi-global matching (BT)	Highway		1	0·35	0·88	0·60	0·64
	Night		1	0·83	0·94	0·94	0·52
Dynamic programming	Highway			1	0·55	0·11	0·05
	Night			1	0·88	0·82	0·40
Graph cut	Highway				1	0·50	0·56
	Night				1	0·97	0·62
Semi-global matching (MI)	Highway					1	0·43
	Night					1	0·66

We see that for many artifacts in uncontrolled image data there is no correlation between matching statistics and stereo performance. These need to be addressed by different methods.

4   Future Work and Conclusions

It is certainly of general interest in computer vision to have some evaluation of stereo data at hand, for judging its complexity, or qualitative relation to other sequences of stereo data (also covering the common case that ground truth is not available). This evaluation is of interest for the following:

Identification of crucial scenarios in large datasets of stereo images: Crucial 3D scenarios, defined by special events in the real world, need to be identified when testing stereo matching in the real world. Such events have to be isolated from a sufficiently diversified database of real world data (e.g., when running a stereo analysis system for days or weeks in real-world traffic). As ground truth is generally not available, our approach helps in identification of these critical datasets.

Realtime check of stereo data in real world applications: In our method, computing feature descriptors and matching depends on the number of detected interest points, which are numerous in highly structured images. Ensuring realtime here requires to limit their number to a fixed upper bound. For SIFT-features such kind of pruning is described in [5]. In its application to image-database retrieval, an insignificant decline in performance was reported even if the number of features is very small. Such realtime checks may be crucial for reliable safety-relevant decisions in, for example, driver assistance systems.

Purposeful design of synthetic sequences for stereo testing: Synthetic data will remain important for testing stereo matching, especially due to having full control about the image formation process. Simulations of interesting situations (rarely appearing in reality, but possible) such as for weather, poor light conditions, or deficiencies in cameras systems, need to come with some evidence of its adequacy for testing stereo vision algorithms.

We have shown that even a simple measure, such as the matching count based on SIFT-features, can provide error measures significantly correlated to a third-view error measure. We pointed out the necessity to benchmark a fairly "huge amount" of stereo image data, and to put those data into qualitative relation to each other.

Future research may aim at more complex measures, allowing to analyze more detailed quality aspects of stereo images. In continuation of the simple count measure as presented here, this could be based on statistics of spatial distributions of matches or mismatches in stereo image pairs. (Note that a simple root-mean square or NCC error value in relation to ground truth does not yet give any information about the spatial distribution of errors.)

Models as presented in [8] may be of very high interest, yet their use is limited due to prohibitive computational costs.

References

1. Aujol, J.F., Gilboa, G., Chan, T., Osher, S.: Structure-texture image decomposition - modeling, algorithms, and parameter selection. Int. J. Computer Vision 67, 111–136 (2006)
2. EISATS: enpeda.. image sequence analysis test site, http://www.mi.auckland.ac.nz/EISATS
3. Felzenszwalb, P.F., Huttenlocher, D.P.: Efficient belief propagation for early vision. Int. J. Computer Vision 70, 41–54 (2006)
4. Förstner, W.: 10 pros and cons against performance characterization of vision algorithms. Machine Vision Applications 9, 215–218 (1997)
5. Foo, J.J., Sinha, R.: Pruning SIFT for scalable near-duplicate image matching. In: Proc. Australasian Database Conf., pp. 63–71 (2007)
6. Hirschmüller, H.: Stereo processing by semiglobal matching and mutual information. IEEE Trans. Pattern Analysis Machine Intelligence 30, 328–341 (2007)
7. Hirschmüller, H., Scharstein, D.: Evaluation of stereo matching costs on images with radiometric differences. IEEE Trans. Pattern Analysis Machine Intelligence 31, 1582–1599 (2009)
8. Hyvärinen, A., Hurri, J., Hoyer, P.: Natural Image Statistics. Springer, Amsterdam (2009)
9. Kolmogorov, V., Zabih, R.: Computing visual correspondence with occlusions via graph cuts. In: Proc. Int. Conf. Computer Vision, pp. 508–515 (2001)
10. Leclerc, Y.G., Luong, Q.-T., Fua, P.V.: Self-consistency, Stereo, MDL, and Change detection. In: Proc. IJCV (2002)
11. Lowe, D.G.: Distinctive image features from scale-invariant keypoints. Int. J. Computer Vision 60, 91–110 (2004)
12. Mikolajczyk, K., Schmid, C.: A performance evaluation of local descriptors. IEEE Trans. Pattern Analysis Machine Intelligence 10, 1615–1630 (2005)
13. Morales, S., Klette, R.: A third eye for performance evaluation in stereo sequence analysis. In: Jiang, X., Petkov, N. (eds.) Computer Analysis of Images and Patterns. LNCS, vol. 5702, pp. 1078–1086. Springer, Heidelberg (2009)
14. Nistér, D., Stewénius, H.: Scalable recognition with a vocabulary tree. In: Proc. IEEE Conf. Computer Vision Pattern Recognition, vol. 2, pp. 2161–2168 (2006)
15. Ohta, Y., Kanade, T.: Stereo by two-level dynamic programming. In: Proc. Int. Joint Conf. Artificial Intelligence, pp. 1120–1126 (1985)
16. Pharr, M., Humphreys, G.: Physically Based Rendering: From Theory to Implementation. Morgan Kaufmann, San Francisco (2004)
17. Scharstein, D., Szeliski, R.: A taxonomy and evaluation of dense two-frame stereo correspondence algorithms. Int. J. Computer Vision 47, 7–42 (2002)
18. Thacker, N.A., Clark, A.F., Barron, J.L., Beveridge, J.R., Courtney, P., Crum, W.R., Ramesh, V., Clark, C.: Performance characterization in computer vision: A guide to best practices. Computer Vision Image Understanding 109, 305–334 (2008)
19. Vedaldi, A., Fulkerson, B.: VLFeat: An open and portable library of computer vision algorithms (2008), http://www.vlfeat.org

Robust Open-Set Face Recognition for Small-Scale Convenience Applications

Hua Gao, Hazım Kemal Ekenel, and Rainer Stiefelhagen

Institute for Anthropomatics
Karlsruhe Institute of Technology
Karlsruhe, Germany
{hua.gao,ekenel,rainer.stiefelhagen}@kit.edu

Abstract. In this paper, a robust real-world video based open-set face recognition system is presented. This system is designed for general small-scale convenience applications, which can be used for providing customized services. In the developed prototype, the system identifies a person in question and conveys customized information according to the identity. Since it does not require any cooperation of the users, the robustness of the system can be easily affected by the confounding factors. To overcome the pose problem, we generated frontal view faces with a tracked 2D face model. We also employed a distance metric to assess the quality of face model tracking. A local appearance-based face representation was used to make the system robust against local appearance variations. We evaluated the system's performance on a face database which was collected in front of an office. The experimental results on this database show that the developed system is able to operate robustly under real-world conditions.

1 Introduction

There is a large demand for building robust access control systems for the safety and convenience of modern society. Among different biometric identification methods, face recognition is a less obtrusive technique which does not require too much cooperation of the users. Due to the absence of user cooperation and due to uncontrolled conditions, building a robust real-world face recognition system is still a challenging task and has attracted broad interest. In real-world systems, there are many sources of variabilities in facial appearance which may significantly degenerate the performance of the system. The major four confounding factors are pose, illumination, expression, and partial occlusion (i.e. glasses or facial hair). In many previous systems, numerous approaches have been proposed to deal with one or two specific aspects of variations [1,2,3].

The active appearance model (AAM) [4] was proposed as a 2D deformable face model for modeling pose changes, facial expression and illumination variations. The shape of the face model is optimized by minimizing the texture representation error. Once the model is fitted on an input image, the corresponding model parameter vector can be used as a feature vector. In [5], linear

M. Goesele et al. (Eds.): DAGM 2010, LNCS 6376, pp. 393–402, 2010.

discriminant analysis (LDA) was utilized to construct a discriminant subspace for face identification. Later in [6], the authors found that the shape parameters of AAMs can be used to estimate the pose angle. A frontal view of an input face image can be synthesized by configuring the shape parameters that control the pose. Face recognition with this pose correction method was evaluated by Guillemaut et al. in [7]. However, they corrected the appearance of the rotated faces with some nonlinear warping techniques instead of synthesis. This texture warping approach has the advantage of preserving the textural information such as moles and freckles contained in the original image, which will be lost in the synthesis-based approach in which small local details may not be modeled.

In this paper, we present a face recognition system which is robust against the aforementioned confounding factors. Three key techniques are employed to achieve the goal of this system: 1) A generic AAM is used to track a set of facial landmarks on the face images. With these facial landmarks, we generate shape-free frontal view faces with a nonlinear piecewise affine warping. The variations in pose and expression are normalized to a canonical shape. 2) A distance metric is employed to assess the quality of AAM fitting. According to this distance metric, we filtered out some frames where the model fitting failed. 3) A local appearance-based face representation is used for face recognition. This representation is considered to be invariant to local appearance changes such as expression, partial occlusion, and illumination changes [8]. Experiments in [9] showed that this approach is also robust against the errors introduced in the face model fitting.

The presented open-set face recognition system is suitable for small-scale convenience applications, which can be easily customized for a small group of people such as family members or laboratory members. The system identifies a person in question and conveys customized information or provides personalized services according to the identity of the person. An example system can be a smart TV set, which is able to show personalized TV programs according to the identity of the person in front of the television. It can also be integrated in a smart household robot so that it can identify the family members and customize the dialogue. The prototype application for this presented system is a visitor interface. The system is mounted in front of an office. A welcome message is displayed on the screen. When a visitor appears in front of the system before knocking on the door, the system identifies the visitor unobtrusively without any special co-operation. According to the identity of the person, the system customizes the information that it conveys about the host. For example, if the visitor is unknown, the system only displays availability information about the host. On the other hand, if the person is known, depending on the identity of the person, more detailed information about the host's status is displayed.

The remainder of this paper is organized as follows. In Section 2, we describe the implementation details for building a robust open-set face recognition system. We present the evaluation procedure and discuss the experimental results in Section 3 and give concluding remarks in Section 4.

2   Methodology

This section explains the processing steps of the developed robust open-set face recognition system.

2.1   Active Appearance Models and Model Fitting

The AAM is a generative parametric model which utilizes both shape and appearance information to represent a certain object such as the human face. A shape in AAM is defined as a set of normalized 2D facial landmarks. An instance of the linear shape model can be represented as $s = s_0 + \sum_{i=1}^{n} p_i s_i$, where s_0 is the mean shape, s_i is the ith shape basis, and $\mathbf{p} = [p_1, p_2, \ldots, p_n]$ are the shape parameters. The appearance model is defined inside the mean shape, which explains the variations in appearance caused by changes in illumination, identity, and expression, etc. It represents an instance appearance as $A = A_0 + \sum_{i=1}^{m} \lambda_i A_i$, where A_0 is the mean appearance, A_i is the ith appearance basis, and $\lambda = [\lambda_1, \lambda_2, \ldots, \lambda_m]$ are the appearance parameters.

Given an input facial image $I(\mathbf{x})$, the goal of fitting an AAM is to find the optimal model parameters such that the synthesized model appearance is as similar to the image observation as possible. This leads to a minimization of a cost function defined as:

$$E = \sum_{\mathbf{x} \in s_0} \left[I(\mathbf{W}(\mathbf{x}; \mathbf{p})) - A(\mathbf{x}, \lambda) \right]^2, \tag{1}$$

where $I(\mathbf{W}(\mathbf{x}; \mathbf{p}))$ is the warped input facial image, and $A(\mathbf{x}, \lambda)$ is the synthesized appearance instance. The minimization problem is usually solved by gradient descent methods, which iteratively estimate the incremental update of the shape parameter $\Delta \mathbf{p}$ and the appearance parameter $\Delta \lambda$, and update the current model parameters respectively. The Inverse Compositional (IC) and Simultaneously Inverse Compositional (SIC) methods proposed by Baker and Mathews [10] formulated the problem in a more efficient way, where the role of the appearance template and the input image is inversed when computing $\Delta \mathbf{p}$. The shape is updated by composing an inverse incremental warping $\Delta W(\mathbf{x}; \mathbf{p})$ which is estimated where $\mathbf{p} = 0$. This framework enables the time-consuming steps of parameter estimation to be pre-computed outside of the iterations. We implemented the SIC fitting algorithm for its better generalization ability to unseen data [11].

It is known that the gradient-descent-based optimization problem usually requires a reasonable initialization. A poor initialization may cause the search to get stuck in a local minimum. We used the responses of a face and eye detector based on Viola & Jones' approach [12] to initialize the face shape with a 2D similarity transformation. This initialization usually suffices for fitting frontal faces. However, when fitting semi-profile faces, part of the initialized shape does not cover the face. Thus the optimization can be affected by the included background pixels. To avoid bad initialization, we adopted a two stage progressive model fitting as used in [9].

2.2 Fitting While Tracking

In the context of tracking AAMs in video sequences, the model parameter $\{\mathbf{p_t}, \lambda_t\}$ at time t can be initialized with the successfully optimized parameter $\{\mathbf{p_{t-1}}, \lambda_{t-1}\}$ at time $t - 1$. To improve AAM fitting in video sequences, Liu [13] extended the SIC algorithm to enforce the frame-to-frame registration across video sequences. The proposed algorithm assumes that the warped images will not change over a few frames. This assumption is considered as a prior to the cost function of the SIC, which constrains the parameter searching to the right direction.

The cost function is then reformulated as follows:

$$\sum_{\mathbf{x}} \left[I_t(\mathbf{W}(\mathbf{x}; \mathbf{p})) - A(\mathbf{x}, \lambda) \right]^2 + k \sum_{\mathbf{x}} \left[I_t(\mathbf{W}(\mathbf{x}; \mathbf{p})) - M_t(\mathbf{x}) \right]^2, \qquad (2)$$

where the first term is the fitting goal of the SIC algorithm. The prior term is defined as the sum of squared error between the current warped image $I_t(\mathbf{W}(\mathbf{x}; \mathbf{p}))$ and the appearance from previous frames, $M_t(\mathbf{x})$. For simplicity, we define $M_t(\mathbf{x})$ as the warped image of the video frame at time $t - 1$:

$$M_t(\mathbf{x}) = I_{t-1}(\mathbf{W}(\mathbf{x}; \mathbf{p}_{t-1})). \qquad (3)$$

The benefit of this term is clear; it presents the specific appearance information of the subject being fitted, which may not be modeled by the generic face models. This information can compensate the mismatch between the face models and the input images being fitted.

2.3 Tracking Quality Assessment

A simple way to verify the result of the fitting is to check the residual error, which is also been considered as the stop criterion for the fitting algorithm. The residual error indicates the reconstruction error of the eigenspace decomposition and the measure is referred to as the "distance from feature space" (DFFS) in the context of "eigenfaces". However, the error of the AAM fitting is composed of the reconstruction error and the search error. The residual error alone is not able to assess the quality of the fitting results. Eigenfaces, especially higher-order ones, can be linearly combined to form images which do not resemble faces at all. In this sense, the coefficients of the eigenfaces should also be taken into consideration. For this purpose we employed a modified DFFS definition which was introduced in [14]:

$$DFFS(\lambda_1, \ldots, \lambda_m, \varepsilon) = K \times \left(\sum_{i=1}^{m} \{ \frac{\lambda_i^2}{\sigma_i^2} \} + \frac{\varepsilon^2}{\sigma_{residue}^2} \right). \qquad (4)$$

Here $\varepsilon = \mathbf{I_x} - (A_0 + \sum_{i=1}^{m} \lambda_i A_i)$ is the residue, and $\sigma_i = \max_{t \in T} |\lambda_{t,i}|$, $\sigma_{residue} = \max_{t \in T} |\varepsilon_t|$, which correspond to the worst outliers of the weights and residue in the training set T. Note that K is an arbitrary constant used as a scale factor.

The modified DFFS value can be used to assess the quality of the AAM fitting result since it yields low values for good face model fitting and high values for poor fitting. It is not exactly zero for a perfect fitting since only the mean face is located precisely in the center of the cloud representing the distribution. All the other face instances have a distance from the center of the cloud and thus have a non-zero value. If the value is larger than a threshold τ, the AAM tracking will be re-initialized.

2.4 Pose Normalization

The most straightforward method to normalize the pose of a face image is the piecewise affine warping which is also used in the fitting algorithm for sampling the texture inside the face mesh. The warp is realized by mapping the pixels in each fitted triangular mesh s to the base mesh s_0. For each pixel $\mathbf{x} = (x, y)^T$ in a triangle in the base mesh s_0, it can find a unique pixel $\mathbf{W}(\mathbf{x}; \mathbf{p}) = \mathbf{x}' = (x', y')^T$ in the corresponding triangle in the mesh s with bilinear interpolation. The implementation for the piecewise affine warp is detailed in [10]. Another nonlinear warping technique based on thin-plate splines (TPS) was also studied in [9]. However, the recognition based on piecewise affine warping outperforms TPS despite its simplicity.

2.5 Open-Set Face Recognition

Face Representation. The pose normalized facial images are masked with the AAM mean shape. All salient facial features are warped to the canonical locations. However, feature points around the chin area might be misaligned, which may create strong edges. As demonstrated in [15], the chin area does not contribute too much discriminative information compared to other facial features. For this reason, we cropped the chin area in the pose normalized facial image. Following the approach in [8], we scaled the cropped images to 64×64 pixels size and then divided them into 64 non-overlapped blocks of 8×8 pixels size. On each local block, the discrete cosine transform (DCT) is performed. The obtained DCT coefficients are ordered using a zig-zag scanning. The first component is skipped because it represents the average pixel intensity of the entire block. The following five low frequency coefficients are retained which yields a five dimensional local feature vector. This local feature vector is then normalized to unit norm. Finally, the feature vectors extracted from each block are concatenated to construct the global feature vector. For details of the algorithm please see [8].

Classification. Open set face recognition is different from the traditional face identification in that it also involves rejection of impostors in addition to identify accepted genuine members that are enrolled in the database. We formulate the open-set face recognition as a multiple verification problem as proposed in [16]. Given a claimed identity, the result of an identity verification is whether the claimed identity is accepted or rejected. Given a number of positive and negative samples it is possible to train a classifier that models the distribution of faces for both cases. Based on this idea, we trained an identity verifier for every one of the n known subjects in the gallery using support vector machines (SVMs). Once a new probe is presented to the system, it is checked against all classifiers; if all of them reject, the person is reported as unknown; if one accepts, the person is accepted with that identity; if more than a single verifier accepts, the identity with the highest score wins. Scores are linearly proportional to the distance to the hyperplane of the corresponding SVM classifier.

Temporal fusion. Since a person's identity does not change during the video capture, we can enforce temporal consistency. In order to make it possible to revise a preliminary decision later on, instead of relying on a single classification result for every frame an n-best list is used. N-best lists store the first n highest ranked results. We choose $n = 3$ in this work. For each hypothesis a cumulated score is stored that develops over time. If the face model tracking fails over multiple frames, the cumulated scores are reset assuming that the person has left or is not facing the camera. Resetting scores allows the whole process to restart once a face is located and the face model tracking is successfully initialized.

3   Experiments

To evaluate the performance of the presented system, we carried out experiments on the database collected in [16]. Totally 54 people were recorded in front of an office, with natural or artificial lighting conditions depending on the time of the day. These recordings were split into two groups, a group of known people and a group of unknown people. Different sets of data were used for training and testing. Known people's recordings were split into training and testing sessions which do not overlap. Unknown subjects used for training are different from those used for testing. Fig. 1 depicts some example frames in the database. The recorded subjects were free to move, even out the sight of the camera. The depicted example frames show different recording conditions as well as subjects with various poses.

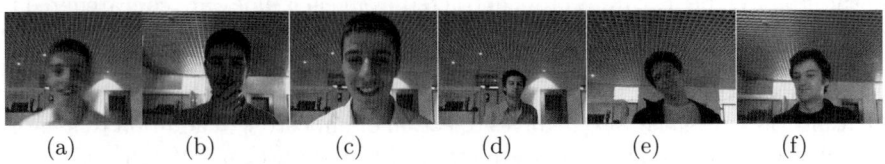

(a)   (b)   (c)   (d)   (e)   (f)

Fig. 1. Recordings from the data set, different illumination and face sizes. (a) Artificial light, motion blur. (b) Day light, dark, partial occluded. (c) Artificial light, bright, near. (d) Artificial light, far away. (e) Head rotate in plane. (f) Head rotate in depth.

3.1 Performance Measure for Open-Set Face Recognition

In closed-set face recognition, the false classification rate (FCR) is a common measure for evaluating the performance of the system. However, in open-set face recognition, there are two more types of error which can occur. The impostors can be erroneously accepted by the system (false accept rate (FAR)), while the genuine members can also be rejected (false rejection rate (FRR)). All the three errors have to be traded-off against each other, as it is not possible to minimize them at the same time. The equal error rate (EER = FAR = FCR+FRR) performance measure is employed to trade off against the three error terms. A system with a lower EER is considered to be more robust and accurate.

SVMs automatically minimize the overall error and try to find the global minimum. To fine tune the system performance to equalize the accept error and reject error, the receiver operating characteristic (ROC) curve for SVM-based classification was created by using a parameterized decision surface. The decision hyperplane $\{x \in S : wx + b = 0, (w,b) \in S \times R\}$ is modified to $wx + b = \Delta$, where Δ allows to adjust the FAR and the CCR (correct classification rate) accordingly. A polynomial kernel with degree 2 is used as in [16].

3.2 Performance Comparison

Table 1 lists the data configuration for training and testing. The unknown training data was down-sampled so that the total number of frames from unknown subjects and each known subject is balanced. Note that only the frames fitted under a certain threshold of the modified DFFS value were accepted for training and testing. The threshold was selected empirically so that it discards all possible failed fittings. Here we choose the threshold $\tau = 10.0$. After face pose normalization through the known training sequences, we obtained approximately 600 known training samples for each subject. For the unknown training, 25 sessions of different subject were used, each session was under-sampled to 30 frames. Sample pose normalized face images are plotted in Fig. 2.

We first started with frame-based classification. The results are listed on the first row of Table 2 where $\Delta = -0.108$ and EER = 3.0%. The ROC curve which plots the correct classification rate against the FAR is illustrated in Fig. 3(a).

Another frame-based test was also carried out on the same data set to verify the effectiveness of the pose correction. Instead of synthesizing a face with a

Table 1. Data set for open set experiments

Training data		
Known	5 subjects	4 sessions and $\approx$ 600 frames per person
Unknown	25 subjects	1 session, 30 frames per subject
Testing data		
Known	5 subjects	3-7 sessions per person
Unknown	20 subjects	1 session per person

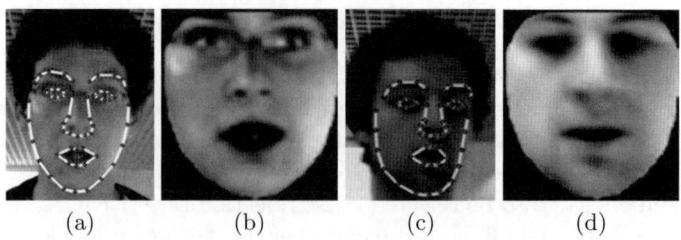

(a)   (b)   (c)   (d)

Fig. 2. Pose normalization. (a),(c) Face images overlaid with tracked AAM shape. (b),(d) Pose normalized face images.

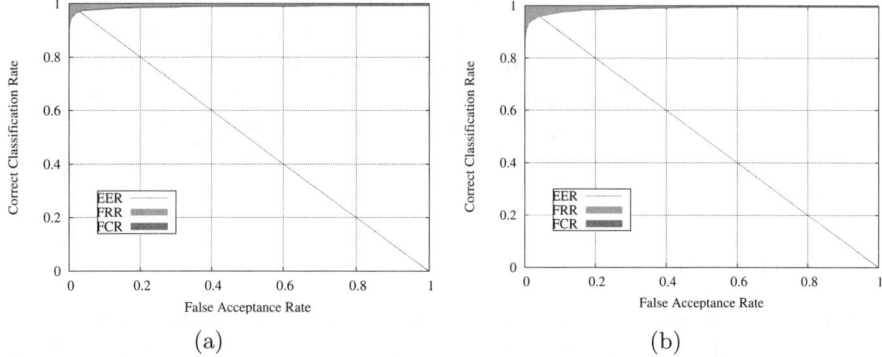

(a)   (b)

Fig. 3. (a) Frame-based ROC curve with pose normalization. (b) Frame-based ROC curve without pose normalization.

piecewise affine warp after AAM fitting, a simple Euclidean transformation was performed according to the eye center coordinates in the fitted AAM shape. The corresponding results are listed on the third row of Table 2 where EER = 4.0% and $\Delta = -0.167$. The ROC curve for this test is depicted in Fig. 3(b).

The frame-based face recognition in video sequences makes a decision on every single frame. The results, therefore, return some insight on the general performance of the registration and classification scheme employed. The EER obtained with pose normalization is 1.0% lower than the one obtained without pose normalization. This means that the AAM-based pose normalization improves the robustness of the system against pose variations. It prevents the system from

Table 2. Classification results with AAM face warping vs. simple alignment

Alignment	Classification	CCR	FRR	FAR	CRR	FCR
AAM	Frame-based	97.1%	2.7%	3.0%	97.0%	0.2%
	Progressive-score	100.0%	0.0%	0.0%	100.0%	0.0%
Euclidean trans.	Frame-based	95.8%	4.1%	4.0%	96.0%	0.1%
	Progressive-score	99.7%	0.3%	0.4%	99.6%	0.0%

accepting unknown identities with similar poses to the enrolled person or rejecting genuine members with unmatched poses. The frame filtering with the modified DFFS metric also improves the robustness of the system as the frames with bad alignment are discarded. Compared to the results reported in [16], the equal error rate decreases by 4.5% even without pose normalization.

The temporal fusion-based classification was also applied as a progressive-score-based approach by accumulating frame scores over time. This can be thought of as classifying every frame as if it were the end of a sequence and taking the final score. The results with progressive-score-based classification are listed on the second and fourth row of Table 2, respectively for the two registration approaches.

Observing the results based on the progressive-score-based classification, we noticed that the results were improved compared to the frame-based scheme. The Euclidean transformation-based alignment achieved 0.4% EER, which is already much better than the frame-based classification. With the AAM-based pose normalization the temporal fusion smoothed out all erroneous decisions and the ERR is 0.0%.[1]

4   Conclusions

In this paper, an open-set face recognition system is presented, in which AAM-based pose normalization is employed to improve its robustness. The system operates fully automatically and runs in near real-time (at 15 fps) on a laptop computer with a 2.0GHz Intel Core 2 Duo processor. It has been observed that normalizing the pose changes improves the recognition performance, because the gallery may not contain the corresponding pose for a given probe. The employed distance metric is able to filter out some misaligned frames, which improved the results further. The local appearance-based face representation makes the system invariant to other confounding factors as well as the misalignment errors.

Currently we only evaluated the system with five known subjects. The performance of the system may decrease as the number of known subjects increases. However, for small-scale convenience applications such as the smart visitor interface, the system is able to operate very robustly with moderate number of group members. In the future, more known subjects will be evaluated and the scalability of the system will be analyzed.

Acknowledgments

This work was realized as part of the Quaero Programme, funded by OSEO, French State agency for innovation.

---

[1] A sample video is available under http://cvhci.anthropomatik.kit.edu/~hgao/dagm-video.zip, which demonstrates the face tracking, pose normalization and open-set face recognition.

References

1. Georghiades, A.S., Belhumeur, P.N., Kriegman, D.J.: From few to many: Illumination cone models for face recognition under variable lighting and pose. IEEE Trans. on PAMI 23(6), 643–660 (2001)
2. Huang, F.J., Zhou, Z., Zhang, H.J., Chen, T.: Pose invariant face recognition. In: Proc. of the IEEE Int'l. Conference on Automatic Face and Gesture Recognition, pp. 245–250 (2000)
3. Zhao, W.Y., Chellappa, R.: SFS based view synthesis for robust face recognition. In: Proc. of the IEEE Int'l. Conference on Automatic Face and Gesture Recognition, pp. 285–292 (2000)
4. Cootes, T.F., Edwards, G.J., Taylor, C.J.: Active appearance models. In: Burkhardt, H., Neumann, B. (eds.) ECCV 1998, Part II. LNCS, vol. 1407, pp. 484–498. Springer, Heidelberg (1998)
5. Edwards, G.J., Cootes, T.F., Taylor, C.J.: Face recognition using active appearance models. In: Burkhardt, H., Neumann, B. (eds.) ECCV 1998. LNCS, vol. 1407, pp. 581–595. Springer, Heidelberg (1998)
6. Cootes, T.F., Wheeler, G.V., Walker, K.N., Taylor, C.J.: View-based active appearance models. Image and Vision Computing 20(9-10), 657–664 (2002)
7. Guillemaut, J., Kittler, J., Sadeghi, M.T., Christmas, W.J.: General pose face recognition using frontal face model. In: Martínez-Trinidad, J.F., Carrasco Ochoa, J.A., Kittler, J. (eds.) CIARP 2006. LNCS, vol. 4225, pp. 79–88. Springer, Heidelberg (2006)
8. Ekenel, H.K.: A robust face recognition algorithm for real-world applications. PhD dissertation, University of Karlsruhe, TH (2009)
9. Gao, H., Ekenel, H.K., Stiefelhagen, R.: Pose normalization for local appearance-based face recognition. In: Tistarelli, M., Nixon, M.S. (eds.) ICB 2009. LNCS, vol. 5558, pp. 32–41. Springer, Heidelberg (2009)
10. Matthews, I., Baker, S.: Active appearance models revisited. International Journal of Computer Vision 60(2), 135–164 (2004)
11. Gross, R., Matthews, I., Baker, S.: Generic vs. person specific active appearance models. Image and Vision Computing 23(11), 1080–1093 (2005)
12. Viola, P., Jones, M.J.: Robust real-time face detection. International Journal of Computer Vision 57(2), 137–154 (2004)
13. Liu, X., Wheeler, F.W., Tu, P.H.: Improved face model fitting on video sequences. In: Proc. of British Machine Vision Conference (BMVC 2007) (2007)
14. Jebara, T.S.: 3D pose estimation and normalization for face recognition. B. Thesis, McGill Centre for Intelligent Machines (1996)
15. Ekenel, H.K., Stiefelhagen, R.: Block selection in the local appearance-based face recognition scheme. In: CVPR Biometrics Workshop (2006)
16. Ekenel, H.K., Szasz-Toth, L., Stiefelhagen, R.: Open-set face recognition-based visitor interface system. In: Fritz, M., Schiele, B., Piater, J.H. (eds.) ICVS 2009. LNCS, vol. 5815, pp. 43–52. Springer, Heidelberg (2009)

Belief Propagation for Improved Color Assessment in Structured Light

Christoph Schmalz[1,2] and Elli Angelopoulou[1]

[1] Pattern Recognition Lab, University of Erlangen-Nuremberg, Germany
[2] Siemens CT T HW 2, Munich, Germany

Abstract. Single-Shot Structured Light is a well-known method for acquiring 3D surface data of moving scenes with simple and compact hardware setups. Some of the biggest challenges in these systems is their sensitivity to textured scenes, subsurface scattering and low-contrast illumination. Recently, a graph-based method has been proposed that largely eliminates these shortcomings. A key step in the graph-based pattern decoding algorithm is the estimation of color of local image regions which correspond to the vertex colors of the graph. In this work we propose a new method for estimating the color of a vertex based on belief propagation (BP). The BP framework allows the explicit inclusion of cues from neigboring vertices in the color estimation. This is especially beneficial for low-contrast input images. The augmented method is evaluated using typical low-quality real-world test sequences of the interior of a pig stomach. We demonstrate a significant improvement in robustness. The number of 3D data points generated increases by 30 to 50 percent over the plain decoding.

1 Introduction

Structured Light is a general term for many different methods for measuring 3D surface data. The main idea is to project a known illumination pattern on the scene. Shape information is then extracted from the observed deformation of the pattern (figure 1). The

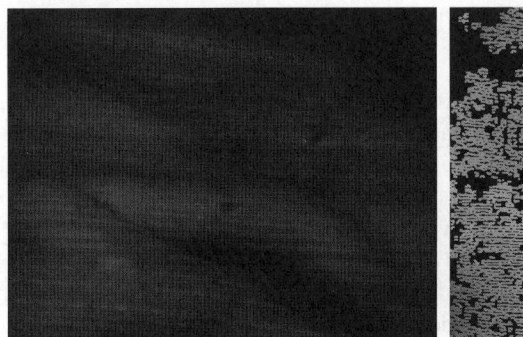
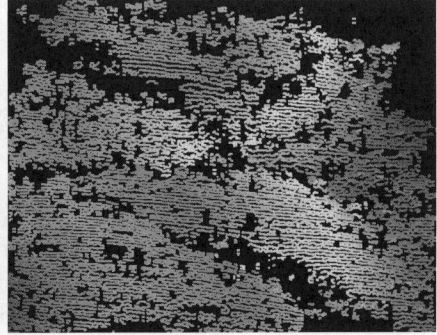

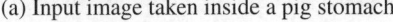

(a) Input image taken inside a pig stomach (b) Result of the proposed decoding method with color enhancement

Fig. 1. Example input image and color coded depthmap result. Range is 142mm to 164mm

M. Goesele et al. (Eds.): DAGM 2010, LNCS 6376, pp. 403–411, 2010.

most basic hardware setup consists of one camera and one projector, but the details of the implementations vary widely. A survey of the various pattern designs that have been proposed in the literature can be found in [1]. Range data is generated by triangulation of the camera ray and the projection ray to a point in the scene. This requires solving the correspondence problem: determining which pairs of rays belong together.

One way to address this issue is temporal encoding, like the Gray Code and the Phase Shifting techniques (e.g. [2]). In these methods, the correspondences are determined by illuminating the scene with a sequence of patterns which is unique for each single pixel. This imposes the limitation that the object may not move while the sequence is acquired. Another approach to solve the correspondence problem is through the use of spatial encoding, where the necessary disambiguating information is encoded in a spatial neighborhood of pixels. This requires that the neighborhood stays connected, which means that the object must be relatively smooth. Nonetheless, spatial encoding has the advantage that only one pattern suffices to generate 3D data. This makes it particularly suitable for moving scenes. It also allows the use of simpler hardware, which in turn results in high scalability from millimeter to meter range. Miniaturization is of high interest in order to build Structured Light-based 3D video endoscopes for medical as well as industrial applications.

We recently proposed a graph-based Single-Shot Structured Light method [3], which shows considerable improvement in robustness in the presence of texture and noise. An essential component of the algorithm is the extraction of the representative color for local regions in the striped image. Ideally, such a color descriptor should be relatively invariant to cross-channel effects and surface reflectivity. The original algorithm used simply the median color of all the pixels in a local region. Though statistically robust, such a measurement does not explicitly address the properties that the region-color descriptor should satisfy. Thus, we propose a belief propagation-based color enhancement step that specifically tries to infer the illuminant color for the particular region using cues from neighboring regions. Thus the influence of the object color is minimized and contrast is enhanced. We evaluate the method with real-world example image sequences, and show an increase of 30% to 50% in the number of data points generated.

2   Single-Shot Structured Light

The performance of a Structured Light-based sensor depends crucially on the pattern that is used. Many different single-shot pattern designs have been proposed. Most of them are based on pseudorandom sequences (1D) or arrays (2D) [4],[5]. They have the property that a given window of size N or NxM occurs at most once. This is known as the *window uniqueness property*. Observing such a window suffices for deducing its position in the pattern. Pattern design involves two trade-offs. One concerns the size of the building blocks of the pattern, the so-called primitives. To achieve a high resolution, small pattern primitives are needed, but the smaller the primitives, the harder it is to reliably detect them. The other one is the alphabet size of the code, i.e. the number of different symbols that are used. Ideally, one wants to use a large alphabet for a long code with a small window size. However, the smaller the differences between individual code symbols, the less robust the code.

A well known single-shot 3D scanning system is the one by Zhang et al. [6]. The color stripe pattern used in that system is based on pseudorandom De Brujin sequences [7]. The decoding algorithm works per scanline and is based on dynamic programming. Its largest drawback seems to be the high processing time of one minute per frame. Koninckx and van Gool [8] present an interesting approach based on a black-and-white line pattern with one oblique line for disambiguation. It runs at about 15Hz and the resolution is given as 10^4 data points per frame, which is also relatively low. A recent paper by Kawasaki et al. [9] uses a pattern of vertical and horizontal lines. It is one of the few articles containing quantitative data about the accuracy of the methodology, which is given as 0.52mm RMS error on a simple test scene. The runtime is 1.6s per frame, but there is no information on the number of points reconstructed per frame. Forster [10] uses a color stripe pattern with scanline-based decoding, running at 20Hz and with up to 10^5 data points per frame. The RMS error of a plane measured at a distance of 1043mm is given as 0.28mm. Our system [3] is also based on color stripes but uses a graph-based decoding algorithm which offers superior robustness. With our method we can generate up to 10^5 data points per frame at 15 frames per second. The accuracy is 1/1000 of the working distance. We improve upon this method by including an additional graph-based inference step to enhance the observed colors of the pattern.

3   Graph-Based Pattern Decoding

In [3] we describe a series of steps for decoding the observed pattern. They are:

1. Finding a superpixel representation of the image: This is achieved with a watershed transform [11].
2. Building the region adjacency graph: Each basin of the watershed segmentation corresponds to one vertex of the graph. Neighboring basins are connected by edges.
3. Assigning edge symbols and probabilities: Edges usually connect vertices of different color. Given the knowledge about the projected pattern, there is only a finite number of possibilities of how color can change between adjacent vertices. The probabilities for each color change are computed.
4. Find a unique path of edges: Use the window uniqueness property of the pattern to solve the correspondence problem.
5. Recursively visit all neighbors in a best-first-search: Once the stripe number of a start vertex is known, propagate this information to all its neighbors, as long as the connecting edges are in accordance with the pattern.

We improved this method by adding an optional additional step 2b: Recover the projected color for each vertex. In the original algorithm the colors of the vertices are determined with a median filter over all image pixels belonging to the corresponding watershed basin. However, this observed color is not the original projected color. There are many alterations introduced by the object texture, scattering, blurring, camera crosstalk and so on. To recover the projected color, we can use an inference algorithm. The output of step 2 and thus the input for the new step 2b is a set of vertices and a set of edges. The color of the vertices is to be re-estimated by explicitly incorporating information about the color changes C across the edges to all neighbors.

$$C = [c_r \, c_g \, c_b]^T \in R^3 \tag{1}$$

The elements of the vector are equalized and normalized so that the maximum absolute value is 1. For details refer to [3]. Each edge also has a scalar edge weight w, which is defined as the L_∞-norm of the original unnormalized color change $\hat{C}$.

$$w = ||\hat{C}||_\infty = max(|\hat{c}_r|, |\hat{c}_g|, |\hat{c}_b|) \tag{2}$$

In the pattern used in [3] there are only eight projected colors (the corners of the RGB cube). This means that the number of labels is rather low and the inference can be performed in real time. Furthermore, the three color channels are independent. Thus we can perform a per-channel inference with binary labels. At a given vertex, a given color channel can only be either on or off.

4   Color Enhancement

We use Belief Propagation [12,13] to implement the color enhancement. BP is an iterative message passing algorithm. Each node of the graph receives messages from its neighbors containing their current beliefs about their state. This incoming information is combined with local evidence and passed on. Assuming pairwise cliques, the update equation for the message from node i to node j at time t is

$$m_{ij}^{t+1}(x_j) = \sum_i f_{ij}(x_i, x_j) g_i(x_i) \prod_{k \in N_i \setminus j} m_{ki}^t(x_i) \tag{3}$$

Here $f_{ij}(x_i, x_j)$ is the smoothness term for assigning labels x_i and x_j to nodes i and j, $g_i(x_i)$ is the data term for assigning x_i to node i and $N_i \setminus j$ is the neighborhood of node i excluding node j. After convergence, the final belief b_i is

$$b_i \propto g_i(x_i) \prod_{k \in N_i} m_{ki}^t(x_i) \tag{4}$$

In our case there is no data term, i.e. $g_i(x_i) = 1$, as we do not judge the absolute color values but only the color changes. Since we split the inference into three binary problems (one per RGB channel), there are only two labels, namely channel on or off. The smoothness term $f_{ij}(x_i, x_j)$ can therefore be written as a 2x2 compatibility matrix $\mathbf{F}$.

$$\mathbf{F} = \begin{bmatrix} p_{constant} & p_{rising} \\ p_{falling} & p_{constant} \end{bmatrix} \tag{5}$$

On the diagonal we have the probability of the channel state being constant, as both nodes have the same label. If node i is in "off" state (index 0) and j in "on" state (index 1) the channel must rise, or fall in the opposite case. The values are computed with a truncated linear model:

$$p = \begin{cases} max(0, 1 - h_{bp} - c_l h_{bp}) & if\,falling \\ max(0, 1 - |c_l| h_{bp}) & if\,constant \\ max(0, 1 - h_{bp} + c_l h_{bp}) & if\,rising \end{cases} \tag{6}$$

Here c_l is an indiviual normalized channel of the color change vector from eq.1 and h_{bp} is the slope of the probability function. This means the that the probability for a falling channel is 1 if c_l is -1 and goes down to 0 as the deviation of c_l from the ideal value approaches $\frac{1}{h_{bp}}$. For the cases of constant and rising channels, the ideal values are 0 and +1. A typical value for h_{bp} is $\frac{3}{2}$.

The most widely used message update equation in BP is the sum-product formula shown in 3. It is used when the focus is to approximate marginals. Other variants, however, have been used. For example, a popular variant is the max-product (or max-sum in the log domain) [12]. In this latter formulation, beliefs no longer estimate marginals. Instead, they are scoring functions whose maxima point to most likely states. In our application, we want a belief estimate that can capture the fact that not all messages are equally reliable. A belief that better captures the influence of the neighboring nodes, and is at the same time more robust to outliers, is one based on weighted sums. Thus we replace the products in eqs. 3 and 4 by weighted sums.

$$m_{ij}^{t+1}(x_j) = \sum_i f_{ij}(x_i, x_j) \sum_{k \in N_i \setminus j} m_{ki}^t(x_i) w_k \qquad (7)$$

$$b_i \propto \sum_{k \in N_i} m_{ki}^t(x_i) w_k \qquad (8)$$

This has two advantages. The first is that we can include our information about the edge weights (eq.2). High weight edges are more reliable as they are less likely to be distorted by noise. The second is that when using products to combine the incoming messages, one "bad" message with a probability of zero makes the product zero. This is especially the case for the so called null edges (see [3]). For this type of edges many entries in f_{ij} are zero and we end up with all-zero messages. In the weighted sum this does not happen. In fact, null edges have only a small influence because of their low weight.

We initialize the messages as $m_{ij}^0(x_j) = 1$, i.e. we make no assumptions whether a given channel is on or off in the beginning. Because of the low number of labels the message passing converges in only two iterations. Afterwards, we can form a belief vector B that gives the probability of each of the color channels being in "on" state. This belief vector can be interpreted as a color again. We call this the enhanced color. Note that since the estimation of B is based solely on the color changes between the superpixels it ideally contains only information on the projected light. The result is shown in figure 2 and 3.

Although the image looks confusing, the contrast between the new colors is better and they are better suited for decoding in the following steps. We therefore compute new color change vectors C for each edge in the graph, this time representing the change in our belief in the colors. Table 1 shows the improvement numerically on the basis of the blue and green regions shown in the center of figure 3c. The enhanced values are much closer to the ideal.

Note that this inference approach can also be applied to patterns with more colors. In that case there are more than two labels per channel and $\mathbf{F}$ is larger. We also experimented with a Graph-Cut optimization [14] to find the optimal labeling. This also works, but the results were inferior, as the output was a "hard" labeling as opposed to the "soft" labeling produced by BP.

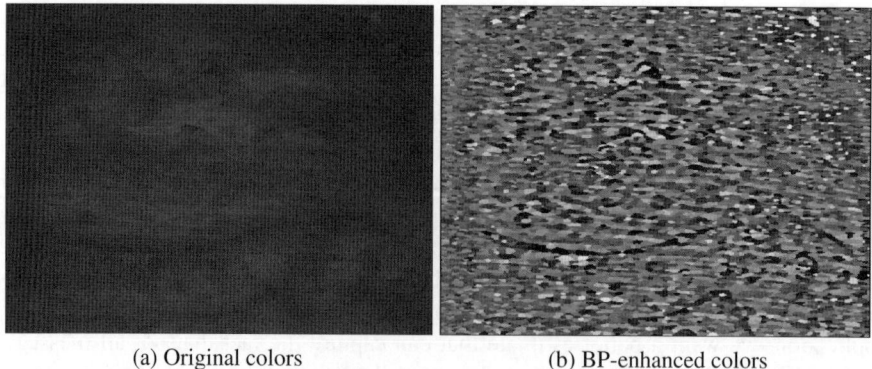

(a) Original colors   (b) BP-enhanced colors

Fig. 2. Color enhancement example

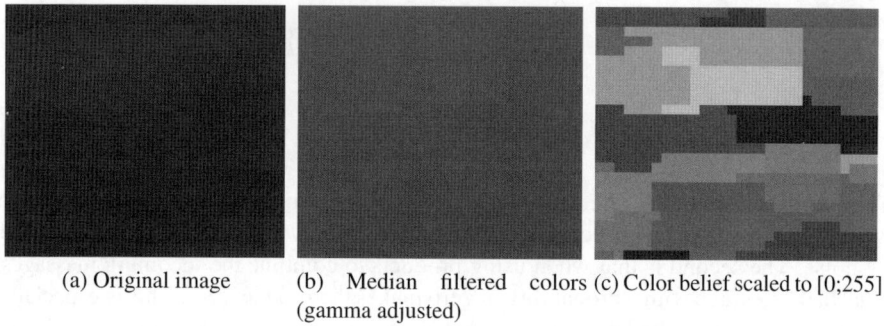

(a) Original image   (b) Median filtered colors (c) Color belief scaled to [0;255]
                            (gamma adjusted)

Fig. 3. Detail view of color enhancement results

Table 1. Example of enhanced region colors. Note that the range of the original colors is [0;255] and the range of the enhanced colors is [0;1]. The color changes are normalized.

	ideal	median color	BP-enhanced color
region color a	(0,0,1)	(15,22,25)	(0.31,0.36,0.92)
region color b	(0,1,0)	(14,24,21)	(0.20,0.87,0.40)
color change	(0,+1,-1)	(-0.20,+0.50,-1.00)	(-0.21,+0.97,-1.00)

5   Results

The proposed decoding method inherits the robustness of [3], which is due to: a) the rank filtering used to assign the superpixel colors, and b) the graph decoding algorithm that allows it to sidestep disruptions in the observed pattern. The BP-based enhanced color deduction further increases the robustness, especially in low-contrast situations, where single edges may be unreliable. In that case integrating the information from all neighbors before making a decision is especially helpful. This is a crucial improvement for medical purposes, where it can counteract the sub-surface scattering in skin and other tissue.

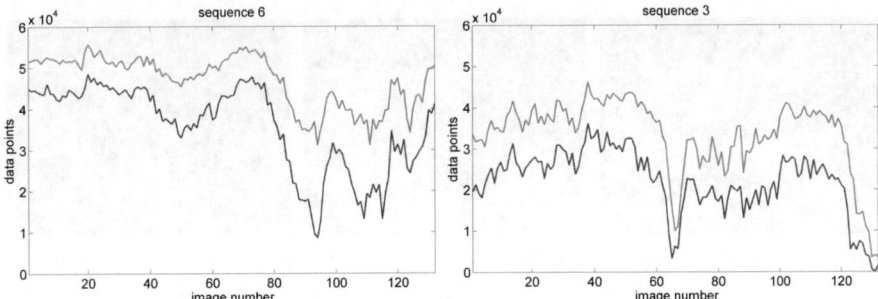

(a) Results for pig stomach sequence 6 with higher image quality.

(b) Results for pig stomach sequence 3 with poor image quality.

Fig. 4. The number of recovered pixels without (red) and with (green) the color enhancement

The biggest benefit of the proposed method is the increase in the number of recovered pixels. The image gradients used for the final triangulation of the distance are unaffected. Experiments with ground truth data have confirmed that the accuracy of the recovered depth map does not change. A detailed analysis on the accuracy of the overall methodology can be found in our prior work [3]. Here we focus on the improvement in the number of data points achieved with the additional color enhancement step. Figure 4 shows the number of data points that could be generated for each frame of two example videos. In sequence 6, which has the better image quality, the overall improvement was 32%, in sequence 3 with very poor image quality we gained 51%. The sequences were recorded with a handheld prototype scanner submersed in a liquid-filled pig stomach.

Figure 5 shows the results for two individual frames from each test sequence. For further comparison we also include the output of a reimplementation of the classic dynamic programming decoding method [6]. As can be seen, [6] is more susceptible to low image quality. Another example image with results is displayed in figure 7. Without the color enhancement [3] generated 29391 data points, with color enhancement we get 40107 points. This is again an improvement of 36%.

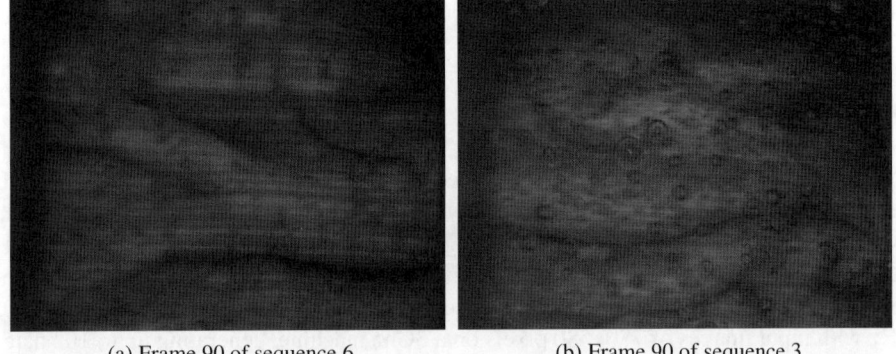

(a) Frame 90 of sequence 6

(b) Frame 90 of sequence 3

Fig. 5. Single frames from sequence 6 and sequence 3

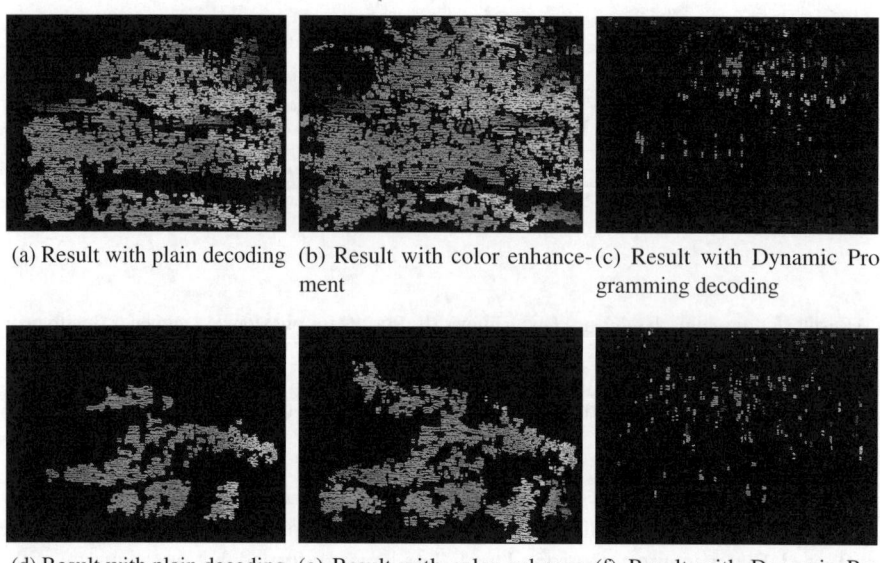

(a) Result with plain decoding (b) Result with color enhancement (c) Result with Dynamic Programming decoding

(d) Result with plain decoding (e) Result with color enhancement (f) Result with Dynamic Programming decoding

Fig. 6. Color coded depthmap results for the image in figure 5a (first row, range is 137mm to 146mm) and the image in figure 5b (second row, range is 148mm to 166mm)

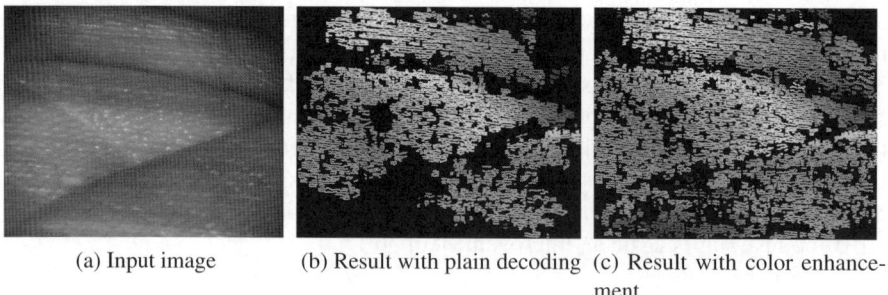

(a) Input image   (b) Result with plain decoding (c) Result with color enhancement

Fig. 7. "Palm" image and color coded depthmap result. Range is 119mm to 134mm.

6   Conclusion and Future Work

We presented an extension to the robust decoding algorithm for Single-Shot Structured Light patterns presented in [3]. It works even under very adverse imaging conditions, where previous methods like Dynamic Programming fail. It improves the data yield in the test sequences by 30% respectively 50% over the plain graph-based decoding. The method can tolerate low contrast, high noise as well as other artifacts and can run at 10 Hz with input images of 780x580 pixels on a 3Ghz machine, generating up to 10^5 data points per frame. As before, the typical accuracy is 1/1000 of the working distance. We have also demonstrated the miniaturization potential with the pig stomach images.

Acknowledgements

We would like to thank Philip Mewes for the chance to record the pig stomach data.

References

1. Salvi, J., Fernandez, S., Pribanic, T., Llado, X.: A state of the art in structured light patterns for surface profilometry. Pattern Recognitio (2010) (in Press) (Corrected Proof)
2. Sansoni, G., Carocci, M., Rodella, R.: Three-dimensional vision based on a combination of gray-code and phase-shift light projection: Analysis and compensation of the systematic errors. Appl. Opt. 38(31), 6565–6573 (1999)
3. Schmalz, C., Angelopoulou, E.: Belief propagation for improved color assessment in structured light. In: 7th IEEE International Workshop on Projector-Camera Systems (PROCAMS) (CVPR 2010) (2010)
4. Paterson, K.G.: Perfect maps. IEEE Transactions on Information Theory 40(3), 743–753 (1994)
5. Mitchell, C.J.: Aperiodic and semi-periodic perfect maps. IEEE Transactions on Information Theory 41(1), 88–95 (1995)
6. Zhang, L., Curless, B., Seitz, S.M.: Rapid shape acquisition using color structured light and multi-pass dynamic programming. In: Proc. First International Symposium on 3D Data Processing Visualization and Transmission, June 19-21, pp. 24–36 (2002)
7. Annexstein, F.: Generating de bruijn sequences: An efficient implementation. IEEE Transactions on Computers 46(2), 198–200 (1997)
8. Koninckx, T.P., Van Gool, L.: Real-time range acquisition by adaptive structured light. IEEE Transactions on Pattern Analysis and Machine Intelligence 28(3), 432–445 (2006)
9. Kawasaki, H., Furukawa, R., Sagawa, R., Yagi, Y.: Dynamic scene shape reconstruction using a single structured light pattern. In: Proc. IEEE Conference on Computer Vision and Pattern Recognition CVPR 2008, pp. 1–8 (June 2008)
10. Forster, F.: A high-resolution and high accuracy real-time 3d sensor based on structured light. In: International Symposium on 3D Data Processing Visualization and Transmission, pp. 208–215. IEEE Computer Society, Los Alamitos (2006)
11. Roerdink, J.B.T.M., Meijster, A.: The watershed transform: definitions, algorithms and parallelization strategies. Fundam. Inf. 41(1-2), 187–228 (2000)
12. Wainwright, M.J., Jordan, M.I.: Graphical Models, Exponential Families, and Variational Inference. Now Publishers Inc., Hanover (2008)
13. Felzenszwalb, P.F., Huttenlocher, D.R.: Efficient belief propagation for early vision. In: Proc. IEEE Computer Society Conference on Computer Vision and Pattern Recognition, CVPR 2004, 27 June-July 2, vol. 1, pp. I-261–I-268 (2004)
14. Boykov, Y., Veksler, O., Zabih, R.: Fast approximate energy minimization via graph cuts. IEEE Transactions on Pattern Analysis and Machine Intelligence 23(11), 1222–1239 (2001)

3D Object Detection Using a Fast Voxel-Wise Local Spherical Fourier Tensor Transformation

Henrik Skibbe[1,4], Marco Reisert[2], Thorsten Schmidt[1,4], Klaus Palme[3,4],
Olaf Ronneberger[1,4], and Hans Burkhardt[1,4]

[1] Department of Computer Science, University of Freiburg, Germany
[2] Dept. of Diagnostic Radiology, Medical Physics,
University Medical Center, Freiburg
[3] Institute of Biology II, Freiburg Institute for Advanced Studies (FRIAS)
[4] Center for Biological Signalling Studies (BIOSS), University of Freiburg
skibbe@informatik.uni-freiburg.de, marco.reisert@uniklinik-freiburg.de

Abstract. In this paper we present a novel approach for expanding spherical 3D-tensor fields of arbitrary order in terms of a tensor valued local Fourier basis. For an efficient implementation, a two step approach is suggested combined with the use of spherical derivatives. Based on this new transformation we conduct two experiments utilizing the spherical tensor algebra for computing and using rotation invariant features for object detection and classification. The first experiment covers the successful detection of non-spherical root cap cells of Arabidopsis root tips presented in volumetric microscopical recordings. The second experiment shows how to use these features for successfully detecting $\alpha-$helices in cryo-EM density maps of secondary protein structures, leading to very promising results.

1 Introduction

With the increasing performance of modern computers and the rapid development of new 3D image recording techniques, the amount of volumetric image data has drastically increased during the last years. Due to this fact, there is a need for adapting existing techniques from 2D image analysis to the third dimension. One major problem in image analysis is the extraction of information which is reduced in size as much as possible while still containing all characteristics necessary to describe, analyze, detect, compare or classify different objects. Many methods widely used for extracting features from 2D images make use of the gradient direction to get rid of the rotation. These approaches can often be directly adapted into the 2D+time domain (e.g. SIFT [1]). However, when working with volumetric images the gradient direction gives us only information about two rotation angles leaving the third angle undetermined.

In this work, we introduce a new method for realizing a fast voxel-wise local spherical Fourier transformation of spherical tensor-valued 3D images. The expansion coefficients are used to compute rotation invariant features in an analytical way. From a practical point of view, our method does exactly this: For

M. Goesele et al. (Eds.): DAGM 2010, LNCS 6376, pp. 412–421, 2010.

each Gaussian windowed surrounding of each voxel of a tensor-valued volume, we simultaneously compute the expansion coefficients of a spherical Fourier tensor expansion up to a certain band. Using spherical tensor algebra (the interested reader is referred to [2,3]), the resulting expansion coefficients can be combined to analytically form rotation invariant features. These voxel-wise features can be used for e.g. object detection, segmentation or object classification. The method proposed here needs a small number of image convolutions followed by successively applying point-wise operations that can run in parallel in a memory efficient way. Outperforming all existing methods we are aware of doing voxel-wise spherical harmonic expansions realized by a huge number of convolutions (e.g. [4]).

This paper is organized as follows: In section 2 we recapitulate the basics and requirements necessary for our mathematical framework. In section 3 we introduce the fast spherical Fourier tensor transformation. Finally, in section 4, two applications are introduced where local rotation invariant features are computed and used for successfully detecting and classifying objects.

2   Preliminaries

We denote scalars in unbold latin face and vectors in latin bold face. Typically, vectors are elements of $\mathbb{C}^{2\ell+1}$ whose basis is written as $\{\mathbf{e}_m^\ell\}_{m=-\ell\ldots\ell}$. Depending on the context we will express the coordinate vector $\mathbf{r} = (x,y,z)^T \in \mathbb{R}^3$ in spherical coordinates (θ, ϕ, r), where $\theta = \arccos(z/\|\mathbf{r}\|)$, $\phi = \operatorname{atan2}(y,x)$ and $r = \|\mathbf{r}\|$. By $Y_m^\ell(\theta,\phi)$ we denote the usual spherical harmonics [2] in Schmidt semi-normalized form. All harmonics for a fixed ℓ are arranged in a vector $\mathbf{Y}^\ell \in \mathbb{C}^{2\ell+1}$. The functions Y_m^ℓ build a complete orthogonal basis for representing functions on the 2-sphere, with $\langle Y_m^\ell, Y_{m'}^{\ell'} \rangle = \frac{4\pi}{2\ell+1}\delta_{\ell\ell'}\delta_{mm'}$. Furthermore, we denote by $\mathbf{R}^\ell : \mathbb{R}^3 \to \mathbb{C}^{2\ell+1}$ the commonly known solid harmonics [2], whose $(2\ell+1)$ components R_m^ℓ are defined by $R_m^\ell(\mathbf{r}) = r^\ell Y_m^\ell(\theta,\phi)$.

2.1   Spherical Tensor Fields

In the following we give a short introduction on spherical tensor algebra based on the definitions and notation used in [5]. The spherical tensor algebra is necessary for expanding higher order tensor fields (e.g. vector fields) in terms of tensor-valued Fourier basis functions. We also use spherical tensor algebra for computing rotation invariant features in an analytical way [6].

The central role of spherical tensor algebra play the Wigner D-matrices $\mathbf{D}_g^\ell \in \mathbb{C}^{(2\ell+1)\times(2\ell+1)}$ which are the unitary irreducible representations of the 3D rotation group. Each D-matrix is associated with an element g of the rotation group. They behave like ordinary rotation matrices in the sense that $\mathbf{D}_g^\ell \mathbf{D}_h^\ell = \mathbf{D}_{gh}^\ell$, but act on the high-dimensional complex Hilbertspace $\mathbb{C}^{2\ell+1}$. A fundamental property of the Wigner D-matrices is their behavior with respect to spherical harmonic expansion coeffcients. Suppose you have expanded some function f in spherical harmonics $\mathbf{a}^\ell = \langle \mathbf{Y}^\ell, f \rangle$. Then the expansion coefficients of the rotated function gf are related to the $\mathbf{a}^\ell$ just by the Wigner D-matrices $\mathbf{a}^{\ell'} = \mathbf{D}^\ell_g \mathbf{a}^\ell$. Spherical Tensor algebra utilizes this behavior in a much more general way. We call a function $\mathbf{f} : \mathbb{R}^3 \to \mathbb{C}^{2\ell+1}$ a spherical tensor field of rank ℓ if it transforms with respect to rotations as

$$\forall g \in SO(3): \quad (g\mathbf{f})(\mathbf{r}) := \mathbf{D}^\ell_g \mathbf{f}(\mathbf{U}^T_g \mathbf{r}) \qquad (1)$$

where $\mathbf{U}_g \in \mathbb{R}^{3\times 3}$ is the corresponding real valued ordinary rotation matrix. The space of all spherical tensor fields of rank ℓ is denoted by $\mathcal{T}_\ell$. Note that for $\ell = 1$ a spherical tensor field is just an ordinary vector field. Interpreting solid harmonics (or spherical harmonics) as spherical tensor fields shows their importance, namely (due to eq. (1)) $g\mathbf{R}^\ell = \mathbf{R}^\ell$, i.e. they are 'fix' with respect to rotations.

Similar to cartesian tensor fields, where Kronecker products connect tensor fields of different rank, there exist spherical products [5,2] that connect spherical tensor fields of different rank. In fact, for two given spherical tensor fields $\mathbf{v} \in \mathcal{T}_{\ell_1}$ and $\mathbf{w} \in \mathcal{T}_{\ell_2}$, there exists a whole set of different products $\circ_\ell$ to build new spherical tensor fields. More precisely, for every $\ell \geq 0$ that obeys the triangle inequality $|\ell_1 - \ell_2| \leq \ell \leq \ell_1 + \ell_2$ there is a bilinear form $\circ_\ell : \mathbb{C}^{2\ell_1+1} \times \mathbb{C}^{2\ell_2+1} \to \mathbb{C}^{2\ell+1}$ that takes two spherical tensors and gives a new one, i.e

$$(\mathbf{D}^{\ell_1}_g \mathbf{v}) \circ_\ell (\mathbf{D}^{\ell_2}_g \mathbf{w}) = \mathbf{D}^\ell_g (\mathbf{v} \circ_\ell \mathbf{w}) \qquad (2)$$

holds for any $\mathbf{v} \in \mathcal{T}_{\ell_1}$ and $\mathbf{w} \in \mathcal{T}_{\ell_2}$. Again the spherical harmonics show a special behavior. In fact, multiplying two spherical harmonics results in another harmonic, i.e. $\mathbf{Y}^{\ell_1} \circ_\ell \mathbf{Y}^{\ell_2} = c_{\ell,\ell_1,\ell_2} \mathbf{Y}^\ell$, where c_{ℓ,ℓ_1,ℓ_2} is a constant related to the Clebsch Gordan coefficients (for details see [2]).

Finally, we present the third important ingredient of spherical tensor calculus: the spherical derivative. In ordinary vector calculus differential operators like the gradient, divergence or the Hessian connect cartesian tensor fields of different rank. There are also spherical counterparts. In the following we need just one type of spherical deriviative, the spherical up-derivative $\boldsymbol{\nabla}^1$, which increases the rank of the spherical field (see [7] for further details and proofs). If $\mathbf{f} \in \mathcal{T}_\ell$ is a tensorfield of order ℓ, then the spherical up-derivative $\boldsymbol{\nabla}^1 : \mathcal{T}_\ell \to \mathcal{T}_{\ell+1}$ maps $\mathbf{f}$ onto a field of rank $\ell + 1$. For multiple application of the spherical derivative we write $\boldsymbol{\nabla}^\ell : \mathcal{T}_{\ell_0} \to \mathcal{T}_{\ell_0+\ell}$. For example, applying $\boldsymbol{\nabla}^1$ on a scalar field gives just the spherical counterpart of an ordinary gradient of the field. The result of applying $\boldsymbol{\nabla}^1$ twice is linearly related to the traceless Hessian of the scalar field.

Relation between Cartesian and Spherical Tensors. The theories of cartesian and spherical tensors are basically equivalent. Up to rank 2 the relations connecting both worlds are well known and reported e.g. in [2] or [8]. To get an impression; a general real cartesian tensor of rank 2 (basically a 3×3 matrix) can be decomposed into a spherical tensor of rank 0 (the trace), of rank 1 (the antisymmetric part) and of rank 2 (the traceless symmetric part).

3   Spherical Fourier Tensor Transformation

In this section, we introduce the Fourier basis which we use for spherical tensor field expansion. This basis can be seen as an extension to [9], replacing the spherical harmonics by tensorial harmonics. With this we are able to decompose spherical tensor fields of any order into basic Fourier patterns. We further show how to expand fast and efficiently by utilizing the spherical derivatives.

3.1   Tensorial Bessel Harmonics

In order to obtain a representation of spherical tensor fields with tensor valued Fourier basis functions having the same convenient rotation properties known from the spherical harmonics, we perform a spherical tensor field expansion based on *tensorial harmonics* [5]. In addition to the tensorial harmonic expansion given in [5] for representing spherical tensor fields on the 2-sphere, we use the spherical Bessel function $j_\ell(r)$ for representing the radial part (see [10] for definition). This directly extends the spherical Fourier basis $\mathbf{B}_k^\ell(\mathbf{r}) := \mathbf{Y}^\ell(\mathbf{r})j_\ell(kr)$ presented in [9] to higher order tensor fields, where $k \in \mathbb{R}_{>0}$ represents the frequency in radial direction. The spherical Fourier tensor field expansion of $\mathbf{f} \in \mathcal{T}_J$ in terms of $\circ$ and the Fourier basis $\mathbf{B}_k^\ell$ is given by

$$\mathbf{f}(\mathbf{r}) = \int_0^\infty \sum_{\ell=0}^\infty \sum_{j=-J}^{j=J} \mathbf{c}_{jk}^\ell \circ_J (\alpha_{\ell jk}^{\frac{1}{2}} \mathbf{B}_k^\ell(\mathbf{r}))dk , \tag{3}$$

where $\alpha_{\ell jk} = \frac{2k^2}{\pi} \frac{2(\ell+j)+1}{2J+1} \frac{2\ell+1}{4\pi}$ are scalar valued normalization factors, and $\mathbf{c}_{jk}^\ell \in \mathbb{C}^{2(\ell+j)+1}$ are the spherical tensor valued expansion coefficients of $\mathbf{f}$.

The expansion coefficients $\mathbf{c}_{jk}^\ell$ can be computed by directly projecting onto tensorial Bessel harmonics, with $c_{jkm}^\ell = \langle \mathbf{f}, \mathbf{e}_m^{\ell+j} \circ_J \mathbf{B}_k^\ell \rangle$. However, it would be quite expensive to do this voxel by voxel in a large volume. According to [8], we suggest to compute the expansion coefficients $\mathbf{c}_{jk}^\ell$ of $\mathbf{f} \in \mathcal{T}_\ell$ in two steps. First, we separately transform all $2J + 1$ components of $\mathbf{f}$ into the harmonic domain, i.e. we express each component of f_M in terms of $\mathbf{B}_k^\ell$, with

$$f_M(\mathbf{r}) = \int_0^\infty \sum_{\ell=0}^\infty \mathbf{a}_k^{\ell M T} \mathbf{B}_k^\ell(\mathbf{r})dk , \tag{4}$$

where $\mathbf{a}_k^{\ell M}$ are the expansion coefficients representing the M-th component of $\mathbf{f}$. Given the coefficients $\mathbf{a}_k^{\ell M}$ we then compute the expansion coefficients $\mathbf{c}_{jk}^\ell$:

$$c_{jkm}^\ell = \frac{2(\ell+j)+1}{2J+1} \sum_M a_{kn}^{\ell M} \langle (\ell+j)m, \ell n \,|\, JM \rangle , \tag{5}$$

where $m = -2(\ell + j), \ldots, 2(\ell + j)$ and $n = M - m$. Until now we have not reached any computational benefit, but we show in the following section that we can use the spherical derivatives for the computation of the expansion coefficients $a_{kn}^{\ell M}$. This avoids explicit convolutions and precomputation of convolution kernels, which makes the computation practical in terms of speed and memory consumption.

3.2 Differential Formulation of the Tensorial Bessel Expansion

In this section we show how to compute the expansion coefficients $\mathbf{a}_k^\ell$ (eq. (4)) with respect to all positions $\mathbf{x} \in \mathbb{R}^3$ of a given 3D image simultaneously by utilizing the spherical derivatives. As a consequence of having a fast transformation for computing the coefficients $\mathbf{a}_k^\ell$ we directly get a fast method for computing the tensorial Bessel harmonic coefficients $\mathbf{c}_{jk}^\ell$ (see eq. (5)).

One possible solution to transform efficiently is separately convolving a function $f \in \mathcal{T}_0$ with all $(2\ell+1)$ scalar valued components $B_{kn}^\ell \in \mathcal{T}_0$ of all $\mathbf{B}_k^\ell \in \mathcal{T}_\ell$. In our scenario, doing a transformation using K different values for k and an angular expansion up to the L-th band, we would need $K(L+1)^2$ convolutions! In contrast, the method proposed here makes use of an iterative differential formulation of the $\mathbf{B}_k^\ell$ for realizing the transformation in angular direction. Hence we only need K convolutions followed by L times applying the spherical derivative operator $\boldsymbol{\nabla}$. In this case, the number of convolutions does not depend on the parameter L. Furthermore, the spherical derivative operator can be implemented efficiently using finite differences, widely used for fast computing derivatives from scalar valued fields which can be executed in parallel in a memory efficient way. This enables us to process huge volumetric images in seconds rather than minutes (e.g. given an image of size 256^3 and doing the voxel-wise expansion up to order 15 (double precision) takes 1.3 minutes by convolutions using the multithreaded fft [11] with planning flag FFTW_MEASURE and 14.1 seconds using our approach. The experiments are run on a 6×quad-core system, each core with 2,7 GHz.). The relation between the convolution based approach and our differential based approach is given by:

$$\mathbf{a}_k^\ell(\mathbf{x}) = \langle f_\mathbf{x}, \mathbf{B}_k^\ell \rangle = \underbrace{(f * \overline{\mathbf{B}}_k^\ell)(\mathbf{x})}_{\substack{(2\ell+1)\ \text{scalar} \\ \text{valued convolutions}}} = \frac{(-1)^\ell}{k^\ell} \langle f_\mathbf{x}, \boldsymbol{\nabla}^\ell \mathbf{B}_k^0 \rangle = \left[\frac{\overline{\boldsymbol{\nabla}}^1}{(-k)} \right]^\ell \underbrace{(f * \overline{\mathbf{B}}_k^0)(\mathbf{x})}_{\substack{1\ \text{scalar} \\ \text{valued convolution}}},$$

where $f_\mathbf{x}(\mathbf{r}) := f(\mathbf{r} + \mathbf{x})$ and $\overline{\boldsymbol{\nabla}}^\ell$ is the complex conjugate of $\boldsymbol{\nabla}^\ell$ (for proof see appendix A). As a result the expansion coefficients $\mathbf{a}_k^0, \ldots \mathbf{a}_k^\ell$ can be computed iteratively by ℓ times applying the spherical derivative operator:

$$\mathbf{a}_k^\ell(\mathbf{x}) = (\tfrac{-1}{k}\overline{\boldsymbol{\nabla}}^1 \ldots (\tfrac{-1}{k}\overline{\boldsymbol{\nabla}}^1 (\underbrace{\tfrac{-1}{k}\overline{\boldsymbol{\nabla}}^1 \underbrace{(f * \overline{\mathbf{B}}_k^0)}_{= \mathbf{a}_k^0})}_{= \mathbf{a}_k^1}))) (\mathbf{x}) , \qquad (6)$$
$$\underbrace{}_{= \mathbf{a}_k^\ell}$$

We finally obtain the expansion coefficients $\mathbf{c}_{jk}^\ell(\mathbf{x})$ of the spherical tensor field by first doing a component-wise transformation of the tensor field (eq. (4)) utilizing the spherical derivatives (eq. (6)) followed by coupling the expansion coefficients according to eq. (5).

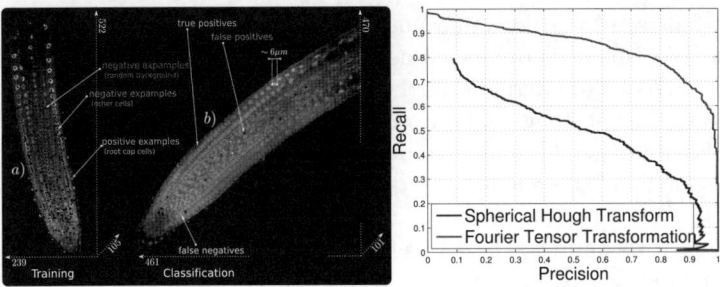

Fig. 1. Left image: a) Training dataset. b) Test dataset. Right PR-graph: Comparing the performance of our detection and classification to the detection rate of the spherical hough transformation.

4   Applications and Experiments

We conduct two experiments demonstrating the performance of our method. In the first experiment we detect nuclei of root cap cells of Arabidopsis root tips. In the second experiment we detect α-helices in secondary protein structures. Since we aim to describe local image structures and further need a finite convolution kernel, we use a Gaussian windowed Bessel function in both experiments. The Gaussian windowed convolution kernel is given by $(g_\sigma(r)j_\ell(kr))\mathbf{Y}^\ell(\theta,\phi) = \mathbf{B}_k^0(\mathbf{r})g_\sigma(r)$ where σ determines the width of the gaussian window function $g_\sigma(r) = e^{-\frac{r^2}{\sigma}}$. Scaling is done by assuming different voxel sizes. Considering the Fourier transform of this function, the parameter k determines the distance of a spherical harmonic from the origin, while the parameter σ determines the size of the Gaussian with which the spherical harmonic is convolved.

There are several ways for obtaining rotation invariant features based on spherical tensor fields (see e.g. [3,9,6]). Similar to [6] we are utilizing the spherical tensor product (eq. (2)) for coupling expansion coefficients of equal rank. By coupling coefficients with themselves we obtain the *power-spectrum* known from ordinary Fourier analysis, with $(\frac{1}{\sqrt{2\ell+1}}(\mathbf{a}_\ell^k \circ_0 \mathbf{a}_\ell^k))^{\frac{1}{2}} = \langle \mathbf{a}_\ell^k, \mathbf{a}_\ell^k \rangle^{\frac{1}{2}} = \|\mathbf{a}_\ell^k\|$. We further can couple expansion coefficients corresponding to Bessel functions $j_\ell(rk_1)$ and $j_\ell(rk_2)$ of different frequencies k_1 and k_2, with $(\frac{1}{\sqrt{2\ell+1}}(\mathbf{a}_\ell^{k_1} \circ_0 \mathbf{a}_\ell^{k_2}))^{\frac{1}{2}} = \langle \mathbf{a}_\ell^{k_1}, \mathbf{a}_\ell^{k_2} \rangle^{\frac{1}{2}}$. In the experiments this feature is called the *Phase*-feature.

First Experiment: Detection and Classification of Cells. In this experiment we aim to detect DAPI[1]-stained nuclei of root cap cells represented in volumetric images of Arabidopsis root tips. The data was recorded using a confocal laser-scanning microscope. Experiments have shown, that, in contrast to inner cells, root cap cells can hardly be detected by strategies suitable for detecting roundish structures, e.g. using the spherical Hough transform [12]. For this scenario a voxel-wise feature computation and classification approach is suitable for first learning the shape and structure of root cap cells using rotation invariant

---

[1] 4'-6-Diamidino-2-phenylindole.

features, followed by a detection and classification of cells in unclassified data sets. The experiment is organized as follows: We select one image for training (size $461 \times 470 \times 101$) and one further image for testing (size $239 \times 522 \times 105$) (depicted in the left image of figure 1 a) and b)). The voxel size of each images is $1\mu m$. Each image contains several hundred cells. The center of the nuclei of the cells were labeled manually and divided into two classes: Root Cap Cells and Inner Cells. We compute rotation invariant voxel-wise features for $k = 1, 3, 5, 7, 9$ and a band-with limit $\ell \leq 5$. σ is set to 2π. The kernel is scaled by a factor of 6 approximately covering a whole cell. We separately normalize each feature dimension with respect to the mean and the variance of the whole set of features computed for a single dataset. For training we select all features representing cells from the training image. We further randomly select features describing locations not belonging to cells representing the background. We train a two-class cSVM [13] using an RBF kernel with $\gamma=1$ and cost$=1$. We first conduct experiments comparing features based on the power-spectrum to the phase-features. For the voxel-wise classification we use the local maxima of the decision values of the SVM. We have a true positive detection if correctly classifying a root cap cell in a $3\mu m$ surrounding of a positive label and a false negative for each root cap cell, which is not detected. All remaining voxels, wrongly classified as root cap cells count as false positives. Results are depicted in the upper left PR-graph shown in figure 2. Surprisingly the phase-feature performs much better than the power-spectrum feature. We belief that this is caused by the textural information of cells in radial direction which is better preserved in the features when coupling coefficients representing different radial frequency components. However, as expected, coupling all possible coefficients leads to the best results (Powerspectrum+Phase). Although we often successfully use the spherical Hough transformation for cell detection, it is not possible using it to detect more than 60% of the cells due to their non-roundish shape. In the right PR-graph of figure 1 we show the performance of our method outperforming the detection rate of the spherical Hough transformation significantly.

We further conduct experiments for different numbers of radial and angular frequency components. As expected the performance increases when considering

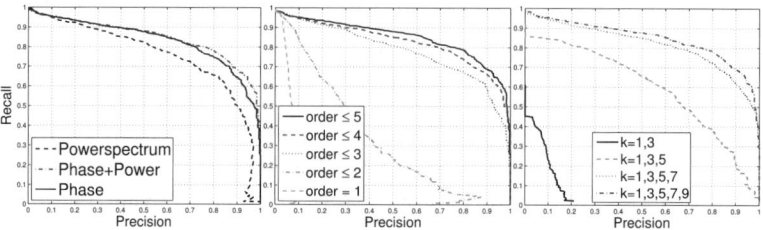

Fig. 2. Left: Comparing the features obtained by only coupling coefficients with themself (power-spectrum), coupling all possible coefficients (phase+power) and finally only coupling coefficients with different values of k (phase). Middle: Performance for different band-width limits ℓ. Right: Performance for different numbers of radial functions.

further higher frequency components. This is true for both increasing the number of spherical Bessel functions and increasing the order of the spherical harmonics. The results are depicted in the middle and right graph of figure 2.

Second Experiment: α-Helices in Secondary Structures of Proteins.
Electron cryomicroscopy is a powerful technique for analyzing the dynamics and functions of large flexible macromolecule assemblies. One major challenge in analyzing such density maps is the detection of subunits and their conformations. One important step in this procedure is the detection of secondary structure elements, mainly the α-helices.

The database for our experiments consists of simulated electron microscopic volumes of 56 polymers with an EM-resolution of 10Å and 1Å per voxel [14]. The data is divided into a training set (4 files) and a test set (52 files). We first try to detect helices using Helixhunter [15], mainly based on an eigen-analysis of the second moment tensor of local structures. We further use a harmonic filter of order 5 [7]. For pre- and post-smoothing we use a Gaussian with $\sigma = 1.5$. Finally we perform experiments using our own rotation invariant power-spectrum-features, based on the coefficients of the Fourier tensor transformation. We compute features directly based on the intensity values. We further compute a second order tensor field by computing the structure tensor at each voxel position. We use eq. 2.1 for representing the traceless, symmetric parts of the resulting cartesian tensor field in terms of a spherical tensor field. We compute features for both the intensity values and the structure-tensor field with $k = 1, 3, 5$ and $\ell \leq 5$. We scale the kernel by a factor of 2 and use $\sigma = 2$ for the Gaussian window function. The features are normalized by weighting the components with respect to their frequency using the weights $k^{\lambda_k} \ell^{\lambda_\ell}$. We obtain the best results when suppressing the lower frequency components by amplifying the higher frequency components using $\lambda_\ell = 3$ and $\lambda_k = 5$. For voxel-wise classification we use a 20KNN-classifier using the $l1$-norm. We only count voxels correctly classified as α-helices as true positives. The results of our experiments are depicted in figure 3. In our experiments Helixhunter has major problems to determine the exact locations of helices. For the experiments based on the harmonic filter, we vary the size of the Gaussian convolution kernels

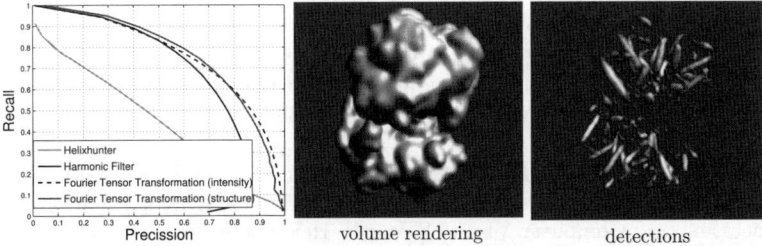

volume rendering   detections

Fig. 3. From left to right: PR-graph showing the performance of the detection procedures used in the experiments. Surface rendering representing the secondary structure with PDB code 1m3z. Corresponding detections of helices using our method.

as well as the order of the filter. The order which works best here is 5. Increasing the order to a higher extent does not noticeable increase the performance. This is caused by the low resolution of the data. The same behavior can be observed for our features, too. Similar to the order of the harmonic filter, the bandwidth limit $\ell \leq 5$ restricts the number of tensorial harmonics representing the signal in angular directions. We experienced that in contrast to the intensity features, it is much easier to obtain good results without having much effort for finding good parameters using the structure-tensor based features.

5   Conclusion

In this paper we extended the spherical Fourier transformation presented in [9] to higher order tensor fields and further presented a new method for performing the transformation in a fast and memory efficient way. We have shown how to utilize the spherical tensor algebra to compute rotation invariant features from the Fourier coefficients in an analytical way. We introduced all details necessary for an implementation, and gave two examples where our rotation invariant local features are used for successfully detecting and classifying objects in volumetric images leading to very promising results.

Acknowledgement. This study was supported by the Excellence Initiative of the German Federal and State Governments (EXC 294).

References

1. Scovanner, P., Ali, S., Shah, M.: A 3-dimensional sift descriptor and its application to action recognition. In: Proc. of the 15th international Conference on Multimedia, pp. 357–360. ACM Press, New York (2007)
2. Rose, M.: Elementary Theory of Angular Momentum. Dover Publications, Mineola (1995)
3. Kazhdan, M., Funkhouser, T., Rusinkiewicz, S.: Rotation invariant spherical harmonic representation of 3d shape descriptors. In: SGP 2003: Proc. of the 2003 Eurographics/ACM SIGGRAPH Symposium on Geometry processing, pp. 156–164. Eurographics Association (2003)
4. Ronneberger, O., Fehr, J., Burkhardt, H.: Voxel-wise gray scale invariants for simultaneous segmentation and classification. In: Kropatsch, W.G., Sablatnig, R., Hanbury, A. (eds.) DAGM 2005. LNCS, vol. 3663, pp. 85–92. Springer, Heidelberg (2005)
5. Reisert, M., Burkhardt, H.: Spherical tensor calculus for local adaptive filtering. In: Aja-Fernández, S., de Luis García, R., Tao, D., Li, X. (eds.) Tensors in Image Processing and Computer Vision. Springer, Heidelberg (2009)
6. Skibbe, H., Reisert, M., Wang, Q., Ronneberger, O., Burkhardt, H.: Fast computation of 3d spherical fourier harmonic descriptors - a complete orthonormal basis for a rotational invariant representation of three-dimensional objects. In: Proc. of the 3-D Digital Imaging and Modeling 3DIM, part of the 12th IEEE International Conference on Computer Vision, ICCV 2009 (2009)

7. Reisert, M., Burkhardt, H.: Harmonic filters for generic feature detection in 3d. In: Denzler, J., Notni, G., Süße, H. (eds.) DAGM 2009. LNCS, vol. 5748, pp. 131–140. Springer, Heidelberg (2009)
8. Skibbe, H., Reisert, M., Ronneberger, O., Burkhardt, H.: Increasing the dimension of creativity in rotation invariant feature design using 3d tensorial harmonics. In: Denzler, J., Notni, G., Süße, H. (eds.) DAGM 2009. LNCS, vol. 5748, pp. 141–150. Springer, Heidelberg (2009)
9. Wang, Q., Ronneberger, O., Burkhardt, H.: Rotational invariance based on fourier analysis in polar and spherical coordinates. IEEE Transactions on Pattern Analysis and Machine Intelligence 31, 1715–1722 (2009)
10. Abramowitz, M., Stegun, I.A.: Handbook of mathematical functions, 1st edn. Dover books on mathematics. Dover Publications, Mineola (1970)
11. Frigo, M., Johnson, S.G.: The design and implementation of FFTW3. Proc. of the IEEE 93(2), 216–231 (2005); Special issue on Program Generation, Optimization, and Platform Adaptation
12. Schulz, J., Schmidt, T., Ronneberger, O., Burkhardt, H., Pasternak, T., Dovzhenko, A., Palme, K.: Fast scalar and vectorial grayscale based invariant features for 3d cell nuclei localization and classification. In: Franke, K., Müller, K.-R., Nickolay, B., Schäfer, R. (eds.) DAGM 2006. LNCS, vol. 4174, pp. 182–191. Springer, Heidelberg (2006)
13. Chang, C.C., Lin, C.J.: LIBSVM: a library for support vector machines (2001), software available at http://www.csie.ntu.edu.tw/~cjlin/libsvm
14. Berman, H.M., Westbrook, J.D., Feng, Z., Gilliland, G., Bhat, T.N., Weissig, H., Shindyalov, I.N., Bourne, P.E.: The protein data bank. Nucleic Acids Research 28(1), 235–242 (2000)
15. Jiang, W., Baker, M.L., Ludtke, S.J., Chiu, W.: Bridging the information gap: computational tools for intermediate resolution structure interpretation. Journal of Molecular Biology 308(5), 1033–1044 (2001)

A Differential Formulation of Spherical Fourier Functions

We obtain $\mathbf{B}_k^\ell$ by ℓ times applying $\boldsymbol{\nabla}^1$ to $\mathbf{B}_k^0$. Proof:

$$\langle e^{i\mathbf{k}^T\mathbf{r}}, B_{k'm}^\ell(\mathbf{r})\rangle = \frac{2}{\pi}\int_0^\infty (i)^{\ell'}(2\ell'+1)\, j_{\ell'}(kr)j_\ell(k'r)r^2 \sum_{\ell'} Y_m^{\ell'}(\mathbf{k})\frac{1}{(2\ell+1)}\delta_{\ell\ell'}dr$$
$$= \frac{2}{\pi}(-i)^\ell Y_m^\ell(\mathbf{k})\underbrace{\int_0^\infty j_\ell(kr)j_\ell(k'r)r^2 dr}_{\frac{\pi}{2k^2}\delta(k-k')} = (-i)^\ell Y_m^\ell(\mathbf{k})\frac{1}{k^2}\delta(k-k')\ . \quad (7)$$

This means that a Bessel function $\mathbf{B}_k^\ell$ in the Fourier domain is a spherical harmonic living on a sphere with radius k. Consider the representation of both the Bessel function $\mathbf{B}_k^0$ and the operator $\boldsymbol{\nabla}^\ell$ in the frequency domain (eq. (7)) and according to [5] $\widetilde{\boldsymbol{\nabla}^\ell} = i^\ell \mathbf{R}^\ell(\mathbf{k})$). In this scenario we can observe, that $\widetilde{\boldsymbol{\nabla}^\ell\mathbf{B}_{k'}^0} = i^\ell \mathbf{R}^\ell(\mathbf{k})\frac{1}{k^2}\delta(k-k')$. Performing the inverse transformation into the spatial domain we obtain

$$\langle e^{-i\mathbf{k}^T\mathbf{r}}, \widetilde{\boldsymbol{\nabla}^\ell\mathbf{B}_{k'}^0}\rangle = (-1)^\ell k'^\ell j_\ell(rk')\mathbf{Y}^\ell(\mathbf{r}) = (-1)^\ell k'^\ell \mathbf{B}_{k'}^\ell(\mathbf{r})\ .$$

It follows, that we obtain higher order Bessel functions $\mathbf{B}_k^\ell$ by iteratively applying the spherical derivative operator $\boldsymbol{\nabla}^1$ to $\mathbf{B}_k^0$, namely $\boldsymbol{\nabla}^\ell\mathbf{B}_k^0 = (-1)^\ell k^\ell \mathbf{B}_k^\ell$ □.

Matte Super-Resolution for Compositing

Sahana M. Prabhu and Ambasamudram N. Rajagopalan

Department of Electrical Engineering
Indian Institute of Technology Madras, Chennai, India
sahana@smail.iitm.ac.in, raju@ee.iitm.ac.in

Abstract. Super-resolution of the alpha matte and the foreground object from a video are jointly attempted in this paper. Instead of super-resolving them independently, we treat super-resolution of the matte and foreground in a combined framework, incorporating the matting equation in the image degradation model. We take multiple adjacent frames from a low-resolution video with non-global motion for increasing the spatial resolution. This ill-posed problem is regularized by employing a Bayesian restoration approach, wherein the high-resolution image is modeled as a Markov Random Field. In matte super-resolution, it is particularly important to preserve fine details at the boundary pixels between the foreground and background. For this purpose, we use a discontinuity-adaptive smoothness prior to include observed data in the solution. This framework is useful in video editing applications for compositing low-resolution objects into high-resolution videos.

1 Introduction

Video matting pulls the matte of a foreground object from a video sequence with a natural background. It enables composition of the object or person seamlessly into a new video. This is different from applying still-image matting methods, such as closed-form matting [1], to each frame. Video matting by spatio-temporal method utilizes information from previous frames and hence is more accurate than matting on a frame-by-frame basis. The video matting problem for complicated scenes was first described and a Bayesian solution proposed in [2]. Mattes with high resolution (HR) are desirable since we can better discern fine details. Note that single-image interpolation is not same as super-resolution, since the former cannot recover the high-frequency components degraded by LR sampling [3]. Due to the limitation of data available in a single image, the quality of the interpolated image is inadequate. It must be emphasized that matting applications especially require accurate edge information.

Multiple image super-resolution deals with the inverse problem of finding high-resolution image from several low-resolution inputs. To overcome the restrictions of the image sensor, signal processing methods can be used to get HR video from the observed low-resolution (LR) sequence. Post-processing has many advantages: savings in computation time, camera cost, memory and bandwidth usage. It is also to be noted that cameras have a trade-off between frame

M. Goesele et al. (Eds.): DAGM 2010, LNCS 6376, pp. 422–431, 2010.

rate and resolution, which can also be avoided by using signal processing. The LR video consists of frames which are down-sampled and warped versions of the same scene. Frequency-domain methods of super-resolution, although simple and efficient, are restricted to global translational motion models. Spatial-domain approaches are preferred, since they can easily incorporate spatial-domain prior information from the observed image for regularization [3]. In a typical video, each of the frames have relative sub-pixel motion due to object motion as well as camera movement. We make the general assumption that the movement between adjacent video frames is smooth and gradual, and contains no sudden jerks. The temporally-correlated LR frames from the video have different local sub-pixel shifts, which implies that each LR image has new information. This additional data must be exploited while reconstructing the super-resolved image [3].

The advances and open issues (such as robustness) in the super-resolution area were described in a survey [4]. Super-resolution using images with global shifts, using iterated conditional modes (ICM) [5], was described in [6]. A motion-compensating sub-sampling observation model, that accounts for both scene and camera motion was considered in [7], where a Huber Markov random field prior was proposed. A MAP approach for joint motion estimation, segmentation, and super resolution appeared as [8]. However, unlike the segmentation problem, matting requires accurate sub-pixel or opacity values at the boundary between the object and the background. Joint estimation of disparity and image intensity at higher resolution for stereo images was described in [9]. The authors of [9] use a discontinuity-adaptive prior which makes HR image estimation robust to errors in disparity. Super-resolution of range images with camera motion was illustrated in [10], which also models the HR range image (representing depth) as a Markov random field (MRF). Super-resolution without parametric constraints on motion between video frames was discussed in [11]. They describe an Expectation-Maximization algorithm to reconstruct the HR image, interleaved with optical flow estimation.

The concept of compositing was utilized in an edge-directed technique for super-resolution using a single image, proposed in [12], which employs a multi-scale tensor voting scheme. Single image super-resolution using a soft-edge smoothness prior, from the alpha matte, was described in [13]. The prior favors smooth edges, which is found to be consistent with human perception. However, they do not utilize the matting equation during HR reconstruction; they simply super-resolve the matte independently, and obtain a visually pleasing super-resolved image using the HR matte alone. Matte super-resolution by defocus matting approach was attempted in [14]. This method uses three cameras, of which one camera must have the desired high-resolution. Besides, this method is learning-based and is bound to propagate matting errors to the prediction stage. One disadvantage of performing matting and then super-resolution independently, is that errors in the matte will get magnified after super-resolution [14].

We discuss multi-frame super-resolution, using frames extracted from a video containing arbitrary motion. Our goal is to implement matte super-resolution, which simultaneously obtains the matte as well as foreground at a higher resolution. The matting equation is included in the HR reconstruction model; hence the solution is optimized from the observed image by keeping the matting constraint. Motion estimation is done on the LR images a priori by using an accurate optical flow method from [15], using the implementation given in [16]. It has already been shown [6] that robustness to small errors in motion estimation is achieved by modeling the image as an MRF. Hence, the original HR image is modeled by a discontinuity-adaptive MRF (DAMRF) prior [17], which serves to regularize the solution as well as to preserve discontinuities at borders between the foreground and background.

The paper is organized as follows. Section 2 describes the observation model used for video matte and foreground super-resolution. In Section 3, we discuss our optimization approach using ICM algorithm. The DAMRF prior used to regularize the solution as well as to obtain distinct edges, is also described in the same section. Finally, the results of the proposed method and the conclusions drawn, are presented in Section 4.

2   Video Matting with Super-Resolution

The alpha matte values indicate the opacity/sub-pixel coverage of the foreground object at every pixel. The compositing equation using natural image matting at a pixel is given as

$$x(j, k) = \alpha(j, k) f(j, k) + (1 - \alpha(j, k)) b(j, k) \qquad (1)$$

where x is the composite image intensity, f is the foreground and b is the background contribution. The range of the alpha matte is $0 \le \alpha \le 1$, where $\alpha = 1$ specifies sure foreground and $\alpha = 0$ specifies sure background. The fractional values of α signify mixture of foreground and background at a pixel. This equation is severely under-constrained as it has three unknowns and only one known quantity, i.e., the observed image. The ill-posed matting problem requires user-specified constraints, provided by trimaps. For videos, trimaps are drawn for a few frames only [2] and rest of the frames can be propagated by optical flow [15]. For simplicity, we consider gray-scale images in formulating our algorithm. The method presented here can be easily extended to color images by super-resolving each color plane independently.

Super-resolution is an inverse problem for which we must first construct a forward model based on motion-compensated sub-sampling. Let the HR images $\mathbf{x} = [x_1, x_2, .., x_M]^T$ be of size $N_1 \mathrm{x} N_2$ each and the LR images $\mathbf{y} = [y_1, y_2, .., y_M]^T$ of size $Z_1 \mathrm{x} Z_2$. The low-resolution images are formed by the following linear observation model

$$\mathbf{y}_m = DW_m \mathbf{x} + \eta_m , \ m = 1, 2..M \qquad (2)$$

where the observed LR image $\mathbf{y}$ and the HR image, $\mathbf{x}$ are arranged lexicographically as column vectors. W denotes the warping matrix, m denotes the frame number of the sequence, and η is random noise. D is the down-sampling factor, which is N_1/Z_1 and N_2/Z_2 in the two spatial directions. We consider blurring only

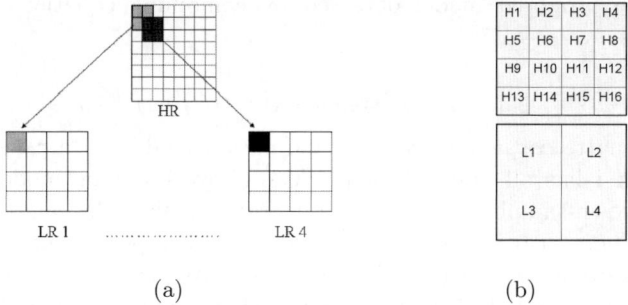

Fig. 1. (a) HR from LR pixels. (b) Down-sampling

by averaging due to down-sampling, so a separate blur matrix is not included in the degradation model. Down-sampling is implemented by averaging four adjacent pixels, as shown in Fig. 1, where $L1 = (H1 + H2 + H3 + H4)/4$, etc. Since all video frames are taken from the same camera, D is common for all frames.

It is important to note that W_m matrix consists of different values not only for each frame but also at each pixel. Unlike many previous methods for super-resolution, we consider non-global motion. Therefore, the relationship between HR and LR frames, as shown in Fig. 1 is valid locally, i.e., within the neighborhood at a pixel. After warping, the pixels of a frame will not maintain the same relative positions, as the motion is not global but arbitrary. The foreground object moves in a different manner from the background. Since the foreground is a non-rigid object or person, the displacement of parts of the foreground will be dissimilar. The warping operation, which is performed on the HR image, is actually estimated from the LR images by a suitable motion estimation method. The final warp matrix is approximated by nearest-neighbor interpolation of the LR warping, as the motion in most videos is smooth. While motion-compensating the LR frames with respect to the reference frame, semantically corresponding pixels should be aligned. The displacement at a pixel can be assumed to be purely translational within the local pixel neighborhood. The warp parameters representing the apparent motion of the scene are computed separately by an accurate and robust optical flow method. The optical flow constraint relates two pixels of images in adjacent frames (m and $m + 1$) of a video as follows

$$x(j, k, m) = x(j + u, k + v, m + 1) \qquad (3)$$

where (u, v) is the displacement vector or flow field between the two frames. The optical flow estimation we use is a multi-scale implementation, with a discontinuity-preserving spatio-temporal smoothness constraint. The image to be reconstructed is fixed as the reference frame, and the displacement velocities of subsequent $M - 1$ frames are defined with respect to the reference.

We solve for the super-resolved matte and foreground simultaneously. First, we need to incorporate the natural matting equation into the HR reconstruction model. The proposed model obtained by combining equations (1) and (2), is as follows

$$\mathbf{y}_m = DW_m(\boldsymbol{\alpha}_m\mathbf{f}_m + (\mathbf{i} - \boldsymbol{\alpha}_m)\mathbf{b}_m) + \eta_m \tag{4}$$

where the matte $\boldsymbol{\alpha}$, the foreground $\mathbf{f}$ and background $\mathbf{b}$ are arranged as column vectors and $\mathbf{i}$ has all unity elements. The above inversion model is valid because the down-sampling and warping operations affect the composite image as a whole. Wherever $\alpha = 0$ or $\alpha = 1$, the motion corresponds to the displacement of the background or foreground, respectively. At places where α is fractional, the displacement of both foreground and background will contribute to the overall apparent motion, although it is difficult to separate the two contributions. Integrating the matting and super-resolution problems leads to better results at the outlines of the foreground, rather than solving them separately, which might introduce errors [14].

3   Regularization by ICM Using DAMRF Prior

We now formulate the method for solving the matte and foreground super-resolution problem. Given the observed video frames $y_1, y_2, ...y_M$, we solve for the maximum a posteriori (MAP) estimate of $\boldsymbol{\alpha}$ and $\mathbf{f}$ within a Bayesian framework. One popular approach for regularized solutions to the super-resolution problem is the MAP estimation. In the MAP procedure, we treat super-resolution as a stochastic inference problem. Observed information is explicitly included in the form of a prior probability density. Bayesian estimation involves maximization of the posterior probability, using the prior and conditional probability. We use Markov Random Field (MRF) model which obeys the Markovian property, i.e., image label at a pixel depends only on its neighbors. We need to minimize energy of the form

$$E = E_1(\boldsymbol{\alpha}, \mathbf{f}) + E_2(\boldsymbol{\alpha}) + E_3(\mathbf{f}) \tag{5}$$

where $E_1(\boldsymbol{\alpha}, \mathbf{f})$ is the data term; $E_2(\boldsymbol{\alpha})$ and $E_3(\mathbf{f})$ are priors corresponding to the matte and foreground, respectively. The solution minimizes the reconstruction error between observed image and generated LR from recovered HR image, which is given by

$$E_1 = \|\mathbf{y}_m - DW_m(\boldsymbol{\alpha}_m\mathbf{f}_m + (\mathbf{i} - \boldsymbol{\alpha}_m)\mathbf{b}_m)\|^2 \tag{6}$$

The minimization is done using iterated conditional modes (ICM) method. We solve for high-resolution matte as well as foreground using double ICM loops. ICM is a deterministic algorithm implemented locally at each clique in a sequential manner [5]. It facilitates faster convergence for maximization of local conditional probabilities for MRF models. It finds widespread applications for image segmentation optimization [8].

Super-resolution is an ill-posed inverse problem due to down-sampling, shifting and noise. We thus need to include image-based priors in the regularization process in order to obtain a physically meaningful solution. Smoothness is a common assumption made in computer vision models [17], which also acts as a noise-removal tool. However, undesirable over-smoothing at edges must be avoided. For the matting problem, the edge information, especially at pixels on the boundary between the foreground and background, are important and must be preserved. We therefore include a smoothness prior which preserves discontinuities [6], to regularize the under-determined problem. We model the prior probabilities for $E_2(\alpha)$ and $E_3(\mathbf{f})$ (in equation (5)) as discontinuity-adaptive Markov random fields (DAMRFs) as follows

$$E_2(j,k) = \gamma_2 - \gamma_2 exp(-(\alpha(j,k) - \alpha(j_1,k_1))^2/\gamma_2)$$

(7)

$$E_3(j,k) = \gamma_3 - \gamma_3 exp(-(f(j,k) - f(j_1,k_1))^2/\gamma_3)$$

where (j_1, k_1) is the first-order neighborhood of the current pixel (j, k), which consists of: $(i-1, j)$, $(i+1, j)$, $(i, j-1)$ and $(i, j+1)$. γ_2 and γ_3 denote smoothness parameters for α and $\mathbf{f}$. The value of γ controls the shape of the function; a large value of γ makes the DAMRF function convex. Different values of γ must be used for estimation of α and $\mathbf{f}$. At every iteration, we find the matte and foreground value at each pixel, by labeling as one of the numbers 1, 5, .. 255 (for f) and 0.1, 0.05, 0.2, .. 1 (for α). Then the energy terms in equation (5) are computed and compared with previous values. If the new energy value is less, then the present labels are accepted, otherwise the previous labels are retained.

3.1 ICM Algorithm

1. Inputs: Initial bilinear interpolated estimates of α, $\mathbf{f}$, and trimap; optical flow velocities of LR images, up-sampled by nearest-neighbor interpolation
2. Compute initial data cost and smoothness costs for α and f
3. for $i = 1 : T$
    for $j = 1 : N_1$; for $k = 1 : N_2$
    old_alpha $= \alpha(j,k)$, new_alpha $= 0$;
    old_fore $= f(j,k)$, new_fore $= 0$;
repeat
    $\alpha(j,k)$ = new_alpha; $f(j,k)$ = new_fore;
    if $E^p(\alpha(new), \mathbf{f}(new)) \leq E^p(\alpha(old), \mathbf{f}(old))$
    $\alpha(old) = \alpha(new)$; $\mathbf{f}(old) = \mathbf{f}(new)$;
    $E^p(\alpha(old), \mathbf{f}(old)) = E^p(\alpha(new), \mathbf{f}(new))$
else
    $\alpha(j,k)$ = old_alpha; $f(j,k)$ = old_fore;
    new_alpha = new_alpha + δ_2; new_fore = new_fore + δ_3;
    until new_alpha ≤ 1 and new_fore ≤ 255
    end
end
4. $\widehat{\alpha} = \alpha(new)$ and $\widehat{f} = f(new)$
Here, $E^p(\alpha, \mathbf{f})$ is the posterior energy function, T is the number of iterations; δ_2 and δ_3 are increments in the labels of α (0 to 1) and $\mathbf{f}$ (0 to 255).

4   Results and Conclusions

In this section, we show two examples to demonstrate the results of the proposed algorithm. Both are frames taken from videos with non-global motion, and are typically used to demonstrate matting (from [18]). We have shown color image examples for better visualization of the foreground and more accurate matte (please see color version of results in the softcopy). We compute HR matte and foreground using four adjacent LR frames, which have local motion. The LR frames were generated by cropping and resizing from the original frames from the video in [18], using Irfanview, which is free-ware graphic viewer. This was done to ensure that we use an unknown resizing method, which may be different from our down-sampling model. Thus, the examples are representative of real cases. The LR matte and foreground can be extracted from any matting method. Displacement vectors are found from the LR observations, using code provided in [16]. The optical flow velocities are up-sampled using nearest-neighbor interpolation for the HR frames. To save time and computations, the trimap is used to determine which pixels are super-resolved. Those pixels which fully belong to the background are not considered. For the alpha matte, only the unknown pixels of the interpolated trimap are super-resolved; whereas for the foreground, both the sure foreground and the unknown region are super-resolved. We require $T = 10$ number of iterations for the ICM-based method. The increments of labels used are: $\delta_2 = 0.05$ for α and $\delta_3 = 5$ for $\mathbf{f}$.

In Fig. 2, the top row shows the first LR frame, extracted LR foreground and the LR matte. The bicubic interpolated matte and foreground (with magnification factor of two) are shown in Figs. 2(d) and (f). The results of our ICM-based super-resolution method are shown in Figs. 2(e) and (g). Comparing Figs. 2(d) and (e), it is obvious that fine details of the hair structure are more prominent in the matte results of the proposed method, than in the interpolated matte. The facial features in Fig. 2(g) are visibly sharper than in Fig. 2(f), where the eyes and lips look more smoothed-out. As a consequence of a more accurate matte, the hair strands also appear more well-defined.

Another example is given by Fig. 3. The first LR frame, extracted LR foreground and the LR matte are shown in Figs. 3(a)-(c). The HR matte and foreground from our approach are shown in Figs. 3(e) and (g). For comparison, again the bicubic interpolated matte and foreground are shown in Figs. 3(d) and (f). It can be seen from the left side of the HR matte and foreground (Figs. 3(e) and (g)), that it shows sharper hair structure than the interpolated matte (Figs. 3(d)). From the interpolated foreground in Fig. 3(f), the right side of the face and neck appears to have white streaks at the edges. This undesirable effect is visibly reduced in the foreground extracted by our method (Fig. 3(g)), as a result of greater matte accuracy (Fig. 3(e)). Besides, the eyebrow appears washed-out in Fig. 3(f), while it is much clearer in Fig. 3(g).

In this paper, we have proposed a joint framework for super-resolving the matte and foreground from a low-resolution video. A discontinuity-adaptive smoothness prior was incorporated to maintain fine edges often encountered in video editing applications. We have demonstrated the effectiveness of our approach on typical matting video examples, which contain both object and camera motion. We are currently working on a faster super-resolution method, using a gradient-descent approach, to obtain the super-resolved matte from the LR trimap itself.

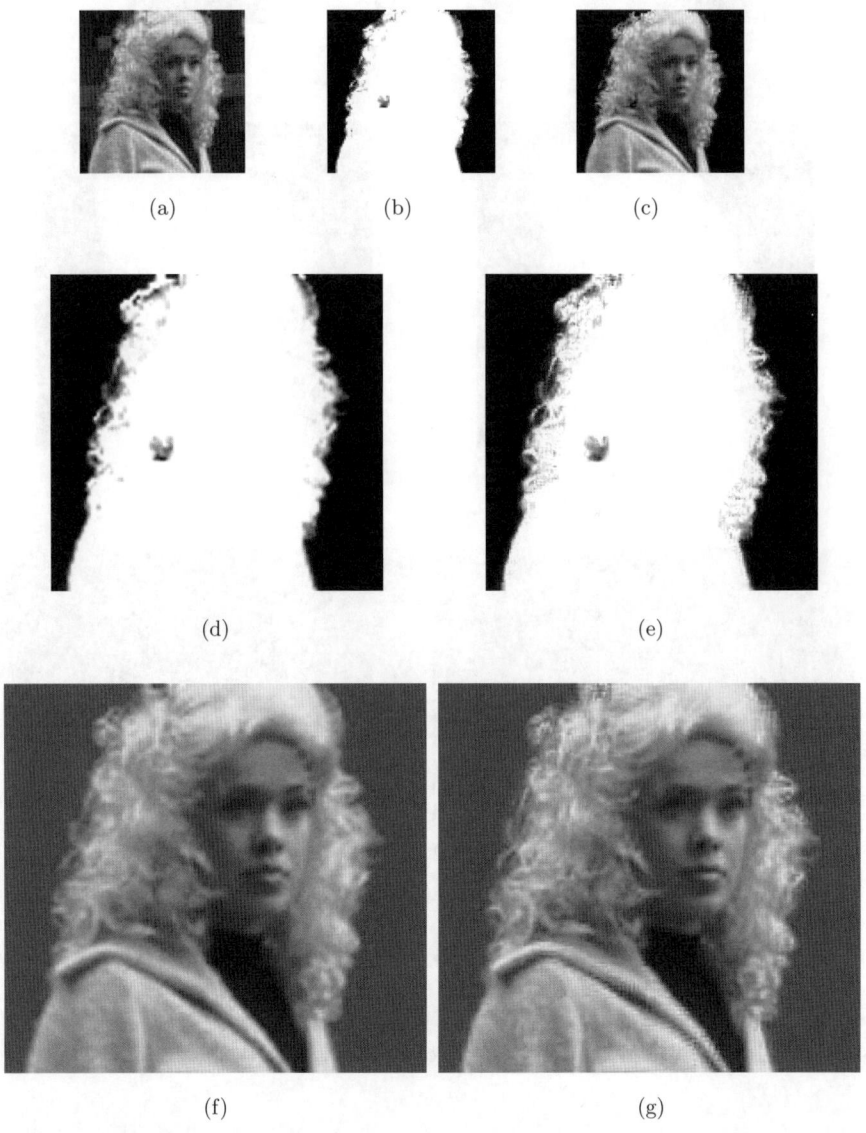

Fig. 2. (a) First LR frame. (b) LR matte. (c) LR foreground. (d) Interpolated matte. (e) HR matte. (f) Interpolated foreground composited. (g) HR foreground composited.

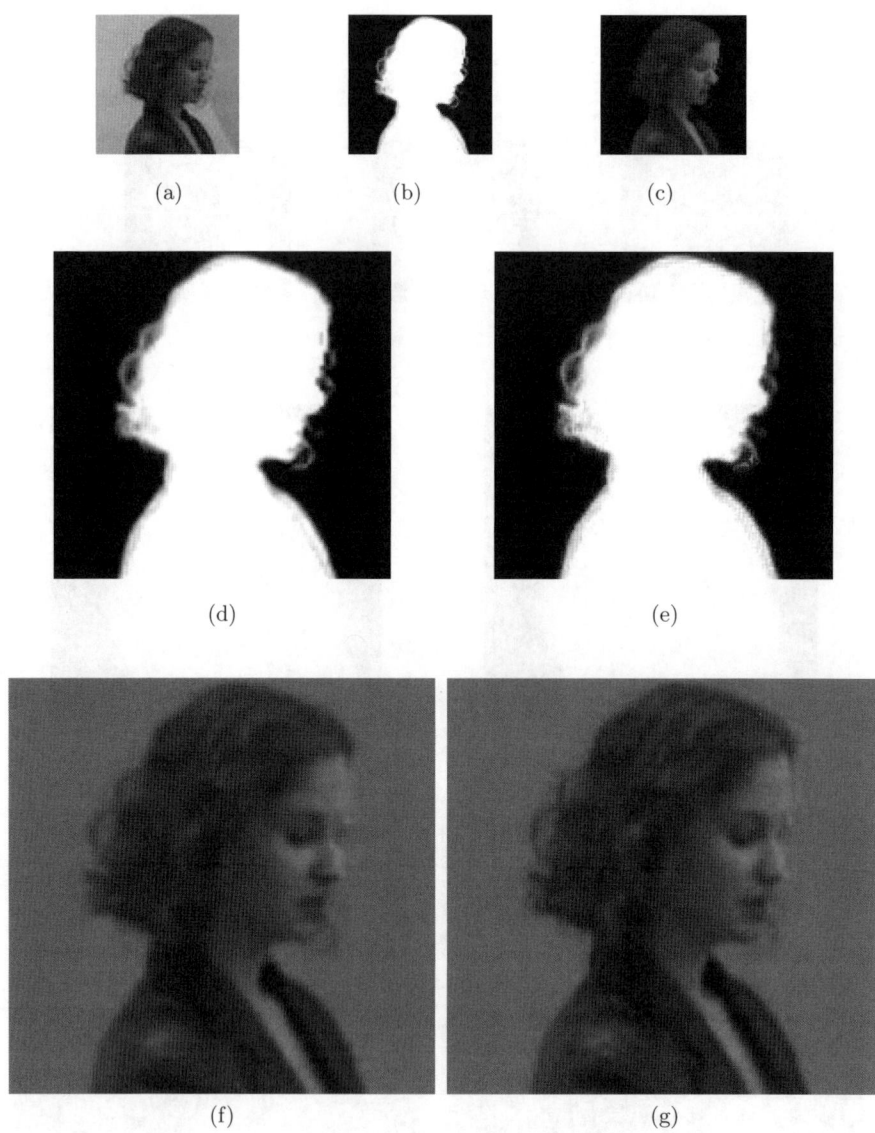

Fig. 3. (a) First LR frame. (b) LR matte. (c) LR foreground. (d) Interpolated matte. (e) HR matte. (f) Interpolated foreground composited. (g) HR foreground composited.

References

1. Levin, A., Lischinski, D., Weiss, Y.: A closed-form solution to natural image matting. IEEE Trans. Pattern Anal. and Mach. Intell. 30(2), 228–242 (2008)
2. Chuang, Y.Y., Agarwala, A., Curless, B., Salesin, D.H., Szeliski, R.: Video matting of complex scenes. ACM Transactions on Graphics, 243–248 (2002)
3. Park, S.C., Park, M.K., Kang, M.G.: Super-resolution image reconstruction: a technical overview. IEEE Signal Processing Magazine 20(3), 21–36 (2003)
4. Farsiu, S., Robinson, D., Elad, M., Milanfar, P.: Advances and challenges in super-resolution. International Journal of Imaging Systems and Technology 14(2), 47–57 (2004)
5. Besag, J.: On the statistical analysis of dirty pictures. Journal of Royal Statistics Society 48, 259–302 (1986)
6. Suresh, K., Rajagopalan, A.: Robust space-variant super-resolution. In: IET International Conference on Visual Information Engineering (2006)
7. Schultz, R.R., Stevenson, R.: Extraction of high-resolution frames from video sequences. IEEE Transactions on Image Processing 5(6), 996–1011 (1996)
8. Shen, H., Zhang, L., Huang, B., Li, P.: A map approach for joint motion estimation, segmentation, and super resolution. IEEE Transactions on Image Processing 16(2), 479–490 (2007)
9. Bhavsar, A.V., Rajagopalan, A.N.: Resolution enhancement for binocular stereo. In: Proc. International Conference on Pattern Recognition, pp. 1–4 (2008)
10. Rajagopalan, A.N., Bhavsar, A.V., Wallhoff, F., Rigoll, G.: Resolution enhancement of pmd range maps. In: Rigoll, G. (ed.) DAGM 2008. LNCS, vol. 5096, pp. 304–313. Springer, Heidelberg (2008)
11. Fransens, R., Strecha, C., Van Gool, L.: Optical flow based super-resolution: A probabilistic approach. Computer vision and image understanding 106(1), 106–115 (2007)
12. Tai, Y.W., Tong, W.S., Tang, C.K.: Perceptually-inspired and edge-directed color image super-resolution (2006)
13. Dai, S., Han, M., Xu, W., Wu, Y., Gong, Y., Katsaggelos, A.K.: Softcuts: a soft edge smoothness prior for color image super-resolution. IEEE Transactions on Image Processing 18(5), 969–980 (2009)
14. Joshi, N., Matusik, W., Avidan, S., Pfister, H., Freeman, W.T.: Exploring defocus matting: Nonparametric acceleration, super-resolution, and off-center matting. In: IEEE Computer Graphics and Applications, pp. 43–52 (2007)
15. Brox, T., Bruhn, A., Papenberg, N., Weickert, J.: High accuracy optical flow estimation based on a theory for warping. In: Pajdla, T., Matas, J(G.) (eds.) ECCV 2004, Part IV. LNCS, vol. 3024, pp. 25–36. Springer, Heidelberg (2004)
16. Chari, V.: http://perception.inrialpes.fr/people/chari/myweb/software/
17. Li, S.: Markov random field modeling in computer vision. Springer, Tokyo (1995)
18. Chuang, Y.Y.: http://grail.cs.washington.edu/projects/digital-matting/video-matting/

An Improved Histogram of Edge Local Orientations for Sketch-Based Image Retrieval

Jose M. Saavedra* and Benjamin Bustos

PRISMA Research Group
Department of Computer Science, University of Chile
{jsaavedr,bebustos}@dcc.uchile.cl

Abstract. Content-based image retrieval requires a natural image (e.g, a photo) as query, but the absence of such a query image is usually the reason for a search. An easy way to express the user query is using a line-based hand-drawing, a sketch, leading to the sketch-based image retrieval. Few authors have addressed image retrieval based on a sketch as query, and the current approaches still keep low performance under scale, translation, and rotation transformations. In this paper, we describe a method based on computing efficiently a histogram of edge local orientations that we call HELO. Our method is based on a strategy applied in the context of fingerprint processing. This descriptor is invariant to scale and translation transformations. To tackle the rotation problem, we apply two normalization processes, one using principal component analysis and the other using polar coordinates. Finally, we linearly combine two distance measures. Our results show that HELO significantly increases the retrieval effectiveness in comparison with the state of the art.

1 Introduction

Due to the progress in digital imaging technology, image retrieval has become a very relevant discipline in computer science. In a content-based image retrieval system (CBIR), an image is required as input. This image should express what the user is looking for. But, frequently the user does not have an appropriate image for that purpose. Furthermore, the absence of such a query image is usually the reason for the search [1]. An easy way to express the user query is using a line-based hand-drawing, a *sketch*, leading to the *sketch-based image retrieval* (SBIR). In fact, a sketch is the natural way to make a query in applications like CAD or 3D model retrieval [2].

Although there are many publications on CBIR, a few authors have addressed image retrieval based on sketches. Some of these works are *Query by Visual Example*(QVE) [3], *Edge Histogram Descriptor* (EHD) [4], *Image Retrieval by Elastic Matching* [5], *Angular partitioning of Abstract Images* [6], and *Structure Tensor*[1], that will be briefly discussed in the next section. Although these methods are applied to SBIR, they still show poor effectiveness under scale, translation, and rotation issues.

---

* Partially funded by CONICYT(Chile) through the Doctoral Scholarship.

M. Goesele et al. (Eds.): DAGM 2010, LNCS 6376, pp. 432–441, 2010.

The main contribution of this work is to propose a novel method based on edge orientations that gets a global representation of both the sketch and the test image. We improve the effectiveness of SBIR by estimating local orientations in a more precise way, obtaining a *histogram of edge local orientations*. The local orientations are computed using a strategy applied for computing directional fields of fingerprints, in the context of biometric processing [7]. Our proposed approach is invariant to scale and translation transformations. To tackle the rotation problem, we apply two different normalization processes, one using principal component analysis and the other using polar coordinates. Finally, we use a combined distance as similarity measure. We experimentally show that our proposed method significantly outperforms the state of the art.

The rest of this paper is organized as following. Section 2 describes the current methods for SBIR. Section 3 describes in detail the proposed method. Section 4 presents the experimental evaluation. Finally, Section 5 presents conclusions.

2   Related Work

There are a few works on sketch-based image retrieval. One of the first proposals is QVE [3]. The test image and the query are transformed into abstract representations based on edge maps. To measure similarity between two abstract representations, this method uses a correlation process based on bitwise operations. To get translation invariance, the correlation is carried out under horizontal and vertical shifts. This method is expensive and not rotation invariant. In addition, this approach does not permit indexing [6].

Another approach was presented by Del Bimbo and Pala [5]. This approach is based on elastic deformation of a sketch to match a test image. The necessary effort to adjust the query to the test image is represented by five parameters that are the input to a multi-layer neural network. This method is also expensive and not rotation invariant, and to get a good performance the query and the test image need to have similar aspect ratios, narrowing its scope.

Other methods use edge information such as edge orientation or density. One of this methods is that proposed by Jain and Vailaya [8]. They proposed a shape descriptor using a histogram of edge directions (HED) among their work on combining shape and color descriptors for CBIR. The idea is to quantize the edge orientation and to form a B-bins histogram. Although this approach may be scale and translation invariant, it is not robust to rotation changes.

Another edge-based approach is the Edge Histogram Descriptor (EHD) that was proposed in the visual part of the MPEG-7 [9]. An improved version of EHD was proposed by Sun Won et al. [4]. The idea is to get a local distribution of five types of edges from local regions of the image. The juxtaposition of local distributions composes the final descriptor. Although this approach is invariant to scale and translation transformations, it is not rotation invariant.

The histogram of distance distribution (HDD) is another descriptor that could also be applied for SBIR. HDD consists in selecting a sample of points from an edge map and then computing distances between random pairs of points. This descriptor has been used for 3D model retrieval [10] and for shape matching like in *Shape Context* [11]. Although this descriptor is invariant to translation, scale, and rotation, it is strongly dependent on the size of the sample.

An important work on SBIR was presented by Chalechale et al. [6]. This approach is based on angular partitioning of abstract images (APAI). The angular spatial distributions of pixels in the abstract image is the key concept for feature extraction. The method divides the abstract image into K angular partitions or slices. Then, it uses the number of edge points falling into each slice to make up a feature vector. To get rotation invariance, the method applies Fourier transform to the resulting feature vector. Although the method is partially invariant to translation, scaling, and rotation, it requires to recover almost 13% from the database to retrieve the correct one, so its effectiveness is low.

Recently, Eitz et al. [1] presented a new approach for SBIR. In this approach, the test image and the query are decomposed into $a \times b$ cells. Then, this method computes gradients at each edge point. To represent a unique orientation in each cell, the method computes the *structure tensor* (ST) over the local gradients. Similarity between a test image and a query is computed comparing corresponding local structure tensors. This approach is not rotation invariant.

We observe that the sketch-based image retrieval is still an open problem, because the current methods show poor effectiveness under scale, translation, and rotation changes. Thus, the main contribution of this work is to improve the effectiveness of image retrieval having as query a line-based hand-drawing.

3   Proposed Method

Our method is based on estimating local edge orientations and forming a global descriptor named HELO (Histogram of Edge Local Orientations). Since noise affects adversely the edge orientation computation [12], its presence in an image may cause descriptors to have low performance for image retrieval. So, we use a local method, which is robust to noise, to estimate edge orientations. In addition, using a local estimation, the sketches do not need to be drawn with continuous strokes.

3.1   HELO Descriptor

Our method works in two stages. The first one performs preprocessing tasks to get an abstract representation of both the sketch and the test image, while the second one make up the histogram. A detailed description is shown below:

- **Preprocessing**: In this stage, the test images are preprocessed off-line. First, the method uses the Canny algorithm [13] to get an edge map from each test image. For the Canny algorithm, we use a 9×9-size gaussian mask and a $\sigma = 1.5$. Then, the method applies a cropping operation to the result using horizontal and vertical projections in a similar way to that applied in the context of text recognition [14].

  The sketch is preprocessed on-line. First, the method uses a simple thresholding to get a binary representation of the sketch. Then, the method applies a cropping operation to the result in a similar way as in the previous case.

- **Histogram Computation**: Here, our approach computes a K-bin histogram based on local edge orientations. We propose to use a method applied for estimating directional fields of fingerprints [7], that allows us to minimize the noise sensitivity by a orientation local estimation. The main idea is to double the gradient angle and to square the gradient length. This has the effect that strong orientations have a higher vote in the local average orientation than weaker orientations [7]. This improves the retrieval effectiveness on the SBIR. The local orientation estimation works as follows:

  - Divide the image into $W \times W$ blocks. We regard each block as a local area where we will estimate the local orientation. In this approach the block size is dependent on the image size to deal with scale changes.
  - Compute gradient respect to x and to y for each pixel in a block, which will be called G_x and G_y, respectively. Here, we use Sobel masks [15].
  - Compute local orientations as follows:
    * Let b_{ij} be a block and α_{ij} its corresponding orientation ($i, j = 1..W$).
    * Let L_x and L_y be the set of local gradients of an image respect to x and y, computed on each block b_{ij} as follows:

    $$L_y^{ij} = \sum_{(r,s)\in b_{ij}} 2G_x(r,s)G_y(r,s) \tag{1}$$

    $$L_x^{ij} = \sum_{(r,s)\in b_{ij}} (G_x(r,s)^2 - G_y(r,s)^2) \tag{2}$$

    here, L_β^{ij} is the gradient on b_{ij} in the direction β.
    * Apply a gaussian filter on L_x and L_y to smooth the components. We use a gaussian filter with $\sigma = 0.5$ and a 3×3-size mask.
    * Calculate the local orientation α_{ij} as follows:

    $$\alpha_{ij} = \frac{1}{2}tan^{-1}\left(\frac{L_y^{ij}}{L_x^{ij}}\right) - \frac{\pi}{2} \tag{3}$$

    At this point, we normalize α_{ij} to the range between 0 and π.
  - Create a K-bin histogram to represent the distribution of the local orientation in the image.
  - Map each local orientation α_{ij} to the corresponding histogram bin to increase it by one. Blocks with a few edge points are neglected. We use a threshold th_{edge} to filter those blocks. We call the resulting histogram the histogram of edge local orientation (HELO). Fig. 1 shows an orientation field of a test image, computed by HELO.

HELO is invariant to translation because the orientation is independent of edge positions. In addition, since the block size depends on the image size, HELO is also invariant to scale changes. Moreover, we measure similarity between two HELO descriptors using the L_1 distance (Manhattan distance).

 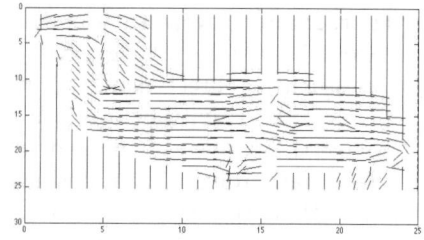

Fig. 1. An image with its corresponding orientation field. Here, $W = 25$.

3.2   HELO under Rotation Invariance

To get rotation invariance, we need to normalize both the sketch and the test image before computing HELO descriptor. We use two different normalization processes and then we compute two HELO descriptors, one for each normalization process. After that, we measure similarity by combining linearly partial distances. For normalization, we use principal component analysis (PCA) and polar coordinates (PC). We present a detailed description of this approach below:

- **Preprocessing**: This stage is similar to the previous one (Section 3.1), except that in this case the cropping operation is performed after the normalization process.
- **Orientation normalization**:
  - **Using PCA**: We compute a 2-d eigenvector v representing the axis with higher variance of the pixel (with value 1) distribution using PCA. We normalize both the sketch and the test image abstract representation rotating them $-\alpha$ degrees around their center of mass. Here, $\alpha = tan^{-1}(v_y/v_x)$.
  - **Using PC**: We transform both the test image and the sketch abstract representation into polar coordinates. In this case, two rotated images containing the same object become similar images only affected by an horizontal shifting.
- **Histogram Computation**: Exactly similar to the previous one (Sect. 3.1).

We compute similarity between a test image I and a sketch S combining PCA-based HELO and PC-based HELO. Let I_{PCA} and S_{PCA} be the PCA-based HELO descriptors computed over I and S, respectively. Let I_{PC} and S_{PC} be the correspondent PC-based HELO descriptors. The similarity measure $sm(I, S)$ is:

$$sm(I, S) = w_{PCA} L_1(I_{PCA}, S_{PCA}) + w_{PC} L_1(I_{PC}, S_{PC}) \tag{4}$$

where, $w_{PCA} + w_{PC} = 1$, $w_{PCA} \geq 0, w_{PC} \geq 0$ and L_1 is the Manhattan distance.

Our proposal is configurable for working with or without rotation invariance. This is an advantage, because the rotation invariance requirement commonly depends on the application. For example, in the context of handwriting recognition rotation invariance may result in confusing the digit 6 with digit 9.

4   Experimental Evaluation

Considering that there is no standard benchmark for SBIR, we have developed one to evaluate different approaches, and to compare them with our proposal. For the test database, we have randomly selected 1326 images. We selected 1285 color images from Caltech101 [16], and we added 46 images containing castles and palaces. Many of the test images consist of more than one object or are cluttered images. For the query database we have chosen 53 images from the database. For each query image, a line-based sketch was hand-drawn. Thus, we have 53 sketches [1]. An example sketch and its corresponding target image appear in Fig. 2.

Fig. 2. A sketch on the left and its corresponding target image on the right

We compare our method with five others methods according to the state of the art. Four of these methods are: APAI [6], ST [1], HED [8], and EHD [4], which were implemented following the specification described in the corresponding papers. Additionally, we compare our method with the *histogram of distance distribution* (HDD) as explained in Section 2.

The evaluation of the methods was performed by querying each sketch for the most similar images and finding the target image rank. We called this rank *query rank*. For measuring our results, we use two metrics. First, we use *Mean of Query Rank* (MQR), for which the average of all *query ranks* is computed. Second, we use the *recall ratio* R_n, which shows the ratio to retrieve the target image in the best n-candidates. R_n is defined as follows:

$$R_n = \frac{\text{target images among first } n \text{ responses}}{\text{total number of queries}} \times 100 \qquad (5)$$

To evaluate translation, scale, and rotation robustness, we divide the experiments in two parts. First, we evaluate our method with sketches having different scale and position from the corresponding target images. Second, we evaluate our method with sketches that have been rotated by three different angles (30°, 60°, and 90°), having 212 sketches.

---

[1] http://prisma.dcc.uchile.cl/archivos_publicos/Sketch_DB.zip

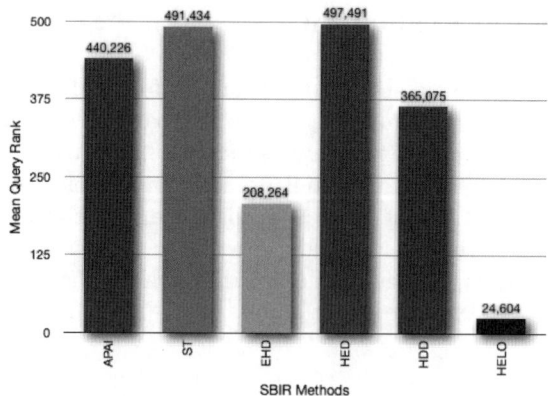

Fig. 3. Mean Query Rank of the evaluated methods

Our method needs three parameters to be specified, the histogram length (K), the number of horizontal and vertical blocks (W), and a threshold (th_{edge}). We fix $K = 72$, $W = 25$, and we set th_{edge} as 0.5 times the maximum image dimension. These parameter values were chosen experimentaly.

4.1 Translation and Scale Invariance Comparison

Fig. 3 shows the MQR for each evaluated method. We observe that our method is more robust than the other methods when scale and position changes exist. We achieve 24.60 as MQR value. This indicates that HELO needs to retrieve less than 25 images from the database to recover the target image. In comparison with the other methods, EHD is the closest to the ours with a significance difference. EHD achieves 208.26 as a MQR, i.e, EHD would require to retrieve almost 208 images to find the target one. Thus, our method improves effectiveness on recall over 8.4 times respect to the state of the art.

Fig. 4 shows the recall ratio graphic. This graphic shows that HELO outperforms the state of the art methods for any value of n. In addition, an example of image retrieval using HELO is shown in Fig. 5.

4.2 Rotation Invariance Comparison

First of all, we evaluate HELO descriptor using separately PCA and PC. Using PCA, we obtain a MQR value of 197.04. The principal axis is computed over the edge point distribution. However, a sketch is a simple rough hand-made drawing without details as those appearing in the target image. Due to these facts, the input sketch and the target image may have very different principal axis affecting the retrieval effectiveness. Using PC, sketches affected by different angular shifts have similar representations in polar coordinates. This is the reason for what PC gives a better MQR value (156.09) than that given by PCA. However, PC changes drastically the edge point distribution decreasing the discriminative power.

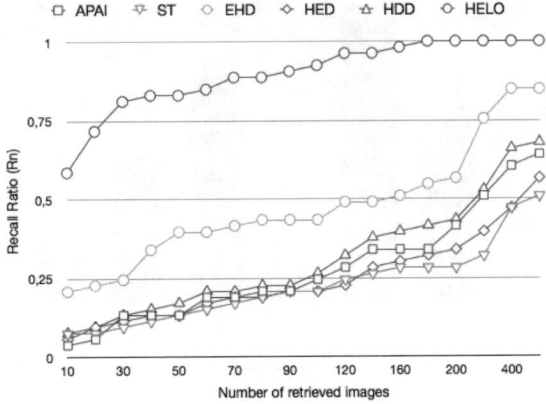

Fig. 4. Recall ratio graphic for the evaluated methods

Fig. 5. Example of the first six retrieved image using HELO. The first is the query

Therefore, to take advantage of each orientation normalization method we propose a linear combination of PC-based HELO and PCA-based HELO, that allows us to improve the retrieval effectiveness. Using our approach we get MQR value to 101.09. We described this method in the Section 3.2. We will refer to the combined-based HELO descriptor as HELO_R. To implement the HELO_R descriptor, we use $w_{PCA} = 0.3$ and $w_{PC} = 0.7$.

Fig. 6 shows the MQR for the evaluated methods under rotation distortions. Clearly, under this kind of changes, our proposal improves the effectiveness on recall over 2.6 times respect to the state of the art. To visualize how many images are needed to retrieve the target image, Fig. 7 shows the recall ratio graphics comparing the six evaluated methods.

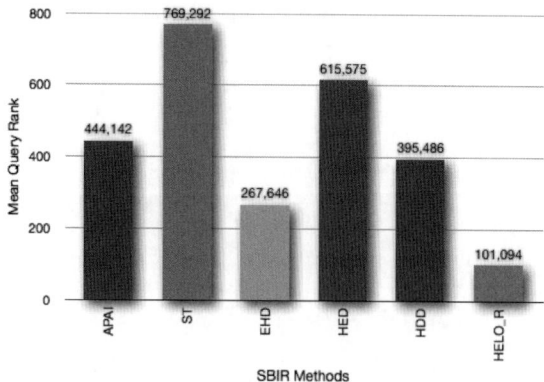

Fig. 6. Mean Query Rank of the evaluated methods under rotation invariance

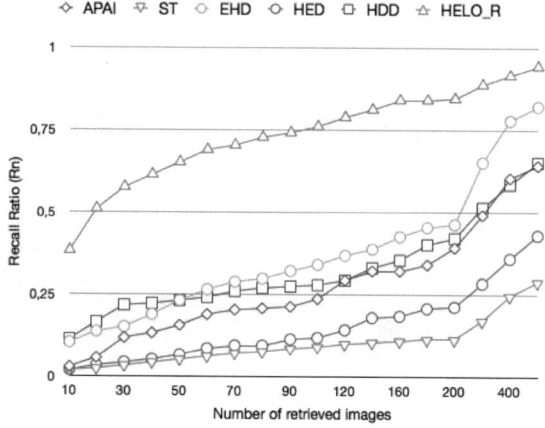

Fig. 7. Recall ratio graphic for the evaluated methods under rotation invariance

5 Conclusions

In this work, we have observed that SBIR is still an open problem, and that the current methods for SBIR do not work well enough. We have presented a novel method for SBIR that uses an efficient algorithm to compute a histogram of edge local orientations. First, we focused on SBIR under scale and translation transformations. Then, we extended our proposed approach to work under rotation invariance. We applied principal component analysis and polar coordinates to get orientation normalization.

Our achieved results show that HELO outperforms significantly the state of the art, improving recall over 8.4 times under scale and translation distortions, and over 2.6 times under rotation distortions. Furthermore, the query sketches do not need to be drawn with continuous strokes.

In our ongoing work, we are analyzing the performance of HELO under different values of its parameters. In addition, SBIR under orientation invariance must be studied in depth. For the future work, we will focus both on the rotation invariance problem and on multi-object sketch queries.

References

1. Eitz, M., Hildebrand, K., Boubekeur, T., Alexa, M.: A descriptor for large scale image retrieval based on sketched feature lines. In: Proc. of the 6th Eurographics Symposium on Sketch-Based Interfaces and Modeling, pp. 29–36 (2009)
2. Funkhouser, T., Min, P., Kazhdan, M., Chen, J., Halderman, A., Dobkin, D., Jacobs, D.: A search engine for 3d models. ACM Transactions on Graphics 22(1), 83–105 (2003)
3. Kato, T., Kurita, T., Otsu, N., Hirata, K.: A sketch retrieval method for full color image database-query by visual example. In: Proc. of the 11th IAPR International Conf. on Computer Vision and Applications, Conf. A: Pattern Recognition, pp. 530–533 (1992)
4. Sun Won, C., Kwon Park, D., Park, S.J.: Efficient use of MPEG-7 edge histogram descriptor. Electronic and Telecomunications Research Institute Journal 24, 23–30 (2002)
5. Del Bimbo, A., Pala, P.: Visual image retrieval by elastic matching of user sketches. IEEE Trans. on Pattern Analysis and Machine Intelligence 19(2), 121–132 (1997)
6. Chalechale, A., Naghdy, G., Mertins, A.: Sketch-based image matching using angular partitioning. IEEE Trans. on Systems, Man and Cybernetics, Part A: Systems and Humans 35(1), 28–41 (2005)
7. Bazen, A.M., Gerez, S.H.: Systematic methods for the computation of the directional fields and singular points of fingerprints. IEEE Trans. on Pattern Analysis and Machine Intelligence 24(7), 905–919 (2002)
8. Jain, A., Vailaya, A.: Image retrieval using color and shape. Pattern Recognition 29, 1233–1244 (1996)
9. Martínez, J.M.: MPEG-7: Overview of MPEG-7 description tools, Part 2. IEEE MultiMedia 9(3), 83–93 (2002)
10. Pu, J., Ramani, K.: A 3d model retrieval method using 2d freehand sketches. In: Sunderam, V.S., van Albada, G.D., Sloot, P.M.A., Dongarra, J. (eds.) ICCS 2005. LNCS, vol. 3515, pp. 343–346. Springer, Heidelberg (2005)
11. Belongie, S., Malik, J., Puzicha, J.: Shape context: A new descriptor for shape matching and object recognition. In: Proc. of the 2000 Neural Information Processing Systems Conference, pp. 831–837 (2000)
12. Davies, E.R.: The effect of noise on edge orientation computations. Pattern Recognition Letters 6(5), 315–322 (1987)
13. Canny, J.: A computational approach to edge detection. IEEE Trans. on Pattern Analysis and Machine Intelligence 8(6), 679–698 (1986)
14. Gatos, B., Pratikakis, I., Perantonis, S.: Hybrid off-line cursive handwriting word recognition. In: Proc. of the 8th International Conference on Pattern Recognition, pp. 998–1002 (2006)
15. Gonzales, R., Woods, R.: Digital Image Processing, 3rd edn. Prentice Hall, Englewood Cliffs (2008)
16. Fei-Fei, L., Fergus, R., Perona, P.: Learning generative visual models from few training examples: an incremental bayesian approach tested on 101 object categories. In: Proc. of the 2004 Conference on Computer Vision and Pattern Recognition, Workshop on Generative-Model Based Vision, p. 178 (2004)

A Novel Curvature Estimator for Digital Curves and Images

Oliver Fleischmann[1], Lennart Wietzke[2], and Gerald Sommer[1]

[1] Cognitive Systems Group, Department of Computer Science
Kiel University, Germany
[2] Raytrix GmbH, Kiel, Germany

Abstract. We propose a novel curvature estimation algorithm which is capable of estimating the curvature of digital curves and two-dimensional curved image structures. The algorithm is based on the conformal projection of the curve or image signal to the two-sphere. Due to the geometric structure of the embedded signal the curvature may be estimated in terms of first order partial derivatives in $\mathbb{R}^3$. This structure allows us to obtain the curvature by just convolving the projected signal with the appropriate kernels. We show that the method performs an implicit plane fitting by convolving the projected signals with the derivative kernels. Since the algorithm is based on convolutions its implementation is straightforward for digital curves as well as images. We compare the proposed method with differential geometric curvature estimators. It turns out that the novel estimator is as accurate as the standard differential geometric methods in synthetic as well as real and noise perturbed environments.

1 Introduction

The estimation of curvature in two-dimensional images is of interest for several image processing tasks. It is used as a feature indicating corners or straight line segments in the case of digital curves [1], in active contour models [2] or for interpolation [3]. In the case of digital plane curves the most common ways to estimate the curvature rely on the estimation of the tangent angle derivative [4], or the estimation of the osculating circle touching the curve [5]. Most of these methods require the segmentation of the curve into digital straight line segments as a preprocessing step [6,7]. Furthermore the application of the these algorithms is limited to digital curves. If it is desired to estimate the curvature of yet unknown curves in images, e.g. isophotes in grayscale images, one has to use the classical definition of curvature known from differential geometry.

We present a curvature estimator based on the idea introduced in [8] which is based on simple convolutions and may be applied to digital curves as well as images.

M. Goesele et al. (Eds.): DAGM 2010, LNCS 6376, pp. 442–451, 2010.

2   Spherical Signal Embedding

We assume a circular signal model in the Euclidean plane with center $\mathbf{m} = r(\cos\theta_{\mathbf{m}}, \sin\theta_{\mathbf{m}})^T \in \mathbb{R}^2$

$$f_{\mathbf{m}}(\mathbf{u}) = \tilde{f}(||\mathbf{u} - \mathbf{m}||) \tag{1}$$

where $\mathbf{u} \in \mathbb{R}^2, \tilde{f} \in L^2(\mathbb{R})$ and $|| \cdot ||$ denotes the Euclidean norm in $\mathbb{R}^2$. The isophotes $\gamma_{\mathbf{m}}(\mathbf{u})$ of f through $\mathbf{u}$ are circles around $\mathbf{m}$ with radius $|| \mathbf{u} - \mathbf{m} ||$ given by

$$\gamma_{\mathbf{m}}(\mathbf{u}) = \{\mathbf{v} \in \mathbb{R}^2 : ||\mathbf{v} - \mathbf{m}|| = ||\mathbf{u} - \mathbf{m}||\}. \tag{2}$$

We will estimate the curvature of an isophote $\gamma_{\mathbf{m}}(\mathbf{u})$ by estimating the radius $r_{\mathbf{m}}(\mathbf{u})$ of the osculating circle touching the isophote $\gamma_{\mathbf{m}}(\mathbf{u})$. Since the isophotes are circles, the radius of the osculating circle at every $\mathbf{v} \in \gamma_{\mathbf{m}}(\mathbf{u})$ is the radius of the isophote itself. The curvature of $\gamma_{\mathbf{m}}(\mathbf{u})$ at $\mathbf{u}$ is then obtained as the inverse of the radius $r_{\mathbf{m}}(\mathbf{u})$ as $\kappa_{\mathbf{m}}(\mathbf{u}) = \frac{1}{r_{\mathbf{m}}(\mathbf{u})} = \frac{1}{||\mathbf{u}-\mathbf{m}||}$ [9]. We seek for a fast and exact method to obtain the radius $r_{\mathbf{m}}(\mathbf{u})$ just from the two-dimensional signal $f_{\mathbf{m}}$. The signal $f_{\mathbf{m}}$ is projected to the sphere $\mathbb{S}^2$ with center $(0, 0, \frac{1}{2})^T \in \mathbb{R}^3$ and radius $\frac{1}{2}$ via the inverse stereographic projection

$$\mathcal{S}^{-1}(\mathbf{u}) = \frac{1}{1 + \sum_{i=1}^{2} u_i^2}(u_1, u_2, u_1^2 + u_2^2)^T. \tag{3}$$

It is well known, that the stereographic projection is a conformal mapping and maps circles in the Euclidean plane to circles on $\mathbb{S}^2$ (see e.g. [10]). Hence the circular signal $f_{\mathbf{m}}$ is mapped to a circular signal on $\mathbb{S}^2$

$$g_{\mathbf{m}}(\mathbf{x}) = \begin{cases} f_{\mathbf{m}}(\mathcal{S}(\mathbf{x})) & \text{if } \mathbf{x} \in \mathbb{S}^2 \subset \mathbb{R}^3 \\ 0 & \text{else} \end{cases} \tag{4}$$

where $\mathcal{S}$ denotes the stereographic projection from the sphere $\mathbb{S}^2$ to $\mathbb{R}^2$.

To illustrate the geometric idea of our method (compare also Figure 1) we fix a single isophote $\gamma_{\mathbf{m}}(\mathbf{u})$ and choose a coordinate system in such a way, that $\mathbf{u}$ is the origin and coincides with the southpole $(0, 0, 0)^T$ of the sphere $\mathbb{S}^2$. Furthermore, we project $\gamma_{\mathbf{m}}(\mathbf{u})$ to $\mathbb{S}^2$ as $\mathcal{S}^{-1}(\gamma_{\mathbf{m}}(\mathbf{u}))$. Since $\gamma_{\mathbf{m}}(\mathbf{u})$ is a circle through $\mathbf{u}$ we know, that $\mathcal{S}^{-1}(\gamma_{\mathbf{m}}(\mathbf{u}))$ is a circle on $\mathbb{S}^2$ passing through the southpole of $\mathbb{S}^2$. Let $\mathbf{v} = (0, 0, 1)^T$ denote the northpole of $\mathbb{S}^2$ and define $\mathbf{w} = \mathcal{S}^{-1}(2\mathbf{m})$. $\mathcal{S}^{-1}(\gamma_{\mathbf{m}}(\mathbf{u}))$ is completely characterized by the intersection of a plane $\mathbf{P}_{\mathbf{m}}$ and $\mathbb{S}^2$ with normal vector $\mathbf{n}_{\mathbf{m}} = (\sin\varphi_{\mathbf{m}}\cos\theta_{\mathbf{m}}, \sin\varphi_{\mathbf{m}}\sin\theta_{\mathbf{m}}, \cos\varphi_{\mathbf{m}})^T$ and distance $d_{\mathbf{m}}$ from the origin. Since $\mathcal{S}^{-1}(\gamma_{\mathbf{m}}(\mathbf{u}))$ passes through $(0, 0, 0)^T$ it follows that $(0, 0, 0)^T \in \mathbf{P}_m$ such that $d_{\mathbf{m}} = 0$. Now we claim that

$$\frac{\mathbf{v} - \mathbf{w}}{||\mathbf{v} - \mathbf{w}||} = \mathbf{n}_{\mathbf{m}}. \tag{5}$$

It is sufficient to show that $\mathbf{w}-\mathbf{v}$ is perpendicular to $\mathbf{u}-\mathbf{w}$ such that $\langle\mathbf{w}-\mathbf{v}, \mathbf{u}-\mathbf{w}\rangle = 0$, where $\langle\cdot, \cdot\rangle$ denotes the inner product in $\mathbb{R}^3$. Since $\mathbf{v} = (0, 0, 1)^T, \mathbf{u} = (0, 0, 0)$

and $\mathbf{w} = \frac{1}{2}(\sin\varphi\cos\theta, \sin\varphi\sin\theta, \cos\varphi + 1)^T$ equation (5) follows immediately. Further by considering the triangle $\mathbf{u}, 2\mathbf{m}, \mathbf{v}$ it follows that

$$\tan\varphi_{\mathbf{m}}(\mathbf{u}) = 2\|\mathbf{m}\| = 2r_{\mathbf{m}}(\mathbf{u}) \Rightarrow \kappa_{\mathbf{m}}(\mathbf{u}) = \frac{1}{r_{\mathbf{m}}(\mathbf{u})} = \frac{2}{\tan\varphi_{\mathbf{m}}(\mathbf{u})}. \tag{6}$$

We conclude that the radius of the osculating circle of $\gamma_{\mathbf{u}}(\mathbf{u})$ can be obtained from the angle $\varphi_{\mathbf{m}}$ which we can obtain from the normal vector of $\mathbf{P_m}$. The problem of estimating the radius of the osculating circle is therefore equivalent to the problem of estimating the normal vector $\mathbf{n_m}$ characterizing the plane which intersects $\mathbb{S}^2$ resulting in $\gamma_{\mathbf{m}}(\mathbf{u})$.

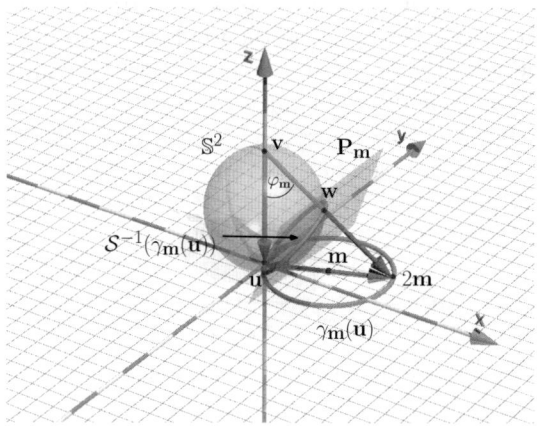

Fig. 1. Illustration of an isophote $\gamma_{\mathbf{m}}(\mathbf{u})$ and its projection $\mathcal{S}^{-1}(\gamma_{\mathbf{m}}(\mathbf{u}))$ to $\mathbb{S}^2$. The radius $\|\mathbf{m}\|$ can be calculated from angle $\varphi_{\mathbf{m}}$ as $\tan\varphi_{\mathbf{m}} = 2\|\mathbf{m}\|$. The vector $\frac{\mathbf{w}-\mathbf{v}}{\|\mathbf{w}-\mathbf{v}\|}$ is equal to the normal vector of the plane $\mathbf{P}_m$. Therefore $\varphi_{\mathbf{m}}$ can be obtained from the normal vector of $\mathbf{P}_m$.

To address the reformulated problem we introduce the Radon transform and its inversion in $\mathbb{R}^3$

$$\mathcal{R}[g](t,\xi) = \int g(\mathbf{x})\delta(t - \langle\xi,\mathbf{x}\rangle)d\mathbf{x} \tag{7}$$

$$\mathcal{R}^{-1}[\mathcal{R}[g]](\mathbf{x}) = \int_{|\xi|=1} h(\langle\mathbf{x},\xi\rangle,\xi)d\xi \quad \text{with} \quad h(t,\xi) = -\frac{1}{8\pi^2}\frac{\partial^2}{\partial t^2}\mathcal{R}[g](t,\xi) \tag{8}$$

with $g \in L^2(\mathbb{R}^3), \mathbf{x} \in \mathbb{R}^3$ and $\xi \in \mathbb{R}^3, |\xi| = 1$. The Radon transform integrates a function g over all two-dimensional hyperplanes in $\mathbb{R}^3$. The hyperplanes are characterized by their normal vectors with orientation ξ and a distance from the origin $t = \langle\xi,\mathbf{x}\rangle$. For a fixed hyperplane orientation ξ, $\mathcal{R}[g](t,\xi)$ describes a one dimensional function in the Radon domain depending on the distance t of the planes from the origin. We refer to these one-dimensional functions as slices.

Consider the projected circular signal $g_{\mathbf{m}}(\mathbf{x})$ at $\mathbf{x} \in \mathbb{R}^3$. If you imagine the integration over all two-dimensional planes in $\mathbb{R}^3$, than there exists exactly one plane $\mathbf{P_m}$, such that the whole projected circle is located in that plane (compare also Figure 1). The angles $(\theta_{\mathbf{m}}, \varphi_{\mathbf{m}})$ of the normal vector characterizing this plane describe the one-dimensional slice in the Radon domain we are interested in. Therefore we seek for a method to obtain the angles describing exactly this slice in a closed form expression. We use the relationship between partial derivatives in the spatial- and the Radon domain given by (see e.g. [11])

$$\mathcal{R}[\frac{\partial}{\partial x_i} g_{\mathbf{m}}](t, \xi) = \xi_i \frac{\partial}{\partial t} \mathcal{R}[g_{\mathbf{m}}](t, \xi) \qquad (9)$$

which states that the Radon transform of every partial derivative with respect to the x_i-axis in the spatial domain is just the partial derivative of the Radon transform of g along each one-dimensional slice in the Radon domain multiplied by the slice angle. Due to our assumed signal model there exists only one slice which is non-constant along t. The slice is exactly the slice described by $(\theta_{\mathbf{m}}, \varphi_{\mathbf{m}})$. If we now apply the inverse Radon transform to Eq. (9) we are able to move the angular components of the normal vector out of the inversion integral such that

$$\frac{\partial}{\partial x_i} g_{\mathbf{m}}(\mathcal{S}^{-1}(\mathbf{u})) = n_{\mathbf{m},i} \mathcal{R}^{-1}[\frac{\partial}{\partial t} \mathcal{R}[g_{\mathbf{m}}]](\mathcal{S}^{-1}(\mathbf{u})). \qquad (10)$$

We gain access to the angles of the normal vector

$$\mathbf{n_m} = (n_{\mathbf{m},1}, n_{\mathbf{m},2}, n_{\mathbf{m},3})^T = (\sin \varphi_{\mathbf{m}} \cos \theta_{\mathbf{m}}, \sin \varphi_{\mathbf{m}} \sin \theta_{\mathbf{m}}, \cos \theta_{\mathbf{m}})^T \qquad (11)$$

by taking the partial derivatives in $\mathbb{R}^3$ without ever actually performing a Radon- or inverse Radon transform. The angles at $\mathbf{u} \in \mathbb{R}^2$ are obtained as

$$\theta_{\mathbf{m}}(\mathbf{u}) = \arctan \frac{n_{\mathbf{m},2} \mathcal{R}^{-1}[\frac{\partial}{\partial t} \mathcal{R}[g]](\mathcal{S}^{-1}(\mathbf{u}))}{n_{\mathbf{m},1} \mathcal{R}^{-1}[\frac{\partial}{\partial t} \mathcal{R}[g]](\mathcal{S}^{-1}(\mathbf{u}))} = \arctan \frac{\frac{\partial}{\partial x_2} g(\mathcal{S}^{-1}(\mathbf{u}))}{\frac{\partial}{\partial x_1} g(\mathcal{S}^{-1}(\mathbf{u}))} \qquad (12)$$

$$\varphi_{\mathbf{m}}(\mathbf{u}) = \arctan \frac{\sqrt{(n_{\mathbf{m},1} \mathcal{R}^{-1}[\frac{\partial}{\partial t} \mathcal{R}[g]](\mathcal{S}^{-1}(\mathbf{u})))^2 + (n_{\mathbf{m},2} \mathcal{R}^{-1}[\frac{\partial}{\partial t} \mathcal{R}[g]](\mathcal{S}^{-1}(\mathbf{u})))^2}}{n_{\mathbf{m},3} \mathcal{R}^{-1}[\frac{\partial}{\partial t} \mathcal{R}[g]](\mathcal{S}^{-1}(\mathbf{u}))}$$

$$\qquad (13)$$

$$= \arctan \frac{\sqrt{(\frac{\partial}{\partial x_1} g(\mathcal{S}^{-1}(\mathbf{u})))^2 + (\frac{\partial}{\partial x_2} g(\mathcal{S}^{-1}(\mathbf{u})))^2}}{\frac{\partial}{\partial x_3} g(\mathcal{S}^{-1}(\mathbf{u}))} \qquad (14)$$

where $\theta_{\mathbf{m}}$ is the orientation angle of the center $\mathbf{m}$ in the Euclidean plane and $\varphi_{\mathbf{m}}$ is the angle describing the radius of the osculating circle as stated in Eq. (6). Note that the above formulas are only valid at the origin. Nonetheless this is no restriction, since we may always treat a point of a plane curve as the origin of a chosen coordinate system, such that the curvature evaluation yields a valid curvature value. For a better understanding of the method introduced above we draw the following analogy: Imagine you want to estimate the curvature of a sampled curve in the Euclidean plane. Then you can estimate the curvature at every sampled point by estimating the osculating circle for a neigborhood of that point. This osculating circle can be estimated by fitting a circle through the points of the neighborhood. The circle fitting is a minimization problem which is, if the geometric distances of the points with respect to the unknown circle are minimized, nonlinear in its nature. By projecting the points on $\mathbb{S}^2$, the nonlinear regression problem turns into a linear one. The circle can now be estimated by fitting a plane through these points. Since the plane has to pass through the origin, the fitting further simplifies. Referring to [12], the minimizing normal vector describing the regression plane is the eigenvector of the moment matrix, obtained from the sample points, corresponding to the smallest eigenvalue. If you further describe this least squares regression as a locally weighted least-squares regression using the Gaussian derivative kernels in $\mathbb{R}^3$, you arrive at the method we introduced by using the relationship of the first order derivatives and the Radon transform in $\mathbb{R}^3$.

2.1 Scale Space Embedding

In general images we want to be able to estimate the curvature of image structures with respect to a certain scale. The embedding of the conformal method in a scale space concept is straightforward. Obvious choices are the Gaussian or the Poisson scale space. Since the curvature is calculated either in terms of partial derivatives, as in this paper, or Riesz transforms as in [8], one may precalculate the convolution kernels resulting in Gaussian derivative kernels or conjugate Poisson kernels (see [13] and [14] for further informations on both scale spaces). The curvature then reads

$$\kappa_s(\mathbf{x}) = 2\frac{G_3^s(\mathbf{x})}{\sqrt{G_1^s(\mathbf{x})^2 + G_2^s(\mathbf{x})^2}} \tag{15}$$

$$G_i^s(\mathbf{x}) = (g * K_i^s)(\mathbf{x}) = \int_{\mathbb{R}^2} g(\mathbf{y}) K_i^s(\mathcal{S}^{-1}(\mathbf{x} - \mathbf{y})) d\mathbf{y} \tag{16}$$

where $\mathbf{x} = \mathcal{S}^{-1}(\mathbf{u}), \mathbf{u} \in \mathbb{R}^2$ and $K_i^s(\mathbf{x})$ either denotes the Gaussian derivative or the conjugate Poisson kernel with respect to x_i in $\mathbb{R}^3$. Further it is possible to implement the method using kernels with bandpass characteristic such as the Difference-Of-Gaussian (DOG) or Difference-Of-Poisson (DOP) kernels, depending on the chosen scale space, as

$$G_i^{s_1, s_2}(\mathbf{x}) = (g * K_i^{s_1})(\mathbf{x}) - (g * K_i^{s_2})(\mathbf{x}). \tag{17}$$

3   Experiments

3.1   Plane Curves

We first evaluate the proposed method for plane curves. Let $\mathbf{l}(t) = (x(t), y(t)), t \in [a, b]$ be a part of a parameterized plane curve. Then we sample $\mathbf{l}$ as $\mathbf{l}_i = (x(i\,d), y(i\,d)), i \in \{1, \ldots, N\}, d = \frac{|a-b|}{N}, N \in \mathbb{N}$. The estimation of the curvature relies on the choice of a scale described by the neighborhood or window size $W \in \mathbb{N}$ with respect to the current point of interest. For each point $\mathbf{l}_i$ we first shift the neighborhood $NB_W(\mathbf{l}_i) = \{\mathbf{l}_{i-W}, \ldots, \mathbf{l}_i, \ldots, \mathbf{l}_{i+W}\}$ to the origin and project it to the sphere $\mathbb{S}^2$ such that $NB'_W(\mathbf{l}_i) = \{\mathcal{S}^{-1}(\mathbf{l}_{i-W} - \mathbf{l}_i), \ldots, (0, 0, 0), \ldots, \mathcal{S}^{-1}(\mathbf{l}_{i+W} - \mathbf{l}_i)\}$. The curvature is then obtained as

$$\kappa_W(\mathbf{l}_i) = 2 \frac{\sum_{j=-W}^{W} K_3^W(\mathcal{S}^{-1}(\mathbf{l}_{i+j} - \mathbf{l}_i)))}{\sqrt{(\sum_{j=-W}^{W} K_1^W(\mathcal{S}^{-1}(\mathbf{l}_{i+j} - \mathbf{l}_i)))^2 + (\sum_{j=-W}^{W} K_2^W(\mathcal{S}^{-1}(\mathbf{l}_{i+j} - \mathbf{l}_i)))^2}} \tag{18}$$

where K_i^W denotes either the Gaussian or the Poisson kernel in the upper half space $\mathbb{R}^3_+$ with respect the scale W. We compare our method to curvature estimation obtained by a circle fitting through the points of the neighborhood $NB'_W(\mathbf{l}_i)$. To fit a circle through these points we use two different distance functions which are minimized, an algebraic distance according to [15] and a geometric distance according to [16]. The distance functions are minimized by solving the corresponding least-squares problems. As a result we obtain the center and the radius r of the fitted circle. The radius serves as a curvature measure due to the already mentioned relation $\kappa = \frac{1}{r}$. Figure 2 shows the comparison of our method with the algebraic and geometric fitting method for three test curves with and without noise. We measured the absolute average error over all curve points for different window sizes as

$$E_W(\mathbf{l}) = \sum_{i=1}^{|\mathbf{l}|} |\kappa(\mathbf{l}_i) - \tilde{\kappa}_W(\mathbf{l}_i)| \tag{19}$$

where $\kappa(\mathbf{l}_i)$ denotes the ground truth curvature and $\tilde{\kappa}_W(\mathbf{l}_i)$ the estimated curvature of the curve at $\mathbf{l}_i$. It turns out that our novel method converges to the true radius of curvature in the case of the assumed signal model, a circle. Compared to the two methods based on circle fittings, it is robust against noise resulting in accurate curvature estimations.

3.2   Digital Images

The method introduced above has the advantage, that it is not limited to digital curves but can also be applied to images, where the curves are not known in advance, e.g. for isophotes in grayscale images. In these cases the curvature is often supposed to serve as a feature indicating corners or straight line segments in the

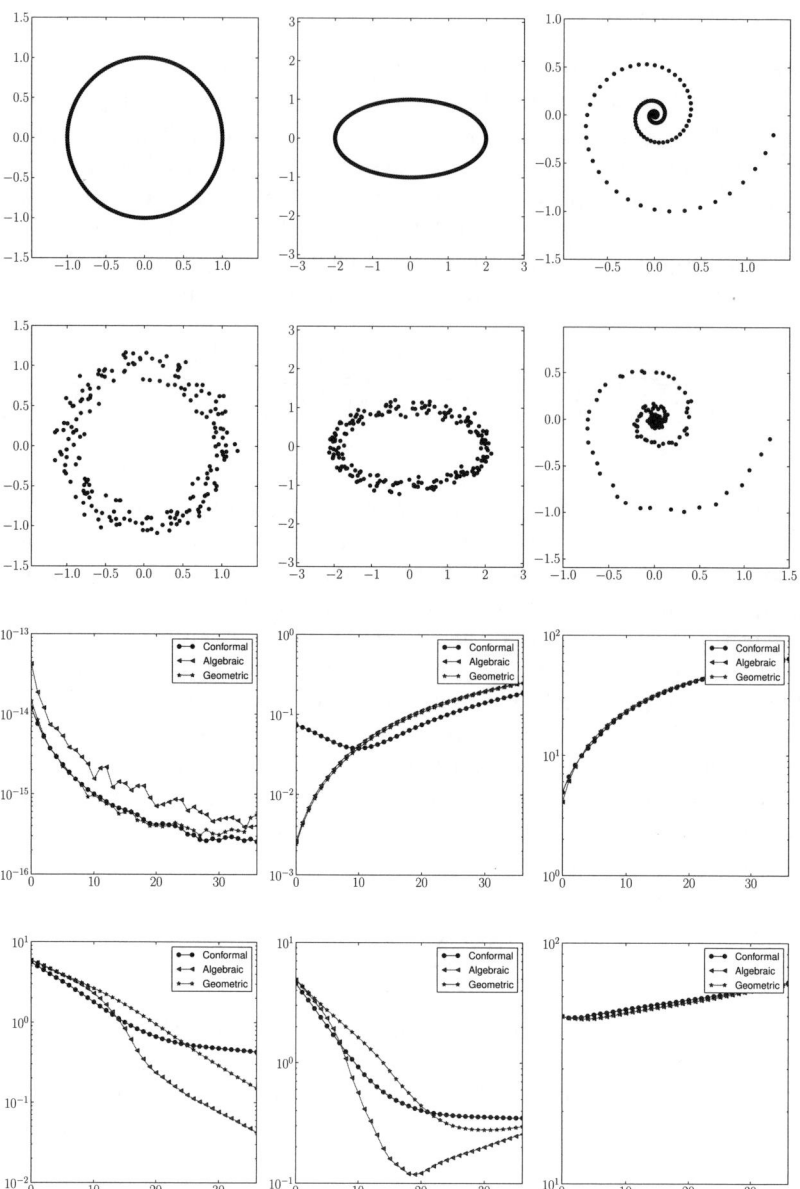

Fig. 2. First row: Test curves sampled at 200 points. Second row: Gaussian white noise perturbed test curves, $\sigma = 0.1$. Third and fourth row: Average absolute curvature errors E_W over all curve points depending on the window size W (abscissa) without and with noise (see also Equ. (19)).

case of high or low curvature. The standard method to obtain the isophote curvature in digital images uses first and second order derivatives. To be comparable to our method, which we introduced in a scale space embedding, we introduce the classical derivative based method to calculate the isophote curvature as [17]

$$\kappa = \frac{2\, G_{1,0}^{s_1,s_2} G_{0,1}^{s_1,s_2} G_{1,1}^{s_1,s_2} - (G_{1,0}^{s_1,s_2})^2 G_{0,2}^{s_1,s_2} - (G_{0,1}^{s_1,s_2})^2 G_{2,0}^{s_1,s_2}}{((G_{1,0}^{s_1,s_2})^2 + (G_{0,1}^{s_1,s_2})^2)^{3/2}} \tag{20}$$

where $G_{i,j}^{s_1,s_2}$ denotes the convolution with the i-th and j-th order derivatives of Difference-Of-Gaussian kernels with scales s_1, s_2 along the x_1 and x_2 axis. To study the accuracy of our estimator we apply it to the artificial signal $f(\mathbf{x}) = \sqrt{x_1^2 + x_2^2}$. Since the test signal depends linearly on the distance from the origin, its ground truth isophote curvature reads $\kappa(\mathbf{x}) = (x_1^2 + x_2^2)^{(-1/2)}$. Figure 3 shows the test signal with and without noise and the average absolute error of both methods for different convolution mask sizes. With increasing convolution mask size the accuracy of our proposed estimator increases. Further it performs better than the derivative based method on the noise perturbed signal even for small convolution mask sizes. Another important aspect of the isophote curvature information is the ability to obtain the ridge curves of an image [17]. The ridge curves are the isophotes for which the gradient vanishes such that the curvature obtained by Equ. (20) is degenerate. Due to their invariance properties concerning translation, rotation and monotonic intensity changes, ridges serve as

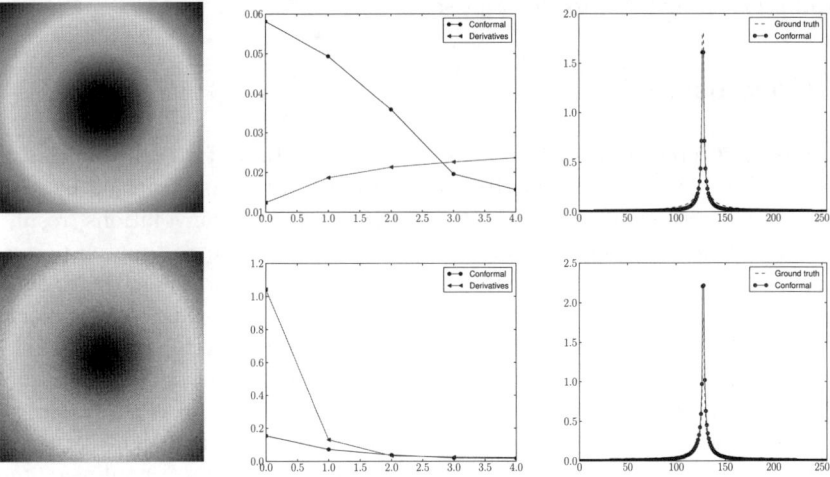

Fig. 3. Left column, top: Ground truth image $f(\mathbf{x}) = \sqrt{x_1^2 + x_2^2}$. Left column, bottom: Ground truth image perturbed with Gaussian white noise, $\sigma = 0.1$. Middle column: Average absolute curvature errors over the whole images for scales $(s_1, s_2) = (2^x, 2^{x+1})$ calculated for the conformal and the derivative based method, where x is the abscissa. Right column: Estimated curvature of the ground truth image for the slice $f(x_1, 0)$ and scales $(s_1, s_2) = (8, 16)$ of the conformal method.

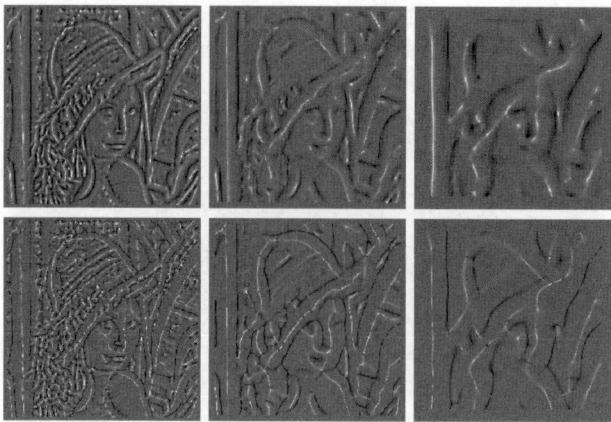

Fig. 4. Top row: Isophote curvatures calculated with the proposed method in Eq. (15) at scales $(s_1, s_2) = (2, 4), (4, 8), (8, 16)$. Bottom row: Isophote curvatures calculated with the classical method in Eq. (20) at scales $(s_1, s_2) = (2, 4), (4, 8), (8, 16)$.

a useful feature, especially if their evolution is considered across multiple scales. Figure 4 shows the ridge curves (degeneracies of the isophote curvature) of the Lenna test-image obtained by the proposed method using Eq. (15) and the curvature obtained according to the classical Eq. (20) using Difference-of-Gaussian convolutions kernels across different scales.

4 Conclusion

We have presented a novel curvature estimator suitable for digital curves and grayscale images. We were able to extract the curvature information by simple linear shift-invariant filters. These filters are applied by convolutions, resulting in a simple and short algorithm. In terms of accuracy our estimator performs at least as accurate as the classical methods. More important is the nature of the construction. Using tools from classical signal processing we transformed the nonlinear problem to a linear one and implicitly developed a method for solving the problem of fitting a circle to a set of points which is classically solved using a least-squares approach. We noticed that our method is equivalent to a corresponding locally weighted least-squares problem. This insight serves as a motivation to construct explicitly the mappings to transform nonlinear image processing problem into linear ones in an appropriate feature space, which was the inverse stereographic projection in this case. The spherical embedding was the first step of investigating certain signal structures in higher dimensional spaces by suitable embeddings.

References

1. Hermann, S., Klette, R.: Global Curvature Estimation for Corner Detection. Technical report, The University of Auckland, New Zealand (2005)
2. Williams, D.J., Shah, M.: A Fast Algorithm for Active Contours and Curvature Estimation. CVGIP: Image Underst. 55(1), 14–26 (1992)
3. Morse, B., Schwartzwald, D.: Isophote-based Interpolation. In: International Conference on Image Processing, vol. 3, p. 227 (1998)
4. Lachaud, J.O., Vialard, A., de Vieilleville, F.: Fast, Accurate and Convergent Tangent Estimation on Digital Contours. Image Vision Comput. 25(10), 1572–1587 (2007)
5. Coeurjolly, D., Miguet, S., Tougne, L.: Discrete Curvature Based on Osculating Circle Estimation. In: Arcelli, C., Cordella, L.P., Sanniti di Baja, G. (eds.) IWVF 2001. LNCS, vol. 2059, pp. 303–312. Springer, Heidelberg (2001)
6. Hermann, S., Klette, R.: Multigrid Analysis of Curvature Estimators. In: Proc. Image Vision Computing, New Zealand, pp. 108–112 (2003)
7. Klette, R., Rosenfeld, A.: Digital Geometry: Geometric Methods for Digital Picture Analysis. Morgan Kaufmann, San Francisco (2004)
8. Wietzke, L., Fleischmann, O., Sommer, G.: 2D Image Analysis by Generalized Hilbert Transforms in Conformal Space. In: Forsyth, D., Torr, P., Zisserman, A. (eds.) ECCV 2008, Part II. LNCS, vol. 5303, pp. 638–649. Springer, Heidelberg (2008)
9. do Carmo, M.P.: Differential Geometry of Curves and Surfaces. Prentice-Hall, Englewood Cliffs (1976)
10. Needham, T.: Visual Complex Analysis. Oxford University Press, USA (1999)
11. Zayed, A.: Handbook of Function and Generalized Function Transformations. CRC, Boca Raton (1996)
12. Kanatani, K.: Statistical Optimization for Geometric Computation: Theory and Practice. Elsevier Science Inc., New York (1996)
13. Lindeberg, T.: Scale-space Theory in Computer Vision. Springer, Heidelberg (1993)
14. Felsberg, M., Sommer, G.: The Monogenic Scale-space: A Unifying Approach to Phase-based Image Processing in Scale-space. Journal of Mathematical Imaging and vision 21(1), 5–26 (2004)
15. Gander, W., Golub, G.H., Strebel, R.: Least-Squares Fitting of Circles and Ellipses. BIT (4), 558–578 (1994)
16. Coope, I.D.: Circle Fitting by Linear and Nonlinear Least Squares. Journal of Optimization Theory and Applications 76(2), 381–388 (1993)
17. Romeny, B.M.: Geometry-Driven Diffusion in Computer Vision. Kluwer Academic Publishers, Norwell (1994)

Local Regression Based Statistical Model Fitting

Matthias Amberg, Marcel Lüthi, and Thomas Vetter

Computer Science Department, University of Basel, Switzerland
{matthias.amberg,marcel.luethi,thomas.vetter}@unibas.ch

Abstract. Fitting statistical models is a widely employed technique for
the segmentation of medical images. While this approach gives impressive
results for simple structures, shape models are often not flexible enough
to accurately represent complex shapes. We present a fitting approach,
which increases the model fitting accuracy without requiring a larger
training data-set. Inspired by a local regression approach known from
statistics, our method fits the full model to a neighborhood around each
point of the domain. This increases the model's flexibility considerably
without the need to introduce an artificial segmentation of the structure. By adapting the size of the neighborhood from small to large, we
can smoothly interpolate between localized fits, which accurately map
the data but are more prone to noise, and global fits, which are less
flexible but constrained to valid shapes only. We applied our method
for the segmentation of teeth from 3D cone-beam ct-scans. Our experiments confirm that our method consistently increases the precision of
the segmentation result compared to a standard global fitting approach.

1 Introduction

Statistical shape models have become a commonly used tool in computer vision,
especially for automated segmentation purposes. Oftentimes statistical models
lack the flexibility to accurately represent all valid shapes, as the the number of
training data-sets is insufficient to learn the shape-space. Many approaches have
been proposed to mitigate that problem. These approaches can be grouped into
three categories: The first possibility is to artificially increase the model flexibility by introducing synthetic variations of the training data at model build time
[1,2,3]. Another option is to relax the model restrictions at fitting time [2,4,5,6,7].
This is achieved either by finding other features in an image and then to restrict
them with plausible model shapes [2,6,7] or by fitting a statistical model which
is subsequently relaxed to match other local information [4,5]. The problem with
the above approaches is that they allow for deviations that are not explained by
the training shapes. The relaxation of the shape model constraint does not guarantee anymore that the resulting shape is a likely instance of the model. Also it is
a delicate matter to define artificial deformations that capture exactly the characteristics of the shape. The third class of methods tries to segment the model either
spatially [8,9,10] or in the frequency domain [11,12,13]. While this increases the
flexibility without above mentioned disadvantages, the main problem here is how

M. Goesele et al. (Eds.): DAGM 2010, LNCS 6376, pp. 452–461, 2010.

to choose the segments. For natural shapes, neighboring points always strongly correlate and therefore any spatial segmentation must be arbitrary. Furthermore no natural decomposition in frequency bands is known.

The method proposed in this paper focuses on fitting a model locally in the spatial domain and thus increasing its flexibility implicitly. The method is inspired by local linear regression which is commonly used in statistics [14]. We fit a complete shape model to a neighborhood around a given point of the image to segment. The fitting result is used to predict the value at this particular point only. By repeating this procedure for every point, we finally obtain a fit of the whole model. The neighborhood size determines how flexible our model is. In the extreme, considering only a single point allows any arbitrary shape to be matched. In contrast, having the neighborhood correspond to the full image leads to the global fit, which strictly adheres to the model constraint. For any local neighborhood we do adhere to the shape constraint, whereas the global shape constraint is nevertheless relaxed. We thus have the advantages of a segmented model without ever actually having to segment the model. Neither do we have to introduce artificial deformations which are not motivated by the data to increase the model's flexibility.

This flexibility comes at the cost of an increased computational overhead. Performing a full fitting at every point becomes infeasible for large images. To lessen the computational burden we further present a method to interpolate between such local fittings, which no longer need to be created for every point but rather once for a region of definable size.

Our work was motivated by a project in which we aimed to perform model based segmentation of teeth from 3D Cone Beam CT data. The manual segmentation of such data-sets is tedious and even human experts are not always able to distinguish the tooth from the surrounding bony structure and to clearly separate neighboring teeth. With the more wide-spread use of this 3D imaging technology to plan surgical interventions, the segmentation of teeth becomes a routine task and automated procedures needs to be employed to be able to perform it efficiently. Due to the difficulty of obtaining good reference segmentations, we did not have enough data-sets available to build a shape model that represents the large anatomical variability of these shapes. Our quantitative evaluation, using a leave-one-out procedure on seven manually segmented data-sets, confirms that our localized fitting nevertheless yields accurate segmentation and consistently improves the segmentation accuracy compared to a global fitting approach.

2 Background

2.1 Statistical Shape and Deformation Models

The idea behind statistical models is to learn the normal shape of an anatomical structure from given example shapes. The resulting model is specific to a given structure and thus can be used to perform image processing tasks, which would not be feasible otherwise. In the area of computer vision and medical image analysis, the main application of statistical models is image segmentation [15]. There

are several variants of statistical shape models, such as the Active Shape model
[16], the Morphable Model [10] or Statistical Deformation Models [17]. They all
apply Principal Component Analysis (PCA) to a number of example data sets
$S_1, \ldots, S_n$ to model typical deformations. The examples are assumed to be suit-
ably discretized and in correspondence. This means that for each example S_i,
there exists a mapping $\phi_i : \Omega \to \mathbb{R}^d$ from a reference domain $\Omega = \{x_1, \ldots, x_N\}$
such that $\phi_i(x)$ and $\phi_j(x)$ denote corresponding points of the examples S_i and
S_j. It is well known that a PCA model can be written as a generative model of
the form:

$$\mathcal{M}[\boldsymbol{\alpha}] : \ \Omega \to \mathbb{R}^d \qquad x \mapsto \mu(x) + \sum_{i=1}^n \alpha_i u_i(x) \qquad (1)$$

where $\mu : \Omega \to \mathbb{R}^d$ denotes the sample mean $\mu(x) := \frac{1}{n} \sum_{i=1}^n \phi_i(x)$ and $u_i : \Omega \to$
$\mathbb{R}^d, i = 1, \ldots, n$ are the principal components, computed from the examples
[18]. Note that the model is completely defined by the parameter vectors $\boldsymbol{\alpha} =$
$(\alpha_1, \ldots, \alpha_n)$. For the case of statistical shape models, the domain Ω is usually
a discretized reference surface, or a parametrization domain. The set of points
$\{\mathcal{M}[\boldsymbol{\alpha}](x) \,|\, x \in \Omega\}$ defines the surface induced by the parameter vector $\boldsymbol{\alpha}$. In the
case of statistical deformation models, Ω is usually an image domain, and $\mathcal{M}[\boldsymbol{\alpha}]$
defines a deformation field that relates the given reference and target image. To
distinguish between these models, we write $\mathcal{M}_S$ for shape models, and $\mathcal{M}_D$ for
the deformation model.

2.2   Statistical Model Fitting

Statistical model fitting aims at finding the set of parameters of the model (1),
such that it optimally explains a given target structure. We assume in the following that the target structure has already been rigidly aligned with the model,
such that only the non-rigid part of the mapping needs to be found.[1] There are
various different methods for shape model fitting (see Heimann et al. [15] for a
recent overview). The most simple case of shape model fitting is to directly fit
a given target surface $\Gamma_T \subset \mathbb{R}^d$. Such a surface representation can often be obtained from an image using simple, intensity based segmentation methods. This
rough first segmentation can then be constrained to a valid shape by fitting the
shape model. The problem is formulated as an optimization problem: The goal
is to find a shape, which for each point x_i minimizes the distance to the closest
point in the target shape Γ_T:

$$\boldsymbol{\alpha}^* := \arg \min_{\boldsymbol{\alpha} \in \mathbb{R}^n} \sum_{x_i \in \Omega} \big(\min_{x' \in \Gamma_T} \|x' - \mathcal{M}_S[\boldsymbol{\alpha}](x_i)\| \big)^2 + \lambda \|\boldsymbol{\alpha}\|^2. \qquad (2)$$

The term $\lambda \|\boldsymbol{\alpha}\|^2$ serves as a regularization term, which penalizes shapes that
strongly deviate from the modeled mean shape. While this approach is simple, its
main problem is that the cost function (2) includes only boundary information of
the modeled shapes. An approach that includes the complete image information

---

[1] This can be achieved, for example, by performing a Procrustes Alignment [19] on a
number of landmark points defined on the reference and target shape.

has been proposed by Rückert et al.[17]. The idea is to directly build a statistical model of the deformation fields $\mathcal{M}_D[\alpha]$, which relate the image intensities of a reference image $I_R : \Omega \rightarrow \mathbb{R}$, to given examples images. The goal of model fitting is to find the deformation represented by this model, which best relates the reference image I_R to a new target image $I_T : \Omega \rightarrow \mathbb{R}$:

$$\alpha^* := \arg \min_{\alpha \in \mathbb{R}^n} \sum_{x_i \in \Omega} (I_R(x_i + \mathcal{M}_D[\alpha](x_i)) - I_T(x_i))^2 + \lambda \|\alpha\|^2. \qquad (3)$$

Note that (3) establishes point-to-point correspondence between the images. It can therefore be used to map labels defined on the reference image onto the target. In particular, given a segmentation of the reference image $B_R : \Omega \rightarrow \{0, 1\}$, the warped image $B_R(x + \mathcal{M}_D[\alpha^*](x))$ yields a segmentation of the target image. Although the Problems (2) and (3) differ in the way they use the image information, their solution depends only on the model coefficients α. The strategy for increasing the fitting accuracy that we are proposing in the next section holds unchanged for both approaches. For clarity of presentation we will discuss our method on the simpler case of shape model fitting (Equation 2). For the practical application that we present in Section 4 we will, however, apply deformation model fitting (Equation 3).

3   Local Shape Model Fitting

The use of model fitting to obtain a segmentation result, which is restricted to valid anatomical shapes, is appealing. However the models are often not sufficiently flexible to represent complicated structures accurately. It has been shown in the literature that spatial segmentation of the model can increase the fitting accuracy [8,9,10]. The reason for the improved accuracy is that each segment only has to represent a local part of the shape, which, by itself, is less complex than the complete global shape. These segments can therefore be accurately represented using fewer example shapes. Our approach exploits the same idea, but instead of partitioning the model we consider local areas of the target structure to which we fit the full model. Similar to a local regression approach known from statistics [20], we fit the model to a local neighborhood around each data point of the target. This strategy avoids completely the problem of having to segment the model into independent parts.

We illustrate the method for the case of shape model fitting using a 2D example of hand shapes. Let $\mathcal{M}_S$ be a statistical shape model and $\Gamma_T \subset \mathbb{R}^d$ a target shape. For each point $x_0 \in \Omega$ we fit the entire shape model, but weight the influence of each point $x \in \Omega$ on the total cost with a weight w_{x_0} depending on its distance to the point x_0:

$$\alpha_{x_0}^* := \arg \min_{\alpha \in \mathbb{R}^n} \sum_{x_i \in \Omega} w_{x_0}(x_i)(\min_{x' \in \Gamma_T} \|x' - \mathcal{M}_S[\alpha](x_i)\|)^2 + \lambda \|\alpha\|^2, \qquad (4)$$

Although the solution $\alpha_{x_0}^*$ defines a full shape, it is only used to determine the result Γ^* at the point x_0:

$$\Gamma^*(x_0) := \mathcal{M}[\alpha_{x_0}^*](x_0) \qquad (5)$$

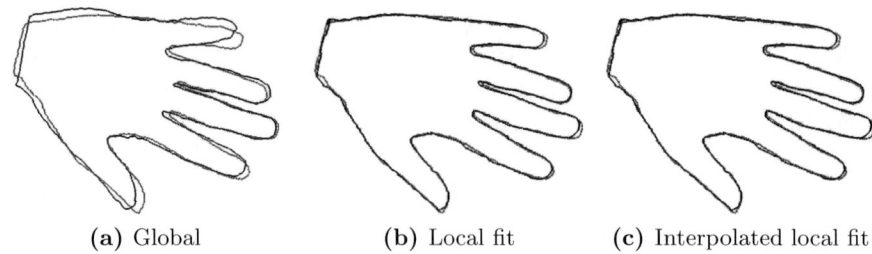

| **(a)** Global | **(b)** Local fit | **(c)** Interpolated local fit |

Fig. 1. A comparison between a global fit (a) and local fitting results (b), (c) for a shape model which was built from 15 hand shapes. The target hand shape was not part of the model's training data. The result shown in (b) has been computed by fitting every point, whereas in (c) only 20 points were fitted and the remaining ones interpolated.

The fitting is performed at every point $x_0 \in \Omega$, and therefore we eventually obtain a result for the whole shape. Every fit strives to minimize the error around x_0, and thus the resulting shape explains the target better than any global fit would. As the local neighborhoods of two nearby points greatly overlap, the resulting fits are similar and the resulting target shape $\Gamma^*(x_0)$ is nevertheless smooth. The problem of discontinuous segments, as observed with segmented models, is completely avoided.

A typical choice for w_{x_0} is the *Epanechnikov kernel* [14]:

$$w_{x_0}(x) := \kappa_\sigma(x_0, x) = D\left(\frac{\text{dist}(x, x_0)}{\sigma}\right) \tag{6}$$

with

$$D(t) = \begin{cases} \frac{3}{4}(1 - t^2) & \text{if } |t| \leq 1 \\ 0 & \text{otherwise.} \end{cases} \tag{7}$$

The weight function κ_σ is compact and its support determined by σ. For surface fitting, the distance $\text{dist}(x, x_0)$ is taken to be the geodesic distance on Ω, as we wish to match neighboring points on the surface. Figure 1 shows an example of how our procedure improves the fitting accuracy.

The fitting procedure is only useful if the shape constraints are still enforced to the degree that artifacts and noise in the data are not fitted. This is determined by the parameter σ in our kernel (6), which acts as a regularization parameter. If σ is small the fitting is local and the target shape is accurately represented. In the extreme case when we fit the model to the point x_0 only, the shape statistics is completely ignored. On the other hand, if σ is large, all points of the shape have nearly the same influence, and we arrive at the global fitting. The effect of this parameter is illustrated in Figure 2, where we fitted a hand shape with a number of manually introduced artifacts. We observe that by increasing σ we can reduce the influence of the artifacts, and still accurately represent the actual target shape.

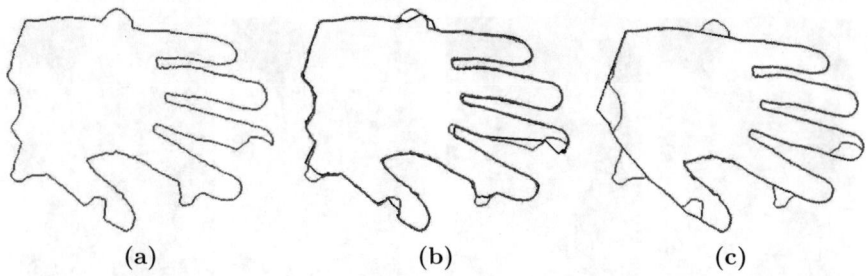

(a)   (b)   (c)

Fig. 2. An example of a local fitting on noisy data. (a) shows the hand with manually introduced artifacts (red line). Fitting only a small neighborhood leads to overfitting (black line). Increasing the size of the neighborhood eliminates the influence of the artifacts almost completely.

3.1 Interpolated Local Shape Model Fitting.

Evaluating Equation 4 at every point $x \in \Omega$ quickly results in an excessive computational burden for densely sampled shapes. To address this problem, we perform the fitting only at a subset of the points $\tilde{\Omega} := \{x_0, \ldots, x_K\} \subset \Omega$. Observe that to define the fitting result Γ^* at point x_k in Equation 5, we used only the single point $\mathcal{M}[\alpha^*_{x_k}](x_k)$, even though α^* defines a full shape

$$\Gamma^*_{x_k} := \mathcal{M}[\alpha^*_{x_k}].$$

Thus, the idea is to combine these local predictions in a smooth way:

$$\Gamma^*(x) := \frac{\sum_{k=1}^{K} \hat{w}_k(x) \Gamma^*_{x_k}(x)}{\sum_{k=1}^{K} \hat{w}_k(x)}, \; x \in \Omega \tag{8}$$

where we choose $\hat{w}_k$ again to be the Epanechnikov kernel (6). Note that since $\hat{w}_k$ is compactly defined, for (8) to be well defined, the support of the kernel needs to be chosen such that for each point $x \in \Omega$ at least one of the weight functions $\hat{w}_k(x)$ is non-zero.

4 Results

In this section we show how our method can be applied for the automatic segmentation of teeth from Cone Beam CT images. Each image has a resolution of $90 \times 71 \times 31$ voxels. Figure 3a shows a sample slice through such a tooth ct-image. The automatic segmentation of such images is a challenging task. Especially at the roots, the tooth is virtually indistinguishable from the surrounding bony structure. Furthermore, neighboring teeth can be touching and are thus difficult to separate. To address these problems, we manually segmented seven data-sets to create a deformation model, which we subsequently used for segmentation. We choose one image as the reference, to which we aligned all the images using

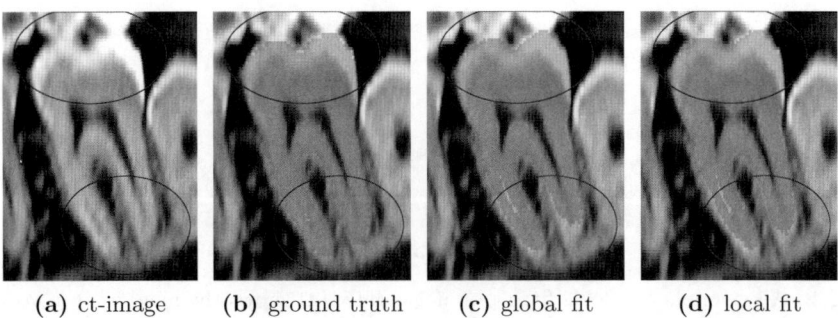

(a) ct-image   (b) ground truth   (c) global fit   (d) local fit

Fig. 3. A typical ct-scan of a tooth is shown in (a) which features typical problems faced in ct-image segmentation. The image is noisy and a neighboring tooth is touching our target tooth (red circle). The local fit (d), while robust enough not to leak into the neighboring tooth at the top, segments the root section better than the global fit (c) (blue circle), compared to the ground truth (b).

Procrustes alignment [19] on eight manually defined landmarks. For solving the optimization problem, we used a standard LBFGS-B optimizer [21].

The shape of the tooth can vary greatly among individuals, and a model built from only seven datasets is not sufficient to span this variation. By using our interpolated local shape model fitting, we get more accurate segmentation results, as shown in Figure 4. Especially at the roots of the tooth, which exhibit most variation, the local fitting clearly leads to a large improvement.

4.1   Distance Measure

For the shape fitting example discussed in Section 3, we used the geodesic distance to determine the local neighborhood. This is not possible for the deformation model, which is defined on the image domain. However, we would still like

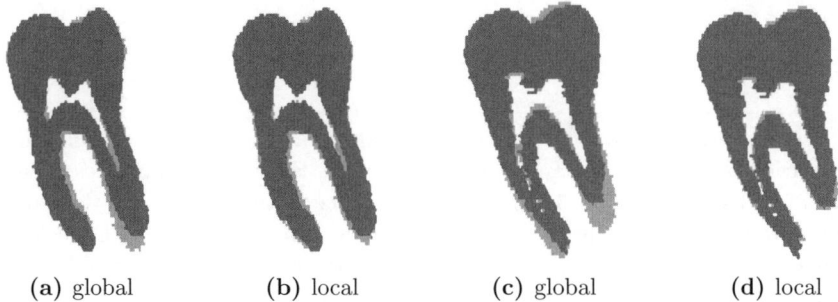

(a) global   (b) local   (c) global   (d) local

Fig. 4. Fitting results (blue) for two sample teeth are compared to ground truth (grey). Especially at the roots, our local approach (b) and (d) is more precise than the global one (a) and (c).

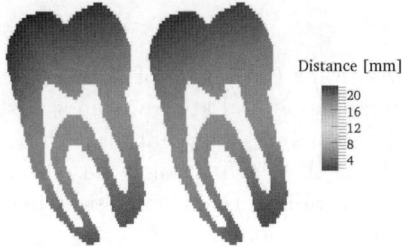

Fig. 5. Comparison of our distance measure (left) to the Euclidean distance (right), measured from a point at the lower right root. Note the difference of the obtained distance in the left root as our distance measure is notably higher than the Euclidean distance in this area.

to quantify the distance in terms of the shape that we model. We therefore define the distance between two points that lie within the structure as shortest path between those points with the constraint that the path always resides within the structure's volume. Figure 5 shows a comparison of the Euclidean distance and our distance function. With the Euclidean distance, the tips of the roots are rather close to each other, in our distance measure they are far apart.

4.2 Global Fit versus Interpolated Local Fit Comparison

We performed a leave-one-out test to asses the fitting quality. We used six manually segmented data sets, similar to the one shown in Figure 3a, for model building. We then fitted the left-out tooth with the global approach as well as our interpolated local fitting method. We used 35 equidistant points within the tooth as our local region defining $\Gamma^*_{x_k}$ (Cf. Section 3.1). In all cases the interpolated local fitting method provided better fitting results than the global method. Table 1 shows the quantitative results of this leave-one-out test. We used the average Hausdorff Distance to measure the quality of our fittings to the ground truth. Informally the average Hausdorff Distance tells us how far away, on average, the other shape is to be expected, if a random point in a shape is chosen. It measures how well two shapes match each other. More precisely the average Hausdorff Distance between two volumes S_1 and S_2 is defined as the total sum of the shortest path of each point in shape S_1 to the closest point in S_2 and vice versa, divided by the total number of points of both shapes.

Table 1. Measured error based on the ground truth of a global fit and an interpolated local regression based fit

Average Hausdorff Distance [pixel]							
tooth #	1	2	3	4	5	6	7
global fitting error	0.084	0.089	0.301	0.221	0.203	0.138	0.151
local fitting error	0.071	0.075	0.240	0.143	0.086	0.119	0.113

5   Discussion

We presented an approach for the fitting of statistical models. Our method is based on the local regression method known from statistics. The core idea is to fit the model to a local region around a point for each point of the model. In this way we obtain a fitting result which is solely based on the model information but still allows for more flexibility than a global fitting method. In contrast to previous methods, no segmentation of the structure needs to be performed, nor do artificial deformations need to be included. The size of the neighborhood that is considered for each fit determines the trade-off between obtaining a fit that strictly adheres to the global shape constraint, and one that accurately explains all the data. This parameter should be chosen such that it reflects the noise properties of the images and the quality of the model.

For large images, fitting a full model at every point is computationally too expensive. To reduce the computational burden of such an approach, we proposed a method to interpolate local shape model fits performed only for a subset of all model points. In this way it becomes feasible to apply the method for the segmentation of large 3D images. We presented an application of our method for the segmentation of teeth from Cone Beam CT images. Our tests confirmed that the local fitting method improves the segmentation results consistently, compared to the global fitting results.

The number of points we choose for the interpolated fitting determines how many times we have to perform the fitting. It would therefore be interesting to choose the points, such they most effectively increase the fitting accuracy. The exploration of strategies for choosing these point optimally, is an interesting problem that will be the subject of future work.

Acknowledgements

This work has been supported by the CO-ME/NCCR research network of the Swiss National Science Foundation (http://co-me.ch).

References

1. Cootes, T.F., Taylor, C.J.: Combining point distribution models with shape models based on finite element analysis. Image Vision Comput. 13(5), 403–409 (1995)
2. Cootes, T.F., Taylor, C.J.: Data driven refinement of active shape model search. In: BMVC, British Machine Vision Association (1996)
3. Loog, M.: Localized maximum entropy shape modelling. In: Karssemeijer, N., Lelieveldt, B. (eds.) IPMI 2007. LNCS, vol. 4584, pp. 619–629. Springer, Heidelberg (2007)
4. Pekar, V., Kaus, M., Lorenz, C., Lobregt, S., Truyen, R., Weese, J.: Shape-model-based adaptation of 3D deformable meshes for segmentation of medical images. In: Proceedings of SPIE, vol. 4322, p. 281 (2001)
5. Shang, Y., Dossel, O.: Statistical 3D shape-model guided segmentation of cardiac images. Computers in Cardiology 31, 553 (2004)

6. Weese, J., Kaus, M., Lorenz, C., Lobregt, S., Truyen, R., Pekar, V.: Shape constrained deformable models for 3D medical image segmentation. LNCS, pp. 380–387. Springer, Heidelberg (2001)
7. Shen, D., Herskovits, E.H., Davatzikos, C.: An adaptive-focus statistical shape model for segmentation and shape modeling of 3-d brain structures. IEEE Trans. Med. Imaging 20(4), 257–270 (2001)
8. de Bruijne, M., van Ginneken, B., Viergever, M.A., Niessen, W.J.: Adapting active shape models for 3d segmentation of tubular structures in medical images. Inf. Process. Med. Imaging 18 (July 2003)
9. Zhao, Z., Aylward, S., Teoh, E.: A novel 3D partitioned active shape model for segmentation of brain MR images. In: Duncan, J.S., Gerig, G. (eds.) MICCAI 2005. LNCS, vol. 3749, pp. 221–228. Springer, Heidelberg (2005)
10. Blanz, V., Vetter, T.: A morphable model for the synthesis of 3d faces. In: SIGGRAPH 1999: Proceedings of the 26th annual conference on Computer graphics and interactive techniques, pp. 187–194. ACM Press, New York (1999)
11. Davatzikos, C., Tao, X., Shen, D.: Hierarchical active shape models, using the wavelet transform. IEEE Trans. Med. Imaging 22(3), 414–423 (2003)
12. Nain, D., Haker, S., Bobick, A., Tannenbaum, A.: Multiscale 3-d shape representation and segmentation using spherical wavelets. IEEE Trans. Med. Imaging 26(4), 598–618 (2007)
13. Knothe, R.: A Global-to-local model for the representation of human faces. PhD thesis, Computer Science Department, University of Basel (2009)
14. Hastie, T., Tibshirani, R., Friedman, J.: Kernel Smoothing Methods. In: The Elements of Statistical Learning. Springer Series in Statistics. Springer, New York (2001)
15. Heimann, T., Meinzer, H.: Statistical shape models for 3D medical image segmentation: A review. In: Medical Image Analysis (2009)
16. Cootes, T., Taylor, C., Cooper, D., Graham, J., et al.: Active shape models-their training and application. Computer Vision and Image Understanding 61(1), 38–59 (1995)
17. Rueckert, D., Frangi, A.F., Schnabel, J.A.: Automatic construction of 3d statistical deformation models using non-rigid registration. In: Niessen, W.J., Viergever, M.A. (eds.) MICCAI 2001. LNCS, vol. 2208, pp. 77–84. Springer, Heidelberg (2001)
18. Tipping, M.E., Bishop, C.M.: Probabilistic principal component analysis. Journal of the Royal Statistical Society 61, 611–622 (1999)
19. Dryden, I., Mardia, K.: Statistical shape analysis. Wiley, New York (1998)
20. Cleveland, W.S., Devlin, S.J.: Locally-Weighted regression: An approach to regression analysis by local fitting. Journal of the American Statistical Association 83(403), 596–610 (1988)
21. Zhu, C., Byrd, R., Lu, P., Nocedal, J.: Algorithm 778: L-BFGS-B: Fortran subroutines for large-scale bound-constrained optimization. ACM Transactions on Mathematical Software (TOMS) 23(4), 550–560 (1997)

Semi-supervised Learning of Edge Filters for Volumetric Image Segmentation

Margret Keuper[1,2], Robert Bensch[1,2], Karsten Voigt[2,3],
Alexander Dovzhenko[2,3], Klaus Palme[2,3,4], Hans Burkhardt[1,2],
and Olaf Ronneberger[1,2]

[1] Lehrstuhl für Mustererkennung und Bildverarbeitung,
Institut für Informatik
[2] Centre of Biological Signalling Studies (BIOSS)
[3] Institut für Biologie II, [4]Freiburg Inst. for Advanced Studies (FRIAS),
Albert-Ludwigs-Universität Freiburg
keuper@informatik.uni-freiburg.de

Abstract. For every segmentation task, prior knowledge about the object that shall be segmented has to be incorporated. This is typically performed either automatically by using labeled data to train the used algorithm, or by manual adaptation of the algorithm to the specific application. For the segmentation of 3D data, the generation of training sets is very tedious and time consuming, since in most cases, an expert has to mark the object boundaries in all slices of the 3D volume. To avoid this, we developed a new framework that combines unsupervised and supervised learning. First, the possible edge appearances are grouped, such that, in the second step, the expert only has to choose between relevant and non-relevant clusters. This way, even objects with very different edge appearances in different regions of the boundary can be segmented, while the user interaction is limited to a very simple operation. In the presented work, the chosen edge clusters are used to generate a filter for all relevant edges. The filter response is used to generate an edge map based on which an active surface segmentation is performed. The evaluation on the segmentation of plant cells recorded with 3D confocal microscopy yields convincing results.

1   Introduction

The segmentation of volumetric data is a difficult, some say ill-posed problem. Depending on the specific application as well as on the imaging technique, the desired object boundary can have very different appearances. Thus, for every new problem setting, the used method needs to be adapted and special prior knowledge about the application has to be included. Important questions can be: What is the appearance of the objects boundary? What edges are we looking for? What is the texture of the object? In the same dataset, e.g. of a plant cell, the user could be looking for either outer (the cell wall) or inner borders (plasmalemma), or intracellular compartments (as the nucleus or chloroplasts).

M. Goesele et al. (Eds.): DAGM 2010, LNCS 6376, pp. 462–471, 2010.

This information can either be acquired by learning from ground truth data (e.g. in [1]), if sufficient labeled data is available, or learned from user interaction. In most cases of 3D image analysis, the generation of ground truth segmentations (needed as input for the learning step) is a very tedious work, because the expert has to draw correct object boundaries in every single slice of the volume. This is why we are presenting a semi-supervised, user-guided segmentation method.

In [2], a user-guided tool for the segmentation of medical data is presented. There, the authors propose a twofold strategy: they create a graph description of contour fragments with a tesselation of the image plane. The actual segmentation is formulated as a path optimization, where the user has to manually select control points on the contour. In [3], a user guided level set segmentation is presented, that allows the user, similarly to our method, to define the edge map before starting a level set segmentation. The edge map is defined by a threshold either on the data itself or on the gradients. Thus, the method works satisfyingly only if the edge information is homogeneous over the whole dataset.

We are presenting a segmentation framework, that uses K-means clustering of the original object edges in order to enable the user to choose between different possible edge appearances in one sample dataset. This information is used to design an edge filter for the entire database, that can handle different appearances of an object's boundary. Then, a first segmentation with active surfaces is performed, using the force field derived from the edge filter response. The filter can be refined by adding more training samples. The needed user interaction is a very simple, quick and intuitive operation.

Since we are working on biological cell data, we have adapted the presented framework to the segmentation of star-shaped objects. The evaluation was performed on 3D confocal recordings of developing plant cells.

2   Framework

The general workflow of the presented method is displayed in figure 1. We assume that in the given database of recorded objects, the object detection step is already solved and for every object, the estimated position of the center c is given. For spherical objects, this detection step can be performed using the Hough transform as e.g. in [4]. Given this set of objects, the first step is to choose a random sample dataset. In this dataset, we find candidate positions at which edge profiles are extracted. These edge profiles are used as features and are grouped into different clusters. The processing up to this step will be presented in detail in 2.1. The result of the clustering is mapped into the original dataset: edges belonging to the same cluster are displayed in the same color. The next and most important step is the user interaction. From the displayed edge distributions presented in a 3D slice viewer, the user can decide which edges lie on the desired object contour. This information is used to design a filter for the specified edges, which is applied to the entire database. The generation of the filter is described in 2.2. The filter response is used to perform a parametric 3D active surface segmentation using spherical harmonics. This step will be described in 2.3. The

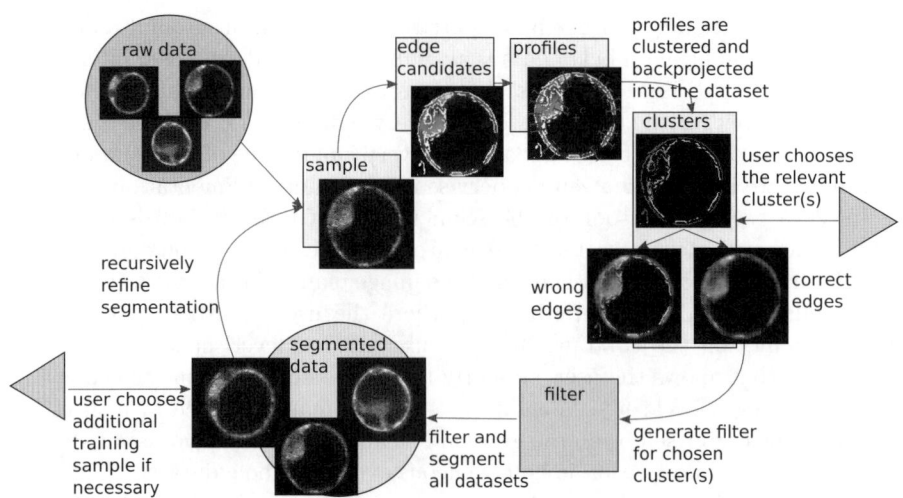

Fig. 1. Schematic overview over the whole workflow

user can now verify the resulting segmentations and, if it is not sufficient for all datasets, choose the next training sample. The edge appearances in this new sample are used to refine the filter and accordingly, to refine the segmentation.

2.1 Profile Extraction and Grouping

In most applications, the user is interested in laying a boundary on certain positions with high gradient magnitude, i.e. image edges. In positions where the information is lacking, the user usually wants a smooth interpolation of the boundary. As candidate positions at which the profiles will be extracted, we thus choose points with high gradient magnitude. To avoid finding too many candidates and to ensure that we are looking at the most important positions in the sample, we perform a non maximum suppression in gradient direction and take all the maxima in gradient magnitude as candidates. At these positions grayvalue profiles are extracted in radial direction from the center. This makes sense because we are assuming that the objects are star-shaped (i.e. there exists a point c such that each line segment connecting c to the object's boundary lies completely within the shape). When looking at more general shapes with spherical topology, one should extract profiles that are normal to the surface at this position, instead. For the extraction of the profiles, two parameters can be adjusted: the step size of the profile and its length. These have to be chosen such that the desired edge appearance can be captured and resolved.

We want to use these profiles as features to describe the appearance at the respective position. For microscopic data we are expecting strong variations in the absolute grayvalues even within the same recording due to absorption. To make our features robust against these variations, we use the derivative of the profile grayvalues, which is invariant against a graylevel offset. The continuous profile derivative p is a function of the radial length $l \in \mathbb{R}$ and the position $\mathbf{x}$. With respect to the center $\mathbf{c}$, $p(\mathbf{x}, l)$ is given by

$$p(\mathbf{x}, l) = \frac{\mathrm{d}}{\mathrm{d}l} I \left(\mathbf{x} + l \cdot \frac{\mathbf{x} - \mathbf{c}}{|\mathbf{x} - \mathbf{c}|} \right), \tag{1}$$

where I is the sample dataset. Thus, the discrete profile vector $\mathbf{p_x}$ is given by $\mathbf{p_x}(i) = p(\mathbf{x}, \lambda \cdot (i - \frac{L}{2}))$, where $0 \leq i < L \in \mathbb{N}$ is the position on the profile, L is the profile length and λ is the stepsize. In order to be also invariant against multiplicative grayvalue changes, we normalize the features by the maximum absolute value.

$$\bar{\mathbf{p}}_\mathbf{x}(i) = \frac{\mathbf{p_x}(i)}{\max_i(|\mathbf{p_x}(i)|)} \tag{2}$$

The $\bar{\mathbf{p}}_\mathbf{x}$ are clustered using K-means clustering (see e.g. [5]). This basic clustering method is suitable for our purpose, because it directly measures the similarity between the profiles and discriminates as soon as the euclidean distance is too large. The number of clusters scales with the number of extracted profiles. In our implementation, there are on average 4000 profiles in one cluster.

2.2 User Specified Filtering

Once the profiles are grouped into different clusters C_j, the user has to decide which of the clusters are relevant for the actual application. Therefore, the data must be presented such that it is easy to distinguish between relevant and non relevant clusters. For every cluster, we generate a 3D overlay plot in which all the points belonging to this cluster are marked in the original 3D sample data. The user can view this overlay and decide, whether the marked points lie on the desired boundary or not. This information is used to generate a Gaussian probability density function (PDF) for every chosen cluster, with

$$f_{C_j}(\bar{\mathbf{p}}) = \frac{1}{(2\pi)^{l/2} |\Sigma_{C_j}|^{1/2}} \cdot e^{-\frac{1}{2}(\bar{\mathbf{p}} - \boldsymbol{\mu}_{C_j})^T \Sigma_{C_j}^{-1}(\bar{\mathbf{p}} - \boldsymbol{\mu}_{C_j})}, \tag{3}$$

where Σ_{C_j} is the covariance matrix of all profiles $\bar{\mathbf{p}}_{C_j}$ in the chosen cluster C_j and $\boldsymbol{\mu}_{C_j}$ the expected value. With these PDFs, the edge filter is already defined and can be applied to all objects in the database. In the filtering step, we have to extract the profile $\bar{\mathbf{p}}_\mathbf{x}$ at every position $\mathbf{x}$ in the dataset. For this profile, we compute the Mahalanobis distance

$$D_{\mathrm{M}}(\bar{\mathbf{p}}_\mathbf{x}, C_j) = \sqrt{\left(\bar{\mathbf{p}}_\mathbf{x} - \boldsymbol{\mu}_{C_j}\right)^T \Sigma^{-1} \left(\bar{\mathbf{p}}_\mathbf{x} - \boldsymbol{\mu}_{C_j}\right)} \tag{4}$$

to every chosen cluster. The filter response is then given by

$$A(\mathbf{x}) = \min_{C_j} \left(D_{\mathrm{M}}(\bar{\mathbf{p}}_\mathbf{x}, C_j) \right). \tag{5}$$

A has low values, where the distance to the closest cluster center is small, i.e. where the profiles are similar to those belonging to the selected clusters. In order to have high responses at these positions, we compute $\bar{A} = 1 - A/\max(A)$. $\bar{A}$ is used to generate the external force field for the parametric active surfaces.

2.3 Parametric Active Surfaces

Active surfaces are a common tool for the segmentation of 3D biological data. Given a rough estimate of the objects position and size, i.e. its center $\mathbf{c}$ and radius r, an accurate fitting of the model to the underlying data can be performed.

Active surfaces classically have internal energies E_{int}, depending only on the shape of the model itself, and are exposed to external energies E_{ext} coming from the underlying dataset. The total energy of an active surface s is thus $E(s) = E_{\mathrm{int}}(s) + E_{\mathrm{ext}}(s)$. The active surface adaptation, i.e. the minimization of $E(s)$, leads to an Euler-Lagrange equation that can be considered as a force balance system $\mathbf{F}_{\mathrm{int}} + \mathbf{F}_{\mathrm{ext}} = \mathbf{0}$ (see [6]). It can be performed in the spatial domain, using a suitable surface mesh as it was done e.g. in [7] or in the Spherical Harmonic domain using parametrically deformable models based on (truncated) spherical harmonic expansions

$$f(\theta, \phi) = \sum_{l=0}^{B} \sum_{m=-l}^{l} \hat{f}_l^m Y_l^m(\theta, \phi), \qquad (6)$$

where

$$Y_l^m(\theta, \phi) = \sqrt{\frac{(2l+1)(l-m)!}{4\pi(l+m)!}} P_l^m(\cos\theta) e^{jm\phi} \qquad (7)$$

and the $\hat{f}_l^m$ are the spherical harmonic coefficients with degree l and order m, B is the maximal bandwidth. The P_l^m are the associated Legendre polynomials, j is the imaginary number. Parametric active surfaces have e.g. been used in [8] and have the advantage that they not only yield smooth surfaces but also a parametric shape description.

Parameterization. The first step of the active surface implementation is the choice of an appropriate parameterization. For the segmentation of star-shaped objects, an easy way of parameterizing a shape is describing it in spherical coordinates (θ, ϕ, r) with the two polar variables θ and ϕ, where $0 \leq \theta \leq \pi$ and $0 \leq \phi < 2\pi$ and $r = s(\theta, \phi)$ (compare [9]). r is the Euclidean distance of the surface from the center. For a so parameterized active surface $s(\theta, \phi)$, we can directly compute the corresponding shape descriptor as $\mathbf{d} = (\hat{s}_0^0, \hat{s}_1^{-1}, \hat{s}_1^0, \hat{s}_1^1, \dots, \hat{s}_l^l)^T$. For a perfect sphere, $s(\theta, \phi) = const.$ and $\hat{s}_l^m = 0$ for all $l, m \neq 0$.

Alternatively, for the more general case of objects with spherical topology, [10] proposes a suitable parameterization that assigns to every pair of angles a three-tuple of coordinates: $\mathbf{s}(\theta, \phi) = (x(\theta, \phi), y(\theta, \phi), z(\theta, \phi))^T$, thus laying a latitude-longitude grid over the shape. This parameterization has been used e.g. in [8] to perform a parametric deconvolution of 3D images. However, for our application, the first and easier parameterization is sufficient because when dealing with cells, we always expect to find star-shaped objects. This easier parameterization also has the advantage that no explicit internal energy is needed. The regularization can be done implicitly by limiting the bandwidth of the spherical harmonic expansion. This is more difficult when the second parameterization is used: this parameterization tends to artificially introduce sharp edges even at low bandwidth values (compare [8]).

External Forces. The external forces $\mathbf{F}_{\text{ext}}$ are computed from the filter response $\bar{A}$. This filter response is usually well representing all positions, where the edges are similar to those chosen by the user in the sample data. Due to the normalization, we can even handle linear gray scale variations. On the other hand, the normalization also causes some spot-like filter responses in the background (compare fig. 3d). Accounting for the fact that we are searching for object surfaces, i.e. locally plane-like structures, we can get rid of these wrong filter responses simply by applying the steerable filter for plane detection described in [11]. The filter response is used as edge map. On the gradients of the edge map, we compute the gradient vector flow (GVF) [6] to get a smooth force field . Then we can start with the surface adaptation.

Active Surface Evolution. As we are initializing the active surface as a sphere, at the beginning we have $s(\theta, \phi) = const.$. For every iteration, we project the forces that act on the surface onto their radial components, and compute their spherical harmonic expansion. The actual surface update can be performed in spherical harmonic domain. To get the new surface positions in the spatial domain, we then need to perform an inverse spherical harmonic transform.

When the process is finished on the whole database, the user can again interact. If the segmentation is not sufficient for all datasets, the user chooses a new sample and runs through steps 2.1 and 2.2. The new appearance clusters are added to the model and all wrongly segmented datasets of the previous iteration are segmented using this new model.

3   Experiments

The evaluation was performed using three sets of 3D recordings of living tobacco leaf protoplasts (cells lacking the cell wall). Plant protoplasts are a unique tool to study e.g. the function of the plasma membrane, cellular reprogramming and development [12]. An exact segmentation of the cells is needed for various applications, such as the description of the cell anatomy itself or of developmental processes in a meaningful anatomical coordinate system.

3.1   Data

Samples containing one to three single cells were recorded by confocal laser scanning microscopy (CLSM). Single cells were detected using a voter-based Hough transform for spheres [4], which provides us with a good estimate of the object's center $\mathbf{c}$ and the radius r, and cropped to separate volumes. The processed data volumes have dimensions ranging from $159 \times 118 \times 71$ voxels for small cells to $509 \times 350 \times 269$ voxels for larger cells. The spatial resolution in xy-direction is $0.28 \times 0.28 \mu m^2$ while the resolution in z-direction is either 0.4 or $0.5 \mu m$. The used imaging technique imposes some special image properties, like artefacts from the point spread function (PSF), noise that is generated at the different

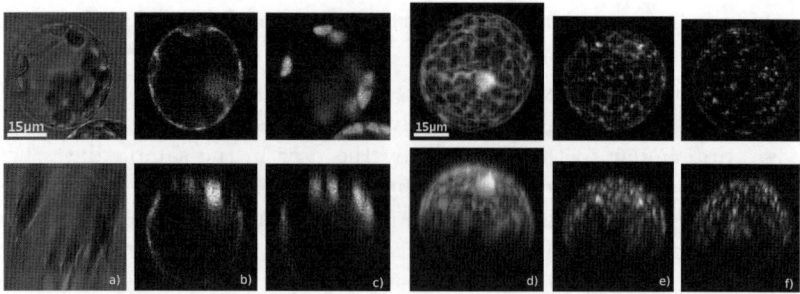

Fig. 2. (a-c) Slices of the recorded channels: a) transmitted light. b) protein pattern (Cyt). c) chloroplasts. (d-e) maximum intensity projections in z-direction (top) and in y-direction (bottom) of the protein stainings: d) Cyt. e) ER. f) GA.

stages of the signal chain and absorption resulting in signal intensity attenuation in recording direction, i.e. z-direction (see bottom row in fig. 2). The cells have been recorded on three successive days resulting in different cell shapes from roundish over elongated to more complex deformed shapes. Three channels have been recorded, a transmitted light channel and two confocal fluorescence channels, one showing the auto-fluorescence of the chloroplasts and another showing the fluorescence of the tagged protein (see fig. 2a-c). Here we used the protein pattern channel for segmentation. Three different protein patterns have been recorded which all have a different appearance (see fig. 2d-f). While the cytoplasm (Cyt, 55 cells in the database) fills the space between the chloroplasts, the endoplasmatic reticulum (ER, 46 cells) forms a mesh structure and the golgi apparatus (GA, 86 cells) is organized in spot-like structures. All protein patterns are located in the outer shell of the cell, i.e. between outer cell membrane and inner vacuole membrane (cf. fig. 2b).

3.2 Segmentation

The whole segmentation process was performed on slightly smoothed data, we applied a Gaussian smoothing with $\sigma = 0.28\mu$m. For the user specified boundary filtering step, we had to specify certain parameters. The chosen profile length is 8 at a stepsize of 0.56μm which is the double voxel size in xy-direction. The steerable filter, which was used for filtering out spot-like filter responses in the background, also has a parameter σ_s that specifies the thickness of the planes it searches for. We have set σ_s to 0.56μm. Finally, the active surfaces were initialized with the estimated radius r from the detection step. The bandwidth was limited to 16 bands. For the cells with stained Cyt, we have displayed the first training sample and the results of the different steps of the presented framework in fig. 3 in two orthogonal views.

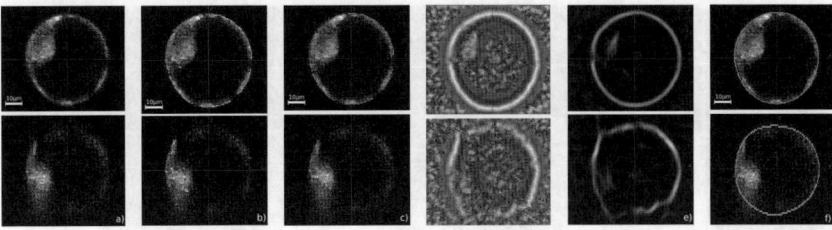

Fig. 3. a) Sample with Cyt staining. b) The clustering result from the K-means clustering with six clusters. Inner and outer boundaries lie, as expected, in different clusters. One can clearly see, that the absorption in z-direction leads to less candidates for edges and thus less training examples for the edge appearance in the lower z-regions. c) The two clusters colored in green were chosen as relevant. d) The filter response $\bar{A}$. e) The used edge map (after the application of the steerable filter). f) The segmentation result.

3.3 Evaluation and Results

To evaluate our method, we applied the segmentation to all 187 cells in our database. For each of the three patterns, one cell was randomly chosen as first training cell. The segmentation results for all cells were visually inspected in a 3D slice viewer by two experts, who gave label 1 if the segmentation was correct, and label 0 if not. For those cells that were not correctly segmented after the first iteration, a second training step was performed: one of the cells with label 0 was chosen for each pattern as training sample. Altogether, we performed three iterations. The results can be seen in table 1. Most of the cells were already correctly segmented after the first iteration. Some results can be seen in fig. 4.

For further evaluation, we compared the segmentation carried out with our method to the results that could be achieved with the ITK segmentation tool ITK-SNAP [3], which is based on 3D geodesic active contours. The internal forces are based on the gradient magnitude in the dataset. The preprocessing as well as the active contour parameters have to be manually adjusted for each dataset, which is why we performed this segmentation only for three datasets. The ITK-SNAP preprocessig parameters are: the scale of the Gaussian blurring σ, which we set to 0.56μm, the edge contrast κ, which we set to 0.1 and the edge mapping exponent, which we set to 1.6. For the geodesic active surfaces, some parameters have to be adjusted as well. Here, we could not use the same parameters for all three cells. We manually initialized the contours from outside,

Table 1. Results of our method after 1, 2 and 3 iterations

Experiment	# of cells	Iteration 1	Iteration 2	Iteration 3
Cytoplasm	55	85.5%	**94.6%**	**94.6%**
Golgi	86	86.1%	88.4%	**96.5%**
ER	46	91.3%	95.7%	**97.8%**

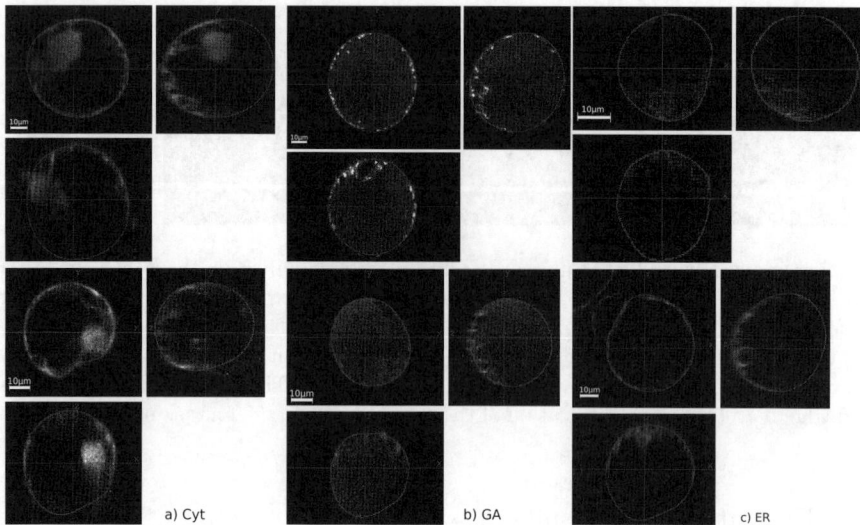

Fig. 4. Segmentation results in three orthogonal views. We have displayed two examples for every stained pattern.

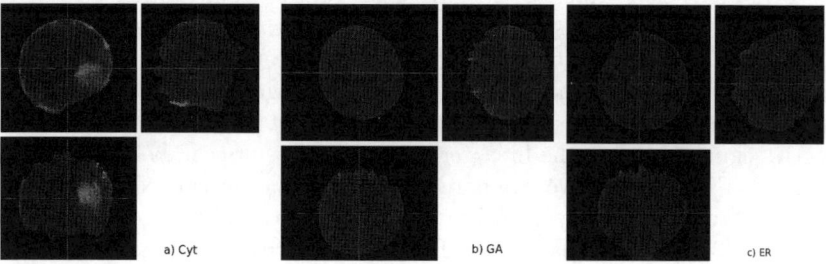

Fig. 5. Segmentation results with ITK-SNAP for the same cells as in fig. 4, second row.

because the internal structures of the cells made an initialization from inside impossible. The balloon force was set to a value between -0.7 and -0.9, the curvature force, that ranges from 0 (detailed) to 1 (spherical) was set to 0.8 and the advection force, that pushes the boundary back as it tries to cross edges, was set to 4.0. Additionally, the iteration has to be stopped manually. We needed between 461 and 791 steps to get the results displayed in fig. 5. As it can be seen, this segmentation tool can, despite all manual interaction, not handle the heterogeneous boundary and the absorption in z-direction.

4   Conclusion

We have presented a semi-supervised segmentation method for volumetric datasets, that can handle heterogeneous edge appearances. In our framework, edge models are learned from user input, while the user interaction is limited to very simple and intuitive operations and no further low-level parameters have to be adjusted. Although current 3D confocal recordings of single plant cells pose numerous challenges, such as inhomogeneous object boundaries, strong gray-value attenuations and noise, the segmentation of the datasets using the proposed method resulted in a highly reliable identification of cell boundaries.

Acknowledgments

This study was supported by the Excellence Initiative of the German Federal and State Governments (EXC 294).

References

1. Cootes, T., Edwards, G., Taylor, C.: Active appearance models. IEEE Trans. on PAMI 23/6, 681–685 (2001)
2. Vehkomäki, T., Gerig, G., Szkely, G.: A user-guided tool for efficient segmenta-tion of medical image data. In: Troccaz, J., Mösges, R., Grimson, W.E.L. (eds.) CVRMed-MRCAS 1997, CVRMed 1997, and MRCAS 1997. LNCS, vol. 1205, pp. 685–694. Springer, Heidelberg (1997)
3. Yushkevich, P.A., Piven, J., Hazlett, C., Smith, H., Smith, G., Ho, R., Ho, S., Gee, J.C., Gerig, G.: User-guided 3D active contour segmentation of anatomical structures: Significantly improved efficiency and reliability. Neuroimage 31/3 (2006)
4. Schulz, J., Schmidt, T., Ronneberger, O., Burkhardt, H., Pasternak, T., Dovzhenko, A., Palme, K.: Fast scalar and vectorial grayscale based invariant features for 3d cell nuclei localization and classification. In: Franke, K., Müller, K.-R., Nickolay, B., Schäfer, R. (eds.) DAGM 2006. LNCS, vol. 4174, pp. 182–191. Springer, Heidelberg (2006)
5. Xu, R., Wunsch, D.C.: Clustering. Wiley, Chichester (2008)
6. Xu, C., Prince, J.: Snakes, shapes, and gradient vector flow. IEEE Trans. Imag. Proc. 7/3, 321–345 (1998)
7. Keuper, M., Padeken, J., Heun, P., Burkhardt, H., Ronneberger, O.: A 3d active surface model for the accurate segmentation of *drosophila* schneider cell nuclei and nucleoli. In: Bebis, G., Boyle, R., Parvin, B., Koracin, D., Kuno, Y., Wang, J., Wang, J.-X., Wang, J., Pajarola, R., Lindstrom, P., Hinkenjann, A., Encarnação, M.L., Silva, C.T., Coming, D. (eds.) ISVC 2009. LNCS, vol. 5875, pp. 865–874. Springer, Heidelberg (2009)
8. Khairy, K., Howard, J.: Spherical harmonics-based parametric deconvolution of 3d surface images using bending energy minimization. Medical Image Analysis 12, 217–227 (2008)
9. Ballard, D.H., Brown, C.M.: Computer vision. Prentice-Hall, NJ (1981)
10. Brechbühler, C., Gerig, G., Kübler, O.: Parametrization of closed surfaces for 3-d shape description. Comput. Vis. Image Underst. 61(2), 154–170 (1995)
11. Aguet, F., Jacob, M., Unser, M.: Three-dimensional feature detection using optimal steerable filters. In: Proc. of the ICIP, pp. 1158–1161 (2005)
12. Dovzhenko, A., Bergen, U., Koop, H.U.: Thin alginate layer (tal)-technique for protoplast culture of tobacco leaf protoplasts: Shoot formation in less than two weeks. Protoplasma 204, 114–118 (1998)

Geometrically Constrained Level Set Tracking for Automotive Applications

Esther Horbert, Dennis Mitzel, and Bastian Leibe

UMIC Research Centre RWTH Aachen University, Germany

Abstract. We propose a new approach for integrating geometric scene knowledge into a level-set tracking framework. Our approach is based on a novel constrained-homography transformation model that restricts the deformation space to physically plausible rigid motion on the ground plane. This model is especially suitable for tracking vehicles in automotive scenarios. Apart from reducing the number of parameters in the estimation, the 3D transformation model allows us to obtain additional information about the tracked objects and to recover their detailed 3D motion and orientation at every time step. We demonstrate how this information can be used to improve a Kalman filter estimate of the tracked vehicle dynamics in a higher-level tracker, leading to more accurate object trajectories. We show the feasibility of this approach for an application of tracking cars in an inner-city scenario.

1 Introduction

Object tracking from a mobile platform is an important problem with many potential applications. Consequently, many different approaches have been applied to this problem in the past, including tracking-by-detection [1,2,3,4], model-based [5,6], template-based [7,8] and region-based [9,10] methods. In this paper, we focus on the latter class of approaches, in particular on level-set tracking, which has shown considerable advances in recent years [9,11].

Level-set tracking performs a local optimization, iterating between a segmentation and a warping step to track an object's contour over time. Since both steps only need to be evaluated in a narrow band around the currently tracked contour, they can be implemented very efficiently [9]. Still, as all appearance-based approaches, they are restricted in the types of transformations they can robustly handle without additional knowledge about the expected motions.

In this paper, we investigate the use of geometric constraints for improving level-set tracking. We show how geometric scene knowledge can be directly integrated into the level-set warping step in order to constrain object motion. For this, we propose a constrained-homography transformation model that represents rigid motion on the ground plane. This model is targeted for tracking vehicles in an automotive scenario and takes advantage of an egomotion estimate obtained by structure-from-motion (SfM).

An advantage of our proposed approach, compared to pure 2D tracking, is that it restricts the deformation space to physically plausible rigid-body motions, thus increasing the robustness of the estimation step. In addition, the 3D

M. Goesele et al. (Eds.): DAGM 2010, LNCS 6376, pp. 472–482, 2010.

transformation model allows us to directly infer the tracked object's detailed 3D motion and orientation at every time step. We show how this information can be used in a higher-level tracker, which models the vehicle dynamics in order to obtain smooth and physically correct trajectories. The additional measurements provided by our geometrically constrained level set tracker make the estimation more robust and lead to smoother trajectories. We demonstrate our approach on several video sequences for tracking cars on city roads under viewpoint changes.

The paper is structured as follows. The next section gives an overview of related work. Section 2 then presents the details of our proposed level-set tracking approach and Section 3 shows how its results can be integrated with a high-level tracker. Section 4 finally presents experimental results.

Related Work. Tracking-by-detection approaches have become very popular recently, since they can deal with complex scenes and provide automatic re-initialization by continuous application of an object detector [1,2,3,4]. However, for elongated objects with non-holonomic motion constraints, the raw detection bounding boxes often do not constrain the object motion sufficiently, making robust trajectory estimation difficult. Model-based tracking approaches try to obtain more information about the tracked objects by estimating their precise pose [5,6]. However, they require a 3D model of the target object, which makes it hard to apply them for complex outdoor settings where many different objects can occur. The complexity can be reduced by limiting pose estimation to a planar region, for which efficient template-based tracking schemes can be used [7]. By decomposing the homography estimated from the template deformation, information about the 3D object motion can be obtained [8]. However, this approach heavily relies on sufficient texture content inside the tracked region, which restricts it mainly to tracking fiducial regions.

In the context of region-based tracking, little work has been done in order to incorporate dedicated 3D scene constraints. [12] explore affine motion models in order to track multiple regions under 3D transformations. [13] and [14] propose different ways of combining level-set tracking with direct 3D pose estimation. However, they both assume a detailed 3D model of the target object to be available, which is not the case in our application. [10] propose a globally optimal approach for contour tracking which is also applied to an automotive scenario, but this approach does not use knowledge about the geometric meaning of the changed contour.

2 Approach

2.1 Level-Set Tracking

We use a probabilistic level-set framework for segmentation and tracking similar to the one introduced by [11]. The target object is first segmented, then tracked through the subsequent image frames. In the following, *background* denotes the area around and *foreground* the area containing the object. The object's contour is represented implicitly by the zero level-set of the embedding function $\Phi(\mathbf{x})$

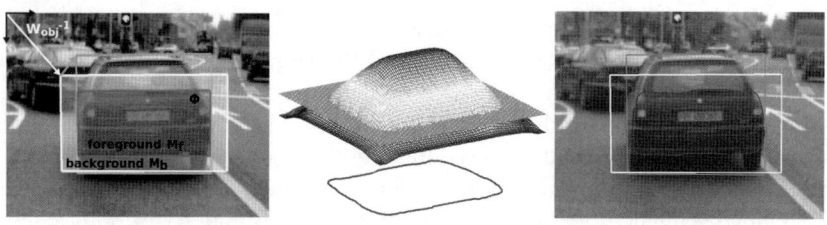

Fig. 1. Detection box (green), foreground initialization (red) and object frame (white) with foreground and background pixels and the corresponding evolved level set embedding function $\mathbf{\Phi}$

(see Fig. 1). The color $\mathbf{y}$ of pixels $\mathbf{x}$ is used to build foreground and background models M_f and M_b, in our case color histograms.

Segmentation. To obtain a segmentation of an object, the level set is evolved starting from an approximate initialization, *e.g.* a bounding box provided by an object detector. We use a variational formulation with three terms which penalize the deviation from M_f and M_b [11], the deviation from a signed distance function [15] (a constraint on the shape of the embedding function), and the length of the contour (to reward a smoother contour, similar so [15]). Eq. 1 shows the gradient flow used to optimize the segmentation:

$$\frac{\partial P(\mathbf{\Phi}, \mathbf{p} | \mathbf{\Omega})}{\partial \mathbf{\Phi}} = \underbrace{\frac{\delta_\epsilon(\mathbf{\Phi})(P_f - P_b)}{P(\mathbf{x} | \mathbf{\Phi}, \mathbf{p}, \mathbf{y})}}_{\substack{\text{deviation from} \\ \text{fg/bg model}}} - \underbrace{\frac{1}{\sigma^2}\left[\nabla^2\mathbf{\Phi} - div\left(\frac{\nabla\mathbf{\Phi}}{|\nabla\mathbf{\Phi}|}\right)\right]}_{\substack{\text{deviation from} \\ \text{signed distance function}}} + \underbrace{\lambda\delta_\epsilon(\mathbf{\Phi})div\left(\frac{\nabla\mathbf{\Phi}}{|\nabla\mathbf{\Phi}|}\right)}_{\text{length of contour}} \quad (1)$$

where $P(\mathbf{x}_i | \mathbf{\Phi}, \mathbf{p}, \mathbf{y}_i) = H_\epsilon(\mathbf{\Phi}(\mathbf{x}_i))P_f + (1 - H_\epsilon(\mathbf{\Phi}(\mathbf{x}_i)))P_b$, ∇^2 is the Laplacian operator, H_ϵ is a smoothed Heaviside step function, δ_ϵ a smoothed Dirac delta function and $\mathbf{\Omega}$ denotes the pixels in the object frame.

P_f and P_b are the pixel-wise posteriors for pixels' probabilities of belonging to the foreground and background. During segmentation, M_f and M_b are rebuilt in every iteration; during the later tracking stage the models are only slightly adapted to achieve high robustness while still adapting to lighting changes.

Tracking. In the following frames the obtained contour is tracked by performing a rigid registration, *i.e.* by warping its reference frame to another position without changing the contour's shape. Similar to inverse compositional image alignment [16] the content of the new frame is warped such that it looks more like the old frame. The inverse of the resulting warp with parameters $\Delta\mathbf{p}$ can in turn be used to warp the contour onto the new frame.

$$\Delta\mathbf{p} = \left[\sum_{i=1}^{N}\frac{1}{2P(\mathbf{x}_i | \mathbf{\Phi}, \mathbf{p}, \mathbf{y}_i)}\left[\frac{P_f}{H_\epsilon(\mathbf{\Phi}(\mathbf{x}_i))} - \frac{P_b}{(1 - H_\epsilon(\mathbf{\Phi}(\mathbf{x}_i)))}\right]\mathbf{J}^\mathsf{T}\mathbf{J}\right]^{-1} \times \sum_{i=1}^{N}\frac{(P_f - P_b)\mathbf{J}^\mathsf{T}}{P(\mathbf{x}_i | \mathbf{\Phi}, \mathbf{p}, \mathbf{y}_i)} \quad (2)$$

with $\mathbf{J} = \delta_\epsilon(\mathbf{\Phi}(\mathbf{x}_i))\nabla\mathbf{\Phi}(\mathbf{x}_i)\frac{\partial\mathbf{W}}{\partial\Delta\mathbf{p}}$, where $\frac{\partial\mathbf{W}}{\partial\Delta\mathbf{p}}$ is the Jacobian of the warp.

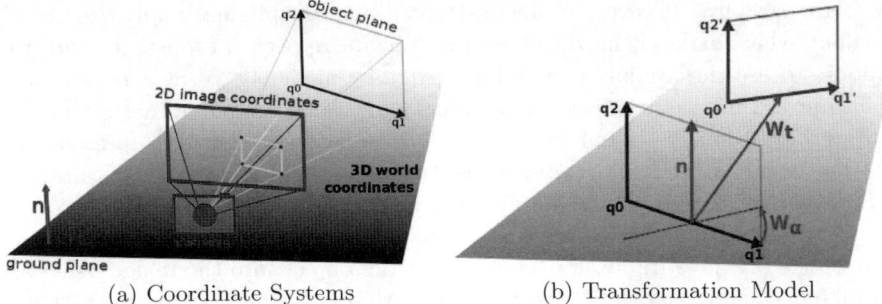

(a) Coordinate Systems   (b) Transformation Model

Fig. 2. Visualization of the coordinate systems and the proposed transformation model used in our approach

2.2 Geometric Transformation Model

In addition to the image based tracking approach as described above, we model the 3D position of a tracked object. This allows us to make assumptions about an object's movement by the projective distortions that arise on the 2D image.

Coordinate Systems. Figure 2(a) shows the used coordinate systems. The image itself consists of a number of pixels with 2D coordinates. The colors of these pixels correspond to points in the world which were projected onto the image plane. The 3D coordinates of those points cannot however be inferred directly from one image without additional depth information. We use a ground plane, which was obtained with structure-from-motion (SfM), to estimate the base point of a detected object. We approximate the object to be a plane in world coordinates that is orthogonal to the ground plane. This object plane can be described with a point $\mathbf{q}_0$ and two direction vectors $\mathbf{q}_1$ and $\mathbf{q}_2$.

$$\mathbf{x}_i = \begin{bmatrix} x_i \\ y_i \\ w_i \end{bmatrix} = \mathbf{P}\mathbf{x}_w = \mathbf{P}\mathbf{Q}\mathbf{x}_o, \quad \text{with } \mathbf{Q} = \begin{bmatrix} \mathbf{q}_1 & \mathbf{q}_2 & \mathbf{q}_0 \\ 0 & 0 & 1 \end{bmatrix}, \quad \mathbf{x}_o = \begin{bmatrix} x_o \\ y_o \\ 1 \end{bmatrix}, \quad \mathbf{x}_w = \begin{bmatrix} x_w \\ y_w \\ z_w \\ 1 \end{bmatrix} \quad (3)$$

where $\mathbf{x}_o$ is a 2D point on the object plane and $\mathbf{x}_w$ are its corresponding world coordinates. The point $\mathbf{x}_i$ in the image that corresponds to this world point can be obtained by projection with the camera matrix $\mathbf{P}$.

3D Transformation Model. The level-set tracking framework requires us to specify a family of warping transformations $\mathbf{W}$ that relate the previous object reference frame to the current one. In the following, we show how this warp can be used to incorporate scene knowledge by enforcing geometric constraints on the object motion.

Our target scenario is an automotive application where the goal is to track other vehicles' motions relative to our own vehicle. In this scenario, we can assume that the tracked object parts are approximately planar and that the target objects move rigidly on the ground plane. This means that their 3D shape will not change between two frames; only their position relative to the camera will. The resulting projective distortions in the image can therefore be modeled by a homography. However, an unconstrained homography has many degrees of freedom, which makes it hard to keep the tracking approach robust. Instead, we propose to use the available scene knowledge by modeling $\mathbf{W}$ as a *constrained homography* that requires fewer parameters and can be estimated more robustly.

Figure 2(b) illustrates our proposed transformation model. We represent object motion by a 3D homography, consisting of a rotation $\mathbf{W}_\alpha$ around an axis orthogonal to the ground plane and a translation $\mathbf{W}_t$ along the vector $\mathbf{t} = [t_x, t_y, t_z]^\mathsf{T}$. In order to compare the object points with the stored level-set contour of the previous frame, we then project the object into the image using an estimated camera matrix $\mathbf{P}$ obtained by SfM. Finally, we compute a 2D homography $\mathbf{W}_{obj}$ which warps the content of the object window (defined by the projections of its four corner points) onto the level-set reference frame.

$$\mathbf{W} = \mathbf{W}_{obj}\ \mathbf{P}\ \mathbf{W}_t\mathbf{W}_\alpha\mathbf{Q}\begin{bmatrix} x_o \\ y_o \\ 1 \end{bmatrix} \tag{4}$$

$\mathbf{W}_\alpha$ can be computed as a sequence of several transformations: a translation $\mathbf{T}_P$ moving the rotation axis into the origin; a rotation $\mathbf{R}_{xz}$ into the xz-plane; another rotation $\mathbf{R}_z$ onto the z-axis; and finally a rotation $\mathbf{R}_z(\alpha)$ about the z-axis with the desired angle α, followed by the inverse of the first three steps.

$$\mathbf{W}_\alpha = \mathbf{T}_P^{-1}\mathbf{R}_{xz}^{-1}\mathbf{R}_z^{-1}\mathbf{R}_z(\alpha)\mathbf{R}_z\mathbf{R}_{xz}\mathbf{T}_P, \qquad \mathbf{W}_t = \begin{bmatrix} \mathbf{I} & \mathbf{t} \\ \mathbf{0} & 1 \end{bmatrix} \tag{5}$$

In the above formulation, we have assumed a general translation $\mathbf{W}_t$. In principle, this could be restricted further to only allow translations parallel to the ground plane. However, the estimated ground plane is not always completely accurate and in any case does not account for uneven ground, especially at farther distances. We have therefore found that allowing a small movement component in the direction of the ground plane normal is necessary to achieve robustness.

Optimizing for the Transformation. The tracking framework uses the Gauss-Newton method to optimize the warp between two image frames. This requires the Jacobian of the overall warp $\mathbf{W}$, which contains the partial derivatives of $\mathbf{W}$ with respect to the parameters α, t_x, t_y and t_z.

$$\frac{\partial \mathbf{W}}{\partial \Delta \mathbf{p}} \quad \text{with} \quad \Delta \mathbf{p} = \begin{bmatrix} \alpha\ t_x\ t_y\ t_z \end{bmatrix}^\mathsf{T} \tag{6}$$

The parameters $\Delta \mathbf{p}$ available for optimization restrict the possible movements of the contour and the gradient $\frac{\partial \mathbf{W}}{\partial \Delta \mathbf{p}}$ indicates the effect a certain parameter value has on the position of the contour in the image. (6) is substituted into (2) and is evaluated for every point $\mathbf{x}$ in the band around the contour which is determined by $\delta_\epsilon(\mathbf{\Phi})$. In this way, pixel locations with a low probability of belonging to the foreground contribute a warp towards the outside of the contour and vice versa. A lower probability results in a larger step and the total step size is thus determined automatically. The algorithm has converged when the step size has become sufficiently small.

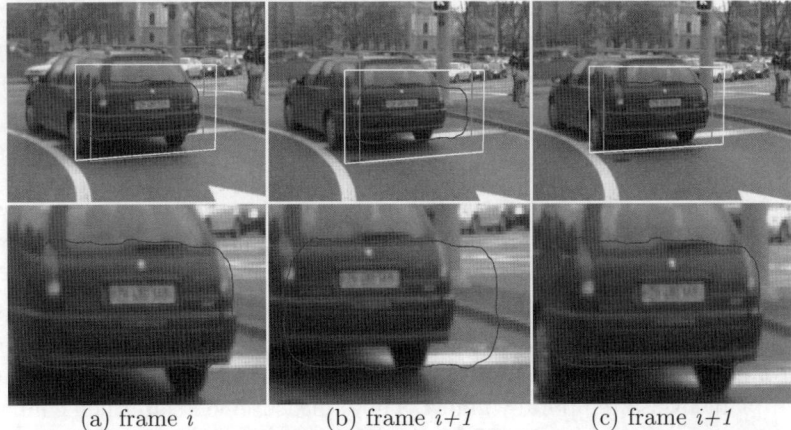

(a) frame i   (b) frame i+1   (c) frame i+1

Fig. 3. (a) 3D position and synthetic view of object frame. (b) Before warp: 3D position as in frame i. (c) After warp: tracked 3D position. Notice how the contour moved in 3D and its projection onto the image plane changed accordingly; its shape did not change.

Final Tracking Algorithm. Putting the above steps together, we can summarize the proposed tracking algorithm as follows:

1. Initialize the object position, *e.g.* using a detection bounding box.
2. Apply the level-set segmentation (in our implementation for 200 iterations).
3. Compute the object plane's world coordinates $\mathbf{Q}$ by projecting the detection box base points onto the ground plane. (This box does not need to be aligned with the image borders and can also be used to initialize rotated objects).
4. For the following frames: Track the object's shape, *i.e.* compute $\Delta\mathbf{p}$ for the warp between two images i and *i+1*:

   (a) Assume the object is still located at the same 3D position. Interpolate synthetic views for both object frames (Fig. 3(a), 3(b)) with $\mathbf{W}^i_{obj}, \mathbf{W}^{i+1}_{obj}$.
   (b) Use eq. (2) with eq. (6) to find a set of parameters $\Delta\mathbf{p}$ such that the contour in the warped object frame *i+1* better matches object frame i.
   (c) Use the inverse of the estimated homography $(\mathbf{W}_t\mathbf{W}_\alpha)^{-1}$ to warp the modeled 3D coordinates of the object and obtain a new 3D position estimate of the object in frame *i+1* (Fig. 3(c)). (*E.g.* if image *i+1* needs to be warped "closer" to the camera in order to look like image i, the object in fact moved to the back.)
   (d) Use the new 3D coordinates to obtain an improved synthetic view of the object in frame *i+1*.
   (e) Repeat steps (b) to (d) until the step size is small enough: $\|\Delta\mathbf{p}\| < \epsilon$.
   (f) Apply the level-set segmentation for 1 iteration to update the contour.

The results of this procedure are a level-set contour and a bounding box for each frame, as well as the estimated 3D position and orientation of the object.

3   Integration with a High-Level Tracker

The level-set tracking approach described in the previous section can robustly follow an individual object over time. However, it requires an initialization to pick out objects of interest, and it does not incorporate a dynamic model to interpret the observed motion. For this reason, we integrate it with a high-level tracker. In this integration, the task of the level-set tracker is to generate independent *tracklets* for individual objects, which are then integrated into a consistent scene interpretation with physically plausible trajectories by the high-level tracker.

System Overview. We apply a simplified version of the robust multi-hypothesis tracking framework by [3]. Given an estimate of the current camera position and ground plane location from SfM, we collect detected vehicle positions on the ground plane over a temporal window. Those measurements are then connected to trajectory hypotheses using Extended Kalman Filters (EKFs). Each trajectory obtains a score, representing the likelihood of the assigned detections under the motion and appearance model (represented as an RGB color histogram). As a result, we obtain an overcomplete set of trajectory hypotheses, from which we select the best explanation for the observed measurements by applying model selection in every frame (Details can be found in [3]).

Motion Model. For modeling the vehicle trajectories, we use an EKF with the Ackermann steering model (*e.g.* [17]), as shown in Fig. 4(a). This model incorporates a non-holonomic motion constraint, enforcing that the velocity vector is always perpendicular to the rear wheel axis. The state vector is given as $\mathbf{s}_t = [x_t, y_t, \psi_t, v_t, \delta_t, a_t]$, where (x, y) is the position of the car, ψ the heading angle, δ the steering angle, v the longitudinal velocity, and a the acceleration. The prediction step of the Kalman filter is then defined as follows:

$$
\mathbf{s}_{t+1} = \begin{pmatrix} x_t + v_t\cos(\psi_t)\Delta t + \frac{1}{2}a_t\cos(\psi_t)\Delta t^2 \\ y_t + v_t\sin(\psi_t)\Delta t + \frac{1}{2}a_t\sin(\psi_t)\Delta t^2 \\ \psi_t + \frac{v_t}{L}\tan(\delta)\Delta t \\ v_t + a_t\Delta t \\ \delta_t \\ a_t \end{pmatrix} + \begin{pmatrix} 0 \\ 0 \\ 0 \\ 0 \\ n_\delta \\ n_a \end{pmatrix}. \tag{7}
$$

L is the distance between the rear and front wheel axes and is set to a value of 3.5m. Multi-vehicle tracking-by-detection using a similar motion model was demonstrated by [4] based on a battery of object detectors with discretized viewing angles. We use a similar coarse discretization of the viewing angle with three separate, HOG-style [18] vehicle detectors in order to initialize our level-set tracker (Fig. 4(b)). However, after this initialization, we only use the observations provided by the low-level tracker and integrate them into the motion model.

Discussion. Our proposed approach has several advantages. Compared to a pure tracking-by-detection approach, the level-set tracker yields much finer-grained measurements of the viewing angle at which the target vehicle is seen. In addition, the level-set tracker can continue tracking objects even when they

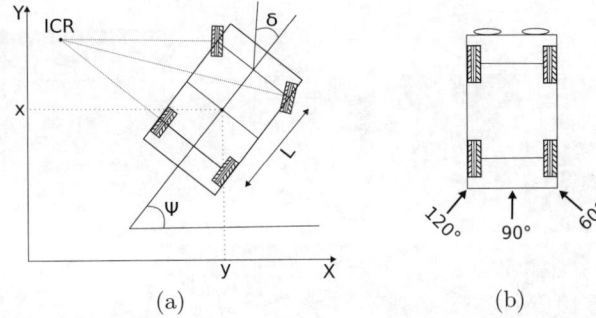

Fig. 4. (a) Ackermann steering model used for modeling the motion of the vehicle (assumes rolling without slippage). (b) Discretization of the the detected viewing angles.

partially leave the image and the object detector would fail. Compared to a level-set tracker with a simpler 2D transformation model (*i.e.*, just using translation and scale, without ground plane constraints), our model has the advantage of being able to estimate the target vehicle's location *and* its current orientation. This orientation estimate is beneficial in two respects. It allows us to extrapolate from the tracked car trunk location and infer the true object center, resulting in better position estimates (which is especially important for elongated objects such as cars). And it enables the use of orientation as *observed quantity* in the motion model, resulting in better predictions. All of those factors contribute to more robust tracking performance, as will be demonstrated in the next section.

4   Experimental Results

Data. We demonstrate our approach on three parts of a challenging sequence from the Zurich Mobile Car corpus, generously provided by the authors of [4]. The sequence was captured using a stereo setup (13-14 fps and 640×480 resolution) mounted on top of a car. We use SfM and ground plane estimates provided with this data set, but restrict all further processing to the left camera stream.

Qualitative Results. Fig. 5 shows qualitative results of our approach on three test sequences which contain cars turning corners, demonstrating its capability to accurately track vehicles under viewpoint changes. (The corresponding result videos are provided on www.mmp.rwth-aachen.de/projects/dagm2010). As can be seen, the estimated vehicle orientation from the level-set tracker enables the high-level tracker to compute smooth vehicle trajectories.

Comparison with Baseline Approach. Fig. 6 presents a comparison of our 3D estimation approach with the results of our level-set tracker using only a 2D (translation + scale) transformation model. As can be seen from those results, our approach achieves better tracking accuracy and manages to closely follow the target vehicles despite considerable viewpoint changes. In contrast, the 2D baseline method slips off the car in all cases, since the 3D position of the car's center is incorrectly estimated, resulting in a wrong trajectory.

Fig. 5. Tracking results of our approach on three test sequences. The integrated 3D estimation results of the high-level tracker show that it is able to accurately follow cars turning corners and to produce smooth trajectories.

Fig. 6. Comparison with the results of a 2D baseline model. (Left columns) Level-set tracking results; (Right columns) High-level tracker's results. The lacking orientation estimate causes the high-level tracker to slip off the vehicles during viewpoint changes.

5   Conclusion

In conclusion, we have presented an approach for incorporating geometric scene constraints into the warping step of a level-set tracker. Our approach allows to estimate both the location and orientation of the tracked object in 3D, while at the same time restricting the parameter space for more robust estimation. As we have shown, the estimation results can be used to improve the performance of a higher-level multi-hypothesis tracker integrating the measurements with vehicle dynamics into physically plausible trajectories. A possible extension could be to incorporate detections for different vehicle orientations, as well as stereo depth information, in order to initialize tracking also for other vehicle viewpoints.

Acknowledgments. This project has been funded, in parts, by the EU project EUROPA (ICT-2008-231888) and the cluster of excellence UMIC (DFG EXC 89). We thank C. Bibby and I. Reid for valuable comments for the level-set tracking and for making their evaluation data available.

References

1. Betke, M., Haritaoglu, E., Davis, L.S.: Real-time multiple vehicle detection and tracking from a moving vehicle. MVA 12, 69–83 (2000)
2. Gavrila, D., Munder, S.: Multi-Cue Pedestrian Detection and Tracking from a Moving Vehicle. IJCV 73(1), 41–59 (2007)
3. Leibe, B., Schindler, K., Van Gool, L.: Coupled Object Detection and Tracking from Static Cameras and Moving Vehicles. PAMI 30(10), 1683–1698 (2008)
4. Ess, A., Leibe, B., Schindler, K., Van Gool, L.: Robust Multi-Person Tracking from a Mobile Platform. PAMI 31(10), 1831–1846 (2009)
5. Koller, D., Daniilidis, K., Nagel, H.: Model-Based Object Tracking in Monocular Image Sequences of Road Traffic Scenes. IJCV 10(3) (1993)
6. Dellaert, F., Thorpe, C.: Robust Car Tracking using Kalman filtering and Bayesian templates. In: CITS (1997)
7. Chateau, T., Jurie, F., Dhome, M., Clady, X.: Real-Time Tracking Using Wavelet Representation. In: Van Gool, L. (ed.) DAGM 2002. LNCS, vol. 2449, p. 523. Springer, Heidelberg (2002)
8. Benhimane, S., Malis, E., Rives, P.: Vision-based Control for Car Platooning using Homography Decomposition. In: ICRA, pp. 2161–2166 (2005)
9. Cremers, D., Rousson, M., Deriche, R.: A Review of Statistical Approaches to Level Set Segmentation Integrating Color, Texture, Motion and Shape. IJCV 72, 195–215 (2007)
10. Schoenemann, T., Cremers, D.: A Combinatorial Solution for Model-based Image Segmentation and Real-time Tracking. PAMI (2009)
11. Bibby, C., Reid, I.: Robust Real-Time Visual Tracking using Pixel-Wise Posteriors. In: Forsyth, D., Torr, P., Zisserman, A. (eds.) ECCV 2008, Part II. LNCS, vol. 5303, pp. 831–844. Springer, Heidelberg (2008)
12. Fussenegger, M., Deriche, R., Pinz, A.: Multiregion Level Set Tracking with Transformation Invariant Shape Priors. In: Narayanan, P.J., Nayar, S.K., Shum, H.-Y. (eds.) ACCV 2006. LNCS, vol. 3852, pp. 395–404. Springer, Heidelberg (2006)

13. Brox, T., Rosenhahn, B., Weickert, J.: Three-dimensional shape knowledge for joint image segmentation and pose estimation. In: Kropatsch, W.G., Sablatnig, R., Hanbury, A. (eds.) DAGM 2005. LNCS, vol. 3663, pp. 109–116. Springer, Heidelberg (2005)
14. Prisacariu, V., Reid, I.: PWP3D: Real-time segmentation and tracking of 3D objects. In: BMVC (2009)
15. Li, C., Xu, C., Gui, C., Fox, M.: Level Set Evolution without Re-initialization: A New Variational Formulation. In: CVPR (2005)
16. Baker, S., Matthews, I.: Lucas-Kanade 20 Years On: A Unifying Framework. IJCV 69, 221–255 (2004)
17. Muir, P., Neuman, C.: Kinematic Modeling of Wheeled Mobile Robots. J. Robotic Systems 4(2), 281–340 (1987)
18. Dalal, N., Triggs, B.: Histograms of oriented gradients for human detection. In: CVPR (2005)

Interactive Motion Segmentation

Claudia Nieuwenhuis[1], Benjamin Berkels[2],
Martin Rumpf[2], and Daniel Cremers[1,*]

[1] Technical University of Munich, Germany
{nieuwenhuis,cremers}@in.tum.de
[2] University of Bonn, Germany
{berkels,rumpf}@ins.uni-bonn.de

Abstract. Interactive motion segmentation is an important task for
scene understanding and analysis. Despite recent progress state-of-the-
art approaches still have difficulties in adapting to the diversity of spatially varying motion fields. Due to strong, spatial variations of the motion field, objects are often divided into several parts. At the same time,
different objects exhibiting similar motion fields often cannot be distinguished correctly. In this paper, we propose to use spatially varying affine
motion model parameter distributions combined with minimal guidance
via user drawn scribbles. Hence, adaptation to motion pattern variations
and capturing subtle differences between similar regions is feasible. The
idea is embedded in a variational minimization problem, which is solved
by means of recently proposed convex relaxation techniques. For two regions (i.e. object and background) we obtain globally optimal results for
this formulation. For more than two regions the results deviate within
very small bounds of about 2 to 4 % from the optimal solution in our
experiments. To demonstrate the benefit of using both model parameters and spatially variant distributions, we show results for challenging
synthetic and real-world motion fields.

1 Introduction

Motion segmentation refers to grouping together pixels undergoing a common
motion. It aims at segmenting an image into moving objects and is a powerful
cue for image understanding and scene analysis. For a semantic interpretation of
a sequence motion is an important feature just like color or texture. For tracking
and video indexing it is often desirable to divide the scene into foreground and
background objects and to perform independent motion analysis for both classes.
Another perspective application is video compression, where several encoding
standards such as MPEG represent a sequence as objects on a series of layers
and, hence, require the objects to be identified before encoding.

Most motion segmentation methods identify objects by grouping pixels with
approximately constant motion vectors. This approach leads to several problems.

---

[*] This work was supported by the DFG SPP 1335 and grant CR250/6-1.

M. Goesele et al. (Eds.): DAGM 2010, LNCS 6376, pp. 483–492, 2010.

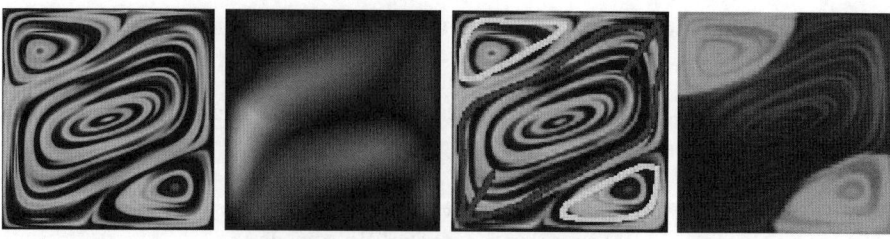

a) Input image   b) HSV Motion Field   c) User Scribbles   d) Interact. Segment.

Fig. 1. Segmentation of a motion field where traditional motion segmentation approaches fail. The proposed algorithm allows to compute interactive image segmentations based on a spatially varying partitioning of the velocity field (motion field input data courtesy of Eberhard Bänsch, University of Erlangen-Nuremberg).

1. Object motion is often characterized by complex motion patterns such as vortices or curls, which are impossible to be segmented based on constant motion vectors (Figure 1 shows a water vortex with motion vectors pointing in all directions along the current). The computation of affine model parameters instead in combination with a spatially varying distribution allows for the grouping of vectors belonging to the same motion pattern.
2. Objects sometimes undergo similar motion as other objects or the background. In such cases, segmentation approaches not taking into account the spatial variance of the motion will fail to separate between similarly moving objects.
3. Moving objects, which are not planar, exhibit different motion in different parts of the object due to changing depth. Also in such cases segmentation based on a constant motion field will fail to recognize all parts belonging to the moving object, e.g. a human with fast moving arms but head and legs almost at rest.
4. Frequently, there are several similar foreground objects which follow different motion patterns, e.g. cars on a road. Similarity based segmentation approaches will not assign all of them to the same class.

To summarize, automatic motion segmentation is often problematic and even for humans it is not clear, where a motion pattern begins and where it ends. Take for example neighboring vortices in water or heat flows (Figure 1) or sequences with several distinct foreground objects belonging to the same object class (Figure 4). By means of minimal user interaction such semantic problems can be overcome.

1.1   Related Work

Non-interactive motion segmentation has been studied in the literature in particular within the scope of optical flow estimation. In [1], Cremers and Soatto introduce the concept of motion competition, i.e. a variational model that, given two consecutive frames of a video, estimates the motion between the given frames and jointly segments the image domain based on the estimated motion. Therein, a parametric motion model is used and particularly the case of piecewise affine motion is considered. Their target functional can be understood as an extension of the Mumford–Shah functional [2] and the applied minimization techniques include a multiphase level set formulation based on the Vese–Chan model [3]. Brox et al. [4] propose a variational approach that combines optic flow estimation with the segmentation of the image domain into regions of similar optical flow, extending the motion competition concept to non-parametric motion and a more elaborate data term for the motion estimation while still using a multiphase level set formulation.

Independently, interactivity has proven itself as a feasible method to facilitate difficult image segmentation tasks. For instance, Bai and Sapiro [5] presented an interactive framework for image and video segmentation. Their technique calculates weighted geodesic distances to scribbles interactively provided by the user, where the weighting is based on spatial or temporal gradients. The segmentation then is obtained automatically from these distances. More related to our approach is the TVSeg algorithm by Unger et al. [6] that also incorporates user interaction in the segmentation of images into foreground and background. The actual segmentation uses an geodesic active contour model [7] that integrates the user input as local constraint and is minimized numerically in a globally optimal manner using a total variation based reformulation.

1.2   Contribution

The contribution of this paper is the introduction of locally adaptive model parameter distributions into a variational motion segmentation approach. Instead of learning a global motion vector distribution for each object, we make two important modifications. First, we do not estimate the probability of the motion vectors directly but of their motion model parameters instead. In this way, the similarity of vectors belonging to the same moving object is preserved and issue 1 solved. Second, as different objects and object parts can still exhibit varying affine motion we model a spatially variant distribution, which allows for changing motion at different image locations. We, thus, solve issues 2 to 4. The locally adaptive parameter distributions are introduced into a variational framework which allows for globally optimal segmentation results in case of two regions and near globally optimal results for more than two regions.

2   A Bayesian Approach to Motion Segmentation

Let $v : \Omega \to \mathbb{R}^2, \Omega \subset \mathbb{R}^b, b \in \mathbb{N}$ denote a given motion field. Motion segmentation is the computation of such a labeling function $u : \Omega \to \{1, .., n\}$ assigning a specific label $u(x)$ to each pixel $x \in \Omega$ based on the motion vector $v(x)$, such that the $\Omega_i = \{x \in \Omega | u(x) = i\}$ are disjoint and $\overline{\Omega} = \bigcup_{i=1}^{n} \overline{\Omega}_i$.

2.1   A Parametric Motion Field Representation

Typical motion vectors resemble specific motion patterns. The easiest pattern would be a constant planar motion, more difficult ones are for example rotations, curls or vortices with spatially varying motion vectors. Only in the first case a simple grouping of motion vectors can be successful. In order to preserve the similarity of different motion vectors belonging to the same object, we describe the motion field by means of model parameters. Similar model parameters then hint at a common motion pattern. In this paper, we assume an affine motion model and compute the affine model parameters $s : \Omega \to \mathbb{R}^6$ by solving the following minimization problem for each pixel $x \in \Omega$

$$s(x) = \arg \min_{s \in \mathbb{R}^6} \int_\Omega G_\sigma(y - x) \, |p(y) \cdot s - v(y)|^2 \, dy, \tag{1}$$

where $p(y) = \begin{pmatrix} y_1 & y_2 & 1 & 0 & 0 & 0 \\ 0 & 0 & 0 & y_1 & y_2 & 1 \end{pmatrix}$ and $G_\sigma(x)$ is a Gaussian function with variance σ and mean 0. In our experiments, we set σ to the pixel size. The optimization problem can be solved by means of a weighted least squares approach. If we only aim at the identification of particular types of affine motion we can replace the general model $p(y)$ by a more specific one. E.g. in case of vortices we consider skew symmetric affine maps, i.e. looking for a vector of five affine parameters $s : \Omega \to \mathbb{R}^5$ and replacing p by $p(y) = \begin{pmatrix} y_1 & y_2 & 1 & 0 & 0 \\ 0 & -y_1 & 0 & y_2 & 1 \end{pmatrix}$. Alternatively, one could keep s and p as they are and penalize the defect from the desired family of affine motion by an additional energy term, e.g. in our case $|s_2(x) + s_4(x)|^2$.

2.2   The Bayesian Formulation

We want to maximize the conditional probability of u in a Bayesian framework given the motion parameter field s

$$\arg \max_u \mathcal{P}(u \,|\, s) = \arg \max_u \frac{\mathcal{P}(s \,|\, u) \, \mathcal{P}(u)}{\mathcal{P}(s)} = \arg \max_u \mathcal{P}(s \,|\, u) \, \mathcal{P}(u). \tag{2}$$

Assuming that all affine parameter vectors are independent of each other – but in contrast to previous approaches not independent of space – we obtain

$$\arg \max_u \mathcal{P}(s \,|\, u) \, \mathcal{P}(u) = \arg \max_u \left(\prod_{x \in \Omega} \left(\mathcal{P}(s(x) \,|\, x, u) \right)^{dx} \right) \mathcal{P}(u), \tag{3}$$

where the exponent dx denotes an infinitesimal volume in $\mathbb{R}^b$ and assures the correct scaling for decreasing pixel size. Preserving the dependence of the model parameters on the spatial position is an indispensable prerequisite to cope with objects effected by different and frequently non constant motion patterns. Such important information is entirely lost in the traditional space-independent formulation. Consequently probability density functions that can be easily separated in parameter-location-space can overlap and make the separation of objects impossible if only the parameter space is taken into account.

Since the probability of a parameter vector is independent of labels of other pixels, we deduce from (3) that

$$\prod_{x \in \Omega} \left(\mathcal{P}(s(x) \,|\, x, u) \right)^{dx} = \prod_{i=1}^n \prod_{x \in \Omega_i} \left(\mathcal{P}(s(x) \,|\, x, u(x) = i) \right)^{dx}. \tag{4}$$

2.3   Spatially Varying Parameter Distributions

$\mathcal{P}(s(x)\,|\,x,u(x)=i)$ denotes the conditional probability of a parameter vector $s(x)$ at location x in the motion field provided x belongs to region Ω_i. These spatially varying probability distributions for each object class i are learned from user scribbles. Let $T_i := \{(x_i^j, s(x_i^j)), j = 1,..,m_i\}$ denote the set of user markings consisting of locations x_i^j and corresponding model parameter vector $s(x_i^j)$ for $x_i^j \in \Omega_i$. We can estimate the probability from user scribbles by means of the Parzen-Rosenblatt [8,9] estimator

$$\hat{\mathcal{P}}(s(x)\,,\,x|u(x)=i) = \frac{1}{m_i}\sum_{j=1}^{m_i} G_\Sigma\left((x,s(x)) - (x_i^j, s(x_i^j))\right).\qquad(5)$$

Here, G_Σ denotes the multivariate Gaussian kernel centered at the origin with covariance matrix Σ. For uniformly distributed samples this estimator converges to the true probability distribution for $m_i \to \infty$ [10]. In case of user scribbles, however, the samples are spatially not uniformly distributed. Therefore, we make use of the separability of the Gaussian kernel and choose Σ such that

$$G_\Sigma\left((x,s(x)) - (x_i^j, s(x_i^j))\right) = G_\rho(x - x_i^j)G_\sigma(s(x) - s(x_i^j))\qquad(6)$$

Commonly, the spatial variance, $G_\rho(x - x_i^j)$, has been neglected so far. We will call this previous approach the spatially invariant approach.

We now introduce a spatially variable kernel function by choosing the spatial kernel width $\rho(x)$ at image location x proportional to the distance from the k-th nearest sample point $x_{v_k} \in T_i, \rho(x) = \alpha\|x - x_{v_k}\|_2$.

$$\hat{\mathcal{P}}(s(x)\,,\,x|u(x)=i) = \frac{1}{m_i}\sum_{j=1}^{m_i} G_{\rho(x)}(x - x_i^j)G_\sigma(s(x) - s(x_i^j)).\qquad(7)$$

Thus, the influence of each sample point in T_i at a given location x is determined by the distance of the k-th nearest neighbor to x. If many sample points are close to x, $\rho(x)$ becomes small and the corresponding kernel becomes peaked. Hence, the influence of the samples further away is reduced. In contrast, if no samples are close by $G_\rho(x)$ tends towards a uniform distribution as in the spatially independent approach. Therefore, the spatially variant approach can be understood as a generalization of the original, spatially independent approach. The spatially variant approach yields a different parameter distribution for each location in the motion field, whereas the original, invariant approach yields the same distribution at all locations. Using

$$\hat{\mathcal{P}}(s(x)\,|\,x,u(x)=i) = \frac{\hat{\mathcal{P}}(s(x)\,,\,x|u(x)=i)}{\hat{\mathcal{P}}(x|u(x)=i)} = \frac{\hat{\mathcal{P}}(s(x)\,,\,x|u(x)=i)}{\int_s \hat{\mathcal{P}}(s,x|u(x)=i)ds}\qquad(8)$$

we can now derive the conditional probability of a parameter vector $s(x)$ given at location x and label i based on user scribbles T_i.

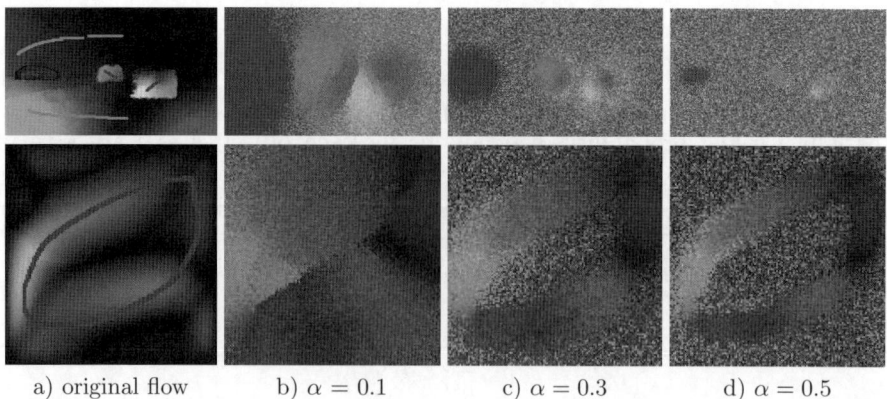

a) original flow   b) $\alpha = 0.1$ c) $\alpha = 0.3$ d) $\alpha = 0.5$

Fig. 2. The influence of the user scribbles on their neighborhood is determined by the parameter α and can be examined by means of motion synthesis. Here, for each pixel we randomly draw a motion vector from the spatially varying distribution. The smaller α the more local is the influence of the user scribbles and the more deterministic is the drawn motion vector.

The parameter α directly determines the variance of the kernel function k and, thus, the locality of the user input. The smaller α the more locally limited is the influence of the user scribbles. This effect can be examined by means of motion synthesis shown in Figure 2. Motion synthesis means that we randomly draw samples from the foreground distribution by means of the inverse distribution function. For all experiments done in Section 3, we set $\alpha = 0.3$ and $k = 10$.

2.4   The Variational Approach

To solve the optimization problem (3) we specify the prior $\mathcal{P}(u)$ favoring shorter boundaries between different regions, i.e. $\mathcal{P}(u) \propto \exp\left(-\frac{\lambda}{2} \sum_{i=1}^{n} \mathrm{Per}(\Omega_i, \Omega)\right)$, where $\mathrm{Per}(\Omega_i, \Omega)$ denotes the perimeter of Ω_i in Ω, cf. [11]. The optimization problem can be solved by minimizing its negative logarithm

$$\mathcal{E}(\Omega_1, \ldots, \Omega_n) = \frac{\lambda}{2} \sum_{i=1}^{n} \mathrm{Per}(\Omega_i, \Omega) + \sum_{i=1}^{n} \int_{\Omega_i} f_i(x)\, dx, \text{ with} \qquad (9)$$

$$f_i(x) = -\log \sum_{j=1}^{m_i} k_{\rho(x)}(x - x_i^j) k_\sigma(s(x) - s(x_i^j)) + \log \sum_{j=1}^{m_i} k_{\rho(x)}(x - x_i^j). \qquad (10)$$

Using the coarea formula in BV, the function space of bounded variation (cf. [11]), we can replace the sum of the perimeters by the total variation of u and arrive at energy minimization problem $\sum_{i=1}^{n} \int_{\Omega_i} f_i(x)\, dx + \lambda \int_{\Omega} |D\,u|\, dx \to \min$. To transform this energy minimization into a convex variational problem we apply the multilabel approach [12] in combination with [13] by Pock et al., which is solved numerically in a primal-dual-minimization scheme. To this end, the multilabel function $u : \Omega \to \{1, \ldots, n\}$ is expressed in terms of its upper level sets, i.e. $\theta_i(x) = 1$ if $u(x) \geq i + 1$ and else 0 for all $i = 1, \ldots, n - 1$, where $\theta \in \mathrm{BV}(\Omega, \{0,1\})^n$ and $\theta_0 = 1$ and $\theta_n = 0$. The final energy to be minimized is

$$\min_{\theta \in \mathcal{B}} \sup_{\xi \in \mathcal{K}} \left\{ -\lambda \sum_{i=0}^{n-1} \int_\Omega \theta_i \ \mathrm{div} \ \xi_i \ dx + \int_\Omega |\theta_i(x) - \theta_{i+1}(x)| \ f_i(x) \ dx \right\} \quad (11)$$

with $\mathcal{B}$ and $\mathcal{K}$ defined as

$$\mathcal{B} = \{\theta = (\theta_1, .., \theta_{n-1}) \in \mathrm{BV}(\Omega, \{0,1\})^{n-1} \ | \ 1 \geq \theta_1 \geq \ldots \geq \theta_{n-1} \geq 0\} \quad (12)$$

$$\mathcal{K} = \left\{ \xi = (\xi_1, .., \xi_{n-1}) \in C_c^1(\Omega, \mathbb{R}^b)^{n-1} \ \left\| \left| \sum_{i_1 \leq i \leq i_2} \xi_i(x) \right| \leq 1 \ \forall i_1 \leq i_2 \right\} \right. \quad (13)$$

where $\xi_i \in C_c^1(\Omega, \mathbb{R}^2)$ denotes the dual variable and C_c^1 the space of smooth functions with compact support.

Proposition 1. *Let $u' \in \mathcal{B}$ be the global minimizer of the original problem (11), $u^* \in \mathcal{B}$ the binarized solution of the relaxed problem and $\tilde{u} \in \tilde{\mathcal{B}}$ the result of the proposed algorithm, where*

$$\tilde{\mathcal{B}} = \{\theta = (\theta_1, .., \theta_{n-1}) \in BV(\Omega, [0,1])^{n-1} \ | \ 1 \geq \theta_1 \geq \ldots \geq \theta_{n-1} \geq 0\}. \quad (14)$$

Then an energy bound $\gamma(u^*, \tilde{u})$ exists such that $E(\tilde{u}) - E(u') \leq \gamma(u^*, \tilde{u})$.

Proof. Since $\mathcal{B} \subset \tilde{\mathcal{B}}$, we have $E(u^*) \leq E(u')$. Therefore,

$$E(\tilde{u}) - E(u') \leq E(\tilde{u}) - E(u^*) =: \gamma(u^*, \tilde{u}). \quad (15)$$

3   Results

In this section we provide experimental results for the interactive segmentation of real and synthetic motion fields. We compare four settings: model-independent and model-based (see section 2.1), spatially invariant and spatially varying distributions (see section 2.3).

3.1   Model Based vs. Non Model Based

Since motion vectors belonging to the same motion pattern often exhibit very different direction and length, it is important to segment model parameter maps instead of the motion field itself. Difficulties arise next to motion boundaries, where different motion models coincide. These situations lead to large residuals in the least squares approach (1) and can, thus, easily be detected. We set all data terms to 0 in these situations. Figure 3 shows a segmentation example, which demonstrates that segmentations based on affine parameter maps usually yield better results than segmentations based on the motion field itself. It displays four planes varying in depth, which strongly influences the speed at different locations of the planes. The parameter map reduces this effect and even reveals underlying structure and, thus, makes an (almost) correct segmentation possible.

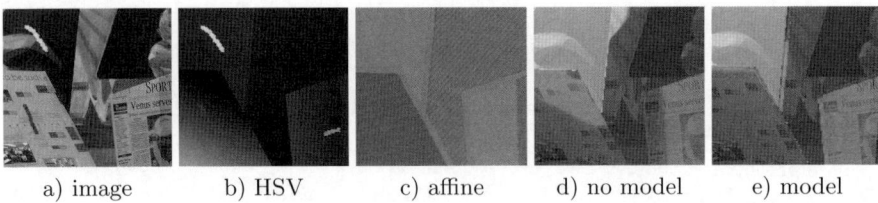

a) image   b) HSV   c) affine   d) no model   e) model

Fig. 3. Comparison of segmentation results based on the original flow field and on affine parameter maps using the spatially invariant dataterm, a) underlying image data, b) HSV-coded motion field with user scribbles, c) affine parameter map, d) segmentation based on motion only, e) segmentation based on affine parameter map

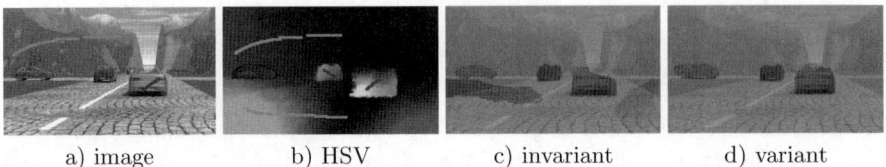

a) image   b) HSV   c) invariant   d) variant

Fig. 4. Segmentation results based on the spatially variant compared to the spatially invariant dataterm, a) underlying image data, b) HSV-coded motion field with user scribbles, c) segmentation based on spatially invariant dataterm, d) segmentation based on spatially variant dataterm

3.2 Spatially Variant vs. Spatially Invariant Distributions

There are several situations where the spatial adaptability of the estimated motion distributions is indispensable, e.g. in case of different objects exhibiting similar motion or in case of one or similar objects exhibiting different motion patterns in different locations. Figure 4 shows results for spatially variant compared to spatially invariant distributions on a dataset with three cars on a road exhibiting very different motion direction and speed. These variations are captured by the spatially variant distribution.

3.3 Model Based Spatially Variant Distributions

In order to allow for spatially changing motion models we combine the spatially variant and the model based approach by computing spatially variant parameter distributions. Figure 5 shows original HSV-coded motion fields with user scribbles, the original segmentation result without parameter maps based on spatially invariant distributions and the improved segmentation result based on parameter maps and spatially adaptive parameter distributions. In case of more than two regions, a global optimal solution cannot be guaranteed.

In our experiments, the energy gap between the binarized relaxed and the optimal solution lies between 2 and 4 % of the original energy (numerically evaluated using Proposition 1) and confirms that the solutions for more than two regions are very close to the globally optimal solution.

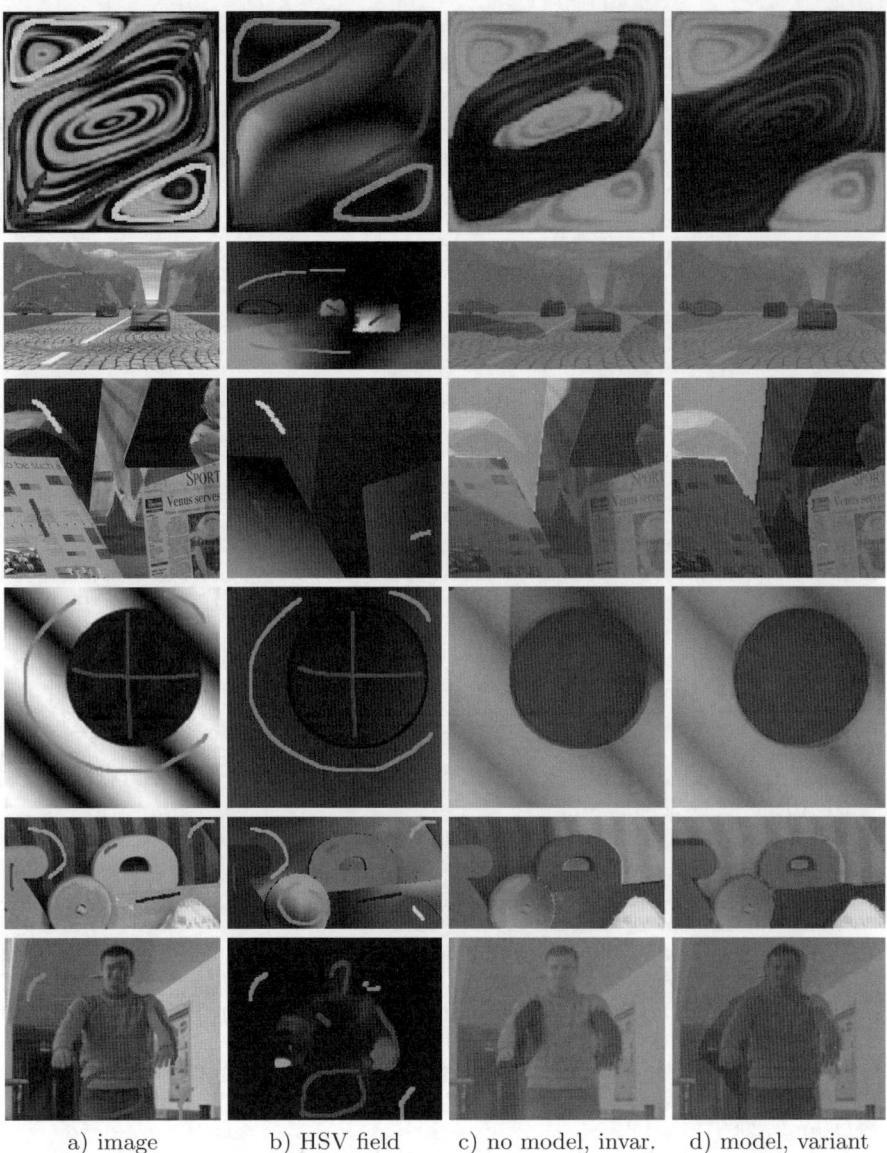

a) image   b) HSV field   c) no model, invar.   d) model, variant

Fig. 5. Segmentation results based on the spatially variant, affine parameter distributions for HSV coded motion fields. a) underlying image data, b) HSV-coded motion field, c) result of non-model based, spatially invariant approach, d) result of model-based, spatially variant approach

4   Conclusion

In this paper, we proposed an algorithm for interactive motion segmentation, which is based on spatially variant motion model parameter distributions. The suggested segmentation algorithm provides two advancements: 1) it reliably detects regions of difficult motion patterns such as vortices or curls due to its operation in the motion model parameter space, 2) it can handle even spatially varying motion patterns due to the spatial adaptivity of the parameter distributions. Few user indications are sufficient to accurately segment objects with strongly varying motion. The approach is formulated as a convex energy minimization problem, which yields the global optimum for two regions and nearly optimal results for more than two regions.

References

1. Cremers, D., Soatto, S.: Motion Competition: A variational framework for piecewise parametric motion segmentation. Int. J. of Comp. Vis. 62(3), 249–265 (2005)
2. Mumford, D., Shah, J.: Optimal approximations by piecewise smooth functions and associated variational problems. Comm. Pure Appl. Math. 42, 577–685 (1989)
3. Vese, L., Chan, T.: A multiphase level set framework for image processing using the Mumford–Shah functional. Int. J. of Comp. Vis. 50(3), 271–293 (2002)
4. Brox, T., Bruhn, A., Weickert, J.: Variational motion segmentation with level sets. In: Leonardis, A., Bischof, H., Pinz, A. (eds.) ECCV 2006. LNCS, vol. 3951, pp. 471–483. Springer, Heidelberg (2006)
5. Bai, X., Sapiro, G.: A geodesic framework for fast interactive image and video segmentation and matting. In: Eleventh IEEE International Conference on Computer Vision (ICCV 2007) (2007)
6. Unger, M., Pock, T., Cremers, D., Bischof, H.: TVSeg - Interactive total variation based image segmentation. In: British Machine Vision Conference (BMVC), Leeds, UK (September 2008)
7. Caselles, V., Kimmel, R., Sapiro, G.: Geodesic active contours. Int. J. of Comp. Vis. 22(1), 61–79 (1997)
8. Rosenblatt, M.: Remarks on some nonparametric estimates of a density function. Annals of Mathematical Statistics 27, 832–837 (1956)
9. Parzen, E.: On estimation of a probability density function and mode. Annals of Mathematical Statistics 33, 1065–1076 (1962)
10. Silverman, B.W.: Density estimation for statistics and data analysis. Chapman and Hall, London (1992)
11. Ambrosio, L., Fusco, N., Pallara, D.: Functions of bounded variation and free discontinuity problems. Oxford Mathematical Monographs. Oxford University Press, Oxford (2000)
12. Pock, T., Chambolle, A., Bischof, H., Cremers, D.: A convex relaxation approach for computing minimal partitions. In: IEEE Conference on Computer Vision and Pattern Recognition (CVPR), Miami, Florida (2009)
13. Pock, T., Cremers, D., Bischof, H., Chambolle, A.: An algorithm for minimizing the piecewise smooth mumford-shah functional. In: IEEE Int. Conf. on Computer Vision, Kyoto, Japan (2009)

On-Line Multi-view Forests for Tracking*

Christian Leistner, Martin Godec, Amir Saffari, and Horst Bischof

Institute for Computer Graphics and Vision
Graz University of Technology, Austria
{leistner,godec,saffari,bischof}@icg.tugraz.at

Abstract. A successful approach to tracking is to on-line learn discriminative classifiers for the target objects. Although these tracking-by-detection approaches are usually fast and accurate they easily drift in case of putative and self-enforced wrong updates. Recent work has shown that classifier-based trackers can be significantly stabilized by applying semi-supervised learning methods instead of supervised ones. In this paper, we propose a novel on-line multi-view learning algorithm based on random forests. The main idea of our approach is to incorporate multi-view learning inside random forests and update each tree with individual label estimates for the unlabeled data. Our method is fast, easy to implement, benefits from parallel computing architectures and inherently exploits multiple views for learning from unlabeled data. In the tracking experiments, we outperform the state-of-the-art methods based on boosting and random forests.

1 Introduction

Tracking of a priori unknown objects is still a big challenges in computer vision. Despite the huge amount of research spent on this task it is still hard to design robust tracking systems that can achieve human-level performance. Visual trackers have to cope with all variations that occur in natural scenes such as shape and appearance changes, different illuminations as well as varying poses or partial occlusions. Numerous methods to approach the tracking tasks have been proposed, such as global template-based trackers, shape-based methods, probabilistic models using mean-shift, particle filtering, local key-point based trackers, or flow-based trackers. See also [1] for a detailed review.

A recently dominating trend is to apply classifiers – trained on object versus background – to track objects because they are able to deliver highly accurate results in real-time. Such tracking-by-detection systems [2] usually train a classifier at the very first frame versus its local background and perform re-detection in the succeeding frames. In order to handle rapid appearance and illumination changes, they use on-line classifiers that learn the target object based on their own predictions, *e.g.*, [3]. However, as these classifiers perform self-learning it is difficult to decide autonomously where exactly to take the positive and negative

---

* This work has been supported by the Austrian FFG project MobiTrick (825840) and Outlier (820923) under the FIT-IT program.

M. Goesele et al. (Eds.): DAGM 2010, LNCS 6376, pp. 493–502, 2010.

updates, respectively. Even if the object is tracked correctly, the alignment may not be perfect, which can lead to slightly wrong updates of the tracker (*a.k.a* label jitter). If these errors accumulate over time and self-reinforce the classifier in its wrong decisions, the tracker can easily drift [4].

Recent approaches try to tackle the drifting problem by formulating the tracking-by-detection task as one-shot semi-supervised learning. For instance, Grabner *et al.* [5] proposed an on-line semi-supervised boosting algorithm (On-line SemiBoost) where supervised updates are only performed at the beginning, *i.e.*, the first frame. All the subsequent frames are considered as unlabeled data used in order to regularize the learner with an unsupervised loss function. Although this method has shown to be less susceptible to drifting and is still more adaptive than a static classifier, it looses the capability of self-learning classifiers to adapt fast in case of rapid appearance changes. Also highlighting this problem of Online SemiBoost, recently Babenko *et al.* [6] formulated the tracking task as a multiple-instance learning (MIL) problem. Using MIL, the classifier in principle is still performing self-learning; however, the allowed positive update area around the current tracker can be increased and the classifier resolves the ambiguities by itself, yielding a tracker that is more robust than a pure supervised learner but less inertial than SemiBoost.

Another semi-supervised learning method that has been recently applied to tracking [7] is co-training, where the main idea is that two classifiers train each other on unlabeled data using distinct views [8]. Co-training can be very powerful but has the main drawback that it requires classifiers which are conditional independent given the class in order to converge, which is hard to fulfill in practice. One way to weaken this condition is to use two different classifiers [9] instead of different sufficient views. However, since this is still often not stable enough [10] showed that for such an approach it is necessary to take at least three classifiers. In practice, using different kinds of classifiers is complicated because it is still an open research problem how to compare the outputs. That is, the classifiers need to yield comparable performance in order to train each other. Also, the computing overhead grows with the number of classifiers and not for all of the learners on-line algorithms exist. Hence, what we need in practice is a single classifier approach that is able to emulate the multi-view robustness of using several classifiers.

In this work, we propose a novel on-line semi-supervised learning approach based on random forests. The method is inherently able to learn from multiple views and is thus called *MVForests*. The motivation for taking random forests [11] for our approach stems from the facts that they are fast and accurate learners, inherently parallel and multiclass capable and less susceptible to class-label noise. We grow a common on-line random forest, similar to the recently proposed method by Saffari et al [12], and hence during evaluation our algorithm is identical to [12]. However, for learning, our method is able to exploit both labeled and unlabeled data, where the latter one is necessary in order to increase the stability of the tracking results. In order to incorporate the unlabeled data, we create a multi-view learning setting for each of the individual trees; that is, each tree is trained individually with a possibly different set of label predictions for the unlabeled data. In particular, each tree is trained by a random sub-set of the remaining trees. Thereby, we guarantee that no single tree is performing self-learning and due to the random selection of trees we further achieve that no single tree is provided with the same label estimates for the unlabeled data set, which preserves the diversity among the trees. We incorporate multiple features into learning by restricting each tree to a subset of feature types. For instance, if we use color features and simple Haar features, trees of the type Haar features are trained by color-trees and vice versa. This setting can be extended to an arbitrary number of features. However, as we will show in the tracking experiments, our method is able to deliver highly accurate results even when using a single feature type. Our algorithm has several advantages: First, it provides an easy, fast an inherent way to learn from multiple views. This is necessary in order to ensure repeatability and real-time performance. Second, since we use more than two learners, we have weaker theoretical conditions in order to show convergence of our method [10]. As we will show in the experiments, our method outperforms the state-of-the-art tracking methods based on boosting and, on average, performs better than using fully self-learned random-forests [12] or off-line random forests [13].

The reminder of this paper is as follows. In the following section, we will introduce the basic notations and shortly review related work. Then, in Section 3, we will introduce our novel on-line learning method. We will evaluate our method on the task of visual object tracking in Section 4. Section 5 concludes the paper and discusses ideas for future work.

2   Notations and Related Work

In supervised learning one deals with a labeled dataset $\mathcal{D}^L \subseteq \mathcal{X} \times \mathcal{Y} = \{(\mathbf{x}_1, y_1), \ldots, (\mathbf{x}_{|\mathcal{D}^L|}, y_{|\mathcal{D}^L|})\}$, where $\mathbf{x}_i \in \mathcal{X} = \mathbb{R}^P$ and $y_i \in \mathcal{Y} = \{+1, -1\}$. In contrast, unsupervised methods aim to find an interesting (natural) structure in $\mathcal{X}$ using only unlabeled input data $\mathcal{D}^U \subseteq \mathcal{X} = \{\mathbf{x}_1, \ldots, \mathbf{x}_{|\mathcal{D}^U|}\}$. Although supervised learners usually yield better results, most of the time unlabeled data can be obtained significantly easier than labeled samples. Hence, there exist increased interest in semi-supervised learning methods [14], such as co-training [8], which are able to exploit both labeled $\mathcal{D}^L$ and unlabeled $\mathcal{D}^U$ data. In co-training, the main idea is that two initial classifiers h_1 and h_2 are trained on labeled data $(\mathbf{x}_i^1, y_i), (\mathbf{x}_i^2, y_i) \in \mathcal{D}^L$, where $\mathbf{x}^1$ and $\mathbf{x}^2$ shows two views of the same data point. Then, these classifiers update each other using the unlabeled data set $\mathcal{D}^U$, if one classifier is confident on a sample whereas the other one is not. Co-training classifiers minimize the error on the labeled samples while increasing the agreement on the unlabeled data. Thus, the unlabeled data helps to improve the margin of the classifiers and to decrease the generalization error [15]. The approach has proven to converge, if two assumptions hold: (i) the error rate of each classifier is low, which means each classifier is in principle able to solve the given task, and (ii) the views must be conditionally independent [8]. Especially the second condition is more of a theoretical requirement and is hard to fulfill in practice. However, the independence condition can be relaxed (*e.g.*, [16,10,15]), for instance, by applying more than two classifiers. If more than two classifiers are used, co-training becomes multi-view learning[1]. For practical usage, this means that co-training can even be applied if the learners are slightly correlated.

Computer vision naturally offers many physical "real-world" views, which can be exploited by co-training and multi-view learning. For instance, [17,18] combined different simple cues based on shape, appearance, or motion to train visual classifiers. Co-training has also been applied to tracking. For instance, Tang et al. [19] used an SVM-based co-training approach that was later extended by Yu *et al.* [20]. Recently [7] presented an on-line boosting approach which outperforms the previous methods based on SVMs.

2.1   On-line Random Forests

Random Forests (RFs) were originally proposed by Amit and D. Geman [21], extended by Breiman [11] and consist of ensembles of T independent decision trees $f_t(\mathbf{x}) : \mathcal{X} \to \mathcal{Y} = \{1, \ldots, K\}$. For a forest $\mathcal{F} = \{f_1, \cdots, f_T\}$ the predictive confidence can be defined as $F_k(\mathbf{x}) = \frac{1}{T} \sum_{t=1}^{T} p_t(k|\mathbf{x})$, where $p_t(k|\mathbf{x})$ is the estimated density of class labels of the leaf of the t-th tree, where sample $\mathbf{x}$ resides. A decision is made by simply taking the maximum over all individual probabilities of the trees for a class k with $C(\mathbf{x}) = \arg\max_{k \in \mathcal{Y}} F_k(\mathbf{x})$. Breiman [11] showed that the generalization error of random forests is upper bounded by

$$ GE \leq \bar{\rho}\frac{1 - s^2}{s^2}, \tag{1} $$

where $\bar{\rho}$ is the mean correlation between pairs of trees in the forest[2] and s is the strength of the ensemble (*i.e.*, the expected value of the margin over the entire distribution). In order to decrease the correlation of the trees, each tree is provided with a slightly different subset of training data by subsampling with replacement from the entire training set, *a.k.a* bagging [22]. Trees are trained recursively, where each split node randomly selects binary tests from the feature vector and selects the best according to an impurity measurement. The information gain after node splitting is usually measured with

$$ \Delta H = -\frac{|I_l|}{|I_l| + |I_r|} H(I_l) - \frac{|I_r|}{|I_l| + |I_r|} H(I_r), \tag{2} $$

where I_l and I_r are the left and right subsets of the training data, respectively. $H(I) = -\sum_{i=1}^{K} p_i^j \log(p_i^j)$ is the entropy of the classes in the node and p_i^j is

---

[1] Note that in the literature the term "multi-view learning" is mainly used for learning from two views or classifiers, respectively. In this work, we distinguish between the two terms in a way that "co-training" only uses two views and is a special case of multi-view learning, where in the latter case always more than two views are used.

[2] The correlation is measured in terms of the similarities of the predictions.

the label density of class i in node j. The recursive training continues until a maximum depth is reached or no further information gain is possible.

RFs have demonstrated to be better or at least comparable to other state-of-the-art methods in both classification [11,23] and clustering [24]. Especially, the speed in both training and evaluation is one of their main appealing properties. Additionally, since the trees are trained and evaluated independently, RFs can easily be parallelized, which makes them interesting for multi-core and GPU implementations [25]. Finally, compared to boosting and other ensemble methods, RFs are more robust against label noise [11]. This resistance to noise, is especially important when learning from unlabeled data where wrong label estimates are an inherent problem. These advantages of random forests have also led to increased interest in the computer vision domain. For instance, recently [26] presented an efficient object detection framework based on random forests, [27] presented a real-time algorithm for semantic segmentation based on randomized trees, and [28] presented state-of-the-art categorization results using RFs. Randomized trees have also successfully been applied to visual tracking, either in batch mode using keypoints [13] or on-line using tracking-by-detection [12].

Random forests, as reviewed above, is an off-line learning method. Recently, Saffari *et al.* [12] proposed an on-line version of RFs, which allows to use them as on-line classifiers in tracking-by-detection systems. Since recursive training of decision trees is hard to do in on-line learning, they propose a tree-growing procedure similar to evolving-trees [29]. The algorithm starts with trees consisting only of root nodes and randomly selected node tests f_i and thresholds θ_i. Each node estimates an impurity measure based on the Gini index ($G_i = \sum_{i=1}^{K} p_i^j(1 - p_i^j)$) on-line, where p_i^j is the label density of class i in node K. Then, after each on-line update the possible information gain ΔG during a potential node split is measured. If ΔG exceeds a given threshold β, the node becomes a split node, *i.e.*, is not updated any more and generates two child leaf nodes. The growing proceeds until a maximum depth is reached. Even when the tree has grown to its full size, all leaf nodes are further on-line updated. The method is simple to implement and has shown to converge fast to its offline counterpart. Additionally, [12] also showed that the classifier is faster and more noise-robust compared to boosting, which makes it an ideal candidate for our tracking system.

3   On-Line Multi-view Training

As we have seen in the previous section, co-training is a popular approach in order to incorporate unlabeled data and has been used in many computer vision tasks. In this section, we will introduce a novel multi-view learning approach called *MVForests*, which extends the idea of co-training to an arbitrary number of views using random forests.

In particular, consider a random forest $\mathcal{F} = \{f_1, \cdots, f_T\}$, where T is the number of trees. Further, assume an on-line setting, where the training samples $\mathbf{x}_i$ arrive sequentially. If $\mathbf{x}_i$ is provided along with its class label y_i we can simply update the forest using [12]. If $\mathbf{x}_i$ is an unlabeled sample, we have to estimate its label $\tilde{y}_i$; however, without using self-learning to reduce drifting. Therefore, we propose the following strategy: For each tree f_t we randomly select with replacement a sub-forest $\mathcal{F}_t^*$, with $|\mathcal{F}_t^*| = T$, *i.e.*, the forest consists of the same amount of trees as the original forest. This strategy can be interpreted as performing bagging on trees and results in forests where some trees of $\mathcal{F}$ are used multiple times, whereas on average one third (see [22]) of the total available trees are left out. We call the sub-forest $\mathcal{F}_t^*$ for the tth tree *parent forest*. Note that for each tree its corresponding parent forest indices are created at the beginning of the learning and are kept fix during the on-line learning. Then, each f_t uses its corresponding parent forest in order to predict the label for $\mathbf{x}_i$; *i.e.*,

$$\tilde{y}_i^t = \arg\max_{k \in \mathcal{Y}} \mathcal{F}_{t,k}^*(\mathbf{x}_i). \tag{3}$$

We further use the confidence-rated predictions of each parent in order to encode uncertainties about a label in form of weight estimates. In particular, we take the confidence of the parent ensemble as weights in form of $\tilde{w}_i = \frac{1}{T}\sum_{t=1}^T p_t(\tilde{y}_i|\mathbf{x})$. For evaluation and testing, we take the original forest $\mathcal{F}$. The overall algorithm is depicted in detail in Algorithm 1.

Algorithm 1. On-line Multi-View Forests

Require: Sequential training example $\langle \mathbf{x}_i, y_i \rangle$ or $\langle \mathbf{x}_i \rangle$
Require: The size of the forest: T
1: // For all trees
2: **for** t from 1 to T **do**
3:    //sub-sample parent tree ensemble
4:    $\mathcal{F}_t^* \leftarrow$ SubSampleTreeIndices(T)
5: **end for**
6: // For each arriving sample $\mathbf{x}_i$
7: **for** t from 1 to T **do**
8:    **if** $\exists y_i$ **then**
9:        $f_t \leftarrow updateTree(f_t, \mathbf{x}_i, y_i)$
10:    **else**
11:        // Estimate label and weight
12:        $\tilde{y}_i^t = \arg\max_{k \in \mathcal{Y}} evalForest(\mathcal{F}_t^*, \mathbf{x}_i)$
13:        $\tilde{w}_i^t = getForestConfidence(\mathcal{F}_t^*, \mathbf{x}_i, \tilde{y}_i^t)$
14:        $f_t \leftarrow updateTree(f_t, \mathbf{x}_i, \tilde{y}_i^t, \tilde{w}_i^t)$
15:    **end if**
16: **end for**
17: Output the forest $\mathcal{F}$.

Discussion. Although a random forest acts from the outside as a single classifier, it consists already of a committee of classifiers, *i.e.*, its trees. This suggests to bring multi-view learning inside a forest. However, there are two important things that have to be considered: first, in order to get reliable label predictions for training each tree, we have to create sub-trees or parents that are strong enough to deliver accurate predictions. It is clear that for a tree f_t the strongest prediction that it can get out of the forest, though excluding itself, consists of the averaged prediction of the rest of the trees, i.e., $\sum_m^T \mathbb{I}(t \neq m)f_t$, where $\mathbb{I}$ is the indicator function. However, it is also clear that if T is a large number, leaving out one tree will not change the overall predictions at all, which means that using this strategy each tree will get the same label estimates for $\mathbf{x}_i$. Therefore, MVForests create the parent forests in form of bagged classifiers from the entire forest, which results in parents where some trees are taken eventually several times and some trees are not taken at all. On average, $1 - \frac{1}{e}$ non-identical trees form a parent ensemble. We enforce the agreement of the trees on the unlabeled data, which overall increases the classification margin and improves the generalization. This strategy ensures that the predictions are reliable but not the same, thus yielding a typical multi-view setting, which overall preserves the diversity among the trees (see also Eq. (1)). To the best of our knowledge, this is the first approach that applies the bagging idea of [22] on sampling from a large amount of classifiers and not data, as in the typical setting.

Our work is related to the tri-training algorithm [10], where the main idea is to take three classifiers h_i and the ith classifier is trained by the remaining two classifiers if they agree on the prediction of an unlabeled datum and simulatenously each h_i has an error below a given threshold. MVForests differ from tri-training in three important aspects: (i) MVForests are not limited to three views but perform on an arbitrary number of views, only limited by the number T of trees that form an ensemble. (ii) Each unlabeled sample is incorporated, regardless of the agreement and the error of concomitant trees, which makes our approach much simpler. (iii) MVForest is an on-line algorithm. A second approach, which is related to MVForests is the recently proposed DAS-RF algorithm [30]; however, in this work an off-line optimization procedure is used which needs several parameters to be set, and it is not designed to learn on-line from multiple views.

4   Experiments

Within this section, we demonstrate the performance of our learning method for the task of object tracking, where we assume no prior knowledge about the object class available except its initial position. We use eight publicly available sequences including variations in illumination, pose, scale, rotation and appearance, and partial occlusions. The sequences *Sylvester* and *David* are taken from [31] and *Face Occlusion 1* is taken from [32], respectively. *Face occlusion 2*, *Girl*, *Tiger1*, *Tiger2* and *Coke* are taken from [6]. All video frames are gray scale and of size 320×240. To show the real accuracy of the compared tracking methods, we use the overlap-criterion of the VOC Challenge [33],

500   C. Leistner et al.

which is defined as $A_{overlap} = R_T \cap R_{GT}/R_T \cup R_{GT}$, where R_T is the tracking rectangle and R_{GT} the groundtruth. We compare MVForests to supervised on-line random forests (On-line RF) [12], off-line random forests (Off-line RF) [13], MILBoost [6], SemiBoost [5] and CoBoost [7]. We skip the related SVM-based co-training approaches as they were all outperformed by CoBoost. All methods are implemented in C++ and run in real-time, *i.e.*, $> 25 fps$. Note that although MVForest are able to incorporate an arbitrary number of features, to ensure fair comparison in our experiments we evaluate the tracking performance of the different approaches using only Haar-features. We use forest sizes of 100 trees, with a maximum depth of 15. For the boosting classifiers, we use 2×50 selectors for CoBoost and the original settings for MILBoost [6]. We initialize the classifiers using virtual samples generated out of the first frame [13], 10 samples for on-line approaches and 500 for off-line approaches, respectively.

As depicted in Table 1, our approach is able to automatically cover the gap between supervised on-line training [12] and off-line training [13]. MVForests perform best in four out of eight sequences, and second best in three. Notably, we frequently outperform MILBoost, which is currently known to be the best performing method on these sequences. We also outperform CoBoost, the current state-of-the-art method for on-line co-training. Please refer to supplamentary material for the result videos.

Discussion. Semi-supervised tracking methods virtually increase the tracking robustness by updating with lower weights in case of reduced confidence. The dilemma, however, arises in case of rapid appearance changes because this also results in lower confidence measurements. In such cases, semi-supervised trackers usually perform inferior to supervised ones [6]. The tracking results suggest that our method is a good compromise in this ambivalent setting, in terms that MVForest reduce their update weights in case of occlusions but due to the multi-view set-up are also adaptive when it comes to appearance changes. See also Figure 1 for a further illustration of MVForest's update behavior.

Table 1. Accuracy comparison of different approaches using single views measured using the Pascal VOC overlap criterion. Best performing method marked bold-face. Second best method marked underlined.

Sequence	MVForest	CoBoost	On-line RF	Off-line RF	MILBoost	SemiBoost
sylv	0.54	0.53	0.53	0.50	**0.60**	0.46
david	**0.71**	0.52	0.69	0.32	0.57	0.31
faceocc2	0.78	**0.79**	0.72	**0.79**	0.65	0.63
tiger1	**0.51**	0.41	0.38	0.34	0.49	0.17
tiger2	0.45	0.13	0.43	0.32	**0.53**	0.08
coke	0.28	**0.41**	0.35	0.15	0.33	0.08
faceocc1	**0.79**	0.78	0.71	0.77	0.60	0.71
girl	**0.77**	0.69	0.70	0.74	0.53	0.69

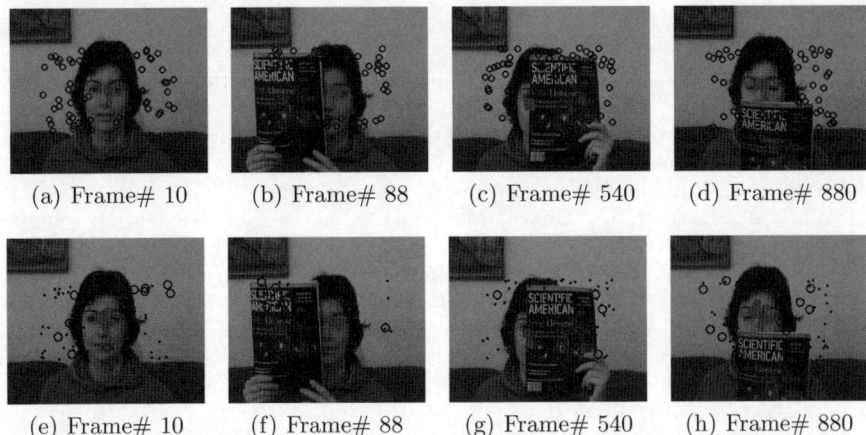

| (a) Frame# 10 | (b) Frame# 88 | (c) Frame# 540 | (d) Frame# 880 |

| (e) Frame# 10 | (f) Frame# 88 | (g) Frame# 540 | (h) Frame# 880 |

Fig. 1. Comparison of supervised updates ((a) to (d)) and MVForest's updates ((e) to (h)) (red circles: positive updates; blue circles: negative updates; circle radius corresponds to sample update weights). MVForests inherently update with smaller weight if the sample is noisy whereas supervised updates are hand-crafted and always weighted equally high (best viewed in color).

5 Conclusion and Future Work

In this paper, we have proposed a novel on-line multi-view learning algorithm using random forests called MVForests. MVForests learn from unlabeled data by emulating a multi-view setting inside the random forests, where each tree receives label estimates by a randomly selected sub-set of the trees forming the forest. We outperform the state-of-the-art learning methods on the task of visual object tracking. It should be noted that our multi-view learning approach is not limited to RFs, and in principle, can be applied to any ensemble of classifiers. MVForests are by no means limited to tracking. Hence, in future work, we plan to apply our method to additional vision problems such object detection and classification.

References

1. Yilmaz, A., Javed, O., Shah, M.: Object tracking: A survey. ACM Comput. (2006)
2. Avidan, S.: Ensemble tracking. PAMI 29(2), 261–271 (2007)
3. Grabner, H., Bischof, H.: On-line boosting and vision. In: CVPR (2006)
4. Matthews, I., Ishikawa, T., Baker, S.: The template update problem. IEEE Trans. on Pattern Analysis and Machine Intelligence 26, 810–815 (2004)
5. Grabner, H., Leistner, C., Bischof, H.: On-line semi-supervised boosting for robust tracking. In: Forsyth, D., Torr, P., Zisserman, A. (eds.) ECCV 2008, Part I. LNCS, vol. 5302, pp. 234–247. Springer, Heidelberg (2008)
6. Babenko, B., Yang, M.H., Belongie, S.: Visual tracking with online multiple instance learning. In: CVPR (2009)
7. Liu, R., Cheng, J., Lu, H.: A robust boosting tracker with minimum error bound in a co-training framework. In: ICCV (2009)

8. Blum, A., Mitchell, T.: Combining labeled and unlabeled data with co-training. In: Proc. COLT, pp. 92–100 (1998)
9. Goldman, S., Zhou, Y.: Enhancing supervised learning with unlabeled data. In: ICML (2000)
10. Zhou, Z.H., Li, M.: Tri-training exploiting unlabeled data using three classifiers. IEEE Transactions on Knowledge and Data Engineering 17(11), 1529–1541 (2005)
11. Breiman, L.: Random forests. Machine Learning (2001)
12. Saffari, A., Leistner, C., Godec, M., Santner, J., Bischof, H.: On-line random forests. In: OLCV (2009)
13. Lepetit, V., Fua, P.: Keypoint recognition using randomized trees. In: CVPR (2006)
14. Zhu, X., Goldberg, A.B.: Introduction to Semi-Supervised Learning, 3rd edn. Synthesis Lectures on Artificial Intelligence and Machine Learning. Morgan & Claypool (January 2009)
15. Abney, S.: Semi-Supervised Learning for Computational Linguistics, 1st edn. Computer Science and Data Analysis. Chapman & Hall/CRC, Boca Raton (2007)
16. Balcan, M.F., Blum, A.: Yang, K.: Co-training and expansion: Towards bridging theory and practice. In: NIPS. MIT Press, Cambridge (2004)
17. Levin, A., Viola, P., Freund, Y.: Unsupervised improvement of visual detectors using co-training. In: Proc. IEEE ICCV, vol. I, pp. 626–633 (2003)
18. Javed, O., Ali, S., Shah, M.: Online detection and classification of moving objects using progressively improving detectors. In: CVPR
19. Tang, F., Brennan, S., Zao, Q., Tao, W.: Co-tracking using semi-supervised support machines. In: ICCV (2007)
20. Yu, Q., Dinh, T.B., Medioni, G.: Online tracking and reacquisition co-trained generative and discriminative trackers. In: Forsyth, D., Torr, P., Zisserman, A. (eds.) ECCV 2008, Part II. LNCS, vol. 5303, pp. 678–691. Springer, Heidelberg (2008)
21. Geman, Y.A.D.: Shape quantization and recognition with randomized trees. Neural Computation (1996)
22. Breiman, L.: Bagging predictors. Machine Learning 2(24), 49–64 (1996)
23. Caruana, R., Karampatziakis, N., Yessenalina, A.: An empirical evaluation of supervised learning in high dimensions. In: ICML (2008)
24. Moosmann, F., Triggs, B., Jurie, F.: Fast discriminative visual codebooks using randomized clustering forests. In: NIPS, pp. 985–992 (2006)
25. Sharp, T.: Implementing decision trees and forests on a gpu. In: Forsyth, D., Torr, P., Zisserman, A. (eds.) ECCV 2008, Part IV. LNCS, vol. 5305, pp. 595–608. Springer, Heidelberg (2008)
26. Gall, J., Lempinsky, V.: Class-specific hough forests for object detection. In: CVPR (2009)
27. Shotton, J., Johnson, M., Cipolla, R.: Semantic texton forests for image catergorization and segmentation. In: CVPR (2008)
28. Bosch, A., Zisserman, A., Munoz, X.: Image classification using random forests and ferns. In: ICCV (2007)
29. Pakkanen, J., Iivarinen, J., Oja, E.: The evolving tree—a novel self-organizing network for data analysis. Neural Process. Lett. 20(3), 199–211 (2004)
30. Leistner, C., Saffari, A., Santner, J., Bischof, H.: Semi-supervised random forests. In: ICCV (2009)
31. Ross, D., Lim, J., Lin, R.S., Yang, M.H.: Incremental learning for robust visual tracking. In: IJCV (2008)
32. Adam, A., Rivlin, E., Shimshoni, I.: Robust fragments-based tracking using the integral histogram. In: CVPR (2006)
33. Everingham, M., Gool, L.V., Williams, C.K.I., Winn, J., Zisserman, A.: The pascal visual object class challenge 2007. In: VOC (2007)

Probabilistic Multi-class Scene Flow Segmentation for Traffic Scenes

Alexander Barth[1], Jan Siegemund[1], Annemarie Meißner[2],
Uwe Franke[2], and Wolfgang Förstner[1]

[1] University of Bonn, Department of Photogrammetry, Germany
[2] Daimler AG, Group Research, Sindelfingen, Germany

Abstract. A multi-class traffic scene segmentation approach based on
scene flow data is presented. Opposed to many other approaches using
color or texture features, our approach is purely based on dense depth and
3D motion information. Using prior knowledge on tracked objects in the
scene and the pixel-wise uncertainties of the scene flow data, each pixel
is assigned to either a particular *moving object* class (tracked/unknown
object), the ground surface, or static background. The global topological
order of classes, such as *objects are above ground*, is locally integrated
into a conditional random field by an ordering constraint. The proposed
method yields very accurate segmentation results on challenging real
world scenes, which we made publicly available for comparison.

1 Introduction

Traffic scene segmentation and categorization is an active field of research in
the computer vision community. Remarkable results on monocular images using
color, intensity, or texture features have been achieved, e.g., by [1], [2], or [3].
Additionally, structure from motion is used for labeling static scenes in [4]. Traffic
scenes are highly challenging since the cameras are (quickly) moving through
an unknown environment with uncontrolled illumination or weather conditions,
highly dynamic interaction of multiple objects, and a variety of different object
classes in the scene. In practice, reliable color information is often not available.

Recent advances in *scene flow* computation allow for the reconstruction of
dense 3D motion fields from stereo image sequences in real-time [5], [6]. With
such methods, depth and motion information is available at almost every pixel in
the image, enabling new opportunities for object detection and scene segmentation. In [7], Wedel et al. use graphcuts to separate moving points from stationary
points in the scene flow data (two class problem).

We extend this idea to a multi-class segmentation problem, replacing the
threshold-based reasoning as in [7] by a probabilistic hypothesis competition.
At this, we focus on traffic scenes where the vision sensor is mounted behind
the windshield of the *ego-vehicle*, which moves in a mainly static, but unknown
structured environment. In our model, the world consists of a ground surface
(typically the road), static elevated obstacles on the ground surface (buildings,
traffic signs,...), as well as a finite number of independently moving objects

M. Goesele et al. (Eds.): DAGM 2010, LNCS 6376, pp. 503–512, 2010.

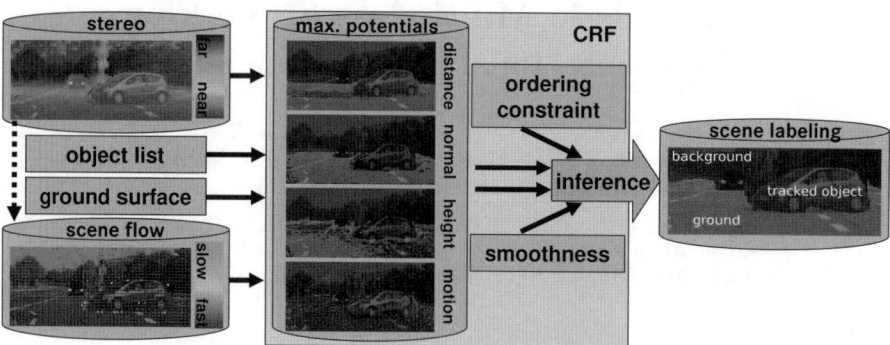

Fig. 1. System overview. Motion, depth, height, and surface normal features are extracted from 3D scene flow data and transferred into CRF class potentials for (known) moving objects, the ground surface, and the static background. Both smoothness and ordering constraints are integrated at the inference step.

(other cars, pedestrians, bicyclists,...). The objective of our approach is to provide a pixel-wise labeling, assigning each pixel in the current image to one of the disjunct classes *static background/obstacle, ground,* or *moving object.*

The moving object class is further separated into a set of *known objects,* which have been tracked before, and an *unknown moving object* class. This means, we directly exploit object information (position, orientation, velocity,...), available from previous time steps. The indiviual likelihood of each pixel belonging to a particular class based on the scene flow data is defined. The interaction of neighboring pixels is incorporated by modeling the problem as a Conditional Random Field (CRF), a widely used representation for segmentation problems. Beside requiring smoothness of the segmentation result, we integrate model knowledge on the scene topology such as **objects are above the ground** into our labeling. Fig. 1 gives an overview on the system.

Defining the potentials based on scene flow features has several advantages compared to similar stereo vision based approaches using gray value distances, for example, [8]. Issues such as robustness to varying illumination or denoising of the flow field are already addressed at the scene flow computation level. The segmentation directly benefits from all improvements at this level without changing the actual segmentation approach. Furthermore, we are able to apply the same segmentation algorithms to scene flow data provided by other sensors.

We will first introduce the generic mathematical framework in Section 2. Then, an exemplary realization of the CRF potential functions is given in Section 3. The system will be evaluated based on challenging real-world scenes in Section 4. Section 5 concludes the results and gives an outlook on future work.

2   General CRF Segmentation Framework

Let $L = \{l_1, \ldots, l_I\}$ denote a labeling for a given image, where the label $l_i \in \{C_1, \ldots C_J\}$ assigns a particular class C_j to the i-th pixel. The objective is to find a labeling L^* from the set of all possible labelings, $\mathcal{L}$, that maximizes the conditional probability $p(L|\boldsymbol{z}, \boldsymbol{\Theta})$, i.e., $L^* = \arg\max_{L \in \mathcal{L}} p(L|\boldsymbol{z}, \boldsymbol{\Theta})$. Here, the feature vector $\boldsymbol{z}$, with $\boldsymbol{z} = [\boldsymbol{z}_1^{\mathsf{T}}, \ldots, \boldsymbol{z}_I^{\mathsf{T}}]^{\mathsf{T}}$, contains the pixel-wise input data for the segmentation process, and $\boldsymbol{\Theta}$ represents a set of global parameters. We model $p(L|\boldsymbol{z}, \boldsymbol{\Theta})$ as CRF [9] aligned to the pixel grid with a maximum clique size of two as

$$\log(p(L|\boldsymbol{z}, \boldsymbol{\Theta})) = \sum_{i=1}^{I} \Phi(l_i, \boldsymbol{z}_i, \boldsymbol{\Theta}) + \sum_{(s,t) \in \mathcal{N}} \Psi(l_s, l_t, \boldsymbol{z}_s, \boldsymbol{z}_t, \boldsymbol{\Theta}). \qquad (1)$$

In our model, the positive function Φ defines the unary potentials for each class C_j. At this point it is assumed that the potential at pixel i depends only on the parameters and the feature data at this position. The potentials between neighboring pixels are given by the positive function Ψ, where $\mathcal{N}$ denotes the set of all pairs of neighboring pixels.

There exist several inference methods, such as graph cuts or loopy belief propagation (LBP) [10], to minimize the energy of a CRF. For a comparative study on these methods see [11]. The segmentation method proposed in this paper utilizes LBP, but is generic in a sense that it does not depend on the actual choice of the inference method. In the following, we will give a concrete realization of the potential functions.

3   Scene Flow-Based Traffic Scene Segmentation

In our approach, the feature vector $\boldsymbol{z}_i$ of the i-th pixel consists of a position and velocity vector of the corresponding 3D point with respect to a static world coordinate system, i.e., $\boldsymbol{z}_i = [X_i, Y_i, Z_i, \dot{X}_i, \dot{Y}_i, \dot{Z}_i]^{\mathsf{T}}$. For each $\boldsymbol{z}_i$ a covariance matrix is computed as in [7]. The parameter set $\boldsymbol{\Theta}$ includes the intrinsic and extrinsic parameters of the camera, ego-motion, as well as a ground surface model Ω with parameters $\boldsymbol{\Theta}_\Omega$, and a list of M tracked objects $O = \{\mathbf{O}_1, \ldots, \mathbf{O}_M\}$.

For the labeling decision, each class provides a certain expectation on particular elements of the feature vector. For example, the ground surface gives a strong constraint on a point's height, while the motion state of a known tracked object forecasts the velocity of a point that belongs to this object. This means, we can extract different criteria based on the feature vector that each are discriminative for a subset of our target classes. Thus, we compose the total potential function Φ by the sum of K single potential functions Φ_k, $1 \leq k \leq K$, that incorporate these criteria:

$$\Phi(l_i, \boldsymbol{z}_i, \boldsymbol{\Theta}) = \sum_{k=1}^{K} \Phi_k(l_i, \boldsymbol{z}_i, \boldsymbol{\Theta}). \qquad (2)$$

These functions could be learned from sufficiently large training data. Alternatively, this concept also allows for an intuitive modeling of the scene. Below we will propose $K = 4$ realizations of unary potentials for traffic scene segmentation based on scene flow, including motion, distance, height, and surface normal criteria. Other knowledge on the expected scene could be easily added accordingly.

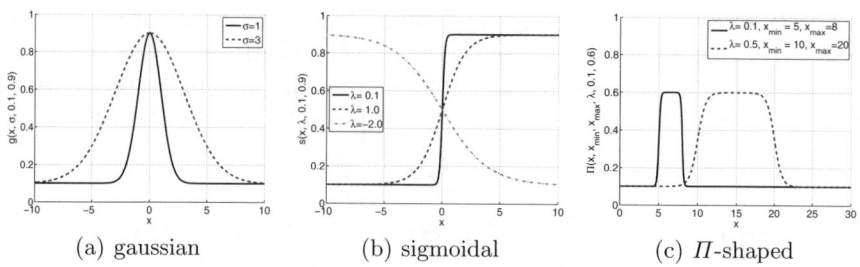

(a) gaussian   (b) sigmoidal   (c) Π-shaped

Fig. 2. Base functions used for defining the potentials

3.1   Basic Functions

The single potential functions Φ_k are defined based on different parametrization of three basic functions scaled to the range $\kappa = [\kappa_{\min}, \kappa_{\max}]$ (see Fig. 2).

Gaussian: A bell-shaped, zero-mean, multi-dimensional Gaussian function g with covariance matrix C_x, defined as

$$g(x, C_x, \kappa) = (\kappa_{\max} - \kappa_{\min}) \exp\left(-1/2\, x^{\mathsf{T}} C_x^{-1} x\right) + \kappa_{\min} \tag{3}$$

The function is scaled in a way that its maximum is $\kappa_{\max}$ and it converges towards a minimum value of $\kappa_{\min}$. For $\kappa_{\max} = (\sqrt{(2\pi)}|C_x|)^{-1}$ and $\kappa_{\min} = 0$ it corresponds to a normal distribution.

Sigmoidal: A one-dimensional sigmoidal function s with width λ and turning point at $x = 0$, scaled to the range κ with

$$s(x, \lambda, \kappa) = (\kappa_{\max} - \kappa_{\min})/(1 + \exp(-x/\lambda)) + \kappa_{\min}. \tag{4}$$

Π-shaped: A gating function Π that is composed of two opposite sigmoidal functions with slope λ

$$\Pi(x, x_{\min}, x_{\max}, \lambda, \kappa) = (\kappa_{\max} - \kappa_{\min})\, (s(x - x_{\min}, \lambda, 0, 1)$$
$$-s(x - x_{\max}, \lambda, 0, 1)) + \kappa_{\min} \tag{5}$$

It has its maximum value $\kappa_{\max}$ within $x_{\min}$ and $x_{\max}$, respectively, and converges towards $\kappa_{\min}$ outside this range. To limit the number of parameters, $\kappa_{\min}$ and $\kappa_{\max}$ will be assigned to one of three basic potential levels κ_{VL}, κ_{UL}, and κ_{DK} for <u>v</u>ery <u>l</u>ikely, <u>un</u><u>l</u>ikely, and <u>d</u>on't <u>k</u>now. Each level can be increased by the constant offset κ_{SP} to be able to <u>s</u>lightly <u>p</u>refer a given class (notation: $\kappa_{\text{XX}}^+ = \kappa_{\text{XX}} + \kappa_{\text{SP}}$).

3.2   Unary Potentials

In the following, the main ideas of the function design are presented. In our approach, the classes $C_1, \ldots, C_J$ are denoted as BG (static <u>b</u>ack<u>g</u>round/ obstacle), GS (<u>g</u>round <u>s</u>urface), O1 (tracked <u>o</u>bject no. <u>1</u>), ..., OM (tracked <u>o</u>bject no. <u>M</u>), and UO (<u>u</u>nknown moving <u>o</u>bject), i.e., $J = M + 3$. Each potential function Φ_k must be defined for all candidate classes C_j.

Motion Potential. The larger the distance of the velocity vector $\boldsymbol{V}_i$ $= [\dot{X}_i, \dot{Y}_i, \dot{Z}_i]^\mathsf{T}$ to the expected velocity $\tilde{\boldsymbol{V}}_i(C_j, \boldsymbol{\Theta})$ at this position, the more un-likely belongs this point to class C_j. If it is very close to the expectation, we do not know whether this pixel belongs to the given class, since there might be another class of similar motion in the scene, but we want to slightly prefer this hypothesis. For all classes beside UO we are able to specify $\tilde{\boldsymbol{V}}_i$. The background and ground are stationary and, thus, move only according to the known camera motion. The velocity vector of tracked objects is also assumed to be known. This yields

$$\Phi_1^{(\text{motion})}\left(l_i = C_j, \boldsymbol{z}_i, \boldsymbol{\Theta}\right) = \log g\left(\boldsymbol{V}_i - \tilde{\boldsymbol{V}}_i(C_j, \boldsymbol{\Theta}), \boldsymbol{C}_{\Delta V}, \boldsymbol{\kappa}_1^{(j)}\right) \quad , C_j \neg \text{UO} \quad (6)$$

where $\boldsymbol{C}_{\Delta V}$ denotes the covariance matrix of the velocity difference and $\boldsymbol{\kappa}_1^{(j)} = [\kappa_{\text{UL}}, \kappa_{\text{DK}}^+]$. For $C_j = \text{UO}$, a constant potential of κ_{UL}^+ is defined.

Distance Potential. Assuming we have an idea on the m-th tracked object's pose and dimension in 3D space, we are able to specify an expected distance range $[\tilde{Z}_{\text{min},i}(\boldsymbol{O}_m), \tilde{Z}_{\text{max},i}(\boldsymbol{O}_m)]$ for the class Om. If Z_i lies outside this range, the i-th point does very unlikely belong to the given object class. On the other hand, if it is within the range, the likelihood for the object class increases. This is modeled by the Π-shaped basic function. For the class GS, we can directly predict the distance $\tilde{Z}_i(\boldsymbol{\Theta}_\Omega)$ of the i-th point based on the surface model Ω. As for the motion potentials, a Gaussian function is used to transform the distance into a potential. There is no expectation on the distance for the classes BG and UO. However, we define points above a maximum distance Z_{max} to be very likely to belong to the background, and unlikely to belong to an unknown object. Points closer than Z_{max} are equally likely to belong to either background or an unknown object based on the distance, which is expressed by a sigmoidal function. The distance potential function $\Phi_2^{(\text{dist})}$ is thus defined as $\Phi_2^{(\text{dist})}\left(l_i = C_j, \boldsymbol{z}_i, \boldsymbol{\Theta}\right) =$

$$\begin{cases} \log s\left(Z_i - Z_{\text{max}}, \lambda_2^{(j)}, \boldsymbol{\kappa}_2^{(j)}\right) & , C_j \in \{\text{BG, UO}\} \\ \log g\left(Z_i - \tilde{Z}_i(\boldsymbol{\Theta}_\Omega), \sigma_{\Delta Z}^2, \boldsymbol{\kappa}_2^{(j)}\right) & , C_j = \text{GS} \\ \log \Pi\left(Z_i, \lambda_2^{(j)}, \tilde{Z}_{\text{min},i}(\boldsymbol{O}_m), \tilde{Z}_{\text{max},i}(\boldsymbol{O}_m), \boldsymbol{\kappa}_2^{(j)}\right) & , C_j = \text{Om} \end{cases} \quad (7)$$

with $\boldsymbol{\kappa}_2^{(j)} : [\kappa_{\text{UL}}, \kappa_{\text{DK}}^+]^{(\text{Om,GS})}, [\kappa_{\text{DK}}, \kappa_{\text{VL}}]^{(\text{BG})}, [\kappa_{\text{UL}}, \kappa_{\text{DK}}]^{(\text{UO})}$; $\lambda_2^{(\text{BG})} > 0$, $\lambda_2^{(\text{UO})} < 0$, and $\sigma_{\Delta Z}^2$ corresponding to the variance of the distance difference.

Height Potential. Analog to the distance potential we can define an expected height range $[\tilde{Y}_{\text{min},i}(\boldsymbol{O}_m), \tilde{Y}_{\text{max},i}(\boldsymbol{O}_m)]$ for a given known object class as well as for the expected ground height $\tilde{Y}_i(\boldsymbol{\Theta}_\Omega)$. For the unknown object class a con-stant height range is assumed. We do not have an expectation on the height of the background class. However, what we know is that points above a maximum height Y_{max} are unlikely to belong to moving objects or the ground surface and, thus, are likely to belong to the background class. The height potential function $\Phi_3(\text{height})$ is given by $\Phi_3^{(\text{height})}(l_i = C_j, z_i, \boldsymbol{\Theta}) =$

$$
\begin{cases}
\log s\left(Y_i - Y_{\max}, \lambda_3^{(j)}, \kappa_3^{(j)}\right) & , C_j = \texttt{BG} \\
\log g\left(Y_i - \tilde{Y}_i(\boldsymbol{\Theta}_\Omega), \sigma_{\Delta Y}^2, \kappa_3^{(j)}\right) & , C_j = \texttt{GS} \\
\log \Pi\left(Y_i, \lambda_3^{(j)}, \tilde{Y}_{\min,i}, \tilde{Y}_{\max,i}, \kappa_3^{(j)}\right) & , C_j \in \{\texttt{Om, UO}\}
\end{cases}
\tag{8}
$$

with $\kappa_3^{(j)} : [\kappa_{\text{DK}}, \kappa_{\text{VL}}]^{(\text{BG})}, [\kappa_{\text{UL}}, \kappa_{\text{DK}}]^{(\text{GS})}, [\kappa_{\text{UL}}, \kappa_{\text{DK}}^+]^{(\text{Om,UO})}$; and $\lambda_2^{(\text{BG})} > 0$.

Surface Normal Potential. In traffic scenes, the class GS differs from all other modeled classes by its surface normal. The predicted surface normal of the ground surface at a given position i is defined by $\tilde{n}_i(\boldsymbol{\Theta}_\Omega)$. The expected normal of any other class is assumed to be perpendicular to the ground surface normal. Thus, we can formulate a separation criteria based on the angle α between $\tilde{n}_i(\boldsymbol{\Theta}_\Omega)$ and the measured surface normal n_i by a sigmoidal function as

$$
\Phi_4^{(\text{normal})}(l_i = C_j, z_i, \boldsymbol{\Theta}) = \log s\left(\alpha\left(\tilde{n}_i(\boldsymbol{\Theta}_\Omega), n_i\right) - 45°, \lambda_4^{(j)}, \kappa_4^{(j)}\right), \forall C_j
\tag{9}
$$

with $\kappa_4^{(j)} = [\kappa_{\text{UL}}, \kappa_{\text{VL}}]$ for all classes, and $\lambda_4^{(\text{GS})} < 0$, $\lambda_4^{(\text{BG,Om,UO})} > 0$.

At pixels with no scene flow data available, e.g., at stereo occlusions, a constant potential is added for all classes that slightly prefers the BG class above the horizon and GS below.

3.3 Binary Potentials

The binary terms Ψ in (1) define the interaction of two neighboring pixels concerning the labeling decision, where the neighborhood structure is defined by the four neighborhood of the image grid. In this contribution the modeling of the binary terms is based on two assumptions. First, we claim smoothness for the labeling result by defining neighboring pixels to be assigned to the same class with a high likelihood τ_1 and to be labeled different with a low likelihood τ_2 (Potts model). Second, prior knowledge on the global topological order of classes in the image is locally integrated by an *ordering constraint*.

Since cars and pedestrians move on the ground surface and are not assumed to fly, pixels representing one of the object classes are likely to be above GS labeled pixels, while BG pixels are likely to be above all other classes with respect to the image rows. Instead of *learning* the order of labels, as for example in [12], our ordering assumption is directly modeled by the relation '$\prec$', defining the strict topological ordering of the class labels $\texttt{GS} \prec \{\texttt{O1}, ..., \texttt{OM}, \texttt{UO}\} \prec \texttt{BG}$ from bottom to top in the image. For two neighboring pixels at image rows v_s and v_t, assuming w.l.o.g. $v_s \leq v_t$, the binary terms are given by

$$
\Psi(l_s = C_{j_s}, l_t = C_{j_t}, z_s, z_t, \boldsymbol{\Theta}) = \begin{cases}
\tau_1 & , j_s = j_t \\
\tau_2 & , j_s \neq j_t \wedge (j_s \prec j_t \vee v_s = v_t), \\
\tau_3 & , j_s \neq j_t \wedge j_s \nprec j_t \wedge v_s < v_t
\end{cases}
\tag{10}
$$

with $C_{j_s}, C_{j_t} \in \{\texttt{BG}, \texttt{GS}, \dots, \texttt{UO}\}$, and $\tau_1 > \tau_2 \gg \tau_3 > 0$, i.e., τ_3 represents the very small likelihood that the ordering constraint is violated.

4   Experimental Results

The proposed segmentation method is tested based on representative traffic scenes with manual ground truth available. The rectified stereo image pairs at two consecutive time steps together with the camera parameters, ego-motion information, as well as the ground truth labeling and prior information on moving objects in the scene is made publicly available.[1] We encourage other researchers in the field of scene flow segmentation to compare their methods based on these examples.

4.1   Data Set and Experimental Setup

Three classes of scenes have been selected (see Fig. 3).

(a) INTERSECTION   (b) STROLLER   (c) LEAD_VEHICLE

Fig. 3. The test scenes (mask: pixels w/o scene flow data, e.g. due to stereo occlusions).

INTERSECTION: An intersection scene with four oncoming cars. This scene contains partial occlusions, distant objects, as well as two nearby objects that move in the same direction with approximately equal velocity.
STROLLER: A pedestrian with a stroller is walking in front of a crossing car. The pedestrian casts a strong *stereo shadow* on the object, i.e., there are large regions that can only be seen from one camera.
LEAD_VEHICLE: The ego-vehicle follows the lead vehicle at approximately the same velocity through dense urban traffic, including two oncoming cars, a slow moving trailer ahead, and one car entering the visible field from the right.

In all scenes, the distance range and velocity of object 01 is known from tracking using a similar method as proposed in [13]. The velocity of the ego-vehicle and the intrinsic and extrinsic camera parameters are also known. The scene flow is computed based on [5], however, any other method could be used alternatively. A flat ground plane surface model is used here for simplicity. The only parameter of this model is the pitch angle of the camera relative to the ground, which is estimated from the measured 3D points. The constant camera height over ground is known in advance. The parameterization of the unary base potential levels is $\kappa_{VL} = 0.9$, $\kappa_{UL} = 0.1$, $\kappa_{DK} = 0.5$, and $\kappa_{SP} = 0.05$. We further use $Z_{max} = 50$ m, $Y_{max} = 3$ m, and $\tau_1 = 0.95$, $\tau_2 = 0.05$, and $\tau_3 = 0.0001$ for the binary terms in all experiments. However, the actual choice of these parameters is uncritical. Even larger changes influence the result only marginally.

---

[1] http://www.mi.auckland.ac.nz/EISATS

4.2 Labeling Results

The segmentation results for the INTERSECTION scene are depicted in Fig. 4 for different configurations. In (a) the final labeling after 40 iterations of message passing is shown, including all proposed unary and binary potentials. The manual ground truth labeling is depicted in (b). As can be seen, the resulting labeling correctly assigns most pixels on the first object to the tracked object class O1. Two of the three remaining cars are correctly assigned to the class UO (non-colored regions). Segments of this class can be used to initialize new object tracks. The white car behind the tracked object is too slow in this scene to be separated from the stationary background and, thus, is labeled as BG. The road surface is reconstructed very well. Only ground regions close to the objects are wrongly identified as O1 or UO due to moving shadows on the ground. The confusion matrices for all investigated scenes are given in Table 1.

In (c), only the unary potentials are considered, yielding several background blobs within the ground surface region and the objects. From (d) to (g) the effect of skipping single unary potentials is demonstrated. Without motion information, the unknown moving objects are assigned to the background, while without the distance information, the two nearby objects are merged to one *tracked object* due to the similarity in motion. The missing surface normal potential in (f) leads

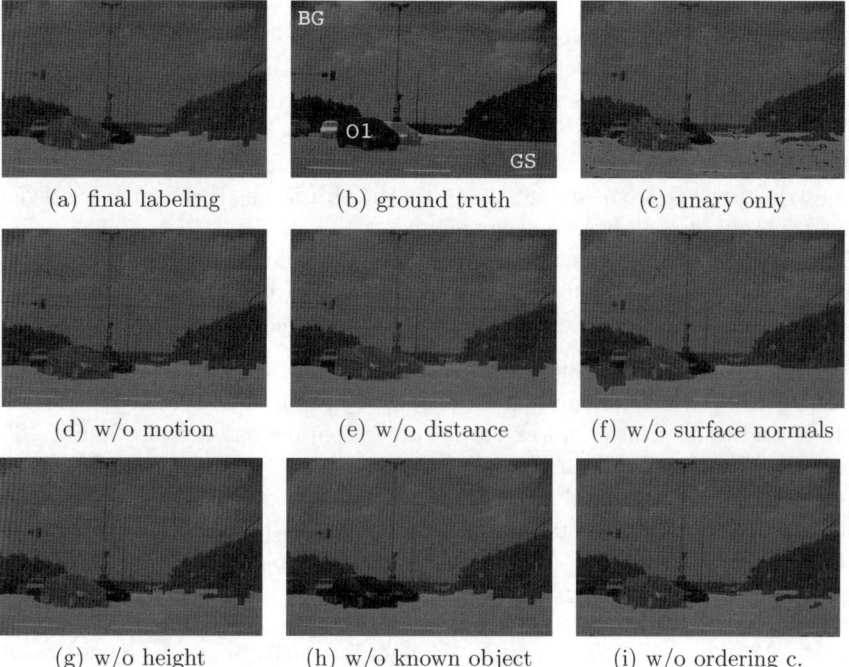

(a) final labeling   (b) ground truth   (c) unary only

(d) w/o motion   (e) w/o distance   (f) w/o surface normals

(g) w/o height   (h) w/o known object   (i) w/o ordering c.

Fig. 4. Labeling results at different system configurations. The colors encode the maximum class potentials at a given pixel (blue=static background, green=ground surface, red=tracked object, black=unknown moving object).

Table 1. Confusion matrices for INTERSECTION, STROLLER, and LEAD_VEHICLE scene. BG=background, GS=ground surface, 01=tracked object, UO=unknown moving object.

GT\Est.	%	BG	GS	01	UO	%	BG	GS	01	UO	%	BG	GS	01	UO
BG	72.9	**99.3**	0.7	0	0	75.5	**99.8**	0.1	0.1	0	61.7	**93.9**	2.4	0.1	3.6
GS	21.3	1.9	**94.3**	2.2	1.6	15.4	11.0	**80.5**	3.1	5.4	25.7	1.2	**96.6**	0	2.2
01	3.6	4.9	0.1	**94.9**	0.1	4.8	14.0	4.4	**74.5**	7.1	6.5	1.4	18.1	**78.5**	2.0
UO	2.2	29.1	0.1	3.3	**67.5**	4.3	29.4	0.2	0	**70.4**	6.1	5.5	8.1	0	**86.4**

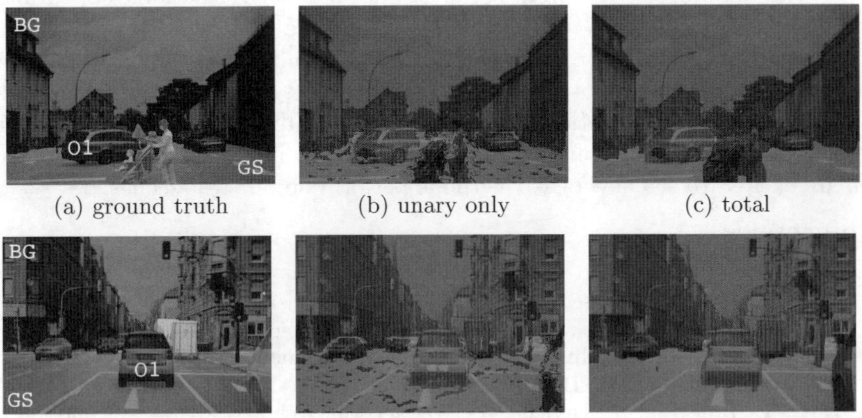

(a) ground truth   (b) unary only   (c) total

Fig. 5. Segmentation results of STROLLER (top) and LEAD_VEHICLE (bottom) scene. Middle: Result if data is evaluated for each pixel independently. Right: Result if smoothness and global ordering constraints are incorporated via local neighborhood inference (result after 40 iterations of loopy belief propagation).

to a degradation for a larger ground region at the left-hand side that is wrongly assigned to background, however, it also indicates that the surface normal is responsible for the discontinuities between ground and background at the horizon in the final labeling. The absence of the height potential alters the segmentation result only marginally in this scene, since there is not much structure about 3 m in the considered distance range. Without the information on the tracked object, all objects are assigned to the UO class in (h) as expected. The ordering constraint eliminates implausible background blobs that would occur within the road surface without this constraint as shown in (i).

In Fig. 5, large parts of the tracked car and the pedestrian with the stroller are correctly labeled as 01 and UO, respectively. Note that the currently stationary leg is assigned to the background, since it is a non moving obstacle. The stereo occlusion is filled with GS from below and BG from the top. The LEAD_VEHICLE results show a very good reconstruction of the ground surface (freespace) and the moving objects in the scene, although the ego-vehicle is also moving.

5   Conclusion

In this contribution a generic framework for precise segmentation of traffic scenes based on scene flow data and object priors has been proposed. This framework is generic in a way that it is independent of the actual scene flow implementation, CRF inference method, or object tracking algorithm. The proposed potential functions represent an intuitive model of traffic scenes, including four class types as well as ordering constraints for these classes. The model can be easily extended by more complex features, other class types, or sophisticated surface models.

The experimental results have shown that the proposed segmentation method performs very well on the considered test scenes. The main problems arise at pixels with missing or error-prone scene flow data. In such situations, appearance features, such as intensity edges or texture information, could provide useful information to further improve the segmentation results, especially at the object boundaries. Appearance potentials could be easily integrated into our framework.

Based on our segmentation algorithm and the published ground truth, it is possible to evaluate and compare different scene flow implementations in future. We are excited to see how other methods perform on our test scenes.

References

1. Wojek, C., Schiele, B.: A dynamic conditional random field model for joint labeling of object and scene classes. In: Forsyth, D., Torr, P., Zisserman, A. (eds.) ECCV 2008, Part IV. LNCS, vol. 5305, pp. 733–747. Springer, Heidelberg (2008)
2. Ess, A., Müller, T., Grabner, H., van Gool, L.: Segmentation-based urban traffic scene understanding. In: BMVC (2009)
3. Brox, T., Rousson, M., Deriche, R., Weickert, J.: Colour, texture, and motion in level set based segmentation and tracking. Image & Vision Comp. 28 (2010)
4. Sturgess, P., Alahari, K., Ladicky, L., Torr, P.: Combining appearance and structure from motion features for road scene understanding. In: BMVC 2009 (2009)
5. Wedel, A., Rabe, C., Vaudrey, T., Brox, T., Franke, U., Cremers, D.: Efficient dense scene flow from sparse or dense stereo data. In: Forsyth, D., Torr, P., Zisserman, A. (eds.) ECCV 2008, Part I. LNCS, vol. 5302, pp. 739–751. Springer, Heidelberg (2008)
6. Rabe, C., Müller, T., Wedel, A., Franke, U.: Dense, robust, and accurate 3D motion field estimation from stereo image sequences in real-time. In: Daniilidis, K. (ed.) ECCV 2010, Part IV. LNCS, vol. 6314, pp. 582–595. Springer, Heidelberg (2010)
7. Wedel, A., Meißner, A., Rabe, C., Franke, U., Cremers, D.: Detection and segmentation of independently moving objects from dense scene flow. In: Cremers, D., Boykov, Y., Blake, A., Schmidt, F.R. (eds.) EMMCVPR 2009. LNCS, vol. 5681, pp. 14–27. Springer, Heidelberg (2009)
8. Bachmann, A.: Applying recursive EM to scene segmentation. In: Denzler, J., Notni, G., Süße, H. (eds.) Pattern Recognition. LNCS, vol. 5748, pp. 512–521. Springer, Heidelberg (2009)
9. Lafferty, J., McCallum, A., Pereira, F.: Conditional random fields: Probabilistic models for segmenting and labeling sequence data. In: ICML, pp. 282–289 (2001)
10. MacKay, D.J.C.: Information Theory, Inference, and Learning Algorithms. Cambridge University Press, Cambridge (2003)
11. Szeliski, R., Zabih, R., Scharstein, D., Veksler, O., Kolmogorov, V., Agarwala, A., Tappen, M.F., Rother, C.: A comparative study of energy minimization methods for markov random fields. In: Leonardis, A., Bischof, H., Pinz, A. (eds.) ECCV 2006, Part II. LNCS, vol. 3952, pp. 16–29. Springer, Heidelberg (2006)
12. Ramalingam, S., Kohli, P., Alahari, K., Torr, P.H.S.: Exact inference in multi-label CRFs with higher-order cliques. In: CVPR, pp. 1–8 (2008)
13. Barth, A., Franke, U.: Estimating the driving state of oncoming vehicles from a moving platform using stereo vision. IEEE Trans. on ITS 10(4), 560–571 (2009)

A Stochastic Evaluation of the Contour Strength

Fernand Meyer[1] and Jean Stawiaski[2]

[1] Mines ParisTech - Centre de Morphologie Mathématique - Fontainebleau, France
[2] Philips Healthcare - Medisys Research Laboratory - Paris, France
Fernand.Meyer@mines-paristech.fr, Jean.Stawiaski@philips.com

Abstract. If one considers only local neighborhoods for segmenting an image, one gets contours whose strength is often poorly estimated. A method for reevaluating the contour strength by taking into account non local features is presented: one generates a fixed number of random germs which serve as markers for the watershed segmentation. For each new population of markers, another set of contours is generated. "Important" contours are selected more often. The present paper shows that the probability that a contour is selected can be estimated without performing the effective simulations.

1 Introduction

Image segmentation aims at extracting from an image the contours of the objects of interest. This task is extremely difficult and problem depending. We propose here a stepwise approach, in which we first extract from the image all contours which may be pertinent. These contours are the frontiers of a fine partition of the image. Each tile represents a region which is homogeneous for some criterion. In general these contours are far too numerous and the image is oversegmented. In a second step one orders the contours according to their importance in the image. A dissimilarity between adjacent tiles is estimated. Coarser partitions are then produced by merging all regions whose dissimilarity is below a given threshold ;every time two regions are merged, one reevaluates their dissimilarity with their neighborhood, and the process is stopped as soon some additional criterion is satisfied. Each new fusion produces a finer partition ; these partitions are nested and may be ranked according their coarseness. The weight of a contour is then simply the first level of coarseness where this contour is no more present.

Such nested partitions are called hierarchies. There a two main classes of methods for extracting the contours of interest from the hierarchy, in order to get the final segmentation. In the first a functional is defined and the set of contours maximizing this functional is extracted from the hierarchy [1,2]. Another approach to segmentation uses seeds or markers for the regions of interest (including the background). Only the strongest contours separating each pair of markers are retained. For the resulting segmentation to be satisfactory, two conditions are to be met : a) the finest partition should contain all contours of interest ; b) the strength of the contours has to be correctly estimated, otherwise, the wrong contours separating markers will be selected.

M. Goesele et al. (Eds.): DAGM 2010, LNCS 6376, pp. 513–522, 2010.

Unfortunately, some contours of objects are intrinsically weak since they correspond to transitions between similar color shades for instance, or objects having almost the same luminance as their background. When such objects are large enough and appear on a clean background, they are nevertheless easily recognized by the human eye, but not easily segmented by the computer. Local methods will estimate these contours as very weak as noticed in [3]. We present in this paper a set of new methods able to produce useful and reliable estimates of the contour strength.

Authors of [4] have described such a method in the context of the watershed segmentation of gradient images. Random germs are spread all over the image and server as markers for the watershed segmentation of a gradient image. Large regions, separated by low contrast gradient from neighboring regions will be sampled more frequently than smaller regions and will be selected more often. On the other hand, high gradient watershed lines will often be selected by the watershed construction, as there are many possible positions of markers which will select them. So the probability of selecting a contour will offer a nice balance between strength of the contours and size of the adjacent regions. The method produces good results for multimedia types of images as well as for 3D granular material but suffers from a major drawback : in order to obtain a robust estimation of the contour strength a relatively large number of simulations has to be made, typically on the order of 50 simulations, implying the construction of 50 watershed. This paper shows how to obtain estimates of the contour strength without simulations. Analyzing under which conditions a given piece of contour will be selected by the watershed makes it possible to compute the contour strength without the need of any simulation. More precisely, one has to determine for each contour the two zones, separated by this contour, where a marker has to be present in order for the contour to be selected.

The paper is organized as follows. In a first section we explain how to produce a hierarchy to start with, obtained with the watershed transform ; we explain why in this case, the strength of the contour is often badly estimated. We then describe an efficient representation of a hierarchy, as a weighted tree. The last part of the paper presents how to implement the stochastic watershed on this tree, in order to estimate a contour strength compatible with the features one desires to stress.

2   Producing and Representing Hierarchies

2.1   Producing a Hierarchy with the Watershed Transform

The watershed associates to each regional minimum of a topographic surface its catchment basin. Morphological segmentation applies the watershed transform to the gradient of the image to segment. Like that, one obtains a fine partition where each region is the catchment basin associated to a minimum of the gradient image.

Suppose now that this same topographic surface is flooded up to some level λ. A number of lakes are created, some of them are still regional minima of the topographic surface, covering one or more minima of the initial surface ; others are "full", in the sense that the level of the lake reaches the lowest pass point leading to another minimum: such lakes are not regional minima anymore. The catchment basins of this flooded relief form a partition which is coarser than the partition associated to the unflooded surface ; a number of adjacent regions of the fine partition will have merged to form larger regions.

For a level $\mu > \lambda$, the same process can be repeated, leading to a yet coarser partition. Hence, the partitions formed by the catchment basins of a topographic surface, for increasing levels of flooding of this surface, form a hierarchy. This hierarchy can be represented by the fine partition formed by the catchment basins of the unflooded surface plus a dissimilarity measure between adjacent regions, equal to the flooding level for which these regions merge.

2.2   Dissimilarity Associated Hierarchies

More generally, we may associate a hierarchy to each partition for which a dissimilarity between adjacent regions has been defined. Merging all regions with a dissimilarity between some level λ produces a coarser partition. For increasing levels λ the partitions become coarser and coarser, producing again a hierarchy.

2.3   Representing a Hierarchy as a Tree

In order to give a visual support to the algorithms presented below, we associate to each hierarchy a topographic surface defined as follows. This surface is completely flat, except along the edges of the tile of the finest partition Π in the hierarchy. A 0 thickness wall is erected along each piece of contour, with a height equal to the dissimilarity between both adjacent regions. Fig.1 illustrates this construction process. The bottom row shows the successive levels of a hierarchy, where from level to level the most similar regions have merged ; the left most image represents the finest partition. The central row of fig.1 presents the construction of a tree representing the hierarchy. In the left most image, this tree is reduced to isolated nodes, representing each a tile of the partition Π. Each region ρ_i is represented by a node ν_i of the tree, weighted by the area of the region.

We then flood this topographic surface in order to construct a tree representing the hierarchy. The upper row shows the topographic surface during flooding. The left most level shows the walls separating the tiles ; the color of each tile being the color of the source which will flood this tile. As the level of the flood increases, it first reaches the level of the lowest wall : the two adjacent lakes are merged and get a uniform color. As these lakes merge for the first time, an edge is created between the corresponding nodes, with a weight equal to the dissimilarity between both regions ; we write e_{ij} for the edge linking the nodes ν_i and ν_j.

At level 2 in fig.1, again two lakes meet for the first time along a wall which separated both lakes and a new edge is created. The same happens at level 3, for which the surface is entirely flooded and the tree which has been constructed spans all nodes. However there exists pieces of walls still emerging from the lakes. As the flood further increases and reaches the level of such a wall, there are not

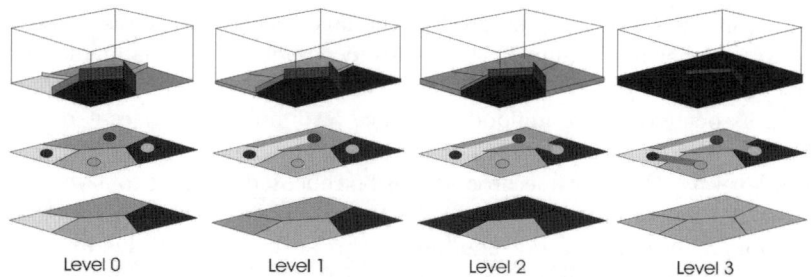

Level 0   Level 1   Level 2   Level 3

Fig. 1. Construction of the minimum spanning tree by flooding a topographic surface

two lakes which meet for the first time, as it is the same lake which is present on both sides of the wall ; in this case no edge is created.

In summary, as the flood reaches the level of a wall separating two regions ρ_i and ρ_j of Π, there are two possibilities : the lakes on each side of the wall are distinct lakes which merge and an edge (e_{ij}) is created between the corresponding nodes ν_i and ν_j ; or both lakes form in reality one and the same lake, created by mergings of lakes at a lower level, in this case, no edge is created between them. This shows that regions may merge at a lower level than the dissimilarity between them : it is sufficient that they belong to a chain of lakes which have merged at lower flooding levels. Based on this remark, we may replace the initial dissimilarity between adjacent regions by the flooding dissimilarity, that is the level for which both regions belong to the same lake during flooding, which is lower (in mathematical terms, this new dissimilarity is a distance, called subdominant ultrametric distance associated to the initial dissimilarity). In Fig.2 we see on the left the initial image and in the center its gradient. The catchment basins of the watershed constitute the finest partition ; the dissimilarity between tiles being the lowest pass point on the gradient image between adjacent regions. The right image shows as dissimilarity the flooding level for which the tiles merge for the first time. The grey tone values on the right are well below the values of the gradient image, specially for large regions, as it is the case for

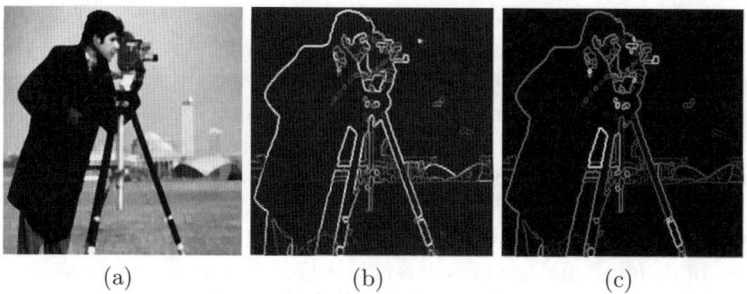

(a)   (b)   (c)

Fig. 2. (a) Initial image. (b) Gradient value on the contour lines of a segmented image. (c) Contours weighted by the level of flooding for which they disappear.

the coat of the cameraman. On the contrary some small contrasted regions are surrounded by extremely bright pieces of contour. This is due to the fact that for larger regions, there are often some parts of the contour which are weaker, leading to early mergings with neighboring regions.

Remark 1. The tree T defined above is the minimum spanning tree of the region neighboring graph defined as follows : each region is represented by a node ; adjacent nodes are linked by an edge with a weight equal to the dissimilarity between both regions. Edges weights along paths of the minimum spanning tree are minimizing the maximum dissimilarity between each pair of nodes [5]. The construction of the flooding tree corresponds also to the single-linkage hierarchy in the context of data clustering.

2.4   Marker Based Watershed Segmentation

The flooding tree also plays an important role in the marker based watershed construction. Some regions, called markers, are selected and play the role of sources from which the topographic surface will be flooded. Their flow is such that they create lakes with a uniform and growing altitude. Consider now the evolution of a particular lake Λ_i when the flooding level increases and reaches the lowest pass point leading to another region. If there is a lake on the other side, there are two possibilities : this lake is a distinct lake Λ_j, produced by another source and these lakes meet for the first time. The pass point where they meet corresponds to an edge of the flooding tree. This edge will be assigned a dissimilarity 1. If on the contrary the lake on the other side is the same lake Λ_i, originating from the same source, the corresponding edge does not belong to the flooding tree. If the region on the other side is still dry, it will be flooded by the overflood of our lake and they will form a unique lake ; in this case, the corresponding edge belongs to the flooding tree, but does not correspond to a contour of the marker based segmentation : it is assigned a dissimilarity 0. It is noteworthy that all significant events such as mergings of lakes and overflood of a lake into its neighbor take place along the tree constructed above.

The new binary distribution of weights on the flooding tree represents the marker based segmentation. Cutting all edges with weight 1 produces a forest. Each tree of this forest has its root in a distinct marker. The union of all regions belonging to a same tree of the forest constitutes a region of the marker based segmentation. In mathematical terms, marker based segmentation results in a minimum spanning forest of the neighborhood graph, in which each tree is rooted in a marker [5].

3   Stochastic Evaluation of the Strength of the Contours

3.1   Stochastic Marker Based Watershed

The stochastic evaluation of the contour strength as defined by Angulo et al. [4] assigns to each piece of contour the probability to appear as contour in a watershed segmentation, with random markers. As we have seen, marker based segmentation results in a forest derived from the flooding tree by cutting some edges of this tree. In order to compute the probability that such an edge becomes a contour we have to understand for which marker distribution this happens. We have defined markers as particular regions of the hierarchy which act as sources. One way to select such regions as markers is by drawing random punctual germs onto the surface. If at least one germ falls in a given region, this region is selected as markers ; a region without a germ is not a marker and will be flooded through sources placed in other regions.

Let us first consider two markers m_1 and m_2. Both markers become sources which pour water. Their flow is such that they create lakes with a uniform and growing altitude. These two lakes keep separated until they finally meet on the lowest edge, at an altitude λ separating them, which becomes a contour edge. Each lake will have covered a number of catchment basins separated by walls with a lower altitude than λ. Both lakes L_1 and L_2 are separated from the rest of the topographic surface by edges higher than λ.

If one of the regions, for instance L_1 is without a marker, it can only be flooded through a neighboring region. The lowest connecting edge to a neighboring region is the edge e_{12} of altitude λ. So if the region L_2 has a marker, it will flood the region L_1 through e_{12}, which is not selected as a contour edge.

If both regions L_1 and L_2 are without markers, then the union of both regions $L_1 \cup L_2$ will be flooded from outside, through a pass point of altitude greater than λ and again the edge e_{12} between both regions will not be selected as contour edge.

The same analysis may now be reformulated using the flooding tree. Consider and edge e_{12} with an altitude λ of the tree, joining two nodes ν_1 and ν_2. Cutting all edges of the tree with an altitude higher than or equal to λ produces a forest. Let us call T_1 and T_2 the trees of the forest containing respectively the nodes ν_1 and ν_2. The edge e_{12} will be a contour edge in a marker based segmentation, if and only if each of the trees T_1 and T_2 has at least one node which is a marker.

The next section will propose several modes for promoting randomly a node to a marker in the tree. For each mode, we then compute the probability of the edges of the tree to become contour edges.

3.2   Contour Strength for Various Random Distribution of Markers

Uniform Poisson distribution of germs on the surface : the surfacic stochastic watershed. We first use points as germs. The simplest distribution of germs is a Poisson distribution. For a fixed number N of germs this reduces to a uniform distribution of N germs on the topographic surface. As soon one or more germs fall into a region R_1 of the fine partition Π, the corresponding node is selected as marker. The probability that a germ falls into a region A of area $\overline{A}$ obeys a binomial distribution of probabilities $p = \frac{\overline{A}}{S}$ and $1 - p$, where S is the area of the domain occupied by the function f. So the probability that out of N germs no one falls into A is $(1 - \frac{\overline{A}}{S})^N$.

Using the same notations as above, we consider an edge e_{12} of altitude λ. We cut all edges higher or equal than λ and consider the trees T_1 and T_2 of the forest adjacent to e_{12}. The edge e_{12} is a contour edge in a marker based segmentation, if and only if each of the trees T_1 and T_2 adjacent to e_{12} has at least one node which is a marker. This means that at least one germ has fallen in each of the regions L_1 and L_2 spanned by both trees. We have to compute the probability of the event {there is at least one germ in L_1} and {there is at least one germ in L_2}. The opposite event is the union of two non exclusive events {there is no germ in L_1} or {there is no germ in L_2}. Its probability is p{there is no germ in L_1} + p{there is no germ in L_2} - p{there is no germ in $L_1 \cup L_2$}, which is:

$$P_{e_{1,2}} = 1 - \left(1 - \frac{\overline{L_1}}{S}\right)^N - \left(1 - \frac{\overline{L_2}}{S}\right)^N + \left(1 - \frac{\overline{L_1} + \overline{L_2}}{S}\right)^N . \qquad (1)$$

As we have assigned to each node ν_i of the tree T the area of the underlying region, the area $\overline{L_1}$ is simply the sum of the weights of the nodes of the tree T_1 in the forest obtained after cutting the edges above λ. We write meas$(T_1) = \overline{L_1}$.

The volumic stochastic watershed. In order to give more importance to the contrast an alternative measure may be used: we suppose that the marker is not thrown on the surface but within the volume of the lakes. Considering again the edge e_{ij} of altitude λ, the adjacent regions spanned by the subtrees T_1 and T_2 may be flooded up to level λ and will then be covered by two lakes L_1 and L_2 with volumes $(V_1 = \lambda \times$ meas$(T_1))$ and $(V_2 = \lambda \times$ meas$(T_2))$. If Λ is the highest dissimilarity between two regions of the hierarchy, the volume occupied by a lake covering the total surface is $(V = \Lambda \times$ meas$(T))$. The probability that e_{ij} is selected as an edge is then:

$$P_{e_{1,2}} = 1 - \left(1 - \frac{V_1}{V}\right)^N - \left(1 - \frac{V_2}{V}\right)^N + \left(1 - \lambda\frac{V_1 + V_2}{V}\right)^N . \qquad (2)$$

The surfacic stochastic watershed with non punctual seeds. In what precedes we have imagined punctual seeds, able to fall at any point of both regions L_i and L_j adjacent to the edge e_{ij}. If the seeds are not points, but a set B, the probabilities will be changed, as the probability that the set B falls within a region X will be proportional, not to the area of X, but to the area $\overline{X \ominus B}$ of the set X eroded by the structuring element B. This value does depend upon the shape of X and we have to measure it on the initial image.

Mutatis mutandis, the area stochastic watershed will weight the edges with the probability:

$$P(e_{1,2}) = 1 - \left(1 - \frac{\overline{L_1 \ominus B}}{S}\right)^N - \left(1 - \frac{\overline{L_2 \ominus B}}{S}\right)^N + \left(1 - \frac{\overline{L_1 \ominus B)} + \overline{L_2 \ominus B}}{S}\right)^N .$$
$$(3)$$

As previously we observe that this probability becomes 0 if a regions becomes too small for containing the set B.

Likewise, the volumic stochastic watershed will weight the edges with the probability:

$$P(e_{1,2}) = 1 - \left(1 - \frac{V_1'}{V}\right)^N - \left(1 - \frac{V_2'}{V}\right)^N + \left(1 - \frac{V_1' + V_2}{V}\right)^N . \qquad (4)$$

where $V_1' = w(e) \times \overline{L_1 \ominus B}$ and $V_2' = w(e) \times \overline{L_2 \ominus B}$.

Results. Fig.3 illustrates the results one obtains for the different methods. Fig.3(a) and (b) show the initial image and the level for which the contours vanish during uniform flooding. Fig.3(c) shows the result of the surfacic stochastic watershed where one uses random points spread over the surface as seeds. If the random points are spread within the volume of the lakes, one obtains Fig.3(d), with large regions and small ones if they are contrasted enough. For balls of a given size taken as random seed, all regions where the ball cannot enter vanish yielding the segmentation of Fig.3(e).

Fig.3(c) and Fig.3(e) compares the stochastic watershed where points are used as markers with the result obtained if one uses disks as seeds. Notice that in this last case, many small regions have vanished, but not all ; some small regions are created as they lie between the contours of larger regions.

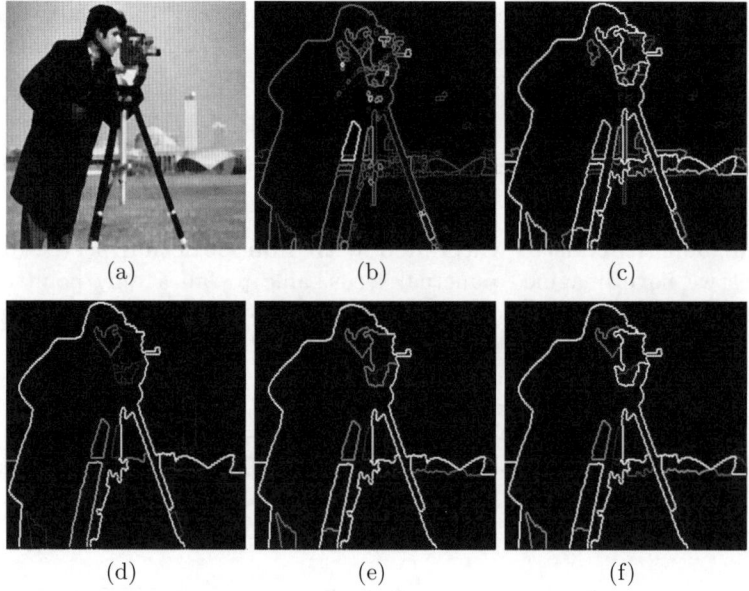

Fig. 3. (a) Initial image. (b) Flooding level for which the contours disappear. (c) Surfacic stochastic watershed with point seeds. (d) Volumic stochastic watershed with point seeds. (e) Surfacic stochastic watershed with disks as seeds. (f) Stochastic watershed with point seeds followed by a stochastic watershed with disk seeds.

Furthermore, the methods presented so far start all with a hierarchy defined by a set of weights on the minimum spanning tree and produce a new set of weights which express a preference for a type of regions compared to others (large or contrasted regions for instance). This homogeneity in the representation of the hierarchies permits to chain the process. Fig.3(f) has been obtained by computing first a surfacic stochastic watershed and on the results compute a stochastic watershed obtained with disks as markers. One sees some difference with Fig.3(e) where only the last stochastic watershed has been used. Figure 4 illustrates some hierarchies of contours obtained on images of the Berkeley Segmentation Dataset [6]. Segmentation results were obtained by thresholding the contour strength map obtained with volumic stochastic watershed with point seeds. The Volumic stochastic measures permits to obtain a good trade-off between size and contrast of the object to be detected.

      (a)   (b)   (c)

Fig. 4. Volumic stochastic watershed with point seeds. Segmentation is obtained by thresholding the contour strength.

4   Conclusion

The stochastic framework is excessively rich as it permits infinite variations : other probability laws for the distribution of seeds, random choice of seeds belonging to a family of shapes, regionalised distribution of seeds according some properties of the domain they will fall [7], etc. An additional nice feature, is that the result always is a probability distribution. That is, whatever the rules which are adopted, the edges get weights between 0 and 1, which makes it easy to combine hierarchies. Given two hierarchies H_1 and H_2 with distinct dissimilarities, it is possible to combine them, by taking for each edge the minimum (resp. maximum) of its dissimilarity in H_1 and H_2.

Furthermore, these reevaluation methods of the contours may be chained: use a first distribution of random germs and on the resulting hierarchy, apply a second and then a third, before, ultimately use a marker based segmentation with markers introduced either in an interactive way or through an automated analysis of the scene.

References

1. Guigues, L.: Modèles multi-echelles pour la segmentation d'images (in french). These de Doctorat de L'Université de Cergy Pontoise (2003)
2. Guigues, L., Cocquerez, J., Men, H.: Scale-sets image analysis. International Journal of Computer Vision 68(3), 289–317 (2006)
3. Najman, L., Schmitt, M.: Geodesic saliency of watershed contours and hierarchical segmentation. IEEE Trans. Pattern Anal. Mach. Intell. 18(12), 1163–1173 (1996)
4. Angulo, J., Jeulin, D.: Stochastic watershed segmentation. In: Int. Symp. Mathematical Morphology, ISMM 2007, pp. 265–276 (2007)
5. Meyer, F.: Minimal spanning forests for morphological segmentation. In: ISMM 1994, Mathematical Morphology and its applications to Signal Processing, pp. 77–84 (1994)
6. Fowlkes, C., Martin, D., Malik, J.: The berkeley segmentation dataset and benchmark (bsdb), http://www.cs.berkeley.edu/projects/vision/grouping/segbench/
7. Noyel, G., Angulo, J., Jeulin, D.: Classification-driven stochastic watershed. Application to multispectral segmentation. In: Proc. of the Fourth European Conference on Color on Graphics, Imaging and Vision (CGIV 2008), pp. 471–476 (2008)

Incremental Computation of Feature Hierarchies

Michael Felsberg

Linköping University, Department of Electrical Engineering, Sweden
mfe@isy.liu.se

Abstract. Feature hierarchies are essential to many visual object recognition systems and are well motivated by observations in biological systems. The present paper proposes an algorithm to incrementally compute feature hierarchies. The features are represented as estimated densities, using a variant of local soft histograms. The kernel functions used for this estimation in conjunction with their unitary extension establish a tight frame and results from framelet theory apply. Traversing the feature hierarchy requires resampling of the spatial and the feature bins. For the resampling, we derive a multi-resolution scheme for quadratic spline kernels and we derive an optimization algorithm for the upsampling. We complement the theoretic results by some illustrative experiments, consideration of convergence rate and computational efficiency.

1 Introduction

The computation of feature hierarchies is an essential step in many state-of-the-art visual object recognition systems. The hierarchical processing is well motivated by observations in biological systems [1]. The present paper proposes an algorithm for incremental computation of feature hierarchies.

Feature hierarchies can be build with respect to abstraction levels or resolution [2], p. 8–9, or a combination of both [3,4]. Here, we focus on the resolution of soft histograms as used in, e.g., [5], where matching is performed on histograms with increasing resolution, i.e., coarse to fine. In this work, increasing spatial resolution goes in hand with decreasing resolution in feature space. This is plausible from a practical (computational effort) and statistical (significance) point of view, and the reciprocal relation of resolution in the spatial and the feature domain has an theoretical upper bound [6].

Computations in the joint spatio-featural space require a common framework for spatial positions and generic features. Biological systems have been observed to use a representation called population codes [7], in earlier work also called channel codes [8,9]. Channel representations as a computational framework, e.g. for object recognition, have been introduced in [10], and are directly related to kernel density estimation [11]. Channel representations of features are basically soft-histograms or Parzen estimators with a smooth kernel function. They are beneficial in many tasks due to their robustness [11,23].

Applying channel representations to spatial coordinates results in low-pass filters or point-spread functions. Subsampled low-pass filters give rise to resolution

M. Goesele et al. (Eds.): DAGM 2010, LNCS 6376, pp. 523–532, 2010.

pyramids [12,13] and multi-resolution analysis. The complementing high-pass filters became very popular in terms of wavelets [14], where signals are decomposed based on a orthonormal basis. The main drawback of discrete wavelets is that if the scaling function (low-pass filter) is smooth, the wavelet becomes highly non-smooth [15]. In contrast to wavelets, framelets can be selected to be smooth, which is beneficial for stability, and contain redundancy, which improves robustness. Similar to wavelets, framelets are compact, which results in limited interaction and thus sparseness and efficiency in computations, e.g. exploited for super-resolution still image extraction using C^0 framelets [16].

In this paper, we extend the existing work in two ways: a) We derive a multi-resolution scheme for quadratic spline channel representations (C^1 kernels) using frame theory. b) We derive an algorithm for incrementally compute spatio-featural hierarchies. Since we consider linear and periodic features, any feature represented as a combination of linear and periodic parameters is covered.

The paper is structured as follows. The second section on methods gives the required background and explains the proposed novel methods. In the subsequent section on experiments and results we explain the performed tests, discuss the results, and analyze the computational complexity. We conclude the paper with a summary of achieved results.

2   Methods

2.1   Channel Representations and CCFMs

The channel representation as a computational framework goes back to [10]. In channel representations features are represented by weights assigned to ranges of feature values, similar to histograms but exploiting smooth bins. The closer the current feature value ξ to the respective feature interval center n, the higher the channel weight f_n (for an example, the reader might refer to Section 3.3):

$$f_n(\xi) = k(\xi - n) \qquad n \in \mathbb{N} \ , \tag{1}$$

where $k(\cdot)$ is a symmetric, unimodal kernel function and where ξ has been scaled such that it has a suitable range (note that the channel centers are integers).

In what follows, we have been using quadratic B-splines as kernel function, since they are smooth and easy to formulate in the z-domain [11]:

$$B_2(\xi) = \begin{cases} 3/4 - \xi^2 & |\xi| \leq 1/2 \\ (|\xi| - 3/2)^2/2 & 1/2 < |\xi| < 3/2 \\ 0 & |\xi| \geq 3/2 \end{cases} \tag{2}$$

Comparing (1) with a kernel density estimator, the only difference is that the kernel function is placed at equidistant positions and not on the samples drawn from the distribution. Since the kernel is symmetric, the estimated coefficient at the discrete position is the same in both cases and the distribution of the stochastic variable ξ, p_ξ, is approximated by f_n in expectation sense [11]:

$$E_\xi\{f_n(\xi)\} = (p_\xi * k)(n) = (p_\xi * B_2)(n) \ . \tag{3}$$

A multi-dimensional channel representation for a set of features is formed by taking the Cartesian product of the respective one-dimensional representations. If the spatial coordinates are contained in the feature set, a channel-coded feature map (CCFM) [17] is generated by local averaging, representing the spatio-featural density. For instance one might consider local orientation, hue, and saturation as local image features, resulting in a 5D CCFM. For practical (computational effort) and statistical (significance) reasons, the number of spatial and featural channels is not independent, but should be chosen reciprocally [6].

As motivated in the introduction, many object recognition approaches require a hierarchical spatio-featural representation, e.g., a pyramid of CCFMs. As an example, let us consider an orientation-based CCFM scale-space. At the finest spatial resolution, we have a minimum number of four orientation channels, representing e.g. positive and negative responses of a Gaussian derivative. On the second level, we obtain eight orientation channels, which, if combined with four by four spatial channels, yields a structure similar to the SIFT descriptor [18], although with quadratic histogram bins instead of linear ones.

Single level descriptors like SIFT are directly computed from filter outputs, but if several different levels are to be considered, a staged process that builds the pyramid successively is beneficial. This means that higher-resolution feature density estimates are estimated from several lower-resolution estimates when traversing the pyramid towards lower spatial resolutions, c.f. Fig.1 left.

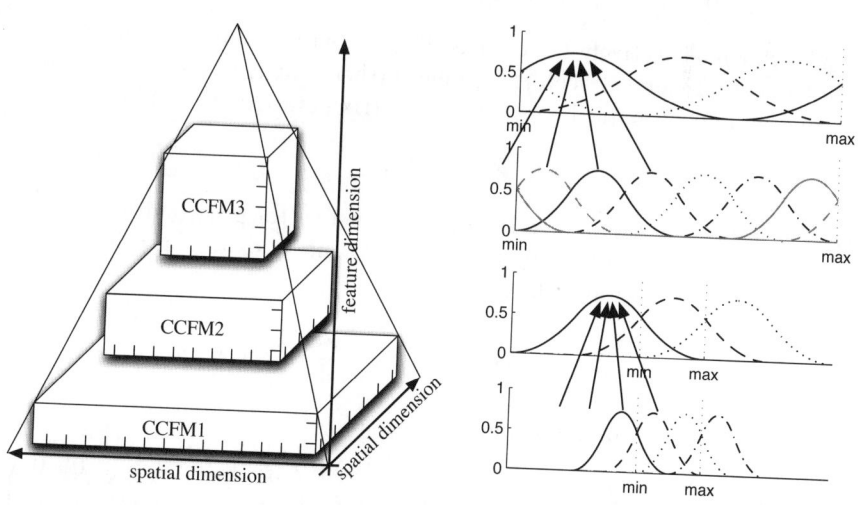

Fig. 1. Left: Going upwards in the spatio-featural pyramid reduces spatial resolution and increases feature resolution. Top right: Downsampling for periodic boundary conditions. The kernel functions are re-entering the domain from the respective opposite side, i.e., the left most connection refers to the solid grey kernel. Bottom right: Downsampling for the zero padded case. The connections outside the existing channels get zero weight. The four connections have the weights 1/8, 3/8, 3/8, 1/8 in both cases.

526   M. Felsberg

2.2   Multi-Resolution Analysis of Density Estimates

The first step to find a staged computation of the CCFM pyramid is to derive the scaling function for quadratic B-splines (2). According to [19] it is given as

$$m_0 = \frac{1}{8}[1,\, 3,\, 3,\, 1] \ . \tag{4}$$

The scaling function allows to compute the scaled quadratic B-spline channel directly from the unscaled B-spline channel coefficients. This is easily verified either in the z-domain or by elementary calculus using (2).

If we combine (4) with a downsampling scheme, we compute new channel values between existing channels and leave out every other channel. This process is illustrated in Fig. 1, right. For periodic features (periodic boundary conditions), the corresponding matrix operator (subscript p) is a circular matrix with every other row left out. For linear features, the channel vector is zero padded, cf. Fig. 1, bottom right. The corresponding matrix operator (subscript l) is a Toeplitz matrix with every other row left out.

$$\mathbf{T}_{p,0} = \frac{1}{8}\begin{pmatrix} 3 & 3 & 1 & 0 & \dots\dots & 0 & 1 \\ 0 & 1 & 3 & 3 & 1 & 0 & \dots & 0 \\ \vdots & & \ddots & & & \ddots & & \vdots \\ 0 & \dots & 0 & 1 & 3 & 3 & 1 & 0 \\ 1 & 0 & \dots\dots & & 0 & 1 & 3 & 3 \end{pmatrix} \quad \mathbf{T}_{l,0} = \frac{1}{8}\begin{pmatrix} 3 & 1 & 0 & \dots\dots & 0 & 0 \\ 1 & 3 & 3 & 1 & 0 & \dots & 0 \\ \ddots & & \ddots & & \ddots & & \ddots \\ 0 & \dots & 0 & 1 & 3 & 3 & 1 \\ 0 & 0 & \dots\dots & 0 & 1 & 3 \end{pmatrix} \tag{5}$$

The subscript p respectively l is omitted if it is obvious from the context.

Let $\mathbf{f}$ denote a channel vector. Assume further that $\mathbf{g}$ is a low-pass filtered (with m_0) and downsampled copy of $\mathbf{f}$. In matrix notation we obtain

$$\mathbf{g} = 2\mathbf{T}_0\mathbf{f} \ , \tag{6}$$

where the factor 2 is required to keep the channel vector $\mathbf{g}$ normalized.

We form tight frame filters by applying the unitary extension principle [20] resulting in the two high-pass filters [21]

$$m_1 = \frac{1}{8}[1,\, 3,\, -3,\, -1] \qquad m_2 = -\frac{\sqrt{3}}{4}[1,\, -1,\, 0,\, 0] \ . \tag{7}$$

The matrix operators corresponding to m_1 read

$$\mathbf{T}_{p,1} = \frac{1}{8}\begin{pmatrix} -3 & 3 & 1 & 0 & \dots\dots & 0 & -1 \\ 0 & -1 & -3 & 3 & 1 & 0 & \dots & 0 \\ \vdots & & \ddots & & & \ddots & & \vdots \\ 0 & \dots & 0 & -1 & -3 & 3 & 1 & 0 \\ 1 & 0 & \dots\dots & & 0 & -1 & -3 & 3 \end{pmatrix} \quad \mathbf{T}_{l,1} = \frac{1}{8}\begin{pmatrix} 3 & 1 & 0 & \dots\dots & 0 & 0 \\ -1 & -3 & 3 & 1 & 0 & \dots & 0 \\ \ddots & & \ddots & & \ddots & & \ddots \\ 0 & \dots & 0 & -1 & -3 & 3 & 1 \\ 0 & 0 & \dots\dots & 0 & -1 & -3 \end{pmatrix}$$

and the matrix operators corresponding to m_2 are formed accordingly. By basic calculations, we verify the reconstruction formula

$$\frac{1}{2}\mathbf{I} = \sum_{j=0}^{2} \mathbf{T}_j^T \mathbf{T}_j \ , \tag{8}$$

where $\mathbf{I}$ is the identity and the factor $\frac{1}{2}$ originates from the downsampling.

2.3   Upsampling Channel Vectors

If we traverse the spatio-featural hierarchy upwards, we downsample spatially after[1] having upsampled the feature dimensions. The downsampling is fully covered in terms of the matrices (5). The upsampling of $\mathbf{g}$ is achieved by combining the reconstruction formula (4.13) in [21] with the iterative scheme in [20]. Plugging (6) into (8) results in

$$\frac{1}{2}\mathbf{f} = \sum_{j=0}^{2} \mathbf{T}_j^T \mathbf{T}_j \mathbf{f} = \frac{1}{2}\mathbf{T}_0^T \mathbf{g} + \mathbf{T}_1^T \mathbf{T}_1 \mathbf{f} + \mathbf{T}_2^T \mathbf{T}_2 \mathbf{f} \ . \tag{9}$$

Using an explicit approach, we obtain the iterative scheme

$$\mathbf{f}^{(k+1)} = \mathbf{T}_0^T \mathbf{g} + 2(\mathbf{T}_1^T \mathbf{T}_1 + \mathbf{T}_2^T \mathbf{T}_2)\mathbf{f}^{(k)} \ . \tag{10}$$

Iterating this equation results in the solution of the underdetermined problem

$$\min_{\mathbf{f}} \|\mathbf{g} - 2\mathbf{T}_0 \mathbf{f}\|_2^2 \ . \tag{11}$$

Unrolling the iteration (10), we obtain

$$\mathbf{f}^{(k+1)} = \Delta^{k+1}\mathbf{f}^{(0)} + (\Delta^k + \ldots + \Delta + \mathbf{I})\mathbf{T}_0^T \mathbf{g} \tag{12}$$

where $\Delta = 2(\mathbf{T}_1^T \mathbf{T}_1 + \mathbf{T}_2^T \mathbf{T}_2)$. The M rows of $\mathbf{T}_0$ are linearly independent and span an M-d space. Let $\mathbf{P}_M$ denote the $N \times N$ projection matrix onto this M-dimensional subspace (non-zero eigenvectors of $\mathbf{T}_0^T \mathbf{T}_0$). We obtain

$$\mathbf{f}^{(k+1)} = \Delta^{k+1}\mathbf{f}^{(0)} + (\Delta^k \mathbf{P}_M + \ldots + \Delta \mathbf{P}_M + \mathbf{I})\mathbf{T}_0^T \mathbf{g}$$
$$= \Delta^{k+1}\mathbf{f}^{(0)} + ((\Delta \mathbf{P}_M)^k + \ldots + \Delta \mathbf{P}_M + \mathbf{I})\mathbf{T}_0^T \mathbf{g}$$

because $\mathbf{P}_M = \mathbf{P}_M^2$ and $\mathbf{P}_M$ commutes with $\Delta = \mathbf{I} - 2\mathbf{T}_0^T \mathbf{T}_0$. In the limit, we obtain

$$\mathbf{f}^{(\infty)} = (\mathbf{I} - \mathbf{P}_M)\mathbf{f}^{(0)} + (\mathbf{I} - \Delta \mathbf{P}_M)^{-1}\mathbf{T}_0^T \mathbf{g} \tag{13}$$

because $\Delta \mathbf{P}_M$ has a spectral radius smaller than one.

This means that the N-dimensional solution $\mathbf{f}$ of our iteration is determined by an M-dimensional constraint given in terms of $\mathbf{g}$. The remaining $N - M$ dimensions, i.e., the null-space of $\mathbf{P}_M$, is determined to have norm zero if we start from $\mathbf{f}^{(0)} = 0$, i.e., we obtain the minimum norm solution of (11). In our particular problem, however, we are not interested in the minimum norm solution, but we require to have a non-negative solution instead, since kernel

---

[1] If we downsampled first, we would lose information.

density estimates are non-negative. Hence, we should choose $\mathbf{f}^{(0)}$ such that $\mathbf{f}^{(\infty)}$ is non-negative everywhere.

For the periodic case, we know that $N = 2M$ and for the linear case, we obtain $N = 2M - 2$ since all channels are doubled except for those at the boundaries. Hence, we need $2M - M = M$ respectively $2M - 2 - M = M - 2$ equations that are not linearly dependent on the rows of $\mathbf{T}_0$. These can be obtained in terms of $\mathbf{I} - \mathbf{P}_M$, but we can easily derive another set of vectors spanning the null-space of $\mathbf{T}_0$. Define the two matrices

$$\mathbf{S}_p = \frac{1}{8} \begin{pmatrix} -3 & 3 & -1 & 0 & \ldots & \ldots & 0 & 1 \\ 0 & 1 & -3 & 3 & -1 & 0 & \ldots & 0 \\ \vdots & & \ddots & & & \ddots & & \vdots \\ 0 & \ldots & 0 & 1 & -3 & 3 & -1 & 0 \\ -1 & 0 & \ldots & \ldots & 0 & 1 & -3 & 3 \end{pmatrix} \quad \mathbf{S}_l = \frac{1}{8} \begin{pmatrix} 1 & -3 & 3 & -1 & 0 & \ldots & 0 \\ \ddots & \ddots & \ddots & & \ddots & & \vdots \\ 0 & \ldots & 0 & 1 & -3 & 3 & -1 \end{pmatrix} .$$

We verify that

$$\mathbf{S}_p \mathbf{T}_{p,0}^T = 0 \quad \text{and} \quad \mathbf{S}_l \mathbf{T}_{l,0}^T = 0 \tag{14}$$

i.e., $\mathbf{S}_p$ ($\mathbf{S}_l$) is in the null-space of $\mathbf{T}_{p,0}$ ($\mathbf{T}_{l,0}$). Furthermore, since $\mathbf{S}_p$ is of rank M and $\mathbf{S}_l$ is of rank $M - 2$, we conclude that they span the null-space of $\mathbf{T}_{p,0}$ respectively $\mathbf{T}_{l,0}$.

In order to obtain a solution according to (11) with non-negative coefficients, a straightforward idea is to simply set all negative coefficients to zero in each iteration of (10). However, this does not lead to stable results in our experiments. Instead, we compute the projection of the negative coefficients onto the null-space. For this purpose, we define the vector $\mathbf{f}_{\text{neg}}$ component-wise

$$f_{\text{neg},n} = \begin{cases} f_n & f_n < 0 \\ 0 & f_n \geq 0 \end{cases} \quad n = 1, \ldots, N . \tag{15}$$

This vector is then projected onto the null-space ($\cdot^\dagger$ denotes the pseudoinverse)

$$\mathbf{f}_{\text{null}} = \mathbf{S}^T \mathbf{S}^{T\dagger} \mathbf{f}_{\text{neg}} . \tag{16}$$

Subtracting this vector from the current solution brings us closer to the non-negative solution without leaving our solution space, but we need to determine the step-length λ. A greedy approach is to use the ratio of the largest negative value of $\mathbf{f}_{\text{neg}}$ and the corresponding coefficient of $\mathbf{f}_{\text{null}}$:

$$n_0 = \arg\min_n f_{\text{neg},n} \quad \lambda = f_{\text{neg},n_0} / f_{\text{null},n_0} . \tag{17}$$

To achieve numerical stability, the coefficient λ must be bounded in the positive and negative range, e.g., by requiring $|f_{\text{null},n_0}| > 10^{-5}$. Finally, we update

$$\mathbf{f}^{(k+1)} \Leftarrow \mathbf{f}^{(k+1)} - \lambda \mathbf{f}_{\text{null}} . \tag{18}$$

3   Experiments

We have applied our algorithm (10,15-18) in three experiments: Convergence tests, image reconstruction from upsampled densities, and orientation pyramids.

3.1   Convergence Behavior

For analyzing the convergence behavior of our upsampling algorithm, we have generated sets of samples from a linear ramp function. One data set consists of the function values without noise and the second contains 5% Gaussian noise. The samples have been collected in soft histograms (channels vectors) with 3, 4, and 6 bins respectively. These vectors have then been upsampled to 4, 6, and 10 bins and compared to the directly encoded noise-free data $\mathbf{h}$, using the Hellinger distance (which is often used in kernel-based matching [22]

$$d^2(\mathbf{f}, \mathbf{h}) = \frac{1}{2} \sum_n (\sqrt{f_n} - \sqrt{h_n})^2 = 1 - \sum_n \sqrt{f_n h_n} \qquad (19)$$

where the right hand-side is obtained since the coefficients of $\mathbf{f}$ and $\mathbf{h}$ sum to one. The right-most term is called Bhattacharyya coefficient [22].

The plots in Fig. 2 show the Hellinger distance as a function of the number of iterations. We can clearly see that the more iterations are required the more channels are to be reconstructed. On the other hand, achieving the same Hellinger distance for a larger number of bins means to achieve a higher accuracy per bin, and thus more information needs to be recovered. If the number of iterations is normalized with the number of bins, convergence speed is about the same.

One conclusion of this observation is that if the upsampling of feature distributions is combined with a downsampling in the 2D spatial domain, the algorithm has constant computational complexity, independent of the actual level in the pyramid. This complexity is linear in the number of pixels and the number of initial channels. This has been confirmed by the observed runtimes, which were all in the sub-second range (Matlab implementation).

Another observation we make in Fig. 2 is that convergence speed seems to be unaffected by noise, but the final error level depends on the noise. Since the reconstruction is compared against the noise-free density estimates, the fixed Gaussian noise has growing influence for decreasing kernel widths.

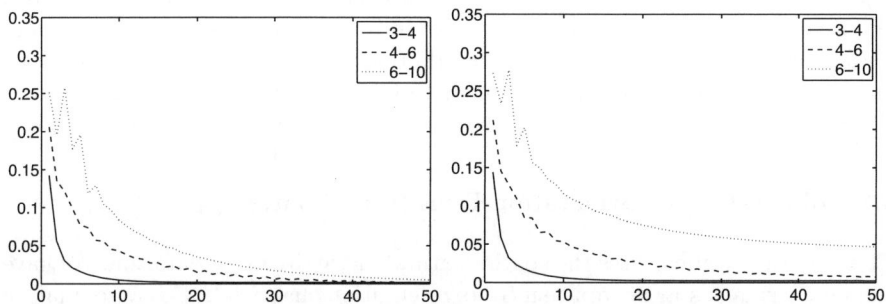

Fig. 2. Convergence of our algorithm: Hellinger distance plotted versus the number of iterations. Left: no noise. Right: Gaussian noise (5% standard deviation).

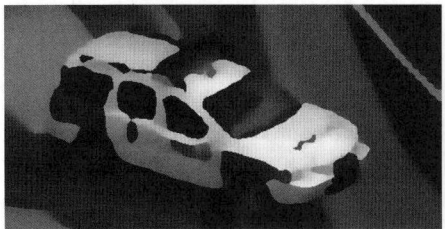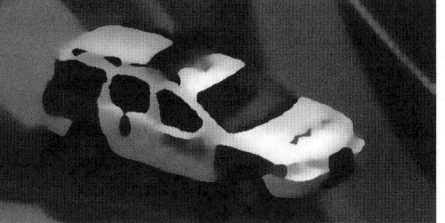

Fig. 3. A car image from [23] reconstructed from CCFMs, clipped to 512×256. Left: reconstruction from direct CCFM encoding. Right: reconstruction from successive encoding using the proposed algorithm.

3.2 Image Reconstruction

In this experiment we visualize the similarities and differences of direct encoding of CCFMs and successiv encoding using the proposed algorithm. The images are taken from [23], size 512×512. We have reproduced the experiment from [6], generating CCFMs with a resolution of $66 \times 66 \times 10$ channels, and reconstructing images with a resolution of 512×512 using the method from [6]. The encoding has been done in two different ways: a) by directly encoding the CCFM at the final resolution and b) by encoding into three channels point-wise and subsequent three-fold upsampling of the feature (greyscale) channel and downsampling of the spatial channels, resulting in the sequence $514 \times 514 \times 3 \rightarrow 258 \times 258 \times 4 \rightarrow 130 \times 130 \times 6 \rightarrow 66 \times 66 \times 10$. The two reconstructions for one example (an image of a police car) are depicted in Fig. 3. In the ideal case, the two images should be identical; the absolute reconstruction quality is not of relevance here.

Up to minor differences, the two reconstructions are identical. The main differences occur at some few edges of medium greyscale difference, which are more crispy in the direct encoding case. The reason for this minor difference is presumably that some information loss is caused by the fact that spatial downsampling is performed in 2D while the feature upsampling is only 1D. However, the level at which edges are blurred is far beyond the original scale of channels. Using three channels to encode the whole range is identical to linear smoothing of the image, i.e., the proposed algorithm has succeeded in recovering robust smoothing from initially uni-modal representations. In addition to that, the striking advantage of the new method is that all intermediate CCFMs are also available, whereas the direct method needs to encode from scratch for any change of resolution.

3.3 Illustration of Orientation Density Estimates

This experiment illustrates the spatio-featural hierarchy for orientation. We have chosen a siemens star as input since its orientation channels are easy to analyze visually. The orientation channels respond on respective antipodal sides and the bow length corresponds to the width of the kernel, see Fig. 4. The first orientation channel (out of four) at level $n = 1$ responds with a quite large variance.

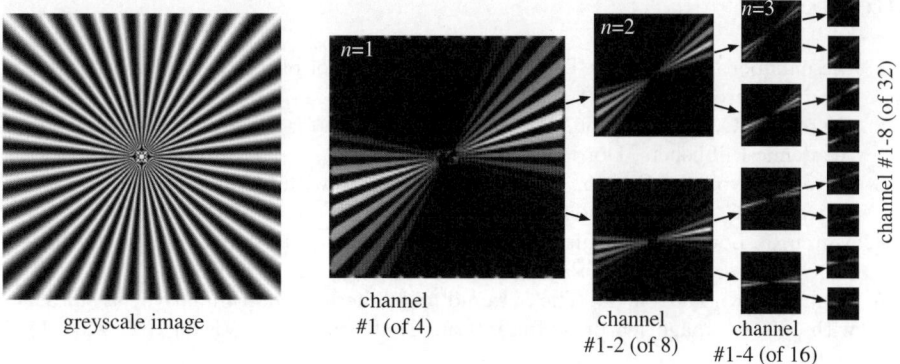

Fig. 4. Orientation pyramid. From left to right: image and hierarchy levels $n = 1, \ldots, 4$

Running our upsampling algorithm results in eight channels and the first two are depicted, together covering about the same range as the previous one. After another run, we obtain 16 channels, of which we show the first four. Finally, we obtain 32 channels of which we show eight.

This illustrates how we obtain increasingly distinct estimates of the orientation by gathering information from a growing spatial support. We can repeat the procedure until we reach a global histogram. The features are not at all restricted to either greyscale or orientation. Any (combination) of features including color, texture, depth, motion, etc. is possible, but more difficult to illustrate.

4   Conclusion

We have presented a framelet-theory based framework for resampling channel-based density estimates up and down. We have further derived an optimization algorithm that produces the required high-pass components for upsampling density estimates with a non-negativity constraint. The algorithm is stable and converges rapidly towards the correct solution. The presented framework is well suited to generate feature hierarchies. Such hierarchies can be traversed up and down, allowing for bottom-up driven detection and top-down driven priming and adaptation of lower levels by simply multiplying prior distributions to the higher-level representations. In some illustrative experiments, we have shown that the derived framework can be applied as intended. The optimization converges rapidly and is efficient to compute. The greyscale reconstruction results are as close to the direct encoding as it can be expected. A periodic feature (orientation) has been illustrated on four levels of the hierarchy. What remains for future work is to apply the new framework in an object recognition system and to verify its benefits on a more applied level.

Acknowledgements

This research has received funding from the EC's 7th Framework Programme (FP7/2007-2013), grant agreements 215078 (DIPLECS) and 247947 (GARNICS).

References

1. Riesenhuber, M., Poggio, T.: Hierarchical models of object recognition in cortex. Nature Neuroscience 2(11), 1019–1025 (1999)
2. Granlund, G.H., Knutsson, H.: Signal Processing for Computer Vision. Kluwer Academic Publishers, Dordrecht (1995)
3. Serre, T., Wolf, L., Poggio, T.: Object recognition with features inspired by visual cortex. In: Computer Vision and Pattern Recognition, pp. 994–1000 (2005)
4. Mutch, J., Lowe, D.G.: Multiclass object recognition with sparse, localized features. In: Computer Vision and Pattern Recognition, pp. 11–18 (2006)
5. Grauman, K., Darrell, T.: The pyramid match kernel: Discriminative classification with sets of image features. In: Intern. Conf. Computer Vision, pp. 1458–1465 (2005)
6. Felsberg, M.: Spatio-featural scale-space. In: Tai, X.-C., Mørken, K., Lysaker, M., Lie, K.-A. (eds.) Scale Space and Variational Methods in Computer Vision. LNCS, vol. 5567, pp. 808–819. Springer, Heidelberg (2009)
7. Pouget, A., Dayan, P., Zemel, R.: Information processing with population codes. Nature Reviews – Neuroscience 1, 125–132 (2000)
8. Snippe, H.P., Koenderink, J.J.: Discrimination thresholds for channel-coded systems. Biological Cybernetics 66, 543–551 (1992)
9. Howard, I.P., Rogers, B.J.: Binocular Vision and Stereopsis. OUP, Oxford (1995)
10. Granlund, G.H.: An associative perception-action structure using a localized space variant information representation. In: Sommer, G., Zeevi, Y.Y. (eds.) AFPAC 2000. LNCS, vol. 1888, pp. 48–68. Springer, Heidelberg (2000)
11. Felsberg, M., Forssén, P.E., Scharr, H.: Channel smoothing: Efficient robust smoothing of low-level signal features. IEEE PAMI 28(2), 209–222 (2006)
12. Granlund, G.H.: In search of a general picture processing operator. Computer Graphics and Image Processing 8, 155–173 (1978)
13. Burt, P.J., Adelson, E.H.: The Laplacian pyramid as a compact image code. IEEE Trans. Communications 31(4), 532–540 (1983)
14. Mallat, S.G.: A theory for multiresolution signal decomposition: the wavelet representation. IEEE Trans. Pattern Analysis Machine Intelligence 11, 674–693 (1989)
15. Daubechies, I.: Orthonormal bases of compactly supported wavelets. Communications on Pure and Applied Mathematics 41(7), 909–996 (1988)
16. Chan, R.H., Shen, Z., Xia, T.: A framelet algorithm for enhancing video stills. Applied and Computational Harmonic Analysis 23(2), 153–170 (2007)
17. Jonsson, E., Felsberg, M.: Efficient computation of channel-coded feature maps through piecewise polynomials. Image and Vision Comp. 27(11), 1688–1694 (2009)
18. Lowe, D.G.: Distinctive image features from scale-invariant keypoints. International Journal of Computer Vision 60(2), 91–110 (2004)
19. Petukhov, A.: Symmetric framelets. Constr. Approx 19, 309–328 (2000)
20. Chan, R.H., Riemenschneider, S.D., Shen, L., Shen, Z.: Tight frame: an efficient way for high-resolution image reconstruction. ACHA 17(1), 91–115 (2004)
21. Chui, C.K., He, W.: Compactly supported tight frames associated with refinable functions. Applied and Computational Harmonic Analysis 8(3), 293–319 (2000)
22. Sonka, M., Hlavac, V., Boyle, R.: Image Processing, Analysis, and Machine Vision. Thomson-Engineering (2007)
23. Vikstén, F., Forssén, P.E., Johansson, B., Moe, A.: Comparison of local image descriptors for full 6 degree-of-freedom pose estimation. In: IEEE ICRA (2009)

From Box Filtering to Fast Explicit Diffusion

Sven Grewenig, Joachim Weickert, and Andrés Bruhn

Mathematical Image Analysis Group, Faculty of Mathematics and Computer Science,
Campus E1.1, Saarland University, 66041 Saarbrücken, Germany
{grewenig,weickert,bruhn}@mia.uni-saarland.de

Abstract. There are two popular ways to implement anisotropic diffusion filters with a diffusion tensor: Explicit finite difference schemes are simple but become inefficient due to severe time step size restrictions, while semi-implicit schemes are more efficient but require to solve large linear systems of equations. In our paper we present a novel class of algorithms that combine the advantages of both worlds: They are based on simple explicit schemes, while being more efficient than semi-implicit approaches. These so-called fast explicit diffusion (FED) schemes perform cycles of explicit schemes with varying time step sizes that may violate the stability restriction in up to 50 percent of all cases. FED schemes can be motivated from a decomposition of box filters in terms of explicit schemes for linear diffusion problems. Experiments demonstrate the advantages of the FED approach for time-dependent (parabolic) image enhancement problems as well as for steady state (elliptic) image compression tasks. In the latter case FED schemes are speeded up substantially by embedding them in a cascadic coarse-to-fine approach.

1 Introduction

Anisotropic diffusion filters with a diffusion tensor instead of a scalar-valued diffusivity offer additional degrees of freedom that allow to steer them according to a task at hand [1]: Coherence-enhancing diffusion filters, for example, are well-suited for processing seismic data sets [2], while edge-enhancing diffusion filters have attractive qualities for lossy image compression [3]. However, since such anisotropic diffusion filters require a diffusion tensor, their efficient implementation is much more difficult than for their isotropic counterparts with a scalar-valued diffusivity such as the Perona-Malik filter [4]. For the latter ones one can use e.g. additive operator splitting (AOS) schemes [5,6], while there is no efficient full operator splitting in the general anisotropic case.

Although there has been a number of proposals for numerical schemes for anisotropic diffusion processes (see e.g. [7,8,9]), probably the two most popular ways to implement anisotropic diffusion filters are explicit and semi-implicit finite difference schemes. Explicit schemes are very simple to implement and allow a direct computation of the values at a new time level without solving linear or nonlinear systems of equations. However, they suffer from severe time step size restrictions which render them inefficient. Semi-implicit schemes, on the other hand, permit to use large time step sizes and can be more efficient than explicit approaches. Unfortunately, they are more difficult to implement and require to solve a large linear system of equations in each time step.

M. Goesele et al. (Eds.): DAGM 2010, LNCS 6376, pp. 533–542, 2010.

Our Contribution. The goal of the present paper is to show that it is possible to combine the advantages of explicit and semi-implicit schemes while avoiding their shortcomings. To this end we introduce a novel class of numerical schemes that we call *Fast Explicit Diffusion (FED) Schemes*. They perform cycles of explicit diffusion schemes with varying time step sizes. Since within each cycle up to 50 percent of all steps may violate the stability condition, one can achieve very large diffusion times. In this way one cycle can become even more efficient than one semi-implicit step. Moreover, we show that one can embed FED cycles within a coarse-to-fine strategy to solve stationary problems in an even more efficient way than with multigrid approaches. These findings are illustrated by applying the FED idea to edge- and coherence-enhancing diffusion filters. The starting point that has led us to the development of FED schemes was the observation that one can factorise a (stable) 1-D box filter into a cycle of explicit linear diffusion schemes with stable and unstable time step sizes. This idea can be generalised in a straightforward way to nonlinear and anisotropic problems in arbitrary dimensions.

Organisation of the Paper. Our paper is organised as follows: In Section 2 we derive the FED idea from the factorisation of a 1-D box filter into explicit linear diffusion steps, and we relate this approach to the so-called Super Time Stepping (STS) method of Gentzsch et al. [10,11]. In Section 3 we show how FED can be generalised to arbitrary diffusion processes, and we show in Section 4 how this can be adapted to edge- and coherence-enhancing diffusion filters. After this, we perform numerical experiments in Section 5, and we conclude the paper in Section 6.

2   Filter Factorisation

2.1   Equivalence between 1-D Discrete Box Filtering and Linear FED

In order to motivate our FED approach, we restrict ourselves to the 1-D case first and consider linear diffusion processes. Since it is well-known that linear diffusion filtering is equivalent to Gaussian convolution and Gaussians can be approximated by iterated box filtering, we explore the connection between a box filter and explicit schemes for linear diffusion.

Let $f = (f_i)_{i \in \mathbb{N}}$ be a discrete 1-D signal given on a grid with mesh size $h > 0$. We define the discrete box filter of length $(2n + 1)h$, $n \in \mathbb{N}$, as well as the discrete second order derivative by

$$\left(B^h_{2n+1}(f) \right)_i := \frac{1}{2n + 1} \sum_{k=-n}^{n} f_{i+k} \quad \text{and} \quad (\Delta_h f)_i := \frac{f_{i+1} - 2f_i + f_{i-1}}{h^2} . \tag{1}$$

The explicit discretisation of the linear heat equation for a function $u(x, t)$,

$$\partial_t u = \partial_{xx} u , \tag{2}$$

evaluated at a spatial-time-grid point (x_i, t_k) with $x_i := \left(i - \frac{1}{2} \right) h$ and $t_k := k\tau$, can then be formulated as

$$u_i^{k+1} = (I + \tau \Delta_h) u_i^k , \tag{3}$$

where I is the identity operator, $\tau > 0$ the time step size and $u_i^k \approx u(x_i, t_k)$ a numerical approximation.

The following theorem states a connection between 1-D discrete box filtering and explicit schemes with different time step sizes:

Theorem 1. *A discrete one-dimensional box filter* B_{2n+1}^h *is equivalent to a cycle with* n *explicit linear diffusion steps:*

$$B_{2n+1}^h = \prod_{i=0}^{n-1} (I + \tau_i \Delta_h) , \qquad (4)$$

with the varying time step sizes

$$\tau_i = \frac{h^2}{4 \cos^2 \left(\pi \frac{2i+1}{4n+2} \right)} \qquad (5)$$

and corresponding stopping time

$$t_n := \sum_{i=0}^{n-1} \tau_i = \frac{h^2}{3} \binom{n+1}{2}. \qquad (6)$$

The corresponding proof can be found in the Appendix.

We call one cycle of this novel scheme a *Fast Explicit Diffusion (FED)* cycle. Because of its equivalence to box filtering, FED is also stable. Interestingly, the time step sizes τ_i in Eq. (5) partially violate stability conditions. Table 1 shows both the smallest three and largest three time step sizes for different n. Since the stability restriction for the time step size of an explicit scheme in one dimension is given by $\tau \leq \frac{h^2}{2}$, it is easy to show that the FED scheme consists of $\lceil \frac{n-1}{2} \rceil$ unstable time steps, where $\lceil a \rceil$ denotes the next largest integer $k \geq a$. Hence, for even n, half of the time steps are unstable. For $n \geq 3$, one FED cycle reaches the stopping time t_n faster than any other explicit scheme with stable time step sizes $\tau \leq \frac{h^2}{2}$.

Since we want to approximate a diffusion process – or equivalently Gaussian convolution – one should use several iterated box filters – or equivalently FED cycles. Let $M \geq 2$ denote this number of FED cycles. This number M of outer cycles should not be confused with the number n of inner steps.

Before we explore extensions of FED to nonlinear, anisotropic and multidimensional problems, let us discuss some related work first.

2.2   Connection to Super Time Stepping

Our FED scheme uses different time step sizes, where some of them may violate stability limits. A similar method has been introduced under the name *Super Time Stepping (STS)* by Gentzsch et al. [10,11]. Contrary to our derivation, they used a direct approach: Gentzsch et al. wanted to find a set of different time step sizes, which keeps stability after each cycle, and at the same time maximises the stopping time of such a cycle. Instead of factorising a box filter, one can show that their method intends to factorise

Table 1. First three and last three step sizes of FED (1-D) with $h = 1$ (rounded). t_n denotes the stopping time of one FED cycle including n inner time steps

n	10	25	50	100	250	500	1000
τ_0	0.251404	0.250237	0.250060	0.250015	0.250002	0.250001	0.250000
τ_1	0.263024	0.252147	0.250545	0.250137	0.250022	0.250006	0.250001
τ_2	0.288508	0.256024	0.251518	0.250382	0.250061	0.250015	0.250004
$\vdots$							
τ_{n-3}	1.33	7.40	28.79	113.79	706.52	2820.19	11269.25
τ_{n-2}	2.88	16.55	64.68	255.93	1589.57	6345.33	25355.72
τ_{n-1}	11.25	65.97	258.48	1023.45	6358.01	25381.06	101422.61
t_n	18.33	108.33	425.00	1683.33	10458.33	41750.00	166833.33

the mask $\left(\frac{1}{2}, 0, \ldots, 0, \frac{1}{2}\right)$. Since this mask is very sensitive w.r.t. high frequencies, they have to introduce an additional damping parameter $\nu \geq 0$ that ensures better attenuation properties of high frequencies. This parameter can be seen as a trade-off between efficiency and damping quality, since larger values for ν scale down the stopping time. In our FED framework, such a damping parameter is not necessary.

While the ordering of the explicit diffusion steps does not matter in exact arithmetic, it can influence the result in practice due to numerical rounding errors when n is large. In order to improve robustness, Gentzsch et al. have proposed to rearrange the explicit steps within so-called $\varkappa$-cycles. We will also use this approach. For further details on STS, we refer to the above cited works and e.g. Alexiades et al., who have done an experimental evaluation [12].

3 Fast Explicit Diffusion (FED) for Arbitrary Problems

3.1 Extension to Arbitrary Diffusion Problems

While the FED scheme has been motivated in the 1-D setting with linear diffusion filtering, it is actually a general paradigm that can be applied to multidimensional, nonlinear and anisotropic diffusion processes. This can be seen as follows.

First, let us reconsider the 1-D diffusion equation (2) and its explicit discretisation (3). By assuming homogeneous Neumann boundary conditions and denoting $\boldsymbol{u}^k \in \mathbb{R}^N$ as the vector with entries u_i^k, Eq. (3) can be written as a matrix-vector product:

$$\boldsymbol{u}^{k+1} = (I + \tau A_h)\,\boldsymbol{u}^k \,, \tag{7}$$

with $\tau \leq h^2/2$. According to Gerschgorin's theorem, the eigenvalues of the matrix $A_h \in \mathbb{R}^{N \times N}$ lie in the interval $[-4/h^2, 0]$. These eigenvalues determine the stability in the Euclidean norm: A stable explicit step requires a time step size τ such that all eigenvalues of the matrix $I + \tau A_h$ lie in the interval $[-1, 1]$.

Keeping this in mind, it is straightforward to replace the matrix A_h by any negative semidefinite matrix P that results from a discretisation of a diffusion process. This process can be one- or multidimensional, linear or nonlinear, isotropic or anisotropic.

In this case, one FED cycle is not any more equivalent to box filtering, but it corresponds to a first order approximation of the above-mentioned diffusion process. All one has to do is to adapt the time step size limit to the largest modulus of the eigenvalues of P. More precisely, let $\mu_i \leq 0$ be the eigenvalues of P and define $\mu_{\max} := \max_i |\mu_i|$. Then the explicit scheme in Eq. (7) with P instead of A_h is stable for time step sizes $\tilde{\tau} := c \cdot \tau$, where

$$c := \frac{4}{h^2 \cdot \mu_{\max}} \tag{8}$$

is the adjustment factor. Since $\mu_{\max}$ can easily be estimated using e.g. Gerschgorin's theorem, this adaptation is no problem at all in practice. Fig. 1 gives a summary of the general FED algorithm. Note that it is essentially an explicit scheme with some overhead that is not time critical.

3.2   Cascadic FED (CFED) for Stationary Problems

So far our FED scheme was designed for diffusion problems where we are interested in the temporal evolution. This refers to parabolic partial differential equations (PDEs) that are used for denoising and enhancement purposes.

However, in the case of inpainting and PDE-based compression problems, one is interested in the nontrivial steady state when Dirichlet boundary data are specified. The corresponding elliptic PDE results from the parabolic evolution for $t \to \infty$. To reach this steady state as quickly as possible, we embed our FED into a coarse-to-fine strategy [13], i.e. we use results computed on a coarse scale as an initialisation for a finer scale. Therefore, we scale down both the image and the reconstruction mask via area-based interpolation to a certain coarse level and apply the FED scheme on this image. Afterwards, we interpolate the corresponding solution and the mask to the next finer level and apply again FED on it. We apply this procedure recursively until the finest

---

1. **Input Data**:
   image f, stopping time T, number M of outer FED cycles, and model parameters

2. **Initialisation**:
   (a) Compute the smallest n such that the stopping time t_n of one FED cycle fulfils $t_n \geq T/M$, and define $q := T/(M \cdot t_n) \leq 1$.
   (b) Compute the time step sizes $\tilde{\tau}_i := q \cdot c \cdot \tau_i$ with c according to (8), and τ_i according to (5).
   (c) Choose a suitable ordering for the step sizes $\tilde{\tau}_i$ according to [10].
   (d) If the diffusivity or diffusion tensor is constant in time, compute the corresponding matrix P.

3. **Filtering Loop**:
   (a) If the diffusivity or diffusion tensor is time-variant, update it and compute the corresponding matrix P.
   (b) Perform one FED cycle with the above ordering of the n explicit time steps $\tilde{\tau}_i$.
   (c) Go back to (a), if the stopping time T is not yet reached.

Fig. 1. General FED algorithm for diffusion filtering

level is reached. To simplify matters, we always use the same parameter settings for the diffusion process on each level. We call this cascadic fast explicit diffusion approach *CFED*. It saves a lot of computational effort, since then a small or midsize stopping time is already sufficient on each level.

4   FED and CFED for Anisotropic Diffusion Filtering

In this section we review two specific two-dimensional anisotropic diffusion filters that we are going to use in our experiments as demonstrators for the potential of the FED and CFED algorithms.

4.1   Edge-Enhancing Diffusion (EED)

Edge-enhancing anisotropic diffusion inhibits diffusion across edges and instead prefers smoothing within the image regions [1]. It follows the evolution equation

$$\partial_t u \;=\; div\left(D\left(\nabla u_\sigma\right)\nabla u\right)\;,\tag{9}$$

where $D \in \mathbb{R}^{2\times 2}$ is the symmetric positive definite diffusion tensor, and u_σ is the image u convolved with a Gaussian of standard deviation σ. Its diffusion tensor is

$$D\left(\nabla u_\sigma\right) \;=\; g\left(|\nabla u_\sigma|^2\right)\cdot\frac{\nabla u_\sigma \nabla u_\sigma^\top}{|\nabla u_\sigma|^2} \;+\; 1\cdot\frac{\nabla u_\sigma^\perp \nabla u_\sigma^{\perp\,\top}}{|\nabla u_\sigma^\perp|^2}\;,\tag{10}$$

where $\cdot^\top$ means the usual matrix transposition and $\binom{a}{b}^\perp := \binom{-b}{a}$. In our experiments we shall use the so-called Charbonnier diffusivity function

$$g\left(s^2\right) \;=\; \left(1 + s^2/\lambda^2\right)^{-1/2}\;.\tag{11}$$

It has proven to be highly useful for image interpolation purposes such as the compression method in [3]. In this case one computes the elliptic steady state solution.

We assume a uniform two-dimensional grid with the mesh sizes $h_x = h_y = 1$ and set the adjustment factor $c = 1/(2h^2)$, which is sufficient for stability with respect to the standard discretisation [14].

4.2   Coherence-Enhancing Diffusion (CED)

Coherence-enhancing diffusion filtering enhances line- and flow-like structures. Its diffusion tensor has the same eigenvectors as the so-called structure tensor

$$J_\rho\left(\nabla u_\sigma\right) \;:=\; K_\rho * \left(\nabla u_\sigma \nabla u_\sigma^\top\right)\;,\tag{12}$$

where K_ρ is a Gaussian of standard deviation ρ, and its eigenvalues are given by

$$\lambda_1 := \alpha \tag{13}$$

$$\lambda_2 := \begin{cases} \alpha, & \text{if } \mu_1 = \mu_2\;,\\[2mm] \alpha + (1-\alpha)\exp\left(\frac{-\lambda}{(\mu_1-\mu_2)^2}\right), & \text{else} \end{cases}\;,\tag{14}$$

where μ_1 and μ_2 are the eigenvalues of the structure tensor such that $\mu_1 \geq \mu_2$. For further details we refer to [1]. As a space discretisation for CED, we have used the one in [9]. It has low dissipativity and allows to use the same c as for the preceding EED scheme.

5   Experiments

In order to evaluate FED for parabolic problems, we enhance a fingerprint test image with CED. First we compute a reference solution by applying a semi-implicit scheme with very small time step sizes. The original image and the filtered result can be seen in Fig. 2.

Fig. 2. Test image and reference image computed by a semi-implicit scheme. **Left**: Original image (finger, 300×300, rescaled to [0,255] for better visualisation). **Right**: CED-filtered reference image ($T = 300$, $\lambda = 1$, $\sigma = 0.5$, $\rho = 4$, $\alpha = 0.001$, $\tau = 0.1$), rescaled to [0,255]

Our error measure is the relative mean absolute error (RMAE), $\sum_i \frac{|u_i - r_i|}{\|r\|_1}$ with $\|r\|_1 := \sum_i |r_i|$. The filtered image is denoted by u, and r is the corresponding reference solution.

Table 2 shows that FED and the semi-implicit method yield comparable results with respect to the RMAE. In some cases, FED is even better than the semi-implicit scheme.

In order to show the efficiency of the novel FED compared to semi-implicit methods, we have conducted an experiment analysing the trade-off between the running time (CPU: Pentium 4, 3.2 GHz) and the RMAE. The result is depicted in Fig. 3. As one can see, the FED scheme shows a better trade-off, i.e. is more efficient than the usual semi-implicit scheme with a conjugate gradient (CG) solver.

Table 2. Comparison between FED and the semi-implicit method for different numbers of FED cycles/semi-implicit steps using the RMAE

cycles/steps	FED	semi-impl.
1	0.028106	0.020914
5	0.010587	0.009639
10	0.007206	0.006638
25	0.003922	0.003731
50	0.002074	0.002234
100	0.001063	0.001265

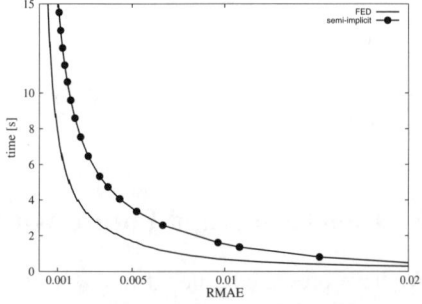

Fig. 3. CPU time (seconds) vs. RMAE

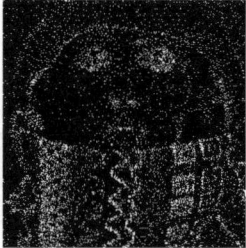

Fig. 4. Test setting for EED-based image reconstruction. **Left**: Original image (trui, 257×257). **Middle**: Inpainting mask where the pixels are specified. **Right**: Reconstruction with EED-based inpainting in the unspecified regions (semi-implicit, $T = 250000$, $\tau = 2.5$, $\lambda = 0.1$, $\sigma = 1.5$)

Let us now consider an elliptic problem, where we evaluate the performance of our FED and CFED scheme. As a testbed we use an interpolation problem that is relevant for image compression with EED [3]. For the coarse-to-fine setting, we use three levels: 257×257, 129×129 and 65×65 pixels.

Fig. 4 depicts the test setting. We use the same error measure as above and compare our results to the reference reconstruction shown in Fig. 4. The comparison concerning the trade-off between the CPU time and the RMAE, which is illustrated in Fig. 5 for the stopping time $T = 5000$, emphasises the superior efficiency of FED and CFED respectively. In both cases, the corresponding semi-implicit schemes are less efficient. Moreover, CFED further improves the efficiency of FED. If one wants to have for example a solution whose RMAE is below 1%, CFED can manage this in less than a quarter of a second, because already a small stopping of $T = 100$ is sufficient.

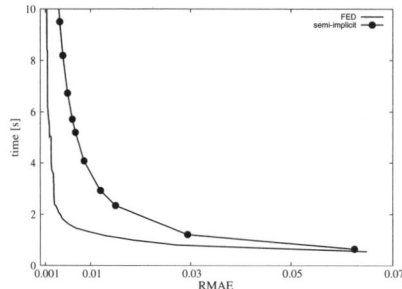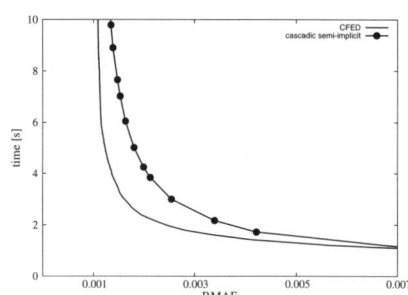

Fig. 5. CPU time (seconds) vs. RMAE for $T = 5000$. **Left**: FED and semi-implicit. **Right**: CFED and cascadic semi-implicit

6   Conclusions and Future Work

We have presented a new framework for explicit diffusion schemes, FED, which has been derived by the theory of one-dimensional box filters. This means we have established an interesting connection between a symmetric linear filter and an explicit scheme with varying time step sizes that partially violates stability limits. FED is very easy to implement, since existing explicit schemes with only few additional code lines can be used. Furthermore, we have successfully applied FED to anisotropic diffusion processes and PDE-based image reconstruction, where we have additionally used a coarse-to-fine strategy. Due to the large time step sizes, explicit schemes can become more efficient than semi-implicit ones, as we have shown in the experimental section. The cascadic strategy CFED can even improve the results of FED with respect to in-painting applications.

In our ongoing work, we are currently working on parallelisation techniques as well as GPU-based implementations. With the help of them, it might be possible to yield even faster anisotropic diffusion filtering and real-time decoding with anisotropic diffusion via explicit schemes. Another research field are higher-dimensional problems, since semi-implicit schemes become cumbersome for such tasks due to the large neighbourhood structure. In this case, the benefit of FED is expected to increase even further.

Acknowledgements. Sven Grewenig gratefully acknowledges funding by the Deutsche Forschungsgemeinschaft (DFG), project WE 2602/7-1.

References

1. Weickert, J.: Anisotropic Diffusion in Image Processing. Teubner, Stuttgart (1998)
2. Höcker, C., Fehmers, G.: Fast structural interpretation with structure-oriented filtering. Geophysics 68(4), 1286–1293 (2003)
3. Galić, I., Weickert, J., Welk, M., Bruhn, A., Belyaev, A., Seidel, H.P.: Image compression with anisotropic diffusion. Journal of Mathematical Imaging and Vision 31(2-3), 255–269 (2008)
4. Perona, P., Malik, J.: Scale space and edge detection using anisotropic diffusion. IEEE Transactions on Pattern Analysis and Machine Intelligence 12, 629–639 (1990)
5. Lu, T., Neittaanmäki, P., Tai, X.C.: A parallel splitting up method and its application to Navier-Stokes equations. Applied Mathematics Letters 4(2), 25–29 (1991)
6. Weickert, J., ter Haar Romeny, B.M., Viergever, M.A.: Efficient and reliable schemes for nonlinear diffusion filtering. IEEE Transactions on Image Processing 7(3), 398–410 (1998)
7. Drblíková, O., Mikula, K.: Convergence analysis of finite volume scheme for nonlinear tensor anisotropic diffusion in image processing. SIAM Journal on Numerical Analysis 46(1), 37–60 (2007)
8. Weickert, J., Scharr, H.: A scheme for coherence-enhancing diffusion filtering with optimized rotation invariance. Journal of Visual Communication and Image Representation 13(1/2), 103–118 (2002)
9. Welk, M., Steidl, G., Weickert, J.: Locally analytic schemes: A link between diffusion filtering and wavelet shrinkage. Applied and Computational Harmonic Analysis 24, 195–224 (2008)
10. Gentzsch, W., Schlüter, A.: Über ein Einschrittverfahren mit zyklischer Schrittweitenänderung zur Lösung parabolischer Differentialgleichungen. ZAMM, Zeitschrift für Angewandte Mathematik und Mechanik 58, T415–T416 (1978)
11. Gentzsch, W.: Numerical solution of linear and non-linear parabolic differential equations by a time discretisation of third order accuracy. In: Hirschel, E.H. (ed.) Proceedings of the Third GAMM-Conference on Numerical Methods in Fluid Mechanics, pp. 109–117. Friedr. Vieweg & Sohn (1979)

12. Alexiades, V., Amiez, G., Gremaud, P.A.: Super-time-stepping acceleration of explicit schemes for parabolic problems. Communications in Numerical Methods in Engineering 12, 31–42 (1996)
13. Bornemann, F., Deuflhard, P.: The cascadic multigrid method for elliptic problems. Numerische Mathematik 75, 135–152 (1996)
14. Weickert, J.: Nonlinear diffusion filtering. In: Jähne, B., Haußecker, H., Geißler, P. (eds.) Handbook on Computer Vision and Applications. Signal Processing and Pattern Recognition, vol. 2, pp. 423–450. Academic Press, San Diego (1999)

Appendix: Proof of Theorem 1

After some calculations, one can represent the box filter as a finite operator series:

$$
B_{2n+1}^h = \sum_{m=0}^{n} \frac{h^{2m}}{2m+1} \binom{n+m}{2m} \Delta_h^m \,, \tag{15}
$$

where $\Delta_h^0 := I$ (identity operator). Replacing Δ_h by $(-z)$ in Eq. (15) defines the polynomial $p_n(z)$. It follows that p_n can be related to the Chebyshev polynomial of first kind,

$$
C_{2n+1}(x) = \frac{2n+1}{2} \sum_{m=0}^{n} \frac{(-1)^m}{2n+1-m} \binom{2n+1-m}{m} (2x)^{2(n-m)+1} \,, \tag{16}
$$

and it holds for $z > 0$:

$$
p_n(z) = (-1)^n \cdot \frac{2C_{2n+1}\left(\frac{h\sqrt{z}}{2}\right)}{(2n+1)h\sqrt{z}} \,. \tag{17}
$$

Hence, the roots z_i of p_n are related to the first n (positive) well-known roots of C_{2n+1}, namely $x_0, \ldots, x_{n-1}$:

$$
z_i = \frac{4}{h^2} x_i^2 = \frac{4}{h^2} \cdot \cos^2\left(\pi \tfrac{2i+1}{4n+2}\right) > 0 \,. \tag{18}
$$

Thus, we can represent p_n as a product of n linear factors $(1 - z/z_i)$, and by the back substitution $(-z) \to \Delta_h$ we finally get

$$
B_{2n+1}^h = \prod_{i=0}^{n-1} \left(I + z_i^{-1} \Delta_h\right) \,. \tag{19}
$$

This shows that B_{2n+1}^h is equivalent to an explicit linear diffusion scheme using the n time step sizes $\tau_i = z_i^{-1}$, and the stopping time t_n is equal to the coefficient of Δ_h ($m = 1$) in Eq. (15).

High-Resolution Object Deformation Reconstruction with Active Range Camera*

Andreas Jordt, Ingo Schiller, Johannes Bruenger, and Reinhard Koch

Multimedia Information Processing, Institute of Computer Science
Christian-Albrechts-University (CAU) of Kiel, Germany

Abstract. This contribution discusses the 3D reconstruction of deformable freeform surfaces with high spatial and temporal resolution. These are conflicting requirements, since high-resolution surface scanners typically cannot achieve high temporal resolution, while high-speed range cameras like the Time-of-Flight (ToF) cameras capture depth at 25 fps but have a limited spatial resolution. We propose to combine a high-resolution surface scan with a ToF-camera and a color camera to achieve both requirements. The 3D surface deformation is modeled by a NURBS surface that approximates the object surface and estimates the 3D object motion and local 3D deformation from the ToF and color camera data. A set of few NURBS control points can faithfully model the motion and deformation and will be estimated from the ToF and color data with high accuracy. The contribution will focus on the estimation of the 3D deformation NURBS from the ToF and color data.

1 Introduction

In this paper we address the problem of reconstruction and tracking of deformable freeform surfaces. If both, the 3D surface geometry and the surface deformation over time need to be analyzed simultaneously, this is a difficult problem. 3D shape analysis with laser scanners, for example, render a high resolution static model, but are not suitable to track deformations over time. Recent range cameras like the Time-of-Flight (ToF) cameras, on the other hand, allow for capturing scene depth with high frame rates of up to 25 fps, but with limited spatial resolution and considerable noise level. In our approach we propose to combine both techniques by first acquiring a high resolution 3D surface model with a laser triangulation system, and then tracking the surface deformation over time with a combined color-depth camera system. 3D surface deformations are modeled by a NURBS spline approximation controlled by 2D image flow and 3D depth measurements from the ToF-camera system in low depth resolution but high color resolution. The smoothing and interpolating properties of the NURBS allow for handling measurement noise. The 3D surface deformation

---

* This work was supported by the German Research Foundation (DFG), KO-2044/3-2 and the EU Interreg A4 Project "Intelligent Robots for Handling flexible Objects" (IRFO), 33-1.2-09

M. Goesele et al. (Eds.): DAGM 2010, LNCS 6376, pp. 543–552, 2010.

can be decomposed into a hierarchy of 3D global object motion and 3D local deformation. These transformations can also be applied to the high resolution surface model, leading to a surface deformation with high spatial and temporal resolution. In the following section we will first review related work, then derive the deformation estimation using the NURBS in section 2, discuss the propagation of the deformation onto the high-resolution model in section 3, and give experimental results in section 4.

1.1   Related Work

There exist many different parametrizations and representations of deformable surfaces. A good survey by Montagnat et al. can be found in [1]. There NURBS surface representation is sorted into the class of explicit polynomial finite support representations. It is stated that these models lead to more stable results if a limited number of parameters is estimated. According to Cohen et al. in [2], who uses NURBS to fit a surface to a scattered data set of 3D points, NURBS are the most efficient way to represent surfaces and additionally implicitly provide a smoothing effect. Most of the work on deformation estimation however, was done using triangle meshes as surface representation [3],[4] which comes with a high number of unkowns that have to be handled by applying additional constraints.

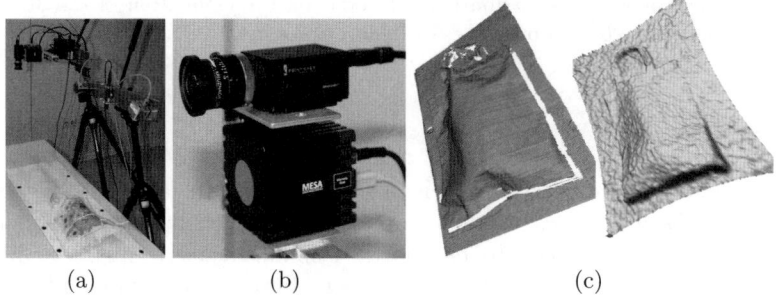

    (a)   (b)   (c)

Fig. 1. (a) Setup for laser triangulation, consisting of a line laser and two CCD cameras. (b) A Swissranger SR4000 ToF-camera, coupled with a CCD-camera. (c) Mesh acquired by laser triangulation (left) and ToF-camera (right)

In a face recognition survey by Browyer et al. [5] p. 11, different modalities (2D/3D data) and acquisition methods are compared regarding their suitability for geometry and deformation capturing. According to this, stereo is in general capable of capturing geometry at high frame rates but suffers from errors on sparsely textured regions. Structured-Light approaches suffer from artifacts due to object motion and spike artifacts frequently occur. It is concluded that it would be optimal to capture the geometry at a single time instant. This matches our motivation to use a ToF-camera, which records the current geometry with a single shot and provides a frame rate of 25 fps at a reasonable noise level.

Zhang et al. use a Structured Light stereo algorithm in [6] to capture the dynamic geometry of faces during deformation. The impressive results of face deformation capturing go along with a highly complicated setup consisting of six cameras and two projectors. A, in point of complexity, comparable system is used by Walder et al. in [7] to record facial expressions and other object deformations. Both approaches are specially designed for these scenarios and are, due to their dimension, not flexible. Our proposed approach, consisting of one ToF- and one CCD-camera is much more flexible and can for example be mounted to a robot arm to capture deformations of objects while they are manipulated by the robot.

2   Low Resolution Deformation Estimation

To expediently analyze complex surface deformations and movements simultaneously, the 3D surface changes are divided into three separate classes of transformations, each handled separately:

- The **rigid body movement**, i.e. the translation and rotation of the whole object. This displacement is also referred to as global pose change $G(\cdot)$
- The remaining **2D deformation** $\mathcal{N}(\cdot, P)$, which is the movement in the image after the global pose change has been compensated.
- The **Z-fitting** $\mathcal{N}(\cdot, C)$, which describes the depth displacement of the object after the two previous deformations have been removed.

To describe and store the deformation acquired in the latter two steps we choose to use NURBS surface functions $\mathcal{N}$. These function come with a set of useful features for the task at hand: A NURBS surface is described by a set of control points, which serves as a distinct deformation descriptor in our system. At the same time NURBS functions are very versatile allowing to approximate all kinds of surfaces. Furthermore, any global pose change can be applied easily to such a surface by simply applying the transformation to its control points. A NURBS function is efficiently fitted into point data because of the linear relationship between a surface point and the control points. This guarantees fast optimization without the need to fear local minima.

2.1   Time-of-Flight Camera

A ToF-camera is an active camera which emits intensity non-coherent modulated near infrared light using special LEDs and calculates the distance of objects to the camera from the reflected signal with a special sensor. Typically a modulation frequency between 10 and 40MHz is chosen for distance measurement with ToF-cameras. Because of the limited operation area and increased accuracy with higher modulation frequencies we use 40MHz in our experiments which results in an operation range of ≈ 3.75 meters. For further details on the operation principle please consult Xu et al. [8] and Lange et al. [9]. To obtain color and depth information we combine the ToF-camera with a standard CCD-Camera and calibrate the two cameras internally and externally using the approach described in [10].

2.2   Global Pose Estimation

In this first step the global pose change, which is independent of local deformation, is estimated. We use a feature-based approach using a set K of 2D KLT-features k_n [11] on the object, where k_n is one feature in multiple images and $k_{n,i} \in [0,1]^2$ is the position of this feature in image $i \in I$. The depth image is not aligned with the CCD image but has to be transferred to the perspective of the CCD camera. Therefor a triangle mesh of the depth image provided by the ToF-camera is generated on the GPU and the mesh is rendered in the perspective of the CCD camera with the corresponding internal and external camera parameters. The corresponding 3D features are then taken from the rendered depth image. To isolate the object from the background, color-segmentation in the HSL color space is applied, removing all none-object features.

The current pose change of the object $G_i(\cdot) : (x,y,z) \mapsto (x',y',z')$ is a global transformation, consisting of a rotation and a translation, which describes the average modification in position and orientation of the object for every 3D coordinate in the initial frame 0 to the current one i. It is estimated from the 2D/3D correspondences using the standard DLT approach as in [12] p.173. The transformation $G_i'(\cdot) : (x,y) \mapsto (x',y')$ unprojects a 2D point in frame 0 to the object surface, applies G_i and reprojects the 3D point to the image. Hence, G_i' is a displacement function approximating the 2D feature movement in the image from frame 0 to frame i, as far as it can be approached by a rigid 3D body movement. The inverse transformations G^{-1} and G'^{-1} to remove the described change in the global pose/image position can be calculated directly from G and G'.

Figure 2 shows three pairs of input images (a)-(c) in which the depth is on top the color images. The darker the closer is the object to the camera. A bag, filled with an object, is observed while the object is removed from the bag. During this operation the bag's movement and deformation estimated. Images (d) and (e) show the textured mesh of the depth values, rendered with G_i^{-1} of the current frame.

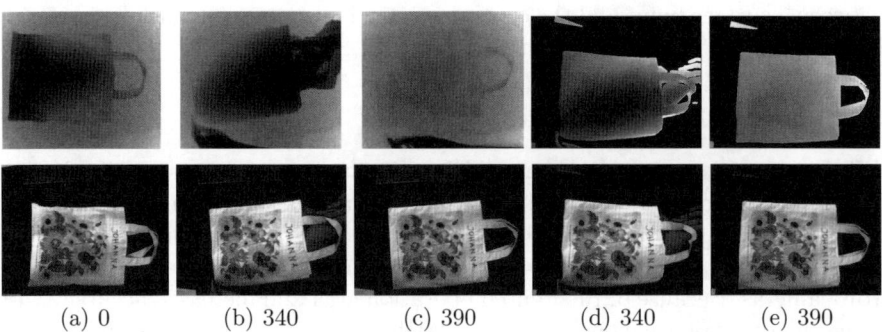

(a) 0   (b) 340   (c) 390   (d) 340   (e) 390

Fig. 2. (a)-(c) Captured depth and CCD images of a bag at time 0, 340 and 390. (d)-(e) Pose compensated rendered and segmented images of frame 340 and 390. Note that the rotation of the bag is reverted (G_i^{-1} is applied) in images (d) and (e) to match the pose in image (a).

2.3   2D Deformation NURBS

The challenging goal to track the object's deformation for every surface point implies that every surface point can be tracked throughout each image. Since such a dense pixel registration is not feasible, we use the KLT features introduced in section 2.2 as the set of "trackable" image points. These features are used to create a dense 2D deformation map, which can be evaluated in every pixel coordinate, by fitting a 2D NURBS function $\mathcal{N}(\cdot, P)$ into the KLT movement data. A NURBS (surface) function of equally weighted control points $p_j \in P$ is defined for m control points by:

$$\mathcal{N}((u,v), P) = \sum_{j=0}^{m} R_j(u,v)p_j \qquad (1)$$

where $R_j(u,v)$ is a function providing the weights defining the influence on the surface point (u,v) for each control point p_j. For the complete definition refer to e.g. [13].

Equation (1) reveals the linear relationship between each surface point and each control point and it is obvious, that the output dimension of the NURBS function is entirely defined by the dimension of the control points.

To interpolate the movement of a set of 2D features K, a control point vector P has to be found such that $\mathcal{N}(\cdot, P)$ defines a 2D deformation map as close as possible to the known deformations $k_{n,0} \rightarrow k_{n,i}$ for each image $i \in I$. This is the case for the minimal argument P_i of the squared error sum

$$P_i = \operatorname*{argmin}_{P \in \mathbb{R}^{3 \cdot m}} \sum_{n \in K} (\mathcal{N}_i(k_{n,0}, P) - k_{n,i})^2 \qquad (2)$$

To ensure contour alignment in surface regions without features, an additional error term for the contour fitting is added to the squared sum. Let B be a set of contour points $b \in [0,1]^2$ in the first image and $\Delta_i(\cdot)$ a function providing the distance of a point to the contour of image i. $\Delta_i(x,y) = 0$ for all border pixels. If (x,y) is inside the contour of the object, $\Delta_i(x,y)$ yields the distance in pixels from the center of mass to the border. If (x,y) is outside the object's contour, $\Delta_i(x,y)$ provides the distance from the center of mass to the corresponding contour border. The NURBS error term (2) is therefore extended by the contour error:

$$P_i = \operatorname*{argmin}_{P \in \mathbb{R}^{3 \cdot m}} \sum_{n \in K} (\mathcal{N}_i(k_{n,0}, P) - k_{n,i})^2 + \sum_{l \in B} \Delta_i(b_l) \qquad (3)$$

We use a Levenberg-Marquardt optimizer to minimize this error function which yields the 2D control point vector P_i^* for each image $i \in I$. Since also the inverse function $\mathcal{N}^{-1}(\cdot, P_i)$ is required in our system, a second control point vector P^{-1} is generated in the same way, such that $\mathcal{N}(\cdot, P_i^{-1}) \approx \mathcal{N}^{-1}(\cdot, P_i)$.

2.4   3D Deformation NURBS

As a result of the two previous steps, a function $\mathcal{N}(G(\cdot), P)$ approximating the dense 2D deformation in the images is available along with the inverse approximation $G'^{-1}(\mathcal{N}(\cdot, P^{-1}))$. To create a full 3D surface deformation function, the global pose data, the 2D NURBS and the depth data remaining after the 2D compensation have to be combined into a 3D NURBS.

Spread function. Up to this point the description of the object contour has not influenced the NURBS shape explicitly, but only through additional constraints ensuring the alignment of the object border. The NURBS parameter domain is usually defined as $[0, 1]^2$. If the contour information is ought to be stored in the NURBS surface, an initial transition from the NURBS domain into the "object shaped domain" has to be defined, such that the squared border of the NURBS domain becomes aligned with the contour of the object. Let $S_i(\cdot)$ be this function to "spread" the object domain into the 2D NURBS domain for every image $i \in I$ and let $S_i^{-1}(\cdot)$ be the corresponding "shrinking" function for the transformation from the 2D NURBS domain into the object domain.

Z-Fitting. Using the inverse function to the global pose change G and the 2D NURBS deformation P, a sequence of images can be generated out of the original image sequence, in which every surface point of the object remains on the same pixel coordinate. Fitting a three dimensional NURBS surface into the depth data processed by G^{-1} and P^{-1} is now straight forward: A uniformly distributed set of points is placed in the bounding box of the object and "shrunk" by S^{-1}.

These points provide the x- and y- image coordinates of the three dimensional control points. The remaining (depth) dimension is fitted into the processed depth image data, analog to the two dimensional fitting process described in 2.3. Let C' be this vector of control points.

Combining the Deformations. The control points C for the global deformation function $\mathcal{N}(\cdot, C)$ can now be defined. The z-fitting provides a 3D NURBS without the global pose change G and 2D deformation $\mathcal{N}(\cdot, P)$. First, the control points C' are moved according to the 2D deformation $\mathcal{N}(\cdot, P)$, and afterwards they are rotated and translated according to the global pose change G:

$$C = G(\mathcal{N}(C', P)) \tag{4}$$

The resulting NURBS function $\mathcal{N}(\cdot, C)$ does not only approximate the surface provided by the segmented depth images, it also maps to the same three dimensional surface point $\mathcal{N}((u, v), C_i)$ in each image i for a constant (u, v), despite its movements in the image.

3   Propagation of Deformation Parameters to High Resolution Model

After estimating the deformation on the low resolution surface measured by the ToF-camera we want to propagate the deformation to a model with higher spatial resolution.

3.1   High Resolution Model Acquisition

The acquisition of the high resolution model is done using a line laser and two CCD cameras. Using a line laser the resolution is only limited by the resolution of the CCD cameras and the thickness of the used laser. Figure 1a shows the used setup for laser triangulation and figure 1c (left) shows a model acquired with the laser triangulation approach which is comparable to [14]. The proposed deformation method is of course able to handle any differently originated high resolution model as well.

3.2   Deformation Application

To apply the detected deformation sequence to the high resolution mesh, a mapping for each high resolution vertex position in 3D to the corresponding two dimensional NURBS coordinate in $[0,1]^2$ has to be found. If chosen carefully, each vertex is assigned to the coordinate in the NURBS domain which is tracing the original surface point throughout all input images.

The most suitable way to create such a mapping is to reproduce the assignment step from the low resolution process in this high resolution case. Let $M : \mathbb{R}^3 \rightarrow \mathbb{R}^2$ be an projection for the high resolution model equivalent to the first deformation image. For this first image, the global pose change is 0, as well as the 2D deformation. Hence, the 2D NURBS coordinates can be acquired directly from the spread function: $(u,v) = S(M'((x,y,z))$.

For image i, a transformed vertex v_i following the deformation is given by

$$v_i = v - \mathcal{N}_0(S(P'(v))) + \mathcal{N}_i(S(P'(v))) \tag{5}$$

The surface registration is constant in respect to the NURBS domain as well as to the high resolution model. This allows to interpolate and smooth C in an arbitrary way without causing unwanted deformations. One way to interpolate and smooth at the same time is the application of dynamic NURBS [15], which include the time domain as a third parameter in the NURBS domain.

4   Results

To evaluate the results quantitatively we chose the following scenario. A bag made of cloth was filled with an object and scanned with the laser scanner. Afterwards the object is removed from the bag while the bag is observed by the ToF- and CCD-camera. After flattening the bag it is again scanned with the laser scanner for comparison of the scanned geometry with the NURBS approximated final geometry. The setup to acquire the results is shown in figure 1a. The NURBS surface representation aims at approximating the real geometry and therefor we rely on a visual validation of the obtained results. The results are presented in figure 3.

Initially the bag is filled (a), then a hand lifts the handle (b), goes inside the bag (c) and removes the object from the bag (d). Finally the empty bag is moved

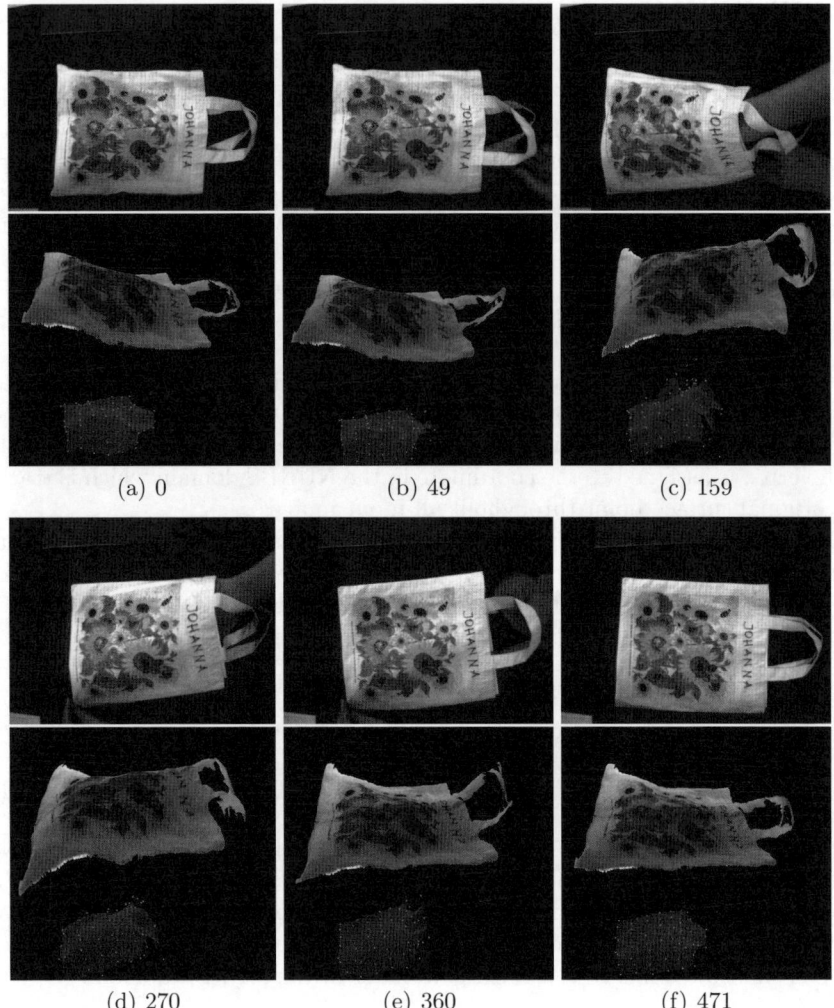

Fig. 3. Deformation of high resolution model (≈ 470000 triangles) of the bag. Images show input color images above the deformed high resolution textured model which is shown above the NURBS surface with control points. Numbers below images indicate frame indices.

to the original position (e) and (f). To quantitatively evaluate the approach, the RMS (root mean squared) deviation of the deformed high resolution model at frame 471 (object completely removed) and the laser scanned empty bag has been measured (figure 4c and d). The size of the filled reconstructed bag was $26.5 \times 40 \times 9.5$cm and the deviation (RMS of distances between surfaces considering each vertex) was found to be 5.86 mm for the presented scene.

The proposed algorithm is applicable to various objects. Figure 5 shows its application to a hand during a movement in a relaxed and a deformed state.

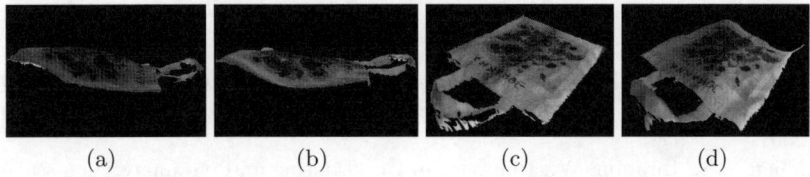

(a)   (b)   (c)   (d)

Fig. 4. Comparison of scanned filled bag (a) with reconstructed filled bag (b) and scanned empty bag (c) with reconstructed empty bag (d)

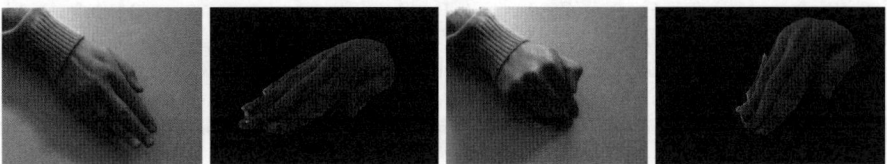

Fig. 5. Deformation applied to a high resolution model of a hand

5   Conclusion

This contribution presents an approach to capture and reconstruct the deformation of objects. We are using a laser scanner to obtain a high resolution 3D model of the object and a ToF-camera to capture the deformation at 25 fps. The choice to use the ToF-camera is motivated by its small size and flexibility, compared to other approaches that use e.g. structured light stereo approaches with projectors. This enables the usage of our approach in less controlled environments and for mounting to robot arms for example. The choice to use NURBS to represent the deformation is motivated by the implicit surface smoothing that is provided by the estimation of the NURBS control points during optimization of the parameters as all points on the object surface contribute to the parameter estimation but the effect of false measurements and outliers is narrowed. Part of our contribution is the decomposition of the object's transformations in several steps. The rigid transformation the object might undergo is estimated by feature tracking and pose estimation. This pose is reverted by rendering the model with the inverse of the estimated pose. The 2D transformation in the image plane the object undergoes is tracked using KLT-features and approximated using a 2D NURBS function. Finally the change in depth is again approximated with a NURBS function. Essential to this processing chain is, that all steps can be reverted easily to map the estimation to the initial shape of the object.

Finally the approximation is applied to the high resolution laser scanned model of the object, by which the deformation of this model is simulated at a spatial and temporal resolution that can not be achieved by other comparable setups and approaches we have knowledge of. Furthermore the recorded deformation could be applied to other objects, making it possible to simulate the deformation of rigid objects.

References

1. Montagnat, J., Delingette, H., Ayache, N.: A review of deformable surfaces: topology, geometry and deformation. Image and Vision Computing 19(14), 1023–1040 (2001)
2. Cohen, F.S., Ibrahim, W., Pintavirooj, C.: Ordering and parameterizing scattered 3d data for b-spline surface approximation. IEEE Transactions on pattern analysis and machine intelligence 22(6), 642–648 (2000)
3. Cagniar, C., Boyer, E., Ilic, S.: Iterative mesh deformation for dense surface tracking. In: 12th International Conference on Computer Vision Workshops (2009)
4. Zhu, J., Hoi, S.C.H., Xu, Z., Lyu, M.R.: An effective approach to 3d deformable surface tracking. In: Forsyth, D., Torr, P., Zisserman, A. (eds.) ECCV 2008, Part III. LNCS, vol. 5304, pp. 766–779. Springer, Heidelberg (2008)
5. Bowyer, K.W., Chang, K., Flynn, P.: A survey of approaches and challenges in 3d and multi-modal 3d+2d face recognition. Computer Vision and Image Understanding 101(1), 1–15 (2006)
6. Zhang, L., Snavely, N., Curless, B., Seitz, S.M.: Spacetime faces: High-resolution capture for modeling and animation. In: ACM Annual Conference on Computer Graphics, pp. 548–558 (August 2004)
7. Walder, C., Breidt, M., Buelthoff, H.H., Schoelkopf, B., Curio, C.: Markerless 3d face tracking. In: Denzler, J., Notni, G., Süe, H. (eds.) DAGM 2009. LNCS, vol. 5748, pp. 41–50. Springer, Heidelberg (2009)
8. Xu, Z., Schwarte, R., Heinol, H., Buxbaum, B., Ringbeck., T.: Smart pixel - photonic mixer device (pmd). In: M2VIP 1998 - International Conference on Mechatronics and Machine Vision in Practice, pp. 259–264 (1998)
9. Lange, R., Seitz, P., Biber, A., Schwarte, R.: Time-of-flight range imaging with a custom solid-state imagesensor. In: EOS/SPIE Laser Metrology and Inspection, vol. 3823 (1999)
10. Schiller, I., Beder, C., Koch, R.: Calibration of a pmd camera using a planar calibration object together with a multi-camera setup. In: The International Archives of the Photogrammetry, Remote Sensing and Spatial Information Sciences, Beijing, China, vol. XXXVII, Part B3a, pp. 297–302. XXI. ISPRS Congress (2008)
11. Shi, J., Tomasi, C.: Good features to track. In: Conference on Computer Vision and Pattern Recognition, Seattle, pp. 593–600. IEEE, Los Alamitos (June 1994)
12. Hartley, R.I., Zisserman, A.: Multiple View Geometry in Computer Vision. Cambridge University Press, Cambridge (2000) ISBN: 0521623049
13. Piegl, L., Tiller, W.: The NURBS Book, 2nd edn. Springer, Berlin (1997)
14. Isgro, F., Odone, F., Verri, A.: An open system for 3d data acquisition from multiple sensor. In: CAMP 2005:7th Int. Workshop on Computer Architecture for Machine Perception, Washington, DC, USA, pp. 52–57. IEEE Computer Society, Los Alamitos (2005)
15. Terzopoulos, D., Qin, H.: Dynamic nurbs with geometric constraints for interactive sculpting. ACM Trans. Graph. 13(2), 103–136 (1994)

Selection of an Optimal Polyhedral Surface Model Using the Minimum Description Length Principle

Tilman Wekel and Olaf Hellwich

Computer Vision & Remote Sensing, Berlin University of Technology
Franklinstrasse 28/29, Office FR 3-1, D-10587 Berlin

Abstract. In this paper a new approach to find an optimal surface representation is described. It is shown that the minimum description length (MDL) principle can be used to select a trade-off between goodness-of-fit and complexity of decimated mesh representations. A given mesh is iteratively simplified by using different decimation algorithms. At each step the two-part minimum description length is evaluated. The first part encodes all model parameters while the second part encodes the error residuals given the model. A Bayesian approach is used to deduce the MDL term. The shortest code length identifies the optimal trade-off. The method has been successfully tested by various examples.

1 Introduction

Detailed surface models are used by various disciplines such as geometric measurement, computer aided design oder scientific visualization. Although a high level of detail is generally required, there is always the need of compact representations for many reasons. The most obvious intention for a simplification is to reduce the amount of data and thus minimize memory and computation costs. Another interesting aspect is roughly stated by Occam's razor saying that things should be described as simple as possible. A very simple solution often captures the major principles of an entity and yields a certain amount of knowledge and understanding.

Consider a geometric scene that basically consists of very simple objects like cubes, pyramids and so forth. If a human is supposed to describe the setup, he intuitively focuses on the general structure in a semantic-oriented matter and his understanding of the given scene influences the way of describing it. A cube can be defined by a few characteristic points rather than by a dense mesh including a high number of vertices and facets. Now, considering that the cube holds some irregularities or small deformations, a human still refers to the cube and just adds that there are some small bumps on the cube's surface. Accordingly, the underlying task is to find laws or regularities in order to describe the data efficiently. If that idea is taken to an extreme and the description is not given verbally but coded in bits, regularities can be used to reduce the number of bits needed to entirely transmit the data. This leads to a generic concept named the

M. Goesele et al. (Eds.): DAGM 2010, LNCS 6376, pp. 553–562, 2010.

minimum description length principle which states, that the model achieving the highest data compression should be used among a specific class of models [1].

This work discusses the application of a rather general principle to the representation of polyhedral surfaces. In section two a short overview of related efforts is given. A Bayesian model for polyhedral surface data is derived in section three. Finally, the two part minimum description length is composed in section four while the evaluation of the presented method can be found in section five. A conclusion and possible applications are given in the last section.

2   Related Work

The simplification of meshes has gained high attention in recent years and there exist several promising techniques. Some approaches focus on a simplification algorithm while others are emphasizing a specific error metric or the approximation quality [2]. However, the automatic selection of an appropriate trade-off between goodness-of-fit and model complexity is often not considered. Most algorithms must be supplied with a certain quality or error parameter. Fidelity-based approaches let the user define some kind of threshold that ensures a minimum approximation quality of the simplified mesh.

Hoppe et al. [3] present a global optimization method using an energy function with a similar structure as the term used in this paper. The function to be optimized is composed of the mesh complexity and the sum of the squared distances from the vertices to the mesh. However, it is shown that the minimum of this function does not necessarily lead to the optimal mesh configuration. The authors face that problem by introducing a spring term representing the sum over all squared edge lengths multiplied by a spring constant. Cignoni et al. [4] present a method to evaluate the quality of a mesh approximation. The method compares two triangular meshes and no further knowledge is required. One of the surfaces, which is called the pivot surface is resampled at a user defined resolution. The normalized surface integral of the shortest distance of all points to the simplified surface is then the desired error measure. The approach by Garland et al. [5] uses an efficient evaluation scheme called quadric error metrics to assign a cost value to each edge. A quadric error measures the squared distance of a given point to a plane. A plane is defined by its normal vector and a point that lies on the plane. The error associated to each vertex is the sum of squared distances to the adjacent faces, weighted by the corresponding area. The algorithm iteratively removes vertices until a user defined number of remaining faces is reached. Lindstrom et al. [6] present an approach that iteratively collapses edges which are then replaced by new vertices. The costs of a replacement are characterized by the change of several geometric properties such as volume, area or shape. The cost scheme only considers local properties and a history of the original geometry is not required which makes this approach very efficient. However, the algorithm does not provide a global error and the process is iterated until the mesh is reduced to a certain number of polygons, which is controlled by the user. Although the algorithm delivers good and reasonable results, it tends to smooth edges and works best for organic models. A slightly modified version is used for the evaluation of the approach presented in this paper.

3   Model Order Selection

If we are looking for a model that explains a given data set appropriately, we try to find a compromise between good fit and small complexity. This problem is known as model selection and formalized in the following. Typically, only a specific class of models are considered. In this context, a model class is defined to be an ordered set of models that are derived from a superior definition and share major properties:

$$\Theta = \{\Theta_0, \Theta_1, \Theta_2 ... \Theta_n\} \ . \tag{1}$$

Each member is assigned with an index that shall equate to the degrees of freedom of that model. The model Θ_i can be seen as a function with i linear independent parameters. In the context of fitting problems we are interested in a model Θ_γ, with $\gamma = \gamma_{opt}$, which gives an optimal trade-off between a good fit and small complexity, that means a small index in the associated set of models. A good fit of a specific model $\Theta_k \in \Theta$ means maximizing the probability of the data given that model:

$$\hat{\boldsymbol{\theta}}_k(D) = \hat{\boldsymbol{\theta}}_k = \arg \max_{\boldsymbol{\theta}_k \in \Theta_k} P(D|\boldsymbol{\theta}_k) \ , \tag{2}$$

where $\boldsymbol{\theta}_k$ is a $k-$dimensional parameter vector and $\hat{\boldsymbol{\theta}}_k(D)$ is a maximum likelihood estimator.

4   Optimal Mesh Representation

Consider that we have measured a number of noisy points which lie on a surface. Such a dense and unstructured point cloud is a typical result of a reconstruction algorithm. The data points are only measured observation but somehow related to hidden variables representing the original geometry. The acquisition process adds noise to the data and we assume the following relation between observation $\boldsymbol{y}_j$ and hidden variable $\boldsymbol{x}_j$:

$$\boldsymbol{y}_j = \boldsymbol{x}_j + \boldsymbol{n}_j, \ \boldsymbol{n}_j \sim \mathcal{N}(\boldsymbol{0}, \boldsymbol{I} \cdot \sigma_j) \ . \tag{3}$$

Our observation $\boldsymbol{y}_j$ is a measured point and $\boldsymbol{x}_j$ is a "hidden" point. The measurement adds noise to the original data. The presented approach is independent from a specific sensor device and we assume a simple Gauss-model. The probability distribution for the observation $\boldsymbol{y}_j$, given $\boldsymbol{x}_j$ turns out to be:

$$P(\boldsymbol{y}_j|\boldsymbol{x}_j) = (2\,\pi\sigma_j^2)^{-\frac{3}{2}} \exp(-\frac{|\boldsymbol{x}_j - \boldsymbol{y}_j|^2}{2\,\sigma_j^2}) \ , \tag{4}$$

where the variance is $\sigma_j{}^2$ in all dimensions. The probability function depends on the Euclidean distance between $\boldsymbol{y}_j$ and $\boldsymbol{x}_j$. The hidden points are not statistically independent. They are related by a surface model that yields several constraints such as smoothness or density. Consider a surface model S_k with k degrees of freedom. According to [7], we can define the probapility space of possible original surfaces as a set of discrete point clouds that has been sampled from our model S_k. It is implicitly assumed that the closest correspondence $\boldsymbol{x}_j \in S_k$ yields the measurement $\boldsymbol{y}_j$. The technical problem of how to find the closest corresponding point is related to orthogonal distance fitting and not focused in this work [8]. It is assumed that there exists a vector-valued function $\boldsymbol{T}(\boldsymbol{y}_j) = \boldsymbol{x}_j$ that associates a measured point $\boldsymbol{y}_j$ to its closest correspondence $\boldsymbol{x}_j \in S_k$ on the surface with respect to the topology. Given the model S_k, we can use the independence assumption and obtain:

$$\log P(D|S_k) = -\sum_{j=1}^{n} \left[\frac{3}{2} \log(2\pi\sigma_j^2) + \frac{(\boldsymbol{x}_j - \boldsymbol{y}_j)^2}{2\sigma_j^2} \right] . \tag{5}$$

If we assume constant variances for all data points, the term is simplified to:

$$\log P(D|S_k) = -\frac{3n}{2} \log(2\pi\sigma^2) - \frac{1}{2\sigma^2} \sum_{j=1}^{n} (\boldsymbol{x}_j - \boldsymbol{y}_j)^2 , \tag{6}$$

which is the probability distribution for the measured data D, given S_k.

4.1   Polygonal Surfaces

In the context of surface simplification, we consider polygonal meshes as surface models. The simplification process iteratively derives a sparse version from the original mesh and the result is again a polygonal mesh. In contrast to parametric models we avoid complex fitting problems including high computation costs. We need to define the function associating a measured point with the closest correspondence on the surface. In this work we use a triangular surface representation. The iterative scheme of common simplification algorithms allows to track the history of each triangle and we can easily find the corresponding triangle of the model for each point [9]. The problem of finding the minimal distance d is then reduced to a closest distance problem between a point and a triangle. We use the definition of closest distance presented in [10]. The modified log-likelihood-function is:

$$-\log P(D|S_k) = \frac{3n}{2} \log(2\pi\sigma^2) + \frac{1}{2\sigma^2} \sum_{j=1}^{n} d(\boldsymbol{y}_j, \hat{\boldsymbol{T}}(\boldsymbol{y}_j))^2 , \tag{7}$$

where $d(\boldsymbol{y}_j, \hat{\boldsymbol{T}}(\boldsymbol{y}_j))$ is the distance between a measured point $\boldsymbol{y}_j$ and $\hat{\boldsymbol{T}}(\boldsymbol{y}_j)$ the associated triangle of the polyhedral surface model $\hat{S}_k$ with respect to the surface topology.

5   Minimum Description Length of a Polyhedral Surface

We want to identify an optimal surface representation. The model that yields a minimum of code-length needed to transmit a given data set D is supposed to be optimal [11]. This approach is based on the two-part description length:

$$L = L(M) + L(D|M) , \tag{8}$$

where $L(M)$ is the code-length needed to encode the model and $L(D|M)$ encodes the data given the model. The MDL principle is used to minimize this term. Even if we will never actually develop a coding scheme or intend to transmit data, the MDL approach can be used to evaluate the compactness of a certain model description [12]. The mapping to a common space such as bytes or a universal code makes both components, data and model comparable. Consider that we want to design an optimal code for a scalar sample drawn from a Gaussian distribution. The data could be coded according to a general converting scheme resulting in constant code lengths for each number. Instead, we encode the values according to their probability in order to minimize the code length. Shannon has shown in [13] that there is always a code which assures:

$$L(X) = - \log(P(X)) . \tag{9}$$

This relation states that high probability values are corresponded to short code lengths and vice versa. Note, that the given relation implies that values with an infinite code-length never occur while values with a probability of one do not need to be transmitted. In practical applications code lengths are integer numbers. However, the requirement of integers can be ignored if the number of bits is sufficiently high. We use non discretized code lengths in this work.

5.1   Model Parameters

Before we start encoding the model, we need to identify all parameters that represent the model completely. A polyhedral surface representation consists of vertices and triangles (V, T), where each vertex is a triplet of real numbers and each triangle is a triplet of integer indices of the corresponding vertices:

$$L(M) = L(V) + L(T) . \tag{10}$$

The configuration of the vertices and triangle indices in a polyhedral mesh can be arbitrary and it is difficult to assume any probability distribution. The optimization process should be independent of specific classes of surfaces or particular applications. If the probability distribution is unknown, the theorem becomes useless. However, Rissanen [14] introduces universal priors for communicating parameters with unknown probability distributions. The length of the corresponding prefix-free code is:

$$L(i) = \log^*(i) = c + \log_2(i) + \log_2(\log_2(i)) + \log_2(\log_2(\log_2(i))) , \tag{11}$$

where $\log_2(i)$ is the encoding of the actual number and $\log_2(\log_2(i))$ is the length of that encoding and so forth. c is a constant included for consistency [12]. The given encoding ensures that the message is decodable without any additional knowledge. For large numbers, $\log^*(i)$ can be sufficiently approximated by the binary logarithm. The representation of real numbers turns out to be more difficult since we need an infinite number of bits to encode a number with infinite precision. If we assume a fixed minimum precision ρ, we can convert a real number r to a corresponding integer i by performing a right shift [12]:

$$i = \lfloor (\frac{r}{\rho}) \rfloor . \tag{12}$$

The remaining fractional part is neglected. Now we can apply the encoding scheme for integer numbers. The resulting code length for all model parameters is then given by the sum of the lengths of all vertices:

$$L(V) = \sum_{i=1}^{n} ((\log_2(\lfloor (x_i \rho^{-1}) \rfloor) + \log_2(\lfloor (y_i \rho^{-1}) \rfloor) + \log_2(\lfloor (z_i \rho^{-1}) \rfloor)) , \tag{13}$$

where we need to consider x_i, y_i and z_i values for each vertex i. Each triangle is represented by three integer numbers and we could encode them with the scheme presented above. It is obvious that there must be an encoding scheme that is significantly more efficient than the simple index-based triangle list. Empirical investigations show, that state of the art compressions usually produce results with $0.5 - 1$ bits per triangle [15]. Assuming a regular structure, we obtain:

$$L(T) = c_{bit} \cdot t , \tag{14}$$

where c_{bit} is a constant of discussed dimension and t is the number of triangles. In order to achieve a maximum compression we use (14) to obtain $L(T)$.

5.2   Encoding of the Data

The data, which represents the residuals between the model and the original surface is encoded in the second part. The length is a measure for the goodness-of-fit of the model. Shannon stated in [13], that there exists a code that assures:

$$L(D|M) = - \log(P(D|M)) \cdot \log(2)^{-1} , \tag{15}$$

where the factor $\log(2)^{-1}$ is added in order to express the description length in bits instead of natural units [16]. The probability function of the data given the model has been derived in section three and the description length for the data turns out to be:

$$L(D|M) = \frac{3n \log(2\pi\sigma^2)}{2 \log(2)} + \frac{1}{2\sigma^2 \log(2)} \sum_{j=1}^{n} d(\boldsymbol{y}_j, \hat{\boldsymbol{T}}(\boldsymbol{y}_j))^2 . \tag{16}$$

Now, L is completely determined up to the variance σ^2 and the precision parameter ρ. The variance is a model parameter and we can maximize the likelihood and minimize $L(D|M)$ respectively by [14]:

$$\sigma^2 = \frac{1}{n} \sum_{j=1}^{n} d(\boldsymbol{y}_i, \hat{\boldsymbol{T}}_i)^2 \; . \tag{17}$$

Making an assumption about the precision is challenging and one of the crucial parts of the approach. One could say, that the precision of our model just needs to be as high as the precision of the original data. The precision of the original data is either obtained through the characteristics of the measuring process or by a naive estimation. In our approach we assume that the measured points came from a surface with a certain smoothness property. If we consider a small epsilon environment of a point $\boldsymbol{x}_i$ including the k-nearest neighbors, we expect only an infinitely small change in the normal direction of the surface that can be classified as noise. Although this assumption only works for areas with low curvature, we obtain a stable value if the average deviation is calculated. Given that, we demand a minimum sampling resolution compared to the level of measured details in order to limit the variance in between small neighborhoods. The estimated noise variance for a point in its corresponding neighborhood N_i is:

$$\hat{\sigma}_i^2 = \frac{1}{|N_i|} \sum_{j \in N_i} (\boldsymbol{n}_i(\boldsymbol{x}_j - \bar{\boldsymbol{x}}_i))^2 \; , \tag{18}$$

where $\boldsymbol{n}_i$ is the normal vector based on the third principle component of N_i and $\bar{\boldsymbol{x}}_i$ is the mean vector of N_i [17]. We consider only neighbours of first order in the triangular mesh. Please note, that σ is a parameter of the gaussian model, while $\hat{\sigma}_i$ describes the estimated variance of a data point. The square root of the averaged variance could be seen as estimated precision which is:

$$\rho = \bar{\hat{\sigma}} = \sqrt{\frac{1}{n} \sum_{i=1}^{n} \hat{\sigma}_i^2} \; . \tag{19}$$

6   Evaluation

Even if this work is rather theoretically motivated, the following investigations show reasonable results in practical applications. The presented scheme is tested on three different examples. The MDL term is evaluated for stepwise simplified meshes. In all cases, a global minimum of the description length can be clearly identified.

The first application example investigates two models with the same number of vertices. The capsule (e) and the augmented model (g) are shown in Fig. 2. We use a slightly modified edge-collapsing scheme to generate the simplified models [6]. The optimal models selected by the MDL criterion can be seen in (f) for the capsule and in (h) for the augmented model. The center plot in Fig. 1 shows the

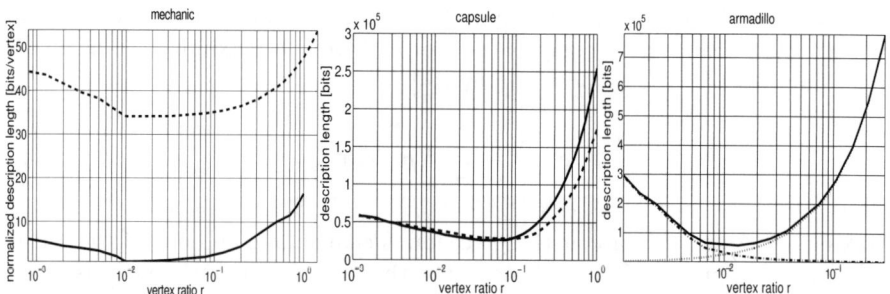

Fig. 1. The left plot shows the normalized description length with respect to the vertex ratio of the mechanical model in low (continuous line) and high resolution (dashed line). The center figure shows the description length of the capsule (continuous line) and the augmented model (dashed line). The right plot shows the description length L (continuous line) as well as $L(D|M)$ (dashed line) and $L(D)$ (dotted line) of the armadillo mesh

minimum description length in bits with respect to the vertex ratio $r = n_{simp}n_{orig}^{-1}$ for both models. n_{simp} is the vertex count of the simplified model, while n_{orig} is the vertex count of the original mesh. Note that the MDL plot of the augmented model (dashed line) has a similar shape but is slightly shifted with respect to the MDL plot of the capsule (continuous line). Apparently, we need to afford more vertices to keep the error sufficiently low. The result shows, that the selection is automatically adapted to higher detailed models.

The second example represents an industrial component with simple shapes and sharp edges. We evaluate the simplification at two different resolutions. The low resolution version consists of 6130 vertices and can be found in (b), Fig. 2. The congruent model with a higher resolution consists of 12260 vertices and is shown in (a) of Fig. 2. The evaluation results are shown in the left plot of Fig. 1, where the vertex ratio r is defined with respect to the vertex count of the smaller mesh. The normalized description length $\hat{L} = Ln_{orig}^{-1}$ is plotted for the mechanical model at a high (dashed line) and at a low resolution (continuous line). In both cases, the MDL criterion selects nearly the same degree of simplification, as can be seen in the right plot of Fig. 1. The image in (c) shows, that a reasonable representation is selected among unnecessarily complex (a, b) or significantly degenerated models (d). This example shows that the MDL criterion is usefull to extract the actual geometry of a given mesh.

While the previous examples investigate particular properties, the mesh shown in (i) of Fig. 2 represents a rather realistic application with complex features and many details. The right plot in Fig. 1 shows L (continuous line), $L(M)$ (dotted line) and $L(D|M)$ (dashed line) in bits with respect to the vertex ratio. The MDL-graph starts at a relatively high level mainly characterized by a high error rate represented by $L(D|M)$. The description length decreases steadily until the number of model parameters become the dominant component. Beyond the minimum, the description length increases rapidly as the vertex ratio converges

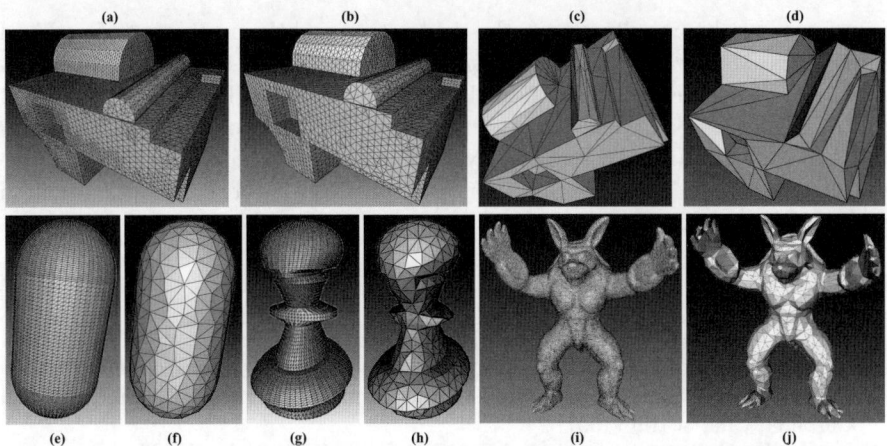

Fig. 2. The figures in the upper row show the result of the simplification of the mechanic model at a high (a) and at a low (b) resolution. Regardless of the initial number of vertices, the MDL criterion identifies a similar model (c) with nearly the same number of vertices among unneccesarily complex (a, b) and too simple models (d). The lower row shows the original mesh of the capsule (e) and of the rather complex model (g) with the same number of vertices. The corresponding simplified versions identified by the MDL criterion can be seen in (f) and (h). The image in (j) shows the optimal model of the armadillo in (i).

to one. The optimal model in terms of MDL can be seen in (j), Fig. 2. Please note that significant features like fingers, toes and ears are well preserved while the number of vertices is reduced drastically ($r \approx 0.013$). The armadillo dataset is a courtesy of the Stanford 3D scanning repository.

7 Conclusion

The minimum description length principle is a convincing and quite elegant way to reasonably identify an optimal model among a set of considered models. In contrast to polygon-budget or fidelity-based approaches, the presented method identifies an optimal model without further knowledge.

If we consider planar shapes, it is intuitive to identify redundant points that can be removed without changing the general geometry. In real world applications we are often faced with rather complex geometry and noisy data. It might be a matter of interpretation or context to decide if a given geometric detail is important or can be neglected in an optimal representation. However, if a small geometric feature is supported by a suffcent number of points, a removal of the corresponding part in the model will lead to a significant increase of the minimum description length. Obviously, we consider a "ratio" of vertex density and amount of details or information, although the model selection does not directly depend on the number of vertices.

In future work, we will improve the model itself and the estimation of required parameters. More complex models like parametric surfaces or geometric primitives such as spheres or cylinders will also be considered. Furthermore, we will try to incorporate simplification and MDL based evaluation in order to formulate a global optimization strategy. Next to simple mesh decimation tasks, we will use the efforts of that work as a theoretical basis for a semantic-oriented analysis of geometric data.

References

1. Hansen, M.H., Yu, B.: Model selection and the principle of minimum description length. Journal of the American Statistical Association 96(454), 746–774 (2001)
2. Luebke, D.: A survey of polygonal simplification algorithms. University of North Carolina, Chapel Hill (1997)
3. Hoppe, H., DeRose, T., Duchamp, T., McDonald, J., Stuetzle, W.: Mesh optimization. In: Proceedings of the 20th annual conference on Computer graphics and interactive techniques, p. 26 (1993)
4. Cignoni, P., Rocchini, C., Scopigno, R.: Metro: measuring error on simplified surfaces. In: Computer Graphics Forum, vol. 17, pp. 167–174 (1998)
5. Garland, M., Heckbert, P.S.: Surface simplification using quadric error metrics. In: Proceedings of the 24th annual conference on Computer graphics and interactive techniques, pp. 209–216. ACM Press/Addison-Wesley Publishing Co. (1997)
6. Lindstrom, P., Turk, G.: Fast and memory efficient polygonal simplification. In: Proceedings of the conference on Visualization 1998, Research Triangle Park, North Carolina, United States, pp. 279–286. IEEE Computer Society Press, Los Alamitos (1998)
7. Jenke, P., Wand, M., Bokeloh, M., Schilling, A., Straer, W.: Bayesian point cloud reconstruction. Computer Graphics forum 25(3), 379–388 (2006)
8. Ahn, S.J.: Orthogonal distance fitting of parametric curves and surfaces. In: Least Squares Orthogonal Distance Fitting of Curves and Surfaces in Space, pp. 55–73 (2004)
9. Velho, L.: Mesh simplification using fourface clusters. In: Shape Modeling International, pp. 200–208 (2001)
10. Eberly, D.: Distance between point and triangle in 3d. Magic Software (2001), http://www.magic-software.com/Documentation/pt3tri3.pdf
11. Gao, Q., Li, M., Vitnyi, P.: Applying MDL to learn best model granularity. Artificial Intelligence 121(1-2), 1–29 (2000)
12. Rissanen, J.: Modeling by shortest data description. Automatica 14(5), 465–471 (1978)
13. Shannon, C.E.: A mathematical theory of communication. SIGMOBILE Mob. Comput. Commun. Rev. 5(1), 3–55 (2001)
14. Rissanen, J.: A universal prior for integers and estimation by minimum description length. The Annals of Statistics 11(2), 416–431 (1983)
15. Szymczak, A., King, D., Rossignac, J.: An edgebreaker-based efficient compression scheme for regular meshes. Computational Geometry 20(1-2), 53–68 (2001)
16. Gruenwald, P.D.: The Minimum Description Length Principle. MIT Press Books, vol. 1. The MIT Press, Cambridge (2007)
17. Gumhold, S., Wang, X., MacLeod, R.: Feature extraction from point clouds. In: Proceedings of the 10th international meshing roundtable, vol. 2001, pp. 293–305 (2001)

Learning of Optimal Illumination for Material Classification

Markus Jehle, Christoph Sommer, and Bernd Jähne

Heidelberg Collaboratory for Image Processing (HCI), University of Heidelberg
{Markus.Jehle,Christoph.Sommer,Bernd.Jaehne}@iwr.uni-heidelberg.de

Abstract. We present a method to classify materials in illumination series data. An illumination series is acquired using a device which is capable to generate arbitrary lighting environments covering nearly the whole space of the upper hemisphere. The individual images of the illumination series span a high-dimensional feature space. Using a random forest classifier different materials, which vary in appearance (which itself depends on the patterns of incoming illumination), can be distinguished reliably. The associated Gini feature importance allows for determining the features which are most relevant for the classification result. By linking the features to illumination patterns a proposition about optimal lighting for defect detection can be made, which yields valuable information for the selection and placement of light sources.

1 Introduction

The illumination of objects is of fundamental importance for many vision tasks. Often, like in the case of automated visual inspection, the placement of light sources can be controlled. By acquiring multiple images of the same object with different illumination settings the properties of objects (like shape or reflectance) can be investigated more robustly. Generally, it is desirable to 1) reduce the number of illumination settings and to 2) obtain information about the optimal placement of light sources. These issues are addressed in this paper.

Appearance of an object can be defined as the visual impression we have. It depends on the object's shape (on various scales), on its material properties, and on the illumination environment. In the absence of subsurface scattering, the material properties can be characterized by the bidirectional reflectance distribution function (BRDF), which defines how light is reflected at an opaque surface. This function specifies the radiance observed in any outgoing direction when the surface is irradiated by light of a certain wavelength from any incoming direction. Appearance can be measured by irradiating a camera sensor. In our work we assume the camera position and orientation to be held constant with respect to the object.

Central to our investigation is the fact, that for given shape and for given material properties the appearance of an object changes if illumination is varied. Acquiring multiple images recorded at different illumination settings allows us to discriminate the materials an object is composed of. The additional information

M. Goesele et al. (Eds.): DAGM 2010, LNCS 6376, pp. 563–572, 2010.

in such an *illumination series* facilitates the classification of materials, which is typically difficult just using a single image. The lighting environment depends on the angular and spectral distribution of the light sources surrounding the object. We implemented a device, which is capable to generate arbitrary extended light sources covering nearly the whole space of the upper hemisphere.

Such illumination series are used as input data for a supervised learning approach. Each object is recorded under various illumination settings, thus spanning a high dimensional feature space. We apply random forests to achieve a pixel-wise classification. For training, data is labeled according to the membership of the different material classes. Then, the trained classifier is used to predict new data samples according to the different material classes. The final segmentation is performed on these probability maps.

The associated Gini feature importance allows for determining the features which are most relevant for the classification result. Since each image in the illumination series is linked to a distinct illumination setting, the process of automatic feature selection allows us to determine the lighting environments being most relevant for a specific problem.

Related Work. Classification of materials based on their reflection properties is a well-studied topic. Exemplarily, [1] use single images to cluster similar materials based on their texture. Recently, [2] presented a set of features and a Bayesian framework for high-level material category recognition using single images.

Multiple images from different viewpoints are exploited in the context of remote sensing by [3], who applied neural networks to classify multispectral and multiangle data. Multiple images recorded under different illumination settings can be used in techniques based on photometric stereo to classify materials (e.g. [4]). Koppal and Narasimhan [5] cluster the appearance of objects by analyzing a scene which is illuminated by a smoothly moving distant light source.

In the field of BRDF measurement [6] apply dimensionality reduction tools for determining reflectance functions. Lensch et. al. [7] optimized both camera and light source placement w.r.t. measuring the BRDF of 3D objects.

Closest related to our work are the material segmentation approaches by [8,9]. The authors use illumination-dependent reflectance properties to enlarge the class of material types that can be separated. In contrast to their work our approach allows us to reduce the number of illumination settings and thus propositions about optimal light source placements can be made.

Organisation. In section 2 the acquisition of illumination series is elucidated. Our classification algorithm is described in section 3. We verify the proposed technique in section 4 with real-world data.

2   Generation of Illumination Series

We are interested in acquiring a series of images, where the camera position is fixed and the angular distribution of the light source $L_i(\theta, \phi)$ is varied, where i stands for the three components of RGB-color space. Debevec et al. [10] acquired

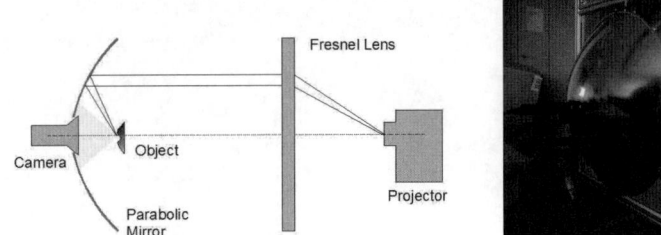

Fig. 1. Sketch and photograph of the parabolic lighting facility. Light emitted by an LCD projector is directed to an object by a parabolic mirror. The reflected light is recorded by a camera aligned to the mirror's rotational axis.

images of a human face under a dense sampling of incident illumination directions using a two-axis rotation system and a directional light source. Instead of using such a mechanical gantry, in our setup a mirror is employed to sample lighting directions. Similar setups have been proposed in the context of BRDF measurement [11,12].

Arbitrary extended, directional light sources can be produced by illuminating a parabolic mirror[1] using parallel light. The light reflected by the mirror is directed to the mirror's focal point. The source of the light is a digital projector[2] which is located in the focal point of a Fresnel lens[3]. We call this setup the *parabolic lighting facility* (see Fig. 1).

By varying the position of the impinging light ray relative to the optical axis one can vary both the polar angle θ and the azimuth angle ϕ. Thus, the illumination angle (θ, ϕ) can be transformed into the distance from the optical axis (x, y) via the following formulas:

$$x = 2f \tan(\theta/2) \cos\phi \quad \text{and} \quad y = 2f \tan(\theta/2) \sin\phi, \tag{1}$$

where f is the focal width. Since the mirror has a central hole of radius 0.75" for camera access, a lower bound for the azimuth angle is $\theta_{\min} = 7.15°$.

For the experiments following basic illumination patterns are used: 1) The whole field of illumination is subdivided into equally spaced *rings*. Here, the polar angle θ is limited, while the azimuth ϕ covers the whole range between 0° and 360°. 2) The whole field of illumination is subdivided into equally spaced *sectors*. Here the polar angle ϕ is limited, while the azimuth θ covers the whole range between 7.15° and 90°. Ring and sector patterns can be combined to produce lighting which is limited both in polar and azimuth angle (see Fig. 2).

---

[1] Edmund Optics NT53-876, diameter 24", focal length 6".
[2] Sanyo PLC-XU101, LCD-technology, resolution 1024×768 pixels, brightness 4000 ANSI-lumen, contrast-ratio 1:400.
[3] Edmund Scientific N31,139, size 31"×41", focal length 40", thickness 3/16".

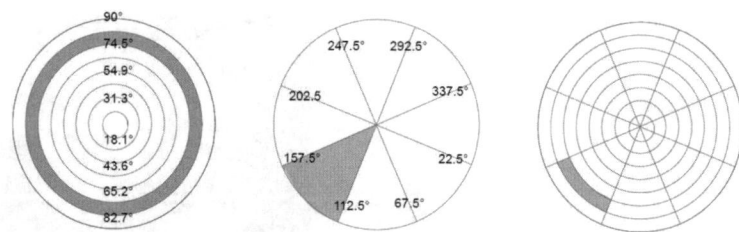

Fig. 2. Illumination patterns. Left: Rings with polar angles. Center: Sectors with azimuth angles. Right: Combination of rings and sectors.

Following issues have to be considered for acquisition:

1. As a photometric technique, our approach is heavily dependent on the correct gray values of the images to be processed. Especially dealing with specularities it is important that the dynamic range of the images is high, so that under- resp. overexposures can be avoided. Thus an HDR-image is generated by combining multiple photographs taken with different exposure times (e.g. $t_{\exp} = \{0.1\text{ms}, 1\text{ms}, 3\text{ms}, 10\text{ms}, 30\text{ms}\}$) using the technique by [13].

2. Because our digital projector exhibits a significant black level (the intensity of a pixel with RGB-value $(0,0,0)$ in the illumination pattern is not perfectly zero), the HDR-images are corrected as follows: We acquire an HDR background image (setting the RGB-value of the whole illumination pattern to $(0,0,0)$) and subtract it from the images in the illumination series.

3. The parabolic mirror setup assumes, that the object is located exactly in the focal point; i.e., the dimensions of the object are negligible compared to the mirror. In our case, the object size is up to 20 mm, which is significantly less than the mirror's diameter (600 mm). However, because the object is still of finite size leading to irregular illumination. To avoid this, the inhomogeneous illumination is corrected by dividing a reference HDR image of a Lambertian object recorded under the same illumination pattern.

3   Analysis of Illumination Series

First, we explain the overall procedure before we have a closer look at the random forest algorithm and its associated variable importance.

Overall Procedure. The starting point is an illumination series composed by N floating point images (which are derived from the acquired HDR-images by taking the logarithm). For each of the N images M feature responses are computed applying generic image descriptors at different scales. The following experiments are performed using simples Gaussian convolutions of adjustable bandwidth σ. The feature space dimension is the number of illumination patterns N times the number of image feature responses M.

Since we deal with supervised learning, the user is requested to label regions of the input object belonging to different materials (which distinguish in BRDF

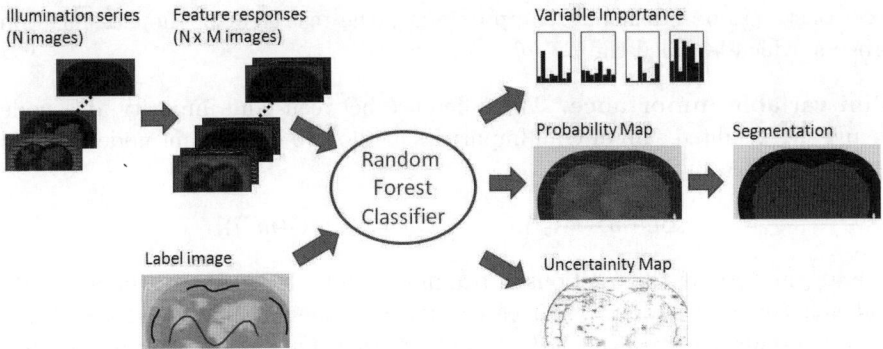

Fig. 3. Overview of our classification approach. For a detailed description we refer to section 3.

and texture). The labeled regions correspond to different classes. These labels are used to train a random forest classifier on all feature responses.

The classifier assigns a soft label (ranging from 0 to 1) to every pixel in the whole image, which can be interpreted as probability map for a specific object class. By thresholding the probability map, each pixel can be assigned to a distinct class, which yields the segmentation result.

The Gini variable importance measures quantifies the role of a feature dimension in discriminating the classes. This measure is useful for automatic feature selection, i.e. to reduce the dimensionality of the classification problem. Which means in our context, to find the *few* illumination environments which are most important for the segmentation task.

Random Forests. Random forest is a procedure that grows an ensemble of N_T decision trees and collects their class votes, injecting several moments of randomness along the way. Random forests were introduced by Breiman [14] and have shown excellent performance in other image processing applications [15,16,17]. We use the Gini impurity criterion (Eq. 2) to compute the best split threshold by applying an exhaustive search over all possible thresholds.

$$Q(m) = \sum_{k=1}^{K} p_{mk}(1 - p_{mk}),\qquad(2)$$

where m is the considered tree node, K the total number of classes, and p_{mk} the fraction of training samples in node m having class k. The procedure is randomized with regard to 1) the selection of candidate samples for training the individual trees (bootstrap sampling) and 2) the random selection of m_{try} candidate features at each specific node among which the best feature is selected (according to Eq. 2). Random forests are suitable for problems with a large number of variables but a small number of observations (due to random feature selection). Each tree is constructed using a different bootstrap sample from the original data. A certain fraction of the data is left out of the bootstrap sample. These out-of-bag samples can be used to evaluate the classifier after each tree construction and therefore approximates the test error of the classification process, which is called the *out-of-bag error*.

Gini variable importance. The difference between Gini impurity at a node m and the weighted sum of Gini impurities at the two descendant nodes m_l and m_r is computed by:

$$\Delta Q(m) = Q(m) - (p_l Q(m_l) + p_r Q(m_r)), \qquad (3)$$

where p_l and p_r are the fractions of training samples belonging to the nodes m_l and m_r. For each node in the tree construction the variable i and thresholds θ_i is determined for which $\Delta Q(m)$ is maximized. One can get an importance score by accumulating the differences of Gini importance from this optimal split $\Delta Q_i(m, T)$ for all nodes m in all trees T in the random forest individually for the variable i.

$$I(i) = \sum_T \sum_m \Delta Q_i(m, T), \qquad (4)$$

This yields a measure $I(i)$ for the mean Gini decrease that variable i achieves and hence indicates its overall discriminative value for the classification.

4   Results

We demonstrate the feasibility of the approach using a mosaic composed of small steel plates. Each plate is a square of 5 mm edge length and its surface is finished in a particular manner: 1) *Unfinished steel plate*, where the isotropic BRDF exhibits a forward scattering lobe of a distinct width. 2) *Polished*, where the BRDF is close to specular. 3) *Blasted*, where the isotropic BRDF exhibits a forward scattering lobe (being wider than in the unfinished steel case). 4) *Anisotropically smoothed*, where the BRDF is clearly anisotropic such that the width of the forward scattering lobe depends on the orientation. The plates can be arranged horizontally or vertically.

To create the *training data set*, three small mosaics are configured, each one consisting of five plates with differently finished surfaces. In each of these mosaics different plates are used and the order of the plates has been varied. The *test data set* is composed of a matrix of 4×4 plates, so that each surface type is used three to four times. From each of the mosaics a series of $M = 8$ HDR-images is acquired using the parabolic lighting facility, each one recorded under a different illumination setting. See Fig. 4 for the illumination series of the test data set.

From each of the images only $N = 1$ feature response is computed using Gaussian smoothing with bandwidth $\sigma = 1$. The materials of the training data set are labeled according to the material classes using "scribbles" via a graphical user interface. For this five-class problem the classifier is trained on the whole set of feature responses using the settings $N_T = 100$ and $m_{\text{try}} = \sqrt{NK}$. The trained classifier is used to predict the probability of the pixels of the *test data set* belonging to the material classes and segmentation is performed afterwards by assigning the pixels to a distinct class according to the highest probability.

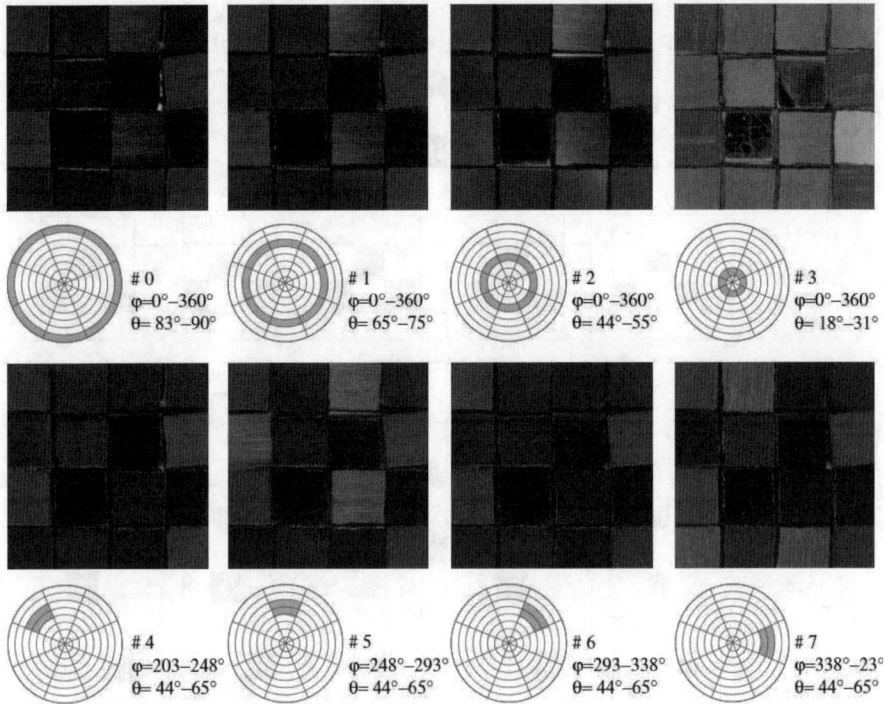

Fig. 4. Test data set. The mosaic is composed of 4 × 4 small quadratic plates of 5 mm edge length having differently finished surfaces. The illumination series consists of 8 HDR-images (logarithmized). Top row: Images recorded under a selection of ring illumination. Bottom row: Images recorded under a selection of combined sector/ring illumination. The specifications of the illumination patterns are given below images.

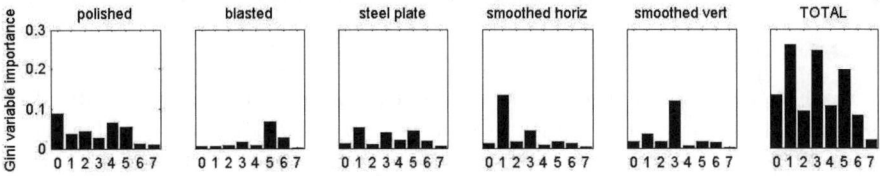

Fig. 5. Variable Importance for the different materials (first five diagrams from left) and overall variable importance (right)

Fig. 6 shows the results of the segmentation. Each column represents a differently finished surface. While the top row represents the ground truth, the second row shows the segmentation outcome considering *all* illumination environments. Our algorithm can classify all materials almost correctly on the test data set, which becomes evident from the misclassification rates listed in Tab. 1.

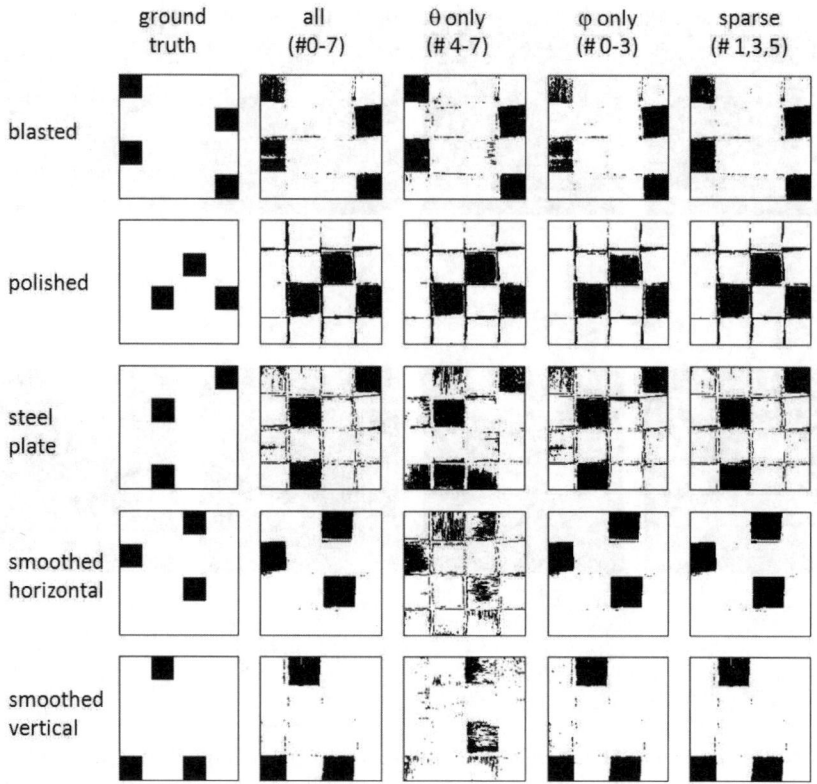

Fig. 6. Segmentation results of the test dataset. For each material a map of the associated segmented regions is given. The left column represents the ground truth which is used to validate the segmentation results. The other columns correspond to the distinct images of the illumination series being used for segmentation (description see text).

Next, we lower the number of the considered illumination environments. If we use only the simulated ring light (*varying polar angle* θ) environments for classification (#4–7), we arrive at a rather bad performance, especially for the correct recognition of the anisotropically finished surfaces. If we use only the simulated ring/sector lights (*varying azimuth angle* ϕ, #0–3), the misclassification rate for the blasted surfaces increases considerably.

By considering Gini variable importance (see Fig. 5), illumination environments can be identified, which are most relevant to the classification result. Thus a *sparse* set of lighting environments can be created (#1,3,5), which works on the test data set as well as the full set. We also performed experiments, where only the *one* illumination environment was used, which is most appropriate for a special material of interest (see the latter four columns of Tab. 1). In all cases the Gini variable importance is capable to propose the optimal lighting.

Table 1. Percentage of pixels classified incorrectly (misclassification rate). The numbers in the first 5 rows correspond to the differently finished surfaces. The columns correspond to the distinct images of the illumination series being used for segmentation (description see text). The latter 4 columns refer to illumination arrangements which are optimized w.r.t. a single material. Also the mean misclassification rate and the out-of-bag error are given.

Configuration	all	θ only	ϕ only	sparse	Polished	Blasted	Stpl./Sm. h.	Sm. v.
Selected channels	#0–7	#4–7	#0–3	#1,3,5	#0	#5	#1	#3
Blasted	2.5%	0.9%	15.8%	1.3%	42.5%	**19.7%**	38.2%	25.4%
Polished	0.6%	0.5%	3.2%	0.8%	**1.7%**	2.7%	24.4%	5.7%
Steel plate	0.3%	4.9%	0.7%	0.1%	18.9 %	40.0 %	**3.9 %**	19.9%
Smoothed horiz.	0.0%	38.0%	0%	0.0%	80.4%	73.1%	**0.1%**	40.7%
Smoothed vert.	0.1%	89.8%	0%	0.2%	80.7%	72.1%	48.6%	**1.7%**
Mean MCR	0.8%	26.8%	3.9%	0.5%	44.8%	41.5%	23.0%	18.7%
Out-of-bag error	0.014%	2.37%	0.012%	0.008%	36.3%	27.9%	1.23%	12.4%

5 Conclusion and Outlook

We demonstrated the feasibility of our technique to material classification: Multiple images were recorded under the same viewpoint but under different illumination conditions. This individual images of the illumination series span a high-dimensional feature space which forms the input of a supervised learning approach. Using Gini variable importance (which is implicitly provided by our classifier) the most discriminative features can be identified. Because these features are linked to illumination environments the number of lighting conditions, which are necessary to classify materials of interest, can be drastically reduced. In our experiment three illumination settings (which are associated to the features with highest variable importance) suffice to yield good classification accuracy. This technique could be used to propose a simple setup for visual inspection tasks, where the lighting is adapted to the objects' properties. While we focused on the material classification in this paper, we plan to extend our approach to objects which differ in their BRDF *and* in their shape properties. We also investigate the use of more elaborated feature descriptors.

Acknowledgments. Markus Jehle and Christoph Sommer gratefully acknowledge funding by Germany's Excellence Initiative through the institutional strategy project of Heidelberg University (DFG ZUK 49/1, TP6) and the industry partners of the HCI. The authors thank Dr. Ralf Zink for helpful discussions and providing the objects of study.

References

1. Varma, M., Zisserman, A.: A statistical approach to texture classification from single images. Int. J. Comput. Vision 62(1-2), 61–81 (2005)
2. Liu, C., Sharan, L., Adelson, E.H., Rosenholtz, R.: Exploring features in a bayesian framework for material recognition. In: Proc. CVPR (2010)

3. Abuelgasim, A., Gopal, S., Irons, J., Strahler, A.: Classification of ASAS multiangle and multispectral measurements using artificial neural networks. Remote Sensing of Environment 57(2), 79–87 (1996)
4. Hertzmann, A., Seitz, S.M.: Example-based photometric stereo: Shape reconstruction with general, varying BRDFs. PAMI 27(8), 1254–1264 (2005)
5. Koppal, S.J., Narasimhan, S.G.: Clustering appearance for scene analysis. In: Proc. CVPR, pp. 1323–1330 (2006)
6. Matusik, W., Pfister, H., Brand, M., McMillan, L.: A data-driven reflectance model. ACM Trans. Graph. 22(3), 759–769 (2003)
7. Lensch, H.P.A., Lang, J., Sa, A.M., Seidel, H.P., Brunet, P., Fellner, D.W.: Planned sampling of spatially varying BRDFs. In: Proc. Eurographics (2003)
8. Lindner, C., Arigita, J., Puente Leon, F.: Illumination-based segmentation of structured surfaces in automated visual inspection. In: Society of Photo-Optical Instrumentation Engineers (SPIE) Conference Series, pp. 99–108 (2005)
9. Wang, O., Gunawardane, P., Scher, S., Davis, J.: Material classification using brdf slices. In: Proc. CVPR (2009)
10. Debevec, P., Hawkins, T., Tchou, C., Duiker, H.P., Sarokin, W., Sagar, M.: Acquiring the reflectance field of a human face. In: SIGGRAPH (2000)
11. Dana, K.: BRDF/BTF measurement device. In: Proc. ICCV (2001)
12. Ghosh, A., Heidrich, W., Achutha, S., O'Toole, M.: BRDF acquisition with basis illumination. In: Proc. ICCV (2007)
13. Robertson, M.A., Borman, S., Stevenson, R.L.: Dynamic range improvement through multiple exposures. In: Proc. ICIP, pp. 159–163 (1999)
14. Breiman, L.: Random forests. Mach. Learn. 45(1), 5–32 (2001)
15. Bosch, A., Zisserman, A., Munoz, X.: Image classification using random forests and ferns. In: Proc. ICCV, pp. 1–8 (2007)
16. Menze, B.H., Kelm, B.M., Masuch, R., Himmelreich, U., Bachert, P., Petrich, W., Hamprecht, F.A.: A comparison of random forest and its Gini importance with standard chemometric methods for the feature selection and classification of spectral data. BMC Bioinformatics 10, 213 (2009)
17. Lepetit, V., Fua, P.: Keypoint recognition using randomized trees. PAMI 28(9), 1465–1479 (2006)

Author Index

Printing: Mercedes-Druck, Berlin
Binding: Stein+Lehmann, Berlin